中国·天津

武清开发区志

天津市武清开发区志编修委员会　编

方志出版社
Publishing House of Local Records

图书在版编目（CIP）数据

中国·天津武清开发区志 / 天津市武清开发区志编修委员会编 .
– 北京：方志出版社，2018.8

ISBN 978-7-5144-3213-8

Ⅰ . ①中 … Ⅱ . ①天… Ⅲ . ①经济开发区 – 概况 – 武清区
Ⅳ . ① F127.213

中国版本图书馆 CIP 数据核字（2018）第 201506 号

中国·天津武清开发区志

编　　者：天津市武清开发区志编修委员会
责任编辑：陈　菁

出 版 人：冀祥德
出 版 者：方志出版社
　　　　　邮址　北京市朝阳区潘家园东里 9 号（国家方志馆 4 层）
　　　　　邮编　100021
　　　　　网址　http://www.fzph.org
发　　行：方志出版社图书经销中心
　　　　　（010）67110500
经　　销：各地新华书店
印　　刷：北京文昌阁彩色印刷有限责任公司

开　　本：787 × 1092　　1/16
印　　张：40.5　　彩页：16
字　　数：718 千字
版　　次：2018 年 8 月第 1 版　　2018 年 8 月第 1 次印刷
印　　数：0001 ～ 5000 册

ISBN 978-7-5144-3213-8　　定　价：300.00 元

首都国际机场
北京
90KM
通州
71KM
北京新机场
45KM
武清
廊坊
35KM
25KM
71KM
100KM
滨海
国际机场
天津港
雄安新区
天津

武清开发区区位图

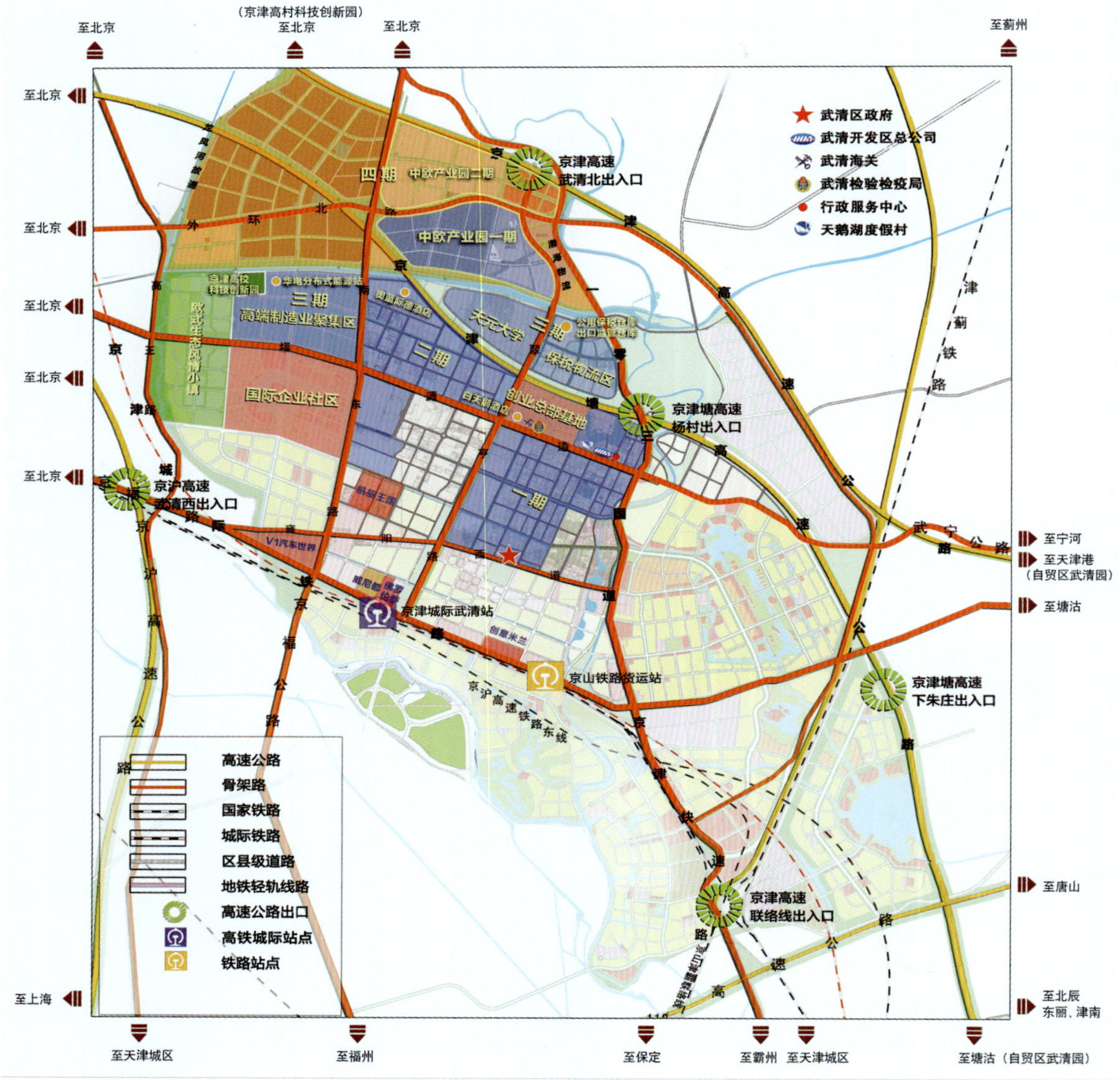
（京津高村科技创新园）
至北京
至蓟州
武清区政府
武清开发区总公司
武清海关
武清检验检疫局
行政服务中心
天鹅湖度假村
京津高速
武清北出入口
四期
中欧产业园二期
中欧产业园一期
京津高校科技创新园
华电分布式能源站
三期
高端制造业聚集区
欧式生态风情小镇
天元大学
公用保税仓库 出口监管仓库
保税物流区
二期
国际企业社区
创业总部基地
京津塘高速
杨村出入口
一期
京沪高速
武清西出入口
V1汽车世界
京津城际武清站
京山铁路货运站
京津塘高速
下朱庄出入口
京津高速
联络线出入口
津蓟铁路
武宁公路
至宁河
至天津港
（自贸区武清园）
至塘沽
至唐山
至北辰
东丽、津南
至上海
至天津城区
至福州
至保定
至霸州
至天津城区
至塘沽（自贸区武清园）
高速公路
骨架路
国家铁路
城际铁路
区县级道路
地铁轻轨线路
高速公路出口
高铁城际站点
铁路站点

武清开发区区域图

园区掠影

社会关注

1992 年 6 月 23 日，市长聂璧初等领导来武清开发区参加奠基仪式。

1995 年 9 月 19 日，武清开发区首家丹麦王国企业开业。

1991 年 5 月 8 日，国家科委副主任李绪鄂考察武清开发区并题词。

1995 年 11 月 27 日，中国工程院领导率专家来武清开发区视察指导。

载体功能

京津城际
铁路武清站

便捷的公路网

金融中心

通信大楼

武清海关

国家检验检疫机构

天鹅湖度假村

国际企业社区

创业总部基地

中欧产业园

留学人员创业园

中国青年创业园

京津高校（武清）科技创新园

企业风采

红日药业技术转化中心

万可电子（天津）有限公司

麦格昆磁（天津）有限公司

天津乐金新型建材有限公司

天津南玻工程玻璃有限公司

丹佛斯（天津）有限公司

可信－国家级孵化器

圣火－国家级孵化器

佛罗伦萨小镇

威尼都商业中心

天狮集团公司

国内外知名企业

艾默生 EMERSON Process Management	LG化学 LG 化学 天津新型建材	亚马逊 亚马逊 amazon.cn
德尔福 DELPHI Innovation for the Real World	马勒东炫 MAHLE Driven by performance	沃尔玛 Walmart 沃 尔 玛
住友集团 T-M	奥钢联 voestalpine ONE STEP AHEAD.	佛吉亚 faurecia
苏伊士 suez	华电 中国华电 CHD	中粮包装 CPMC
绫致 BESTSELLER	丹佛斯 Danfoss	麦格昆磁 Magnequench Leading Magnet Innovation
戴纳派克 Atlas Copco	欧德亮法尔宝 odelo Farba LIGHTING GROUP	尼得科 Nidec All for dreams
格兰富 GRUNDFOS	万可电子 WAGO INNOVATIVE CONNECTIONS	日进汽车 ILJIN

基伊埃	普洛斯物流	维益食品
格立莫农机	欧文托普	群英汽车饰件
光宝电子	米勒纺织品	柯菲凯博
合宜锻造	阿玛松	佛罗伦萨小镇
红日药业	天狮集团	铁科院
信义玻璃	南玻集团	奥克斯
日丰	伊利	娃哈哈
凯涛奇	诺禾致源	诚通人力

《中国·天津武清开发区志》编修委员会

主　　任： 张绍锋

副 主 任： 张福旺　张书月

《中国·天津武清开发区志》编修人员

主　　编： 张书月

副 主 编： 高元勃　王　毅　杨振关

编修人员： 闻　琪　魏建东　王　玉　许　贤　苑广伟
王小萌　王金祥　裴洪亮　刘文香　杨少海
孙　波　崔洪年　杨　英　王福东　李　杰
王秀丽　丁　丽　王付华　张秀启　赵　岩
殷绍峰　王永苹　王树柠　刘福伟　李洪宇
王凤刚　聂光炎　杨　超　杨　雷

责任编辑：张立华　张春燕　李　萍　王凤俊
封面设计：王春晶
校　　对：席炳田

序　言

一部记录中国天津·武清开发区（以下简称武清开发区）建设发展历史、展示武清人改革开放以来精神风采的志书——《中国·天津武清开发区志》，经过一年多的努力，编纂工作结束并将付梓出版，令人振奋，可喜可贺！

武清开发区自 1991 年经国家有关部门批准建立，至今已有 27 年。在近三十年的发展经历中，在一片荒芜的土地上，国内外四千余家知名企业入驻，一座建设规模宏大、管理现代、功能完备的现代化园区，迅速崛起于京津走廊之间。开发区已经成为武清引领创新、带动转型、支撑发展的龙头和主发动机。在把武清建成京津之间最具竞争力和最具实力地区，以及“京津卫星城　美丽新武清”建设的历史进程中做出了积极贡献，书写了武清发展史上最为辉煌的篇章。武清开发区的建设发展与辉煌成就，得益于党和国家改革开放的政策机遇；得益于从中央到地方各级领导及社会各界的关注与支持；得益于历届武清区（县）委、区（县）政府带领全区干部群众的长期奋进与拼搏；得益于武清开发区人的辛勤耕耘。

盛世修志。编写志书是我们中华民族不断总结自己、发展自己的优良传统。真实记录历史沿革、发展脉络、时代变迁、重大事件、重要人物，总结人类进步发展的经验教训，既是一种史料积累与文明传承，也是推动未来发展的精神动力。编纂一部记录武清开发区建设发展历程的志书，是许多武清人多年来的愿望，更是我们这些正在开发区工作同志的历史责任。

《中国·天津武清开发区志》全书共分 11 篇 38 章，文字总量达 70 多万字。书中通过大量史料和图片，较为全面、科学地记录了武清开发区建设的历程、重大事件、重要人物、发展成果，是一部反映武清开发区时代风貌、物质文明与精神文明建设成果的史书，也是存史传世、推动未来建设发展之作。

在编纂过程中，我们得到了广泛的关注与支持。天津经济技术开发区、天津高新技术产业园区，武清区委、区人大、区政府、区政协等领导机关，及区档案局、文广局、国土局、规划局、《天津日报·武清资讯》等部门也给予了多方面的帮助与支持。区内许多企业在史料搜集、文稿撰写等方面，都给予了大力支持。尤其是参与此志书编纂的工作人员，精心策划、深入挖掘、细心采写编辑，做出了积极努力。在此书出版之际，一并深表诚挚的谢意。

目前，按照县镇行政区域所属的地方志编修较多，而为开发区修志的较少，编纂《中国·天津武清开发区志》可借鉴的经验不多。同时，由于本书记录的史实资料年代较长，搜集整理的时间较短，加之我们的写作、编辑水平所限，难免有疏漏和不妥之处，敬请谅解。

张绍锋

2018年8月

（作者：中国天津·武清开发区工委书记、管委会主任）

Preface

"Records of Wuqing Development Zone" is a book to record history of the construction and development of China Tianjin Wuqing Development Area (UDA), and a book to demonstrate the spirit of local people since the reform and opening up of China. We are so happy and exciting, that the book writing is finishing, and ready to be printed after more than one year' s effort.

UDA was approved by the relevant national department in 1991. During 27 years development, UDA came from a barren land to a new technology city with big scale, modern administration and high economic performance. With more than 2000 domestic and international well-known companies, UDA grows fast along Beijing-Tianjin corridor.

As the window for opening up of Wuqing, UDA promotes area' s economy and even the whole district development, and becomes the base of social employment and re-employment. UDA makes the active contribution during the historical process of being competitive and strong region between Beijing and Tianjin, and during the historical process of building "satellite city to Beijing and Tianjin, beautiful new Wuqing". Thanks to the opportunities by Party and State' s reform and opening up policy, the consideration and support by the central and local leaders and all social circles, the long-term effort and hard work by Wuqing District (county) Commission, district (county) government and general public and the ploughing and weeding by the local common people.

Writing when prosperity. Recording or book writing is Chinses tradition of summing up and developing ourselves. Real historical records, development context, changes in the times, major events, important figures, and lessons learned from the progress and development are not only the accumulation of historical records and inheritance of civilizations, but also the spiritual driving force for future development. The compilation of a chronicle of UDA is our wish for years, furthermore it is a historic responsibility for us as the staff worker in UDA.

"Records of Wuqing Development Zone" includes 33 chapters with about 500,000 words. Through a large number of historical materials and pictures, the book records comprehensively and scientifically the construction process, major events, important figures, and the development result in UDA. It is not only a reflection of the ages appearance, material and spiritual civilization construction, but also a history book of history existence and to promote the future construction and development.

In the process of compiling, we received a lot of attention and support, including Tianjin Economic and Technological Development Zone, Tianjin High–Tech Industrial Park, Wuqing District Committee, District People's Congress, District Government, District Political Consultative Conference and other leading organizations, as well as the District Archives Bureau, Culture and Broadcast Bureau, Land Planning Bureau, "Tianjin Daily Wuqing Information" and other departments. Many departments in UDA and many existing enterprises have given strong support in collecting historical materials and writing drafts. In particular, the staff members involved in the compilation of this book planned carefully and made active efforts. At the time of publication, we would like to express our sincere gratitude.

Due to the lack of example, we can' t receive experiences to prefect the compilation. We can find some local editorials in the administrative regions, but fewer for the development zones like UDA. At the same time, due to long time ago historical record, urgent compiling work, combined with our limited abilities of writing and editing, we expect that there are inevitable omissions and inappropriate. We apologized for the inconvenience that may cause to you.

ZHANG ShaoFeng

Author, Secretory of the Working Committee of the Management Committee and Director of UDA

凡　例

一、以马克思列宁主义、毛泽东思想、邓小平理论、“三个代表”重要思想、科学发展观、习近平新时代中国特色社会主义思想为指导，坚持辩证唯物主义和历史唯物主义的立场、观点和方法，运用现代科学理论和方法，全面客观地记录武清开发区的自然风貌、经济发展的历史与现状，以期达到总结经验，推动未来发展的目标。

二、坚持详近略远、详独略同的原则，反映时代特点，突出地方特色。为认识武清开发区建设发展历程，及其在武清区域中建设发展的作用，产生的影响力、推动力，提供翔实可靠的依据。

三、全书结构层次，一般以篇、章、节、目、子目为框架。采用述、记、志、传、图、表、录等体裁，横分门类，竖写史实，以志为主，述而不论。

四、记述地域以现行武清开发区为主。记述时限从1991年12月28日开始至2016年12月止，个别特殊情况有所突破。

五、采用规范的语体文，各种名称首次出现用全称，再次出现用简称。简化字使用均以国家语言文字工作委员会正式公布的为准。

六、统计数字以统计部门公布的数字为准，属于单位或科室提供的，以单位统计核定数字为准。外币注明币种，人民币不注明币种。

七、“大事记”以编年体为主，一事一记，辅之以纪事本末体。

八、入志人物名录，收录武清开发区历届工委、管委会、总公司党政领导成员、高级职称人员，当选区级人大代表、政协委员、市级以上劳动模范，及从武清开发区调出担任正处级以上领导职务的人物等。客籍人物为在本区域或国内外有重要影响的贤达名人。

九、计量单位使用，依据国务院1984年2月发布的中华人民共和国法定计量单位执行。考虑到社会使用习惯，全书中亩不统一换算。

十、附录设置。除全志的总附录外，个别章节之后亦适当设附录，与章节正文相辅相成。

Guide for reading

Ⅰ. the book is based on Marxism–Leninism, Mao Zedong Thought, Deng Xiaoping Theory, the important thought of Three Represents and the scientific outlook on development. It implements the spirit of General Secretary Xi Jinping's important speech and the new ideas, new ideas and new strategies for managing state affairs. It uses modern scientific theories and methods to record objectively and completely the history and current situation of natural landscape and economic development of UDA, so as to achieve the goal of summing up experience and promoting future development.

Ⅱ. based on th principle of being slightly more detailed and more detailed than others, it reflects the characteristics of the times and highlighting local characteristics. In order to understand the construction and development of UDA, and its active role, its influence and driving power in development of Wuqing district, the book also provides detailed and reliable basis.

Ⅲ. The book structure includes generally article, chapter, section, head, subheading as the framework. Adoption of the narrative, recording, biography, charts, tables and other genres, horizontal categories, vertical writing historical facts, mainly engaged in objective recording instead of writing.

Ⅳ. the book records mainly the area to the existing UDA. The narrative time limit began on 28th December, 1991 and ended in December 2016 except some special cases.

Ⅴ. except "cover (title page)", "Preface" (Guide for reading) and "Overview" providing Chinese and English version, the rest content is in Chinese. The writing is in the spoken styles. The various names appearing in the book are written firstly in full name, but follow with the abbreviation. The simplified Chinese Characters are subject to the official announcement by the

State Language Working Committee of China.

Ⅵ. The statistics are based on the figures published by the statistical departments. For some number by the companies or departments, the unit statistics approved data shall prevail. Foreign currency indicates the currency name, Chinses RMB is not indicated with "RMB".

Ⅶ. "Memorabilia" in the book is mainly chronological, one Memorabilia with one record, and assisted by the Chronicle.

Ⅷ. the recorded figures in the book includes senior staff, elected district–level deputies and CPPCC members, city or above city level model workers, and the figures redeployed from UDA with division or above division rank from UDA management Committee and General Corporation of Party and Government. The rest figures are celebrities with significant domestic and international influence in UDA.

Ⅸ. The units using is implemented in accordance with the statutory units of measurement in the People's Republic of China promulgated by the State Council in February 1984. Considering the social habits, the unit "MU" in the book is not converted

Ⅹ. Appendix. In addition to the general appendix, some chapters are also added with appendices, with complements the text with each other.r.

目　录

第一篇　申建启动

第二篇　开发建设

第三篇　招商引资

第四篇　行业　企业

第五篇　金融

第六篇　经济综合管理

第七篇　党政群团

第八篇　科技　教育　文化

第九篇　政法

第十篇　商务区

第十一篇　人物

附　　录

Contents

Article Ⅰ Application and Start

Article Ⅱ Exploitation and Construction

目录

Article Ⅲ Investment Promotion

Article Ⅳ Industries and Enterprises

Article Ⅴ Finance

Article Ⅵ Comprehensive economic management

Article Ⅶ Party, Government, Alliance and Group

目录

Article Ⅷ Technology, Education and Culture

Article Ⅸ Politics and Law

Article Ⅹ Central Business District

Article Ⅺ Figures

Appendix

概　　述

概　述

早在20世纪80年代末，随着京津之间首条高速公路的竣工通车，国内外众多经济专家就通过各种新闻媒体发出预言：京津塘高速公路的建成通车，必将引发这里区域经济的大发展，京津塘高速公路将成为中国经济发展的又一硅谷，而武清开发区就是这一硅谷中崛起的一座科技新城。

1991年12月28日，经国务院批准，建立天津市高新技术产业园区武清开发区（以下简称“武清开发区”）。2010年12月，经国务院批准为国家级经济技术开发区，2014年年底纳入天津国家自主创新示范区核心区。武清开发区隶属于天津市武清区。武清古称泉州、雍奴，建制于西汉，唐天宝元年（公元742年）定名武清，2000年6月13日撤县建区。武清开发区的建设发展经历，是改革开放以来，武清百余万人民在历届区（县）委、政府的领导下，抢抓机遇、团结奋进、努力拼搏、创新发展的真实写照，也是书写在武清两千多年发展史上最为辉煌的篇章。

区域现状

武清开发区从建区到2016年25年的建设发展过程中，其总体区域发展规模已经从建区初期的3平方公里，逐步发展到近期的规划面积55平方公里。其中，40平方公里已建成，15平方公里正在规划、开发之中。

武清开发区区位优势得天独厚。地处京津走廊之间，是京津冀协同发展京津城市主轴的中间节点。坐落在古老的京杭大运河（北运河）畔、世界瞩目的京津塘高速公路“经济硅谷”之地。距北京市区71公里，天津市区25公里，北京首都国际机场90公里，北京新国际机场45公里，天津滨海国际机场35公里，天津港71公里。

区域交通体系开放便捷。周边10分钟车程范围内，有京津塘、京津、京沪、滨保等高速公路4条、高速公路出入口5个；有京津城际铁路经停站1处，京山铁路客、货运站各1处；规划的京、津地铁将在武清驳接；103、104国道在区内通过；武清自建的九横九纵立体化交通网络通达。

自然生态环境良好。开发区东临京杭大运河，北有龙凤新河，西有龙凤河故道，中间镶嵌着美丽的天鹅湖。区内绿化率达40%以上，空气和水质优于国家标准。多年来，无环保不达标企业入驻，是国家有关部门通过的ISO 14001环境管理体系认证的单位。

服务环境优质高效。始终秉承“服务他人就是发展自己”理念，坚持服务立身、服务致胜，对开发区实行“封闭式”管理，设有开发区行政服务中心、海关、检验检疫局和保税物流区，为企业提供“一站式”办公、“一条龙”服务。金融、法律、财务等商务服务机构齐全，特别是与普华永道、世邦魏理仕等国际知名咨询机构建立战略合作，可为企业提供政策、管理、工程、技术、金融、法律等高水平咨询和培训服务，成为有关部门通过的ISO 9001质量管理体系认证单位。

配套功能设施完备。基础功能设施达到“十一通一平”，建有大型商务写字楼、星级酒店、温泉公寓、人才公寓、国际学校、三甲医院、主题乐园、奥特莱斯购物小镇等。

科技创新体系完善。获批国家专利试点园区、国家知识产权质押融资试点园区、天津市双创示范基地、天津市留学生创业园。现有国家级科研院所近30个，企业、工程技术中心11个，检验检测机构5个，国家级和市级孵化器3个、市级众创空间1个，科技型中小企业1000余家，超亿元科技型企业100余家，市级以上高新技术企业80家。产业基金、融资平台等科技金融服务完善。建有武清开发区博士后科研工作站、院士工作站和专家服务基地。建成天元大学一期，规划建设国家大学创新园区，高端人才、创新人才加速聚集。

多重政策优势叠加。入区企业可享受国家级高新技术产业园区、国家级经济技术开发区、滨海国家自主创新示范区、京津冀协同发展等叠加政策，并享受武清区“六层次”人才引进、培养和奖励政策，促进科技型中小企业发展政策，以及天津市企业转型升级、民营经济发展等扶持政策。

建区以来，共吸引投资1400亿元，其中外资80多亿美元，引入50个国家和地区的企业4000余家，其中有美国艾默生、亚马逊、德尔福，法国苏伊士、家乐福、佛吉亚，日本东棉、住友，韩国LG，新加坡丰树，澳大利亚沃利帕森，中国中粮、中交、中电投等世界500强企业34家；有丹麦绫致、丹佛斯、艾尔姆、格兰富，德国GEA、万可，英国哈克尼斯，瑞典戴纳派克、贝格，芬兰玻石，西班牙海斯坦普，比利时哈蒙，法国库恩，美国麦格昆磁、维益，土耳其欧德亮法尔宝，突尼斯柯菲凯博，韩国日进等国外龙头企业50余家；有天狮集团、红日药业、诺禾致源、信义玻璃、娃哈哈饮品、伊利、奥克斯、畅联等国内龙头企业50余家。

形成了高端制造、生物医药、总部经济三大主导产业。高端制造业以智能制造、轨道交通、汽车及零部件、电子信息为主；生物医药以基因测序、中药颗粒、医疗器械、诊断试剂为主；总部经济以总部结算、金融服务、研发转化、文化创意为主。

武清开发区是武清区对外开放的窗口，引领创新、带动转型、支撑发展的龙头。建区以来，累计实现地区生产总值2491亿元，税收763亿元；吸引直接就业12万人。

至2016年年底，开发区正以打造“协同创新门户、生态科技园区”为目标，着力提升发展的质量和效益，重点开发3个载体功能区：中欧产业园。与商务部投促局共建，规划9.5平方公里。发展定位是为欧洲企业打造发展平台载体，建成高端产业发展基地。主要发展高端制造、生物医药、新材料产业。目前为欧洲企业量身建设5万平米环保节能厂房和中欧园服务中心已投入使用，正在规划建设环保节能厂房二期和生活配套区。创业总部基地。规划1.26平方公里，包括6个区域，建筑面积120万平方米。主要发展金融服务、研发转化、文化创意等现代服务业，提升武清开发区功能环境，促进产业结构调整升级。京津高校（武清）科技创新园。占地161亩，建筑面积11.5万平方米，发展定位是立足加强与京津高校和科研机构的产学研用合作，建设高新项目研发平台、高端产业孵化平台、传统产业升级助推平台、国家级重大研究课题创新成果转化平台和高层次人才集聚平台。

发展历程

武清高新区是全国首个县域所属的国家级开发区，它的创建历程，是武清人在我国改革开放日益深入发展的形势下，抢抓机遇、不断创新、历尽艰辛、奋进拼搏的结果。

武清地处京津冀核心地带、京津走廊之间。优越的区位给这片热土赋予了社会经济文化发展的诸多优势。早在20世纪90年代初，随着改革开放、农村家庭联产承包责任制的实行，作为津郊农业大县的武清，耕地面积占整个天津农业区县的四分之一，粮食产量占三分之一，且有了“津沽粮仓”的美誉和“全国粮食生产先进县”的桂冠。但是，只步入了“温饱型”境地，想要实现经济更快更好发展、让人们跨入小康生活，还只是个追寻的梦幻。武清经济要实现大踏步跨越发展，靠种粮、种菜的传统农业不行；靠满腔热情地跑贷款、抓项目，自己办乡镇企业也不行。此时，深圳特区的崛起，珠江三角洲、长江三角洲经济的迅速发展，乃至全国部分地区开发区的建立，给苦苦追寻发展的武清人带来了启示。1990 年 10 月 8 日，天津市委常委、市科委主任王成怀在到武清参加“全国乡镇企业商品展销会”期间，带来了国家“火炬计划”要批准一批省市建立国家级高新技术产业园区，同时将建一个县域国家级高新区的利好消息。武清的决策者们即刻意识到这是武清发展中千载难逢的机遇，果断做出了想方设法、积极争取建设高新区的决策，很快组建了武清高新区申报办公室。于 1991 年年初踏上了艰难的申办征程。

机遇与挑战并存。创建县属国家级高新区，不仅需要领导者远见卓识的果断决策，还要具备明显的条件优势、较好的发展基础。要得到国家有关部门的认可批准，建立县域国家级高新区又谈何容易？但是，武清人硬是凭着加快发展的强烈责任感，紧紧抓住国家“火炬计划”建立高新技术产业园区的机遇、积极申办，并为此做出了一系列的努力。1991 年 12 月 28 日，经国家科委批准建立“天津市高新技术产业园区武清开发区”，武清高新区从此成为全国第一个办在县域的国家级高新开发区。

武清开发区起步区域面积 3 平方公里，地处刚刚建成通车的京津塘高速公路杨村站出口。万事开头难。建设一个高标准、高起步的国内外瞩目的高新区，首先是需要数亿元的资金投入。然而，当时的武清财政收入不足亿元，各项基础设施建设的投资只能靠银行贷款、群众筹资、外出拆借来解决。很快实现了水、电、路、气、通信等“五通一平”的建设投资标准。基础设施建设完成后，又迅速展开了强大的招商引资攻势。首先在首都人民大会堂召开了有世界各国驻中国使节、新闻媒体记者参加的“武清高新区招商引资推介会”，相继在国内外建起了招商引资办事处，组建了由县党政主要领导、高新区专业人员组成的招商引资组团，到国内外推介自己、开展了卓有成效的招商引资。历尽艰难，实现了三年借债投入起步、五年初具规模可看、十年盈利有余的发展目标。

精彩纷呈

如果把改革开放说成是中国人创造了一个精彩时代的话，那么，武清人则在自己的土地上以武清开发区为平台，也创造了精彩华章。纵观武清开发区近二十几年发展经历，从 1991 年 12 月 28 日国家科委批准建立的“天津市高新技术产业园区武清开发区”，到 2010 年 12 月 30 日国务院批准的“国家经济技术开发区”；从 3 平方公里的起步区，到二期、三期、四期的 35 平方公里的宏大区域；从一号标准厂房的建设，到国内外 4000 余家国内外知名企业入驻发展，无不体现了武清人在历届区（县）委、政府的领导下，利用自己的聪明才智，举全区（县）之力，创造了一个又一个精彩。

之一：让武清融入了世界。武清开发区的建立打开了武清长期以来封闭的区域窗口，让武清人眼界大开，走向世界。为了招商引资，从县（区）级领导到有关工作人员纷纷走出国门，考察国际市场、宣传武清、广交朋友、洽谈项目。同时，也在坚持高质量、高标准夯实基础设施，努力实现“十一通一平”，打造“生态型、环保型、服务型”环境的基础上，让武清开发区成为世界瞩目的一片热土，把武清推向了世界。到 2016 年年底，已吸引国内外企业 4000 余家。其中，世界 500 强就有 34 家，有美国艾默生和英格索兰、日本东棉和住友、韩国 LG、中粮等，国内外龙头企业百余家，有天狮、丹佛斯、南玻、信义玻璃、娃哈哈饮品、伊利奶制品、红日药业、戴纳派克、奥克斯、玉柴重工等。这些企业的入驻也使武清名声远扬，逐步形成智能制造、生物医药、总部经济三大优势支柱产业。特别是近年来随着创业总部基地、高端制造业集聚区、保税物流区、金融商务区等项目建设，更为世人瞩目。

之二：用占全区不足 2% 的土地，换来了占全区 50% 的经济发展效益。年度实现税收总额、一般预算收入，连续多年占全区的一半以上。到 2016 年，武清开发区累计实现地区生产总值 2491 亿元，实现税收 763 亿元。成为武清经济发展成果的“半壁江山、重中之重”。

之三：搭建了就业再就业平台。近些年来，许多城市就业难成为社会发展的一大问题，既涉及民生又关系到区域社会的稳定。而武清由于开发区的建立，却从没有出现过就业难的问题，许多从国营、集体下岗的职工，都能及时得到就业安置。武清开发区从建设之初，就明确了经济、就业两个指标一起抓的思路。开发区积极与区人才市场、劳动力市场、驻区企业联系，想方设法利用多种形式，为城乡劳动力搭建就业再就业平台。到 2016 年年底，开发区安置就业再就业人员超过 12 万人。为区域城乡居民增收、维护社会稳定，做出了积极贡献。

之四：拉动了全区其他园区经济发展。武清是全市园区经济发展较好的区县之一，不仅发展快，而且质量高效益好，在推动武清经济快速发展的同时，也间接促进了其它园区的发展。其中，京津科技谷产业园、京津电子商务产业园、汽车零部件产业园、京滨工业园先后获批市级示范园区。这些经济园区的蓬勃发展均得益于武清开发区的示范带动作用，它们从申办到建设管理，几乎都是借鉴武清开发区建设发展的模式。

之五：促进了宜居城市建设。按照生态型、环保型、现代化宜居城市的建设思路，把武清开发区与武清城区建设同谋划、同建设、同发展，是武清历届区（县）委、政府恪守的一项原则。在招商引资建厂的同时，把环保作为铁门槛，绝不允许污染企业进入；在加强基础设施建设的同时，与增强城市载体功能一起建设；在布局安排上，既考虑行业特点，又注重休闲、生活、文化娱乐配套；在环境建设方面，既注重生产环境，又兼顾城市居民生活绿化、美化，使开发区处处皆美景，企业均呈现“花园”式效果。

之六：为武清跨入天津经济发展第一集团军行列助力。过去武清在天津发展中位置处于一市区、二四郊、三塘汉大、四五县的位置，而武清在老五县中也不占优。近年来，武清跨越发展，其各项经济发展指标除滨海新区外，连续几年居全市区县之首，稳步进入天津经济发展的“第一集团军”行列。而这一跃升，也得益于有了武清开发区的建立与发展。

之七：成为培育发展人才的摇篮。事业的发展需要人才，人才是在事业发展的熔炉中锻炼成长的。武清开发区在近 30 年发展过程中，从建区初期的“18 棵青松”到现在百余名“特别能战斗”的队伍，不仅培育了“武清开发区人”精神，建起了一支高素质的工作团队，而且为武清乃至省市建设发展培育了许多干部。这些人，有的走上了省、市级、区县级领导岗位，有的担当了乡镇（街道）的主要领导职务，不少人在乡镇经济园区领班带岗。他们走出开发区，在各自不同的岗位上，为全区、乃至全国各省市的发展做出自己新的贡献。

宝贵经验

经过近 25 年的艰辛努力，武清开发区已经成为武清全区对外开发开放的窗口、产业升级的龙头，经济发展的引擎，京津冀协同发展带上一颗璀璨的明珠，京津走廊崛起的科技新城。武清开发区所以取得这样令世人瞩目的成就，它的基本经验何在?

经验之一：新机制。在建设发展过程中，他们按照现代企业管理的要求，适应国际化发展的需要，从实际出发，逐步建立并完善了一整套新的管理机制。开发区采取的工委、管委会与总公司三块牌子、一套人马的领导机制，既体现了它的权威性，又实现了指挥协调发展的一致性；人员使用的聘任制的实施，使他们逐步建起了高效、高质的特别能战斗的团队；工程建设的招投标制，不仅堵塞了经济漏洞、节约了大量建设资金，同时保证了工程建设质量。封闭式管理，任何职能管理部门、执法部门工作人员都不允许进入区内企业“吃、拿、卡、要”，既避免了腐败现象发生，又为入区企业创造了良好的投资环境。这些，无疑为开发区建设发展奠定了坚实的基础。

经验之二：新理念。武清开发区在建设发展过程中，形成了从“投资者是上帝，上帝没有错”要求的提出，到“服务他人就是发展自己”的科学完备的服务理念。从一站式办公、一条龙服务体系的建立，到每一项具体工作，无不体现着他们的诚心诚意的服务，开发区内哪一家企业的入驻，哪一家企业的发展壮大，都渗透着开发区人辛勤的汗水。

经验之三：借助京津冀协同发展之力。国家关于京津冀协同发展的大计，给武清开发区的发展带来了千载难逢的良好机遇。武清地处京津走廊，有着强劲的区位发展综合优势，世界瞩目、国内瞩目、京津冀更加瞩目。随着京津冀协同发展战略的逐步落实，首先使武清开发区招商引资向着现代化、高科技、高端化、高效益发展方向迈进，一大批国内外知名企业涌入开发区，年引资规模达数百亿元。坐落在开发区核心地带的“创业总部基地”应运而生，给武清开发区带来了高质量、高水平、高效益的标志性发展的新态势。其次是一大批科研部门、大院大所及高端科技人才大量涌入，为武清开发区今后发展备足了后劲。

经验之四：领导关注。武清开发区的发展，离不开从中央到市委、市政府及有关部门领导的关注与支持。党和国家领导人胡锦涛、张高丽、孙春兰、李鸿忠、王光英、朱光亚等相继到此视察。1994 年 6 月 22 日，中共中央政治局常委、书记处书记胡锦涛在市县领导的陪同下，视察了武清开发区。视察期间，胡锦涛认真听取了武清县委、县政府领导的汇报，详细询问了武清开发区的建设发展经历、成果、经验。胡锦涛对武清开发区建设发展给予高度评价，对武清开发区未来建设发展寄予厚望。历任天津市委书记、市长都多次到开发区检查指导工作。科技部和市科委及有关部门领导多次到开发区具体帮助指导建设发展工作。1992 年，天津市委副书记、市长聂璧初亲自到武清为开发区奠基，这无疑给武清开发区以极大鼓舞和力量。尤其是历届区（县）委、政府领导，更是始终不渝地把开发区作为全区发展的重中之重，从谋划、指挥到身体力行，经常现场办公，帮助开发区解决发展建设中遇到的各种困难。

经验之五：社会支持。武清开发区建设成就的取得，是“举全区之力”的结果。

这里有全区各职能部门热情服务的脚印；有驻区企业辛勤耕耘的辛劳；有驻军指战员参与建设留下的汗水；有附近数万居民群众主动出让土地、撤村建居的鼎力支持。在开发区建设发展史上，无不体现着武清人识大体、顾大局、海纳百川的博大胸怀，及迎难而上、奋发努力、不断创新发展的时代风采。

经验之六：开发区人努力。规模宏大、高质量、高效益的武清开发区，也是众多参与开发区建设者不断努力奋斗的结果。从历届工委书记、副书记，管委会主任、副主任，总公司总经理、副总经理，到每个员工，都以他们强烈的责任感、尽职尽责的行动，构筑了开发区发展的大厦。从建立到发展的六年间，开发区 18 人以良好的精神状态和优异的工作成绩，赢得了“18 棵青松”的赞誉。留下了一次招商谈判 16 小时不间断工作的佳话，创造了许多为开发区建设发展舍小家为大家生动感人的故事。

辛勤的耕耘必将有丰硕收获。昨天，辉煌已经记入武清发展的史册。今天，实现中华民族伟大复兴的祖国正在改革开放更加深入的康庄大道上前行，武清和武清开发区定将与祖国发展同行。明天，武清开发区会不断续写出更加辉煌、美妙的新篇章！

Summary

As early as the late eighties of last century, with the opening of the first expressway between Beijing and Tianjin, many domestic and international economic experts predict through various news media that the Beijing–Tianjin–Tanggu Expressway will surely trigger the dramatic economic development of near regions, the areas along this Expressway will become another economic development of China's Silicon Valley, and Wuqing Development Zone (UDA) is the Technology city in the Silicon Valley.

The State Council approved the establishment of Tianjin High–tech Industrial Park Wuqing Development Zone (UDA) on 28th December 1991. The State Council approved further UDA as a state–level economic and technological development zone in December 2010. By the end of 2014 UDA was under the core area of Tianjin National Innovation Demonstration Zone. As a result, UDA has been the only development area under County level in China so far, which has two state–level titles. UDA is under the Wuqing District of Tianjin. Wuqing, formerly known as Quanzhou Yongyang, was built in the Western Han Dynasty, and in Tang Tianbao the first year (AD 742) named Wuqing. On 13th June 2000 Wuqing became a district to Tianjin instead of County. The construction and development of UDA is not only the results of leading of the successive district (County) committees and governments, seizing opportunities, forging ahead in unity, hardworking and innovative development, but also the most brilliant chapter in Wuqing history of more than two thousand years.

Regional Status

During the construction and development process of 25 years till 2016, UDA came from the initial 3 sq.km to recent 50 sq.km gradually.35 sq.km is the mature region, the rest 35 sq.km is under planning and constructing.

UDA has unique geographic advantage, it is located in the middle point of Beijing and Tianjin main axel of Beijing Tianjin coordinated development, and along the Beijing Tianjin corridor. It is located in the ancient Beijing–Hangzhou Grand Canal (North Canal), and famous Jingjintang Expressway "economic Silicon Valley". It' s 71 km to Beijing downtown, 25 km to Tianjin downtown, 90 km to Beijing International Airport, and 45 km to Beijing second international Airport, 35 km to Tianjin Airport and 71km to Tianjin Seaport.

With strong local transport network, it takes within 10 minutes to reach one highway entrance of the 4 existing Highway, including Jingjintang highway, Jingjin highway, Jinghu highway, or Binbao highway. There are Wuqing Station for Beijing Tianjin intercity train connecting Beijing and Tianjin railway station, JingShang Railway for passengers and cargos. The subway in Beijing and Tianjin is planned to connect in Wuqing. There are also the state road number 103 and number 104. Wuqing also has the key regional traffic network of "Nine horizontal and nine vertical" leading to all directions.

Natural ecological environment is good. UDA is to east by Beijing–Hangzhou Grand Canal, to North by Longfeng new river, to west by old Longfenghe river, in the middle with the Swan Lake. The greening rate is more than 40%, air and water quality is better than the national standard. Over the years, the enterprises, who can' t meet environmental protection standard, have been not allowed to enter UDA. UDA is the certified region meeting the requirement of ISO14001 environmental management system certification by the relevant state departments.

Adhering to the concept of "Serving others as self–development", we provide quality and efficient services. UDA adopts the "closed–end" management, there are Administrative Service Center, Customs, Inspection and Quarantine Bureau and Logistics Zone, and provides "One–stop" comprehensive services, including finance, legal, financial services and other concerning business possibilities. In particular, we have established strategic cooperation with internationally renowned consulting agencies like PWC and CBRE, who provide high–level consultation on policies, management, engineering, technology, finance and law, to make the enterprises to achieve ISO9001 quality management system certification.

UDA has completed supporting facilities. The basic functional facilities reaches "eleven through and a flat", there are a large office buildings, star hotels, various apartments, international schools, hospitals, theme parks, shopping outlets and so on.

Scientific and technological innovation system is perfect. UDA is approved as the National Pilot Patent Park, National Pledge Financing with Intellectual Property Pilot Park, Tianjin Demonstrative Base of Double Innovation, Tianjin Pioneering Park for Foreign Students. There are nearly 30 state–level scientific research institutes, 11 enterprises and engineering centers, 5 testing and testing institutes, 3 state–level and city–level incubators, 1 municipal–level Maker space, more than 1,000 high–tech SMEs, More than 100 million yuan enterprises, 80 high–tech enterprises above the municipal level. Industrial funds, financing platforms and other science and technology improve financial services. UDA has a post–doctoral research station, academician workstation and expert service base. The constructing TIENS International University plans to build National University Innovation Park to attract various excellent talents.

The enterprises in UDA can enjoy the concerning multi preferential policies including the policies from the national high–tech industrial park, economic and technological development area, Tianjin Free Trade Zone, Binhai National Independent Innovation Demonstration Zone, Beijing–Tianjin–Hebei coordinated development and other related. Furthermore, there are "six levels" talents attraction, training and reward policies, science and technology development policies for the promotion of small and medium–sized enterprises, as well as the transformation and upgrading of enterprises in Tianjin, private economy and other supporting policies.

Since its establishment, the total investment in UDA has reached about 140 billion yuan, including over 8 billion U.S. dollars. 2100 existing enterprises come from 50 different countries and regions. Among them, there are 34 companies belong to top 500 in the world including Emerson, Amazon, Delphi, Suez, Carrefour, Faurecia, East Japan Cotton, Sumitomo, Korea LG, Maple Tree Singapore, Australia Wally Parsons, China's COFCO, China Communications,

China Power Investment. Other foreign leading companies include Bestseller, Danfoss, LM Power, Grundfos, Germany GEA, WAGO, Harkness Screens, Sweden Dynapac, Begg, Finland Bollard, Spain Gesamp, Harmon, Kuhn, Molycorp, Rich' s, Odelo, Coficab, ILJIN and so on, the domestic key companies include Tiens Group, Chasesun Pharmaceutical, Novogene, Xinyi Glass, Wahaha drinks, Yili, Aux, Chang Union and so on.

Three existing leading industries are high–end manufacturing, biomedicine and headquarters economy. High–end manufacturing mainly focuses on intelligent manufacturing, rail transportation, automobiles and parts, and electronic information. Biomedicine focuses on genetic analysis, Chinese medicine particles, medical devices and diagnostic reagents. The headquarters economy is based on headquarters settlement, financial services, transfer of research and developing, culture and innovation.

UDA is the window of opening up in Wuqing District. It leads the innovation and transformation, supports the local development. Since the establishment, UDA has reached the total GDP of 249.1 billion Yuan, the total tax revenue of 76.3 billion Yuan, and has provided 120 thousand direct jobs.

UDA is aiming to make itself to be the portal of coordinated development, and ecological, science and technological park, and focus on improving the quality and efficiency of development. The key is to develop the following 3 functional areas,

1. Sino–European Industrial Park

Co–builded with the Investment Promotion Agency of Ministry of Commerce, the Park is 9.5 sq.km. It is the platform for European enterprises of High–end products. The main industries focus on high–end manufacturing, biomedicine and new materials. At present, the tailor–made European enterprises with total area of 50,000 sq. meters has been put into use, we are planning and constructing the second phase of energy–saving workshops and living facilities area.

2. Startup Headquarter Base

With the planning area of 1.26 sq.km, the base includes six parts, with the construction area of 1.2 million sq.m. The main focus are financial services, research and development transformation, cultural and creative and other modern services, which can promote the functional environment of UDA, and industrial restructuring and upgrading.

3. Beijing&Tianjin University (Wuqing) Technology Innovation Park

The Park has the area of 161 MU with the construction area of 115 thousand sq.m, the development orientation is based on strengthening cooperation with Beijing, Tianjin universities, research institutes and universities, build research and development platform for high-tech projects, high-end industry incubator, traditional industry upgrade boost, national major research innovation for transformation and talents gathering platform.

Development History

Wuqing High-tech Area is the first national-level development Area under the jurisdiction of the county in China. The process of setting up is the result of opportunity seizing, constant innovating, hardworking and forge ahead under the national policy of deepening the reform and opening up.

Hard Start 1, the decision

Wuqing is located in the heart of Beijing-Tianjin-Hebei, and between Beijing-Tianjin corridor. The superior location benefits Wuqing many advantages of potentialities for social, economic and cultural development. As early as the begin of 1990, with the implementation of the reform and opening-up and the household contract responsibility system in rural areas, Wuqing was mainly engaged in the agricultural industry, the cultivated area accounts for one quarter of the total agricultural area in Tianjin, and the grain yield accounts for one-third of the total yield in Tianjin. Therefore Wuqing was also known as "Granary" of Tianjin, and titled as "National Agricultural Advanced County".

However, it could simply have adequate food and clothing. To realize the faster and better economy and well off, it seems still to be a dream. How to make the dream come ture, it didn' t work to rely on agriculture, enthusiastic loans applications, projects or setting up enterprises in townships.

At this point, the rise of the Shenzhen Special Economic Zone, the rapid economic development in the Pearl River Delta and the Yangtze River Delta, and even the establishment of development zones in various regions in China brought enlightenment to the Wuqing who has been struggling for developing. On 8th October 1990, Wang ChengHuai, the member of Standing Committee of Tianjin Municipal Party Committee and director of Tianjin Municipal Commission of Science and Technology, came to Wuqing to participate the activity of "National Township Enterprises Commodity Fair". He brought the news that the "Torch Plan" will approve not only a batch of provincial and municipal high–tech Technology Industrial Parks, but also a county–level high–tech area.

The decision makers realized immediately that this was a golden opportunity for the development, and decided to make effort to actively apply for the approval to set up Wuqing High–tech Area, and organized the Application Office. In the early 1991, we embarked on the journey of application.

Hard Start 2, fight for

Opportunities and challenges co–exist. The establishment of the national hi–tech area under township not only requires decisive decision–making by the leaders on a farsighted basis, but also the applicator with outstanding conditions and a decent development foundation. It is never an easy job to get the approval by the relevant state departments. However, due to the strong sense of responsibility, We firmly seized the opportunity of setting up a hi–tech industrial park by the State's "Torch Plan". On 28th December 1991, with the approval by the State Science and Technology Commission, Wuqing established the "Tianjin High–tech Industrial Park Wuqing Development Area", and became the national first county–level high–tech development area.

Hard Start 3, begin

UDA began with 3sq.km, and was located at YangCun Station exit of JingJinTang Expressway, which was just put into operation. Everything is hard in the beginning. To build a high standard high-tech Park with decent beginning requires firstly the investment. However, at that time, Wuqing's fiscal revenue was less than 100 million yuan. The investment in various infrastructure can only be solved by bank loans, public financing and out-borrowing. But soon we realize the construction standard of "five access and one flat", namely water, electricity, roads, gas, and telecommunications. After the Infrastructure construction, we launched the investment promotion immediately. Firstly, we organized the "Wuqing High-tech Zone Investment Promotion Seminar" in the Great Hall of the People in Beijing, which was attended by ambassadors and news media from all over the world, and then set up offices for investment promotion at home and abroad. We also organized the delegation consist of the main leaders of Party and government and professionals to promote the area. After years of hard work, we realized the initial investment of three years in debt, began to take shape in five years and won profit in 10 years.

Hundreds of High Lights

If the reform and opening up created a wonderful time for the Chinese people, then Wuqing, based on in their own land and UDA as a platform, also created a brilliant chapter. Throughout the nearly 20 years of development experience UDA, from 28th December 1991 being approved of establishment of the "Tianjin High-tech Industrial Park Wuqing Development Zone" by State Science and Technology Commission to 30th December 2010 being approved of the "National Economic and Technological Development Zone" by the State Council; from the starting area of 3 sq.km to 35 sq.km of phase two, three, four; from the construction of No. 1 standard factory to more than two thousand domestic and foreign well-known enterprises, all were the brilliant chapter under the leadership of the government, with intelligence and the county power.

Chapter 1, Wuqing integrated itself into the world

The establishment of UDA opened the window of Wuqing district, which has been close for a long time, it broadened the vision of local people, and helped us to approach the world. In order to attract investment, leaders from the county level to the relevant staff had to go abroad to visit the international market, promote Wuqing, make friends, negotiate the project. At the same time, based on the principle of "high quality, high standard", we strived to build solid foundation to realize "eleven access and one flat" and create "ecologically friendly, environment-friendly and service-oriented" environment, to build UDA to be a highlight in the world. UDA has attracted more than 2000 enterprises domestically and internationally, including 17 companies from the top 500 in the world, like Emerson and Ingersoll Rand from USA, East cotton and Sumitomo from Japan, LG from Korea, COFCO etc, and over 100 leading companies like Tien Group, Danfoss, CSG, Xinyi Glass, Wahaha Drinks, YiLi, Chasesun Pharmaceutical, Dynapac, Aux, Yuchai Heavy Industries, Blue Cat cartoon media and so on. These enterprises investment enabled Wuqing to be renowned all around the world, and helped Wuqing form three major industries, namely intelligent manufacturing, biomedicine, headquarters economy. Especially in recent years, with the coming projects in the areas of startup headquarter base, high-end manufacturing cluster, bonded logistics, financial business district, cultural industry park.

Chapter 2, 50% economic contribution with less than 2% land of Wuqing

Furthermore, the yearly total tax revenue and the general budget revenue accounted for more than half of whole Wuqing district. By 2016, the total output value of UDA has reached 244.1 billion yuan and the tax revenue has reached 76.3 billion yuan, which is also regarded as most important area in Wuqing district.

Chapter 3, set up the platform for employment.

The low employment rate emerged recently in many cities, which impacted people' s livelihood and endanger the social stability. Thanks to UDA, Wuqing district would not face the same issue like others. Even some employees who had to leave the state-owned or collectively enterprises could find another job in time. From the beginning, UDA confirmed two main tasks, namely economic development and employment opportunities. The HR Department in UDA contacts actively with the district talent market, labor market and existing enterprises, and try various forms to build the platform to provide job chances for urban and rural labor force. Up to now, more than 120 thousand people works in UDA, which increase the income of the masses and enhance the social stability.

Chapter 4, promote the economic development of other parks in Wuqing

Wuqing is one of the districts in Tianjin with outstanding economic development, whose features is fast and effective, the booster of Wuqing economic development,also indirectly promote the development of other park. Now Jing-Jin Technology Valley, Carpet Industrial Park, Tianjin Wuqing Auto Industrial Park and Jinbin Industrial Park become the municipal demonstration park. The rapid development of above parks has benefited and learned from UDA, including the Park applications, construction, management and so on.

Chapter 5, promote the construction of the livable city

It' s the principle of the successive Wuqing government, that UDA and Wuqing Urban Area should be designed and planed, constructed and developed together in line with the construction ideas of eco-friendly, environment-friendly and modern livable cities.

The enterprises with pollution can not enter UDA, infrastructure building should be builded together with city functions, the layout considers both industries specialty and other supporting facilities including leisure , Living and cultural and entertainment, In terms of environment construction, both the production environment and the greening and beautification of urban residents are taken into consideration, which shows beautiful pictures in UDA everywhere, and the enterprises are like being in the "garden".

Chapter 6, assist Wuqing district to be in the first group of the economic development in Tianjin

In the past, Wuqing ranked embarrassed at last among different regions in Tianjin in terms of the economic development. Recently Wuqing realized the leapfrog development, except BinHai New Area Wuqing has been the Nr. 1 for several years in a row in Tianjin, and steady entered the first group of the economic development in Tianjin, which thanks to the set up and development of UDA.

Chapter 7, cradle for talents

The development requires talents, people must be forged to be a talent. During about 30 years development, UDA calculated, from the beginning of "18 pines" to current hundreds strong fighters, the Wuqing spirit and constructed a high quality working team. Furthermore, the people from us also make contributions to the development of Wuqing and even Tianjin. Some of these people embarked on the leading posts at the provincial, municipal and district / county levels, and some took the key leadership positions in towns and villages. Many people took posts in the township and town economy parks. Although they left UDA, they made new contributions to the development of Wuqing and other provinces and cities in their respective posts.

Precious Experience

After about 30 years hardworking, UDA became the windows of opening up in Wuqing, leader of industrial updating, engine of the economic development, brilliant pearl on the belt of JingJinJi coordinated development and technology new city on JingJin corridor. Why can UDA make this achievement? What is the basic experience?

Experience 1, new mechanism

UDA follows the requirements of the modern company management, and adopts itself to internationalized development in the process of construction and development. We come from the reality to build gradually a complete management mechanism. UDA has the system of two titles with one team, two titles are management committee and general corporation. The system not only reflects the authority, but also realizes the consistency of command and coordinate development. Staff contracting employment makes the working team effective and powerful. The construction bidding system not only blocks the economic loopholes, saves a lot of construction funds, but also ensures the construction quality. Closed management method, don' t allow any so called officers to enter the existing enterprises to hinder the operation, which avoid the corruption, and create a good business environment as well. These will undoubtedly lay a solid foundation for the development and construction of UDA

Experience 2, new concept

During the process of construction and development, from the initial concept of "Investors are God, God will never wrong" to "serving others is self-development" UDA can always see the benefits. From one-stop service to every specific work in detail, all reflects our sincerity. All the new enterprises or its growth in UDA are achieved with our effort.

Experience 3, take the advantages of the JingJin coordinated development

The plans of JingJin coordinated development brought a golden opportunity for UDA. Located in the Beijing–Tianjin corridor, Wuqing has the strong comprehensive advantage of development. With the gradual implementation of the coordinated development strategy of Beijing–Tianjin–Hebei region, UDA attracted a large number of well–known domestic and foreign enterprises, whose total investment reached ten billions RMB.it also leads the investment promotion of UDA to the direction of modernization, high–tech, high–end and high efficiency. As a result, the "Startup Headquarter Base" was set up, and brought new trend of development with high quality, level and efficiency. Furthermore, a large number of the scientific research departments, universities and the talents of high–end scientific and technological fields influx in UDA, providing sufficient stamina for the future development of UDA.

Experience 4, leader's attention

UDA development is connected with the attention and support of leaders from the central government, city commission, city government and concerning leading departments. The leader of the party and country, Hu JinTao, Wang GuangYing and Zhu GuangYa visited Wuqing. The former President Hu JinTao, accompanied with leaders from Tianjin and Wuqing, visited UDA, heard report and learn the history of construction, development, results and experience. President Hu Jintao spoke highly of the construction and development of UDA, and placed great hopes on the future of UDA. The successive leaders from Tianjin municipal Party committee, municipal government visited repeatedly to UDA and provided construction suggestions. The Ministry of Science and Technology, the Municipal Science and Technology Commission and other relevant departments also visited many times, and helped guide the construction and development work. In 1992, the former Vice secretory of Tianjin Municipality, Nie Bichu, personally came to Wuqing to lay the foundation stone for UDA. These undoubtedly gave us great encouragement and strength. In particular, all the successive leaders in Wuqing have always taken UDA as the top priority in the development of the entire district, and tried to solve the issues during the development in the process of planning, commanding, construction and development.

Experience 5, social support

Achievements in UDA are the result of "strength of the whole district". There are footprints of enthusiastic service of all functional departments in Wuqing, the hardworking of the existing enterprises, sweat left by military officers and soldiers participating in the construction, the support by tens of thousands of residents nearby selling land, withdrawing the village and setting up the facilities. In the history of the UDA development, everything reflects local people's great mind, and times features of forging ahead and continuously innovation.

Experience 6, self–efforts

To achieve big scale, high quality and efficiency is the result of UDA constructors' great efforts. Everyone in UDA, from the successive directors, deputy directors, general and deputy general managers, to ordinary employees, takes effort with their strong sense of responsibility. During the 6 years from the establishment to development, 18 people in UDA have won the title of "18 Pine" with spirit and outstanding working achievements. They created many stories of sacrificing, like 16 hours undisrupted meeting, someone continued to work with the sickness.

Hard work will be rewarded with golden harvest. The glory in the past has been recorded. Today we are on the way to new times, face the challenge of full scale well off to realize the great rejuvenation of China, and move toward the in–depth road of reform and opening up. Wuqing district and UDA will set foot alongside motherland, and continue to write more brilliant, wonderful new chapter!

大 事 记

大事记

1991年

12月28日　国家科委审议批准天津新技术产业园区武清开发区。新建区的区域范围为3平方公里。即南起五支，北至七支，东起京津公路，西至1500米处。

12月31日　县委常委的几位领导听取园区专题汇报（起步区规划、明年要上的配套设施、园区办机构、优惠政策、问题与打算等）。

1992年

1月17日　县长李树宏召集交通、电力、邮电、建委等部门研究园区规划建设和拆迁等问题。

1月29日　县委常委扩大会专题讨论园区的建设，听取各单位关于“五通一平”的建设规划方案。

2月13日　国家科委副主任李绪鄂到武清县视察园区工作。县长梁文忠、县委副书记王成全、常务副县长邵久武、县人大常委会副主任杨作莹等领导参加接待。

2月16日　市委常委、市科委主任王成怀，市科委副主任梁肃等市科委的一些领导在市科委听取武清县园区工作汇报。参加汇报会的有县长梁文忠，县人大常委会副主任杨作莹，县政府办公室主任王树培，县园区办公室副主任张建国、丁连喜等。

2月24日　天津冶建新技术发展中心被市园区办认定为武清开发区首个高新技术企业。

2月26日　到武清参加市人大代表视察活动的副市长李盛林，听取武清高新技术产业开发区的情况汇报后，实地视察开发区建设发展情况。

2 月 20 日至 27 日　县长梁文忠，县人大常委会副主任杨作莹及政府办、园区办一行 6 人，到广东省中山市就科技园区建设进行学习考察。

3 月 4 日　在市科委二楼会议室，市委常委、市科委主任王成怀主持召开武清园区工作研究会。梁文忠、杨作莹、王树培等县和开发区领导参加。

3 月 8 日　县长梁文忠在县政府第二会议室主持召开第三次县长办公会议，并就开发区建设的有关具体问题进行研究。

3 月 10 日　在县政府二会议室由副县长李乃彦主持召开园区征地工作协调会议。

3 月 14 日　县长梁文忠在政府第二会议室主持召开各银行行长会议。会议就开发区起步区第一期工程投资问题进行了议定。

3 月 16 日　县长梁文忠在政府二会议室主持召开开发区“五通一平”建设协调会和开发区优惠政策协调会。

3 月 26 日　市委常委、市科委主任王成怀及有关部门负责人一行 9 人到武清了解指导开发区工作。

3 月 30 日　在政府大会议室由县长梁文忠主持召开“武清开发区工作情况通报会”，各部委办、县直各单位及驻武清单位、驻武清部队的领导参加会议。

4 月 9 日晚　在县政府第二会议室召开武清开发区管委会全体成员会议。会议听取开发区总公司总经理王树培关于开发区近期工作情况、存在问题和下步工作想法的汇报。

4 月 21 日　市委常委、市科委主任王成怀带领市有关部门领导、美国星达生物公司总裁叶庄华先生，到武清开发区实地考察，并就在该区投资亿元、中美合资兴建酶制剂厂达成初步意向。

4 月 18 日　在天津新技术产业园区高技术创业服务中心，市长聂璧初主持召开市人民政府第八十七次常务会议。会议原则同意市科委提出的关于组建天津新技术产业园区管理委员会的请示、天津新技术产业园区暂行管理办法和天津新技术产业园区环境建设初步方案。

5 月 3 日　市委常委、市科委主任王成怀，在天津新技术产业园区创业中心召开天津新技术产业园区新区情况汇报会。会议汇报了武清开发区起步区的详细规划。

5 月 20 日　市长聂璧初主持会议，听取市科委、市规划局和武清县政府关于天津新技术产业园区规划、建设等问题的汇报。会议要求适时举行新技术产业园区招商信息发布会，扩大宣传、公开招商。

6月23日　国家级新技术产业园区——天津新技术产业园区授牌及天津新技术产业园区武清开发区奠基仪式，在武清开发区举行。市领导聂璧初、王成怀、张好生，国家科委副主任李效时，秘书长宋必信及国家、市等有关部门的领导出席授牌及奠基仪式。

8月7日　武清县人民政府在北京人民大会堂召开“天津新技术产业园区武清开发区及天津市武清经济开发区新闻发布会”。县长梁文忠，县人大常委会主任刘金铎，县政协主席程振江，县委副书记王成全，县委常委、宣传部部长何俊田，县人大常委会副主任杨作莹，县长助理王树培及开发区管委会的全体成员参加。会议邀请新华社主任李继成及中央人民广播电台、中央电视台、《人民日报》等二十余家新闻单位的记者30余人。会上，县长梁文忠就武清的投资环境作简要介绍，县长助理、开发区管委会副主任王树培作了两区情况的说明。与会记者对武清开发区的投资环境表示极大关注。

9月18日　县政府、开发区管委会、县委统战部邀请天津市各民主党派及社会团体负责人到武清县视察指导工作，市政协副主席肖元、赵今生出席并讲话。

10月8日　美籍华人江源先生第一次到武清考察建立科学园区有关环境等方面的事宜。市委常委、科委主任王成怀，副主任梁肃，县政府王树培等领导参加接待。

10月13日　日本冲绳县“福州—北京3000公里踏查团”一行80人到武清访问。

12月4日至8日　应天津市市长聂璧初的邀请，美国开放系统控制公司董事长拉森博士和原台湾新竹科学管理局局长、台湾著名实业家何宜慈博士访问天津。其间，参观了武清新技术产业园区和武清逸仙科技工业园。

1993年

2月8日　总公司办公地点从县政府院内迁至开发区内京津公路东侧曹园村租楼办公。

3月4日　总公司在北京保利大厦设立驻京招商处。

3月12日　开发区内水厂临时供电。

4月5日　标准厂房主体竣工。4月8日在开发区举行验收仪式。

4月7日　市规划局局长赵友华率队到武清县就开发区土地出让有关事宜进行现场

办公。武清县领导徐景树、邵久武、王树培及有关部门负责人参加。

4月16日 台湾杰麦乐器集团公司在武清经济开发区举行兴工动工仪式。副市长陆焕生、市农委主任朱连康、王武敬及杰麦集团总裁谢武弘等出席。

4月18日 天津大学开元制药公司在武清新技术园区举行奠基仪式。

5月23日 印尼客商张志华先生和新加坡客商李福才先生到开发区考察生活区。并就100亩别墅区开发达成意向，签署了土地预留协议。

5月26日 总公司与北京地雅公司就中心区912.5亩土地（含水面495亩）成片开发事宜达成一致意见，草签了土地预留意向书。

5月26日 总公司与北京华成科协开发公司草签了2万平方米标准厂房的出售协议。

7月9日 武清开发区招商座谈会在雍阳宾馆召开。市计委、外经贸委、外国投资服务中心、台办、侨办、台联、侨联及市园区的主要领导20余人应邀参加。

7月20日 杰麦富工艺有限公司土地使用权出让签字仪式在武清开发区总公司举行。

8月4日 武清开发区第二栋标准厂房开标会在总公司举行。武清县第一建筑公司中标。

8月8日 天津新技术产业园区武清开发区又一家高新技术企业——天津市宏瑞机械电子公司举行开业典礼仪式。

8月14日 武清开发区电力规划初步方案论证会在雍阳宾馆召开。经过讨论和充分论证，确定了开发区的电力规划方案。

8月14日至15日 武清开发区"首都新闻记者俱乐部"成员一行10人，到武清开发区进行了为期两天的专题采访。

8月22日 全国人大常委会委员、国家科委原副主任李绪鄂到武清开发区考察指导工作。

9月8日 北京地雅开发公司在天津新技术产业园区武清开发区举行中心区开发奠基典礼。

9月9日 台湾室内设计装饰商业同业公会、全国联合会成员一行24人，到武清开发区考察投资环境。

9月11日 中国中小企业国际合作协会和韩国振兴公团组织的中小企业投资调查团一行20人，专程到武清开发区考察投资环境。

10月2日 中共天津市委书记高德占在市委秘书长郑质英陪同下视察武清开发区。

10月8日 全国民盟主席陶大镛，北京市民盟、天津市民盟的主要领导一行6人，专程到武清开发区考察投资办学条件。

10月19日 台湾高雄市社会行为研究投资考察团一行20余人，到武清开发区考察。

10月22日 在京的部分政协委员参观团80余人，在天津市政协副主席黄炎智、陆焕生及县主要领导陪同下参观武清开发区。

10月25日 台湾中国发展基金管理公司广树诚先生一行6人到武清开发区，进行为期两天的投资考察和高科技园区规划发展论证活动。

11月24日 老挝国家总理府副部长、省、司局级官员及驻华大使、参赞等20余人到武清开发区参观考察。县委书记、开发区管委会主任梁文忠，副县长、管委会副主任王树培会见了考察团。

12月9日 武清开发区一号地热井进行试井调试，次日正常供水、供热。每小时出水量达80至100立方米，水温达74℃。

12月16日 参加第二届友谊之夜中外人士新年联欢晚会的中外朋友，应邀由北京来开发区参观考察。随同前来的有：国家广电部副部长刘习良，国际台台长张振华，副台长魏建群，中央人民广播电台副台长王建儒，广播艺术团团长，老艺术家谢添、赵子岳、陈强、谢芳夫妇，及外国专家、外国驻京商会等要员共110余人。

1994年

1月3日 总公司一号供热站通过验收，向区内企业鸿发电子有限公司供热。该供热站由三台4吨锅炉组成，蒸发量达12吨/每小时，可满足7万平方米范围的取暖需求。

1月14日 武清开发区35千伏变电站启动前期准备会在武清县农电培训中心召开。会议就武清开发区35千伏变电站启动前期的未尽事宜及准备工作做了具体安排，并决定于1994年1月31日启动试运行。

1月24日 在津全国人大代表科技教育组成员十一人到县了解武清开发区建设发展情况。

1月25日 天津市人大代表30余人视察武清开发区。

1月29日 武清开发区总公司由京津公路东侧曹园村租住的原办公地点，迁至开发区内福源道与泉州路交口北端的别墅楼内。

2月17日 武清开发区发展及控制规划经第三次县长办公会研究通过。自此，武清开发区总面积扩大为24.8平方公里，范围是：东起北运河；西至京福公路西500米平行线；北起龙凤新河；南至雍阳西道并与逸仙科学工业园和杨村镇接壤。

2月24日 市人大常委会副主任王成怀、武善谋等领导带领市人大代表40余人，就如何配合园区立法问题到武清开发区考察。

3月5日 武清开发区又一项大型基础设施工程—泉发路排水工程开工。该工程由武清县市政工程公司承建，需动土方50000立方米，铺设雨污管道1032米。

3月15日 武清开发区泉兴路、泉旺北路道路工程开标。武清县交通局、天津市南开区道路管理所、天津市公路三所、天津市政二公司四单位参加投标。武清县交通局中标。

3月30日 国家计委主任陈锦华，国家计委办公厅陆主任在天津市计委主任陈浩东，市政府副秘书长、市农委主任陈钟槐陪同下，到武清开发区视察天宝电子有限公司。

3月31日 武清开发区35千伏变电站正式启动，主变及全套配电设备经试验运转正常。

4月2日 由韩国地域局局长朴滨守率领的韩国仁川市赴津代表团一行60余人，到武清开发区参观考察。

4月14日 中国国家足球队总教练克劳斯·施拉普纳先生与他的两个儿子一起到武清开发区考察投资环境。

4月28日 台商独资企业——杰麦诗乐器有限公司举行开业庆典，民政部副部长严明复，国务院台办副主任孙晓郁，海峡两岸关系协会副秘书长刘刚奇，天津市副市长叶迪生及武清县委、县政府、县人大、县政协、纪检主要领导及有关委办局负责人参加。

5月3日 武清开发区总体规划方案研讨会在总公司二楼会议室举行。清华大学建筑学院院长赵炳时，天津大学建筑系主任荆其敏、方威孚，天津市规划设计院副院长王德俊和规划二所所长赵纯正及武清县有关部门负责人参加了论证会。

5月11日 天津市人大常委会主任聂璧初率领在津全国人大代表和市人大代表100余人视察武清开发区。

5月10日至13日 国家科委火炬办在青岛组织召开全国高科技产业园区工作研讨会。武清开发区应火炬办邀请参加。

5月25日 在总公司举行二号热力站设备安装招标会。会上铁道部第十八工程局在六家单位共同竞标中，以带资100%，提前预交保证金20万元的条件一举中标。

5月27日　由台湾投资企业协会组织的台湾工商企业访问团一行40余人，到武清开发区考察。

5月30日　由日本大真空和东棉共同投资创立的天津大真空有限公司举行开业庆典。

6月22日　中共中央政治局常委、书记处书记胡锦涛在天津市委书记高德占陪同下，到武清开发区考察。

6月25日　由新加坡佳福公司投资建设的加迪尼面包食品（天津）有限公司，在武清开发区正式签订土地使用权出让合同。

6月25日　建设部组织京津两地城市规划专家召开以“规划发展”为主题的座谈会。与会专家就武清开发区两年来的规划建设情况以及今后的发展畅谈了各自的想法和建议。

7月8日　韩国中小企业投资调查团一行20人，在团长朴英濬带领下到武清开发区参观考察。

7月18日　原日本雅马哈集团总裁董事长川上浩等一行四人就天津成立“日本工业园地”事宜对武清开发区投资环境进行考察。

7月25日　由国家科委、计委和外经贸委及其他有关部门人员组成的“京津塘高速公路高科技产业带”发展研究课题组一行13人，到武清开发区进行考察论证。

8月18日　石家庄市新技术产业园区管委会主任等三人到武清开发区参观考察。

8月18日　旅美专家郎氏蛋白糖公司董事长与武清开发区签订项目协议。

8月19日　中国民盟天津市委中青年学习研讨班在雍阳宾馆举行。听取了县委副书记李乃彦关于武清社会发展现状的介绍。副县长、开发区管委会副主任王树培详细介绍开发区的建设发展情况。并参观了武清开发区建设现场。

9月11日　由京津两市市委研究室的领导以及中科院、北京大学、人民大学等有关学者组成的京津联合会研讨会成员一行14人，到武清开发区参观考察。

9月23日　天津市政府组织的由全国在津的人大代表、政协委员、先进个人等组成的少数民族国庆参观团一行百余人参观武清开发区。

10月6日　市人大常委会主任聂璧初、鲁学政等领导以及市人大代表、市土地局有关人员百余人到武清开发区视察。

10月23日　民政部司长张文范一行30人，在常务副县长冯祥生陪同下到武清开发区考察。

11月8日 世界银行一行六人就京津塘高速公路建成后对周边经济的影响专题，到武清开发区考察。

11月15日 武清开发区总公司二号供热站供热典礼在二号供热站门前举行。至此，武清开发区起步区65万平方米的供热问题全部解决。

12月2日 原中央顾问委员会常委、北京市委第一书记段君毅，原中央顾问委员会委员、国务院秘书长杜星恒一行6人，在天津市委副秘书长王树良陪同下到开发区考察。

12月10日 天津中央电子有限公司举行开业庆典。

12月17日 由国家贸促会和韩国商工会共同组织的韩国驻京代表团20余人到武清开发区考察。

1995年

1月9日至14日 在开发区总公司二楼会议室召开"天津大真空有限公司"二期工程、天津三英焊业有限公司工程、天津力生公司工程的设计审查会。

3月4日 天津市政协副主席李长兴等到武清开发区考察指导工作。

3月24日 西藏自治区党委常委、昌都地委书记李光文率领西藏昌都地委芒康、八宿、江达、类乌、蔡雅等县委领导，在邵久武、李乃彦、夏俊田等县领导陪同下，到大真空有限公司参观。

4月11日 日本住友株式会社、住金物产株式会社和日本伊都锦株式会社，分别与武清开发区总公司签订《土地预留协议》。

4月26日 天津市副市级以上的老干部30余人，在县委书记邵久武，县长李树宏等五大机关主要领导和市政协常委徐景树的陪同下到武清开发区参观指导。

4月18日至5月5日 开发区管委会副主任、副县长王树培带领开发区总公司总经理虞东文等一行4人，赴韩、日两国招商，共接触两国工商界人士116人，达成新的投资意向10余个。

5月6日 外交部亚欧司一行50余人到武清开发区考察参观。

5月31日 天津警备区退休老干部200多人在警备区政委、政治部主任和县武装部有关人员的陪同下到武清开发区参观指导。

9月7日 天津市副市长朱连康，市农委副主任王武敬带领市各有关部门、天津十二区县的领导和开发区管委会主任一行40余人到武清县开发区参观指导。

9月19日 武清开发区第一家丹麦独资企业——HYDRO–X（天津）工业水处理有限公司举行开业仪式。丹麦王国大使及国家、市有关部门负责人200多人参加开业典礼。

10月5日 以联合国粮农组织驻华代表库瑞西为首的参加天津市农业投资环境报告会的16个国家驻华使馆官员一行70余人，在副市长朱连康和农委副主任王武敬的陪同下，到武清开发区参观考察。

10月20日至11月1日 以邵久武为代表的武清开发区招商团一行3人赴澳大利亚悉尼市、柏斯市进行为期9天的考察招商工作。

11月9日 海关总署领导到开发区考察。县委书记邵久武、县长李树宏、副县长王树培接待。

11月14日 泰国高新技术考察团在泰国工业部工业经济司司长的带领下一行8人，在国家科委国际合作司和国家科委火炬办的负责人陪同下到武清开发区参观考察。

11月27日 全国政协副主席、中国工程院院长朱光亚在市政府、市园区管委会有关负责人以及县委书记邵久武、县长李树宏、县政协主席程振江、副县长王树培等有关领导的陪同下，到武清开发区视察。朱光亚为武清开发区题词："开拓高新产业，发挥区位优势。"

12月5日 在津的全国政协委员一行20余人到开发区视察。

12月21日 武清开发区总公司在全体员工会议上宣布：成立城市管理部，撤销物业管理部，以适应开发区城市管理日益发展的需要。

12月23日 在紫薇宫康好酒店为区内企业外籍员工举办圣诞酒会。副县长、开发区管委会副主任王树培代表县政府和总公司向参加酒会的外籍员工送上良好的祝愿。

1996年

1月19日 国家贸促会原会长、中国国际贸易促进委员会特邀顾问、海峡两岸关系协会顾问、全国政协委员郑鸿业到开发区视察。

1月29日 天津市委副书记、常务副市长李盛霖到武清开发区考察并与市、县部分人大代表进行座谈。

2月3日 海关总署的有关领导在天津海关关长赵桂芬、副关长杜琨陪同下，到开发区就天津海关武清分关的工程建设问题与县领导进行协商洽谈。天津海关武清分关是海关总署根据武清开发区发展的实际需要于1995年批准在武清设立的。位于武清开发区广源道南，泉州路西，包括天津海关武清分关和国家海关总署培训基地，总占地25800平方米。

2月7日 新华社记者刘志杰，《经济日报》记者童之奇，《经济参考报》记者肖德木，《人民日报》记者王惠敏到武清开发区进行采访。

2月8日 京津两地经济联合考察团一行40余人，在天津市委常委、秘书长罗远鹏和北京市委干部欧阳文安的率领下到武清开发区考察。

2月29日 天津市委常委、副市长曲维枝，园区管委会主任宣栋生及天津市政府有关人员一行10人到武清开发区检查指导工作。

3月13日 常州市委常委、副市长李林生，副市长吴春生一行22人到开发区参观考察。

3月18日 香港力生（天津）工业发展有限公司宗明工业园在天津武清开发区举行奠基仪式。

3月21日 在武清开发区2700余米的泉旺路上，来自武清驻军某师2200名指战员到开发区植树。

3月26日 国家科委副主任徐万华一行10人，在天津科委主任梁肃的陪同下到武清开发区视察。

4月9日 武清开发区首届企业信息发布会在紫薇宫一康好酒店召开。来自武清县内的27家企业参加会议，到会达80人，其中有22家企业涉及十类产品，初步与丹佛斯公司达成合作意向。

5月9日 以捷克教育、青年及体育部副部长埃马努尔·翁德拉契克为团长的捷克访中代表团一行4人到武清开发区参观考察。

5月25日 坐落在武清开发区的韩国天津沈劳乐器有限公司举行开业典礼。

6月7日 以王树培为领队的武清招商考察团一行3人圆满结束了对丹麦、美国14天的招商考察。

6月23日 武清开发区奠基四周年。已实现入区企业192家，协议投资额30.19亿元，外资额2.7亿元，出让土地2885亩，实现税收2664万元，实现劳动就业21880人。

6月25日 以执行长王友剑为首的台湾农村发展基金会一行17人到武清开发区

考察。

7 月 10 日 参加市第九届政协十九次会议的 200 名政协委员参观开发区。市政协主席刘晋峰，副主席李长兴、黄炎智、陆焕生、陈培烈、王积涛、张昭若、陈树勋、张永根，驻津的全国政协委员及天津市 10 个区县的政协主席参加。

7 月 23 日 日本天津伊都锦有限公司举行奠基动工典礼。

7 月 30 日 天津民盟全委会主委、市政协副主席王积涛带领天津市民盟委员 70 余人到武清开发区参观。

8 月 1 日 武清开发区韩国独资企业三富电子（天津）有限公司举行开业典礼。

8 月 26 日 总公司召开全体会议，任命任瑞才、谭听二人为开发区总公司总经理助理。

8 月 28 日 坐落在武清开发区泉州路西的武清海关举行奠基典礼仪式。

9 月 5 日 坐落在泉旺路北的东炫（天津）有限公司举行开业典礼。东炫株式会社建于 1982 年，担当着韩国汽车行业发展的主导力量，主要生产汽车三滤产品。

9 月 11 日 韩国 LG 化学株式会社副会长上城在甲到武清开发区进行投资项目考察。

9 月 18 日 丹麦最大的精密机械制造集团——丹佛斯集团世界各地的高层管理人员，在武清开发区丹佛斯（天津）有限公司举行为期四天的采购工作会议。

9 月 19 日 以全国政协委员、贵州省政协主席龙志毅为团长的全国政协委员考察团一行 30 余人，到武清开发区视察参观。

10 月 18 日 经县长办公会议批准，武清开发区成立劳动就业部。

10 月 28 日 首家开业的德资企业百兴畜产品天津有限公司举行开业典礼。

10 月 30 日 河北省 25 个开发区的 50 余名负责人在省对外开放办副主任吕力的带领下到武清开发区参观学习。

11 月 8 日 天津华住金属制品有限公司举行开业典礼。

11 月 20 日 陕西省政府办公厅秘书长带领陕西省考察团到开发区考察学习。

11 月 21 日 天津市人大常委会主任聂璧初、市人大常委会副主任王成怀及市有关部门领导，到武清开发区视察。

11 月 22 日 以冯祥生为团长的武清招商考察团一行完成对韩国及国内城市大连、烟台、威海的访问。

11 月 28 日 开发区企业可乐马天津有限公司举行开业典礼。

12 月 2 日 开发区正式成立供水公司、热力公司、物业公司。

12月10日 市人大武清代表团一行30余人在主任王德成的带领下，到开发区参观考察。

1997年

1月10日 市政协常委徐景树与开发区总公司总经理虞东文一行4人赴日本进行为期10天的考察。

2月18日 日本食品流通研究会成员一行十余人在国内贸易部秘书长孙玉环的带领下到开发区考察。

3月6日 被誉为我国大型方便面生产基地之一的珠海华丰工业（集团）股份有限公司，在武清开发区就其投资建设的俄罗斯食品饮料项目举行《国有土地使用权出让合同》签字仪式。

3月9日 国务院台办副主任李炳才、海峡两岸关系协会秘书长张金成、国务院台办经济局副局长何七忠等人，在市台办主任曲耕莘的陪同下到武清开发区参观。

3月11日 新疆维吾尔自治区副主席一行10人到武清开发区参观考察。

3月12日 肯达工贸（集团）公司与开发区总公司举行了《土地预留协议》签字仪式，将在武清开发区投资8000万元，兴建食品饮料项目。

4月16日 俄罗斯国防部长夫人在中国国防部部长迟浩田夫人姜青萍女士的陪同下到开发区参观。

6月23日 “庆祝武清开发区奠基五周年大会”在县体育馆举行。市人大常委会副主任王成怀，国家科委火炬办副主任刘振堂，国家科委、市有关部门负责人，京津两地新闻单位和驻京使馆、商会有关人员及全县有关部门1500余人参加会议。

10月18日 武清开发区管委会大楼破土动工。该大楼占地14108.5平方米，建筑面积6400平方米，预计投资1500万元。

10月23日 日本独资企业——天津伊都锦时装有限公司举行开业仪式。

10月23日 芬兰独资企业瑞特格散热器（天津）有限公司成立，《国有土地使用权出让合同》签字仪式在天津喜来登天津厅举行。副市长叶迪生出席签字仪式并接待瑞特格散热器集团公司执行总裁芬·博格先生。

10月30日 市政府秘书长张惯文带领市政府办公厅以及天津市人民政府政策研究

室7名领导到开发区内调研。

11月11日 中央党校全国人大常委会机关培训班一行15人到开发区考察。

11月11日 瑞士驻中国大使希克到开发区考察。

12月28日 中华人民共和国武清海关举行开关庆典，正式对外办理业务。副市长朱连康、海关总署副署长黄汝凤，武清县委书记李乃彦，天津海关关长赵桂芬出席并讲话。

1998年

1月6日 由开发区总公司牵头，市公用局、县建委、县规划土地局、县自来水公司等单位就筹建武清县引滦水处理厂事宜进行研究、磋商。

3月15日 副市长夏宝龙在县委书记、开发区管委会主任李乃彦，县委副书记、县长、开发区管委会副主任王树培，县委常委、常务副县长袁桐利等陪同下到开发区视察。

4月9日 天津市外经贸委主任王述祖率市外经贸委各处处长一行10余人到开发区内光宝电子（天津）有限公司、天宝光碟有限公司调研。听取了企业负责人的情况汇报。

4月14日 中科集团总裁张云岗、执行董事刘作鉴一行4人到武清开发区考察。

4月24日 丹麦经济与发展合作部部长保罗·尼尔森、丹麦驻华大使白慕申一行20余人到开发区考察。

5月8日 中共中央台湾工作办公室副主任、国务院台湾事务办公室副主任、海峡两岸关系协会常务副会长唐树备到开发区台资企业光宝电子（天津）有限公司考察。

5月26日 波兰军队总长夫人维·舒姆斯卡到武清开发区参观访问。

6月16日 由台湾光宝集团独资兴建的光宝电子（天津）有限公司举行新厂落成暨投产仪式。市委书记张立昌、市长李盛霖在典礼前后分别会见光宝集团董事长宋恭源一行，对光宝电子（天津）有限公司新厂落成和投产表示祝贺。国务院台湾事务办公室副主任李炳才，信息产业部副部长曲维枝，副市长王述祖，县委书记李乃彦、县长王树培参加庆典仪式。

6月23日 德资企业万可电子（天津）有限公司举行开业仪式。副市长王述祖及市县有关领导参加。

7月14日 天津市委副书记、市政协主席房凤友，市政协原主席刘晋峰，市委常委、组织部部长邢军到武清开发区视察。

7 月 17 日 全国人大常委会副委员长王光英在市委副书记、市政协主席房凤友的陪同下到武清开发区视察。

9 月 19 日 市长李盛霖在市政府秘书长陈洪江、县长王树培陪同下到天狮集团调研。

10 月 9 日 天津市政协港澳台侨委员会参观考察团一行 12 人在市政协副主席蔡世彦带领下，到开发区视察。

10 月 20 日 美国独资企业麦格昆磁国际有限公司与武清县规划土地管理局在县雍阳宾馆举行《国有土地使用权出让合同》签字仪式。

12 月 28 日 武清开发区建区七周年联谊会在开发区总公司新址举行。全国人大常委会文教卫委副主任李绪鄂、天津市科委原主任王成怀、国家科委火炬中心原主任王瑞明出席联谊会并分别讲话。

1999 年

2 月 4 日 参加市政协十届二次会议的港澳委员到武清开发区大真空公司和西湖橡塑公司视察。

5 月 20 日 武清县举办第四届高新技术项目转让、难题招标及人才招聘洽谈会。清华大学、中科院等 46 家大专院校、科研单位的 137 位专家和科研人员参加。

7 月 1 日 卧龙潭净水中心举行落成通水仪式。晚上，天津市市长李盛霖到净水中心察看供水设施，并和工作人员交谈。

8 月 31 日 人事部部长宋德福在中共天津市委副书记、市政协主席房凤友、副市长孙海麟、中共武清县委书记李乃彦、县长王树培陪同下到开发区视察。

11 月 12 日 波黑共和国驻中国大使斯维蒂拉夫、巴尼亚卢卡市市长乔治 . 乌米切维奇一行 4 人，到武清县开发区参观。

11 月 20 日 天津市市长李盛霖、副市长孙海麟到武清县调研。

11 月 28 日 中共中央政治局常委、中央纪委书记、全国总工会主席尉健行和全国总工会副主席、书记处第一书记张俊九，在市有关领导的等陪同下，到武清县开发区考察。

2000年

4月13日 内蒙古自治区政府主席云布龙，副主席傅守正、郝益东率领内蒙古自治区考察团一行53人，在市领导杨新成、孙海麟、陈洪江等陪同下参观武清开发区。

4月28日 由市人大常委会副主任潘义清、张毓环率领的天津市人大考察团一行32人，视察武清开发区。

5月9日 丹麦丹佛斯公司董事会议首次在丹佛斯（天津）有限公司举行。县长王树培会见丹麦丹佛斯公司总裁雍根·克劳斯先生及其他董事会成员。

6月15日 开发区区内企业斯维达拉工业（中国）有限公司举行动工奠基典礼。

6月23日 “腾飞新世纪——庆祝武清开发区奠基八周年各界人士联谊会”在武清开发区管委会举行。科技部、市农委、市纪检委、市园区、县五大机关、县直各部门的有关领导和负责人以及开发区的招商关系单位、新闻单位、区内企业代表300余人参加。

8月28日 由武清开发区投资创办的以民营方式运作的天津英华学校（小学部）举行开学典礼仪式。

9月10日 以全国人大常委会委员顾金池为团长的全国人大刑诉法检查团一行20余人到开发区参观视察。

10月18日 “中国天津武清开发区之窗”—www.tjuda.com改版开通。开发区之窗包括“开发区概览”“投资指南”“管理服务”等背景资料以及“新闻”“公告”“配套信息”“统计公报”等动态信息栏目。

12月5日 全国及天津市部分政协委员到开发区视察。

12月15日 武清海关保税工厂批准颁证仪式在武清开发区总公司举行。沈劳乐器有限公司、麦格昆磁有限公司、西湖橡塑有限公司三家企业被批准为保税工厂。

2001年

2月28日 “创建全国科普示范区工作检查验收小组”一行13人到开发区参观考察。

3月13日 天津中天高科特种车辆有限公司投资协议签订仪式在武清开发区总公司举行。

4月10日 “创建全国科普示范区”中国科协暨华北组检查团一行15人到开发区

参观考察。

4月26日 “天津武清难题招标人才引进洽谈会第六届年会”在武清开发区举行。副市长孙海麟、市农业办公室主任崔士光等，李乃彦、王树培等区领导以及来自国内各大专院校、科研单位的专家教授、科研人员和大公司、大企业的负责人共500多人出席。

5月12日 “大红鹰全民健身万里行申奥大签名”活动在武清开发区举行。

5月18日 区内企业环球（天津）药业有限公司举行奠基仪式。副市长俞海潮出席。

6月8日 吉通网络通信天津有限公司宽带网接入武清开发区签约仪式在武清开发区总公司举行。

6月14日 在本市第五届外商投资企业“服务月”活动期间，主管外经外贸副市长王述祖带领市外经贸委、经委、国税局、工商局、海关、外汇管理局、电子仪表局和市园区的有关领导，到武清开发区参观考察。

7月13日 市人大执法检查团一行50余人在市人大常委会副主任罗远鹏的带领下，到武清开发区检查《天津新技术产业园区管理条例》执行情况。

7月13日 由中国五金交电化工公司和中商国际旅行社共同投资5000万元举办的“中商津通科技发展有限公司”在武清开发区落户。

9月 开发区厦门办事处设立并展开工作。至此，开发区驻外招商办事机构已有天津、北京、上海、广州和厦门5个。

10月2日 全国政协副主席宋健一行在市政协主席、市委副书记房凤友等领导的陪同下，到开发区视察。

10月 英华中学选址在雍阳西道与泉兴路交口处。

11月7日 市公安局六处四科、武清分局主管户籍工作的领导在开发区派出所的协助下，召开部分区内企业负责人座谈会并现场办公，当场为麦格昆磁、华美等公司办理蓝印户口41例。

12月28日至29日 在天鹅湖度假村多功能厅召开中国天津武清开发区建区十周年招待会，科技部领导、市领导、市有关部门领导、区委常委扩大会领导、区级离退休老干部、区直各有关部门、有关街道、京津乡友会成员和区内企业、招商业务单位、新闻单位，计300余人参加。

2002 年

3 月 天津中天高科特种车辆增资 1.45 亿元人民币。

4 月 11 日 投资 700 万美元的瑞典 LM 公司举行开业庆典。

4 月 16 日 芬兰瑞特格公司新厂奠基。

5 月 7 日 市老同志聂璧初、吴振、刘晋峰、张再旺在市委副书记、市政协主席房凤友陪同下到开发区调研。

5 月 31 日 丹麦工业联合会、北欧联合会、北欧航空公司和丹麦驻中国大使馆共同组织丹麦广播公司等 6 家丹麦新闻单位记者一行 16 人，到武清开发区参观访问。

6 月 11 日 市委书记张立昌、副市长孙海麟、市委秘书长王文华到开发区视察。

6 月 21 日 重庆市委副书记和沙坪坝区区委副书记一行 5 人到武清开发区考察。

6 月 22 日 副市长孙海麟及各区县的区长、县长到武清开发区考察并参观麦格昆磁公司。

6 月 30 日 天津新技术产业园区一行 80 余人到武清开发区参观考察。

7 月 2 日 在武清开发区总公司举行南玻集团《国有土地使用权出让合同》签字仪式。

7 月 9 日 市政协副主席张永根率市政协医卫文体委员会部分委员一行 25 人，到武清开发区调研。

7 月 15 日 沈阳市一行 8 人到武清开发区考察。

10 月 8 日 全国人大常委会副委员长司马义 · 艾买提到武清开发区视察。副市长夏宝龙，区领导李乃彦、王树培陪同。

11 月 12 日 副市长孙海麟在市农委有关负责人陪同下到武清开发区调研。

2003 年

1 月 15 日 市委副书记、市长戴相龙，市委常委、常务副市长夏宝龙，副市长孙海麟，市政府秘书长何荣林等市领导，到武清开发区调研。

1 月 16 日 天津武清开发区企业协会第一届会员大会在天鹅湖度假村国际会议中心召开。

2 月 28 日 农行开发区支行隆重举行成立揭牌仪式。

3 月 11 日 开发区 “外商之家” 在紫薇宫挂牌成立 。

3月17日 瑞一(天津)科技发展有限公司在二期新区举行奠基仪式。

6月23日 纪念武清开发区奠基十一周年茶话会在开发区总公司举行。

7月28日 区政府举行仪式，向为武清发展做出贡献的外资企业负责人颁发荣誉市民证书。绫致时装公司董事长王沛德、丹佛斯(天津)有限公司总裁克劳斯·托尼森、LG新型建材公司总经理朴炫信成为开发区首批获此殊荣的外资企业负责人。

8月30日 国家五部委督查组及市国土资源局、市监察局、市审计局等一行18人到武清开发区检查工作。

10月10日 在津全国人大代表11人到武清开发区考察。

10月12日 参加第十四届乡友联谊会的在京武清籍乡友来到开发区访问。

10月16至17日 贵州省在津挂职干部一行15人到武清参观考察。

11月28日 市部分人大代表一行30余人到开发区参观英华中学、天津完达山乳品有限公司、天津南玻工程玻璃有限公司。

2004年

1月5日 天津市委、市政府领导带领市有关部门负责人到武清检查指导工作。

2月17日 副市长孙海麟一行到开发区南玻集团、完达山乳品有限公司、中天特车三家企业考察。

3月22日 在武清开发区总公司会议厅召开A类企业颁证仪式暨企业分类调整情况通报会。武清A类企业达到10家，其中A升AA1家，B升A9家。

4月9日 市级老领导及随行80余人考察中天高科特种车辆有限公司和天津英华国际学校。

5月18日 丘比克(天津)转印有限公司举行开业庆典。

5月21日 瑞一（中国）科技发展有限公司举行开业仪式。

6月15日 丹麦丹佛斯有限公司董事会及丹佛斯家族全体成员汇聚到武清开发区，主持丹佛斯中国四期新工厂奠基仪式及三期新厂房开业典礼。来自世界各地的丹佛斯的合作伙伴、中国前驻丹麦大使夫妇、丹麦驻中国大使馆经济参赞、天津市人大常委会副主任王德惠、天津市政协副主席王家瑜及武清区委、区政府领导共计350余人参加。

10月23日 团中央书记处第一书记周强一行在团市委有关领导陪同下到武清开发

区，与区委、区政府、团区委和开发区总公司的领导进行了座谈交流。

11 月 9 日至 11 日　全国民营企业文化建设工作会议在天鹅湖度假村召开，全国政协副主席、全国工商联主席黄孟复，全国工商联副主席程路、天津市人大常委会副主任张元龙、副市长崔津渡出席并讲话。

11 月 30 日　武清选区的市人大代表 40 余人到艾尔姆玻璃纤维制品（天津）有限公司视察。

12 月 6 日　天津市城市总体规划纲要评审组一行 30 余人到武清开发区进行考察。

2005 年

3 月 30 日　国家档案局局长毛福民及有关负责人，市档案局、有关区县和部分机关、企、事业单位档案工作负责人一行 30 余人参观武清开发区中天特车有限公司、英华国际学校，并到开发区总公司进行了座谈。

4 月　武清开发区取得 ISO 9001：2000 质量管理体系和 ISO 14001：1996 环境管理体系证书 。

5 月 12 日　中央督导组一行在市委常委、组织部部长史莲喜陪同下检查武清区保持党员先进性教育活动开展情况。

6 月 11 日　华一集团威斯克（天津）精密五金有限公司在武清开发区奠基。

6 月 25 日　丹麦独资丹佛斯（中国）有限公司举行第四期新工厂投产和第五期厂房奠基仪式。丹麦王国副首相本特森先生及丹麦王国驻华大使米磊先生，副市长陈质枫，区委书记王树培，副区长苗玉刚，丹佛斯公司总裁柯劳森及相关负责人参加仪式。

8 月 3 日　天狮天津国际健康产业园奠基仪式在武清开发区举行。

8 月 30 日　河北省霸州市委书记辛绍杰、市长杨杰一行 50 余人到武清开发区进行考察。

9 月 12 日　奥帕汽车配件（天津）有限公司在武清开发区举行奠基仪式。

11 月 18 日　武清开发区总公司举行栖仙温泉公寓西区高层住宅楼主体封顶仪式。

11 月 26 日　中央纪委、中央组织部巡视组领导和市委办公厅有关负责人一行 8 人到武清开发区考察。

12 月 16 日　在开发区总公司举行蜡笔小新（中国）产业基地和休闲食品项目落户

武清开发区签字仪式。

2006 年

2 月 22 日 武清开发区高新公寓正式开工建设。高新公寓是专门服务于开发区企业外来务工人员的配套生活服务设施，坐落于开发区二期内。高新公寓占地 110 亩，总建筑面积 8 万多平方米，包括宿舍楼 13 栋共 7 万平方米，公建楼 3 栋共 1.2 万平方米，整个工程预计投资 1 亿元。该公寓宿舍楼包括男、女单身宿舍和夫妻宿舍三种房型，共 1997 套住房，可容纳近 7500 人住宿。公建配套设施有食堂、超市、公共浴池、图书阅览室、文化活动室、诊所等，可提供餐饮、文化娱乐、医疗等基本生活服务。

3 月 21 日 印度 EKC 工业公司与武清开发区正式签订入区建设协议。这是武清开发区建区以来引入的首家印度企业。

3 月 31 日 天津市副市长孙海麟陪同中信（香港）投资公司、美国投资基金公司有关负责人一行 7 人，到武清开发区考察。

4 月 20 日 欧利生涂料（天津）有限公司举行开业庆典。

5 月 28 日 天津市市长戴相龙在武清开发区管委会会见中国粮油食品进出口（集团）有限公司董事长宁高宁一行。

5 月 29 日 中粮包装（天津）有限公司在武清开发区举行奠基仪式。

6 月 8 日 丹佛斯（天津）有限公司举行成立十周年庆典活动。丹麦王国二王子约阿希姆、丹佛斯企业创始人的妻子碧藤夫人、丹麦王国驻华大使麦克森、天津市人大常委会副主任陈洪江及武清区有关领导出席。

9 月 19 日 内蒙古武清籍支边老同志回乡探访团一行 30 余人，到武清开发区参观访问。

10 月 19 日 中国国民党中央常委连胜文率领台湾青年企业家代表团一行 10 人到武清开发区进行考察。

10 月 20 日 金红叶纸业（天津）有限公司举行开业庆典。

10 月 20 日 由武清开发区总公司、天狮集团协办的 2006“天狮国际”杯中国国家女排与波兰国家女排对抗赛在武清区体育馆举行。

11 月 3 日 万可电子（天津）有限公司举行新厂房落成庆典仪式。

11月8日 天狮国际健康产业园正式动工建设。

11月16日 欧瑞康巴尔查斯涂层（苏州）有限公司天津分公司举行开业庆典仪式。

12月14日 来自新华社、《人民日报》、中央电视台、《中国日报》、《香港大公报》、《天津日报》等23家新闻媒体的编辑、记者云集武清，参加为庆祝武清开发区成立15周年举办的新闻发布会。

12月15日 在天鹅湖度假村举行庆祝武清开发区成立15周年招待会，副市长只升华，市级老同志聂璧初、王成怀、梁肃，区领导王树培、袁桐利、李宝锟、李学鹏、钟书明、苗玉刚、李伯怀及市、区有关部门负责人，开发区内各企业负责人、外国投资服务机构和著名中介机构代表以及众多新闻界的朋友300余人参加。

12月28日 在武清区广播电视中心一号演播厅举行纪念武清开发区成立15周年大会。

2007年

3月12日 丘比克（天津）转印有限公司举行新增生产线投产典礼。

3月23日 市委、市政府领导到武清开发区调研。

4月6日 上海英格索兰压缩机有限公司天津客户中心举行开业庆典。

4月10日 市级老领导聂璧初、王成怀等一行8人到武清开发区考视察。

4月12日 戴纳派克（中国）压实摊铺设备有限公司举行新厂房落成庆典仪式。

4月12日 奥帕汽车配件（天津）有限公司举行开业庆典。

5月18日 泰姆玻璃（中国）有限公司举行开业典礼，芬兰共和国驻华大使郭安祺，中国硅酸盐学会会长张人为，芬兰克拉斯涛集团总裁和CEO米卡等中外嘉宾300多人出席。

5月29日 朝鲜民主主义人民共和国妇女代表团到武清开发区参观考察。

6月5日 艾默生过程管理武清园区举行开业典礼。

7月11日 天津市台湾同胞投资企业协会会长韩家宸一行来到武清开发区考察，就加强台资企业与武清合作关系同区领导进行座谈。

8月28日 “武清开发区综合商贸物流园”项目经市发改委批准备案。项目包括保税商贸物流区、普通商贸仓储区、出口加工区、商务服务区和综合办公区，建有公共型保税仓库、出口监管仓库、加工厂房、货场、商务综合楼等配套和公共设施，总建筑面积60万平方米。

9月19日 万可电子天津有限公司派代表为开发区总公司送来锦旗，感谢总公司多年来在企业发展中给予的有力保障和优质服务。

10月11日 丹麦丹佛斯公司全球总裁雍根·克劳森、丹佛斯公司中国地区总裁鲍尔森先生一行到武清开发区进行专题考察。

10月30日 中粮包装（天津）有限公司举行开业庆典。副市长只升华、中粮集团总裁于旭波及市区有关领导参加。

11月9日 信义集团董事局主席李贤义先生一行8人到武清开发区进行专题考察。

12月6日 天津市新20项重大工业项目之一的奥克斯天津高新技术产业园项目在天鹅湖度假村国际会议中心举行签约仪式。

2008年

3月5日 天津市2008年武清区重大建设项目现场推动会在开发区天狮国际生命研究中心工程现场召开。

4月21日 武清开发区泉兴公用保税仓库和出口监管仓库（以下简称“两库”）举行颁证揭牌仪式。“两库”占地120亩，建筑面积1.2万平方米，投资3000万元，是“武清无水港”建设的起步工程。“武清无水港”即 武清国际保税物流园区，占地2.61平方公里，预计投资50亿元，将用5年时间建成立足天津、服务京冀、辐射环渤海的现代化物流基地。该项目被列为2008年天津市重点建设项目。

5月8日 天津日进汽车系统有限公司举行竣工仪式。

6月21日 副市长王治平带领市有关部门负责人一行10人到武清视察重大项目建设情况。

6月29日 被列为天津市新20项重大工业项目之一的奥克斯天津高新技术产业园项目正式开工建设。该项目总投资30亿元，占地1430亩，建筑面积30万平米，主要生产新型家用空调，商用中央空调、嵌入式软件、智能马达及其他家电产品。

8月21日 市委书记张高丽，市委常委、组织部部长史莲喜率有关部门负责同志到武清开发区调研。

10月24日 户田麦格昆磁磁性材料（天津）有限公司开业仪式暨麦格昆磁（天津）

有限公司开业十周年庆典在武清开发区户田新厂区举行。区领导袁桐利、李宝锟、苗玉刚及区内相关职能部门负责人出席并表示祝贺。

10 月 30 日 财政部部长谢旭人，天津市委常委、副市长崔津渡在区领导李宝锟陪同下到武清开发区调研，参观天狮健康产业园并听取情况汇报。

12 月 2 日至 3 日 区领导袁桐利、李宝锟、钟书明、李建成分别带领有关部门开展学习实践科学发展观活动，深入开发区企业走访，同企业负责人一起探求应对金融危机、加快发展的对策和措施，为企业办实事、解难题。

12 月 17 日 中国产业发展促进会第一届理事会第四次会议在天狮集团国际会议中心召开。区领导李宝锟、李学鹏、李建成应邀出席会议。会上开发区总公司进行招商宣传。

2009 年

3 月 31 日 “绿色北欧——安徒生产业创意园”规划建设发布会在天狮国际会议中心举行。发布会吸引了来自北欧五国使馆官员和商会负责人，部分欧美企业代表、有关招商机构负责人及多家新闻单位的记者 300 余人参加。

6 月 10 日 天津出入境检验检疫局武清办事处挂牌成立。天津出入境检验检疫局武清办事处位于武清开发区源泉路，设立工业品科、动植食科、检务科、综合科 4 个科室，将全面负责武清区所辖进出口企业的检验检疫业务。

7 月 9 日 天津市委理论学习中心组读书会暨“保增长、渡难关、上水平”活动现场交流推动会，到武清中华自行车王国、三宇车体制造、中国艺术家聚集区等项目进行现场交流考察。市领导张高丽、刘胜玉参加。

7 月 2 日 天津赛诺制药有限公司在武清开发区举行奠基仪式。

7 月 10 日 伊利集团董事长兼总裁潘刚一行到武清参观考察。

7 月 30 日 武清区人民政府与中国水利水电建设集团公司、天津亿卓投资有限公司武清新区开发项目投资合作签约仪式在武清开发区总公司举行。

8 月 6 日 天津滨海高新技术产业开发区管委会副主任余学林等一行到武清开发区考察。

8 月 18 日 市政协副主席、市委统战部部长刘长喜一行到武清开发区部分企业进行专题调研。

9月7日 湖南株洲高新技术产业开发区管委会副主任马立恒一行，到武清开发区就健康产业及直销企业发展进行参观考察。

9月8日 大港石化产业园区管委会主任徐延琥一行到武清开发区参观考察。

10月16日 贝科斯高性能涂料（天津）有限公司举行开业典礼仪式。

10月25日 北京住总集团举行武清开区软件创意园专家公寓项目奠基仪式。专家公寓组团北临广源道，东邻天鹅湖度假村，西、南为景观湖水系，占地293.7亩，建筑总面积27.6万平方米。将建成集独栋、联排公寓、情景洋房等为一体的复合型低密度一流居住社区。

10月27日 天津康尔克生物科技有限公司举行开业庆典。

10月30日 天津红日药业股份有限公司在深交所创业板挂牌上市，是上市28家企业中唯一一家天津企业。

11月2日 软件创意园湖心岛和五星级酒店项目投资协议签订。该项目由广东玉圭园房地产有限公司投资，占地200亩，投资总额5亿元。

11月2日 主题公园项目投资协议签订，该项目位于104国道西侧、京津城际铁路北侧、雍阳西道南侧，占地654亩，投资总额30亿元，主要发展游乐及住宅、商业项目。

11月3日 伊利酸奶、奶酪华北生产基地项目投资协议签约仪式在开发区总公司举行。

2010年

1月10日 武清开发区总公司和广东玉圭园集团举行现代服务业项目投资协议签约仪式。

2月23日 市政协副主席张大宁带队到武清开发区总公司就落实市政府“解难题、促转变、上水平”精神对天狮集团调研。

2月28日 武清区土地整理中心与海南兰海集团投资控股有限公司，在武清开发区总公司举行泉州新城土地一级整理项目投资协议签约仪式。

3月10日 副市长任学锋带领市相关部门负责人到光宝电子（天津）有限公司等武清台资企业调研。

3月12日 市委、市政府主要领导带领市发改委、市规划局等单位负责人到武清就解难题活动开展情况进行调研。

3月25日 市委常委、市委教育工委书记苟立军，副市长李文喜带领市农委及有关部门负责人一行到武清调研。

4月8日 丹佛斯制冷设备（天津）有限公司在开发区举行开业庆典。丹麦驻华大使叶普，市政协副主席陈质枫，市级老同志王德惠、曹秀荣，区委书记袁桐利，区长李宝锟等出席。

4月22日 国务院侨务办公室副主任许又声一行在市侨办主任哈文龙陪同下到武清参观考察并走访天狮国际健康产业园。

4月27日 以全国政协委员、香港中国商会主席兼会长、经纬集团主席陈经纬为团长的香港中国商会代表团到武清考察，并参观开发区。

5月14日 如乐（天津）钢结构部件有限公司举行开业典礼。

5月26日 台湾科学工业园区同业公会理事长谢其嘉先生一行到武清进行商业考察洽谈并参观开发区。

6月3日 市委书记张高丽到武清考察，并考察了京津总部基地、麦格昆磁（天津）有限公司、东蒲洼还迁小区施工现场。

6月9日 开发区总公司与湖南蓝猫卡通传媒有限公司、深圳市陶君实业有限公司在天鹅湖度假村举行天津武清蓝猫动漫科技园项目投资协议签约仪式。

6月13日 武清开发区总公司与中国华电集团公司在天鹅湖度假村举行天津华电武清燃气分布式能源站项目、华电水务武清污水处理厂项目合作协议签约仪式。

6月29日 海南省委副书记、省长罗保铭带领省政府代表团一行60余人，在副市长任学锋、市政府秘书长李泉山的陪同下到武清考察。

7月9日 武清开发区创业总部基地招商推介会在天鹅湖度假村举行。

7月15日 天津市区县示范工业园区暨区县重大项目建设现场推动会在武清召开，市委常委、市委教育工委书记苟利军，副市长李文喜到武清开发区考察。

7月19日 天津市津能双鹤热力设备有限公司举行扩建奠基仪式。

7月22日 副市长只升华一行到武清调研，先后察看了开发区三期、创业总部基地、天狮国际健康产业园等项目。

7月22日 武清开发区总公司与中粮包装（天津）有限公司就新包装线项目举行签约仪式。

7月24日 中组部干部监督局巡视员、部巡视工作联络办公室主任王金兰一行到武清考察，现场察看了创业总部基地、高端制造业聚集区等项目。

7月31日 市级老同志吴振、石坚、孙海麟等到武清调研，先后考察了创业总部基地、开发区西区、天狮国际健康产业园等项目。

8月2日 市委市政府领导到武清调研，察看了开发区三期、创业总部基地、天狮国际健康产业园等项目。

8月7日 滨海新区区长宗国英一行到武清参观考察，参观了高端制造业聚集区、天狮国际健康产业园、创业总部基地等项目。

8月25日 武清开发区总公司与广西玉柴重工有限公司，在开发区总公司举行营销结算中心、融资租赁项目签约仪式。

8月28日 武清开发区与大连机床集团在市迎宾馆举行研发制造基地项目签约仪式。市领导苟利军、李文喜，区领导袁桐利、张勇与大连机床集团董事长陈勇开一行座谈，共同出席签约仪式。

8月29日 落户武清开发区的尼波齿轮（天津）有限公司举行开业庆典。

9月25日 康业钢丝（天津）有限公司举行开业仪式。

9月27日 开发区总公司与基伊埃韦斯伐里亚分离制造（中国）有限公司就分离机制造项目举行签约仪式。

9月28日 开发区总公司与天津市建工集团控股有限公司就“北欧绿色产业园一期和招商中心项目”举行签约仪式。“北欧绿色产业园一期”项目占地320亩，建筑面积22万平方米，将建成以环保、节能为主的特色产业园区。

9月29日 “泉兴出口监管仓库入仓退税功能授牌仪式”在开发区总公司举行。

10月14日 丹佛斯制冷设备（天津）有限公司举行百福马生产线投产仪式 。

10月20日 天狮集团投资70亿元建设的天狮国际健康产业园正式开园，天狮集团总部、生产中心、研发中心、物流中心正式迁入产业园内，成为天狮集团的全球总部基地。产业园内投资2.5亿元、建筑面积2.8万平方米的泰济生国际医院同日启动试运营。

10月22日 泰坦爱迪姆机械制造（天津）有限公司举行开业典礼。

11月30日 由广西玉柴集团投资成立的玉柴重工（天津）有限公司和天津银德融资租赁有限公司举行开业典礼。

12月28日 中国武清开发区总公司与天津日进汽车系统召开联席会议。会上，开发区总公司进行了招商宣传。

12 月 30 日　国务院办公厅复函天津市人民政府、商务部，国务院同意武清经济开发区升级为国家级经济技术开发区，定名为武清经济技术开发区，实行现行国家级经济技术开发区的政策。

2011 年

1 月 21 日　开发区总公司与香港敏华实业有限公司在开发区总公司会议室举行敏华工业城项目签约仪式。区委书记袁桐利，区委常委、开发区工委书记钟书明，敏华控股有限公司董事局主席黄敏利及有关方面负责人出席仪式。该项目由香港敏华集团投资建设，位于武清开发区三期高端制造业聚集区，占地 723 亩，投资总额 3 亿美元。

2 月 18 日　副市长任学锋一行到武清就全区经济建设发展情况进行调研，区领导袁桐利、张勇、钟书明、李建成陪同。

3 月 11 日　天狮集团被商务部正式授予中华人民共和国直销经营许可证。武清区委书记袁桐利、区长张勇、区人大常委会主任刘万明、区政协主席李学鹏等武清区委常委扩大会领导向企业表示祝贺。

3 月 23 日　国能飞腾科技有限公司高性能纤维项目工程举行奠基典礼。区领导张勇、钟书明、杨中东等出席。该项目位于武清开发区高端制造业聚集区，投资 6.3 亿元，占地 225 亩，建筑面积 13 万平方米。

4 月 22 日　武清开发区总公司与中国纺织科学研究院举行中纺院高新技术园项目签约仪式，区委书记袁桐利，区委常委、开发区工委书记钟书明出席签约仪式。

4 月 26 日　武清开发区总公司与北京圣火科贸有限公司举行租赁与代理招商签约仪式。

4 月 28 日　武清开发区与北京美加投资有限公司举行“天津坝上春秋”艺术园项目签约仪式，武清区委书记袁桐利，区长张勇，区委常委、开发区工委书记钟书明，美国世纪发展集团、北京美加公司董事长于学文出席签约仪式。项目位于武清区文化产业园区内，投资总额 30 亿元人民币。

2012 年

2 月 9 日　武清开发区与中国中投证券有限责任公司举行投资合作签约仪式。

2月18日 天津新知生产力促进中心举行开业典礼。

2月19日 武清开发区总公司与信义玻璃控股有限公司就信义汽车玻璃总部项目举行签约仪式。

3月3日 天津可信科技企业孵化器有限公司在武清开发区举行开业庆典。

3月26日 亚马逊－普洛斯物流园举行开业典礼。

4月2日 中国武清开发区总公司与浙江森马服饰股份有限公司，举行森马服饰北方物流结算中心项目签约仪式。

4月8日 中国武清开发区总公司与天地融科技股份有限公司，举行天地融研发中心和生产基地项目签约仪式。

4月18日 中国武清开发区总公司与陕西同力重工股份有限公司，举行天津同力生产基地项目签约仪式。

4月18日 天马筛得力工艺设备（天津）有限公司举行奠基典礼。

4月26日 武清开发区总公司与远东宏信有限公司，举行远东宏信天津项目签约仪式。

4月27日 亿农农资有限公司举行开业庆典。

5月16日 武清开发区总公司与广州摩拉网络科技有限公司、嘉民集团三方举行梦芭莎电子商务北方仓储物流运营结算中心项目签约仪式。

6月9日 万国食品包装（天津）有限公司举行开业典礼。

6月28日 维益烘焙产品（天津）有限公司举行开业庆典。

8月1日 武清开发区总公司与保定冀中药业有限公司，举行冀中药业研发中心和生产基地项目签约仪式。

9月27日 中国武清开发区总公司与广东日丰投资控股有限公司，举行日丰管业北方建材生产基地项目签约仪式。

10月19日 中国投资协会外资委员会及所属美国美亚电力、沃尔沃公司等16家国际知名企业代表应邀到武清开发区考察并举行座谈。

11月21日 武清开发区总公司与北京网库互通信息技术有限公司，举行中国网库“天津电商谷”项目签约仪式。

2013年

1月29日 武清开发区与德国 Hay Holding GmbH 公司举行 HAY 项目签约仪式。

2月18日至3月1日 武清开发区工委书记、总公司总经理刘东海带队一行4人，赴德国、瑞士、英国举行系列招商活动。

3月29日 武清开发区与广州西翠实业有限公司举行天津日化产品生产基地项目签约仪式。

4月15日 梦达驰汽车系统（天津）有限公司举行开业典礼。

5月8日 中投证券投资有限公司举行开业典礼。

5月10日 武清开发区在北京举行外资企业投资环境说明会。

5月14日 武清开发区与华电工程（集团）有限公司举行华电水务工程有限公司、华电水务投资有限公司、华电膜科技、华电污水厂工程项目签约仪式。

6月17日 日丰建材（天津）有限公司举行奠基典礼。

6月18日 天津信恒餐饮管理有限公司举行开业典礼。

6月26日 “携手发展、共赢未来”2013年中国·天津·武清开发区创业总部基地投资环境推介会在天狮国际健康产业园奥蓝际德宴会中心举行。

7月9日 武清开发区举行天津泰阳生物医药项目签约仪式。

7月16日 部分国家级经济技术开发区座谈会在武清开发区成功举行。

7月22日 武清开发区总公司与中投汇鑫保险经纪有限公司举行签约仪式。

8月9日 武清开发区与天津泰阳制药有限公司举行签约仪式。

9月9日至18日 武清区委、区政府组成欧洲招商工作组，由区委书记张勇带领开发区总公司总经理刘东海、区长助理余元堂、区招商局局长萧庆东、区科委主任杨文玉等一行，赴欧洲德国、瑞士、英国3国开展了为期10天的招商工作。

9月22日 人社局、全国博士后管理委员会批准天津市武清经济技术开发区管理委员会设立博士后科研工作站，开展博士后工作。

10月14日 畅联国际华北区总部项目举行签约仪式。

10月18日 宾得科机械设备（天津）有限公司举行开业典礼。

10月22日 得利满奥宗尼亚环保技术（天津）有限公司举行开业典礼。

10月23日 澳普林特集团总部举行开业典礼。

10月24日 丘比克（天津）转印有限公司举行10周年庆典。

10月24日 凯士比泵阀技术服务（天津）有限公司项目落户武清开发区。

11月12日 莱斯安全阀门（天津）有限公司举行开业典礼。

12月10日 武清开发区管理委员会与普华永道共同签署《战略合作框架协议》。

12月12日 武清开发区在京举办欧盟产业园投资环境说明会。

12月13日 天津市武清区举行博士后科研工作站授牌仪式。

2014年

1月15日 武清开发区与德国迈恩德电子有限公司（MD）举行MD项目签约仪式。

1月23日 武清开发区与韩国苏明公司举行中国总部及结算中心项目签约仪式。

2月21日 武清开发区与日本瑞穗银行股份有限公司、瑞穗银行（中国）有限公司共同签署《战略合作框架协议》。

3月4日 武清开发区与怡和嘉业医疗科技有限公司举行无创通气治疗设备制造、研发和销售总部项目签约仪式。

3月25日 武清开发区举办了“2014年中国·天津·武清开发区欧盟产业园投资环境说明会”。

3月26日 武清开发区在深圳举行投资环境说明会。

3月28日 武清开发区与上海巴克斯酒业举行克斯锐澳鸡尾酒项目签约仪式。

3月31日 康瑞普（天津）冶金设备有限公司举行奠基典礼。

4月18日 武清开发区总公司与中国电力投资集团公司华北分公司举行中电投武清开发区分布式光伏发电项目签约仪式。

4月26日 武清开发区与世界500强美国德尔福汽车线束签约。

5月15日 武清开发区在北京君悦酒店参加“葡萄牙产业园区投资建设推介会”，在推介会上作为全国两家开发区之一（武清开发区、秦皇岛开发区）进行主旨演讲，重点对欧盟产业园做了宣传推介。

5月16日 武清开发区举行人民调解委员会启动仪式。

5月27日 悦居（天津）有限公司创意米兰项目举行动工仪式。

5月28日 远东宏信有限公司宏信设备天津基地举行奠基典礼。

6月13日 全市“互看互比互学”活动到武清开发区调研并考察华电分布式能源站、京津高校（武清）科技创新园，考察后市领导对2个项目给予高度评价。

7月3日 武清开发区在北京举办“2014年天津·武清开发区创业总部基地投资环

境说明会”。

7月10日 外交后勤服务保障基地项目落户武清开发区。

7月15日至24日 武清开发区组成欧洲招商代表团赴德国、法国、意大利3国开展了为期10天的招商工作，拜访推动新项目7个，获取10个项目信息，拓展招商渠道5个。

7月31日 “协同京津冀、决战大数据”2014论坛暨京津·高村科技创新园推介会在北京举办。

8月6日 武清开发区总公司与山水文园集团举行山水六旗文旅小镇项目签约仪式。

8月19日 武清开发区总公司与南开大学生命科学学院举行南开大学吸附分离技术工程中心项目签约仪式。

8月29日 武清区人民政府与金融街控股股份有限公司举行战略合作签约仪式。

9月1日 武清开发区总公司与天津欧诺仪器仪表有限公司举行欧诺急救医学产业园项目签约仪式。

9月3日 德国米勒纺织品项目落户武清开发区。

9月16日 凯士比泵阀技术服务（天津）有限公司举行开业仪式。

9月27日 天津君歌环保设备项目举行奠基典礼。

10月11日 武清开发区与北京交控科技有限公司举行科技轨道交通高科产业园项目签约仪式。

10月16日 玻石机械(天津)有限公司举行二期扩建奠基典礼。

10月16日至17日 深圳市外商投资企业协会暨深圳市国际投融资商会在武清开发区开展了为期2天的招商对接活动。

10月17日 天津市合宜锻造有限责任公司举行开业典礼。

10月21日 基伊埃机械设备(天津)有限公司举行开业典礼。

10月22日 武清开发区总公司与美国EPC公司举行易派驰凸轮轴制造项目签约仪式。

10月28日 武清开发区工委召开党的群众路线教育实践活动总结大会。

11月4日 英格尔检测技术服务(天津)有限公司项目落户武清开发区。

11月12日 华电分布式能源站第二套燃气蒸汽联合循环机组正式并网发电。

11月17日 哈沃科技(天津)有限公司举行开业典礼。

11月18日 天津怡和嘉业医疗科技有限公司举行开业典礼。

11 月 19 日 尼森冷却系统（天津）有限公司举行五周年庆典和新厂房启动仪式。

11 月 20 日 柯菲凯博汽车线束天津武清项目举行签约仪式。

11 月 24 日 武清区政府与天津外国语大学举行合作框架协议签约仪式。

12 月 3 日 天津薇美资电子商务公司落户武清开发区。

12 月 5 日 天津光彩圣火科技企业孵化器有限公司升级为国家级孵化器。

12 月 10 日 丹佛斯（天津）有限公司举行第三百万只 T2 热力膨胀阀下线庆典仪式。

12 月 12 日 武清开发区与北京吉诺沃生物科技公司举行天津吉诺沃生物科技项目签约仪式。

12 月 18 日 武清开发区与南开大学校友会举行南开大学校友会创业孵化园项目签约仪式。

12 月 19 日 京津高村科技创新园、GAM 嘉丰达、清科集团在北京金融街共同举办了高村助力产业升级——2014 智慧城市产业链与生态圈建设研讨会。

12 月 25 日 武清开发区与金融街控股股份有限公司举行签约仪式。

12 月 27 日 武清开发区与美国布瑞奇科技孵化器有限公司签署合作协议。

2015 年

1 月 20 日 欧文托普暖通空调系统项目举行签约仪式。

2 月 26 日 天津国家自主创新示范区在天津滨海高新技术产业开发区挂牌，示范区包括“一区二十一园”，用地总面积 244.67 平方公里，其中，核心区用地面积 55.24 平方公里，武清开发区是核心区的一部分。

3 月 22 日 北京瑞健科技项目举行签约仪式。

3 月 29 日 天津市首家“创意影像艺术产业园”落户武清开发区。

4 月 11 日 武清开发区博士后科研工作站增设“天津大学前沿技术研究院有限公司”和“天津国民天房资产管理有限公司”两个分站 。

4 月 14 日 瑞士创新（北方）中心落户武清开发区。

4 月 16 日 武清开发区与北京化工大学生命科学与技术学院签署北京化工大学天津科研孵化基地项目合作备忘录。

4 月 21 日 中国天津自由贸易试验区正式挂牌，标志着自贸区武清园招商活动全面展开。

4月28日 武清开发区成功举办创业总部基地投资环境说明会。

4月29日 天津诗兰姆汽车零部件有限公司落户武清开发区。

5月5日 天津麦点餐饮管理有限公司落户武清开发区。

5月14日 盈可泰北京农业技术天津生产基地项目落户武清开发区。

5月29日 天津新媒体科技众创基地举行开园仪式。

6月1日 大华同安财务管理咨询（天津）有限公司落户武清开发区。

6月10日 天津西马格特宝机械有限公司举行“提升技术研讨会”开幕活动。

6月12日 穆勒纺织品（天津）有限公司举行开业仪式。

6月14日 天津佳视智晶科技有限公司落户武清开发区。

6月24日 天津诗兰姆汽车零部件有限公司举行开业仪式。

7月3日 欧蒙(天津)医学诊断技术有限公司举行奠基仪式。

7月9日 金唯智基因检测项目举行签约仪式。

7月15日 新皇冠玻璃制品项目落户武清开发区。

7月22日 武清开发区在北京中关村举办“京津协同发展创新创业研讨会”。

7月23日 保利资产文化传媒项目落户武清开发区。

7月23日 武清开发区与北京天肽生物科技有限公司举行天肽生物结算总部项目签约仪式。

8月19日 武清开发区与澳大利亚沃利帕森集团举行沃利帕森天津设计服务中心项目签约仪式。

8月21日 天赋前沿众创空间通过全市首批众创空间认定。

8月29日 天津财经大学与武清开发区共同设立的天津市京津冀协同创新发展研究院举行成立仪式。

9月13日 2015年天津武清开发区杯国际马拉松赛在武清区政府前广场鸣枪开赛。本届比赛是武清区连续第四年举办天津国际马拉松赛，也是武清开发区第四次冠名赞助马拉松赛。

9月25日 上海畅联国际物流股份有限公司华北物流中心基地举行奠基。

9月28日 英国哈克尼斯银幕（中国）总部项目落户武清开发区。

10月15日 武清开发区与北京航空航天大学签署协议共建北航（天津武清）智能

制造研究院。

10月16日 美源集团总部项目举行签约仪式。

10月16日 中禾种业项目举行签约仪式。

10月30日 “2015年武清开发区中欧产业园投资环境说明会暨欧盟商协会领袖与企业家对话会”在武清开发区举行。

11月3日 沃斯坦热力设备(天津)有限公司举行二期开业典礼暨沃斯坦氟塑料烟气余热回收系统产品展示会。

11月15日 光大环球医药中间体研发、销售总部项目举行签约仪式。

11月22日 天津普瑞华盛医学检验所项目落户武清开发区。

11月28日 达伦多跨境商品直购体验中心举行开业仪式。

11月30日 天津华创瑞风空调设备有限公司落户武清开发区。

12月1日 家乐福(中国)华北区物流中心正式运营。

12月7日 武清开发区举行第二届天津(武清)北美高科技项目与资本对接会。

12月9日 武清开发区与天津大学生物医学工程专业研究团队签署合作协议，建立天津物理医学与健康产业技术研究院。

12月18日 天津万达影城威尼都店正式开业。

2016年

1月7日 武清开发区与天津大学生物医学工程专业研究团队签署共建天津物理医学与健康产业技术研究院协议。

1月8日 天通泰国际双创产业园项目举行协议签约仪式。

1月15日 三英超精密运动控制项目举行签约仪式。

1月22日 自贸区武清园举行集中签约仪式。易汇资产管理(天津)有限公司、美投资产管理(天津)有限公司、天津中腐科技有限公司、天津兑瑞资产管理有限公司、丽水婴乐乳业有限公司进出口贸易结算总部5家企业落户自贸区武清园。

2月9日 北京天马网视科技结算项目落户武清开发区。

2月17日 医疗健康产业项目举行集中签约仪式。北京迪玛克医药科技有限公司、北京浦菲特精密模具有限公司、福路明精密管材(北京)有限公司、海克力斯(北京)

贸易有限公司、北京平海康健科技有限公司5家企业落户开发区。

2月19日 中际联合高空安全装备项目举行签约仪式。

3月25日 林格贝生物研发结算总部项目落户武清开发区。

4月1日 海鸟城跨境电子商务项目落户武清开发区。

4月1日 加拿大迪诺孚抗癌基因检测项目落户武清开发区。

4月7日 世界500强法国佛吉亚汽车部件项目落户武清开发区。

4月14日 武清开发区与中国饭店协会举行战略合作签约仪式。

4月27日 美国艾达康基因检测和测序项目落户武清开发区。

5月12日 转化医学产业创新平台项目落户武清开发区。

5月15日 2016天津武清开发区杯国际马拉松赛暨全国马拉松锦标赛(第3站)在天津市武清区行政中心前正式鸣枪开跑。武清开发区连续第五次冠名天津国际马拉松赛。

5月18日 在北京人民大会堂举行武清开发区转化医学平台“院士专家工作站”共建协议签约仪式。

5月20日 丹麦格兰富水处理设备项目落户武清开发区。

6月8日 武清开发区与北京康立生医药技术开发有限公司举行合作签约仪式。

6月26日 武清开发区举行北京企业集中签约仪式，中海外控股、新希望、汇中财富、史莱福灵、ESM、加拿大迪诺孚、阿芙精油、中机科仪、信立方、翼龙影业10家北京优质企业落户。

6月28日 武清开发区获批2016年天津市专利试点园区。

6月30日 开发区获批天津市留学人员创业园。

7月1日 武清金泰苏河汇众创空间项目举行签约仪式。

7月6日 武清区举办投资环境恳谈会暨重点项目签约仪式。开发区集中签约世界500强沃尔玛、奥美3D打印、汇元网科技结算、华策影视、雷默传动、贝塔鹰人工智能系统研发、薇美姿7个项目。

8月4日 西班牙海斯坦普汽车零部件项目举行签约仪式。

8月12日 大自然(台湾)环保生态循环经济总部项目举行签约仪式。

8月26日 三博远致医学检验所项目举行签约仪式。

8月29日 开发区获批国家知识产权质押融资试点园区。

9月8日 迈克博生物科技项目落户武清开发区。

9月13日 宜安普惠融资租赁（天津）有限公司落户自贸区武清园。

9月23日 中盈科创科技成果交易中心项目举行签约仪式。

9月24日 创意米兰购物广场开业。

9月29日 开发区获批天津市级专利导航项目（基因工程产业专利导航）。

10月18日 开发区中医联合实验室举行签约仪式。

10月28日 文化创意产业园“思库·武清”项目举行签约仪式。

11月15日 日本友成汽车模具及车灯项目落户武清开发区。

11月24日 2016中国区域协调发展与投融资创新论坛暨中国区域投资营商环境榜发布典礼在北京举行，开发区获评2016年中国区域最佳投资营商环境园区。

12月16日 武清开发区铁科院项目一期进入试生产阶段。

12月25日 安赛医疗器械生产基地项目落户开发区。

12月26日 开发区获批国家知识产权试点园区。

第一篇

申建启动

第一章 决策 定址

第一节 建区决策

武清县委、县政府关于建设武清开发区的决策酝酿，于20世纪90年代初，起步于邓小平南方谈话后。

当时，武清虽然在全国改革开放不断深入，全县农村家庭联产承包责任制取得显著成果、乡镇企业迅速发展、农民收入增加，跨入全国农村综合实力百强县之列。但是，全县经济发展仍处于以传统产业发展为主、现代化技术水平低、经济效益差、发展速度缓慢的状况。为寻求全县经济的更快更好发展，借助国家实施《火炬计划纲要》，拟在全国建立一批高新技术产业园区的发展机遇，结合本地区经济社会发展发展实际，武清开始酝酿打破瓶颈、创新发展的决策。

1990年10月8日，在武清县秋季商品交易会上，前来参加交易会开幕式的天津市委常委、市科委主任王成怀在与县长梁文忠谈话间透露：国家正在实施的《火炬计划纲要》中要在全国各省市自治区建一批高新技术产业园区，同时批准建设一个县属国家级高新区做基层开发试点，目前全国许多省市自治区都在积极争取，天津也准备申办。并提出，武清如果有想法，可以考虑一起申办。梁文忠得知此消息后，当天立即向县委书记徐景树汇报了这一情况。

作为武清县党政主要领导的徐景树、梁文忠，经过认真思考很快形成了共识。一致认为：改革开放给武清带来经济发展、人民生活水平提高的好形势。但是，传统产业落后、技术水平低、经济发展滞后，是不争的事实，成为制约快速发展难以逾越的瓶颈。而“火炬计划”是一项国家实施科技兴国的战略部署，是发挥我国技术力量的优势和潜力，以市场为导向，促进高新技术成果商品化、产业化、国际化的重要载体。它的重点发展领域是，电子信息、新材料、生物技术、光机电一体化、新能源、高效节能与环保。而建立武清高新技术产业园区，正是破解武清发展瓶颈千载难逢的机遇。

不久，县委书记徐景树主持召开县委常委扩大会议，深刻阐述了申办开发区的想法，统一了决策层的思想，确定了申办建立武清开发区的决策。

当年11月8日，县政府正式组建申办开发区专门机构，即园区领导小组、园区办公室。11月28日，县政府责成副县长冯祥生带领部分人员到江苏昆山经济技术开发区学习考察，为申办积累经验。12月28日，在县政府第二会议室召开园区领导小组成员会议，研究了部门任务与人员分工，提出了必须跑步前进，全面迅速开展工作的要求。从此，紧锣密鼓般地拉开了申办武清开发区的序幕。

1991年3月，武清县委常委扩大会议在坐落于武清城区雍阳东道的县委大院西会议室召开，会议在进一步统一全县县级领导建立武清开发区思想的基础上，决定在原园区申办机构的基础上，从县直各有关部门抽调力量，充实了申办办公室工作人员，决定抽调县人大常委会副主任杨作莹主持负责申办办公室的工作。

申办手续的规划资料等基础工作，在市有关部门的大力支持下，经过工作人员夜以继日的努力，很快完成了逐级审批、上报工作。并很快与负责国家火炬计划审批实施的国家科委副主任李绪鄂取得了联系，详细汇报了武清建立高新区的优势、条件、规划、决心等，希望得到国家科委的帮助与支持。

5月7上午，国家科委副主任李绪鄂应武清县委、县政府的邀请，到武清进行首次实地考察。在市长聂璧初，市委常委、市科委主任王成怀等市有关领导和武清县委书记徐景树、县长梁文忠的陪同下，首先详细向李绪鄂一行汇报了创建武清开发区的具体规划。而后，陪同李绪鄂一行实地察看了拟建开发区规划区的地理位置、环境条件等情况，还考察了武清的杨村第二小学、县医院、商业大厦等城区基础设施建设情况。

当年6月，国务委员兼国家科委主任宋健一行到天津，在天津高新技术产业园区筹建处会议室，听取市有关部门负责人汇报。当市有关部门负责人介绍武清也在积极申办开发区时，宋健当即指出："国家科委暂不批准县级建科技园区。如果允许区县申办，天津的塘沽有港口和开发区的优势，还可以考虑"。市有关部门的负责人听后忙插话说："塘沽目前还没有提出要求，武清倒要求很迫切"。宋健听了没有表态，也没有做出任何解释。面对情况，武清锲而不舍，坚持继续做好申办的各项工作，争取得到批准。

11月5日，开发区申办工作进入了关键期，当听到国家科委副主任李绪鄂正在河北省沧州地区考察的消息后，按照县委书记徐景树的安排，县长梁文忠、县人大常委会副主任杨作莹及有关工作人员，在市委常委、市科委主任王成怀，副主任梁肃带领下，于当天晚上11点多钟赶到河北沧州，再次汇报武清创建开发区的筹备情况，并邀请李绪鄂一行在返京途中到武清停留一天。

1991年12月24日，将修改、补充的文件资料送到国务院有关部门。

1991年12月28日，国家有关部门正式批准全国25个省、市、自治区的26家国家级开发区的建立。而天津市高新技术园区武清开发区，则是此次批准的全国高新区中唯一县属的国家级开发区。园区区域范围为3平方公里。

第二节 区域定址

最初，国家科委审议批准的天津新技术产业园区武清新建区的区域范围为3平方公里。即南起杨村五支渠，北至七支渠，东起京津公路，西至1500米处。

在武清开发区起步区选址过程中，开发区筹建办曾在讨论提交县委常委会确定起步区选址方案的会议上，提出了两种意见：一种意见主张将起步区建在城区附近的杨村四支渠以北（即现在杨村街道办事处附近）。理由是这里距离城区较近，有利于县里各部门就近检查指导工作，有利于城区在企业上班工人的就近上下班方便。另一种意见则认为，把起步区放在京津塘高速公路杨村出口附近。理由有三：一是交通便利。区内企业出门就能上京津塘高速、京津公路，有利于企业运输、职工出行。二是开发区选在交通要道附近，往返人流集聚，企业建成后本身就是活广告，有利于扩大武清开发区的影响力。三是工业区建在城区以外，避免噪音污染，有利城区居民生活。在两种意见一时不能达成一致的时候，县长、开发区管委会主任梁文忠当即提议，请参会人员到大家争议的两个地点实地察看“现场办公”，再做决断。参会人员实地察看后，觉得起步区建在京津塘高速公路杨村出口附近更好些。这次现场办公，统一了思想、初步定下起步区的地址。

1991年12月31日上午，县委常委的几位领导听取园区专题汇报（起步区规划、要上的配套设施、园区办机构、优惠政策、明年问题与打算），原则同意武清开发区起步区的选址。

1992年6月23日上午，国家级新技术产业园区——天津新技术产业园区授牌及天津新技术产业园区武清开发区奠基仪式，在武清开发区选定的起步区内举行。市领导聂璧初、王成怀、张好生，国家科委副主任李效时，秘书长宋必信及国家、市有关部门的领导出席授牌及奠基仪式。

1992 年 8 月 7 日上午，武清县人民政府在北京人民大会堂召开“天津新技术产业园区武清开发区及天津市武清经济开发区新闻发布会”。县长梁文忠，县人大常委会主任刘金铎，县政协主席程振江，县委副书记王成全，县委常委、宣传部部长何俊田，县人大常委会副主任杨作莹，县长助理王树培及开发区管委会的全体成员参加。会议邀请新华社主任李继成及中央人民广播电台、中央电视台、《人民日报》等二十余家新闻单位的记者，及各国驻中国使领馆有关人员近百人参加。会上，县长梁文忠就武清的投资环境作了简要介绍，县长助理、开发区管委会副主任王树培作了两区情况的说明。与会记者和各国使节对武清开发区的投资环境表示了极大关注，拉开了武清开发区建设发展、招商引资的序幕。

第三节　办公地址

武清开发区管委会、总公司的办公地址，从建立至 2016 年年底，办公地址共 4 处，历经三次迁址。

1991 年 12 月 28 日从国家批准建立至 1993 年 2 月，办公地点仍设在筹备申办时期的武清县政府院内。

1993 年 2 月 8 日，办公地址由武清县政府院内，迁到武清开发区起步区附近的京津公路东侧曹园村租楼办公。

1994 年 1 月 29 日，办公地址由曹园村的出租楼内迁往开发区起步区内福源道与泉州路交口北端的别墅楼内。

1997 年 10 月 8 日，武清开发区管委会、总公司办公大楼破土动工。1998 年 12 月，在武清开发区建区 7 周年前夕，迁入新址办公。新建成的办公楼占地面积 14108.5 平方米，建筑面积 6400 平方米。

第二章　自然状况

武清开发区坐落在武清城区（杨村）北侧，东依京津公路（103 国道）、北运河畔，北靠京津塘高速公路、京津塘高速公路二线、龙凤河，西至 104 国道，南至城区雍阳西道。武清开发区与武清的周边环境为：地处京津冀核心区域，位于天津市西北部，海河水系中下游，东与天津市宝坻区、宁河县毗邻，南与天津市北辰区、西青区相连，西与河北省霸州市、廊坊市接壤，北与北京市通州区搭界，与河北省廊坊市香河县隔青龙湾相望。地理坐标为北纬 39° 07 ' 05 " ~ 39° 42 ' 20 "，东经 116° 46 ' 43 " ~ 117° 19 ' 59 "。境域北阔南狭，东西宽 41.78 公里，南北长 65.22 公里，面积 1574 平方公里。武清城区距北京市区 71 公里，距天津市区 25 公里。

第一节　地质 地貌

据武清有记载的地质资料证明，武清开发区所处的武清境内，地层分布范围、厚度及岩性等相差悬殊，但从距今 18 亿 ~ 8.5 亿年的元古界依次到距今 6 亿 ~ 2.25 亿年的古生界，距今 2.25 亿 ~ 0.7 亿年的中生界、距今 0.7 亿年至今的新生界等均有分布。

境内大面积分布有中生界地层和新生界地层。

境内地质构造是中生代以来长期持续沉降的地区，幅度大于天津市其他区县，在华北及全国均不多见。地下有北北东和北西西两组断裂带影响着武清的地层变动。

境内地貌是华北大平原的一部分，奠基于中生代燕山运动形成的华北凹陷盆地，处于海河流域的下游。由于以下降为主的下沉运动及河流冲积物的填充，形成了微度起伏的冲击平原，所以地面倾斜平缓，海拔高差不大，境内地势自西、北、南三面向东南方向倾斜。西北部海拔 13.5 米，北部 11 米左右，南部 5 米左右，东南部 2 米左右。地面自然纵坡 1∶6500。

武清的地貌类型按其成因可分为冲积平原和海积冲积平原；按成因、形态及地表组成物质又分为微斜平地、低平地、缓岗、洼地、河漫滩和人为地形。冲击平原区即由这些形态组成。

第二节　气候

武清开发区位于中纬度，欧亚大陆东岸，北依燕山，东近渤海，主要受季风环流影响。夏季主要受副热带高压影响，多偏南风，湿润多雨；冬季受蒙古冷高压控制，盛行西北风，干燥寒冷。区域季节变化明显，介于大陆性气候和海洋性气候的过渡带上，属暖温带半湿润大陆性季风气候。

区域冬夏季长，春秋季短，日照时长，辐射也强，可满足作物一年两熟之需。

一、气温

区域处于中纬度，夏季太阳仰角高，地面吸收太阳辐射热能多，气温高；冬季太阳仰角低，地面吸收太阳辐射热能少；春秋两季是过渡季节，冷热适中。

1. 平均气温

据20世纪90年代资料记载，武清年平均气温为11.6° C（市记录11.8° C），最暖年是1983年为12.7° C，最冷年是1957年为10.2° C。与2014年资料相比，年均气温为14.2° C，较20世纪平均气温高出2.6° C，比最高暖年还高出1.5° C，出现明显偏高的发展趋势。

每年最热月份是7月，多年月均气温为26.4° C；最冷月份是1月，多年平均值是 –5.1° C。春4月平均气温为12.8° C，秋10月平均气温是12.8° C。

2. 极端气温

自1957年有气象纪录以来的30余年气温对照，1964年6月出现的极端最高气温达到39.9° C，其主要原因是日照时间长、天空云量少，高温一般出现在6月，少数年份由于特殊气候出现在5、7、8月。2014年5月29日，出现了年极端高温39.9° C，平了历史纪录。

极端最低气温高达 –22° C，出现在1966年2月。极端最低气温多数出现在1月，少数出现在12和2、3月，主要和强冷空气活动有关。一年有5个月（11—3月）极端最低气温稳定在0° C以下；4月、10月在0° C左右，5–9月均在0° C以上。

3. 无霜期

天津地区无霜期平均一般为 190 天左右，武清的无霜期多年平均为 207 天。据 20 世纪统计：1968 年无霜期为最长的 244 天，1957 年为无霜期最短的 171 天。历年初霜平均日期为 10 月 25 日，最早为 1957 年的 10 月 3 日：最晚为 1979 年的 11 月 10 日：终霜平均日期为 3 月 30 日，最早为 1967 年的 2 月 16 日，最晚为 1978 年的 4 月 26 日。2016 年无霜期为 210 天。

二、降水

据资料统计，武清区在 20 世纪多年降水量平均值为 578.3 毫米。最多年份在 1977 年为 1080 毫米，高出平均值的 87%；最少年份在 1972 年的 285.2 毫米，低于平均值 51%。多少年份之差为 794.8 毫米，是造成干旱与洪涝的主因。至 21 世纪，市统计年均降水量为 596.7 毫米，增长 18.4 毫米，降水量有所增加。但 2016 年年降水量仅为 423.9 毫米，未达到年均降水水平。

武清的降水量四季不均衡。有“春雨贵如油”的说法，春季降水一般不足全年的 10%，多年平均降水量仅 55.6 毫米。个别年份如 1964 年 4 月降水量较大，为 114.2 毫米。

夏季降水强度大，是出现洪涝的季节。6—8 月降水总量 434.8 毫米，占全年降水量的 75%；6—9 月为汛期，历年降水总量为 482 毫米，占全年的 83%。1977 年 6—8 月降水量最大为 850.6 毫米，最小为 1972 年的 174.6 毫米。

秋季降水量略多于春季，多年平均值为 77.6 毫米，占全年降水量的 13%。

冬季往往降水稀少，12—2 月为 10.4 毫米。个别年份如 1973 年 1 月为 24.1 毫米，1979 年 2 月为 30.5 毫米。

区内全年降雨日为 63 天，其中春季 12 天，夏季 33 天，秋季 13 天，冬季 5 天。雨季最早始于 6 月 4 日，最晚始于 7 月 23 日，平均始于 7 月 3 日前后；最迟结束于 9 月 30 日，平均结束于 8 月 23 日前后，持续时间约为 2 个月。雨季的降水量占全年的 70% 以上。

夏季降水强度大、多暴雨，月最大降水量 437.4 毫米，出现在 1977 年 7 月，占全年降水的 75%；日最大降水量为 265.1 毫米，出现在 1984 年 8 月 10 日，占全年降水量的 45%；一小时最大降水量为 87.8 毫米，出现在 1984 年 8 月 10 日 5 至 6 时。

日降雨量≥ 50 毫米的暴雨日数每年平均 2 次，最多年份 1977 年为 6 次。暴雨日出现以 7 月最多，占 52%；8 月次之，占 31%。

日雨量≥ 25 毫米的大雨日数每年平均为 6.5 次，最多年份 1977 年达 13 次。出现在7月的占40%，8月占31%。11月至3月没有大雨。

三、日照与辐射

区内天候晴多于阴，平均晴天年日数为283.9天，阴天为81.1天，年日照数平均为2752.2小时，日照率为62%。一年中以5、6月份日照时数为最多，7、8月份进入雨季，日照时数降低，11、12月份为最低值。

太阳辐射年均实测为125.9千卡/平方厘米；月均实测太阳辐射以5、6月份最强，分别为16.3千卡/平方厘米和15.2/千卡/平方厘米；冬季辐射最弱，12月为5.7千卡/平方厘米，1月为6.4千卡/平方厘米。

四、风

在季风环流的支配下，冬夏风向随季节变换更替。冬季风常发源于高纬度的蒙古、西伯利亚高气压中心地区，对流层低空盛行寒冷干燥的偏北风；夏季风来自低纬度的北太平洋副热带高气压中心地区，多刮高温、高湿的偏南风。所以，武清地域秋冬多西北风，春夏多西南风。冬春西北风和夏季雷雨大风时风力较大。月平均风速以4月最大，为4.2米/秒，8月最小，为2.2米/秒。多年最大风速达24米/秒。

五、相对湿度 蒸发 干燥度

相对湿度。年平均相对湿度为62%。一年中四季相对湿度，以夏季最大，7月平均相对湿度为79%；冬春季最小，1月平均相对湿度为51%，4月平均相对湿度为57%；秋季10月平均相对湿度为67%。

蒸发。历年平均为1164.4毫米，各月分布不均以5月最大，为308.2毫米/月；最小是12月，为53.1毫米/月；年平均蒸发量149.8毫米。

干燥度。年平均干燥度为2。年内变化，以冬、春较大，冬季1月平均干燥度为14.7，春季4月平均干燥度为6；夏季较小，7月平均干燥度为0.6，秋季10月平均干燥度为3.1。

历年各月平均蒸发量统计表

表1　　　　单位：毫米

月份	1	2	3	4	5	6	7	8	9	10	11	12	年
历年各月蒸发量	57.6	67.5	137.2	226.0	308.2	278.2	203.4	177.1	167.0	137.5	76.5	53.1	149.8

第二篇

开发建设

第一章　区域规划与管理

第一节　发展定位

武清开发区在建设发展过程中，主动按照国家高新技术产业园区、经济开发区发展的要求，借鉴广东深圳、广西北海等开发区建设发展的经验与做法，紧密结合发展实际，思路清晰、定位准确、规划高端、管理到位、稳步发展、效益显著。从 1991 年、1992 年国家批准建立的高新区和天津市政府批准的武清经济开发区共计 6.9 平方公里，至 2016 年年底建成区域已达 35 平方公里。

一、总体发展及在武清发展中的定位

1992 年建区初，武清县委、县政府组织带领有关部门负责人赴广东、广西、珠江三角洲等我国东南沿海地区率先建起的开发区参观考察。1992 年 3 月，在学习借鉴先进地区开发区建设经验的基础上，县委召开常委扩大会，专题研究武清开发区建设发展规划，结合实际，确定了武清开发区的总体发展思路的定位，即“着眼长远，适度超前，综合起步，滚动开发”的 16 字方针。“着眼长远”，是指制定发展规划一定要把眼光放远。做到前十年不怕让人骂，后十年让人夸，三十年不落伍。“适度超前”，是指区域内基础设施建设一定要超前，坚持高标准、高质量，适应国内外各种现代化企业发展需要，搞好配套设施建设。“综合起步”，是考虑到起步时期开发区资金紧缺的现状，集中建设“高端区”与“普通工业区”基础设施，入区企业集中在两个区域综合发展，待经济基础雄厚了再细致分区扩建。滚动开发，是指土地开发建设“征收一片，开发一片；出让一片，收益一片”。避免土地盲目开发，保证开发区稳步发展。

开发区建设发展规划还提出，经过努力，逐步把武清开发区建成武清对外开放的窗口，全区经济发展的引擎、就业再就业的基地，为把武清建成京津之间最具竞争力

和最具实力的地区，做出积极的贡献。

二、自我管理机制定位

武清开发区建立后，本着现代化、科学化、规范化管理的原则，逐步建立起一整套管理机制，其主要内容及定位分别是：

（一）组织领导机制。本着精干、高效的原则，由国家批准建立的天津市高新技术产业园区武清开发区，以及由市政府批准建立的武清经济开发区，两个开发区一块牌子、一套人马，统称武清开发区。开发区设管委会，管委会主任、副主任由县主要领导兼任，开发区总经理兼任管委会办公室主任。这一组织机构及其领导机制的形成，既体现了开发区在全局发展中的地位与权威性，又实现了开发区在贯彻执行县委、县政府决策谋略与建设发展步伐，以及在对外交往等方面的一致性。同时，开发区的群团组织暂时不设，只设综合部、招商部、城管部、建设部、财务部。呈现出一心一意搞管理、抓建设的组织管理格局。

（二）工作人员聘任制。开发区建区后，除特殊人才外，在用人上始终采取企业管理式的聘任制，根据工作需要招录人员，一律采取自愿报名、统一考试、集体决定、择优录用的原则，任何部门、任何领导都无权安插工作人员。开发区建区 20 年来，从区级领导机关到开发区总公司领导，无一人擅自安排子女或亲属到开发区上班。同时在区内工作人员灌输“职工没有退路，开发区才有出路”的理念，制订了“廉诚守信，务实进取”的区训。实行能上能下、能进能出、不适应辞退的用人机制，确保了每个工作人员尽职尽责、奋发向上的良好精神状态。

（三）分配激励机制。即“模糊工资”。开发区工作人员每月的工资收入，除每人统一的生活费公开外，其他一律根据工作质量好差、贡献大小，由部门负责人排队、主管经理核定发放奖金福利数额，总公司核心领导集体讨论决定，率先在全区砸了“铁饭碗”，不再吃“大锅饭”。解决了干多干少、干好干坏一个样的问题。

（四）招投标机制。一切工程都实行招投标，并坚持“最低标价中标”的原则，从此避免了工程浪费和腐败现象的滋生。

（五）封闭式管理。为了让入区企业一心一意抓生产、搞经营，县委、县政府制定文件，明确规定开发区内企业实行“封闭式管理”，任何部门、单位都不许以任何理由私自对开发区所属各企业从事检查工作、收取费用等项活动。确需进入企业工作的，必须在开发区总公司工作人员带领下进行。凡必须收取的行政事业性费用，一律由开发区年内一次性统一付给。封闭式管理，真正让区内企业有了宽松的生产经营环境。

三、发展理念定位

武清开发区在建设发展过程中，坚持为投资者服务是永恒的主题，并逐步建立了独具特色的建设发展理念。开发区建设初期，从提高工作人员素质入手，首先提出了“投资者是上帝”的理念。要求每个工作人员充分认识到“上帝是没错的，如果有错误就是我们”的道理。同时提出，每个工作人员面对投资者不许说“不”“不行”“不能”，要想方设法、满腔热情、周到细致地为投资者搞好服务。2000 年后，武清开发区进一步深化服务，提出了“服务他人就是发展自己”的理念。这一理念的实施，使开发区服务质量进一步得到提升，对全区园区经济建设乃至全区各项工作开展起到了带头示范作用。

四、开发建设定位

在基础设施建设方面分步实施，武清开发区建设初期，受资金等条件制约影响，先是围绕入驻企业急需的土地、道路、水电通信等达到“五通一平”标准。以后随着建设发展需要逐步增加基础设施建设，逐步完善，增强载体功能。到 2016 年，区内基础设施建设已经达到了“十一通一平”标准。在环保方面，坚持严格按照国家环保要求招商引资，对于不符合国家环保要求的企业，一律不准入区开发建设。在土地转让方面，坚持批准一块、建设开发一块。绝不空卖空买，严格防控土地荒芜、闲置、浪费。

五、产业发展定位

武清开发区建设初期，按照国家高新产业园区建设发展的要求，主要发展电子信息、机械制造、生物医药、汽车零部件、新材料、新能源等六大支柱产业。后来随着国内外经济发展、市场变化，逐步发展仓储物流、文化产业、总部经济等高端产业，并最终形成高端制造、生物医药、总部经济三大优势支柱产业。

六、建设与民生定位

一是区域内原居住居民安置方面。建区初期，对于出让土地的杨村街道、东蒲洼街道的失地农民，将涉及农民卖地资金全部存入银行，用利息支付农民每年不低于 300 公斤小麦的标准享受生活补贴，不足部分，由开发区补足，确保农民生活无后顾之忧。2003 年起，区委、区政府对于出让土地农民所在村实施撤村建居，在建设还迁房的基础上，让失地农民由农业户口转为城镇户口，帮助中青年实现就业再就业，为失去劳动能力的老人上养老保险，彻底解决了人们的后顾之忧。二是对在开发区外来打工者的生活安置，则建设“高新公寓”，解决了外来打工者的饮食起居问题。

第二节　规划编制

按照从实际出发、超前发展的原则，做好规划设计，描绘发展蓝图，为区（县）委、政府领导机关以及开发区领导提供决策发展的有力依据，成为武清开发区建设发展历程的一项重要工作。

一、规划设计部机构及职责

规划设计部主要职能包括设计管理、产业项目服务及管理、内勤管理三部分内容。

设计管理

主要包括园区规划编制及自建工程方案及施工图管理两部分。

1. 负责园区总体规划、控制性详细规划、城市设计导则、土地细分导则的制订、报审及控制管理工作。

2. 负责园区内远景、产业、市政、景观、室内等各专项规划制订及控制管理工作。

3. 负责园区自建项目方案及施工图设计管理，负责组织方案汇报、设计对接、拨款及组织施工图联审工作。

4. 负责协调设计单位为园区自建项目提供现场服务并办理相关手续。

5. 负责搜集整理设计前期资料及最终图纸等相关资料，建立设计专项档案。

6. 责起草设计任务书及配合设计项目招投标。

7. 配合法务审查、签订设计合同，协调拨付各阶段设计进度款。

产业项目服务及管理

1. 负责为招商各部及入区企业提供用地红线图、能源接口图、规划设计条件等相关资料和咨询服务。

2. 负责对企业新建、扩建总平图、鸟瞰图、外立面效果图实施规划审批。

3. 负责对企业报送的路由申请、厂区开口申请等实施规划审批。

4. 负责对开发区新建及扩建企业进行巡查，对发现问题的企业下发整改通知并责令完成整改。

5. 负责对开发区企业开工前，联系相关单位进行控制点、定桩、放线、验线工作，并在企业竣工后组织相关部门进行规划竣工验收。

6. 负责协助二次开发部、行政许可中心出具分证方案图纸。

内勤管理

1. 负责部内的印章管理。

2. 负责部内“一企一档、一项目一档”档案管理。

3. 负责设计进度款、履约保障金、投标保证金等款项的拨款申请、支付、审核、记录工作。

4. 负责周计划、周总结、月计划、月总结及年度总结的撰写。

二、阶段性规划设计历程

在武清开发区建设发展的过程中，经历了逐步摸索、循序渐进、不断提高的过程。

（一）建设初期

武清开发区于 1992 年 6 月 24 日奠基，宣布建设开发正式启动。此前，在开发区建设筹备过程中，就参照国内开发区建设发展的经验，结合本地区的实际，对开发区的建设发展做了规划设计，并在县委常委扩大会议上做了汇报，得到了同意批准。

（二）建设中期

2002 年，随着台湾 200 余家企业到武清开发区做投资建厂前期考察，武清开发区对园区二期建设发展进行了规划设计，经区委、区政府研究，报请市、国家有关部门。为武清开发区二期建设发展的土地征用、建设开发起到了积极推动作用。2009 年，武清开发区在天鹅湖度假村西侧启动总部基地建设项目前，相继邀请清华大学城市建设设计院、上海 DC 国际建筑设计事务所等部门做了规划设计，为建设高标准的总部基地建设，提供了指导性文件。

（三）近期规划

近年来，武清开发区在规划设计组织健全、管理制度逐步完善的基础上，坚持对每一个重大步骤、重点项目，都邀请国内外高等规划设计部门帮助规划设计，为园区建设发展决策的科学化、民主化，提供了更多的规划设计方案。

第三节　规划设计类型

中国天津武清开发区于 1991 年 12 月 28 日设立，是国家级经济技术开发区和国家级高新技术产业园区，2014 年年底纳入天津国家自主创新示范区核心区。近期规划面积 55 平方公里，其中，40 平方公里已建成，15 平方公里正在规划、开发。远期规划面积 80 平方公里。

产业方面，开发区产业发展形成了高端制造、生物医药、总部经济三大主导产业。高端制造业以智能制造、轨道交通、汽车及零部件、电子信息为主；生物医药以基因测序、中药颗粒、医疗器械、诊断试剂为主；总部经济以总部结算、金融商务、研发转化、文化创意为主。

交通方面，开发区周边 10 分钟车程范围内，有京津塘、京津、京沪、滨保等高速公路 4 条、高速公路出入口 17 个；有京津城际铁路经停站 1 处，京山铁路客、货运站各 1 处；规划的京、津地铁将在武清驳接；103、104 国道在区内通过；武清自建的"九横九纵"立体化交通网络通达。

生态环境方面，开发区东临京杭大运河，北有龙凤新河，西有龙凤河故道，中间镶嵌着美丽的天鹅湖。区内绿化率达 40% 以上，空气和水质优于国家标准。

用地功能布局，开发区内以工业用地为主，约占总用地面积 40%，分布于开发区一二三四期，仓储物流用地主要集中在三期北区。居住用地位于创业总部基地、四期内，现有尚清湾、天鹅湖一号、翡翠半岛、畔水庭院等居住项目。商业用地集中于创业总部基地及天狮产业园中，主要为总部经济。开发区内有新建的天元大学、职教中心、天狮学院等教育科研用地约占总用地面积 7%。

重点规划领域，建区以来开发区规划建成中欧产业园、创业总部基地、京津高校（武清）科技创新园等一批优质招商载体。其中中欧产业园是为欧洲企业打造的发展平台载体。发展定位是建成高端产业发展基地，主要发展高端制造、生物医药、新材料产业。至 2016 年，为欧洲企业量身建设的 5 万平方米环保节能厂房和中欧园服务中心已投入使用，正在规划建设环保节能厂房二期和生活配套区。创业总部基地规划 1.26 平方公里，包括 6 个区域，建筑面积 120 万平米。主要发展金融商务、研发转化、总部楼宇和文化创意等现代服务业，提升武清开发区功能环境，促进产业结构调整升级。京津高校（武清）科技创新园占地161亩，建筑面积11.5万平米，发展定位是立足加强与京津高校和科研机构的产学研用合作，建设高新项目研发平台、高端产业孵化平台、传统产业升级平台、创新成果转化平台和高层次人才集聚平台。

第四节 主要规划设计工作成果

武清开发区规划设计部自成立以来始终坚持突出规划引领作用，积极引智借力，通过与高水平设计单位合作、聘请相关领域专家指导，先后高水平完成了开发区远景规划、四期总规、综合交通规划、四期产业规划、城市家具导视系统等几十项的总体及专项规划。完成了涵盖开发区35平方公里控规的编制及日常调整维护工作。

开发区规划设计部始终坚持精细化管理及服务，规范设计流程，完善施工图管理制度，先后制定了施工图启动、联审等一系列体制机制。完成了总部基地等自建项目建筑、院区管网、景观、室内装修等各阶段设计总计面积达200万平方米。

在产业项目服务及管理方面，开发区规划设计部始终坚持“服务他人就是发展自己”的发展理念，自主编制了开发区规划管理服务机制，明确服务流程及时限，积极在企业建厂规划、管线路由等方面为企业提供帮助，完成了200余个项目修详规、工程证审核，完成了180余项管线路由审批，联合其他部门完成了对150余次企业的规划验收，为超过200家企业提供了前期规划咨询服务。

重大规划项目一览表

表2

序号	规划项目	设计单位
1	开发区远景规划设计	天津市城市规划设计研究院
2	开发区CBD及主要道路城市设计	上海同济城市设计研究院
3	开发区综合交通规划	天津市城市规划设计研究院
4	开发区绿地系统规划	天津泰达园林建设有限公司
5	开发区城市家具及标示导视系统规划	彼路国际咨询（北京）有限公司

续表 2

序　号	规划项目	设计单位
6	总部基地总部区规划建筑方案	上海 DC 国际建筑设计事务所
7	开发区四期景观规划	北京土人景观规划设计有限公司
8	开发区四期产业规划	中国通用咨询有限公司
9	开发区四期市政基础设施规划	中国市政工程东北设计研究总院有限公司
10	京津高校（武清）科技创新园规划建筑方案	天津冶金规划设计院
11	自贸区武清产业园东疆港商贸地块规划建筑方案	天津市天友建筑设计股份有限公司
12	中欧产业园服务中心及生活配套区规划建筑方案	波捷特 (北京) 建筑设计顾问有限公司
13	中欧产业园高端装备制造基地标准厂房规划建筑方案	天津冶金规划设计院
14	服务外包区规划建筑方案	机械工业第六设计研究院
15	开发区招商中心规划建筑方案	上海 DC 国际建筑设计事务

第二章 土地使用与管理

武清开发区在土地使用与管理方面，始终按照国家及市和区土地管理政策、法规征用土地，合理有效进行土地开发，严格有序地搞好土地使用管理，使有限的土地得到了充分利用。到2016年年底，武清开发区建成区面积35平方公里。区域范围包括：东临京津公路（103国道）；南靠武清城区的南财源道、泉州路、光明道、南东路；西部地界为福源道、新兴路、龙凤河、南东路；北部地界为外环北路、翠亨路、龙凤河等。

第一节 土地征用

武清开发区土地征用总体原则是，按照国家和市有关部门批准的开发面积，由武清开发区和区土地规划管理部门做出规划，待区政府批准后再报请国家有关部门审批。获得批准开发的土地征用，则由区政府统一制定土地征用补偿、人员安置、开发建设办法，并负责协调所涉及街道乡镇做好村民的工作。

首期土地征用，分别于1992年和2006年，按照国家批准的天津市高新技术园区武清开发区建设面积，以及天津市政府批准的天津市武清经济开发区的范围，相继在京津公路以西、京津塘高速公路以南地域，征用了杨村街道与东蒲洼街道部分村街的土地。2007年至2009年，再次征用土地涉及杨村与东蒲洼街道大部分街村、南蔡村镇的部分村。

征用土地后对失地农民的补偿安置，最初是按照国家对土地征用补偿的标准由武清开发区一次性补偿到村街。为确保失地街村群众生活不受影响，区里明确规定补偿款由村街统一管理存入银行。银行把每年的利息补贴给村民作为生产、生活费用的支出。为保证失地村民的基本生活，区政府还明确规定，银行每年发给村民的利息补贴，每亩补偿费的利息按照当地市场价格购买300公斤小麦，不足部分由各级政府部门出资补齐差额，以解决群众的后顾之忧。从2003年起，根据开发区征用土地造成大面积的村街村民没有土地的现状，按照农村城市化建设发展的思路，武清区委、区政府决定开展撤村建居工程。就土地征用、补偿，撤村建居等做了一系列详细的政策规定。从此，开发区占用土地的杨村、东蒲洼街道和部分镇的村民，相继迁入了新建的环境优美、设施齐备、功能齐全"花园"式的居民小区。其中杨村、东蒲洼街道新建的社区就达数十个。其中东蒲洼街道新建社区20多个，不仅解决了原有界域内的3万多村民的居住问题，还吸引了附近乡镇大量居民的入驻，使街道居民总量增至近10万人。与此同时，失地村民都由过去的农村户口转为城镇户口，生活水平、居住环境得到了根本性提升。中青年居民基本实现了就业、再就业，有了稳定的经济收入，政府部门还为相关人员上了养老保险，解决了失地居民生活上的后顾之忧。

第二节　土地开发

武清开发区从建立至今的土地开发，大体分为四期。

首期的开发区域为京津公路（103国道）以西、京津塘高速公路以南，城区四支渠以北。在这片5平方公里的区域内，一是加强了基础设施的建设。先是实现了供电、供水、供热、通信、土地的"五通一平"，后来又增加到"十一通一平"，为武清开发区的创建与发展奠定了基础，增强了载体功能。二是建起了标准厂房，供外来企业入驻经营。通过招商引资，香港天宝电子有限公司、日本大真空、台湾杰麦集团公司、韩国LG、红日药业、天狮集团公司等一批国内外企业投资建厂。三是建起了天鹅湖度假村，引入了一批金融机构，建起了"武清海关"等一批服务型单位、机关，为企业入驻、发展增添了配套功能。

二期开发建设区域主要是翠亨路以西，龙凤河以南。吸引了南玻集团、丹麦节能环保企业、韩国三星、中粮集团等企业入驻。

三期开发区域主要是福源道以北、天鹅湖度假村以西。开发建设的项目是"创业总部基地"。面积1.26平方公里，建筑面积120万平方米。功能布局为6个区域，包括企业总部区、服务外包区、综合办公区3个功能区；中心服务区、商务酒店区和专家公寓区3个配套区。其发展定位：主要发展总部结算、商务办公、研发转化、文化创意等现代服务业和总部楼宇经济，提升武清开发区功能环境，促进产业结构调整升级。

四期开发区域为京津高速公路武清北站出口以南，以“中欧产业园”为主体。规划面积 9.5 平方公里。其中一期 5 平方公里，二期 4.5 平方公里。发展定位：由国家商务部投促局和武清开发区共建，为欧洲企业搭建的发展载体平台。以生物医药、先进制造业、新材料为主导产业。将建成具有绿色生态特点的欧洲产业聚集发展基地。截至 2016 年，园内为欧洲企业量身建设的 5 万平方米环保节能厂房和中欧园服务中心已投入使用。规划建设的环保节能厂房二期和生活配套区正在建设之中。

第三节　土地管理

严格遵守国家及有关部门对土地使用管理的法规，科学合理使用土地，让有限的土地发挥最大的效益，是武清开发区始终恪守的土地管理原则。

在土地开发使用布局方面，坚持规划先行。自开发区起步至 2016 年，始终坚持科学规划、产业布局有序、合理使用土地。即使在开发区招商引资的初期，也没有急功近利、盲目安排使用。在地处天鹅湖度假村西侧、福源道北侧黄金段开发建设的“创业总部基地”地址，就是开发区创业起步区预留的一片土地。起步区最初建设的项目是工业企业，而引进国内外现代高端产业总部、建设科技孵化基地、发展楼宇经济，成为武清开发区建设发展的追求，并多次邀请国内外设计部门帮助设计规划，直到 2009 年才投入建设，并收到了显现的效果。到 2016 年年底，这一基地已吸引数百家国内外知名企业入驻。

在土地转让方面，坚持公开公平公正，实行土地转让招拍挂。开发区区域内每出让一块土地，都通过媒体发布公告，并邀请有关专业部门严格按照程序开展招投标。这一做法，既规范了土地转让的管理办法，又防止了土地转让过程中腐败现象的滋生。

控制两条底线，防止土地出让后环境污染或者荒芜。武清开发区自建立至 2016 年，始终把住环境污染这一关，即使在开发区创建初期招商引资十分困难的情况下，也不允许任何有污染企业入驻。20 世纪 90 年代初，国内一批本无企业项目且无开发能力的单位和个人，也以兴业建厂为名低价购买囤积土地，以期地价上涨后转让获利，造成大量出让的土地长期闲置，甚至杂草丛生，出现大面积荒芜的现象。武清开发区坚持凡无项目来区购买转让土地者一律不予转让。对于一些暂时获得土地转让权又较长时间不能开工建设的，则按照国家有关规定动员其将土地收回，避免土地的浪费、荒芜。

第四节　地域名称

由于在开发建设过程中以道路骨架，沿路安排入区企业入驻路的建设与形成，武清开发区内的地名以路名为主。而路的命名，考虑到国内外投资者向往吉祥、兴旺的心理，根据地域特色，一般以当地的古泉州，以及兴旺发达、惠风和畅等成语字头确定道路名称。其路名如下：

光明道、北财源道、南财源道、广源道、开源道、新源道、旺源道、来源道、浩源道、源和道、源明道、源春道、源景道、环湖路、禄源道、禄财道、福源道、翠湖路、翠源道、三号路、丰和路、兴旺路、凤湖路、发达路、和畅路、巢湖路、引湖路、新创路、新兴路、新平路、新开路、旺发路、来湖路、汇丰路、泉丰路、泉兴路、泉华路、泉发路、泉和路、泉州路、泉旺路、泉明路、泉春路、泉月路、泉汇路、泉秀路、泉秋路、泉达路、泉锦路、泉雨路、筑湖路、金湖路。

第三章　市政建设及管理

第一节　道路

武清开发区内道路宽敞、四通八达、安全便捷。截至2016年年底，区内建有公路53条，总长度达102456米。路河桥28座，长度921米。

武清开发区自建立以来，高度重视区域内道路交通建设。一是根据入区企业建设发展需要，主动投资建设四通八达的路网。二是坚持高质量建设。施工建设过程中，坚持高标准，聘请高水平施工队承担工程建设。三是建立强有力的道路管理养护队伍，常态化做好道路养护工作。截至2016年，基本完成对建园初期铺设道路翻修，确保了区内道路交通高速、快捷、安全运行，大大方便了驻区企业及员工的生产、生活。

与此同时，为了筑造交通发展优势，抢占京津冀协同发展的制高点，武清区委、区政府在2003年至2007年京津城际轨道、103国道改造期间，借势在全区范围内打造以“九横九纵”为道路骨架的“路网建设工程”。争取了京津城际轨道武清站及途经境内的高速公路在武清设立的17个出入口。武清交通优势的凸显，也给武清开发区的建设发展创造了良好的交通环境。

开发区道路一览表

表3

道路名称	建设时间	长度（米）	宽度（米）	路面结构	备　注
福源道	1992年	10123	40	沥青混凝土路面	
泉州路	1992年	2094	30	沥青混凝土路面	
泉旺路	1992年	2960	38	沥青混凝土路面	
泉达路	1992年	2034	40	沥青混凝土路面	

续表 3

道路名称	建设时间	长度（米）	宽度（米）	路面结构	备　注
源泉路	1992 年	2024	20	沥青混凝土路面	
光明道	1992 年	1570	20	沥青混凝土路面	
兴旺路	1992 年	158	14.5	沥青混凝土路面	
发达路	1992 年	610	30	沥青混凝土路面	
三号路	1992 年	951	20	沥青混凝土路面	
旺发路	1992 年	376	14.5	沥青混凝土路面	
泉兴路	1992 年	1162	25	沥青混凝土路面	
泉发路	1992 年	2034	30	沥青混凝土路面	
开源道	2002 年	2504	30	沥青混凝土路面	
浩源道	2003 年	4029	30	沥青混凝土路面	
来源道	2005 年	952	25	沥青混凝土路面	
南财源道	2005 年	2900	20	沥青混凝土路面	
北财源道	2005 年	2900	20	沥青混凝土路面	
新源道	2006 年	1650	30	沥青混凝土路面	
旺源道	2006 年	1660	40	沥青混凝土路面	
禄源道	2006 年	2900	25	沥青混凝土路面	
禄财道	2006 年	337	16	沥青混凝土路面	
广源道	2006 年	8600	30	沥青混凝土路面	
翠湖路	2009 年	965	18	沥青混凝土路面	
翠源道	2009 年	1706	30	沥青混凝土路面	

续表 3

道路名称	建设时间	长度（米）	宽度（米）	路面结构	备　注
环湖路	2009 年	2760	24	沥青混凝土路面	
和畅路	2011 年	916	30	沥青混凝土路面	
丰和路	2011 年	527	30	沥青混凝土路面	
新兴路	2011 年	1148	40	沥青混凝土路面	
新创路	2011 年	1300	30	沥青混凝土路面	
新平路	2011 年	1200	30	沥青混凝土路面	
新开路	2011 年	1280	40	沥青混凝土路面	
汇丰路	2011 年	1360	30	沥青混凝土路面	
泉丰路	2011 年	2661	40	沥青混凝土路面	
泉华路	2011 年	1240	30	沥青混凝土路面	
泉汇路	2011 年	1246	40	沥青混凝土路面	
泉秀路	2011 年	1360	40	沥青混凝土路面	
泉和路	2011 年	1436	40	沥青混凝土路面	
泉锦路	2011 年	1823	30	沥青混凝土路面	
泉明路	2014 年	1550	17	沥青混凝土路面	
泉春路	2014 年	1118	16	沥青混凝土路面	
泉月路	2014 年	1542	22	沥青混凝土路面	
泉秋路	2014 年	1660	16	沥青混凝土路面	
泉雨路	2014 年	1285	22	沥青混凝土路面	
源和道	2014 年	2814	25	沥青混凝土路面	

续表 3

道路名称	建设时间	长度（米）	宽度（米）	路面结构	备　注
源明道	2014 年	2950	24	沥青混凝土路面	
源春道	2014 年	3000	16	沥青混凝土路面	
源景道	2014 年	3045	22	沥青混凝土路面	
筑湖路	2016 年	234	24	沥青混凝土路面	
金湖路	2016 年	240	18	沥青混凝土路面	
凤湖路	2016 年	240	24	沥青混凝土路面	
巢湖路	2016 年	234	18	沥青混凝土路面	
引湖路	2016 年	294	24	沥青混凝土路面	
来湖路	2016 年	283	18	沥青混凝土路面	
凤湖路	2016 年	240	24	沥青混凝土路面	
巢湖路	2016 年	234	18	沥青混凝土路面	
引湖路	2016 年	294	24	沥青混凝土路面	
来湖路	2016 年	283	18	沥青混凝土路面	

2016 年开发区道路统计表

表 4

项目	道　路				
	条数	长度（米）	面积（平方米）		
			合计	车行道	人行道
快速路					
主干路	13	48200	1432530	899648	532882

续表 4

次干路	32	54258	1567654	927300	640354
支路					
合计	45	102458	3000184	1826948	1173236

2016 年开发区桥梁统计表

表 5

项目	桥 梁		
	座数	长度（米）	面积（平方米）
立交桥			
跨河桥	28	912.28	18876.32
人行天桥			
合计	28	912.28	18876.32

第二节 灯 光

本着有利夜间企业生产、员工出行的原则，武清开发区着力打造遍布全区的路灯、夜景照明体系。到 2016 年，全区总灯杆数量 3072 座。其中：一期灯杆 1103 座，二期灯杆 610 座，三期北区灯杆 232 座，三期西区灯杆 589 座，四期灯杆 345 座。总部基地灯杆 193 座。

区内路灯建设由开发区负责，建成后交由电力部门管理，以确保路灯、夜景灯光正常运行。

2016 年武清开发区灯杆一览表

表 6

序号	区域	路名	路段	数量（套）	备注
1	一期	泉旺路	雍阳西道至福源道	163	
2		泉发路	雍阳西道至福源道	77	
3		泉达路	雍阳西道至福源道	73	
4		财源道	泉兴路至翠亨路	110	
5		来源道	泉兴路至泉达路	37	
6		光明道	泉兴路至翠亨路	62	
7		兴旺路	禄源道至光明道	32	
8		源泉路	禄源道至广源道	34	
9		泉州路	五支桥至广源道	90	
10		泉兴路	福源道至北财源道	36	
11		禄源道	津京公路至翠亨路	65	
12		发达路	禄源道至北财源道	10	
13		禄财道	泉旺路至泉发路	12	
14		福源道	津京公路至翠亨路	140	
15		三号路	开源道至广源道	18	
16		开源道	津京公路至泉州路	25	
17		泉旺北路	福源道至广源道	40	
18		广源道	三号路至翠亨路	79	
19	总部基地			193	
20	二期	福源道	翠亨路至南东路	103	
21		开源道	南东路至翠亨路	88	

续表 6

序号	区域	路名	路段	数量（套）	备注
22		广源道	翠亨桥至南东路	97	
23		新源道	泉丰路至南东路	38	
24		泉汇路	福源道至高新路	59	
25		汇丰路	福源道至高新路	34	
26		泉丰路	福源道至高新路	72	
27		泉和路	福源道至新源道	49	
28		和畅路	开源道至新源道	27	
29		高新路	泉汇路至泉丰路	25	
30		丰和路	开源道至广源道	18	
31	三期西区	福源道	南东路至高王路	253	
32		广源道	南东路至新兴路	82	
33		浩源道	新创路至新兴路	80	
34		新开路	福源道至浩源道	46	
35		新平路	福源道至浩源道	43	
36		新兴路	福源道至浩源道	40	
37		新创路	广源道至浩源道	45	
38	三期北区	旺源道	津京公路至翠亨路	47	
39		翠源路	泉华路至泉锦路	62	
40		浩源道	泉华路至泉锦路	29	
41		泉华路	翠源道至浩源道	41	
42		泉秀路	翠源道至浩源道	53	
43	四期	源春路		18	

续表 6

序号	区域	路名	路段	数量（套）	备注
44		源和路		18	
45		源景路		101	
46		源明路		70	
47		泉明路		48	
48		泉月路		71	
49		泉秋路		19	
50	翠亨路		雍阳西道至二线出口	382	开发区干
总计	开发区一期灯杆 1103 座，二期灯杆 610 座，三期北区灯杆 232 座，三期西区灯杆 589 座，四期灯杆 345 座。总部基地灯杆 193 座。 开发区总灯杆数量 :3072 座				

2016 年开发区 LED 节能路灯一览表

表 7

序号	区域	道路名称	节能路灯盏数	功率	备注
1	三期西区	福源道	249	220W	
2		开源道	39	180W	
3		广源道	80	180W	
4		浩源道	78	180W	
5		新创路	49	180W	
6		新开路	50	180W	
7		新平路	47	180W	
8		新兴路	46	180W	
合计			638		

续表 7

序号	区域	道路名称	节能路灯盏数	功率	备注
9	三期北区	翠源道	61	180W	
10		旺源道	47	180W	
11		浩源道	27	180W	
12		泉锦路	55	180W	
13		泉秀路	41	180W	
14		泉华路	40	180W	
合计			271		
15	四期	源春道	18	220W	
16		源和道	18	220W	
17		源景道	101	220W	
18		源明道	70	220W	
19		泉明路	48	220W	
20		泉月路	71	220W	
21		泉秋路	19	220W	单侧双灯头
合计			345		
共计			1254		

说明：LED 节能路灯节能模式为路灯开启后前 3 小时为全功率工作，3 小时后转为半功率工作，直至路灯关闭

第三节 排水

武清开发区区域地势较为低洼，为确保雨季道路、厂区排水，建设较为完善的排

水系统。

排水设施简介

1. 开发区 22v 雨水泵站。建成时间：2004 年。坐落位置：开发区二期汇丰路与福源道交口，占地面积约 0.4 亩。排水能力：装机 3 台轴流泵、总功率为 66 千瓦、总流量为 0.51 立方米 / 秒；收水范围：翠亨路以西、泉丰路以东、福源道以北、广源道以南，收水面积约 1.25 平方公里。该面积内雨水经泵站提升排入六支渠。

2. 开发区后河淤雨水泵站。建成时间：2009 年。坐落位置：开发区二期高新北路天狮北门附近，占地面积约 0.75 亩。排水能力：装机 4 台轴流泵，总功率为 500 千瓦、总流量为 3.7 立方米 / 秒。收水范围：泉汇路以西、高新西路以东、广源道以北、高新北路以南，收水面积约 3.9 平方公里。该面积内雨水经泵站提升排入龙凤新河。

3. 开发区南玻雨水泵站。建成时间：2004 年。坐落位置：开发区二期南玻玻璃厂内，占地面积约 0.4 亩。排水能力：装机 3 台轴流泵、总功率为 55 千瓦、总流量为 0.68 立方米 / 秒。收水范围：泉丰路以西、南东路以东、福源道以北、广源道以南，收水面积约 1.2 平方公里。该面积内雨水经泵站提升排入六支渠。

4. 开发区北区雨水泵站。建成时间：2010 年。坐落位置：开发区三期翠亨路与保税北路交口，占地面积约 1.2 亩。排水能力：装机 4 台轴流泵、总功率为 800 千瓦、总流量为 1.4 立方米 / 秒。收水范围：京津公路以西、翠亨路以东、广源道以北、龙凤河以南，收水面积约 2.4 平方公里。

5、畦疃雨水泵站。建成时间： 2010 年。坐落位置：开发区三期新开路与浩源道交口，占地面积约 1.8 亩。排水能力：装机 6 台轴流泵，总功率为 2130 千瓦、总流量为 18 立方米 / 秒。收水范围：南东路以西、新兴路以东、福源道以北、浩源道以南，收水面积约 3.9 平方公里。该范围内雨水经泵站提升后排入龙凤河。

第四节　污水处理

根据建设发展需要，开发区主动规划设计，高标准建设了污水处理系统。该项目按照 BOO 的模式建设，由中国华电工程（集团）有限公司负责投融资建设并永久经营。华电水务（天津）有限公司为该项目法人单位，负责该厂的运营管理。

武清开发区三期西区污水厂及中水厂项目。该项目位于新开路与浩源道之间，北临浩源道，占地60亩，项目建设总规模5.5万吨/日，分两期建设。一期设计处理规模1万吨/日，采用（改良A/O工艺+高效澄清+机械过率+消毒工艺）。2012年7月开始建设，2013年5月建成，开始通水、调试，2013年10正式运营，2013年12月获得环评验收文件。二期设计处理规模4.5万吨/日，采用"A/A/O+高效澄清+砂率+消毒工艺"，2015年3月开始建设，2015年年底建成，开始通水、调试、运营，2016年8月通过环评现场监测，年底正在办理环评验收手续。

该厂原设计出水水质为《城镇污水处理厂污染物排放标准》（GB18918-2002）一级A标准，出水作为福源电厂冷却水使用，多余部分用来补充河道景观水。2016年，公司按照地方管理要求，对本厂实施提标改造，将出水水质标准提高到天津市地标A类水标准。提标改造工作于2016年12月完成。

第五节　园区绿化

武清开发区建区以来，始终以打造"绿色生态园区"为目标，以着力建设水绿、天蓝、景美的生态环境，大手笔布绿。从组织领导、规划建设、资金保证等方面高度重视，取得了显著成效。截至2016年年底，绿化生态景观建设累计投资2.65亿元。已建成公共绿地382万平方米。绿化覆盖率达42%以上，绿地率达40%以上。2016年投资4780万元，对福源道等重点道路进行了绿化景观综合提升。三季有花，四季常绿，水荫相映，鸟语花香的生态园区体系已经形成。武清开发区先后被评为天津市绿化先进单位、天津市花园式单位、天津市城市绿化先进集体、天津市城市绿化广场建设优秀奖、庭院小区绿化建设优秀奖等荣誉称号。开发区的绿化工作，不仅美化了环境，而且在全区绿化、美化及开展全民义务植树活动中，起到了带头引领作用。

一、建设发展历程

（一）规划先行、精心组织设计。武清开发区坚持对绿化工作超前科学规划，合理布局。规划设计之初，将绿化景观环境作为重要组成部分，纳入总体规划设计方案。所有道路和项目建设均预留足够的绿化空间，根据功能特点，进行重点突出设计，如创业总部基地以"一环一岛两轴线"为设计重点，以湖心岛为中心，实现了水绿融合、错落有致的景观效果，体现了人与生态的和谐。按照超前设计分步实施的原则，随市政道路工程的延伸，绿化建设同步跟进，实现了绿随路走，项目建成绿化景出。

在绿化景观建设过程中，开发区成立了由管委会主要领导负总责的工作领导小组，下设专业绿化管理公司，配备专职技术管理人员 7 名，其中具备中级以上职称 3 名，绿化工作管理制度及督查考核机制完善，分工明确、责任到人。每年制定科学的绿化工作实施方案，纳入开发区年度重点工作计划，每周对工程进度、工程质量以及整体环境进行专项督查。

（二）突出特色，坚持建管结合。武清开发区在绿化景观环境建设上突出体现多样化、立体化，根据功能的不同，建设风格各异。如高端制造业聚集区以道路绿化为特点，乔木、花灌木、地被花卉、草坪分层配置，企业透视围墙栽植藤本花卉；总部办公区、休闲居住区则体现出人景合一的公园模式特点，清新和谐，水、绿、凉亭等景观有机的融为一体。体现了一路一景、步移景异，点、线、面、立体绿化的景观效果。在苗木的选用上，以乡土树种为主，适量引进外地名贵花木。景观乔木有法桐、国槐、白蜡、银杏、千头椿等 22 个品种，23 万余株；常绿景观苗木有雪松、造型油松、龙柏等 11 个品种，2 万余株；透视围墙栽植藤本月季、蔷薇等 12 万株；景观花灌木有红枫、五角枫、海棠、紫叶李、樱花、榆叶梅等 46 个品种，27 万余株；模纹、地被花卉、水生植物等 30 余个品种，30 余万平方米；草坪总面积 350 余万平方米。

在绿化工程方面，是否能够满足人们的宜业宜居及审美要求，方案设计、施工管理固然重要，但绿化养护更为重要，俗话说“三分种，七分管”。如果绿化养护不到位，设计意图就不能得到充分的体现。只有做到建、管并举，才能将绿化景观建设的生态、减灾、教育等功能得到最大限度的发挥。在此方面，开发区建立了绿化养管标准、督查考核等完善的管理制度，实行单位自查、专人巡查、领导抽查、联查考核等监管机制，规范管理。按技术规范进行修剪、施肥、浇水、打药等管护作业，特别是狠抓病虫害、火灾的监测预警，从未发生过大规模的病虫害及火灾事件。各种苗木成活完好率达 98% 以上，绿地管护良好。

（三）注重生态，加强宣传引导。武清开发区义务植树登记卡和考核制度完善，职工每年 3·12 植树节期间都积极参加义务植树活动，至 2016 年年底，共建设生态防护林 300 余亩，义务植树 2.2 万株。自建温室大棚 600 平方米，苗圃 70 亩，用于培育苗木花卉。重视对古树名木的保护，开发区有古树国槐 2 株，设立有标志牌、编号及 GPS 定位，古树名木档案资料齐全，责任部门、责任人明确，养护措施到位。

二、基础绿化简介

公路绿化。区域内公路绿化属绿化公司统一施工建设管理。园区公路两侧有树木草坪、鲜花装点绿化，路中间设有绿化隔离带。其中，公路两侧栽种的树木，一般采用大树木移栽的方法，使公路短时间内就有绿树成荫之感。正如许多到此参观考察的人们所说："看武清开发区，路像路、树像树、项目像项目，处处形象可观。"路的绿化隔离带均是由树木、草坪、花卉相间，高低不同的层次感极强的绿化景观，令人赏心悦目。被人们称为"花园大道""景观大道"。在连续举办的5届"中国天津武清开发区杯国际马拉松赛"中，主跑道就设在翠亨路上，翠亨路也随着央视体育频道的向国内外数十家媒体直播，对国内外展示了翠亨路靓丽的风采。

生活区绿化。园区坚持生态宜居、景观优美，高标准、高质量，推动了园区绿化建设，栖仙公寓、卧龙潭、高新公寓等成为人们公认的"花园式"小区。其中，栖仙公寓成为全国生态环境的示范区，吸引了全国各地的参观者。坐落在开发区内的"天鹅湖度假村"，环境优美、设施完备、服务一流，成为武清对外接待的最佳之地、全国各地游客休闲度假的乐园。

厂区绿化。厂区外由开发区绿化公司负责，厂区内由厂家负责。厂区绿化，坚持厂家自愿原则，在开发区绿化公司指导下进行绿化。大多数厂区重视绿化、美化建设，在建厂的同时规划建设好环境，使工厂呈"花园式"景区。

第六节　高新公寓

武清开发区高新公寓是开发区针对园区各层次人才专门兴建的公益性配套服务设施，旨在为入区各层次人才提供舒适、便捷的良好居住环境。公寓坐落在武清开发区二期104国道以东，占地16.06万平方米，建筑面积16.8万平方米，可出租房屋3885间。高新公寓分为三期建设，总投资5.2亿人民币，至2016年年底已全部建成投入使用。可容纳1万余名各层次人才居住和生活。

公寓物业管理工作由武清开发区工业物业有限公司负责。公寓各项服务价格低廉，6人间床位费每人每月租金100元，夫妻一室每月租金600元，夫妻二室每月租金800元，单身2人间每月租金720元。公寓配套设施完善，食堂、公交站点、公共浴室、图书馆、社区医院、银行、超市、网吧、体育健身场所等一应俱全。

第四章　能源供应

第一节　供水

开发区自来水公司系武清开发区总公司下属企业，成立于1993年，占地面积1万平方米，日供应地下水能力1.5万立方米，负责对开发区企业和栖仙公寓提供生产生活用水服务，为开发区早期的发展奠定了供水基础。

为解决武清城区及开发区地下水源匮乏，保护环境，进一步提升水质，改善投资环境，1999年3月武清区实施了“引滦入杨”工程，并于1999年7月建成地表水（滦河水）处理厂——卧龙潭净水中心，占地面积拓展到12.2万平方米，一期日供水能力3万立方米。为保障企业供水的稳定和安全，推动园区可持续发展，净水中心于2008年年初开始实施二期扩建工程，并于年底竣工投入使用，日供水能力6万立方米，供水服务面积达30平方公里。武清开发区自来水公司地表水处理工艺成熟，出厂水质各项指标优于国家标准。近年来，公司奉行“强有力保障，零缺陷服务”服务宗旨，主动为区内企业、员工、居民提供足够的高质量水源，保证了区内企业生产、生活的需要。

第二节　供电

武清开发区把电力基础设施建设作为重点工作，与电力部门紧密配合，加大投资力度，建设高标准、高质量的电力供应体系。

一、开发区内电力现状

2016年，武清开发区内共有110千伏公用变电站4座，主变8台，容量为363兆伏安；35千伏变公用电站2座，主变4台，容量为72兆伏安；35千伏变专用电站6座，主变 20 台，容量为 105.15 兆伏安。

2016 年开发区电站一览设

表 8

序号	变电站	电压等级	主变编号	主变容量（兆伏安）	变电站性质	位置
1	郑楼	110	1#	31.5	公用	一期
			2#	31.5	公用	
2	泉丰	110	1#	50	公用	二期
			2#	50	公用	
3	信义	110	1#	50	公用	三期西
			2#	50	公用	
4	广源	110	1#	50	公用	三期西
			2#	50	公用	
5	泉旺	35	1#	16	公用	一期
			2#	16	公用	
6	泉发	35	1#	20	公用	一期
			2#	20	公用	
7	LG 乐金	35	1#	10	专用	一期
8	南玻	35	1#	16	专用	二期
			2#	16	专用	
9	日进	35	1#	20	专用	三期
10	EKC	35	1#	3.15	专用	二期

续表 8

序号	变电站	电压等级	主变编号	主变容量（兆伏安）	变电站性质	位置
11	天狮园	35	1#–14#	32	专用	二期
12	佛罗伦萨	35	1#	8	专用	前进道

武清开发区内企业基本均为 10 千伏用户，开发区各条道路两侧都分布了 10 千伏主干线路，且线路之间均具备联络功能，为园区用户的可靠用电提供了保障。部分企业为 35 千伏用户，包括 LG、南玻、日进、EKC、天狮、佛罗伦萨小镇等，这些用户的电源均取自开发区内的武清 220 千伏变电站。

二、开发区周边电力状况

武清开发区周边共有 110 千伏公用变电站 5 座，主变 10 台，容量为 500 兆伏安；其中位于武清城区 3 座，南蔡村镇 1 座，豆张庄镇 1 座。35 千伏公用变电站 1 座，主变容量 2*20 兆伏安，位于徐官屯街。

2016 年开发区周边电站一览表

表 9

序号	变电站	电压等级	主变编号	主变容量（兆伏安）	变电站性质
1	雍西	110	2#	50	公用
			3#	50	公用
2	前进	110	1#	50	公用
			2#	50	公用
3	河东	110	2#	50	公用
			3#	50	公用

续表 9

序号	变电站	电压等级	主变编号	主变容量（兆伏安）	变电站性质
4	南蔡	110	2#	50	公用
			3#	50	公用
5	周立营	110	1#	50	公用
			2#	50	公用
6	徐官屯	35	1#	20	公用
			2#	20	公用

三、开发区用电分析

武清开发区内电网由郑楼站、泉丰站、信义站、广源站、泉发站、泉旺站 6 个变电站做支撑，各变电站之间通过 10 千伏线路联络，供电方式灵活；周边有南蔡站、徐官屯站、河东站、前进站、雍西站、周立营站，这些变电站与园区内的部分 10 千伏线路有联络，可负担部分负荷，以减轻园区内变电站的压力。这种“6+6”的配比方式完全可以满足近期开发区内企事业单位的用电需求。

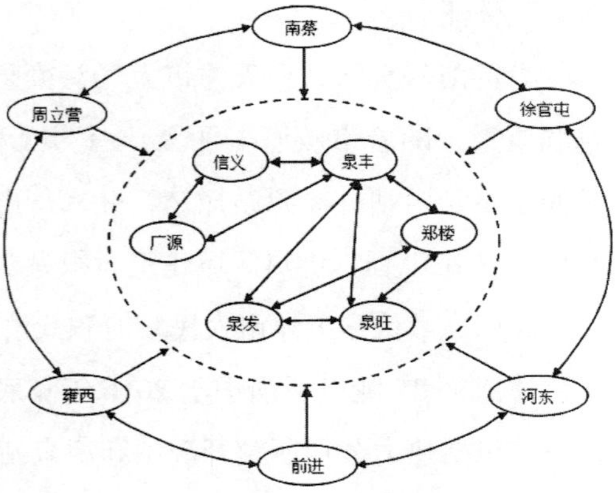

图 1　开发区电网结构

第三节　供 热

一、公司建设

开发区热力有限公司是武清开发区总公司下属企业，公司坐落于武清开发区源泉路 11 号，是武清开发区总体规划及配套设施的重要组成部分。

在此之前，开发区的供热工作分别隶属于开发区规划建设部、开发区物业部及开发区城市管理部。随着开发区的不断发展，园区集中供热事业也得到了长足的发展，从1993开始建设一号供热站到1997年建设栖仙供热站，安装11台锅炉、两口地热井，供热外网40多公里，因此，迫切需要专业公司对供热工作进行管理。1997年1月1日总公司正式宣布成立武清开发区热力公司，至此热力公司开始挂牌服务。

截至2015年3月底，热力公司拥有固定资产1.9亿元，年产值4000万元。下设5个锅炉房供热站点（源泉站、禄源站、栖仙东站、栖仙西站、开源站），17台锅炉，热水锅炉供热能力157兆瓦，蒸汽锅炉供热能力100吨/小时，热水锅炉供热总量80.43万吉焦，蒸汽锅炉供热总量35.86万吉焦。采暖面积总负荷为184万平方米，管网总长度达100公里。居民供热户数达5000余户，企业供热户数达200余户，企业用蒸汽户数达40余户。热力公司一直践行开发区总公司“服务他人就是发展自己”的理念，在服务入区企业供暖、供蒸汽及居民小区供暖等方面做了大量工作，分别在2011年、2012年、2013年年度采暖季获得了天津市供热办颁发的“天津市稳定优质供热先进集体”荣誉证书。

为贯彻落实国家和天津市大气污染防治工作要求，有效控制燃煤污染，提高环境空气质量，随着市政府美丽天津一号工程的建设，从2015年4月始，热力公司所辖栖仙东站、西站、禄源站撤销，并入华电供热网，实现煤改燃。武清区将此项目列为2015年惠民工程，供热区域建筑面积为78万平方米。

2016年，依据天津市人民政府和武清区人民政府签订的煤改燃责任书中相关内容：武清建成区35吨以下锅炉于2016年年底前全部完成煤改燃。涉及到热力公司的改燃任务，包括热力公司所辖开源站和源泉站。从2016年采暖季，开源供热站撤销，并入华电供热网，实现煤改燃，供热区域建筑面积为80万平方米。源泉供热站拆除原有的三台燃煤蒸汽锅炉，购置三台20吨燃气蒸汽锅炉，继续为所辖供热区域4万平方米用户提供供暖和20户企业用蒸汽用户提供服务。

二、运营服务

源泉站建于1993年，于1994年11月10日正式为企业提供冬季采暖和全年生产用蒸汽服务。

禄源站建于1995年，属于集资建站，于1995年11月10日正式为企业提供冬季采暖服务。

栖仙东站建于1997年，于1997年11月15日正式为企业及栖仙东区居民小区提供冬季采暖服务。

栖仙西站建于2000年，于2000年11月15日正式为企业、栖仙中区和栖仙西区居民小区提供冬季采暖服务。

开源站建于2003年，于2003年11月10日正式为企业提供冬季采暖和全年生产用蒸汽服务。

创业总部基地C区建于2010年，有四台地源热泵空调机组，主要为用户提供冬季采暖和夏季制冷服务。创业总部基地B1、B3及北区建于2015年，有15台空调机组，主要为用户提供夏季制冷服务。

中欧产业园建于2014年，有四台地源热泵空调机组，主要为用户提供冬季采暖和夏季制冷服务。

三、机构编制

2016年，热力公司有职工88名。办公室管理人员5名，源泉供热站24名，创业总部基地28名，中欧产业园6名，维修队11名，栖仙东站、栖仙西站、禄源站及开源站共14名。

热力公司有源泉供热站、创业总部基地和中欧产业园3个站所。

源泉站位于武清开发区源泉路11号，2016年有三台20吨天然气蒸汽锅炉，为区内22家企业提供冬季供暖服务，供暖面积约4万平方米。为14家企业提供生产用蒸汽服务。年供蒸汽量8万吨，高峰时供汽量40吨/小时。

创业总部基地站位于创业总部基地C区，有地源热泵空调机组4台，为创业总部基地96家企业提供夏季制冷和冬季供暖服务，面积约16万平方米。创业总部基地B1、B3及北区，15台空调机组为创业总部基地30家企业提供夏季制冷服务，面积约32万平方米。

中欧产业园站位于开发区四期，组4台地源热泵空调机为产业园内7家企业提供夏季制冷和冬季供暖服务，面积约6万平方米。

热力公司有5座换热站。源泉站一座、创业总部基地四座（创业总部基地C区一座、B1区块一座、B3区块一座、北区一座）。

热力公司有WQ-01和WQ-02号两口地热井。WQ-01号地热井建于1993年，位于福源道与泉州路西。年开采量4万立方米，为开发区总公司及尚清湾小区居民提供热水服务。WQ-02 号地热井建于 1994 年，位于泉旺路东。年开采量 10 万立方米，为栖仙东区、栖仙中区、栖仙西区及英华学校提供热水服务。

第四节 燃气

1996 年起，投资一亿元开建了“陕气入杨”工程，来自全国各地的“百川燃气”“滨达燃气”“天津大燃气”等专营公司，相继进入开发区运营，为燃气供应提供热情周到、安全优质的服务。

百川燃气有限公司

天津武清百川燃气销售有限公司位于开发区泉州公路西侧，公司成立于 2005 年，注册资金 5000 万元。隶属于百川能源（股票代码：600681），公司专营天然气管道管网输配、燃气经营、天然气灶具、热水器、计量表销售、安装、维修服务、会展策划。为武清开发区燃气供应企业之一。

截至 2016 年，公司管网现已覆盖 1 个中心城区，14 个乡镇，气源来自中石油武清翁羊坊分输站，设计日供气能力 200 万立方米，累计居民用户达 12 万余户，工商业用户 500 余户。

公司人员共计 120 人，年收入 21265.78 万元。2016 年纳税近 2000 万元。公司成立以来，本着服务用户、服务企业的宗旨为武清城区及部分乡镇提供优质天然气，在公司全体员工的努力下，业务迅速发展，合作的知名企业包括比亚迪、伊利乳业、红日药业、天狮大学、唯品会、酒仙网、亚马逊、佛罗伦萨小镇、RIO、三全食品等，为雍鑫信杰、凯森热力、久久热力、开发区热力等供热企业及东蒲洼、南蔡村、黄庄、后巷、下朱庄等还迁区提供用气保障，工程施工及供气服务建立了良好的口碑。

滨达燃气有限公司

天津滨达燃气实业有限公司武清公司建于 1996 年 6 月。注册资金 1.5 亿美元。坐落在武清开发区广源道 1 号。为武清开发区生产生活燃气供应企业之一。

2016 年公司有员工 78 人，武清公司经营范围：城区、武清开发区、逸仙园、梅厂镇、徐官屯、曹子里、南蔡村、景瑞，主管网长度 59.733 公里，庭院管网 145.1869 公里。截至 2016 年年底，合同户数 52955 户，通气点火户数 27767 户，2016 年度气体销量 3293 万立方米。

营运与安全管理部负责运营管理，客户服务部负责民用户、工服用户的抄表收费、卡表开卡、落户、工单录入等工作。公司有专职安检人员 7 人，管网巡检人员 7 人，维修人员 18 人，专职安全管理人员 1 人。

截至 2016 年年底，燃气居民合同用户 58 个小区，共 52779 户，通气户数 27555 户，工业服务用户 212 户，年度气体销量 3293 万立方米。其中工业用户包括武清开发区内的三星视界、中粮包装、丹佛斯、南玻、完达山、浦项世亚等国内外知名企业。

此外，为武清开发区供应燃气的还有坐落在武清开发区内的天津大燃气有限公司。

第五章　市容与环卫管理

走进武清开发区，一种绿化美化、花园式、生态文明之感油然而生，京津走廊之间一座现代化的科技新城正在崛起。

第一节　综合执法移交

2015 年 4 月 25 日，为深化行政执法体制改革，提升行政执法效能和社会综合管理水平，按照《天津市街道综合执法暂行办法》规定和《天津市人民政府关于推进街镇综合执法工作的实施意见》的部署要求，按照属地管理、条块结合的原则和缩短执法半径、提高管理效率的工作思路，下移执法重心，在街（镇）组建综合执法队伍，实施“一支队伍管执法”的行政执法新模式，切实提升基层社会综合管理能力和水平，武清开发区根据地域分别纳入杨村街、东蒲洼街、徐官屯街、南蔡村镇综合执法范围。

第二节　市容管理

武清开发区的市容管理属城市管理部负责，下设市容管理队伍。

其主要工作：一是加强区内日常市容市貌管理，提升城市形象和品位。自建区以来，逐步健全管理网络，完善管理制度，分解管理片区，确保定人、定岗、定职责，使违法行为得到及时有效处置，为市容管理工作奠定了组织保障。同时，区内市容管理实行 24 小时全天候管理。对早中晚易形成管理空档的时间段，实行早中晚班制，即早上 6∶00 上班，晚上 12∶00 下班，进行不间断巡查管理。二是不断开展集中市容环境整治活动。认真落实精细化管理，积极开展市容市貌集中整治活动。集中整治主要分为两个方面：一是重点对主干道两侧的占道经营、流动摊点、乱停乱放等进行集中整治，规范整理城区市容市貌。二是重大节日前，进行市容环境集中整治，为节日增添浓烈氛围、靓丽色彩。三是加强区内广告、霓虹灯管理，规范城区美化亮化秩序。市容管理部门对户外广告许可上注重从源头抓起。对新设置的广告牌确立规划先行理念，明确广告牌制作标准、规格、材质等。对不合格广告牌进行集中拆除，使开发区户外广告设置有了质的提高，进一步美化城区市容市貌。与此同时，不断加大对霓虹灯广告设施的管理，对区域内的霓虹灯广告设施进行拉网式排查，晚间根据亮化情况登记亮化问题，白天针对排查问题逐一进行督促整改。

第三节　环卫管理

健全管理机制，强化制度建设，不断改进环卫管理，确保区内环境干净整洁。自建区以来，环卫管理建设工作，经历了由简单到精细、从人工到机械的过程。

随着开发区道路基础设施建设的不断完善，清扫保洁道路面积也在逐年扩大。到2016年，区内的清扫保洁总面积已达到300多万平方米。在垃圾清理、路面与环境等方面，坚持每一条路段都能落实“保洁全天候、管理无缝隙、责任全覆盖”的总体要求和具体标准。对一些“亮点、难点、重点”地段增添清扫保洁人员，增加巡回保洁趟次；主干道路充分利用道路冲洗车、道路清扫车工作效率高，机动性强的特点，充分做好人、机配合清扫保洁工作。

为减轻清扫保洁人员工作强度，不断提升区内保洁质量，开发区对环卫工作加大投资力度，不断从国内外购买环境清扫保洁机械设备。到2016年，已先后购置洒水车2辆、洗扫车8辆、干扫车5辆。开发区市容环境管理部门机械化水平日益提高，充分利用道路清扫车、道路冲洗车工作效率高，机动性强的特点，配合人工做好清扫保洁工作。

第三篇

招商引资

第一章　招商组织

第一节　园区招商部

1992年3月9日，武清县开发区管理委员会成立，梁文忠任主任，邵久武、杨作莹任副主任，王树培、武文宏、李本贵、甄玉鑫为成员。成立开发区总公司，王树培任总经理，下设综合部、招商部、建设部。

1996年12月，任命安友霞为招商部副部长。

1998年12月，任命王泉洪为招商部副部长。

2000年11月，任命杨宜峰为招商部部长，黄玉广为招商部副部长。

2001年9月，任命尹国华为招商部副部长。

2005年11月，任命崔秀杰为招商部部长。

2006年3月，任命黄巨山为总公司招商部副部长，暂时主持工作。

2006年9月，经总经理办公会议研究决定：聘任黄巨山为总经理助理，兼任总公司招商部部长。王洪亮任总公司招商部副部长。

2007年5月，任命安友霞为总公司招商部副部长。总公司招商部由副部长王洪亮主持工作。

2008年11月，任命王洪亮为招商部部长。

2009年，任命郎聪为招商部副部长。

2010年4月，任命王继宾为招商部部长。

2010年10月，任命杜瀛涛为招商部部长。

2010年11月，任命郎聪为招商部部长。

2012年3月，总公司招商部拓展为招商一部、二部、三部、四部和创业拓展中心5个部门，相关部门人员调整如下：郎聪任招商一部部长；韩洪斌任招商二部部长；王金祥任招商三部副部长，主持工作（试用期一年）；许贤任招商四部副部长，主持工作（试用期一年）。

2013年，任命孙竹为招商二部副部长，主持工作（试用期一年）；任命王玉为招商五部副部长，主持工作（试用期一年）；王金祥试用期满，任招商三部副部长，主持工作；许贤试用期满，任招商四部副部长，主持工作。

2014年4月，任命王金祥为招商三部部长；任命许贤为招商四部部长。

2014年10月，成立招商六部，任命王金祥为招商一部部长；任命许贤为招商二部部长；王玉试用期满，任招商三部副部长，主持工作，免其招商五部副部长职；苑广伟任招商四部副部长，主持工作（试用期一年）；王小萌任招商五部副部长，主持工作（试用期一年）。

2014年12月，任命刘福伟为招商部副部长，负责侨梦苑招商工作（试用期一年）；李杰任招商六部副部长，主持工作（试用期一年）。

2015年7月，任命王玉为招商三部部长。

2016年3月，东疆武清产业园筹备工作领导小组办公室更名为东疆招商部；刘福伟任招商六部副部长，主持工作；李伟任东疆招商部副部长，主持工作，试用期一年。

2016年8月招商部部门调整，招商部下设五个部门，包括招商一部、招商二部、招商三部、招商四部及自贸区武清园招商部。王玉任招商一部部长，沈晓菁任招商一部副部长；许贤任招商二部部长；苑广伟任招商三部部长；王小萌任招商四部部长；王金祥任自贸区（武清园）招商服务中心主任。

招商部门主要职责：负责招商引资工作；负责招商队伍管理，建设高效、专业、廉洁团队；负责制定招商引资相关政策及办法；负责拓展招商引资渠道，搜集项目信息；负责项目接待，洽谈、考察、追踪、落地；负责投资协议、房屋租赁合同等合作文件起草；负责牵头并会同其他部门对项目进行综合评审，对达标项目提出入区意见和申请。

自贸区（武清园）招商服务中心职责：负责自贸区、天津港、东疆港有关部门协调工作；负责自贸区武清园筹备期内运营主体的设立、变更工作；负责自贸区相关项目的引进及服务，确保高标准完成年度任务；负责自贸区相关政策研究，并提供政策咨询；处理与自贸区武清园相关的其他事项。

引资情况：建区以来，共吸引投资1400亿元，其中外资80亿美元以上，引入50个国家和地区的企业2200余家，其中世界500强投资企业35家，国内外行业龙头企业200余家。世界500强投资企业包括美国艾默生、亚马逊、沃尔玛，法国苏伊士、佛吉亚、家乐福，日本住友，韩国LG，新加坡丰树，澳大利亚沃利帕森，奥地利奥钢联，中国中粮，中化集团，中国水电，国家电投，中交集团，华电集团，太平洋建设等；国外龙头企业包括丹麦绫致、丹佛斯、艾尔姆，瑞典戴纳派克、贝格，德国GEA、万可、HAY、格立莫、阿玛松、米勒、欧文托普，美国麦格昆磁，维益食品，法国库恩，英国哈克尼斯，芬兰玻石机械，土耳其欧德亮法尔宝，韩国日进汽车，突尼斯柯菲凯博，澳大利亚嘉民物流等；国内龙头企业包括天狮、南玻、信义玻璃、娃哈哈饮品、伊利酸奶、完达山乳业、红日药业、三全食品、奥克斯、畅联物流、诺禾致源、汉氏联合、阿芙精油、妈妈壹选、薇美姿等。

第二节　智能制造产业重大项目工作组

2016年8月1日，开发区成立智能制造产业重大项目工作组，张绍锋任组长，李鹏程任副组长，王树柠为组员，聘任雷彦斌为顾问，日常工作由李鹏程负责。

智能制造产业重大项目工作组部门职责：

一、深入研究《中国制造2025》等国家关于智能制造产业发展的相关政策文件。

二、负责制定武清开发区智能制造产业发展规划，并统筹推进智能制造产业发展。

三、负责智能制造产业创新平台规划和运营管理，遴选和引进智能制造产业核心技术产业平台。

四、负责制定武清开发区智能制造产业扶持政策，助推产业发展。

五、加强与国家、天津市、武清区相关部门的对接，组织开发区智能制造企业申报享受各项扶持政策。

六、充分利用开发区产业引导基金支持智能制造企业发展。

2016年年底，完成《武清开发区智能制造产业发展规划》整体方案。主要通过8个企业链条板块（机车车辆板块、通信信号板块、新型材料板块、四电系统板块、工务工程板块、教育认证板块、节能环保板块、客货运输板块）对今后开发区的发展和招商目标作出细致规划。对开发区今后的招商引资、园区建设、平台搭建、科技创新、国际合作与保障措施上提出专业性建议。

2016年成立智能交通园，围绕打造开发区特色优势产业，按照有基础、有特色，代表京津冀开发区水平的要求，谋划建设武清开发区智能交通园区。

智能交通园产业定位充分发挥铁科院、北交控实力雄厚、规模巨大、带动能力强的优势，配套引进上下游企业，完善轨道交通装备制造产业链条，实现科技创新成果产业化，形成特色和优势突出、产业链协同高效、核心竞争力强、公共服务体系健全的智能交通产业集群，拉动武清开发区经济增长。经过近1年的时间，铁科院已完成一期建设并投产，二期工程正在建设当中。北交控也已经准备进行建设。

第三节　生物医药产业重大项目工作组

2016年8月1日，开发区成立生物医药产业重大项目工作组，郭新华任组长，孙浩任副组长，王永苹为组员，日常工作由孙浩负责。

生物医药产业重大项目工作组部门职责：

一、负责生物医药产业规划统筹和整体推进，制定产业发展顶层设计方案。

二、负责推进生物医药产业聚集区物理空间的对接及整体方案的规划。

三、负责生物医药产业创新平台的规划和运营，打造生物医药产业优势的核心技术平台。

四、负责生物医药产业扶持政策的制定和执行，与相关主管部门对接生物医药产业支持政策的申报、评审及后期兑现等相关工作，尤其是国家支持的重大专项研发课题的申报及国家工程技术中心、重点实验室的申报和后期服务工作。

五、负责生物医药产业招商引资统筹协调，负责高校院所、科研机构等资源及国际科技合作项目的引进，同时推动重大项目的对接与落地。

六、协助推进生物医药引导基金的设立、管理及使用。

七、完成领导交与的其他事宜，配合公司内其他部门完成整体工作协调。

2016年年底，制定完成了生物医药聚集区的顶层设计、工作方案以及产业促进政策；完善生物医药产业领域“引进育留”的人才支持政策，搭建生物医药产业的科技创新创业领军人才服务平台，形成适应产业发展需要的高端领军人才支撑队伍；完成国际健康产业示范区的选址及整体框架设计，对接专业设计院对该起步区进行整体板块的布局设计，并配合规划设计部门进行招投标工作；对接武清区人民政府、天津市科委、天津市投促办三方共建武清生物医药产业合作协议，并完成合作协议签署前期准备工作。

第四节 驻外办事机构

一、驻京办事处

驻京办事处（In Peking office；BJO）是经过国务院机关事务管理局批准，由其下设的驻京办事处管理司直接负责管理的机构。驻京办是涵盖省、直辖市、自治区以及特区的驻京机构。

武清开发区驻京办设立于 2013 年 8 月，源于天津市政府驻京办武清区首都工作部的设立。主要组成人员包括：区政府办副主任张朝阳任首都工作部主任；武清区招商局招商科常威；武清开发区管委会总公司招商一部项目经理苑广伟；武清区招商局招商科张耀方。首都工作部主要职责是面向北京及京津冀，深挖北京优势企业资源，维护渠道资源，以支持天津，支持武清的各项事业发展，尤其是经济发展。

2013年是首都工作部设立的第一年，联系机构、维护渠道等事宜作为主要工作内容，招商引资工作处于紧锣密鼓的基础筹备阶段。

2014 年 5 月，苑广伟结束首都工作部的派驻工作，调回开发区负责招商一部的引资工作。在此期间加强与区招商局，北京相关渠道的联系沟通，宣传推介开发区，并完成领导安排的各项工作，为驻京办未来的工作开展打下了坚实的基础。

2016 年，李鸿忠任天津市委书记，并在走访调研武清区工作的过程中提出武清要在京津冀协同发展中“当先锋，当猛将，唱重头戏”。因此武清开发区工委研究决定，成立京津冀协同发展办公室及武清开发区驻京办。驻京办由自贸区（武清园）招商服务中心段然牵头主要工作。办事处定位为：项目招商、渠道拓展、信息储备的全功能前沿阵地。旨在响应协同发展号召，同时加强与首都产业经济的联动发展，对接非首都功能产业转移。

段然于 2016 年 12 月 19 日正式到位，前期派驻区招商局首都工作部，招商局副局长韩艳涛任主任，武清商务区等其他园区均有人员派驻。

2017 年，武清开发区北京办事处考核指标为：全年引进实体及结算类项目 20 个，实现税收 2000 万元。

截至 2017 年第一季度，累计引进项目 10 个，引资额 1.21 亿元人民币，其中总部结算类项目 6 个，外资项目 1 个，超亿元项目 1 个，参加产业会议论坛，项目对接等活动41次，积累了一批优质的在谈项目，并与北京市科委、朝阳区商务委、通州区投促局、中国国际技术智力合作公司、中欧商协会、首都股权投资协会等渠道建立了良好的合作关系。

通过驻京办现有阶段的工作和各方面资源的积极拓展，下一步计划通过市场化手段，探索在京组建独立招商团队的可行性，以期更好地服务于京津冀协同发展，更好地宣传推介武清开发区，打造好武清开发区对接首都产业外迁的前沿阵地。

二、珠三角办事处

珠三角办事处于2016年8月5日成立。刘福伟任珠三角办事处主任，主持工作。

珠三角办事处工作职责主要包括作为开发区驻珠三角区域窗口，积极与当地政府、企业及高校院所等交流互动，做好开发区宣传推介工作，推动开发区在珠三角区域的战略布局；负责办事处招商队伍管理，建设高效、专业、廉洁团队；负责开发区在珠三角区域的招商引资工作，追踪考察重点项目、组织珠三角区域有拓展意向企业赴开发区考察交流，促进企业投资落户开发区；负责为开发区制定珠三角区域招商引资相关政策及办法提供参考信息；负责拓展珠三角区域招商引资渠道，搜集项目信息。

珠三角办事处引资成果丰硕，吸引包括影儿时尚集团、露乐母婴用品、薇美姿持股平台等优质项目落户武清开发区。

三、德国代表处

德国代表处于2014年年底成立。劳津任代表处主任。

德国代表处工作职责主要为配合商务部投促局搭建德国中心平台；加强武清开发区在德在欧宣传；收集项目信息，跟进在谈项目，推动项目落户武清开发区。

德国代表处引资成果丰硕，主要成果包括推动商务部投促局批准中国国际投资促进中心与武清开发区合作共建“中欧产业园”；推动德国农业机械项目克罗尼和德国跨境电商项目 kidsroom 落户武清开发区。

第二章 招商活动

第一节 招商理念

一、主要理念

武清开发区始终秉承“服务他人就是发展自己”的理念，把满足企业发展需要作为核心目标，精心打造具有国际标准的投资服务环境。通过建设布局合理、功能齐全、环境优美的服务设施，打造全面、过硬、完善的服务体系，让所有投资者在这里感到家的舒适与温暖。

以目标市场中投资者所需的价值为中心，优化投资环境，优选招商项目。用有效的招商引资策略解决投资者的问题，满足投资者的需求。树立亲商服务意识；创造优惠投资政策，打造配套法制环境，建设完善基础设施。

制定人才、技术、资本等专项扶持政策，吸引创业“种子”，培植发展“土壤”，大力引进高等院校和科研院所研究机构、产学研合作项目、高科技成果转化项目、国家重点实验室、留学生项目和科技服务业，以及“互联网 +”、智能制造、生物技术等前沿产业。年内引进研发、孵化、转化等高端院所项目、科技型中小企业，推动企业申报市级、国家级高新技术企业。推动制造业价值链向研发设计、市场开拓“微笑曲线”两端延伸。

第二节 招商方式

开发区主动开拓招商方式方法，运用多途径多渠道开发创新，争取效益最大化。

一、商务拜访

招商人员及时联系项目投资方，通过登门拜访、邀请来区、电话、邮件等方式，介绍开发区投资环境等情况，深入了解项目投资计划和实际需求，就双方关注问题进行洽谈沟通。

二、市场化招商

加强与新兴中介机构的合作，利用其紧贴市场、熟悉企业、熟悉政策等优势，创新激励保障机制，成立市场化招商部门，实施专业化招商。建立招商大使聘任制度，聘请社会及企业知名人士为招商大使，充分利用优势资源，发挥桥梁纽带作用。建立与产业联盟、行业协会的合作机制。利用其行业主导地位，适时举办峰会、论坛等活动。扩大开发区影响力，引进优质项目。

三、政府组团招商

轰动效应，参加人员多，气氛热烈，有时能产生连锁反应。

四、小组专业招商

优点：行动灵活，针对性强，效率较高。这是目前招商最常用的一种方式。

五、驻点招商

派出专业人员到外商较为集中和资金积累较早的地区实行驻点招商。针对性和连续性较好，可以做很深入细致的工作。

六、以商招商

通过投资客商的现身说法，实行以商招商。

七、借助网络“窗口”虚拟招商

一是网上发布项目信息，把项目推向全国、全世界；二是积极搜寻网上信息，特别关注大集团、大企业的网页，寻找商机。三是利用微博、Q群，发展与各大公司和知名企业高管的联系，主动接洽和推介，开展全方位、多层次、宽领域的交流与合作，为今后争取和引进项目奠定基础。

第三章　招商载体

第一节　创业总部基地

一、设置

创业总部基地项目占地1.26平方公里，建筑面积120万平方米，总投资达60亿元人民币，功能定位为主要发展商务、办公、创意、动漫、研发、IT、服务外包、企业总部等现代服务业，其中共规划6个区域，包括3个功能区，分别是企业总部区、服务外包区和综合办公区；3个配套区，分别是中心服务区、商务酒店区和专家公寓区，各种生产、生活配套功能齐全，为入驻企业提供最为优质高效的办公服务体验。

功能区之一：企业总部区。基本情况和发展定位：位于基地西北部，占地260亩，共有21栋楼宇，建筑面积32万平米，是承接企业总部、地区总部、分支机构及研发中心、采购中心、物流中心、营销中心、结算中心和管理中心等的高水平载体平台。至2016年，项目已全面竣工，项目招商同步进行。已入驻华电水务总部、中铁22局、威莱日化北方销售总部、星期六鞋业销售总部、诺禾致源生物科技、惠尔丰信息系统等30余个优质高端项目；并与腾讯孵化器、华纳音乐、中铁24局等50余家深入进行洽谈，部分达成入驻意向。

功能区之二：服务外包区。基本情况和发展定位：位于基地南部，占地160亩，共14栋建筑，建筑面积16万平米。主要承接服务外包产业、创意产业、科技型中小企业及其孵化平台。项目于2010年年底投入使用，已入驻中投证券投资、中体竞赛集团总部、中国亿农科技结算中心、卓越亚马逊呼叫中心、中兴云计算、玉柴重工全球营销结算中心、娃哈哈采购中心、银乐保销售总部、阿芙精油销售总部等100余个优质项目。

功能区之三：综合办公区。基本情况和发展定位：位于基地东南部，占地200亩，是承接金融产业、商务办公等的载体平台，规划建成商务综合组团。至2016年，项目已基本完成建设。

配套区之一：中心服务区。基本情况及功能定位：位于基地中部湖心岛，占地130亩、建筑面积6万平米。为入驻功能区项目提供展览展示、信息服务、文化娱乐、高档餐饮和生态观光等功能于一体的配套服务支撑体系。至2016年，项目已基本建成，近期部分将投入使用。

配套区之二：商务酒店区。基本情况和功能定位：位于基地西南部，占地70亩、建筑面积18.6万平米。包括五星级酒店、水疗中心、娱乐中心和快捷酒店，可提供中高档住宿、娱乐休闲等相关配套服务。至2016年，项目正进行内外檐装修，年内投入使用。

配套区之三：专家公寓区。基本情况和发展定位：位于基地东北部，占地300亩，总建筑面积40万平方米。为入驻功能区项目高管打造的复合型、低密度、高品位居住社区，包括独栋别墅、联排公寓、情景洋房、高层等高档滨水住宅，可购买、可租住。项目已建成可入住。

二、管理

创业总部基地由武清开发区下属物业公司——天津市武清开发区物业公司进行园区物业服务管理，园区物业将为入驻企业提供以下服务内容：

严密的治安防范服务：根据园区每栋楼宇的实际运营情况，规划、设计出严密、高效的秩序维护体系，辅以先进的安全监控系统、超前的安全管理理念、严格的队伍管理制度、高素质的秩序管理队伍，确保每一家入驻企业办公环境的安全舒适。

高效的环境维护服务：专业的清洁、消杀和绿化养护队伍，精心打理、修饰园区每一寸空间，确保楼内卫生整洁清新，园区绿化草常绿、树常青、花常开，着力为每一名工作在创业总部基地的企业员工创造一个亲近自然的工作生活环境。

完善的设施管理服务：科学、严格的设备管理和高素质的专业技术人员，为园区企业提供全天候24小时公共设施保障服务，确保园区办公、生活舒适便利。定岗定位定时的各类专业维修服务，时刻保证入驻企业各项设施的运行顺畅。

专业的小区工程完善服务：凭借工程技术优势，提供园区专业化工程维修维护服务，以人为本，从处处方便园区企业运行的角度出发，不断改善园区整体办公服务水平。

优质的首问负责制服务：首先受到来访、来电、咨询或投诉的任一工作人员即为首问责任人，要负责给予对方必要的指引、介绍或答疑等服务，对于不属于本部门业务范围的要负责引导入驻园区企业与相关部门进行接洽，督促、协助相关部门做好接待，并跟进业务办理结果，使每一家入驻园区企业得到便捷、满意的优质服务。

周到的定期走访服务：针对已入住的企业，企业服务部将定期对其进行走访，听取企业相关人员在园区办公中遇到的问题，记录企业对园区服务的意见建议以及个性化要求，针对业主提出的建议，持续进行改进，为业主提供更加优秀高效的服务。

第二节　中欧产业园

2015年10月30日，由中国商务部投资促进事务局和武清开发区管委会主办的“2015年武清开发区中欧产业园投资环境说明会暨欧盟商协会领袖与企业家对话会”在武清开发区举行。商务部投资促进事务局、中国国际投资促进中心、天津市商务委、武清区各职能部门、德国商界领袖及企业家代表、开发区已入区企业、意向客户、服务机构负责人共80余人参加。武清开发区总公司副总经理王继宾主持会议。

会上，武清区副区长刘东海从区位交通、生态环境及经济社会发展等方面介绍了武清区基本情况。他强调，当前天津面临着京津冀协同发展、建设自由贸易试验区、加快滨海新区开发开放、建设国家自主创新示范区和“一带一路”等五大战略机遇，为武清抢占战略制高点、实现转型发展新突破提供了千载难逢有利条件。借助区位、交通、生态、产业和服务等方面综合优势，武清将加快建设京津国家级创新主轴重要节点、京津冀协同发展示范区、改革开放先行区。他表示，多年来武清高度重视与各国合作，先后有50个国家和地区的280余家外资企业落地发展，武清与其一直保持着紧密而良好的交流合作关系。在商务部投资促进局的支持和帮助下，围绕为外资企业创造更优的发展环境，商务部投资促进事务局和武清开发区共建中欧产业园，通过打造便捷的交通、优美的环境和高效的服务，为更多外资企业特别是欧洲企业加快发展创造了良好的载体平台。武清将秉承“服务他人就是发展自己”的理念，为投资者提供强有力的商业及公共事业配套、金融等支持，扶持企业成长成功，使武清成为各界朋友未来投资发展蓝图的一部分。

商务部投资促进事务局副局长王旭致辞，他表示，中欧经贸关系是世界上规模最大、最具活力的经贸关系之一。双向投资成为促进中欧各自经济发展和创新的主要动力，而“一带一路”倡议的提出又为中欧更加紧密的合作创造了机遇。近年来，武清高度重视与欧洲各国企业合作，目前已有英国、德国等14个欧洲国家的100余家企业在武清投资，与武清保持紧密良好的合作关系。武清经济技术开发区中欧产业园的启动，标志着武清与欧洲企业之间的合作将会进入一个全新的阶段，为武清将自身打造成为京津走廊最具竞争力的经济区域带来更多的机遇。商务部投资促进事务局作为负责“引进来”和“走出去”双向投资促进工作的国家级投资促进机构，一直致力于依托自身合作网络，通过现有各类精品投资促进活动及双向投资项目信息资源，为中欧园区、企业之间搭建交流与对接的平台。此外，商务部投资促进事务局也高度重视海外投资促进分支机构的拓展和建设，目前已在欧洲设立了两个驻外机构—德国中心及匈牙利中心。武清开发区是德国中心的共建合作单位，过去的一年，双方密切配合，合力在德做了大量卓有成效的对德对欧投资促进工作。今后，商务部投资促进事务局驻欧的两个机构还将继续发挥平台和窗口作用，为包括武清在内的国内外园区、企业拓展双边资源，提供信息资源和渠道支撑。

随后，举行中欧产业园揭牌仪式。中国国际投资促进中心(德国)(上文:“德国中心”)主任徐遥君介绍共建中欧产业园有关情况，他讲到，德国中心是商务部投资促进事务局落实中德两国政府有关“推动在德设立投资促进机构”共识而在德国设立的中方机构，以“立足德国，面向欧洲，服务全国”为宗旨，与国内6省市商务主管部门和开发区建立合作关系，为拓展中德双边资源、开展合作提供信息和渠道支撑。2014年底武清开发区作为德国中心共建单位之一在德国法兰克福注册成立德国代表处，并派驻专员赴德长期开展投资促进工作。武清开发区规划建设的中欧产业园落实《国务院办公厅关于促进国家级经济技术开发区转型升级创新发展的若干意见》(国办发〔2014〕54号)文件精神，促进园区转型升级创新发展的重要举措，通过打造京津之间承接欧洲企业的载体平台，体现德国中心与武清开发区共建的实质性成果。经商务部投资促进事务局研究同意由中国国际投资促进中心与武清开发区共建中欧产业园。仪式上，刘东海与王旭为“武清经济技术开发区中欧产业园”揭牌。

接下来，武清开发区工委委员、开发区副总经理郎聪围绕中欧产业园的基本情况、投资环境和投资解决方案等方面进行详细介绍。他指出，中欧产业园位于武清开发区四期，规划面积9.5平方公里，其中一期5平方公里，二期4.5平方公里。为欧洲企业打造的发展平台载体，以生物医药、先进制造业、新材料为主导产业，建成高端产业发展基地。其中，生物医药主要引进诊断试剂、仿制药、保健药项目，先进制造业主要引进高端设备制造和关键零部件制造项目，新材料主要引进生物医药材料、电子信息材料、节能环保材料项目。产业园内一期、二期分别体现3个产业各自聚集，相关项目可以直接入驻一期，二期为项目未来扩展预留空间。中欧产业园是水绿特色鲜明的生态园区，毗邻龙凤河，依托先进节能环保技术，实现绿色建筑推广、太阳能与建筑一体化、地源热泵等应用；建有再生水厂，实现水资源循环利用。目前已完成一期开发，已经引入了欧文托普、伍尔特、哈尼克斯、克罗尼、格立莫、阿玛松等一批欧洲产业项目。为欧洲企业量身建设环保节能标准厂房，规划建设占地150亩，建筑面积20万平方米的标准厂房，其中5万平米已投入使用。产业园全部建成后，预计引进欧洲项目100个以上，每年实现税收40亿元以上。

随后，“欧盟商协会领袖与企业家对话会”举行。德国中小企业联合会中国区主席波茨曼先生介绍了德国中小企业发展经营情况和经验，欧文托普（天津）暖通空调设备有限公司副总经理朱国林先生介绍了企业在武清开发区的投资生产情况，德国《企业家》杂志社主编盖茨纳先生与嘉宾交流了德国企业营销网络和企业文化，德国西蒙顾和公司中国区总裁王裕治先生介绍 “隐形冠军”企业的发展理念和对华合作前景，华韵尚德国际文化总监张家富先生就中国园区在德推介经验进行了发言。随后，与会来宾就中欧相关热点问题进行讨论。

第四章　招商成果

第一节　撤县建区前招商

开发区遵循“着眼长远，适当超前，综合起步，滚动开发”的发展思路，自1992年4月正式启动以来，坚持基础设施和招商引资两手抓，在实际运作中做到“选用一片，开发一片，建成一片，收益一片”，由小到大，滚动发展。建区的当年即完成“四通一平:（给水、排水、电力、供热通信和土地平整）。吸引中外企业43家引资9.2亿元，其中外资9100万美元。至1993年，“五通一平”面积扩大到2.5平方公里。发展国内外招商代理机构，设立北京招商部，并与国家及京津两地侨联、台联等十几个团体及涉外机构建立协作关系，吸纳了一批规模大、起点高的企业入驻。1993年新增入区企业68家，协议投资15亿美元。经过多年的开发建设，至2000年，开发区吸引了来自国内和世界各地119个国家和地区的330家企业入区，投资总额60亿元，其中外资5.2亿美元。产业涉及电子信息、新型材料、生物医药、机电一体化、服装、食品等。区内投资企业以外商投资为主，知名企业有：投资7000元美元，生产发光二极管的台湾光宝公司；投资5000万美元，生产水晶振动子的日本大真空公司；投资3700万美元，生产磁性材料钕铁硼的美国麦格昆磁公司；投资3000万美元：生产西洋乐器的杰麦集团；投资2400万美元，生产温控器的丹麦丹佛斯公司；投资2300万美元，生产女士时装的日本伊都锦有限公司；投资1886万美元，生产环保型化学地板砖和地垫的韩国LG新型建材有限公司；投资1200万美元，生产压路机械设备的瑞典斯维达拉公司；投资1000万美元，生产精制钢铁剪板的华住金属制品有限公司。此外还有生产药芯焊丝的天津大学三英焊业公司和主要生产高钙素等健康产品的国内民营企业天狮集团等。

第二节　进入 21 世纪以后引资成果

进入 21 世纪以来，开发区不断扩大招商力度，引资成果逐年递增。

2002 年，积极利用优惠政策和中介人奖励政策招商。学好、吃透《武清开发区入区项目部分优惠政策修订意见》，积极向社会各界宣传，通过奖励政策调动各方面人士招商引资的积极性。极大鼓舞了全区人士的招商积极性。有 47 名获奖中介人得到区政府拨给的奖金。

采取灵活手段招商引资。通过新区展示、媒体宣传、项目追踪、专业会议、网站宣传、网络沟通、贷款担保、补贴租房费用等手段，围绕电子信息、新材料、生物医药、机械制造四个主导产业开展有针对性招商，促使形成产业群，发挥规模效应。以我国加入 WTO 及申奥成功为契机，盯住北京设施建设跟进北京建筑建材、建筑机械制造等项目。充分发挥开发区地缘优势，追踪、洽谈、引进，搞好服务，加快建设投产速度，促进项目入区落户。

截至 2003 年 11 月底，新增投资项目 70 家，协议利用外资老口径 7932.4 万美元，完成全年任务的 49.6%，同比增长 23.2%，新口径 4035.14 万美元，完成全年任务的 50.4%，同比增长 16%。内资企业注册资本 8. 2 亿元，完成全年任务的 102.5%，同比增长 84.2%。到 2003 年底，协议利用外资老口径可实现 13887 万美元，新口径 6201.6 万美元。

2004 年，引进新项目 44 家，企业增资 24 家，投资总额达到 32.6 亿元人民币，比 2003 年同期增长 80%，其中外资 2.4 亿美元，比 2003 年同期增长 126%；注册资本 17 亿元人民币，比 2003 年同期增长 35%(区政府工作报告中增幅为 54%)，其中外资 1.1 亿美元，比 2003 年同期增长 168%。2016 年，尚有后备项目 14 家，其中外资 12 家，注册资本均在 300 万美元以上，累计投资总额 1.6 亿美元，注册资本 7000 万美元；内资 2 家，投资总额 5.2 亿元，注册资本 3 亿元。

2005 年，强化高标准、高水平招商。全年引进新项目 28 家，投资总额达到 33 亿元人民币，同比增长 2.8%，其中外资 3.8 亿美元，同比增长 58.3%；注册资本 13.2 亿元，同比减少 18.1%，其中外资 1.2 亿美元，同比增长 13.8%。招商举措：一是明确主导产业和发展重点，扩大产业招商成果。年内引进的企业大多数为主导产业，其中汽车及零部件、电子信息、新型材料、生物医药、机械制造等五大主导产业的企业有 11 家，占新入区企业的 60%，占投资总额的 85%。二是进一步提高入区门槛。年内主要引进消耗资源特别是土地资源少，具有高科技含量和高附加值的“一少双高”企业，投资强度达到每亩100万元以上。年内共劝退不符合标准企业20余家，投资总额达到3亿元。

2007年，全年共引进企业64家，其中新批企业44家，增资企业20家；引资总额45亿元，其中外资2.4亿美元；注册资本30亿元（同比增长50%），其中外资1.45亿美元。5年间，开发区共引进企业339家，其中新批企业237家，增资企业102家；吸引投资总额157亿元，其中外资12亿美元；注册资本85亿元，其中外资5.3亿美元。

2008年，开发区招商工作走在了全市各区县的前列，全年共引进企业57家，吸引投资总额70.8亿元，同比增长101%；吸引注册资本50.2亿元，同比增长81%。年初确定的目标顺利实现。2008年开发区招商工作主要特点有：第一，外资引进取得较大突破。全年共引进外资企业29家，投资总额5.5亿美元，同比增长113%；注册资本4亿美元，同比增长142%。这两项主要指标都在全市同类开发区中名列前茅。第二，项目质量明显提高。全年开发区共引进投资超过5000万元的项目16个，购地建厂和租用厂房的项目绝大多数为外资。这些项目的共同特点：一是技术领先，均为国际同行业龙头；二是产品附加值高，市场前景和预期经济效益都非常好。同时，总部经济发展步伐加快，引进了一批投资规模大、税收前景好的商贸、地产及管理咨询类公司，其中单个项目注册资本在5000万美元以上的有4家。第三，全区招商资源整合平台作用明显。创业拓展中心以高效、快捷的服务赢得投资者和乡镇街道的认可。全年拓展中心共引进注册项目99个，吸引注册资本27.7亿元；其中外资项目8个，注册资本2.43亿美元。各乡镇街特别是一些基础薄弱的单位以拓展中心为平台，积极开展招商工作。共有18个乡镇街利用拓展中心引进73个项目，注册资本11.1亿元，产生税收5155万元。另外，开发区全年还向乡镇街推荐项目20个，注册资本15亿元以上。

2009年，妥善应对金融危机的不利影响，百倍珍惜土地资源，严格坚持招商标准，强化项目包装推介，加大跑和争的力度，特别是敢于在竞争中打硬仗、打胜仗，促进招商引资继续保持良好势头。第一，引资成果在全市同类开发区中名列前茅。全年共引进企业64家，其中外资企业24家。吸引投资总额51.7亿元，其中外资3亿美元。吸引注册资本39.39亿元，其中外资1.66亿美元。第二，项目质量进一步提高。引进项目中投资超过1亿元的19家，均为技术领先、附加值高、市场前景好的优质项目。

其中，佛罗伦萨小镇、韦史伐里亚分离机、三宇车体等3个项目投资均在10亿元左右，预计年税收均在1亿元以上。娃哈哈原材料采购中心预计年销售额200亿元、税收5000万元以上。同时，信义玻璃增资17.5亿元，主题公园项目投资总额30亿元。还引进了加拿大马泰克、法国赛诺制药、意大利爱迪姆机械制造和马克菲尔钢纤维、美国嘉吉、日本酉岛泵、丹麦新能源设备，以及国内的伊利酸奶、康普瑞机械制造、华圣蓝金等一批高质量项目。第三，全区招商平台作用更加突出。拓展中心全年引进项目107家，其中17个乡镇（街道）78家；吸引注册资本21.1亿元，其中乡镇街13.3亿元；实现税收1.65亿元，其中乡镇（街道）8704万元。全年，总公司共向乡镇（街道）推荐项目11个，投资总额4.2亿元。

2010年，共引进项目91个，投资总额105.75亿元，增长74.3%；注册资本65.8亿元，增长67%。其中，内资项目47个，投资总额67.6亿元，注册资本44.4亿元；外资项目44个，投资总额5.45亿美元，注册资本3.05亿美元。其中，投资超亿元优质项目共19个。第一，现代服务业招商实现高起步。引进了一批高质量的旅游、动漫、高档服务业和企业总部项目。其中有投资10亿元的玉圭园五星级酒店和投资30亿元的凯旋王国项目，投资10亿元的蓝猫卡通传媒，投资20亿元玉柴重工全球营销中心和融资租赁公司，分别投资7亿元的台湾华纳集团、香港俊安集团商务办公项目，以及上市公司九安医疗结算中心，商联总部基地等。第二，先进制造业引进一批大项目好项目。其中，信义节能环保玻璃生产基地投资30亿元、占地1008亩；伊利酸奶奶酪生产基地投资3亿元、占地200亩；中工马泰克投资2亿元、占地305亩；三全食品投资6亿元、占地278亩；大连机床投资2亿元、占地78亩；广州威莱日化用品投资1000万美元、占地82亩；美国维益食品投资1200万美元、占地28亩；国能飞腾对位芳纶投资6亿元、占地251亩；卡秀堡辉工业涂料投资500万美元、占地35亩；信堡节能玻璃投资2.2亿元、占地78亩；亚宝药业投资2亿元、占地63亩；韦斯伐里亚投资4800万欧元、占地240亩；敏华工业城投资3亿美元、占地723亩；以及比利时哈蒙国际热交换器、荷兰稳砜风电配套紧箍件等。第三，现代物流业招商开局良好。引进了深圳人人乐连锁超市物流配送中心，投资4亿元，占地300亩；以及上海佳吉物流项目。第四，现有企业增资扩产踊跃。天狮生命源、中粮包装、艾尔姆、南玻、信义玻璃、丹佛斯、大真空等企业共增加投资总额45.3亿元，其中外资3.28亿美元；增加注册资本34.57亿元，其中外资1.75亿美元。其中，中粮包装两片罐项目增加投资总额9000万美元，建成后将成为中粮集团国内最大的包装生产基地。第五，全区招商平台作用更加突出。

创业拓展中心引进项目 90 个，其中 16 个乡镇街的项目 64 个；吸引注册资本 38 亿元，其中乡镇街 2.2 亿元；实现税收 3.46 亿元，其中乡镇街 4618 万元。共向乡镇街推荐项目 16 个，其中规模较大的有，向汽车零部件产业园推荐的中建装饰和北京高速铁路玻璃项目，向地毯产业园推荐的中建钢构和硅酸钙造纸项目，向京滨工业园推荐的台湾亚克力项目，向豆张庄乡推荐的界龙纸业项目等。

2011 年，共引进项目 113 个，投资总额 82.7 亿元，增长 25.7%。引进投资超亿元优质项目 24 个，其中总投资超 30 亿元的 1 个，天津坝上春秋艺术园；总投资超 20 亿元的项目 2 个，敏华家具和普亚物流；总投资超过 10 亿元的项目 4 个，日进第二工厂、中纺院高新技术园、亚马逊电子商务运营中心、奥克斯二期。特别是，引进了亚马逊、普洛斯和国机重工等 3 个世界 500 强项目。第一，高端制造业聚集区基本招满项目，引进高端制造业项目 17 个。主要有敏华家具、国能飞腾、国机重工、日进第二工厂、韦史伐里亚、大连机床、中纺院高新技术园、美国维益食品、德国天马筛得力分离机、德国西马格矿山机械、德国大都克电触头、奥克斯数码电器、天加空调、凯涛奇第二工厂、恒通源水处理、嘉林药业、法国 BEIRENS 工业排风系统项目等项目。第二，依托创业总部基地平台，促进总部楼宇经济取得突破性发展，共引进项目 18 个。有中国亿农营销结算中心、天津振戎国际能源、奥克斯研发中心、完达山液态奶总部、可信科技有限公司、坝上春秋设计创意总部、圣火科技园、天盛鼎和通信工程有限公司、奥帕蒂玛软件有限公司、信邦科技创业投资公司、奥峰文化传媒、与众科技（天津）有限公司、天津雅歌科技有限公司、天津尚思科技有限公司、天津三和工业电器科技有限公司、安科科技发展（天津）有限公司、龙沙集团、融鑫汇、创达投资咨询等。截至 2016 年，创业总部基地共引进总部楼宇经济项目 40 余个。第三，保税物流区基本招满项目，引进现代物流项目 4 个。主要有普亚物流园、玉柴重工国际服务中心、玉柴物流中心、人人乐物流等。第四，原有企业增资扩产形式较好。2011 年开发区企业增资共 23.33 亿元。其中，较大增资项目包括信义玻璃增资 5.02 亿元、陶润置业 3.77 亿元、蜡笔小新 2.45 亿元、天狮生命科学 1.98 亿元、佛罗伦萨小镇 1.58 亿元。第五，加大项目信息追踪，储备一批优质项目。2016 年，主要在谈项目 39 个。其中在谈制造业项目有熔盛重工、陕西同力重工、丹麦格兰富工业泵等 21 个；在谈总部类项目有珠海振戎投资公司、汇通宏宇小额贷款、中材集团研发设计管理总部、中科博晓软件服务中心、亚马逊北方呼叫中心等 13 个；在谈物流项目有迪卡侬北方仓储物流分拨中心、艾格服装、北京探路者户外用品股份有限公司、森马物流等 5 个。第六，招商宣传推介工作不断加强。

以招商引资为核心，抓住升级国家级开发区和建区20周年两大契机，精心策划组织了系列宣传推介活动，借助媒体扩大了知名度和影响力。圆满完成了20周年发展高峰论坛和建区20周年纪念大会，得到各界一致好评。整理编辑了30余万字的开发区20周年发展纪实文集和开发区建区20周年纪念邮册。加强网站建设、运行与管理，充分发挥了其宣传平台和招商平台作用。

2012年，全年新引进项目共129个，注册资本85亿元。其中，完成注册手续的114个，注册资本82.99亿元。第一，一批大项目好项目落地。引进了投资25亿元的中投证券投资；超10亿元项目信义汽车玻璃、同力重工和日丰管业等3个；超亿元项目劲家庄食品、天地融电子、森马物流等15个。特别是，引进了世界500强项目美国国际纸业，及法国苏伊士、中化集团等3个。第二，重点区域招商顺利推进。一是高端制造业聚集区摆满项目。引进项目25个、投资总额134亿元，其中亿元以上优质项目有敏华家具、同力重工、远东宏信等14个。二是保税物流区完成招商。引进项目16个、投资总额56亿元，其中亿元以上优质项目有亚马逊、梦芭莎、森马物流等11个。三是创业总部基地引资成果显著。引进现代服务业和总部楼宇经济类项目37个。四是四期起步区招商态势良好。引进了超10亿元项目日丰管业，正抓紧洽谈投资超10亿元项目3个。五是加强了大院大所的追踪和引进。目前中纺院、天津建科院已落户，正在追踪的2个。第三，科技型中小企业发展顺利。截至2016年，开发区共有科技型中小企业336家。其中销售收入超亿元的“小巨人”企业56家，超“十二五”期间总任务数6家。积极落实扶持政策，99家次企业享受贷款贴息、创新项目、专利奖励等各种扶持资金2486万元。挖掘“上市源”企业，6家正加紧进行上市准备。加强银企对接，协助6家企业融资1.52亿元。强化产学研对接，以京津高校创新园为载体引进了天津大学前沿院。第四，招商宣传推介不断加强。一是首次在外地成功举办“投资环境北京推介会”，承办了“中欧经贸合作与可持续城镇化发展论坛”，扩大了知名度和影响力。二是区“两台一报”集中宣传报道了开发区，香港商报、人民政协报等10余家知名媒体对开发区进行了广泛宣传。第五，项目信息储备优质丰富。2016年，主要在谈项目有56个，其中，制造业项目32个、总部经济类项目10个、物流项目5个、现代服务业项目9个。另外，获取并正在追踪的项目信息29个。

2013年，创新招商工作机制。一是海外招商。先后2次赴德国、英国、瑞士等欧洲3国开展系列招商活动，首次在国外成功举办大规模投资说明会，首次成功参展国际高端展会——法兰克福2013年全球车展，拓展了中国驻德使馆法兰克福总领事馆、瑞中经济协会、英中贸易协会等新渠道7个，有力提升了武清区特别是开发区的知名度和影响力，获得我驻外使、领馆和国外企业、协会、商会等各界的一致好评。二是专项推介。全年在北京、上海、广州、福建、深圳、香港及区内举办了15场大、中型招商推介会。三是专业化和产业链招商。制定了欧盟产业园产业发展规划，明确生物医药、先进制造业和新材料为主攻方向，按照产业为主、兼顾区域原则专业化、产业链招商。

2014年，招商引资实现新突破。全方位拓展引资深度和广度，全年引进项目202个，引资到位额112亿元。一是大项目好项目招商。引进了中电投、中交建、美国德尔福等3个世界500强项目；投资200亿元的山水六旗文旅小镇；投资超亿元的维克空调、巴克斯酒业等19个。二是借重首都资源招商。引进了首都项目60个，其中有北交控、外交部后勤基地等实体项目10个，中投中财文化投资基金、欧华美科等楼宇经济项目50个。承担的全区借重首都资源重点项目伟嘉生物、云游总部等5个签约。三是重点平台招商。欧盟产业园以生物医药、先进制造业和新材料为重点，引进了迈恩德、柯菲凯博、格力莫、阿玛松等优质外资项目23个。创业总部基地以科技创新和结算中心为重点，引进了诺禾致源、阿芙精油结算中心等总部楼宇项目119个。高村科技创新园以大数据和生物医药为重点，引进项目151个，包括嘉丰达、亦昭生物等优质实体项目23个。

2015年，招商引资保持良好态势。开发区围绕主导产业，共引进项目240个，到位额120亿元，主要包括澳大利亚沃利帕森、法国家乐福等世界500强2个，政银合盈、信通瑞银等超10亿元项目3个，中铁五州、中禾种业等超亿元项目15个，网动科技、盈可泰农业技术等首都项目93个，中国科学院遗传所、北化工天津科研基地等院所类项目6个；光效影业、天下粮仓等总部类项目50个，以及格立莫、瑞士中心等优质外资项目15个。自贸区武清园围绕跨境电商、现代物流、融资租赁、商业保理和贸易结算产业，引进鲁西集团、海陆川贸易等项目151个。高村创新园围绕京津冀协同发展，依托区位、交通和环境优势，引进项目162个，引资到位额100.6亿元，主要有投资30亿元的搜房网总部和投资8亿元的新兴重工国际贸易总部项目。着力实施立体化招商宣传，举办创业总部基地、中欧产业园等集中推介活动10余次，参加相关领域专项活动30余次。发挥德国代表处和美国布瑞奇孵化器作用，赴欧洲、美洲开展2次海外招商，获得优质项目信息20余个。深入开展政策研究，结合京津冀协同发展、自创区、自贸区等叠加政策，制定了产业链招商规划和招商引资扶持政策，完善落实了项目预案、洽谈、会商、追踪回访、代理合作等招商工作机制。

2016年，在国际国内经济新常态大背景下，武清开发区认识、适应新常态，充分发挥同时享有国家经济技术开发区和国家高新技术产业园区、国家自主创新示范区、自由贸易园区政策优势，主动谋划，奋力攻坚，抢抓当前面临的推进京津冀协同发展、建设自由贸易园区、加快滨海新区开发开放、建设国家自主创新示范区和"一带一路"建设多重叠加历史机遇，利用得天独厚的地理位置和多年积聚的产业优势服务优势环境优势，推动形成"多元化、精细化、产业化"招商新模式，对外开放成绩显著，抢占了京津冀协同发展制高点、实现了开发区转型发展新突破。厉兵秣马，拼博实干，武清开发区在"十三五"开局之年经济运行持续稳步增长，协同发展取得积极进展，招商引资态势良好，创新驱动能力显著增强，载体平台不断优化，经济社会发展取得丰硕成果。

全年共引进项目265个，引资到位额101亿元，已超额完成全年任务。主要有佛吉亚、沃尔玛等世界500强项目3个，台湾大自然环保、中盈科创等超亿元项目18个，奥瀚科技、中文投等北京项目100个，海斯坦普、博思美等外资项目14个，新希望、美源星等总部项目36个，三英精控等亿元楼宇项目2个。自贸区武清园引进融资租赁、商业保理、资产管理类项目101个，注册资本82.6亿元。至2016年12月30日，共引进内资企业1873家，涉及12大类，其中：现代服务业519家，电子信息229家，生物医药121家，房地产业95家，机械制造业76家，批发零售业48家，新能源44家，新材料36家，汽车零部件20家，建筑业11家，电子商务2家，其它636家。

至2014年6月19日，引进外资企业253家，其中投资总额在1000万美元以上的（含1000万美元）67家，1000万美元以下100万美元以上的（含100万美元）75家，100万美元以下的111家。

第三节　2016年重点工程

2016年重点工程分为区级重点工程、开发区重点工程和产业项目三部分。其中区级重点工程2个大项，7个子项；开发区重点工程24个大项，101个子项；产业项目46个大项，46个子项。

一、2016 年区级重点工程（共 2 大项、7 子项）一览表

表 10

序号	项目名称	主要内容	完成时间	阶段性目标
1	主要指标	(1) 税收：在 2015 年基础上增长 30%。	年底	6 月实现任务过半；年底完成全年任务。
		(2) 固定资产投资：完成 285 亿元。	年底	6 月实现任务过半；年底完成全年任务。
		(3) 引资到位额：完成 100 亿元。	年底	每个招商部门上半年完成引资到位额 9 亿元；年底完成 17 亿元。
2	重点项目建设	(1) 天狮大学：完成一期建设。	年底	6 月完成主体；11 月完成外檐装修；年底完成一期建设。
		(2) 红日康仁堂：完成一期建设。	年底	3 月完成主体；6 月完成装修；11 月完成设备安装；年底完成一期建设。
		(3) 铁科院: 完成一期建设。	年底	4 月完成基础 ;10 月完成主体 ; 年底完成一期建设。
		(4) 北航智能制造研究院：投入运营。	6 月	4 月完成装修设计。
				6 月完成装修。
			年内	年内引进孵化企业 1 家，争取 1 家实验室挂牌。

二、2016 年开发区重点工程（共 24 大项、101 子项）一览表

表 11

序号	项目名称	主要内容	完成时间	阶段性目标
1	经济指标	(1) 地区生产总值：实现增长 15%。	年底	6 月实现任务过半；年底完成全年任务。
		(2) 工业总产值：实现增长 15%。	年底	6 月实现任务过半；年底完成全年任务。

续表 11

序号	项目名称	主要内容	完成时间	阶段性目标
2	创新创业平台	(1) 推进众创空间建设。	年内	1 月完成工作方案；年内推动市级众创空间认定工作，为企业和创新创业人才搞好各项服务。
		(2) 生物医药产业研究院：投入运营。	年内	2 月完成合作协议签订；6 月完成场地装修及设备购置；8 月确定方案，年底投入运营。
		(3) 京津冀协同创新发展研究院。	年内	年内协助做好京津冀产业定位相关工作。
		(4) 国际双创产业园。	9 月	9 月投入运营。
		(5) 中文投文化产业园。	9 月	9 月投入运营。
		(6) 物理医学与健康产业技术研究院。	10 月	10 月投入运营。
		(7) 团中央中国青年创业社区：完成装修。	6 月	1 月完成施工图设计。
				6 月完成装修。
			年内	成立专项小组跟进服务，强化项目监督把关，年内引进创业团队 15 个。
3	创新创业主体	(1) 依托院士工作站、博士后工作站、专家服务基地，引进高层次人才和海外留学人才 400 名以上。	年内	全年做好企业对接以及博士进出站工作；协助企业引进高层次人才和海外留学人才 400 名以上。
		(2) 积极宣传落实人才政策，加强本土人才培养。	年内	全年组织各级人才政策宣传，培训 1500 人次。
		(3) 建立有利于出创新成果、有利于创新成果产业化的新机制，完善科技创新体系和扶持政策。	年内	3 月制定新机制；年内抓好各项任务落实。

续表 11

序号	项目名称	主要内容	完成时间	阶段性目标
4	科技招商引领	(1) 制定人才、技术、资本等专项扶持政策。	年内	年内协同就业、企管、财务共同研究制定扶持政策。
		(2) 引进研发、孵化、转化等高端院所项目 10 个以上。	年底	每个招商部门上半年引进 1 个；年底引进 2 个。
		(3) 引进科技型中小企业 150 家以上。	年底	每个招商部门上半年引进 13 家；全年引进 25 家。
		(4) 新增“小巨人”企业 10 家、打造科技小巨人升级版。	年底	上半年新增 5 家；年底新增 10 家。
		(5) 推动 45 家企业申报市级、国家级高新技术企业。	年底	上半年组织政策宣传培训；下半年组织 45 家企业集中申报。
5	自主创新示范区	以产业精准定位争取政策，以独特的政策优势聚集产业，加强调研论证，全方位向上争取，逐步建成“双创”特区。	年内	5 月制定生物医药产业扶持政策体系; 年内制定高端制造扶持政策体系，完成顶层设计，积极向上争取；全年推动《“6+4”政策》《天津高新区加快创新创业载体建设的若干举措（试行）》《津领七条》等政策落地实施。
6	服务骨干企业稳定增长	(1) 做好规上企业“一对一”服务，确保有效增长。	年内	贯彻落实服务企业体制机制，每月普访，每双月召开联席会议，每季度班子成员走访企业。
		(2) 落实中小微企业融资贷款服务。	年内	全年宣传中小微贷款政府担保政策，组织银企对接会等方式推动政策落实。
		(3) 推动 40 家企业完成转型升级。	年底	上半年完成 20 家；年底完成 40 家。
		(4) 企业高管培训。	年内	每季度组织 1 次高管培训，全年 4 次。

续表 11

序号	项目名称	主要内容	完成时间	阶段性目标
		(5) 企业上市挂牌工作。	年内	年内推动区内 2 家有上市意向的企业上市挂牌。
		(6) 劳动就业工作。	年内	全年组织招聘会 260 场；组织校企联合招聘 4 次，年内与 2 家中介机构建立联系。年内普访企业 4 次以上，重点企业每月走访 1 次，及时解决涉稳问题。每季度进行针对性走访，重点关注前 50 家和后 30 家企业。
7	主导产业集群发展	(1) 搞好产业细分，加强产业链招商，引进关联度高、带动力强的项目 240 个。	年底	每个招商部门上半年引进项目 20 个；年底引进项目 40 个。
		(2) 着眼打造两个“千亿级”产业集群，大力引进智能制造和生物医药相关项目。	年内	年内引进智能制造和生物医药相关项目各 12 个。
8	总部企业增值发展	(1) 促进 10 个现有企业的总部或区域总部、结算中心、采购中心、销售中心落户武清。	年内	上半年落户 5 家；全年 10 家。
		(2) 新引进总部类项目 60 个。	年底	每个招商部门上半年引进项目 5 个；年底引进项目 10 个。
		(3) 打造亿元楼宇 2 个。	年底	每个分管招商领导各打造亿元楼宇1个。
9	优势平台跨越发展	(1) 自贸区武清园引进跨境电商、融资租赁、商业保理、国际贸易等项目 80 个以上，实现税收 2 亿元。	年内	6 月引进项目 40 个以上，实现税收 1 亿元；年底引进项目 80 个以上，实现税收 2 亿元。
		(2) 中欧产业园引进外资项目 6 个以上。	年底	每个招商部门年底前引进项目 1 个。

续表 11

序号	项目名称	主要内容	完成时间	阶段性目标
10	载体平台建设	(1) 中欧产业园一期剩余市政设施建设。	年底	配合南蔡村镇完成拆迁扫尾；拆迁完成后 6 个月内完成道路、渠系工程。
		(2) 中欧产业园标准厂房消防手续。	9 月	3 月完成招标 ;7 月竣工 ;9 月完成消防竣工验收。
		(3) 四期供热管线施工及换热站安装。	10 月	4 月完成设计招投标定队 ;6 月完成施工图设计 ;8 月开标定队并施工 ;10 月完成建设。
		(4) 中欧产业园服务中心装修及市政院区工程。	8 月	6 月完成市政院区施工，8 月完成服务中心内部装修。
		(5) 中欧产业园服务中心布展方案及施工。	3 月	3 月完成布展内容谋划。
			2 月	2 月完成布展方案及施工图设计。
			9 月	9 月完成布展施工。
		(6) 中欧产业园服务中心绿化景观工程。	5 月	2 月进场 ;5 月竣工。
		(7) 新增动漫科技园、商联、行政审批中心等楼宇载体面积 18.5 万平米。	年底	年底新增竣工楼宇面积 18.5 万平米。
		(8) 实施企业空地动态监管和供地项目证后监管，推动企业开工 5 家，竣工 5 家，证后监管企业不少于 100 家。	年内	施行项目季度走访推动机制，年内推动企业开工 5 家，竣工 5 家；证后监管企业不少于 100 家。
		(9) 建立违法用地监管机制，杜绝违法用地。	年内	2 月建立机制，全年抓好落实。根据区里要求做好违规用地整治工作。
		(10) 盘活闲置厂房、楼宇资源。	年内	2 月建立闲置厂房、楼宇数据库；年内推动资源盘活。

续表 11

<table>
<tr><th>序号</th><th>项目名称</th><th>主要内容</th><th>完成时间</th><th>阶段性目标</th></tr>
<tr><td rowspan="8">11</td><td rowspan="8">功能项目建设</td><td rowspan="7">(1) 行政审批中心建设。</td><td>9 月</td><td>9 月完成装修方案设计调整。</td></tr>
<tr><td>9 月</td><td>9 月完成整修、院区、景观相关工程立项手续办理。</td></tr>
<tr><td>11 月</td><td>9 月完成消防和建委竣工验收；11 月装修进场施工。</td></tr>
<tr><td>11 月</td><td>11 月完成冬植施工。</td></tr>
<tr><td>9 月</td><td>7 月地热井工程进场；9 月完成施工。</td></tr>
<tr><td>年底</td><td>年底完成党建展厅相关设计工作。</td></tr>
<tr><td>9 月</td><td>5 月展馆进场施工 ;9 月完成建设。</td></tr>
<tr><td>(2) 泉丰路下穿高速工程竣工通车。</td><td>年底</td><td>8 月完成通道工程箱体施工，开始恢复高速通行，11 月底完成北侧 U 型槽施工，南侧 U 型槽待中轮与天狮达成一致后，2 个月内通车。</td></tr>
<tr><td>12</td><td>重大项目服务保障机制</td><td>产业项目综合评审机制。</td><td>年内</td><td>1 月制定机制 ; 全年抓好落实。</td></tr>
<tr><td rowspan="3">13</td><td rowspan="3">物业管理市场化</td><td rowspan="3">引进国家级资质物业公司，制定行政审批中心物业、餐饮管理工作方案，将开发区自有物业全部推向市场。</td><td>年内</td><td>行政审批中心入住前 6 个月内启动招标。</td></tr>
<tr><td>年内</td><td>推动创业总部基地物业管理市场化。</td></tr>
<tr><td>年内</td><td>建立市场化物业公司参与自建工程规划设计、建设装修、设备采购、验收等全过程机制。</td></tr>
</table>

续表 11

序号	项目名称	主要内容	完成时间	阶段性目标
14	资金需求	全年融资 60 亿元。	年底	上半年完成 30 亿元；年底完成 60 亿元。
15	资本效益	(1) 完善资本运行部内部职能划定。	年内	3 月完成职能制定；年内做好资本运营工作。
		(2) 扩增资本，提高融资能力。	年内	年内协调国资委通过合规方法增资 20 亿元。
		(3) 完善财务管理制度。	年内	年内规范完善下属公司财务管理制度、会计核算体系。
		(4) 自贸区武清园轻资产公司三板上市筹备工作。	年内	年内确定上市服务中介机构。
		(5) 去库存，降风险。	年内	8 月制定完成去库存，降风险总体方案。
			年内	10 月完成栖仙住宅小区库存房屋处置；10 月完成还迁小区库存房屋处置。
			年内	9 月完成栖仙住宅小区煤改燃供热东站、西站拆迁地块房产开发规划方案设计；11 月完成施工图设计。
16	基础功能建设	(1) 开发区核心区和主要道路沿线城市设计：包括核心区提升改造、京津公路沿线区域城市设计、光明道及福源道街道风貌整治、重点地块城市设计和服务业功能布局研究。	6 月	6 月完成方案设计。
		(2) 开发区综合交通规划：包括交通整治、货运系统、公交系统、停车系统和智能交通。	4 月	4 月完成方案设计。

续表 11

序号	项目名称	主要内容	完成时间	阶段性目标
		(3) 开发区 CBD 城市设计。	4 月	4 月完成方案设计。
		(4) 道路大中修工程。	8 月	8 月竣工。
		(5) 路灯汰旧换新工程。	10 月	10 月底竣工。
		(6) 创业总部基地夜景灯光提升改造。	10 月	8 月完成招标;10 月完成改造。
17	生态环境建设	(1) 开发区核心区和主要道路沿线城市设计：包括核心区提升改造、京津公路沿线区域城市设计、光明道及福源道街道风貌整治、重点地块城市设计和服务业功能布局研究。	6 月	6 月完成方案设计。
		(2) 开发区综合交通规划：包括交通整治、货运系统、公交系统、停车系统和智能交通。	4 月	4 月完成方案设计。
		(3) 开发区 CBD 城市设计。	4 月	4 月完成方案设计。
		(4) 道路大中修工程。	8 月	8 月竣工。
		(5) 路灯汰旧换新工程。	10 月	10 月底竣工。
		(6) 完成“一污”拆迁。	10 月	5 月确定方案;10 月完成拆迁。
		(7) 三期西区污水厂扩建。	年内	全年做好华电三期西区污水处理厂运营,确保处理达标。
		(8) 四期供水管网续建规划、工程和管网运行管理。	年内	全年配合做好供水管网现场施工管理,并做好验收交接工作。

续表 11

序号	项目名称	主要内容	完成时间	阶段性目标
		(9)天狮大学污水管网对接。	10 月	督促天狮大学 9 月完成施工图设计，10 月开工。
		(10) 完成 25.1 万平米绿化工程（四期起步区 23.7 万平米、行政审批中心 1.4 万平米）。	年内	四期起步区随市政道路施工进度，完成相关绿化施工 ;11 月完成行政审批中心绿化冬植施工。
		(11) 国家级、市级生态工业示范园区创建。	年内	跟踪并落实国家级、市级生态工业示范园区申报及创建要求。在积极完成申报工作的基础上组织好创建工作。
18	商务环境建设	城区产城融合功能环境建设，大力增加服务功能，引进培育科技服务、会计税务、咨询评估等新型服务业态。	年底	每个招商部门全年引进 2 个，共 12 个。
19	安全环境建设	(1) 安全服务外包。	年内	1 月制定安全服务外包方案；年内抓好落实。
		(2) 安全生产工作。	年内	2 月签订目标责任书，做好春节安全生产；6 月安全月，夏季安全生产大检查 ;10 月国庆安全生产；12 月冬季安全生产大检查；4—10 月特种作业人员和企业管理人员培训；每月宣传教育和不定期监督整改；确保无安全责任事故发生。
		(3) 加强重要部位安全防范，提高处突应急能力。	3 月	3 月制定防范方案。

续表 11

序号	项目名称	主要内容	完成时间	阶段性目标
		(4) 建立劳资纠纷调处机制，落实劳动保障书面审查，推进和谐劳动关系，及时解决劳动争议。	年内	2 月建立机制；每季度组织召开 1 次人力资源经理联席会议，8—10 月进行企业劳动保障书面审查，做好和谐劳动关系宣传等工作。
		(5) 建立施工单位准入、建筑工地管理、农民工权益保障机制，做好农民工工资清欠工作。	2 月	2 月建立机制。
		(6) 安全开发区建设。	年内	在开发区出入口建立卡口，全域布控高清摄像头，污水泵站、自来水厂、人才公寓等重点区域加强重点监管，确保安全。
20	先进生产力促进计划	(1) 加强非公企业党建，严格规范党员发展；做好党员教育管理工作。	年内	年内新增非公有制党组织 20 个，全年做好党员发展工作；加强每季度积极分子信息库更新工作；全年组织党支部书记培训 2 次；做好党员 7.1 表彰。
		(2) 强化党组织的先进性、党的工作认同感和共产党员自豪感。	年内	1 月制定党建工作要点;2 月形成工作方案，明确党员示范岗、党员责任区、党员技术攻关小组、党员双创竞赛、党建工作联查等多种形式工作程序。
21	完善管理体制	(1) 适应管理体制新变化，完善领导体制和工作机制。	1 月	1 月理清工委、管委会和总公司职责，建立以党工委为领导核心、管委会为决策机构、总公司为执行机构的领导体制和工作机制。

续表 11

序号	项目名称	主要内容	完成时间	阶段性目标
		(2) 完善开发区行政管理制度。	8 月	8 月完成修订。
		(3) 建立与税务并行的统计机制，防范开发区税收外流。	年内	年内制定并行统计机制。
		(4) 规范招投标管理。	3 月	3 月完善招采评审程序。
22	调整机构设置	(1) 调整机构设置，明确内部分工。	3 月	3 月完成机构设置并明确职能分工。
		(2) 规范下属公司管理。	年内	3 月形成科学高效管理机制；全年抓好落实。
23	干部队伍保障力执行力	(1) 解放思想大讨论。	6 月	3 月完成方案制定;6 月完成。
		(2) 组织员工培训 4 次，拓展训练 2 次。	年内	每季度组织 1 次培训，全年 4 次；上半年组织拓展训练 1 次，全年组织 2 次。
		(3) 绩效考核工作。	年内	6 月根据实际完善方案；全年抓好落实。
		(4) 修订宣传资料。	8 月	2 月完成投资指南和招商 PPT 基准版修订;7 月启动宣传片招标；8 月完成制作。
		(5) 做好《协同先锋报》编辑发行工作。	年内	每月出版 1 期。
		(6) 做好微信服务平台宣传和推广。	年内	1 月确定宣传和推广方案；年内抓好落实。
		(7) 开发区招商推介活动。	年内	年内在国内组织集中推介活动 2 次；在海外组织集中推介活动 2 次；每个招商部门围绕高端制造、生物医药和新材料产业，以及总部、大院所、知名中介机构各组织招商活动 2 次。

续表 11

序号	项目名称	主要内容	完成时间	阶段性目标
24	服务企业10件实事	(1) 完成智慧园区一期建设，提高管理服务水平。	年底	在行政审批中心装修或智慧楼宇招标时，同步启动智慧园区招标，招标定队后，3个月完成系统深化调研，6个月完成系统开发和硬件安装，9个月完成系统测试。
		(2) 建立三支基金，服务中小微企业发展。	年底	年底设立引导基金、天使基金和创投基金。
		(3) 完成英华中学改造提升，改善国际教育办学条件。	年内	年内确定补办方案。
			10月	8月完成公寓提升；10月完成空调；10月完成提升改造设备类项目。
		(4) 完成人才公寓改造提升，创造温馨宜人的家居环境。	6月	6月完成人才公寓一期内外檐粉刷。
			9月	4月进场，8月完成装修，9月完成人才公寓二期5号楼装修、保洁及物业移交。
			10月	10月完成金侨人才公寓过户手续。
			10月	8月完成金侨人才公寓装修方案设计;10月完成施工图设计。
			年底	年底完成金侨人才公寓装修招投标。
			10月	10月完成人才公寓二期消防提升改造施工图设计。
			年内	年内完成施工图设计审核。
			9月	9月完成施工许可证办理。

续表 11

序号	项目名称	主要内容	完成时间	阶段性目标
		(5) 按照现代清新、人性化标准，完成道路标识、公交站点、公厕、城市家具等新建改造。	8 月	7 月确定方案深化设计，8 月完成施工图设计。
			年底	年底完成新建改造。
		(6) 完成迎宾道规划改造，提升整体形象。	6 月	6 月完成工程改造。
		(7) 理顺行政服务中心与区审批局的关系，减少中间环节，提高办事效率。	年内	全年完善问题汇总、一次性提醒和轮岗培训制度；7 月完成审批人员培训；年内成立开发区行政审批分中心并运行。
		(8) 引进知名餐饮品牌，合理布局便企商业网点，增加园区服务功能和活力。	9 月	9 月完成功能布局规划设计。
		(9) 建立园区公交系统，对接交通主要枢纽，畅通对外联系主渠道。	年底	7 月确定运行方案；8 月确定运营主体；9 月完成审批手续；年底开始试运行。
		(10) 实施企业发展“一三五十”计划（税收 1000、3000、5000、10000 万元），通过精准服务，打造一批重量级增长点。	年内	1000 万元企业新增 10 家，达到 29 家；3000 万元企业新增 3 家，达到 5 家；5000 万元企业新增 2 家，达到 6 家；10000 万元企业新增 1 家，到达 8 家。

三、2016年产业项目（共46大项、46子项）一览表

表12

序号	项目名称	主要内容	完成时间	初步阶段性目标安排
1	奥克斯工业三期	竣工。	3月	3月竣工。
2	坝上春秋美术馆	取得土地证。	年内	5月取得土地指标，启动征地手续；年内完成地上物招拍挂取得土地证。
3	权健	完成主体。	年内	待取得土地指标后3个月完成招拍挂，7个月完成工程证，9个月完成施工证。
			年内	待取得施工许可证后进场施工，4个月内完成基础，8个月内完成主体。
4	畅联物流	竣工。	年底	3月复工；10月完成主体；年底竣工。
5	美森乳业	竣工。	年底	3月复工；年底竣工。
6	柯菲凯博	进场施工。	年底	9月完成工程证；年底完成施工证。
			年底	年底进场。
7	商联	竣工。	年底	3月复工；6月完成主体；8月完成装修；年底竣工。
8	中纺院二期	竣工。	6月	6月竣工。
9	中化远东宏信	竣工。	6月	3月复工；6月竣工。
10	卡秀堡辉	竣工。	6月	3月复工；6月竣工。
11	冀雅电子	收回全部地块。	9月	9月完成洽谈，签署协议。
12	敏华二期	完成主体。	年底	3月进场；5月完成基础；年底完成主体。

续表 12

序号	项目名称	主要内容	完成时间	初步阶段性目标安排
13	赛孚制药	完成部分主体。	7 月	7 月完成施工证。
			年底	8 月进场;年底完成部分主体。
14	海石花物流	竣工。	年底	3 月复工;7 月完成主体;年底竣工。
15	拉谷谷服饰	竣工。	年底	3 月复工;年底竣工。
16	共速达	竣工。	年底	3 月复工;7 月完成主体;10 完成装修;年底竣工。
17	欧蒙诊断试剂	竣工。	年底	3 月复工;8 月完成主体;年底竣工。
18	北方博业	竣工。	年底	3 月复工;年底竣工。
19	丰树物流	竣工。	年底	3 月复工;年底竣工。
20	嘉林药业	竣工。	6 月	3 月复工;6 月竣工。
21	北交控	完成基础。	年内	待取得土地指标后,3 个月完成招拍挂,7 个月完成工程证,9 个月完成施工证。
			年内	待取得施工证后,3 个月完成基础。
22	格立莫	完成主体。	5 月	3 月完成工程证;5 月完成施工证。
			年底	5 月进场;7 月完成基础;年底完成主体。

续表 12

序号	项目名称	主要内容	完成时间	初步阶段性目标安排
23	尤纳斯	完成主体。	年内	待取得土地指标后 3 个月完成招拍挂，6 个月完成工程证，8 个月完成施工证。
			年内	取得施工许可证后进场施工，4 个月内完成基础，8 个月内完成主体。
24	中业园	完成主体。	年底	3 月复工；年底完成主体。
25	晟鸿空调	完成基础。	9 月	3 月完成泵站注销；5 月完成招拍挂；10 月完成工程证；12 月完成施工证。
			年底	9 月进场；年底完成基础。
26	华电膜科技	竣工。	年底	3 月复工；年底竣工。
27	伟嘉生物科技	完成主体。	年内	待取得土地指标后 3 个月完成招拍挂，6 个月完成工程证，8 个月完成施工证。
			年内	取得施工许可证后进场施工，4 个月内完成基础，8 个月内完成主体。
28	齐正二期	完成主体。	年内	待取得土地指标后 3 个月完成招拍挂，6 个月完成工程证，8 个月完成施工证。
			年内	取得施工许可证后进场施工，4 个月内完成基础，8 个月内完成主体。

续表 12

序号	项目名称	主要内容	完成时间	初步阶段性目标安排
29	洋马科技(汇智光华动力科技)	完成施工证。	12 月	12 月完成工程证。
30	外交部服务中心工业(千代福)	完成施工证。	12 月	9 月完成工程证，12 月完成施工证。
31	飞鹰聚力	完成基础。	年底	8 月完成工程证;10 月完成施工证。 10 月进场;年底完成基础。
32	安徽安华(君安华天机械)	年底进场。	年底	10 月完成工程证；12 月完成施工证。 年底进场。
33	东湖俱乐部二期	实现资产盘活。	年底	年底实现资源盘活。
34	动漫科技园	完成土建、院区和市政工程。	8 月	8 月完成土建、院区和市政工程。
35	玉圭园酒店	投入运营。	年内	6 月实现资源盘活。 5 月复工;年内投入运营。
36	麒麟尚岛水榭(湖心岛)	投入运营。	年内	6 月实现资源盘活。 5 月复工;年内投入运营。
37	原国能地块	办理分证手续。	8 月	8 月完成分证。
38	伊利二期	完成施工证。	10 月	8 月完成工程证;10 月完成施工证。
38	豪威生物二期	完成施工证。	12 月	10 月完成工程证;12 月完成施工证。

续表 12

序号	项目名称	主要内容	完成时间	初步阶段性目标安排
40	瑞一扩建	完成主体。	5 月	5 月完成施工证。
			年底	6 月进场；年底完成主体。
41	海迈扩建	完成主体。	5 月	5 月完成施工证。
			年底	6 月进场；年底完成主体。
42	宇钢(老厂)	完成施工证。	7 月	7 月完成施工证。
43	维益扩建	完成主体。	3 月	3 月完成施工证。
			年底	4 月进场；年底完成主体。
44	乐金扩建	完成施工证。	5 月	5 月完成施工证。
45	铁科院二期(150亩)	取得土地证	11 月	11 月取得土地证。
		完成土地平整	10 月	10 月完成土地平整。
		完成临水、临电、雨水和污水，到达项目用地红线。	10 月	10 月完成临水、临电、雨水和污水，到达项目用地红线。
		取得施工许可证，开工建设。		12 月取得施工许可证。
46	格兰富水泵	完成厂房改造提升。	10 月	10 月完成厂房改造。

第四篇

行业　企业

第一章　行业概况

武清开发区于1991年12月28日设立，是国家级经济技术开发区和国家级高新技术产业园区，2014年年底纳入天津国家自主创新示范核心区。1992年开发区起步引进34家企业，1993年引进企业超过百家。1997年，在遭遇亚洲地区项目萎缩的情况下，把招商区域由亚洲向欧美地区扩展，使入区企业达到了243家。2000年，有19个国家和地区的330家企业入区，投资额60亿元，其中外资5.2亿美元，实现税收2亿元，占县财政收入三分之一强，就业人员达3万人。发展到2002年，区内企业项目出现了行业集群的趋势。开发区根据自己的规划和现状，进行有针对性的招商，直到2007年这五年间，形成了电子信息、新型建材、机械制造、生物医药、汽车及零部件五大主导产业，销售收入达135亿元；较2006年同期增长19%，对整体经济贡献率过半达54%；实现税收13亿元，占总量的57%。到2009年，新能源产业也发展为主导产业之一，合并号称六大主导产业，营业收入达190亿元，同比增长30%；实现税收14.6亿元，增长13%。2010年，高端制造产业、企业总部产业、科技型产业和现代服务产业异军突起，不断引进大项目、好项目，包括多个“世界500强”企业。

建区以来，共吸引投资1400亿元，其中外资80亿美元以上，引入50个国家和地区的企业2200余家，其中有世界500强投资企业35家，包括美国艾默生、亚马逊、德尔福、法国苏伊士、家乐福、佛吉亚，日本东棉、住友，韩国LG，新加坡丰树，澳大利亚沃利帕森，奥地利奥钢联，中国中粮、中交、国电投等；有国外龙头企业100余家，包括丹麦绫致、丹佛斯、艾尔姆、格兰富，德国GEA、万可，英国哈克尼斯，瑞典戴纳派克、贝格，芬兰玻石，西班牙海斯坦普，比利时哈蒙，法国库恩，美国麦格昆磁、维益，土耳其欧德亮法尔宝，突尼斯柯菲凯博，韩国日进等；有国内龙头企业100余家，包括天狮集团、红日药业、诺禾致源、信义玻璃、娃哈哈饮品、伊利、奥克斯、畅联等。

到2016年，全区企业行业整合，形成了高端制造、生物医药、总部经济三大主导产业。高端制造业以智能制造、轨道交通、汽车及零部件、电子信息为主；生物医药以基因测序、中药颗粒、医疗器械、诊断试剂为主；总部经济以总部结算、金融商务、研发转化、文化创意为主。

武清开发区是武清区对外开放的窗口，引领创新、带动转型、支撑发展的龙头，2016年实现税收140亿元，同比增长26%，一般预算收入47亿元，同比增长29%；地区生产总值491亿元，同比增长15%；工业总产值1459亿元，同比增长13%；固定资产投资完成238亿元。建区以来，累计实现地区生产总值2491亿元，税收763亿元；吸引直接就业12万人。

第一节　高端制造

武清开发区的高端制造产业主要以智能制造、轨道交通、汽车及零部件、电子信息为主。代表企业包括北交控、铁科院、丹佛斯、德尔福、佛吉亚、三英精控、艾默生、LG、戴纳派克、基伊埃、奥宗尼亚、万可、麦格昆磁、信义玻璃、马勒等310家。该产业于2010年初见规模；2012年引进项目25个，投资总额达134亿元，其中亿元以上项目有敏华家具、同力重工、远东宏信等14个。

轨道交通装备产业具有行业关联度高、技术资金密集、产业链条长、发展潜力大等特点，是国家战略性新兴产业重点发展方向，也是天津市确定的“十三五”期间重点打造的十个高端产业之一。为迎接全球轨道交通产业新一轮增长周期，抢抓国家大规模实施铁路和城市轨道交通建设的重大机遇，武清开发区编制《智能制造产业暨轨道科技城重大项目产业发展规划（2017—2020）》，作为今后指导智能制造产业发展的纲领性文件。

未来四年轨道交通市场容量约为8.1万亿元，是一个具有巨大发展空间的产业。轨道交通装备产业受国家政策扶持，将享受巨大政策红利。未来十年，中国轨道交通装备智能制造业发展前景光明。“十三五”期间天津市面临京津冀协同发展、自由贸易试验区建设、国家自主创新示范区建设、“一带一路”建设、滨海新区开发开放等重大国家战略，享受诸多政策倾斜。天津市《建设全国先进制造研发基地实施方案（2015—2020）》明确指出发展地铁、轻轨、城际列车以及轨道交通大型施工和养护装备任务，武清开发区是该专项任务的承接者之一。武清开发区成立二十余年来，培育了大量优秀制造类企业，具备良好的发展条件及比较优势，能够为发展壮大轨道交通装备制造产业体系奠定坚实基础。

入驻武清开发区的铁科院是轨道交通领域综合性研究机构，作为国家科技龙头引领轨道交通领域车、机、工、电各专业技术创新和产业发展，形成了强大的原始创新能力、轨道交通标准制定话语权、引入铁路产品检验认证资质，有望取得城市轨道交通产品检验认证资质，享受五个国家实验平台资源利用，是轨道交通领域权威教育培训机构。武清开发区依托铁科院，加快建设轨道交通产业园，强化“一个产品就是一个产业”的帮扶引导，带动现有企业配套发展。引导外资企业设立研发部门，提升发展阀门、压缩机、离心机等技术和产品。依托重大项目，培育发展智能传感器、智能计量仪表、伺服电机等智能制造关键部件。发展壮大叶片、轴承、齿轮等风力发电装备领域，布局增材制造、智能机器人等新兴领域。到2020年，预计产业产值达1000亿元，建成产学研结合的千亿级产业集群。

重点企业简介

北交控轨道交通高科产业园

北京交控科技有限公司是2009年为落实北京市政府对自主创新CBTC研究成果产业化与示范工程建设而成立的掌握核心技术的信号系统供应商。为积极推进科技创新成果的应用工作，推动中国轨道交通的新技术、新产品的推广和产业化发展，加速推进中国轨道交通产业化的建设，实现专业化和规范化生产，提升国家工程中心及交控科技的核心竞争力，将在天津武清区建立中国轨道交通中试基地和产业化基地，建立800米长的轨道交通试验线，建立完善的设计中心、制造中心、测试中心、维护中心与培训中心等全生命周期的产业链。

项目位于武清开发区四期，占地200亩，总投资12亿元，达产后年纳税不低于7500万元。主要业务为城市轨道交通领域高端设计咨询、核心技术研发与精密制造、全场景测试、全系统中试、国际领先认证与评估、高端专业化培训、基于大数据与预警的维保等。

中国铁道科学研究院轨道交通产业科技创新和成果转化基地

铁科院始建于1950年，是我国铁路唯一的多学科、多专业的综合性研究机构。目前已发展成为集科技创新、技术服务、成果转化、咨询监理、检测认证、人才培养等业务为一体的大型科技型企业。

建院60余年来，铁科院立足铁路运输主战场，围绕铁路建设及运输生产重点领域，开展了大量重大、关键技术攻关与试验研究，取得了3300多项科研成果，获得825项各类科技成果奖，其中国家级科技奖176项，省、部级科技奖649项，为推动中国铁路科技进步做出了重要贡献。

铁科院拟在武清开发区内投资项目的投资总额不低于22亿元，主要经营以下业务：一期：金化所的新材料产品，电子所的电子信息产品等；二期：环保所的节能环保产品、通号所的电子信息产品、铁建所的工务工程产品和机辆所的移动装备产品等。

丹佛斯（天津）有限公司

丹麦独资企业，成立于1996年10月，丹麦最大的工业生产企业丹佛斯国际有限公司在武清开发区先后注册成立了丹佛斯（天津）有限公司、丹佛斯森科（天津）消防设备有限公司两家公司，是该公司亚太地区最大的生产基地。目前公司在开发区一、二期拥有两个厂区，总投资1.8亿美元，注册资本4206万美元，总占地275亩，总建筑面积7.5万平米。主要生产热力膨胀阀、温控阀、水阀、冷凝机组、商用压缩机、制冷压缩机等制冷设备以及消防设备，其拳头产品热力膨胀阀占有全球40%的市场份额。丹佛斯的产品成功的应用于水立方奥运游泳馆、人民大会堂、国家大剧院、北京首都国际机场、中央电视台新址等项目。

德尔福派克电气系统有限公司天津分公司

美国德国合资企业，成立于2014年10月，由美国德尔福投资设立。美国德尔福公司成立于1890年，总部设在美国俄亥俄州沃伦，是全球最大的汽车线束系统制造厂商，世界500强企业。德尔福是全球最大的汽车零部件供应商之一，产品供给包括通用汽车、福特、丰田、日产、雷诺、大众等全球最大汽车厂家。除发动机、变速箱、外壳、座椅、轮胎外，德尔福几乎能提供其它所有的汽车零配件，在全球汽车零部件市场占有率高达15% ~ 20%。德尔福目前在全球41个国家设了176家全资制造厂、42家合资厂、53个客户服务中心和销售代表处以及32个技术中心。

德尔福武清汽车线束项目由德尔福派克电气系统有限公司投资设立，位于武清开发区四期，由武清开发区订制建设标准厂房，占地60亩，建筑面积2.2万平方米，总投资1亿元，主要生产汽车各类线束制品，产品应用于汽车线束系统、车载电话、车载娱乐系统等设备领域。主要客户为戴姆勒奔驰、长城汽车等。2016年实现销售收入4.28亿元，纳税528万元，吸纳就业1175人。

宝沃佛吉亚汽车部件中国总部项目

中外合资企业，成立于2016年6月，由佛吉亚（中国）投资有限公司投资设立，佛吉亚是法国汽车零部件企业，全球第六大汽车零部件供应商，世界500强企业。在汽车座椅、排放控制技术系统、汽车内饰和外饰四大业务领域居业界领先地位。其中座椅业务排名全球第二，欧洲第一。在全国共有38家工厂，4个研发中心，客户主要有大众集团、标致雪铁龙、长安福特、东风日产、通用汽车、现代、长城汽车、福田汽车。

一期项目由佛吉亚在武清开发区投资2000万人民币建设汽车部件北方生产基地，租赁中欧产业园厂房从事汽车座椅装配业务，现已顺利投产。二期项目由佛吉亚集团与宝沃集团合资成立，投资1.25亿人民币，建设宝沃佛吉亚中国区总部、研发中心、管理中心、生产基地，并具备对外投资功能，定制3万平方米厂房，预计在2018年10月投入使用，从事汽车座椅装配、座椅骨架、发泡填充物生产及汽车内饰等相关业务。

三英精控（天津）科技有限公司

内资企业，成立于2015年12月，注册资本1000万元，租赁武清开发区创业总部基地3000平方米楼宇。专注于超精密运动控制技术和产品的开发，并致力于为科学研究、创新研发及高端仪器、设备的制造等提供系统的技术解决方案与集成，满足市场对超精密运动控制技术需求的专业制造商。该公司在纳米运动控制技术方面具有国际领先的技术和经验，并具有完全的自主知识产权。公司核心技术集精密传感、精密驱动、精密机械、精密控制、精密集成等各领域的技术于一体，整体技术指标已达到国际领先水平。公司产品涵盖大行程高精度运动平台、纳米和亚纳米运动控制平台、精密运动控制集成系统等系列产品。

公司创始人兼董事长须颖博士，英国Warwick大学博士、国际知名纳米运动控制专家、国家“千人计划”特聘专家及“十二五”国家重大科学仪器专项及国家科技部“863”、“科技支撑”等重大研究的项目负责人。

艾默生过程管理（天津）阀门有限公司

美国独资企业，成立于2003年10月，由艾默生电气公司投资设立，投资总额955万美元，注册资本560万美元。产品全球市场占有率达25%，中国市场占有率达16%。该公司主要从事生产、组装、销售新型电子、气动阀门控制系统及相关配套零配件，并提供售后服务，研究、开发和测试验证市场所需的新产品并提供相应的技术支持，采购、零售、批发非自产新型电子、气动控制阀门产品，设计研究开发新产品改进现有产品设计，产品的零售批发以及进出口业务。2015年销售收入8.96亿元，利润1.68亿元，纳税9445万元。2016年销售收入5.78亿元，利润7719万元，纳税3661万元。吸纳就业311人。

LG化学（天津）工程塑料有限公司

韩国独资企业，成立于2004年12月，2005年10月正式投产，公司总占地面积8万余平方米，建筑面积2万余平方米，公司注册资金1800万美元，一期工程总投资额1200万美元。公司主要设备均从国外引进，采用共混改性方法生产各种型号的EP树脂(PC、PC.ABS合金、PP改性、PBT改性、Nylon等)，年产各种工程塑料5万吨。产品用途广泛，主要应用于汽车、家电、电气、IT等行业。公司的生产包装设备全部从国外进口，并采用世界一流的韩国LG化学先进的工艺流程和生产管理方法，生产高性能高品质的工程塑料。2016年销售收入5.5亿元，纳税3309万元，吸纳就业190人。

戴纳派克（中国）压实摊铺设备有限公司

瑞典独资企业，成立于1999年8月，由阿特拉斯科普柯公司投资设立，戴纳派克是全球最大的压实摊铺设备制造商之一，制造厂分布于瑞典、德国、法国、巴西和中国，于2007年7月加入阿特拉斯·科普柯集团，隶属于阿特拉斯.科普柯集团建筑和矿山技术事业部。阿特拉斯.科普柯集团是一家全球领先的工业生产解决方案供应商。其提供的产品和服务从压缩空气及气体设备、发电机、建筑及采矿设备、工业工具及安装系统到相关售后服务及专业租赁，一应俱全。集团总部位于瑞典斯德哥尔摩，业务遍及150多个国家和地区。

戴纳派克（中国）压实摊铺设备有限公司作为戴纳派克在中国投资的第一家独资生产厂成立于1999年8月，投资总额1200万美元，注册资本500万美元，占地60亩（40000平方米），建筑面积5万平方米。负责道路的压实摊铺设备和技术的市场发展、施工咨询、施工设计及产品销售与售后服务。主要生产道路工程用压路机、摊铺机、轻型混凝土设备。产品采用进口散件及国产部件，在国内进行组装，与瑞典、德国生产的产品具有相同的质量和性能。2016 年实现销售收入 4.8 亿元，纳税 2099 万元，吸纳就业 180 人。

基伊埃韦史伐里亚分离设备（天津）有限公司

德国独资企业，成立于 2011 年 1 月，由德国 GEA 集团投资设立。投资总额 4050 万美元，注册资本 1350 万美元。占地面积 120 亩。主要从事生产、销售碟片式离心机、卧式螺旋离心机、食品及水处理分离设备以及相关辅助设备、零部件，并提供技术咨询及售后服务。其离心分离技术全球领先，产品主要用于船舶舱底水处理等。2016 年销售额 4.79 亿元，年纳税 1682 万元，吸纳职工 163 人。

奥宗尼亚环保技术（天津）有限公司

法国独资企业，成立于 2012 年 7 月，由得利满水处理系统（北京）有限公司投资设立，位于武清开发区三期京津高校（武清）科技创新园内，总投资 2400 万元，租赁厂房 3000 平方米。主要生产臭氧发生器和臭氧尾气破坏器等设备，产品主要用于饮用水、污水处理等领域，其技术具有全球领先水平。2016 年销售收入 9451 万元，纳税 361 万元，吸纳就业 42 人。

信义玻璃（天津）有限公司

香港独资企业，成立于 2004 年 4 月，投资总额 19800 万美元，注册资本 12600 万美元，占地面积 1596 亩，主要从事开发、生产、销售汽车玻璃和工程玻璃。其投资方信义玻璃集团于香港主板上市，是集浮法玻璃生产、汽车玻璃和建筑玻璃深加工、幕墙设计施工于一体的综合性大型玻璃企业。60 % 的产品出口欧洲、北美、日本、澳洲等 100 多个国家和地区。2016 年销售收入 21.16 亿元，利润 4 亿元，纳税 1.74 亿元，吸纳就业 1957 人。2017 年 1—5 月营业收入 9 亿元，利润 1.2 亿元，纳税 6679 万元。

麦格昆磁（天津）有限公司

美国独资企业，成立于 1998 年 8 月，投资总额 4998 万美元，注册资本 1666 万美元，占地 96.68 亩。是世界粘结钕铁硼磁粉行业的龙头企业，公司主要产品—钕铁硼磁粉占有全球市场份额的80%以上。其产品广泛应用于计算机、通讯产品、办公自动化设备、工业自动化、家用电器、电机应用、核磁共振仪等高科技领域。2016年营业收入6.17亿元，利润4222万元，纳税5407万元，吸纳就业408人。2017年1—5月营业收入3.1亿元，利润2320万元，纳税5230万元。

马勒东炫滤清器（天津）有限公司

德国独资企业，成立于1995年7月，投资总额1767万美元，注册资本622万美元，占地18亩，于2012年另租厂房7680.42平米。主要从事生产、销售汽车滤清器、工业滤清器、汽车零部件及相关咨询服务。主要产品为进气歧管、空气滤清器。主要客户是宝马汽车、奔驰汽车。2016年营业收入8.96亿元，利润8797万元，纳税8167万元，吸纳就业397人。2017年1—5月营业收入3亿元，利润1922万元，纳税2481万元。

万可电子（天津）有限公司

德国独资企业，成立于1997年2月，投资总额1938万欧元，注册资本813万欧元，占地面积119.58亩。主要开发、加工、制造、销售电动机械、电子连接元件、电子交叉组件、成套电子系统、机床、压缩工具、铸型工具以及相关元件及辅助产品。主要生产线路连接端。其投资方德国万可连接技术有限公司，专业从事以独创的弹簧压力技术为特征的电连接器、电子模块和现场总线输入输出系统的跨国公司。其创建于1951年，总部坐落于德国的MINDEN市。在全球拥有50多家子公司及分销商，目前公司的业务遍布欧洲、北美、拉丁美洲和亚洲等国家和地区。2016年营业收入6.73亿元，利润4281万元，纳税3887万元，吸纳就业1366人。2017年1—5月营业收入3亿元，利润1293万元，纳税2149万元。

第二节　生物医药

截至2007年，武清开发区引进的生物医药项目已成为区内的五大主导产业之一。主要以基因测序、中药颗粒、医疗器械、诊断试剂为主。代表企业包括天狮集团、红日药业、华大蛋白、诺禾致源、金唯智、怡和嘉业、赛诺、普光、和治等125家。

2016年，武清开发区依托武清开发区院士工作站、博士后工作站、专家服务基地和京津高校武清科技创新园，共引进院士30人、博士70人、硕士746人、本科3296

人，同时红日药业、天狮集团、天大前沿院等企业建有各类重点实验室、企业技术中心、工程中心等科研平台 10 个，为医药产业群奠定了有力的支撑。

2016 年，天津（武清）国际健康产业示范区揭牌，近期规划建设国际健康产业园和国际健康产业研究院，进行 GMP 车间定制、产学研项目孵化转化、创新公共服务平台建设。示范区的打造，对于推动武清区生物医药产业的项目聚集、平台聚集和人才聚集，打造“千亿级”生物医药产业链条具有重要意义。

武清开发区着力打造生命健康产业。加强品牌塑造，提升中药、保健品等优势产品领域。吸引重大项目，发展疫苗、重组蛋白质药物、治疗性抗体等生物制品和抗肿瘤、乙肝、糖尿病等新药产品，培育高端医学影像设备、临床监护设备、体外诊断仪器和试剂等医疗器械产品。引入高端医疗和健康管理机构，发展医学检测、健康管理、养老保健等。培育精准医疗、生物 CRO 等新业态，布局干细胞与再生医学、分子靶向治疗等前沿领域。“十三五”期间，武清开发区将发挥集合优势实现产学研政企相结合，推动生物医药产业发展。到 2020 年，生命健康产业产值达到 1000 亿元，成为京津冀竞争优势领先的具有国际化功能的生物医药产业聚集区。

重点企业简介

天狮集团

民营企业，成立于 1993 年 12 月。主要研发生产营养保健食品、保健用品、美容护肤品、家居用品等多元化产品，涉足零售、旅游、金融、国际贸易、电子商务等诸多领域。2016 年实现销售收入 30 亿元，利润 4 亿元，纳税 3.5 亿元。

一是天狮国际健康产业园。占地面积1200亩，总投资70亿元，天狮集团总部所在地，是集产品研发、中试、生产制造、国际物流、国际营销、国际教育与培训、国际旅游与研讨、国际康复、养生保健、健康管理为一体，产、学、研紧密结合，可实现生产及物流分拨自动化、仓储立体化、运营现代化、管理人性化、发展环保化的多功能产业园区。二是天狮学院。2008 年 4 月经教育部批准成立全日制普通本科高校。2016 年学校有学生 3392 人，毕业生就业率保持在 95% 以上。三是在建天狮国际大学。总投资 100 亿元，占地 3000 亩，总建筑面积 210 万平方米，将整合天狮学院建成教育理念先进、办学特色鲜明、教学设施精良、师资队伍一流、管理规格严格，符合经济和社会发展需要的国际化教育平台，将设置 11 个学院、55 个专业，在校学生可达 2.5 万人。

项目将分两期建设，其中一期有33栋建筑，目前完成理学院主体建设7万余平方米，正在进行外檐工程，预计2017年能够完成理学院全部建设并投入使用。

天津红日药业股份有限公司

民营企业，始建于1996年，是一家横跨现代中药制剂、中药配方颗粒、化学合成药、生物技术药、医疗器械、互联网医疗等诸多领域，融投资、研发、生产、资本于一体的高科技医药健康产业集团。红日药业研发的创新产品血必净注射液，为现代中药攻克世界医学难题，建人类脓毒症治疗史上里程碑。在“全成分®”配方颗粒领域，作为行业领先者，企业拥有中国最大的中药指纹图谱标准库和业内唯一“全成分®”配方颗粒工艺专利体系。企业围绕“发现新靶点、新适应症”这一核心点设立创新药品研发项目，通过运用研发中心技术资本与人力资源，力争开创抢仿、争做国内首仿的研发项目，为企业后续发展储备强劲动力。在合作模式上也有所创新，科学家可以选择技术转化、合资公司或独立公司三种方式在红日药业进行工程化研究。在此期间红日会有风险投资提供资金支持。在完成工程化研究之后，将进入红日产业基地进行技术产品化，形成的产品可以是合资公司产品、红日产品，也可以是新公司产品。产品可以利用红日的市场覆盖及红日的学术营销进入国内乃至国际市场，实现产品的市场化。

天津诺禾致源生物信息科技有限公司

内资企业，成立于2014年2月，总投资1.8亿元，位于创业总部基地C07、08、09号楼，建筑面积1.9万平方米，2016年有员工900余人，来自国内顶尖大学和科研院所，硕士博士比例占80%以上。该公司搭建了目前国际上最先进、全国第一个Hiseq X-Ten高通量基因测试平台；医学检验实验室已完成建设，正在报批。公司专注于开发生物科技和信息技术在优生优育、遗传疾病和癌症个体化诊疗领域的应用，开发具有预防措施和治疗方案的筛查和诊断产品。

其投资方北京诺禾致源生物信息技术有限公司成立于2011年3月，注册在北京中关村生命科学园，发展方向为基因组学研究与应用开发，为国家高新技术企业，双软企业、北京市科技研究开发机构、北京市博士后流动站、北京市企事业专利试点单位。公司汇聚了大批在基因组学和生物信息学领域有多年研究经验的多科学人才，具有对基因组和生物信息领域前沿和发展趋势的良好把握能力，开发了一系列生物信息新方法新软件，开创了测序技术在人类疾病与健康、微生物、动植物研究与现代农业育种等领域的诸多新应用，多项研究成果发表于 Nature、Science 等科学期刊。团队在生物信息研发的部分领域，特别是衡量研发水平的最核心领域之一——复杂基因组组装，保持全球领先地位。

北京华大蛋白质研发中心有限公司

民营企业，成立于 2003 年 4 月，总投资 1 亿元，先期租赁武清开发区国际健康产业技术研究院 5000 平米物理空间，主要从事蛋白质临检、抗体生产 2 大业务，并与开发区共建质谱第三方检测平台，满足园区企业及京津冀相关检测需求。该项目入驻将大幅提升武清国际健康产业示范区产业链配套水平，对开发区精准医疗产业聚集起到自发聚拢和整合效用，推动开发区在“十三五”期间加速形成生物医药千亿级产业集群。

苏州金唯智生物科技有限公司天津分公司

美国独资企业，成立于 2015 年 9 月，租用开发区创业总部基地楼宇，主要从事生物技术的技术研发、咨询。其投资方为美国 GENEWIZ Inc，1999 年成立于美国，创始人孙中平博士和廖国娟博士都是国家“千人”。该公司 10 余年来始终致力于基因诊断试剂的研发和生产，旗下有两大品牌，分别为 ADMERA（阿德美亚）和 GENEWIZ（金唯智）。ADMERA（阿德美亚）主要为个人消费者和医院提供基因检测、取样和精准用药服务；金唯智主要针对药厂和科研机构提供基因测序服务。目前在昆山和昌平各建有一家公司，两家公司的主要客户均为药厂和科研机构。金唯智每年的产值均保持在 30—40% 的增长速度。

天津怡和嘉业医疗科技有限公司

内资企业，成立于 2014 年 4 月 8 日，注册资本 1000 万元，主要生产呼吸机等相关医疗器械，现租用津京高校创新园厂房 4000 平方米，7 条生产线，预计年产能 10 万台以上。目前刚刚在开发区四期购买 50 亩土地，用于建立生产基地。2015 年 1—10 月实现销售收入 4910 万元，纳税 154 万元，吸纳就业 100 人。

其母公司北京怡和嘉业医疗科技有限公司专注于睡眠呼吸领域，2006 年公司通过了国家高新技术企业和重点软件企业的认定，同时公司还是医疗器械质量管理示范企业。2008 年通过 CE 认证，产品正式进军国际。公司推出拥有自主知识产权的全新智能无创呼吸机系列，临床医学方面覆盖了从初筛检查、常规多导睡眠监测、确定治疗方案、到睡眠呼吸科研等，产品研发采用了最先进的智能传感控制技术和国际化的设计控制流程，Iso-9000.13485的质量控制体系贯穿了整体工艺设计和全部生产控制流程，保证了所有产品的一流品质，已成为诊疗产品研发、制造和销售服务为一体的行业领军企业。

天津赛诺制药有限公司

公司与法国兰花公司共同投资兴建，中外合资企业，成立于2009年6月，由天津中新药业集团股份有限公司的中方股东天津中新药业集团股份有限公司是在新加坡股票交易所和上海证券交易所上市的两地上市公司，下属分公司和参控股公司40余家。具备完整的中药产业链，在化学原料药、制剂和生物工程领域同样实力雄厚。外方股东兰花公司投资业务广泛，包括欧洲时报、美国泛华研究所、时装等各个领域。

公司分别从意大利IMA和ROMACO公司、德国VTA公司、美国密理博公司引进粉针分装机和粉碎机、真空刮膜浓缩仪和超滤系统，建有国家级一流的中药粉针剂生产基地，公司全面实施标准化程序管理和严格的质量监督机制，并已经通过国家GMP认证。

主要产品中药粉针剂——注射用黄芪多糖是由美国泛华公司和山西中医药研究院历经数载共同研制的国家中药二类新药，已在美国和中国多个国家申请了发明专利，产品的投产填补了天津市中药粉针剂生产的空白。注射用黄芪多糖是我国首个全面改善放、化疗病人血象的中药粉针剂，作为肿瘤辅助治疗药物具有纯度高、副作用小、作用机制确切、疗效显著而独特的特点。

天津赛诺制药有限公司投资总额2050万美元，注册资本979.9万美元，占地面积40000.91平方米，主要从事采用生物工程技术及其它新技术、新工艺提取天然药物有效成分，进行相关丸剂、粉针剂及保健品的研制、生产、销售，提供相关技术咨询技术服务。主要产品为治疗癌症药物——黄芪多糖。2009年被认定为高新技术企业。

天津市普光医用材料制造有限公司

内资企业，成立于2001年9月，注册资本9297.96万元，占地面积56.1亩（37400平方米），是一家集医疗用品的研究、开发、销售为一体的高新技术企业。主要生产医用高分子制品。主要产品包括医用消毒片、消毒棉棒、消毒筒、急救毯、湿片原材料等系列产品，产品谱系宽用途广，并享有多项专利，可按客户要求生产不同规格、不同种类的相关产品，全部采用自动化生产线完成。产品销往欧洲、北美、澳大利亚、中东、东南亚等30多个国家和地区，占有30%国际市场份额。2011年销售收入6870.4万元，利润1126.2万元，纳税422.07万元，2012年1—11月实现销售收入6073.9万元，利润931.5万元，纳税568.45万元。吸纳就业355人。

天津和治药业有限公司

内资企业，成立于2002年5月，注册资本3800万元，主要从事口服液、片剂、颗粒剂、硬胶囊剂、酒剂、酊剂生产；保健食品的生产、外加工。2016年有中药车间、化药车间、保健品车间、医疗器械车间十条生产线，具有中药提取及口服液、片剂、胶囊剂、颗粒剂、酒剂、酊剂、软胶囊剂、丸剂、茶剂十种剂型的生产能力，拥有百余个品种。主要合作伙伴有天津天士力制药股份有限公司、天津天狮集团、天津星运生物科技发展有限公司等，生产产品在同类产品中认知度较高。保健食品主要销往东南亚、欧洲、南非的十几个国家地区。2003年一次通过国家级GMP认证，2008年再次通过GMP再认证。

第三节 总部经济

总部经济是以总部结算、金融商务、研发转化、文化创意为主的一个行业，其代表企业包括绫致、天狮、中国华电水务、中铁22局、亚马逊呼叫中心、阿芙精油结算中心、威莱日化、欧莎服饰、小狗电器等40余家。

2010年，开发区完成了创业总部基地的规划方案和基础设施、景观绿化工程的竣工；2011年总部基地楼宇建设全面提速。依托创业总部基地平台，促进总部楼宇经济取得突破性发展，共引进项目18个。有中国亿农营销结算中心、天津振戎国际能源、奥克斯研发中心、完达山液态奶总部、可信科技有限公司、坝上春秋设计创意总部、圣火科技园、天盛鼎和通信工程有限公司、奥帕蒂玛软件有限公司、信邦科技创业投资公司、奥峰文化传媒、与众科技（天津）有限公司、天津雅歌科技有限公司、天津尚思科技有限公司、天津三和工业电器科技有限公司、安科科技发展（天津）有限公司、龙沙集团、融鑫汇、创达投资咨询。2013年，32万平方米企业总部区竣工；2015年，基地10万平方米的服务外包北区和综合办公区北区基本建成，商联项目完成基础。

从 2011 到 2015 年的“十二五”规划的五年间，总部经济发展迅猛，到 2015 年已发展成为高端制造、生物医药并列的开发区三大主导产业之一。2016 年，又有新希望、美源星等总部经济项目 36 个，三英精控等亿元楼宇项目 2 个。总部经济的载体平台也在不断优化发展中。

重点企业简介

绫致时装（天津）有限公司

丹麦独资企业，成立于 1997 年 2 月，由欧洲最大的时装集团之一的绫致集团设立，总投资 9490 万美元。公司主要从事服装，服饰、鞋帽、家具等产品的生产、加工和销售，主要经营 ONLY（奥利）、JACK&JONES（杰克 & 琼斯）、VERO MODA（维莎曼）SELECTED（思莱德）和金·林德伯格品牌。2016 年，在全国有近 7000 家专卖店，为全国 5 万多人提供就业岗位。

该公司在三期北区投资建设了绫致物流园，建筑面积 12.5 万平方米。建有自动化仓库和办公楼，其中自动化仓库配有先进的自动化分拣系统、VNA 全自动高位叉车仓库等，整套系统由奥地利、英国、德国设计团队研发，将传统物流与新兴电商平台有机结合，实现电商全国线上配发以及北方零售门店仓储配发。2016 年营业收入 288 亿元，利润 30 亿元，纳税 24.28 亿元，吸纳就业 5.3 万人。2017 年 1—5 月营业收入 116.37 亿元，利润 12.81 亿元，纳税 14.71 亿元。

天津天狮集团有限公司

民营企业，成立于 1993 年 12 月。主要研发生产营养保健食品、保健用品、美容护肤品、家居用品等多元化产品，涉足零售、旅游、金融、国际贸易、电子商务等诸多领域，2005 年正式进入美国主板证券市场。一是天狮国际健康产业园。占地面积 1200 亩，总投资 70 亿元，天狮集团总部所在地，是集产品研发、中试、生产制造、国际物流、国际营销、国际教育与培训、国际旅游与研讨、国际康复、养生保健、健康管理为一体，产学研紧密结合，可实现生产及物流分拨自动化、仓储立体化、运营现代化、管理人性化、发展环保化的多功能产业园区。二是天狮学院。2008 年 4 月经教育部批准成立全日制普通本科高校。学校现有学生 3392 人，毕业生就业率保持在 95% 以上。三是在建天狮国际大学。占地 3000 亩，总建筑面积 210 万平米，总投资 100 亿元，将整合天狮学院建成教育理念先进、办学特色鲜明、教学设施精良、师资队伍一流、管理规格严格，符合经济和社会发展需要的国际化教育平台，将设置 11 个学院、55 个专业，在校学生可达 2.5 万人。2016 年营业收入 982 亿元，利润 199 亿元，纳税 2.95 亿元，吸纳就业 1 万人。2017 年 1—5 月营业收入 468 亿元，利润 562 亿元，纳税 9585 万元。

北京世纪卓越信息技术有限公司天津分公司

美国独资企业，成立于 2011 年 10 月，由世界 500 强美国亚马逊集团投资设立。项目由全球最大的工业及物流基础设施提供商和服务商普洛斯公司和全球最大的电子商务公司亚马逊公司合作开发、运营。项目位于武清开发区保税物流区内，规划占地 391 亩，建筑面积 19 万平方米，总投资 10 亿元。由世界 500 强企业美国普洛斯集团建设，美国最大的网络电子商务平台公司亚马逊承租经营，将建成亚马逊集团全球最大的仓储物流枢纽、电子交易平台和培训中心，涉及商品 200 万种，辐射中国北方地区。将建设全球一流的绿色、环保、高标仓储空间以及集网上销售、订单处理、支付、客服、采购管理、仓储与配送等模块于一体的电子商务平台。2016 年销售收入 5.8 亿元，纳税 147 万元，吸纳就业 146 人。

华电水务投资

内资企业，成立于 2013 年 5 月，由中国华电集团投资设设立。注册资本 2 亿元，主要从事城市饮用水处理、市政污水处理、海水淡化及资源化利用、水利工程等水务领域、以及城市污泥处理、固体废弃物处理、沼气开发、生态环境治理等国内及国外的投资、建设及运营。

小狗电器

民营企业，成立于 1999 年 7 月。2007 年之前与蓝岛、西单、燕莎等金字招牌的百货商场合作，之后入驻国美、大中、苏宁、永乐、五星电器系统。2007 年 6 月，小狗电器入驻淘宝，2010 年 8 月 6 日获得淘宝电器行业 " 淘品牌 " 荣誉称号；2008—2013 年连续六年居淘宝吸尘器类目销量第一；2012 年 5 月 18 日吸尘器新品 D–968 万人团期间售出吸尘器 29416 台，创品牌记录新高；其中 D–968 央视广告片获广告界最高奖项——中国国际广告节银奖；2013 年 3 月上市新品，智能扫地机器人 V–M600 上市，26 小时售罄 10000 台；小狗吸尘器 D–928 全网累计销量 673681 件，人气积聚，火爆异常。

欧莎世家

欧莎世家是香港欧莎工艺制品有限公司旗下品牌，大陆业务办事处坐落于“家居建材集散中心”——佛山，是专业家居饰品的生产商和经营商，欧莎世家专业承接家具、灯饰、装饰品三大系列产品生产及批发零售。产品集生活化、功能化、个性化、艺术化、融装饰性、实用性、观赏性于一体，一千多个款式；2016年欧莎世家拥有全国各地的地产商、设计及软装配饰公司、装修装饰公司、酒店宾馆、别墅会所、贸易商、批发零售商等合作伙伴，和国内多个陶瓷、卫浴品牌展厅合作。

梦想城堡（天津）电子商务有限公司

内资企业，成立于2014年6月17日，注册资金500万元。主要从事阿芙精油的线上以及线下销售，“AFU阿芙”品牌，进入中国短短几年时间，迅速覆盖全国一二线城市的顶级商场，全国设有300家形象专柜。2016年营业收入3.39亿元，利润5849万元，纳税6515万元。

截至2016年年底，武清开发区正以打造协同创新门户、生态科技园区为目标，着力提升发展的质量和效益，重点开发4个载体功能区：

1. 中欧产业园。与商务部投促局共建，规划9.5平方公里，是为欧洲企业打造的发展平台载体。发展定位是建成高端产业发展基地，主要发展高端制造、生物医药、新材料产业。目前为欧洲企业量身建设5万平方米环保节能厂房和中欧园服务中心已投入使用，正在规划建设环保节能厂房二期和生活配套区。

2. 创业总部基地。规划1.26平方公里，包括6个区域，建筑面积120万平方米。主要发展金融商务、研发转化、总部楼宇和文化创意等现代服务业，提升武清开发区功能环境，促进产业结构调整升级。

3. 京津高校（武清）科技创新园。占地161亩，建筑面积11.5万平方米，发展定位是立足加强与京津高校和科研机构的产学研用合作，建设高新项目研发平台、高端产业孵化平台、传统产业升级平台、创新成果转化平台和高层次人才集聚平台。

4. 自贸区武清园。位于天津自贸区东疆保税港区，规划335亩。搭建武清对外开放的更高平台，享受自贸区相关政策。发展定位是规划建设跨境物流和楼宇经济项目的招商载体，主要发展跨境电商、融资租赁、商业保理等重点行业。

第二章 知名企业

第一节 开发区世界 500 强企业

北京世纪卓越信息技术有限公司天津分公司

美国独资企业，成立于 2011 年 10 月，由世界 500 强企业之一的美国亚马逊集团投资设立。项目由全球最大的工业及物流基础设施提供商和服务商普洛斯公司和全球最大的电子商务公司亚马逊公司合作开发、运营。项目位于武清开发区保税物流区内，规划占地 391 亩，建筑面积 19 万平方米，总投资 10 亿元。由世界 500 强企业美国普洛斯集团建设，美国最大的网络电子商务平台公司亚马逊承租经营，将建成亚马逊集团全球最大的仓储物流枢纽、电子交易平台和培训中心，涉及商品 200 万种，辐射中国北方地区。将建设全球一流的绿色、环保、高标仓储空间以及集网上销售、订单处理、支付、客服、采购管理、仓储与配送等模块于一体的电子商务平台。2016 年销售收入 5.8 亿元，纳税 147 万元，吸纳就业 146 人。

北京世纪卓越信息技术有限公司天津第二分公司

美国独资企业，成立于 2001 年 10 月，由世界 500 强美国亚马逊集团投资成立。

中粮包装（天津）有限公司

内资企业，成立于 2006 年 3 月，由中国粮油食品（集团）有限公司投资兴建的大型综合包装制造企业。该公司坐落在中国武清开发区二期，投资总额 1.5 亿美元，注册资本 5000 万美元，占地 183 亩，于 2006 年 6 月破土动工，2007 年 10 月竣工投产。企业主要生产和销售各类粮食、食品储藏容器及包装制品，拥有十余条高速制罐、制盖、印涂生产线，主要涵盖印涂铁、饮料罐、喷雾罐、食品罐、番茄酱罐、奶粉罐、杂罐、皇冠盖等产品，在华北地区拥有红牛、枪手、哈啤、华润、好利来等优质的客户群。为建成中粮包装在华北地区规模最大、产品竞争力最强的生产基地，2010 年年底该公司开始建设两条自动化程度非常高的两片罐生产线，及塑胶、化工罐生产线。2016 年实现销售收入 10.4 亿元，利润 1.4 亿元，纳税 9381 万元，吸纳就业 658 人。

天津中粮制桶有限公司

内资企业，成立于 2013 年 6 月，是由中国粮油食品（集团）有限公司投资兴建的大型综合包装制造企业。2016 年实现销售收入 9987 万元，纳税 798 万元，吸纳就业 92 人。

中粮包装（成都）有限公司天津分公司

内资企业，成立于 2011 年 4 月，是由中国粮油食品（集团）有限公司投资兴建的大型综合包装制造企业。

艾默生过程管理（天津）阀门有限公司

美国独资企业，成立于 2003 年 10 月，由艾默生电气公司投资设立，投资总额 955 万美元，注册资本 560 万美元。产品全球市场占有率达 25%，中国市场占有率达 16%。公司主要从事生产、组装、销售新型电子、气动阀门控制系统及相关配套零配件，并提供售后服务，研究、开发和测试验证市场所需的新产品并提供相应的技术支持，采购、零售、批发非自产新型电子、气动控制阀门产品，设计研究开发新产品改进现有产品设计，产品的零售批发以及进出口业务。主要生产电气控制阀门。2015 年销售收入 8.96 亿元，利润 1.68 亿元，纳税 9445 万元。2016 年销售收入 5.78 亿元，利润 7719 万元，纳税 3661 万元，吸纳就业 311 人。

艾默生过程管理阀门自动控制（天津）有限公司

美国独资企业，成立于 2006 年 3 月，由艾默生电气公司投资设立。2016 年销售收入 2.29 亿元，纳税 2040 万元。吸纳就业 112 人。

LG 化学（天津）工程塑料有限公司

韩国独资企业，成立于 2004 年 12 月，是由 LG 化学投资设立。建筑面积 2 万余平方米，公司注册资金1800万美元，一期工程总投资1200万美元。公司主要设备均从国外引进，采用共混改性方法生产各种型号的EP树脂（PC、PC.ABS合金、PP改性、PBT改性、Nylon等），年产各种工程塑料5万吨。产品用途广泛，主要应用于汽车、家电、电气、IT等行业。公司的生产包装设备全部从国外进口，并采用世界一流的韩国LG化学先进的工艺流程和生产管理方法，生产高性能高品质的工程塑料。2016年销售收入5.5亿元，纳税3309万元，吸纳就业190人。

乐金华奥斯（天津）有限公司

韩国独资企业，原天津乐金新型建材有限公司，成立于1996年12月，总投资额3900万美元。是由世界500强企业、韩国最大的化学企业——LG化学株式会社投资建立的独资企业。天津乐金塑钢门窗有限公司于2002年5月正式成立，总投资额2375万美元，是LG化学株式会社的独资企业。2007年7月，新型建材和塑钢门窗两家公司合并，合并后名称为天津乐金新型建材有限公司，现改名为乐金华奥斯（天津）有限公司合并后投资总额达到6942万美元，注册资本达到3450万美元，占地282亩（188000平方米）。为韩国独资企业。主要生产产品：塑钢型材；合成地板、PVC地砖；高光膜；亚光膜；汽车用卷材等。2016年销售收入1845万元，纳税43万元，吸纳就业12人。

戴纳派克（中国）压实摊铺设备有限公司

瑞典独资企业，成立于1999年8月，由阿特拉斯科普柯公司投资设立，戴纳派克是全球最大的压实摊铺设备制造商之一，制造厂分布于瑞典、德国、法国、巴西和中国，于2007年7月加入阿特拉斯·科普柯集团，隶属于阿特拉斯·科普柯集团建筑和矿山技术事业部。阿特拉斯·科普柯集团是一家全球领先的工业生产解决方案供应商。其提供的产品和服务从压缩空气及气体设备、发电机、建筑及采矿设备、工业工具及安装系统到相关售后服务及专业租赁，一应俱全。集团总部位于瑞典斯德哥尔摩，业务遍及150多个国家和地区。

其产品的设计及制造基于70年以上的压实技术经验。戴纳派克（中国）压实摊铺设备有限公司作为戴纳派克在中国投资的第一家独资生产厂成立于1999年8月，投资总额1200万美元，注册资本500万美元，占地60亩（40000平方米），建筑面积5万平方米。负责道路的压实摊铺设备和技术的市场发展、施工咨询、施工设计及产品销售与售后服务。主要生产道路工程用压路机、摊铺机、轻型混凝土设备。产品采用进口散件及国产部件，在国内进行组装，与瑞典、德国生产的产品具有相同的质量和性能。2016 年实现销售收入 4.8 亿元，纳税 2099 万元，吸纳就业 180 人。

基伊埃韦史伐里亚分离设备（天津）有限公司

德国独资企业，成立于 2011 年 1 月，由德国 GEA 集团投资设立。投资总额 4050 万美元，注册资本 1350 万美元。占地面积 120 亩。主要从事生产、销售碟片式离心机、卧式螺旋离心机、食品及处理分离设备以及相关辅助设备、零部件，并提供技术咨询及售后服务。其离心分离技术全球领先，产品主要用于船舶舱底水处理等。2016 年销售额 4.79 亿元，年纳税 1682 万元，吸纳职工 163 人。

天津华住金属制品有限公司

日本独资企业，成立于 1995 年 4 月，由世界 500 强企业——日本住友商事株式会社投资设立。投资总额 7125 万美元，注册资本 2580 万美元，占地面积 100 亩（66667 平方米），主要从事生产、加工、销售新型金属零件材料及相关技术的开发、服务。主要产品为热轧酸洗板、冷轧板、电镀锌、热镀锌、不锈钢、矽钢片、铝板、马口铁、彩色钢板、三元合金、ZAM 材以及其他镀合金材料等。日本住友集团拥有 400 多年历史，是日本最古老的企业集团之一。旗下多家企业进入世界 500 强的行列。2016 年销售收入 12.68 亿元，利润 3895 万元，纳税 2640 万元。吸纳就业 277 人。

中农立华（天津）农用化学品有限公司

日本独资企业，成立于 1997 年 3 月，由世界 500 强企业——日本住友商事株式会社投资设立。主营氮肥增效剂生产，生产、加工、销售叶面肥、有机硅助剂、聚醚逐级、农药及相关技术咨询服务业务，位于武清区杨村南（北方射击场旁），注册资本 450 万元，投资总额 600 万元。2016 年销售收入 8947 万元，利润 846 万元，纳税 407 万元。吸纳就业 120 人。

奥宗尼亚环保技术（天津）有限公司

法国独资企业，成立于 2012 年 7 月，由得利满水处理系统（北京）有限公司投资设立，位于武清开发区三期京津高校（武清）科技创新园内，总投资 2400 万元，租赁厂房 3000 平方米。主要生产臭氧发生器和臭氧尾气破坏器等设备，产品主要用于饮用水、污水处理等领域，其技术具有全球领先水平。2016 年销售收入 9451 万元，纳税 361 万元，吸纳就业 42 人。

天津大真空有限公司

日本独资企业，成立于 1993 年 5 月，由日本东棉株式会社投资设立，位于武清开发区福源道 8 号，注册资本 4867.3 万美元，投资总额 1.4 亿美元，占地面积 67.5 亩（45000 平方米），主要从事生产、销售水晶制品、陶瓷制品和光学制品；五金电子产品及上述商品的批发零售及进出口，制造水晶制品，陶瓷制品，光学制品，五金、电子产品所需的原材料，消耗品的批发、零售及进出口。主要产品为水晶振动子、水晶片。已通过 ISO 系列认证。2016 年销售收入 1.6 亿元，纳税 604 万元，吸纳就业 814 人。

德尔福派克电气系统有限公司天津分公司

美国德国合资企业，成立于 2014 年 10 月，由美国德尔福投资设立。美国德尔福公司成立于 1890 年，总部设在美国俄亥俄州沃伦，是全球最大的汽车线束系统制造厂商，世界 500 强企业。德尔福是全球最大的汽车零部件供应商之一，产品供给包括通用汽车、福特、丰田、日产、雷诺、大众等全球最大汽车厂家。除了发动机、变速箱、外壳、座椅、轮胎外，德尔福几乎能提供其它所有的汽车零部件，在全球汽车零部件市场占有率高达 15% — 20%。德尔福目前在全球 41 个国家设了 176 家全资制造厂、42 家合资厂、53 个客户服务中心和销售代表处以及 32 个技术中心。

德尔福武清汽车线束项目由德尔福派克电气系统有限公司投资设立，位于武清开发区四期，由武清开发区订制建设标准厂房，占地 60 亩，建筑面积 2.2 万平方米，总投资 1 亿元，主要生产汽车各类线束制品，产品应用于汽车线束系统、车载电话、车载娱乐系统等设备领域。主要客户为戴姆勒奔驰、长城等。2016 年实现销售收入 4.28 亿元，纳税 528 亿元，吸纳就业 1175 人。

天津宏信设备租赁有限公司

内资企业，成立于 2012 年 7 月，由中化集团投资设立，注册资本 10000 万元，占地 550 亩，主要从事工程机械设备及零部件、金属结构件租赁、制造、维修、销售、加工、安装，机械设备技术开发、转让、咨询服务，房屋建筑工程、公路工程、地基与基础工程、钢结构工程施工，工程项目管理，商务信息咨询，陆路、海上、航空国际货运代理。

主要产品包括：高空升降车、路面机械、基坑支架等。其投资方为中国化工集团控股的上海宏信设备工程有限公司，该投资方已在香港上市。2016 年销售收入 9244 万元，纳税 106 万元。吸纳就业 453 人。

国际纸业（天津）包装有限公司

美国独资企业，成立于 2000 年 9 月，由国际纸业集团投资设立。投资总额为 500 万美元，注册资本 250 万美元。主要从事采用专利技术、综合利用再生纸，生产和销售纸垫板及相关纸制品，开发包装类新产品。主要生产纸箱、纸板。2011 年销售收入 1.46 亿元，利润 213.4 万元，纳税 786.27 万元，2012 年 1—11 月实现销售 1.24 亿元，利润 415 万元，纳税 663.86 万元。吸纳就业 154 人。其投资方国际纸业（亚洲）有限公司成立于 1898 年是世界 500 强企业。是世界最知名的、规模最大的专注于为全球客户提供造纸、包装、印刷和森林产品的公司之一。业务遍及全球 40 个国家和地区，产品销往全球 120 个国家。

万国食品包装（天津）有限公司

美国独资企业，成立于 2012 年 2 月，由国际纸业集团投资设立。投资总额 970 万美元，注册资金 570 万美元。其投资方是世界 500 强企业、全球最大的纸业集团国际纸业。生产和销售纸杯、纸餐具、纸容器，上述产品和塑料制品的批发、进出口并提供相关配套服务，包装装潢印刷品印刷。公司具有先进的淋膜工艺、高速柔性印刷工艺和高速的纸杯成型工艺，产品主要包括冷、热饮纸杯、冰淇淋杯、双层杯、铝箔杯、食品盛放杯、外带全家餐桶等高质量的纸制食品包装容器，与国内外知名企业肯德基、麦当劳、星巴克、百事、可口可乐、雀巢、吉野家、德克士、味全、和路雪、汉堡王等保持长期良好的合作关系。2016 年销售收入 4079 万元，纳税 12 万元。吸纳就业 64 人。

上海英格索兰压缩机有限公司天津客户中心

美国独资企业，于 2006 年 8 月成立，由英格索兰压缩机有限公司投资设立，注册资本 765 万美元，年销售额 10.7 亿元人民币。主要从事销售和租赁本公司生产的压缩机及其后处理设备（冷干机、过滤器等），移动式灯塔，提供上述产品的安装、售后服务及现场供应压缩空气的业务。2011 年销售收入 1.01 亿元，利润 4254.2 万元，纳税 1534.32 万元，2012 年 1—11 月实现销售收入 1.21 亿元，利润 6336.9 万元，纳税

1278.96万元。吸纳就业12人。

其投资方英格索兰公司成立于1871年，总部设在美国纽约，于1906年在美国纽约证券交易所上市，年收入近100亿美元，在全球42个国家设立450多个分支机构，拥有近4万名员工，为世界500强企业之一。是全球建筑机械和工业设备工具制造产业的龙头，主要产品包括空气压缩机、建筑五金产品、汽车零部件和建筑设备、高尔夫用汽车工具和工具温度传送控制设备等。1922年，在上海设立办事处。截至2016年，在中国已经拥有8个合资企业、1个独资企业、3个代表处和1个投资公司，年销售额6亿多美元。

奥钢联金属部件（天津）有限公司

奥地利独资企业，成立于2017年3月，由奥钢联金属部件（沈阳）有限公司投资设立，总部设在奥地利林茨，旗下拥有钢铁冶炼、铁轨系统、汽车用钢、管材等四家分公司。奥钢联在世界5大洲50多个国家拥有500家集团分公司和生产基地。特别是用于汽车、铁路和航空以及能源等技术密集型产业的高要求钢铁产品的生产、加工和深度开发等方面，奥钢联是全球领先的供应商。

奥钢联金属部件（沈阳）有限公司是一家外商独资企业，计划在武清开发区投资设立奥钢联金属部件生产基地项目，租赁中欧产业园4号厂房，从事航空、航天、汽车、摩托车轻量化及环保型新材料研发与制造。预计2018—2022年5年内累计营业额约为3000万欧元，约合21948万元人民币；税收累计约为150万欧元，约合1097万元人民币。

宝沃佛吉亚汽车部件中国总部

中外合资企业，成立于2016年6月，由佛吉亚（中国）投资有限公司投资设立，佛吉亚是法国汽车零部件企业，全球第六大汽车零部件供应商，世界500强企业。在汽车座椅、排放控制技术系统、汽车内饰和外饰四大业务领域居业界领先地位。其中座椅业务排名全球第二，欧洲第一。在全国共有38家工厂，4个研发中心，客户主要有大众集团、标致雪铁龙、长安福特、东风日产、通用汽车、现代、长城汽车、福田汽车。

一期项目由佛吉亚在武清开发区投资2000万元人民币建设汽车部件北方生产基地，租赁中欧产业园厂房从事汽车座椅装配业务，现已顺利投产。二期项目由佛吉亚集团与宝沃集团合资成立，投资 1.25 亿元人民币，建设宝沃佛吉亚中国区总部、研发中心、管理中心、生产基地，并具备对外投资功能，定制 3 万平方米厂房，预计在 2018 年 10 月投入使用，从事汽车座椅装配、座椅骨架、发泡填充物生产及汽车内饰等相关业务。预计 2018 年实现营业额 8 亿元，税收 4100 万元，2019 年实现营业额 12 亿元，税收 6200 万元，2020 年实现营业额 13 亿元，税收 6800 万元。

沃尔玛购物广场

独资企业，成立于 2016 年 8 月，由沃尔玛（天津）商业零售有限公司投资设立，沃尔玛（中国）投资有限公司，沃尔玛百货有限公司的全资子公司。沃尔玛由美国零售业的传奇人物山姆·沃尔顿先生于 1962 年在阿肯色州成立。经过五十多年的发展，沃尔玛公司已经成为世界最大的私人雇主和连锁零售商，多次荣登《财富》杂志世界 500 强榜首及当选最具价值品牌。目前沃尔玛在中国经营多种业态和品牌，包括购物广场、山姆会员商店等。山姆会员商店是沃尔玛旗下的高端会员制商店，已有超过 30 年的历史。至今山姆在全球已拥有 800 多家门店，成为全球最大的会员制商店之一。

沃尔玛购物广场项目设立在武清开发区荔隆广场，租赁 18000 平方米载体。预计项目建成并投入运营后年营业额约 3 亿元，年税收总额约 3000 万元。

丰树集团

新加坡独资企业，成立于 2013 年 2 月，由淡马锡集团投资设立，丰树产业公司是一家侧重于亚洲地产开发、投资和资本管理的龙头企业，其总部位于新加坡。丰树的战略重点是投资在亚洲地区具有良好增长潜力的市场和房地产板块。结合了作为开发商，投资公司和资本管理经理人的关键优势，集团已在新加坡成功地建立了一系列屡获大奖的房产项目，并在亚洲地区通过不同的房地产类别提供持续丰厚的回报。

截至 2011 年 9 月 30 日，丰树拥有和管理总值 187 亿新元的写字楼、物流、工业、住宅及零售、生活娱乐物业。集团管理着三家在新加坡上市的房地产投资信托和三个私募房地产基金，其投资信托和私募基金在新加坡和亚洲各地涉及广泛的房地产平台。集团也在新加坡、中国、印度、日本、马来西亚、韩国和越南建立了广泛的网络机构以支持集团在该区域的扩展。丰树的资产组合包括在新加坡屡获奖项的怡丰城和丰树商业城，以及区域性的综合开发项目，如在中国的未来城和南海富丰新城。

丰树计划在武清投资 2 亿元 ~ 3.7 亿元人民币建设物流基地设施以满足京津区域的

客户需求。项目总投资2亿元～3.7亿元，其中建设投资1.7亿元～3.4亿元。本项目建成后，年均经营收入为4300万元，年均利润为3200万元，投资利润率为9%。丰树京津区域商品配送中心位于天津武清开发区内，项目一期总占地面积为133400平方米（200亩）；项目建（构）筑占地80000～145000平方米；主要服务于京津地区的物流，零售，电子商务企业。

国能飞腾科技有限公司

内资企业，成立于2011年1月，由中国大唐集团投资设立，国能飞腾科技有限公司位于武清开发区三期西区，投资6.3亿元，占地225亩，建筑面积13万平方米。将建设集高性能纤维自主研发、生产、销售于一体并拥有自主知识产权的高新技术企业。主要产品对位芳纶是具有高强度、高模量、耐高温、耐酸碱、密度低等特点的高性能纤维，其强度是优质钢材的5～6倍、韧性是钢材的2倍，重量仅为钢材的1.5%。主要应用于航空航天、国防军工、防护装甲、高级轮胎、交通电力、结构工程、通讯光纤、海底输油管道、土木结构工程和特高压输电线路等领域。该项目填补了我国新材料领域空白，是一项重大新兴材料科技项目。七年，吸纳就业60人。

中工马泰克路面机械（天津）有限公司

合资企业，成立于2010年5月，由国机重工投资设立，（CCMC-Martec）公司是由加拿大马泰克国际再生公司与中国工程机械总公司合资成立的中外合资企业，总部位于中国天津武清经济技术开发区。中工马泰克拥有加拿大马泰克国际再生公司所有热再生机的技术与专利，并在加拿大温哥华设有分支机构。中工马泰克公司面向全球市场，致力于沥青热再生设备、就地冷再生机、铣刨机等公路养护设备的开发、制造与服务。

中电投武清开发区分布式光伏发电站

中电投武清开发区分布式光伏发电站是中国电力投资集团在华北地区设立的区域公司，主要立足华北，面向全国，高效发展新能源，定位以风、光新能源发电为主，以燃气、生物质、垃圾等清洁可再生能源发电为补充的综合型能源企业。中电投集团是国有五大发电集团之一，是集电力、煤炭铁路等产业于一体的综合性能源公司，全国唯一同时拥有水电、火电、核电的新能源资产，是国家三大核电开发建设运营商之一、有强劲的投融资能力，每年的投资额在 800 亿元以上。

中电投采取总体规划、分期开发、示范现行的步骤，将现有可利用的 200 万平方米屋顶建设分布式光伏电站，总投资约 14.08 亿元。

中交四公局第六工程有限公司

内资企业，成立于 2014 年 7 月，由中交建设集团投资设立，主要从事道路、桥梁工程施工等相关业务，公司坐落于武清开发区创业总部基地 B11 号楼 10 层，1652 平方米，预计自公司成立起，第三年纳税不低于 1000 万元。

中水电津城投资发展有限公司

内资企业，成立于 2010 年 2 月，由中水电集团投资设立。中水电津城投资发展有限公司（简称“中水电津城公司”）是由中国水电建设集团路桥工程有限公司、中国水电建设集团房地产有限公司、中国水利水电第四工程有限公司、中国水利水电第十一工程局有限公司、中国水利水电第十三工程局有限公司、中国水利水电第十四工程局有限公司和天津新技术产业园区武清开发区总公司共同出资组建。公司主要负责完成天津市武清新城开发 BT 项目的投资建设，项目总投资约 80 亿元，总工期六年。

华电水务投资

内资企业，成立于 2013 年 5 月，由中国华电集团投资设立。注册资本 2 亿元，主要从事城市饮用水处理、市政污水处理、海水淡化及资源化利用、水利工程等水务领域、以及城市污泥处理、固体废弃物处理、沼气开发、生态环境治理等国内及国外的投资、建设及运营。

华电水务工程

内资企业，成立于 2013 年 5 月，由中国华电集团投资设立。注册资本 1.01 亿元，从事水处理和环保技术的研究和应用，为全球用户提供方案咨询、工程设计、设备制造、工程总包、安装调试、技术培训等系统解决方案。

华电水务膜分离科技（天津）有限公司

内资企业，成立于 2013 年 12 月，由中国华电集团投资设立。注册资本 5000 万元，主要业务为膜分离技术，水处理设备技术开发、咨询、转让，膜分离装置、水处理设备制造、销售、安装、维修，水处理工程设计、施工。

天津沃利帕森工程技术有限公司

澳大利亚独资企业，成立于2015年8月，由沃利帕森集团投资设立。澳大利亚沃利帕森集团是世界500强企业、国际知名的跨国国际工程承包商，也是资源与能源领域、复杂工业领域处于世界领先地位的专业工程公司，主要为油气炼化、矿山冶金、化工石化等领域的中外客户提供工程设计和项目交付服务。该集团在中国的执行子公司——沃利帕森中国，已执行项目500余个，拥有2500余名员工，是中国最大的国际工程设计、采购、咨询、施工管理服务提供商之一。此次签约的沃利帕森天津设计服务中心项目位于创业总部基地，办公面积3000平方米，将承接北京设计总部和天津办公室的职能。

伟信（天津）工资咨询有限公司

合资企业，成立2011年12月，由美国URS集团投资设立，伟信顾问是一家国际著名的工程顾问公司，在全球工程顾问公司综合排名一直居于前50名之列，在世界80多个地区均有办事机构或分公司。通过伟信在全球各地区子公司的网络，我们无论在工程设计、管理、施工以至环境评估及其他有关专业范畴，都能提供独立、整体及完善的服务。伟信（天津）工程咨询有限公司是伟信顾问集团（前称史伟高）在天津成立的一家合资工程设计、顾问公司。

天津伟信以伟信集团的国际经验和分布在世界各地的专家资源为后盾，提供城市规划，景观设计，建筑设计、港口工程、环境和市政工程的设计、咨询服务。配合20多年来参与中国项目的经验和国际专业技术及项目管理的水平，积累了丰富的当地知识，建立了良好的关系网，保证能为客户提供优质和符合实际情况的咨询服务，解决问题。

天津真和实业有限公司

日本独资企业，成立于1996年3月，由日本伊藤忠株式会社投资设立，注册资本50万美元。经营范围为生产、销售皮革制品及鞋类，坐落于武清区大孟庄镇师范学校北侧。

天津三之星机带有限公司

日本独资企业，成立于1998年3月，由日本三井物产株式会社投资设立。注册资本50000万日元，公司主营开发、生产、销售机械用橡胶带和相关的技术咨询服务，公司位于武清开发区3号路12号。

第二节　国家级高新技术企业

截至2016年，开发区拥有国家级高新技术企业54家，其中，2008年认定7家，2009年认定2家 ，2011年认定1家，2012年认定4家，2013年认定4家，2014年认定10家，2015年认定12家，2016年认定14家。自2014年起，每年都在10家以上，且逐年增多。

开发区国家级高新技术企业一览表

表13

序号	镇街园区	企业名称	认定年份
1	开发区	丹佛斯（天津）有限公司	2008
2	开发区	天津红日药业股份有限公司	2008
3	开发区	天津市普光医用材料制造有限公司	2008
4	开发区	天津市世纪恒通科技有限公司	2008
5	开发区	天津天狮生物发展有限公司	2008
6	开发区	中纺新材料科技有限公司	2008
7	开发区	中天高科特种车辆有限公司	2008
8	开发区	麦格昆磁（天津）有限公司	2009
9	开发区	天津达祥精密工业有限公司	2009
10	开发区	思科普压缩机（天津）有限公司	2011
11	开发区	可信（天津）科技有限公司	2012
12	开发区	天津澳普林特通讯器材组件有限公司	2012

续表 13

序号	镇街园区	企业名称	认定年份
13	开发区	天津南玻节能玻璃有限公司	2012
14	开发区	信义玻璃（天津）有限公司	2012
15	开发区	天津日进汽车系统有限公司	2013
16	开发区	天津市建电实业有限公司	2013
17	开发区	天津市津能双鹤热力设备有限公司	2013
18	开发区	天津赢达信科技有限公司	2013
19	开发区	天地融电子（天津）有限公司	2014
20	开发区	天加空调（天津）有限公司	2014
21	开发区	天津君歌分子蒸馏设备有限公司	2014
22	开发区	天津三卓韩一橡塑科技股份有限公司	2014
23	开发区	天津尚思科技有限公司	2014
24	开发区	天津市海正泰克塑胶制品有限公司	2014
25	开发区	天津中敖生物科技有限公司	2014
26	开发区	天津逐鹿信息技术有限公司	2014
27	开发区	信义汽车部件（天津）有限公司	2014
28	开发区	与众科技（天津）有限公司	2014
29	开发区	邦盛福祉科技（天津）有限公司	2015
30	开发区	歌思（天津）低温设备有限公司	2015
31	开发区	天津富禄通信技术有限公司	2015
32	开发区	天津海迈医用科技有限公司	2015
33	开发区	天津宏信科技开发有限公司	2015
34	开发区	天津华迈科技有限公司	2015
35	开发区	天津极欧科技股份有限公司	2015

续表 13

序号	镇街园区	企业名称	认定年份
36	开发区	天津梦祥原科技有限公司	2015
37	开发区	天津欧恒祥科技有限公司	2015
38	开发区	天津星微软件开发有限公司	2015
39	开发区	维克（天津）有限公司	2015
40	开发区	颐和美林（天津）生物科技有限公司	2015
41	开发区	艾默生过程管理（天津）阀门有限公司	2016
42	开发区	百米马（天津）有限公司	2016
43	开发区	滴滴集运（天津）科技股份有限公司	2016
44	开发区	华电水务膜分离科技（天津）有限公司	2016
45	开发区	美泰克（天津）矿物有限公司	2016
46	开发区	启联（天津）科技有限公司	2016
47	开发区	世纪天云科技（天津）有限公司	2016
48	开发区	泰济生健康管理有限公司	2016
49	开发区	天津博耐特电子有限公司	2016
50	开发区	天津大学前沿技术研究院有限公司	2016
51	开发区	天津怡和嘉业医疗科技有限公司	2016
52	开发区	天津运城制版有限公司	2016
53	开发区	沃斯坦热力设备（天津）有限公司	2016
54	开发区	天津鸿新企业管理咨询有限公司	2016

第三章　企业名录

第一节　开发区国企、央企企业名录

表 14

序号	企业名称	国企投资方
1	中体产业集团股份有限公司	国家体育总局
2	天津中体影视有限公司	
3	天津中体经纪管理有限公司	
4	中体传播网有限公司	
5	天津中体明星俱乐部有限公司	
6	中体竞赛管理有限公司	
7	天津金佰利投资发展有限公司	
8	天津塞力斯特建筑安装有限公司	
9	天津国民天房资产管理有限公司	天津市房地产开发经营集团
10	天津天房融华资产管理有限公司	
11	天津天房城镇化建设投资合伙企业（有限合伙）	
12	天津天房金汇投资中心（有限合伙）	
13	天津天房融汇投资管理有限公司	
14	中投证券投资有限公司	中国中投证券有限责任公司
15	中投中财基金管理有限公司	

续表 14

序号	企业名称	国企投资方
16	中投汇鑫保险经纪有限公司	中国中投证券有限责任公司
17	中投中财（天津）文化产业股权投资基金合伙企业（有限合伙）	
18	天津市中投汇鑫投资管理有限公司	
19	中粮包装(天津)有限公司	中粮集团
20	中粮制桶（天津）有限公司	
21	杭州中粮美特容器有限公司天津分公司	
22	中粮包装（成都）有限公司天津分公司	
23	中纺新材料科技有限公司	中国纺织科学研究院
24	中纺院（天津）科技发展有限公司	
25	中纺院（天津）滤料技术检测有限公司	
26	保利（天津）房地产开发有限公司	保利房地产（集团）股份有限公司
27	保利广州物业管理有限公司天津分公司	
28	广州保利地产代理有限公司天津分公司	
29	玉柴重工（天津）有限公司	广西玉柴重工有限公司
30	天津玉柴国际物流有限公司	
31	天津银德融资租赁有限公司	
32	中农住商（天津）农用化学品有限公司	中国农业生产资料集团公司
33	天津市中农化农业生产资料有限公司	
34	天津天大领先制药有限公司	天津大学
35	天津大学前沿技术研究院	
36	天津华电福源热电有限公司	中国华电集团
37	华电水务（天津）有限公司	

续表 14

序号	企业名称	国企投资方
38	华电水务膜分离科技（天津）有限公司	中国华电集团
39	天津华电科工环保技术有限公司	
40	天津松江创展投资发展有限公司	天津松江集团有限公司
41	天津运河城投资有限公司	
42	中水电津城投资发展有限公司	中国水电建设集团
43	中国水利水电第二工程局有限公司天津分公司	
44	北京住总集团有限责任公司天津武清分公司	北京住总集团
45	北京住总市政工程有限责任公司天津武清分公司	
46	天津伊利乳品有限责任公司	内蒙古伊利实业集团股份有限公司
47	天津完达山乳品有限公司	黑龙江农垦集团
48	天津宏信设备租赁有限公司	中化集团
49	天津振戎国际能源有限公司	珠海振戎公司
50	可信（天津）科技有限公司	武清开发区总公司
51	中工马泰克路面机械（天津）有限公司	中国国机重工集团有限公司
52	舍尔特工业（天津）有限公司	武清区工经委
53	天津武清一商友谊百货有限公司	天津一商集团有限公司
54	天津市五一阳光投资发展有限公司	天津市总工会
55	金锐丽城（天津）置业投资有限公司	金泰地产集团
56	天津京津高速公路有限公司	北京首都创业集团有限公司
57	天津市武清开发区全发电力工程有限公司	武清电力公司
58	天津市武清区汇才人力资源开发服务有限公司	武清区北方人才
59	天津市武清区信邦科技创业投资发展有限公司	天津市科委

续表 14

序号	企业名称	国企投资方
60	天津永安有限责任公司	天津市武清区国有资产监督管理委员会
61	天津远恒有限公司	
62	天津市普光医用材料制造有限公司	中新药业
63	天津市国环置业有限公司	
64	天津大学前沿技术研究院有限公司	天津大学资产经营有限公司
65	天津大学技术转移有限公司	天大科技园有限公司
66	天津海石花物流有限公司	外交部
67	千代福国际信息技术有限公司	
68	天津交控科技有限公司	北京交控科技有限公司
69	中铁五州控股集团有限公司	中铁中基控股集团有限公司
70	铁科纵横（天津）科技发展有限公司	铁科院
71	天津市建筑工程质量检测中心	建科院
72	天津宏信设备租赁有限公司	中化远东
73	中交四公局第六工程有限公司	中交第四公路工程局有限公司
合计	73	38

第二节 开发区外资企业名录

表 15

序号	企业名称	国别	投资总额	注册资本	取照时间
1	天津阿托兹精细化工有限公司	中国、美国	500 万元	400 万元	1995.9.18
2	天津澳普林特通讯器材组件有限公司	加拿大	780 万美元	780 万美元	2006.12.28
3	沃克空间（天津）商贸有限公司	中国(香港)	70 万元	50 万元	2010.3.25
4	EKC 工业（天津）有限公司	印度	5000 万美元	1667 万美元	2006.3.30
5	天津杰麦多乐器有限公司	中国(台湾)	7570 万美元	3056.4 万美元	1992.11.11
6	功学社（天津）商贸有限公司	中国(台湾)	280 万美元	200 万美元	2005.8.8
7	天津天朝葡萄酿酒有限公司	美国	240.02 万美元	240.02 万美元	1993.5.21
8	天津国荣食品工业有限公司	中国(台湾)	14 万美元	10 万美元	1993.6.7
9	天津旭升制衣有限公司	日本	48 万美元	34 万美元	1994.7.5
10	天津鸿佳地毯有限公司	中国(台湾)	650 万美元	477 万美元	1994.8.22
11	新艺美工艺制品(天津)有限公司	新加坡	395 万美元	280 万美元	1994.12.9

续表 15

序号	企业名称	国别	投资总额	注册资本	取照时间
12	天津镒利工程机械有限公司	新加坡	360 万元	360 万元	1996.5.13
13	可乐马家具（天津）有限公司	中国（香港）	43 万美元	43 万美元	1996.8.21
14	天津欧亚服装有限公司	韩国	22 万美元	22 万美元	1996.11.8
15	绫致时装（天津）有限公司	丹麦	16855 万美元	8180 万美元	1997.2.28
16	金林德伯格（天津）有限公司	新加坡	1400 万美元	1000 万美元	2011.12.23
17	天津光瑞服装服饰有限公司	中国（台湾）	14 万美元	10 万美元	1997.6.25
18	天津多捷制衣有限公司	中国（香港）	72 万美元	60 万美元	2000.11.10
19	祥尔瑞（天津）服装服饰有限公司	加拿大	39 万美元	28 万美元	2001.4.23
20	天津松本包装制品有限公司	日本	14 万美元	10 万美元	2001.11.16
21	智波合金（天津）有限公司	英国	20 万美元	14 万美元	2002.6.19
22	天津大渊机电有限公司	韩国	56 万美元	40 万美元	2002.7.17
23	天津同心同友机电有限公司	韩国	12 万美元	10 万美元	2002.8.26
24	天津晶弘太阳能科技有限公司	日本 加拿大	120 万美元	100 万美元	2003.4.1
25	天津嘉琪仪表电子有限公司	中国（香港）	20 万美元	15 万美元	1992.12.7

续表 15

序号	企业名称	国别	投资总额	注册资本	取照时间
26	天津大真空有限公司	日本	241.6 亿日元	81.7 亿日元	1993.5.17
27	福运泉（天津）野酸枣开发有限公司	中国（香港）	138.5 万美元	98.5 万美元	1993.5.18
28	天津立发医疗用品有限公司	中国（香港）	40 万美元	40 万美元	1993.7.19
29	华美（天津）电镀技术有限公司	中国（香港）	670 万元	570 万元	1993.12.30
30	天津中央电子有限公司	韩国	378.4 万美元	265 万美元	1994.2.24
31	天津泰永电机有限公司	韩国	80 万美元	80 万美元	1994.5.24
32	天津瑞科建设工程有限公司	中国（香港）	665 万美元	535 万美元	1994.6.15
33	海德罗奥（天津）工业水处理有限公司	丹麦、泰国	51 万美元	36 万美元	1994.12.5
34	天津磁化电子有限公司	韩国	1631 万美元	1280 万美元	1995.3.9
35	天津华住金属制品有限公司	日本、中国（香港）	7125 万美元	2580 万美元	1995.4.12
36	天津沈劳乐器有限公司	韩国	134 万美元	130 万美元	1995.5.12
37	天津豪晶电子材料有限公司	马来西亚	200 万美元	189.7 万美元	1995.6.15
38	天津富禄通信技术有限公司	韩国	3500 万美元	2250 万美元	1995.6.16
39	马勒东炫滤清器（天津）有限公司	德国、韩国	1344 万美元	1044 万美元	1995.7.24

续表 15

序号	企业名称	国别	投资总额	注册资本	取照时间
40	天津伊都锦时装有限公司	中国（香港）、天津	2300 万美元	1416.22 万美元	1995.9.11
41	光宝电子（天津）有限公司	中国（香港）	19950 万美元	6650 万美元	1995.9.15
42	丹佛斯（天津）有限公司	丹麦	8108.9043 万美元	4206.4043 万美元	1995.9.29
43	井上（天津）机械制造有限公司	日本	28400 万日元	21400 万日元	1995.11.8
44	乐金华奥斯（天津）有限公司	韩国	6942 万美元	3446.14 万美元	1995.12.27
45	莱生（天津）天然保健品开发有限公司	美国	250 万美元	180 万美元	1996.7.1
46	万可电子（天津）有限公司	德国	5158 万欧元	1720 万欧元	1997.2.28
47	瑞特格（中国）有限公司	芬兰	2000 万美元	1550 万美元	1997.10.20
48	天津海特磁性材料有限公司	美国	140 万美元	100 万美元	1997.10.24
49	西湖（天津）橡塑制品有限公司	新加坡	500 万美元	175 万美元	1998.3.27
50	天津天狮生物发展有限公司	中国（香港）	2130 万美元	1000 万美元	1998.3.27
51	麦格昆磁（天津）有限公司	美国	4998 万美元	1666 万美元	1998.8.28
52	麦格昆磁国际贸易（天津）有限公司	巴巴多斯	110 万美元	80 万美元	2010.5.20
53	禾丰（天津）卫生用品有限公司	中国（台湾）	948 万元	674.3348 万元	1998.9.23

续表 15

序号	企业名称	国别	投资总额	注册资本	取照时间
54	利安隆（天津）实业有限公司	中国（香港）	350 万美元	350 万美元	1998.10.23
55	天津亨达地毯有限公司	美国	128 万元	90 万元	1999.5.5
56	戴纳派克（中国）压实摊铺设备有限公司	瑞典	3900 万美元	1300 万美元	1999.8.26
57	中成中药加工工艺（天津）有限公司	韩国	250 万美元	200 万美元	2000.3.8
58	山依耐神建材（天津）有限公司	韩国	70 万美元	50 万美元	2000.3.23
59	星宝电机（天津）有限公司	韩国	1048 万美元	496 万美元	2000.5.26
60	汇科琪（天津）水质添加剂有限公司	中国（香港）	24 万美元	20 万美元	2000.8.2
61	美善家具（天津）有限公司	美国	990 万美元	840 万美元	2000 年 8.18
62	合众创亚（天津）包装有限公司	新加坡	500 万美元	250 万美元	2000 年 9.29
63	真明农化（天津）有限公司	日本	14 万美元	10 万美元	2000.10.25
64	欣烨机电科技（天津）有限公司	韩国	67 万美元	57 万美元	2000.11.2
65	天津爱莱克电子有限公司	日本	38.57 万美元	27 万美元	2001.1.17
66	艾尔姆风能叶片制品（天津）有限公司	丹麦	2793.25 万美元	1175 万美元	2001.2.21
67	爱姆卡（天津）工业五金有限公司	德国	34 万美元	30 万美元	2001.3.14

续表 15

序号	企业名称	国别	投资总额	注册资本	取照时间
68	天津北口电子部材有限公司	日本	1750 万日元	1250 万日元	2001.5.10
69	玻石机械（天津）有限公司	芬兰	35 万美元	25 万美元	2001.5.30
70	联泰石材（天津）有限公司	中国（台湾）	40 万美元	30 万美元	2001.5.30
71	富阳水泥装备（天津）有限公司	丹麦 维尔京群岛	143 万元	100 万元	2001.7.26
72	山阳（天津）机械有限公司	日本	8.3 亿日元	4.2 亿日元	2001.11.30
73	巴哈斯－桑索霍芬（天津）机械有限公司	德国	420 万美元	210 万美元	2001.11.30
74	巴哈斯（天津）商贸有限公司	德国	14 万美元	10 万美元	2011.8.2
75	伟信（天津）工程咨询有限公司	中国（香港）	82.85 万美元	82.85 万美元	2001.12.19
76	雅丽达阀门（天津）有限公司	马来西亚	1572 万元	1100 万元	2002.3.22
77	天津宝特金属材料有限公司	美国	56 万美元	40 万美元	2002.5.30
78	天津光精工精密机械有限公司	日本	290 万美元	233.7 万美元	2002.6.6
79	通用咨询（天津）有限公司	中国、美国	50 万美元	50 万美元	2002.10.10
80	天津乾命畜牧机械有限公司	韩国	14 万美元	10 万美元	2002.10.31
81	天津澳普林特电子印务有限公司	澳大利亚	74 万美元	70 万美元	2002.11.15

续表 15

序号	企业名称	国别	投资总额	注册资本	取照时间
82	瑞一（中国）科技发展有限公司	韩国、印尼	1470 万美元	600 万美元	2003.1.14
83	丘比克（天津）转印有限公司	日本、韩国、萨摩亚、中国（香港）	1181 万美元	660 万美元	2003.5.19
84	天津达祥精密工业有限公司	萨摩亚	13190 万美元	4400 万美元	2003.6.12
85	天津三卓韩一橡塑科技股份有限公司	新加坡		1783 万元	2003.7.11
86	优派克精密机械（天津）有限公司	马来西亚	840 万美元	420 万美元	2003.9.27
87	艾默生过程管理（天津）阀门有限公司	美国	395 万美元	280 万美元	2003.10.10
88	艾默生过程管理阀门自动控制（天津）有限公司	美国	560 万美元	280 万美元	2006.11.21
89	西斯密（天津）电机有限公司	意大利	420 万美元	210 万美元	2004.1.30
90	信义玻璃（天津）有限公司	中国（香港）	19800 万美元	12600 万美元	2004.3.3
91	三晶电子(天津)有限公司	韩国	448 万美元	230 万美元	2004.6.1
92	欧利生涂料（天津）有限公司	日本、中国（台湾）	1098 万美元	585 万美元	2004.7.21
93	那美钢（天津）汽配有限公司	日本	1000 万美元	500 万美元	2004.9.1
94	天津维纳科技发展有限公司	中国、中国（香港）	600 万元元	466 万元	2004.2.24
95	LG 化学（天津）工程塑料有限公司	韩国及其中国投资公司	1800 万美元	855 万美元	2004.12.29

续表 15

序号	企业名称	国别	投资总额	注册资本	取照时间
96	天津天狮生命科学有限公司	英属维尔京群岛	14900 万美元	10900 万美元	2005.4.29
97	天津天狮生命源有限公司	英属维尔京群岛	12500 万美元	6500 万美元	2005.4.29
98	玻石机械（中国）有限公司	芬兰	1097 万美元	600 万美元	2005.5.11
99	奥帕汽车配件（天津）有限公司	韩国	1250 万美元	500 万美元	2005.6.17
100	天津和信昌工业有限公司	萨摩亚	3423 万美元	1540 万美元	2005.6.27
101	金红叶纸业（天津）有限公司	中国	2750 万美元	1500 万美元	2005.8.24
102	赫英木结构制造（天津）有限公司	中国（香港）	560 万美元	400 万美元	2005.8.29
103	蜡笔小新（天津）有限公司	英属维尔京群岛	90000 万港元	52808 万港元	2006.1.19
104	诺威尔（天津）燃气设备有限公司	中国（香港）	3056 万港元	2160 万港元	2006.1.10
105	美泰克（天津）矿物有限公司	美国	300 万美元	220 万美元	2006.3.30
106	中粮包装（天津）有限公司	英属维尔京群岛	14950 万美元	5000 万美元	2006.3.30
107	天津中粮制桶有限公司	中国（香港）	4500 万美元	1500 万美元	2013.6.24
108	栢诚（天津）建筑设计有限公司	中国（香港）	600 万元	600 万元	2006 年 3.14

续表 15

序号	企业名称	国别	投资总额	注册资本	取照时间
109	天津圆圆电机有限公司	韩国	15 万美元	15 万美元	2006.6.14
110	NCO 咨询（天津）有限公司	英属维尔京群岛	73.53 万美元	73.53 万美元	2006.7.25
111	天津科威金属制品有限公司	中国（台湾）	1385 万美元	1135 万美元	2006.6.29
112	欧瑞康巴尔查斯涂层（苏州）有限公司天津分公司	瑞士（研发中心）	0	0	2006.8.7
113	天津南玻节能玻璃有限公司	中国（香港）	23600 万人民币	12800 万元 33600 万元	2006.9.26
114	天津日进汽车系统有限公司	韩国	10500 万美元	3500 万美元	2006.11.13
115	柯蒂斯怀特（天津）流体控制有限公司	美国	278 万美元	195 万美元	2007.1.25
116	天津娃哈哈食品有限公司	英属维尔京群岛	4230 万美元	1700 万美元	2007.2.13
117	中轮企业（天津）有限公司	捷克	2200 万美元	1300 万美元	2007.4.13
118	户田麦格昆磁磁性材料（天津）有限公司	中国（香港）、日本	600 万美元	450 万美元	2007.4.16
119	尼得科压缩机（天津）有限公司	日本、荷兰	9900 万美元	5994.39 万美元	2007.7.20
120	天津三富电子有限公司	韩国	605 万美元	415 万美元	2007.3.22
121	朗森电热设备配件（天津）有限公司	丹麦	20.4 万欧元	20.4 万欧元	2007.7.25

续表 15

序号	企业名称	国别	投资总额	注册资本	取照时间
122	西西延森过滤器（天津）有限公司	丹麦	4.2 万欧元	3 万欧元	2007.7.25
123	天津永思企业投资管理咨询有限公司	中国（香港）	1000 万美元	800 万美元，220 万美元	2007.12.19
124	味千食品发展（天津）有限公司	中国（香港）	5000 万美元	2500 万美元	2008.6.6
125	天津领先餐饮有限公司	中国（香港）	200 万美元	200 万美元	2008.7.7
126	英能科冷却系统（中国）有限公司	匈牙利	1500 万欧元	750 万欧元	2008.6.19
127	贝格高性能涂料（天津）有限公司	瑞典	560 万美元	280 万美元	2008.7.7
128	金红叶纸业集团有限公司天津武清分公司	印度尼西亚			2008.6.2
129	檀亚电子（天津）有限公司	韩国	40 万美元	28 万美元	2008.9.12
130	马克菲尔（天津）柔性支挡有限公司	中国(香港)、卢森堡	1200 万美元	580 万美元，880 万美元	2008.10.16
131	马克菲尔（天津）钢纤维有限公司	卢森堡	800 万美元	400 万美元	2009.3.3
132	天津英力科技发展有限公司	荷兰、中国	10245 万元人民币	5122.8057 万元	2004.2.26
133	天津天鹅湖房地产开发有限公司	中国（香港）	5000 万美元	5000 万美元	2008.10.24
134	莱斯勒斯风电科技（天津）有限公司	丹麦	10 万欧元	10 万欧元	2009.1.21
135	泰坦爱迪姆机械制造（天津）有限公司	意大利	589.2 万欧元	312.5 万欧元	2009.2.12

续表 15

序号	企业名称	国别	投资总额	注册资本	取照时间
136	佛罗伦萨小镇（天津）有限公司	中国（香港）	12200 万美元	6100 万美元	2009.5.27
137	天津圣朗商业有限公司	中国（香港）	50 万美元	50 万美元	2010.9.14
138	西岛泵（天津）有限公司	中国、日本	1220 万美元	610 万美元	2009.6.29
139	天津赛诺制药有限公司	中国、卢森堡	2279.14 万美元	1210 万美元	2000.3.23
140	尼森冷却系统（天津）有限公司	丹麦	450 万欧元	225 万欧元	2009.9.2
141	飞搏来复合材料（天津）有限公司	中国（香港）	300 万美元	210 万美元	2009.10.22
142	洸美（天津）科技有限公司	中国（香港）、日本	71.3 万美元	57 万美元	2009.12.8
143	尼波齿轮（天津）有限公司	丹麦	1250 万美元	500 万美元	2009.12.21
144	满孚首成（天津）实业有限公司	中国（香港）	9800 万美元	5341.9846 万美元	2008.9.3
145	信置房地产开发（天津）有限公司	英属维尔京群岛	6520 万美元	3260 万美元	2010.1.26
146	天津满致商贸有限公司	中国（香港）	14 万美元	10 万美元	2010.11.1
147	嘉洛尼（天津）国际贸易有限公司	中国（香港）	14 万美元	10 万美元	2010.11.1
148	天津柯特尼商贸有限公司	中国（香港）	14 万美元	10 万美元	2010.11.1
149	乐和高（天津）商贸有限公司	丹麦	24.900477 万元	24.900477 万元	2010.3.31

续表 15

序号	企业名称	国别	投资总额	注册资本	取照时间
150	迪普勒（天津）商贸有限公司	英国	70 万元	50 万元	2010.12.6
151	康赛斯（天津）空调有限公司	中国（香港）	105 万美元	75 万美元	2011.2.12
152	天津普亚仓储有限公司	新加坡	7680 万美元	3540 万美元	2011.7.19
153	天津西马格特宝机械有限公司	德国	640 万欧元	330 万欧元	2011.11.2
154	惠尔丰（中国）信息系统有限公司	中国（香港）	5000 万元	5000 万元	2011.11.22
155	国艾斯（天津）商贸有限公司	丹麦	15 万欧元	10.5 万欧元	2010.3.15
156	合发兄弟机电（天津）有限公司	新加坡	214 万美元	150 万美元	2010.4.21
157	迪发密封技术（天津）有限公司	丹麦	92.85 万美元	78 万美元	2010.4.20
158	中工马泰克路面机械（天津）有限公司	加拿大、中国天津	2.4 亿人民币	8000 万元	2010.5.24
159	哈蒙冷却系统（天津）有限公司	中国（香港）	1460 万美元	730 万美元	2010.6.23
160	丹佛斯森科（天津）消防设备有限公司	丹麦	100 万欧元	100 万欧元	2010.7.28
161	群英（天津）汽车饰件有限公司	德国	1375 万欧元	550 万欧元	2010.9.29
162	德凯罗金属（天津）有限公司	巴拿马	67.3 万美元	43 万美元	2010.10.18

续表 15

序号	企业名称	国别	投资总额	注册资本	取照时间
163	天津银德融资租赁有限公司	广西、中国（香港）	2500 万美元	1000 万美元	2010.10.13
164	维益烘焙产品（天津）有限公司	毛里求斯	2500 万美元	1100 万美元	2010.10.21
165	天津妈妈壹选健康产品有限公司	中国（香港）	1000 万美元	500 万美元	2010.11.22
166	天津市圣伟房地产开发有限公司	中国（香港）	500 万美元	500 万美元	2010.12.1
167	信义光伏产业（安徽）控股有限公司天津分公司	中国（香港）	0	0	2011.1.7
168	基伊埃机械设备（天津）有限公司	德国	4050 万欧元	1350 万欧元 /1748 万欧元	2011.1.21
169	奥帕蒂玛软件（天津）有限公司	意大利	25 万元	25 万元	2011.3.1
170	意桥食博餐饮管理（天津）有限公司	中国（香港）	70 万美元	70 万美元	2011.2.28
171	亿农农资有限公司	美国	5000 万元	5000 万元	2011.6.13
172	敏华家具（中国）有限公司	中国（香港）	9800 万美元	6000 万美元	2011.6.10
173	安可科技发展（天津）有限公司	中国（香港）	285 万美元	200 万美元	2011.7.13
174	威莱（天津）贸易有限公司	中国（香港）	280 万港币	200 万港币	2011.11.7
175	天马筛得力工艺设备（天津）有限公司	德国、荷兰	672 万欧元	336 万欧元	2011.8.12

续表 15

序号	企业名称	国别	投资总额	注册资本	取照时间
176	万国食品包装（天津）有限公司	美国	970 万美元	570 万美元	2012.2.14
177	天津融阳小额贷款股份有限公司	天津、江西、百慕大	10000 万元	10000 万元	2012.2.6
178	麦锡金属处理技术服务（天津）有限公司	美国	500 万美元	250 万美元	2012.2.20
179	闻绮（天津）商贸有限公司	意大利	329 万欧元	232.5 万欧元	2011.8.24
180	天津嘉武仓储有限公司	中国（香港）	8106 万美元	2703 万美元	2012.3.29
181	彩欧家具（天津）有限公司	丹麦	605 万元	565 万元	2012.3.21
182	和进（天津）液压机械有限公司	韩国	200 万元	140 万元	2012.5.30
183	信义汽车部件（天津）有限公司	中国（香港）	9900 万美元	5715 万美元	2012.5.22
184	天津卡秀堡辉涂料有限公司	中国（香港）	700 万美元	400 万美元	2012.6.21
185	创喜（天津）餐饮管理有限公司	中国（香港）	14 万美元	10 万美元	2012.7.10
186	欧德亮法尔宝汽车灯系统科技（天津）有限公司	土耳其	2000 万欧元	800 万欧元	2012.10.9
187	梦达驰汽车系统（天津）有限公司	新加坡	6000 万元	3000 万元	2012.8.28
188	企业银行（中国）有限公司天津武清支行	韩国	0	0	2012.12.4
189	沃斯坦热力设备（天津）有限公司	德国、荷兰、中国	500 万美元	250 万美元	2012.12.18

续表 15

序号	企业名称	国别	投资总额	注册资本	取照时间
190	宾德科机械设备（天津）有限公司	奥地利	213 万欧元	150 万欧元	2013.1.16
191	哈沃科技（天津）有限公司	德国	772 万欧元	386 万欧元	2013.1.29
192	天津俊融发展有限公司	中国（香港）	5000 万美元	5000 万美元	2013.1.25
193	天津库恩农业机械有限公司	法国	714 万元	500 万元	2013.1.6
194	天津汉泉环保科技有限公司	英属维尔京群岛	285 万港币	200 万港币	2013.3.7
195	天津市合宜锻造有限责任公司	德国	7500 万欧元	2500 万欧元	2013.5.30
196	赛模杰隔热产品（天津）有限公司	美国	85 万美元	60 万美元	2013.1.17
197	天津何思教育信息咨询有限公司	加拿大、新加坡	42 万美元	30 万美元	2013.8.6
198	莱斯安全阀门（天津）有限公司	德国	1200 万欧元	480 万欧元	2013.7.17
199	嘉吉饲料（天津）有限公司	美国	2000 万美元	800 万美元	2013.7.31
200	天津正美玻璃科技有限公司	中国（香港）	11400 万港币	3800 万港币	2013.11.15
201	银乐宝（天津）商贸有限公司	中国（香港）	3000 万港币	1700 万港币	2014.2.17
202	悦居（天津）有限公司	中国（香港）	8 亿元	4.5 亿元	2012.9.17
203	劲家庄（天津）健康食品有限公司	中国（香港）	9000 万美元	3000 万美元	2012.2.22

续表 15

序号	企业名称	国别	投资总额	注册资本	取照时间
204	丰泉仓储（天津）有限公司	中国（香港）	12000 万元	6000 万元	2014.4.16
205	斯密特（天津）商务信息咨询有限公司	美国、中国	1000 万元	1000 万元	2014.6.19
206	科蓝泰克（天津）科技有限公司	中国、加拿大	50 万元	50 万元	2014.2.11
207	天津苏明交通装备有限公司	韩国	1400 万元	1000 万元	2014.3.19
208	易派驰（天津）凸轮轴制造有限公司	美国	350 万美元	250 万美元	2014.9.11
209	天津市吼吼网络信息技术有限公司	韩国	500 万元	500 万元	2014.12.6
210	格立莫农业技术（天津）有限公司	德国	18767 万元	7506.8 万元	2015.1.5
211	科斐凯博线缆（天津）有限公司	卢森堡	5160 万美元	1720 万美元	2015.4.14
212	恒丰晟泰国际贸易（天津）有限公司	中国（香港）	9998 万美元	3888 万美元	2015.4.28
213	阿玛松农业机械（天津）有限公司	德国	112 万欧元	80 万欧元	2014.11.17
214	德尔福派克电气系统有限公司天津分公司	新加坡	11235 万元	0	2014.10.28
215	大都克电接触科技（中国）有限公司	德国	800 万美元	800 万美元	2012.8.17
216	苏州金唯智生物科技有限公司天津分公司	美国	0	0	2015.9.6
217	天马荷斯筛分系统（天津）有限公司	德国	600 万欧元	300 万欧元	2006.5.31
218	欧华美科（天津）医学科技有限公司	中国（香港）	18618.5 万元	7447.4 万元	2014.5.12

续表 15

序号	企业名称	国别	投资总额	注册资本	取照时间
219	富优仕（天津）国际贸易有限公司	刚果	1000 万元	1000 万元	2015.12.25
220	伍尔特（中国）有限公司天津分公司	瑞士			2016.2.17
221	科罗尼（天津）机械有限公司	德国	3000 万元	1500 万元	2016.4.25
222	爱伊医美（天津）美容有限公司	中国、韩国	100 万元	100 万元	2016.6.23
223	史莱福灵传输科技（天津）有限公司	德国	400 万欧元	200 万欧元	2016.6.23
224	宝沃佛吉亚（天津）汽车部件系统有限公司	法国	3000 万元	1500 万元	2016.6.12
225	博思美科技（天津）有限公司	中国（香港）	10 万欧元	7 万欧元	2016.9.12
226	海斯坦普汽车组件（天津）有限公司	西班牙	100 万欧元	100 万欧元	2016.8.23
227	天津德尔汽车零部件有限公司	中国、中国（香港）、韩国	500 万元	500 万元	2016.12.30
228	致海通达（天津）商务信息咨询有限公司	中国（香港）	10 万元	10 万元	2016.12.22
229	天津迈克维环保科技有限公司	美国	100 万美元	100 万美元	2016.12.22
230	天津市歌奥篮商贸有限公司	广东、中国（香港）	100 万元	100 万元	2016.12.19
231	天津果敢时代国际贸易有限公司	中国（香港）	100 万美元	100 万美元	2016.11.22

续表 15

序号	企业名称	国别	投资总额	注册资本	取照时间
232	宜思曼振动技术（天津）有限公司	德国	850 万元	600 万元	2017.6.9
233	莫图泰克筛分系统（天津）有限公司	南非	1400 万元	700 万元	2017.2.17
234	宜居家具（天津）有限公司	中国（香港）	200 万元	100 万元	2017.3.30
235	友成机工（天津）有限公司	日本	16000 万元	8000 万元	2017.2.17
236	景岳生物科技（中国）有限公司	中国（台湾）、北京	20000 万元	5000 万元	2017.4.12
237	雷特莱恩（天津）科技有限公司	美国	30 万元	30 万元	2017.7.20
238	天津大昌教育信息咨询有限公司	中国（台湾）	100 万元	100 万元	2017.6.9
239	奥宗尼亚环保技术（天津）有限公司	法国	699.5284 万美元	349.7642 万美元	2012.7.31
240	笛卡儿教育信息咨询有限公司	中国（台湾）	3000 万元	3000 万元	2017.10.26
241	奥多莱克斯（天津）生物科技发展有限公司	德国、中国	1000 万元	1000 万元	2017.11.16
242	天津阿爱姆科技有限公司	奥地利	100 万元	100 万元	2017.9.16
243	格兰富水泵（苏州）有限公司天津分公司	丹麦	0	0	2016.7.26
244	穆勒纺织品（天津）有限公司	德国	1000 万元	1000 万元	2014.10.30

第三节　开发区内资企业名录

表 16

序号	企业名称	注册资本（万元）	取照时间
1	天津市天鹰塑胶工业公司	300	1993.4.10
2	天津市科威实业公司	200	1993.6.21
3	天津天狮生物工程公司	1800	1993.12.7
4	天津地雅房地产开发公司	3000	1993.12.28
5	天津市三英焊业有限责任公司	1600	1994.8.9
6	天津市跃奇特自行车厂	50	1995.8.11
7	天狮集团有限公司	5000	1996.11.1
8	天津天大领先制药有限公司	1372.5	1997.5.20
9	天津网络广告有限公司	500	1997.7.9
10	中体产业集团股份有限公司	73000	1998.3.13
11	天津市中农化农业生产资料销售有限公司	500	1998.4.6
12	天津市华琛散热器有限公司	3200	1998.5.11
13	天津市京辰电控设备有限公司	50	1998.5.15
14	天津中体影视有限公司	2000	1998.6.25
15	天津市跃天工贸发展有限公司	50	1998.9.23
16	天津中体经纪管理有限公司	600	1998.12.17
17	天津红日药业股份有限公司	100445.398	1999.3.19
18	天津市宇刚保温建材有限公司	10000	1999.6.24
19	天津洪福药业有限公司	1800	1999.6.28
20	天津天狮药业有限公司	4009.46	1999.7.2
21	天津市武清区天源工贸有限公司	300	1999.7.22

续表 16

序号	企业名称	注册资本（万元）	取照时间
22	天津名门动物食品有限公司	500	1999.7.26
23	天津市美联环保设备有限公司	50	1999.8.16
24	天津市陆阳自动控制系统有限公司	100	1999.8.19
25	天津市津能电缆有限公司	3363	1999.10.20
26	天津豹鸣股份有限公司	1058.5	1999.11.1
27	天津市昌海物资有限公司	50	1999.11.22
28	天津市环普自动控制新技术有限公司	50	1999.12.15
29	天津国财有限责任会计师事务所	50	1999.12.28
30	天津武清区天鹅湖温泉度假村有限公司	1500	2000.1.1
31	天津市清平工贸有限公司	100	2000.1.26
32	天津新技术产业园区中加科技发展有限公司	3000	2000.6.1
33	天津中体明星俱乐部有限公司	1000	2000.9.5
34	天津星驰工业品有限公司	3000	2000.11.28
35	中纺新材料科技有限公司	3000	2001.5.24
36	康业钢丝（天津）有限公司	3000	2001.6.20
37	天津市顺德蓄热式电锅炉有限公司	100	2001.7.12
38	天津再发隔音墙有限公司	1000	2001.10.18
39	天津市津能双鹤热力设备有限公司	230	2001.11.1
40	天津万润达科贸有限公司	3000	2001.11.16
41	天津市宝利德空调设备有限公司	550	2001.11.19
42	天津市逸海商贸有限公司	100	2001.11.27
43	天津市世纪恒通科技有限公司	50	2001.11.30
44	天津力神大通传媒广告有限公司	50	2001.12.13
45	天津武清开发区信诚置业发展有限公司	1000	2001.12.24
46	天津武清开发区新中大置业发展有限责任公司	1100	2001.12.24

续表 16

序号	企业名称	注册资本（万元）	取照时间
47	天津伟家精密塑胶有限公司	50	2002.1.21
48	天津再发隔音墙安装有限公司	1000	2002.1.23
49	天津市金锐鑫科贸发展有限公司	1000	2002.1.30
50	天津市保农捷农药商贸有限公司	1000	2002.1.31
51	天津市国环置业有限公司	5000	2002.2.8
52	天津博仕德机械制造有限公司	1800	2002.3.12
53	天津市武清报关行	150	2002.3.12
54	天津市海正泰克塑胶制品有限公司	500	2002.3.13
55	天津油联石油化工有限公司	50	2002.4.1
56	天津市宝源科工贸有限公司	500	2002.4.11
57	天津东方广厦钢结构工程有限公司	2800	2002.4.18
58	天津市恒和电控成套工程有限公司	60	2002.4.25
59	天津集福家园家居装饰制造中心	500	2002.4.29
60	天津和治药业有限公司	3800	2002.5.23
61	天津全达铝塑装饰材料有限公司	400	2002.5.27
62	天津格瑞新金属材料有限责任公司	1000	2002.5.30
63	天津市三焱电渣钢有限公司	300	2002.6.11
64	天津市雅佳制冷工程有限公司	350	2002.6.26
65	天津完达山乳品有限公司	4600	2002.8.6
66	天津市惠普科技有限公司	1000	2002.8.9
67	天津安博万皮革制品有限公司	260	2002.9.3
68	天津众朋机电技术有限公司	300	2002.9.19
69	天津顺通置业有限公司	1500	2002.9.27
70	天津豹鸣建筑工程材料有限责任公司	50	2002.10.30
71	天津市浩达金属制品有限公司	200	2002.11.7
72	天津市吉泰方洲信息技术工程有限公司	600	2002.11.7
73	天津市中迪暖通工程有限公司	150	2002.11.18

续表16

序号	企业名称	注册资本（万元）	取照时间
74	天津世昇水治理有限公司	200	2002.11.19
75	天津英华教育投资管理有限责任公司	1000	2003.1.17
76	天津帅博纸业有限公司	150	2003.3.3
77	中体竞赛管理有限公司	6200	2003.3.5
78	天津仁济和科技有限公司	100	2003.3.11
79	天津市晶恒太阳能灯具有限公司	120	2003.3.14
80	天津中敖生物科技有限公司	2000	2003.4.10
81	天津港集船务代理有限公司	100	2003.4.16
82	天津市博洋工贸有限公司	100	2003.4.25
83	天津市菲林时装有限公司	200	2003.6.16
84	天津市宇鹏科技发展有限公司	50	2003.7.23
85	天津海迈医用科技有限公司	1200	2003.8.8
86	天津金佰利投资发展有限公司	6850	2003.8.25
87	天津中敖畜牧集团有限公司	5000	2003.9.9
88	天津润雅科技发展有限公司	500	2003.9.19
89	天津市锐凯橡塑制品有限公司	50	2003.11.7
90	天津市华盛科技发展有限公司	100	2003.12.10
91	天津龙甲特种门窗有限公司	1500	2003.12.11
92	天津市大华电力器材有限公司	2000	2004.1.1
93	天津百兴钢结构有限公司	10000	2004.2.16
94	天津世纪高速公路建设发展有限公司	20000	2004.2.24
95	天津华迈科技有限公司	3000	2004.2.27
96	天津市宇航帆布有限公司	200	2004.3.25
97	天津中信广场科技有限公司	5000	2004.4.29
98	天津经汇工贸有限公司	50	2004.6.2
99	天津博世达电力设备制造有限公司	1500	2004.6.22
100	天津京津高速公路有限公司	275000	2004.7.2

续表 16

序号	企业名称	注册资本（万元）	取照时间
101	天津龙兴肠衣有限公司	1000	2004.7.5
102	天津市真泰塑业包装有限公司	1020	2004.7.15
103	天津东方医药投资有限公司	2000	2004.9.8
104	天津市嘉轩羊绒制品有限公司	100	2005.2.2
105	天津武清百川燃气销售有限公司	2000	2005.4.26
106	天津武清一商友谊百货有限公司	3000	2005.5.11
107	天津信诚能源设备有限公司	60	2005.6.9
108	天津凯德恒业置地有限公司	3000	2005.7.1
109	天津金海源环保设备有限公司	1250	2006.3.6
110	天津泉兴国际物流有限公司	3000	2006.3.7
111	天津市星恒时代广告有限公司	50	2006.4.6
112	天津市智慧数据技术有限公司	10	2006.4.24
113	天津华琛星宇散热器有限公司	400	2006.5.22
114	天津正尚金属制品有限公司	3000	2006.6.6
115	天津塞力斯特建筑安装有限公司	100	2006.7.4
116	天津东方鑫跃节能设备有限公司	3400	2006.7.7
117	天津市欣苑后勤服务有限公司	10	2006.8.1
118	天津市强源飘香食品有限公司	10000	2006.8.23
119	天津正通墙体材料有限公司	5000	2006.10.12
120	天津久川方源国际贸易有限公司	15000	2006.11.3
121	天津碧澜天钢结构有限公司	200	2006.11.24
122	天津博德电气制造有限公司	1200	2006.12.4
123	天津天狮环球国际贸易有限公司	5000	2006.12.7
124	天津兴达伟业汽车模具有限公司	200	2006.12.31
125	天津中房雍阳置业有限公司	2000	2007.1.17
126	天津市坤海商务信息咨询有限公司	100	2007.1.17
127	天津奥蓝际德国际旅行社有限公司	50	2007.4.6

续表 16

序号	企业名称	注册资本（万元）	取照时间
128	天津翠亨纸业有限公司	2000	2007.4.10
129	湖北九州建设项目咨询管理有限公司天津分公司	0	2007.4.28
130	天津市宇正工贸有限公司	800	2007.5.6
131	天津斯维克阀业有限公司	4000	2007.6.6
132	天津浔兴拉链科技有限公司	10000	2007.7.10
133	天津红日医药科技有限公司	6000	2007.8.10
134	天津荣石基进出口有限公司	100	2007.9.29
135	天津盛宏房地产投资有限公司	1000	2007.11.15
136	保利（天津）房地产开发有限公司	20000	2008.1.16
137	天津市兴和源磁性材料有限公司	600	2008.1.17
138	天津市武清区汇才人力资源开发服务有限公司	20	2008.2.28
139	绫致时装销售（天津）有限公司	3000	2008.3.4
140	天津金色网络工程有限公司	50	2008.3.12
141	天津奥克斯电气有限公司	50000	2008.3.24
142	天津东方远景节能科技有限公司	30	2008.3.24
143	天津市众智房地产经纪有限公司	10	2008.3.26
144	诺德（天津）传动设备有限公司	3000	2008.4.11
145	天津翠金湖房地产开发有限公司	20000	2008.4.17
146	天津生泰科技有限公司	100	2008.4.17
147	广州富利建筑安装工程有限公司天津分公司	0	2008.5.13
148	上海申联建筑设计有限公司天津分公司	0	2008.5.20
149	天津渤海绿都投资有限公司	1000	2008.7.14
150	天津马丁森人才测评软件开发有限公司	50	2008.7.14
151	保利广州物业管理有限公司天津分公司	0	2008.7.22
152	天津市泉塑塑料制品有限公司	50	2008.11.5

续表 16

序号	企业名称	注册资本（万元）	取照时间
153	天津永唐秦能源投资有限公司	200	2008.12.1
154	广州保利地产代理有限公司天津分公司	0	2008.12.12
155	天津市天元创业发展有限公司	5000	2009.1.20
156	天津市盛金投资咨询有限公司	3	2009.1.21
157	奥蓝际德酒店管理（天津）有限公司	500	2009.2.13
158	天津动听广告传媒有限公司	50	2009.2.13
159	北京住总市政工程有限责任公司天津武清分公司	6000	2009.2.19
160	天津瀚桥车体制造有限公司	30000	2009.3.5
161	天津市五一阳光投资发展有限公司	14000	2009.3.11
162	天津生力源科技有限公司	100	2009.3.11
163	宗源投资（天津）有限公司	1000	2009.3.19
164	天津瑞驰通宇实业有限公司	10000	2009.3.24
165	天津时间文化传媒有限公司	50	2009.5.27
166	天津融通瑞丰资产管理有限公司	100	2009.6.3
167	天津艺景园林工程有限公司	100	2009.6.3
168	天津博一堂广告有限公司	50	2009.6.4
169	汇力（天津）股权投资基金管理有限公司	10000	2009.6.5
170	天津爱雪酒店管理有限公司	100	2009.6.16
171	天津娃哈哈宏振食品饮料贸易有限公司	501	2009.6.18
172	天津松江创展投资发展有限公司	10000	2009.8.6
173	天津市人人乐商品配销有限公司	5000	2009.8.23
174	呼和浩特市外建项目管理有限公司天津武清分公司	0	2009.8.28
175	华圣蓝金（天津）膜科技有限公司	8000	2009.9.1
176	天津至永胜医疗器械有限公司	200	2009.9.15
177	天津京睿城投资有限公司	5000	2009.9.16

续表 16

序号	企业名称	注册资本（万元）	取照时间
178	天津市昕晨投资发展有限公司	1000	2009.11.18
179	玉圭园（天津）投资有限公司	5000	2009.11.23
180	天津市晨曦阳光科技发展有限公司	1000	2009.11.23
181	深圳市中安信业创业投资有限公司天津分公司	0	2009.11.30
182	天津尚尊科技有限公司	500	2009.12.8
183	天津运河城投资有限公司	10000	2009.12.15
184	北京住总集团有限责任公司天津武清分公司	0	2009-3-31
185	天津康普瑞钢缆有限公司	25000	2009-6-5
186	天津市众意达热力有限公司	100	2009-8-12
187	天津盛庆房地产投资有限公司	20000	2009-9-28
188	天津东方远景园林工程有限公司	100	2009-12-25
189	中水电津城投资发展有限公司	30000	2010-2-4
190	天津海世富通园林绿化有限公司	100	2010-3-9
191	宁波奥克斯物业服务有限公司天津分公司	0	2010-3-11
192	兰海泉洲水城（天津）发展有限公司	167100	2010-3-23
193	天津亚泰兰海投资有限公司	10000	2010-6-28
194	天津伊利乳品有限责任公司	27000	2010.1.29
195	天津诚安天下物业服务有限公司	60	2010.3.10
196	天津东方顺强门窗有限公司	100	2010.3.10
197	天津信堡玻璃股份有限公司	2000	2010.3.19
198	天津盛众房地产投资有限公司	20000	2010.3.29
199	天津奥光机械配件有限公司	100	2010.4.2
200	天津亚宝药业科技有限公司	10000	2010.4.6
201	天津市远达置业发展有限公司	1000	2010.4.9

续表 16

序号	企业名称	注册资本（万元）	取照时间
202	安泽西（天津）商贸有限公司	100	2010.4.30
203	泰济生健康管理有限公司	5000	2010.5.4
204	平岩（天津）机械设备有限公司	100	2010.5.25
205	玉圭园（天津）文化娱乐有限公司	5000	2010.6.9
206	奥蓝际德国际大酒店有限责任公司	5000	2010.6.11
207	中国水利水电第二工程局有限公司天津分公司	0	2010.6.11
208	天津亚格科技发展有限公司	500	2010.6.30
209	天津蓝猫置业投资有限公司	13000	2010.7.7
210	天津联众置业投资有限公司	4000	2010.7.20
211	天津金汇工业投资有限公司	1000	2010.7.27
212	天津中纺凯泰特种材料科技有限公司	2000	2010.7.29
213	天津蓝猫卡通传媒有限公司	1000	2010.8.3
214	天津全津食品有限公司	10000	2010.8.13
215	玉柴重工（天津）有限公司	20000	2010.10.9
216	天津东湖房地产投资有限公司	3000	2010.10.19
217	天津建武置业投资有限公司	1000	2010.10.27
218	天津英虞商贸有限公司	100	2010.11.2
219	天津政通建设发展有限公司	76000	2010.11.24
220	天津比朗实验仪器制造有限公司	50	2010.11.29
221	富莱恩（天津）保健用品有限公司	100	2010.11.29
222	天津市鸿驰油脂有限公司	600	2010.12.10
223	赛亚斯（天津）投资有限公司	500	2010.12.14
224	天津星微软件开发有限公司	10	2011.1.11
225	天津嘉銮商贸有限公司	100	2011–11–25
226	天津金侨城投资有限公司	5000	2011–9–28
227	天津大连机床机械制造有限公司	20000	2011.1.14

续表 16

序号	企业名称	注册资本（万元）	取照时间
228	天津新韩自动门有限公司	100	2011.1.14
229	天津天盛鼎和通信工程有限公司	500	2011.1.18
230	国能飞腾科技有限公司	10000	2011.1.20
231	天津江汉科技有限公司	35	2011.2.12
232	天津陶润置业投资有限公司	48666	2011.2.17
233	天津市新知科技咨询服务有限公司	3	2011.3.15
234	天津振戎国际能源有限公司	6000	2011.4.7
235	可信（天津）科技有限公司	1000	2011.4.15
236	天津紫晶兴益广告有限公司	3	2011.4.15
237	天津中讯股权投资基金管理有限公司	100	2011.4.22
238	中纺院（天津）科技发展有限公司	15000	2011.5.3
239	天津市天狮生命科学与技术研究院	1000	2011.5.5
240	金锐丽城（天津）置业投资有限公司	10000	2011.5.17
241	天津市武清区信邦科技创业投资发展有限公司	10000	2011.5.23
242	天津可信科技企业孵化器有限公司	500	2011.5.25
243	嘉杰（天津）置业投资有限公司	33000	2011.5.27
244	与众科技（天津）有限公司	50	2011.5.27
245	天加空调（天津）有限公司	6000	2011.5.30
246	天津中泰华隆供应链管理有限公司	500	2011.5.31
247	天津光彩圣火科技企业孵化器有限公司	1000	2011.6.1
248	天津中讯创业投资合伙企业（有限合伙）	6010	2011.6.9
249	天津市嘉鹏科技发展有限公司	10	2011.6.27
250	坝上春秋投资有限公司	20000	2011.6.29
251	天津尚思科技有限公司	50	2011.7.1
252	全球商品博览汇（天津）有限公司	5000	2011.7.22
253	天津三骏奇商贸有限公司	10	2011.7.27

续表 16

序号	企业名称	注册资本（万元）	取照时间
254	经纬城市绿洲（天津）置地有限公司	5000	2011.7.28
255	天津天德建筑装饰工程有限公司	100	2011.8.25
256	天津泰里酒店管理有限公司	200	2011.8.25
257	融鑫汇（天津）租赁有限公司	20000	2011.8.26
258	天津拉斐庄园商贸有限公司	100	2011.8.30
259	天津天拓工程造价咨询有限公司	200	2011.9.1
260	华电水务（天津）有限公司	3760	2011.9.5
261	天津嘉林科医有限公司	10000	2011.9.7
262	天津森纳尔投资有限公司	5000	2011.9.14
263	天津奥克斯数码电器有限公司	40000	2011.9.16
264	天津天创盈讯创业投资合伙企业（有限合伙）	11000	2011.9.26
265	天津赢达信科技有限公司	500	2011.10.11
266	天津博梵科技有限公司	100	2011.10.14
267	中衍期（天津）投资管理有限公司	1000	2011.10.14
268	天津华益维新企业管理咨询有限责任公司	10	2011.10.17
269	北京世纪卓越信息技术有限公司天津分公司	0	2011.10.25
270	天津百财易文化传播有限公司	10	2011.10.28
271	天津信堡实业有限公司	5000	2011.11.2
272	天津市梓博科技发展有限公司	2000	2011.11.14
273	天津业之峰诺华装饰有限公司	200	2011.11.21
274	天津市泽博科技发展有限公司	100	2011.11.30
275	天津黑马行云物联网科技有限公司	150	2011.12.12
276	天津征鸿网络科技有限公司	100	2011.12.20
277	天津军盛空调配件有限公司	100	2012.1.5
278	天津鸣鼎投资管理有限公司	480	2012.1.12

续表 16

序号	企业名称	注册资本（万元）	取照时间
279	北京裕昌置业集团天津投资有限公司	30000	2012.1.12
280	北京世纪博爱医学研究所有限公司天津分公司	0	2012.1.31
281	北京世纪卓越信息技术有限公司天津第二分公司	0	2012.2.13
282	天津欧恒祥科技有限公司	500	2012.2.22
283	天津国能飞腾国际贸易有限公司	1000	2012.3.2
284	北京北方人瑞教育咨询有限公司天津分公司	0	2012.3.5
285	天津华电福源热电有限公司	25700	2012.3.6
286	营伸（天津）汽车零配件有限公司	3	2012.3.6
287	天津市虹石网络技术有限公司	3	2012.3.6
288	天津乐活城生物科技有限公司	100	2012.3.12
289	天津德驰汽车零部件有限公司	5000	2012.3.12
290	天津兆盛房地产投资有限公司	15000	2012.3.15
291	中投证券投资有限公司	250000	2012.3.28
292	金穗（天津）投资管理有限公司	300	2012.4.1
293	赛顿新能源技术（天津）有限公司	200	2012.4.9
294	邦盛福祉科技（天津）有限公司	500	2012.4.17
295	天地融电子（天津）有限公司	15000	2012.4.18
296	天津铜人数控设备制造有限公司	2000	2012.4.20
297	天津东标科技有限公司	100	2012–5–3
298	天津同力重工有限公司	30000	2012.5.4
299	天津双旺科技发展有限公司	2200	2012.5.7
300	天津诺科生物科技企业孵化器有限公司	100	2012.5.14
301	森马（天津）物流投资有限公司	14000	2012.5.17
302	天津文创投资有限公司	3000	2012.5.31
303	天津奥源骏康科技发展有限公司	500	2012.6.14

续表 16

序号	企业名称	注册资本（万元）	取照时间
304	天津三宜信息技术有限公司	50	2012.6.15
305	天津人瑞教育信息咨询有限公司	50	2012.6.19
306	天元建设集团有限公司天津分公司	0	2012.6.20
307	天津市合广科技有限公司	100	2012.7.6
308	天津高丽亚娜科技有限公司	80	2012.7.9
309	天津信恒餐饮管理有限公司	2000	2012.7.10
310	天津寓言数码科技有限公司	100	2012.7.15
311	天津爱格临床营养食品开发有限公司	100	2012.7.19
312	天津绿鑫园林绿化有限公司	200	2012.7.24
313	天津宏信设备租赁有限公司	10000	2012.7.27
314	天津优标技术检测服务有限公司	300	2012.7.30
315	奥宗尼亚环保技术（天津）有限公司	800	2012.7.31
316	天津市德诺工程技术有限公司	300	2012.8.8
317	豪威生物科技有限公司	9000	2012.8.14
318	天津金勘矿业投资有限公司	50	2012.8.14
319	天津异域风情装饰有限公司	100	2012.8.28
320	天津旭堃科技有限公司	100	2012.9.7
321	天津成辉科技有限公司	30	2012.9.21
322	天津禾奇信息技术有限公司	100	2012–7–11
323	天津市久固装饰工程有限公司	30	2006.3.15
324	景裕科技（天津）有限公司	200	2012.9.27
325	天津冠一节能科技有限公司	500	2012.9.28
326	天津豪君科技有限公司	100	2012.10.11
327	兴天投资咨询（天津）有限公司	2000	2012.10.26
328	天津豪威传动科技有限公司	2000	2012.5.15
329	中国纺织科学研究院纤维新材料分院	0	2012.12.20
330	爱特驰商贸（天津）有限公司	500	2011.7.18

续表 16

序号	企业名称	注册资本（万元）	取照时间
331	歌思（天津）低温设备有限公司	100	2012.11.26
332	颐和美林（天津）生物科技有限公司	100	2012.9.17
333	兴天通讯技术有限公司	2000	2012.9.25
334	天津莱蒙天寿股权投资基金合伙企业（有限合伙）	10500	2012.12.19
335	天津莱蒙天贵股权投资基金合伙企业（有限合伙）	23400	2012.12.19
336	天津网库电商谷信息技术有限公司	1000	2013.1.5
337	天津路德房地产咨询有限公司	50	2013.1.6
338	天地融软件（天津）有限公司	1000	2013.1.23
339	日丰企业（天津）有限公司	6000	2013.1.14
340	天津爱之莱特科技有限公司	3200	2013.1.25
341	天津科能机械配件有限公司	1000	2012.12.19
342	天津逐鹿信息技术有限公司	10	2012.12.14
343	天津博腾科技有限公司	160	2013.1.6
344	天津博力仟禧物联网科技有限公司	100	2012.10.29
345	天津市丰汇电子商务有限公司	100	2013.1.5
346	海南椰国食品有限公司天津分公司	0	2009.6.16
347	天津文达信息技术有限公司	10	2013.1.31
348	天津宏信科技开发有限公司	300	2013.2.1
349	天津市华杰装饰工程有限公司	80	2012.12.19
350	天津森联科技发展有限公司	1000	2013.1.29
351	天津金恩斯科技有限公司	30	2013.1.16
352	壹叁科技（天津）有限公司	100	2013.3.7
353	天津昱弘企业管理咨询有限公司	3	2013.1.10
354	天津天房融汇投资管理有限公司	1000	2013.3.22
355	天津百威电气设备有限公司	300	2012.11.7

续表 16

序号	企业名称	注册资本（万元）	取照时间
356	天津伟舜科技有限公司	100	2013.3.28
357	天津天房金汇投资中心（有限合伙）	11000	2013.4.10
358	天津中业园净化工程有限公司	7000	2013.4.8
359	天津市中投汇鑫投资管理有限公司	1000	2013.1.18
360	天津九保行机械科技有限公司	1000	2013.4.3
361	天泽恩源（天津）制药有限公司	6000	2012.9.5
362	天津科艾机械科技有限公司	2000	2013.3.29
363	天津中铁五新钢模有限公司	2400	2013.4.15
364	天津市优商科技有限公司	50	2013.1.23
365	天津如真电子商务有限公司	200	2013.2.22
366	天津市大华伟业置业有限公司	5000	2013.4.17
367	途牛保险经纪有限公司	5000	2013.5.20
368	天津西翠精细化工实业有限公司	12000	2013.6.7
369	友元办公联盟（天津）有限公司	6000	2013.6.9
370	天津元天重机配件有限公司	200	2013.4.17
371	天津永安有限责任公司	50000	2013.6.27
372	天津信地建筑工程有限公司	100	2013.6.7
373	天津市力维建筑工程有限公司	100	2013.7.30
374	天津荣全企业管理咨询有限公司	10	2013.7.20
375	天津莫泰克石油科技有限公司	100	2013.8.9
376	天津美森科技有限公司	12000	2013.8.12
377	天津国能清源科技有限公司	50	2013.7.9
378	天津优达投资有限公司	30000	2013.8.15
379	天津长红汇通企业管理咨询有限责任公司	100	2013.7.30
380	小狗电器（天津）有限公司	500	2013.7.26

续表 16

序号	企业名称	注册资本（万元）	取照时间
381	天津市信通新家园资产管理合伙企业（有限合伙）	50005	2013.10.16
382	天津天房城镇化建设投资合伙企业（有限合伙）	1100000	2013.10.16
383	中投中财基金管理有限公司	5000	2013.10.12
384	天津易利恒科技股份有限公司	5000	2013.10.28
385	天津骏科电子有限公司	20000	2013.10.25
386	天津君润承科技有限公司	180	2013.10.28
387	天津畅联供应链管理有限公司	6000	2013.11.14
388	中模创通（天津）工程技术有限公司	50	2013.11.15
389	天津富润房地产开发有限公司	10000	2013.10.23
390	天津天房融华资产管理有限公司	10000	2013.5.28
391	天津红日康仁堂药业有限公司	15000	2013.11.18
392	天津国民天房资产管理有限公司	500	2013.11.27
393	天津正兴财商贸有限公司	100	2013.12.13
394	乐金华奥斯（天津）门窗有限公司	400	2013.12.19
395	天津奇正科技有限公司	400	2013.12.23
396	伊利特化工贸易（天津）有限公司	10	2013.12.30
397	天津灏德教育信息咨询有限公司	30	2013.12.25
398	天津市万瑞科技有限公司	20	2012.5.1
399	天津北方博业科技发展有限公司	3000	2014.1.6
400	现代富博（天津）智能装备科技有限公司	1000	2014.1.23
401	天津丰业新能源科技有限公司	300	2014.1.28
402	天津科思科技有限公司	50	2014.1.2
403	天津七彩跃华科技有限公司	100	2014.1.15
404	天津君歌环保设备有限公司	5000	2014.1.16
405	天益京（天津）生物科技有限公司	6800	2014.1.30

续表 16

序号	企业名称	注册资本（万元）	取照时间
406	天津雅致盛强广告有限公司	3	2014.1.21
407	天津诺禾致源生物信息科技有限公司	1000	2014.2.18
408	天津中泰市政工程有限公司	2000	2014.2.12
409	天津信义新能源管理有限公司	1000	2014.2.11
410	华电水务膜分离科技（天津）有限公司	5000	2013.12.6
411	天津大学前沿技术研究院有限公司	500	2013.12.13
412	维克（天津）有限公司	5000	2014.3.13
413	天津万豪京伦国际贸易有限公司	100	2014.1.20
414	欧蒙（天津）医学诊断技术有限公司	2500	2014.2.20
415	天津市赋泽建筑工程有限公司	2000	2014.3.4
416	天津盈丰企业管理咨询中心（有限合伙）	10	2014.3.6
417	天津销雨田科技有限公司	20	2014.3.5
418	天津鑫荣国际工程管理咨询有限公司	200	2014.3.10
419	天津博耐特电子有限公司	300	2014.3.10
420	天津彭利建筑科技有限公司	600	2014.3.6
421	天津汝和企业管理咨询有限公司	10	2013.9.24
422	天津旭日旧机动车经纪有限公司	5	2014.3.18
423	天津金顺发旧机动车经纪有限公司	5	2014.3.18
424	天津众友机动车销售有限公司	5	2014.3.18
425	天津美斯泰服装贸易有限公司	100	2014.3.5
426	天津天锂能源科技有限公司	2500	2014.3.5
427	天津红日康仁堂药品销售有限公司	1000	2014.1.24
428	天津量子企业管理咨询有限公司	10	2014.3.18
429	天津众鑫企业管理咨询有限公司	100	2014.3.18
430	天津金桥通达商务信息咨询有限公司	10	2014.3.20
431	天津润枫文化传媒有限公司	10	2014.3.20
432	天津越思企业管理咨询有限公司	50	2014.3.13

续表16

序号	企业名称	注册资本（万元）	取照时间
433	天津晟鸿净化设备有限公司	3000	2014.3.19
434	天津九洲博信科技有限公司	100	2014.3.24
435	天津君歌分子蒸馏设备有限公司	500	2012.6.7
436	永顺通达科技（天津）有限公司	100	2014.3.28
437	天津三和机械设备租赁有限公司	500	2014.3.31
438	天津天合春晖文化传媒有限公司	100	2014.3.31
439	天津市奥骊进出口贸易有限公司	50	2014.4.3
440	天津迪高医疗设备有限公司	50	2014.3.24
441	天津骏信通博商贸有限公司	500	2014.3.26
442	天津慧百惠众文化传播有限公司	10	2014.3.18
443	巴克斯酒业（天津）有限公司	5000	2014.4.3
444	百米马（天津）有限公司	10000	2014.3.18
445	天津市昊鸿翔宇投资有限责任公司	10000	2013.3.11
446	天津众志滨成科技有限公司	100	2013.8.5
447	中国水电建设集团十五工程局有限公司天津分公司	0	2012.4.18
448	天津苦水玫瑰科技有限公司	50	2014.4.14
449	天津东汇国际贸易有限公司	5160	2014.4.16
450	博大（天津）信息技术有限公司	100	2014.4.9
451	天津骄子营销策划有限公司	50	2014.4.18
452	天津火凤凰装饰有限公司	100	2014.4.21
453	天津黑马科技有限公司	50	2014.4.29
454	天津顺全隆企业管理咨询有限公司	100	2014.4.2
455	天津柏源科技有限公司	100	2014.4.23
456	众飔（天津）科技有限公司	10	2014.4.25
457	天津勤业双诚商贸有限公司	500	2014.4.8
458	天津壹德行房地产咨询有限公司	200	2014.4.9

续表 16

序号	企业名称	注册资本（万元）	取照时间
459	天津远恒置业有限公司	5000	2014.2.27
460	天津怡和嘉业医疗科技有限公司	1000	2014.4.8
461	天津泰益德置业有限公司	3000	2014.2.19
462	古艺都（天津）家具销售有限公司	100	2014.4.18
463	天津海视影视文化传媒有限公司	600	2014.5.4
464	天津众鑫农牧科技有限公司	100	2014.5.4
465	天津优尼卡特科技有限公司	500	2014.4.25
466	天工筑（天津）展览有限公司	300	2013.3.20
467	康瑞普（天津）冶金设备有限公司	3500	2013.6.17
468	天津力孚生物科技有限公司	2500	2014.5.9
469	天津天鑫蓬通国际贸易有限公司	200	2014.5.13
470	天津拉谷谷服饰有限公司	5000	2014.4.29
471	泰来商务信息咨询（天津）有限公司	10	2014.4.23
472	天津晨升源泰国际贸易有限公司	100	2014.5.19
473	天津市晔彤科技发展有限公司	50	2014.5.20
474	华津科技（天津）有限公司	100	2014.5.20
475	天益阳（天津）生物分离工程技术有限公司	500	2014.5.19
476	天津市潘达商务信息咨询有限公司	10	2014.5.19
477	天津市国预网络科技有限公司	50	2014.5.23
478	天津一诺金洋商贸有限公司	50	2014.5.4
479	天津桐森商贸有限公司	10	2014.4.24
480	天津鹏尧国际贸易有限公司	100	2014.3.28
481	天津萨格科技有限公司	100	2014.4.18
482	天津星期六鞋业有限公司	1000	2014.5.22
483	天津君安阳光智慧科技发展有限公司	1500	2014.5.23
484	天津市荭雅五方环保科技有限公司	35	2014.5.23

续表 16

序号	企业名称	注册资本（万元）	取照时间
485	欧华美科东投（天津）医学科技有限公司	500	2014.5.27
486	欧华美科北投（天津）医学科技有限公司	500	2014.5.27
487	欧华美科南投（天津）医学科技有限公司	500	2014.5.27
488	天津盛昌联金属材料销售有限公司	50	2014.5.30
489	天津源利通达金属材料销售有限公司	50	2014.5.30
490	通领全擎（天津）科技有限公司	50	2014.5.21
491	天津伟嘉盛邦生物科技有限公司	10000	2014.6.10
492	天津广修堂科技有限公司	50	2014.6.3
493	富峻电子设备（天津）有限公司	100	2014.5.5
494	天津克瑞斯自行车贸易有限公司	50	2014.6.5
495	天津东科意诚装饰材料销售有限公司	200	2014.6.3
496	天津明亮旧机动车销售有限公司	5	2014.6.11
497	天津载极信息科技有限公司	10	2014.6.13
498	天津华榕科技有限公司	50	2014.6.16
499	天津瑞祥货架有限公司	20	2014.6.9
500	天津圣安天逸科技有限公司	50	2014.6.9
501	天津远恒汇通环境建设投资有限公司	20000	2014.2.27
502	天津世纪盛辉货架贸易有限公司	20	2014.6.3
503	天津东朔开拓科技有限公司	20	2014.6.13
504	天津达奇水利设备安装有限公司	10	2014.6.9
505	欣达仁和医学科技（天津）有限公司	100	2014.6.17
506	天津诚融企业管理咨询有限公司	100	2014.6.23
507	天津市瑞鹏装饰装修工程有限公司	1000	2014.6.23
508	天津市宏顺通达钢材销售有限公司	100	2014.6.24
509	天津诚信管道工程有限公司	100	2014.6.24

续表 16

序号	企业名称	注册资本（万元）	取照时间
510	天津安盾视达科技有限公司	10	2014.6.24
511	天津驰程宇自行车贸易有限公司	50	2014.6.24
512	天津广翼天鸿科技有限公司	200	2014.3.26
513	纽茵茨（天津）商贸有限公司	100	2014.5.13
514	天津雯清健康咨询有限公司	10	2014.6.26
515	天津渤海中睿新能源科技有限公司	1000	2014.4.2
516	中交四公局第六工程有限公司	10100	2014.7.7
517	天津飞华信息技术有限公司	10	2014.7.3
518	哈林秀王（天津）体育文化传播有限公司	100	2014.7.3
519	天津万方工程设计咨询有限公司	50	2014.6.30
520	天津轻游信息技术有限公司	100	2014.6.20
521	天津奥德瑞齐科技有限公司	100	2014.6.16
522	天津晟奥电气有限公司	2000	2014.5.28
523	天津服梓商贸有限公司	100	2014.6.12
524	爱义信科技（天津）有限公司	60	2014.6.4
525	天津凯斯诺自行车有限公司	200	2014.6.5
526	天津金赤钢铁销售有限公司	100	2014.7.9
527	天津泡芙科技有限公司	100	2014.7.1
528	艾睿企业管理咨询（天津）有限公司	200	2014.7.9
529	天津东瑞教育咨询有限公司	3	2014.7.15
530	天津六合东瑞生物科技有限公司	10	2014.7.15
531	天津津力弘源建筑工程有限公司	600	2014.7.10
532	天津鑫宏泰商贸有限公司	100	2014.7.10
533	天津诚之城建筑安装工程有限公司	100	2014.6.17
534	天津隆浩商贸有限公司	100	2014.7.8
535	天津益亚商贸有限公司	100	2014.7.8

续表 16

序号	企业名称	注册资本（万元）	取照时间
536	天津赛普设备安装有限公司	10	2014.7.8
537	天津百灵鸟餐饮管理有限公司	100	2014.7.11
538	百联金网（天津）信息科技有限公司	500	2014.7.15
539	天津翰晟浩天商务信息咨询有限公司	505	2014.4.8
540	天津丹信商贸有限公司	50	2014.7.21
541	天津俊恺门窗销售有限公司	50	2014.7.21
542	天津百胜顺通二手车销售有限公司	200	2014.7.18
543	波士轮利特天极（天津）网络技术有限公司	300	2014.7.16
544	天津渤润文化发展有限公司	20	2014.7.15
545	天津普菲特环保科技有限公司	100	2014.7.17
546	天津华泰友发钢铁销售有限公司	100	2014.7.14
547	中天华易信息科技（天津）有限公司	3000	2014.8.4
548	天津莱玩网络科技有限公司	1000	2014.8.4
549	天津赛阳节能科技有限公司	100	2014.3.5
550	天津市甲昊橡胶科技有限公司	100	2014.3.13
551	克莱尼（天津）科技有限公司	500	2014.4.4
552	天津大唐宏运文化传播有限公司	50	2014.4.30
553	天津禾佳农业科技有限公司	1000	2014.4.16
554	天津市金富通科技有限公司	500	2014.4.23
555	天津市高迪食品科技有限公司	200	2014.5.7
556	天津逸致教育信息咨询有限公司	10	2014.4.9
557	天津大学技术转移有限公司	280	2014.4.16
558	天益成（天津）企业管理咨询有限公司	50	2014.6.11
559	天津君源企业管理咨询有限公司	50	2014.6.9
560	天津远恒有限公司	50000	2014.1.27
561	逸景瑞德绿化工程（天津）有限公司	500	2014.6.18

续表 16

序号	企业名称	注册资本（万元）	取照时间
562	天津市正燊商贸有限公司	10	2014.8.13
563	天津惠通津源科技有限公司	1000	2014.8.1
564	世纪天云科技（天津）有限公司	500	2014.8.6
565	天津卓美物业服务有限公司	100	2014.8.12
566	天津巨涛教育信息咨询有限公司	50	2014.8.12
567	天津市亚泰建筑工程有限公司	1000	2014.8.6
568	天津华辰环保科技有限公司	500	2014.7.30
569	天津莲臻企业管理咨询有限公司	10	2014.7.08
570	天津博立恩阀门有限公司	2000	2014.8.08
571	天津华跃恒朗商贸有限公司	100	2014.8.6
572	天津泰泽电子商务有限公司	3000	2014.8.4
573	天津华安鑫源科技合伙企业（有限合伙）	1000	2014.8.4
574	天津纤佰度化妆品销售有限公司	10	2014.8.6
575	天津思韵堂教育信息咨询有限公司	20	2014.8.12
576	天津贝叶斯科技有限公司	3	2014.8.18
577	天津塑铂络科技有限公司	200	2014.8.5
578	天津欧莎世家电子商务有限公司	1000	2014.8.4
579	天津清联能源工程有限公司	2000	2014.8.22
580	天益康（天津）医院管理有限公司	2000	2014.8.26
581	天津启源电力设备制造有限公司	5100	2014.8.18
582	中纺院（天津）滤料技术检测有限公司	200	2014.6.11
583	兰佑时代（天津）商贸有限公司	100	2014.8.22
584	维新环保科技（天津）有限责任公司	2000	2014.8.27
585	天津大厨小灶餐饮管理有限公司	50	2014.8.26
586	天津鑫泽伟嘉业钢材销售有限公司	200	2014.8.25
587	梦想城堡（天津）电子商务有限公司	500	2014.6.17
588	天津诚品购商贸有限公司	10	2014.6.16

续表 16

序号	企业名称	注册资本（万元）	取照时间
589	天津协鼎科技有限公司	50	2014.8.27
590	金立信（天津）装饰有限公司	10	2014.9.2
591	天津亿仟科技有限公司	50	2014.8.2
592	天津森昌文化传播有限公司	10	2014.9.1
593	光明云（天津）科技有限公司	1000	2014.9.9
594	天津郕昇建筑装饰工程有限公司	1060	2014.9.4
595	天津恒祥发商贸有限公司	10	2014.9.5
596	天津盛骄商贸有限公司	10	2014.9.11
597	天津拉卡拉超市有限公司	100	2014.9.19
598	德高（天津）环保科技有限公司	100	2014.9.12
599	天津祥瑞文化传播有限公司	100	2014.9.01
600	天津鼎和鑫商贸有限公司	500	2014.8.22
601	天津龙腾佳业科技有限公司	50	2014.9.17
602	天津中隧科技有限公司	1000	2014.9.25
603	泰之道（天津）国际贸易有限责任有限公司	50	2014.9.17
604	天津蜜思密商贸有限公司	100	2014.9.22
605	天津祺瑞医学科技有限公司	3000	2014.10.11
606	天津市天清二手车销售有限公司	50	2014.9.22
607	天津市菁才教育信息咨询有限公司	10	2014.9.16
608	天津文博乐医疗科技有限公司	500	2014.7.30
609	中仪睿科（天津）人工环境工程技术有限公司	500	2014.8.22
610	天津东昇伟业科技有限公司	100	2014.8.11
611	天津创信合益科技有限公司	100	2014.9.10
612	天津小资生活广告有限公司	30	2014.10.9
613	网臬科技（天津）有限公司	100	2014.10.15

续表 16

序号	企业名称	注册资本（万元）	取照时间
614	欧华美科（天津）医疗器械销售有限公司	500	2014.10.15
615	天津欧兰制冷设备有限公司	200	2014.10.23
616	天津嘉传科技有限公司	1000	2014.10.15
617	鑫材泰克（天津）复合材料有限公司	500	2014.9.28
618	天津诺亮生物科技有限公司	5	2014.7.23
619	天津诺润生物科技有限公司	5	2014.7.23
620	天津诺格生物科技有限公司	5	2014.9.11
621	天津创海生物工程技术有限公司	300	2014.9.11
622	北京天驰洪范企业咨询有限公司天津分公司	0	2014.10.20
623	天津中汇付科技有限公司	10	2014.10.20
624	天津久瑞安佳农业科技有限公司	3000	2014.10.21
625	天津鑫明扬商贸有限公司	500	2014.10.24
626	天津万博益弘商贸有限公司	200	2014.10.10
627	天津绘程达科技有限公司	100	2014.10.21
628	天津天润华装饰工程有限公司	100	2014.10.29
629	天津微瑞博科技发展有限公司	100	2014.5.22
630	天津聚化合化工科技有限公司	200	2014.10.29
631	天津和仁泰商贸有限公司	100	2014.10.30
632	天津中天远景商贸有限公司	100	2014.10.28
633	天津西贝文化传播有限公司	100	2014.10.28
634	天津市圣百龙家居销售有限责任公司	100	2014.10.30
635	天津腾安恒商贸有限公司	500	2014.11.11
636	天津德驰二手车销售有限公司	30	2014.06.12
637	天津市金聚中通信息咨询有限公司	10	2014.11.14
638	天津市聚融屹金商贸有限公司	10	2014.11.14
639	天津日昇建筑劳务有限公司	200	2014.11.13

续表 16

序号	企业名称	注册资本（万元）	取照时间
640	天津東绮生物科技有限公司	100	2014.11.11
641	天津天坤劳务服务有限公司	200	2014.11.25
642	天津飞鹰聚利科技有限公司	6000	2014.11.18
643	天津中正东泰建材销售有限公司	120	2014.11.14
644	英格尔检测技术服务（天津）有限公司	1000	2014.11.18
645	铁科纵横（天津）科技发展有限公司	4966	2014.11.18
646	天津舌尖上餐饮管理有限公司	200	2014.11.19
647	天津立通轨道交通科技有限公司	500	2014.11.26
648	天津简学教育信息咨询有限公司	100	2014.11.27
649	天津神州鹰电子科技有限公司	100	2014.12.02
650	鑫亿垣（天津）餐饮管理有限公司	100	2014.12.01
651	天津一磨香成油脂销售有限公司	500	2014.12.1
652	立方通达实业（天津）有限公司	5000	2014.12.11
653	金世生（天津）生物科技有限公司	100	2014.12.15
654	天津武清泰济生医院有限公司	5000	2014.3.20
655	天津诺金生物科技有限公司	5	2014.08.05
656	天津市燕安建筑工程有限公司	2000	2014.12.10
657	天津市诺泰建筑装饰工程有限公司	100	2014.8.27
658	天津诺龙生物科技有限公司	5	2014.9.12
659	天津冠腾科技发展有限公司	50	2014.12.24
660	捷科阀业（天津）有限公司	500	2014.12.18
661	天津鑫隅建材销售有限公司	100	2014.11.10
662	天津府宁建筑工程有限公司	2000	2014.11.24
663	天津金鼎财务咨询有限公司	50	2014.12.2
664	天津市泉达健康管理咨询有限公司	600	2014.12.29
665	天津市和济健康管理咨询有限公司	480	2014.12.31
666	天津鑫海拓达科技有限公司	100	2014.12.9

续表 16

序号	企业名称	注册资本（万元）	取照时间
667	天津中谊慧诚国际贸易有限公司	1000	2014.12.31
668	天津中谊慧诚广告有限公司	1000	2014.12.31
669	天津中谊慧诚科技有限公司	1000	2014.12.31
670	天津冠恒科技有限公司	100	2014.12.31
671	天津海石花物流有限公司	2000	2014.9.12
672	壹玖捌柒（天津）电子商务有限公司	100	2014.8.22
673	天津唯尚广告传媒有限公司	50	2014.10.23
674	天津鑫庆餐饮管理有限公司	8	2014.12.17
675	天津爱琴海餐饮管理有限公司	10	2014.12.24
676	天津纳尚科技发展有限公司	100	2014.12.25
677	行知天下教育科技（天津）有限公司	100	2014.12.26
678	天津伍克洛商贸有限公司	500	2014.12.29
679	天津恒世宁科技有限公司	10000	2014.12.30
680	天津中澳国际贸易有限责任公司	2000	2014.7.21
681	天津中澳嘉喜诺生物科技有限公司	1000	2014.7.21
682	富友（天津）科技有限公司	10	2014.11.21
683	卡友（天津）科技有限公司	10	2014.11.21
684	广州佛朗斯机械有限公司天津武清分公司	0	2014.12.2
685	天津大通速达商贸有限公司	100	2014.12.9
686	天津快捷通达商贸有限公司	100	2014.12.15
687	天津天创顺和科技有限公司	100	2014.3.4
688	启联（天津）科技有限公司	1000	2013.6.21
689	天津市阔山二手车销售有限公司	100	2014.11.13
690	天津诺海生物科技有限公司	5	2014.10.15
691	天津凯翔生物科技有限公司	300	2014.9.19
692	天津诺轩生物科技有限公司	5	2014.9.16

续表 16

序号	企业名称	注册资本（万元）	取照时间
693	天津木精科技有限公司	200	2014.10.13
694	北京威申视讯视频科技有限公司天津分公司	0	2015.1.9
695	天津福杰商贸有限公司	100	2015.1.12
696	天津薇美姿科技有限公司	100	2015.1.9
697	致炫国际贸易（天津）有限公司	100	2015.1.4
698	北京市正一味快餐管理有限公司天津第四分店	0	2015.1.5
699	千代福国际信息技术有限公司	1000	2015.1.14
700	天津通海赢州国际贸易有限公司	1000	2015.1.13
701	天津市特斯伦商贸有限公司	3100	2015.1.15
702	天津奥特科技有限公司	30	2015.1.15
703	天津盛鑫隆达商贸有限公司	100	2015.1.13
704	天津康宝餐饮管理有限公司	5	2015.1.13
705	维克环保设备（天津）有限公司	1000	2015.1.13
706	天津华信互动网络科技有限公司	1000	2015.1.15
707	天津众意佰德商贸有限公司	50	2015.1.20
708	天津金源茂丰科技发展有限公司	200	2015.1.23
709	天津星蕾悦网络科技有限公司	100	2015.1.22
710	天津东盛轩辕建筑工程有限公司	500	2015.1.21
711	北京强坤顺达劳务派遣有限公司天津分公司	0	2015.1.21
712	天津裕江源金属材料有限公司	100	2015.1.26
713	英泰商务信息咨询（天津）有限公司	50	2015.1.27
714	天津交控科技有限公司	500	2015.1.9
715	天津华电科工环保技术有限公司	1000	2015.1.29
716	天津中天金麒商贸有限公司	100	2015.1.29
717	天津伊森餐饮服务有限公司	100	2015.1.23

续表 16

序号	企业名称	注册资本（万元）	取照时间
718	天津市鑫鸿宇科技有限公司	100	2015.2.3
719	天津天信商务信息咨询有限公司	100	2015.2.2
720	天津联信天嘉科技有限公司	200	2015.2.3
721	天津慧商国际贸易有限公司	100	2015.2.3
722	天津优兔科技有限公司	100	2015.1.21
723	天津市天竺网络科技有限公司	100	2015.1.21
724	天津王冠久晟科技有限公司	100	2015.2.4
725	天津亚西科技有限公司	100	2015.1.20
726	津刘香（天津）科技有限公司	50	2015.2.6
727	天津海创企业管理咨询有限公司	5100	2015.2.9
728	天津龙涛建筑装饰工程有限公司	1000	2015.2.10
729	天津宝旺通餐饮管理有限公司	100	2015.2.10
730	北京川百汇餐饮管理有限公司天津第一分公司	0	2015.1.13
731	天津吉诺沃生物科技有限公司	100	2015.2.12
732	天津联东兴达科技有限公司	400	2015.3.2
733	天津润通泰钢材销售有限公司	500	2015.3.2
734	天津扬子之家健康咨询有限公司	100	2015.2.28
735	天津市联创佳业汽车销售有限公司	50	2015.3.2
736	天津市成发玉通科技有限公司	100	2015.3.5
737	天津光效影业管理有限公司	1000	2015.3.5
738	天津大路环科科技有限公司	500	2015.3.9
739	天津市奥思商业管理有限公司	2000	2015.3.5
740	天津市天财同创科技发展有限公司	100	2015.3.9
741	恒创一族科技（天津）有限公司	50	2015.3.2
742	天津市环津钢结构有限公司	200	2015.3.9
743	天津市政银合盈股权投资基金合伙企业（有限合伙）	600400	2015.3.19

续表 16

序号	企业名称	注册资本（万元）	取照时间
744	天津广浩机电设备有限公司	200	2015.3.19
745	天津林荣鑫农业科技有限公司	100	2015.3.19
746	天津莱克美商贸有限公司	100	2015.3.13
747	天津欣广企业管理咨询有限公司	500	2015.3.18
748	天津佰礼轩餐饮管理有限公司	50	2015.3.18
749	万兆（天津）科技有限公司	50	2015.3.23
750	天津武清祥云瑞博口腔门诊部（普通合伙）	200	2015.3.20
751	天津道顺商贸有限公司	200	2015.3.26
752	中天新科（天津）农业科技有限公司	100	2015.3.30
753	天津市荣泽天一科技有限公司	200	2015.3.31
754	天津盛饰堂装饰工程有限公司	100	2015.3.30
755	玛德毅（天津）国际贸易有限公司	500	2015.3.31
756	运亮科技（天津）有限公司	100	2015.4.1
757	天津发祥瑞锦科技有限公司	800	2015.3.26
758	贵利道通（天津）科技有限公司	800	2015.3.30
759	天津艳利芳兴科技有限公司	700	2015.3.30
760	保合安通（天津）科技有限公司	810	2015.3.30
761	博士通（天津）科技有限公司	500	2015.4.1
762	天津盈嘉乐科技有限公司	810	2015.3.30
763	天津市瑞柏康科技有限公司	200	2015.3.31
764	天津卓同物业管理有限公司	500	2015.3.27
765	天津腾亮环保科技有限公司	50	2015.4.7
766	天津萨姆特环保科技有限公司	50	2015.4.7
767	天津柯尼达科技有限公司	100	2015.4.7
768	天津国志通运科技有限公司	600	2015.4.2
769	天津祥云佛运科技有限公司	700	2015.3.27

续表 16

序号	企业名称	注册资本（万元）	取照时间
770	天津东海明泽科技有限公司	700	2015.3.26
771	吉乐祥龙（天津）科技有限公司	800	2015.3.26
772	盈嘉阳光（天津）科技有限公司	700	2015.3.26
773	天津东天泰祥科技有限公司	600	2015.3.25
774	天津嘉艺隆装饰装修工程有限公司	500	2015.4.8
775	维联财富（天津）商务信息咨询有限公司	10000	2015.4.9
776	天津广德利商贸有限公司	500	2015.4.9
777	天津心也文化传播有限公司	500	2015.4.8
778	天津好押互联网科技有限公司	500	2015.4.9
779	天津佳盈鼎盛化工贸易有限公司	500	2015.4.8
780	天津德百斯特国际贸易有限公司	500	2015.4.9
781	红桂祥荣（天津）科技有限公司	820	2015.3.31
782	天津市泰强联仁科技有限公司	700	2015.3.31
783	春赞乐扬（天津）科技有限公司	700	2015.4.1
784	天津凤翔德仁科技有限公司	600	2015.4.1
785	天津龙泰通润科技有限公司	800	2015.4.3
786	天津伟合立达科技有限公司	800	2015.4.2
787	天津和协仁通科技有限公司	600	2015.4.3
788	润华龙云（天津）科技有限公司	800	2015.4.3
789	天津英通联合科技有限公司	600	2015.4.3
790	天津香艳明合科技有限公司	600	2015.4.8
791	天津昌天福欣科技有限公司	600	2015.4.8
792	天津佰付通科技发展有限公司	50	2015.4.15
793	天津五零五九科技有限公司	50	2015.4.15
794	天津宝双金商贸有限公司	60	2015.4.16
795	锦程方合（天津）科技有限公司	760	2015.1.20

续表 16

序号	企业名称	注册资本（万元）	取照时间
796	天津红福涞科技发展有限公司	100	2015.4.16
797	中财万鑫（天津）科技有限公司	500	2015.4.16
798	天津诗兰姆汽车零部件有限公司	500	2015.4.20
799	天津其特尼电子科技有限公司	100	2015.4.20
800	天津华潜泵业有限公司	100	2015.4.20
801	天津博峰纵横文化传播有限公司	50	2015.4.16
802	天津帛玺邦科技有限公司	100	2015.4.17
803	天津武清泉达医院有限公司	600	2015.4.20
804	天津国图民宏科技有限公司	600	2015.4.10
805	天津天润利德科技有限公司	700	2015.4.8
806	天津昊月润名科技有限公司	800	2015.4.8
807	天津荣合立达科技有限公司	600	2015.4.15
808	天津宏明运通科技有限公司	600	2015.4.15
809	天津熙姝阳商贸有限公司	100	2015.4.22
810	中晟盈达（天津）国际贸易有限公司	200	2015.4.21
811	天津可朗奇餐饮管理有限公司	100	2015.4.27
812	天津金港盛通科技有限公司	500	2015.4.27
813	金鑫杰（天津）科技有限公司	500	2015.4.27
814	天津智安通科技有限公司	100	2015.4.23
815	天津市陆腾餐饮管理有限公司	50	2015.4.29
816	天津卓邦东正国际贸易有限公司	1000	2015.4.29
817	天津富通碧海科技有限公司	100	2015.4.29
818	天津闯千里科技有限公司	1000	2015.4.29
819	天大前沿科仪（天津）科技有限公司	200	2015.4.30
820	天津华天建筑工程有限公司	200	2015.3.25
821	奥宜丝卫生用品（天津）有限公司	500	2015.3.10
822	天津颂伟网络科技有限公司	1000	2015.3.25

续表 16

序号	企业名称	注册资本（万元）	取照时间
823	万山同顺（天津）科技有限公司	800	2015.1.16
824	秀华（天津）科技有限公司	810	2015.1.19
825	绿光（天津）商业管理有限公司	100	2015.4.30
826	天津雅丽富通商贸有限公司	100	2015.4.30
827	天津市麦点餐饮管理有限公司	5000	2015.5.5
828	天津云漫神游网络科技有限公司	200	2015.3.17
829	天津志鑫盛明商贸有限公司	50	2015.5.8
830	天津龙源泰富商贸有限公司	50	2015.5.8
831	天津市昌盛商务信息咨询有限公司	200	2015.5.12
832	天津鼎瑞驰商贸有限责任公司	50	2015.5.11
833	天津良宜筑商贸有限公司	50	2015.5.11
834	天津美林谷环保科技有限公司	500	2015.5.12
835	天津聚宝盆装修有限公司	500	2015.5.11
836	天津龙江涛科技发展有限公司	100	2015.5.12
837	网动科技（天津）有限公司	100	2015.5.11
838	天津达摩影视制作有限公司	1000	2015.5.13
839	天津佳视智晶光电科技有限公司	1000	2015.5.12
840	翱飞世（天津）商贸有限公司	1000	2015.5.13
841	天津艳晟富蓝商贸有限公司	100	2015.5.11
842	兆亿润达（天津）科技企业孵化器有限公司	10000	2015.3.19
843	天津一简一家纺织品销售有限公司	100	2015.1.28
844	天德轩信息技术（天津）有限责任公司	100	2015.3.16
845	天津味道信息科技有限公司	100	2015.3.30
846	维百偲特（天津）企业管理咨询有限公司	100	2015.4.1
847	天津启洲信息科技有限公司	100	2015.4.2

续表 16

序号	企业名称	注册资本（万元）	取照时间
848	天津市来点儿网络科技有限公司	100	2015.4.27
849	天津品味科技有限公司	100	2015.4.27
850	天津环宇融创科技有限公司	100	2015.4.27
851	天津京参科技有限公司	100	2015.5.13
852	天津市双馨彩印有限公司	300	2015.5.20
853	天津弘康科技有限公司	200	2015.5.14
854	天津鑫嘉华商务信息咨询有限公司	100	2015.5.19
855	欧文托普（天津）暖通设备有限公司武清分公司	0	2015.5.19
856	天津川流科技发展有限公司	150	2015.5.19
857	天津瑞庆祥珠宝有限公司	1	2015.5.19
858	康百（天津）生物医药科技有限公司	100	2015.5.19
859	大华同安财务管理咨询（天津）有限公司	500	2015.5.20
860	天津福泽亨达科技有限公司	100	2015.5.18
861	澳宇（天津）畜产制品有限公司	315	1999.3.19
862	天津诺禾医学检验所有限公司	1000	2014.8.22
863	天津日吉科技有限公司	3000	2014.11.26
864	天津诺晶生物科技有限公司	5	2014.9.23
865	天津诺宏远生物科技有限公司	5	2014.10.20
866	天津绣远生物技术有限公司	1200	2014.9.28
867	天津诺唯生物科技有限公司	5	2014.9.18
868	天津舒曼迪生物科技有限公司	3	2014.10.16
869	天津诺涵生物科技有限公司	5	2014.10.8
870	天津诺沃生物科技有限公司	5	2014.9.18
871	天津艾未电子商务有限公司	100	2015.5.21
872	天津博惠兴业科技有限公司	100	2015.5.25

续表 16

序号	企业名称	注册资本（万元）	取照时间
873	卓泰财富（天津）财务咨询有限公司武清分公司	0	2015.5.22
874	润德科丰（天津）科技有限公司	100	2015.5.21
875	天津恒友装饰工程有限公司	500	2015.5.25
876	天津外大多语言服务有限公司	10	2015.1.30
877	凌波微步（天津）科技有限公司	100	2015.5.25
878	天津市安盛立达房地产经纪有限公司	50	2015.5.18
879	天建绿洲（天津）科技有限公司	500	2015.5.27
880	天津通力包装制品有限公司	1000	2015.5.25
881	天津悦易通达科技有限公司	100	2015.5.27
882	天津时讯科技有限公司	100	2015.5.27
883	天津随付科技有限公司	100	2015.5.27
884	天津易付时通科技有限公司	100	2015.5.27
885	天津乐畅科技有限公司	100	2015.5.27
886	天津海通时代商务信息咨询有限公司	100	2015.6.1
887	中隆租赁（天津）有限公司	20000	2014.12.26
888	天津明德轩文化传播有限公司	100	2015.4.23
889	天津翰博企业管理咨询有限公司	100	2015.4.21
890	天津九为企业管理咨询有限公司	500	2015.4.17
891	天津金仕诺翻译服务有限公司	20	2015.4.30
892	天津金池电子商务有限公司	200	2015.2.5
893	天津市宏福天源科技有限公司	200	2015.4.29
894	天津汇佳装饰工程有限公司	50	2015.5.15
895	天津雍泽房地产经纪有限公司	500	2015.5.20
896	天津润汇兴生物科技有限公司	200	2015.5.5
897	天津汇泉行科技有限公司	50	2015.4.8
898	天津市如家房地产经纪有限公司	200	2015.5.6

续表 16

序号	企业名称	注册资本（万元）	取照时间
899	天津领航财务咨询有限公司	10	2015.6.1
900	山里人（天津）科技有限公司	100	2015.6.1
901	天津浩泽鑫盛不锈钢有限公司	1000	2015.5.21
902	天津亿丰钛不锈钢有限公司	1000	2015.5.18
903	微爱在线（天津）科技有限责任公司	100	2015.5.27
904	天津天下粮仓餐饮管理有限公司	5000	2015.6.3
905	天津盈聚科技有限公司	5000	2015.6.3
906	天津狗不理餐饮管理有限公司	50	2015.3.11
907	天津恒鼎盛房地产经纪有限公司	500	2015.6.9
908	翼凌瀚森（天津）家具有限公司	300	2015.6.9
909	天津思跃达企业管理咨询有限公司	300	2015.6.11
910	天津三众合康商贸有限公司	100	2015.6.11
911	峰汇旺（天津）科技有限公司	780	2015.1.19
912	神燕（天津）科技有限公司	860	2015.1.19
913	天津宸泰创想国际贸易有限公司	600	2015.6.15
914	天津大庆义凤科技有限公司	100	2015.6.15
915	中城房地产经纪（天津）有限公司	1000	2015.6.16
916	天津聚津财务咨询有限公司	10	2015.6.19
917	天津金旺不锈钢有限公司	1280	2015.6.17
918	天津鑫汇天通科技有限公司	100	2015.6.24
919	清江（天津）文化传媒有限公司	300	2015.6.10
920	天津市久兴不锈钢有限公司	1000	2015.6.10
921	天津万利达金属材料有限公司	1000	2015.6.10
922	盈可泰（天津）农业技术有限公司	500	2015.6.25
923	欧文托普（天津）暖通设备有限公司	1000	2014.10.14
924	天津凤翔生物科技有限公司	3	2011.11.11
925	天津绣康生物科技有限公司	200	2014.11.4

续表 16

序号	企业名称	注册资本（万元）	取照时间
926	天津鑫远生物科技有限公司	5	2014.11.10
927	天津信旭生物科技有限公司	5	2014.11.4
928	天津鸿坤房地产开发有限公司	5000	2014.2.12
929	天津市优加智慧网络科技发展有限公司	400	2015.6.26
930	天津炙焱科技有限公司	30	2015.6.26
931	天津威富达信商贸有限公司	100	2015.6.30
932	天津焦点文化传媒有限公司	100	2015.6.30
933	祥龙（天津）科技有限公司	780	2015.1.26
934	时传泽丹（天津）科技有限公司	850	2015.1.9
935	天津基业不锈钢有限公司	1800	2015.7.3
936	天津优尔特不锈钢有限公司	1000	2015.7.1
937	天津中亿不锈钢有限公司	1000	2015.7.1
938	天津企钛不锈钢有限公司	1000	2015.7.3
939	天津万信不锈钢有限公司	1000	2015.7.3
940	天津明源医疗器械销售有限公司	500	2015.7.3
941	天津枭鹰新能源科技有限公司	500	2015.7.3
942	天津中电特种电缆有限公司	6000	2015.7.3
943	天津市中捷市政工程有限公司	900	2015.7.3
944	天津市洪昌市政工程有限公司	900	2015.7.3
945	天津佛佩入凡商贸有限公司	100	2015.7.7
946	天津晟源泰商贸有限公司	100	2015.7.7
947	北京志霖恒远知识产权代理事务所（普通合伙）天津分所	0	2015.7.7
948	河北北方环保工程有限公司天津分公司	0	2015.7.1
949	中城建（天津）投资有限公司	10000	2015.7.13
950	盛传文化传播（天津）有限公司	50	2015.7.13

续表 16

序号	企业名称	注册资本（万元）	取照时间
951	安徽省振远保安服务集团有限公司天津分公司	0	2015.7.13
952	天津菊花兰建材销售有限公司	100	2015.7.10
953	天津鑫华胜不锈钢有限公司	1000	2015.7.6
954	天津永信达不锈钢有限公司	1000	2015.7.6
955	天津中金钢联商贸有限公司	1000	2015.7.6
956	天津丰立不锈钢有限公司	1000	2015.7.6
957	天津市久桓装饰工程有限公司	1000	2015.7.09
958	天津市久桓供电有限公司	5000	2015.7.15
959	天津市久桓供热有限公司	1000	2015.7.9
960	天津市久桓环境工程有限公司	5000	2015.7.9
961	天津鲁艺装饰工程有限公司	100	2015.7.17
962	天津中核电缆有限公司	6000	2015.7.16
963	天津支点电动汽车技术服务有限公司	500	2015.7.23
964	天津捷兰达自行车有限公司	50	2015.7.23
965	天津郎艺建筑装饰工程有限公司	100	2015.7.23
966	欧茂（天津）科技有限公司	300	2015.7.24
967	天津津通万达建筑工程有限公司	200	2015.7.24
968	天津普利斯康生物技术有限公司	10	2015.7.24
969	天津中信钢联商贸有限公司	1000	2015.7.16
970	天津华宇钢联商贸有限公司	1000	2015.7.13
971	天津中盛钢联商贸有限公司	1000	2015.7.13
972	天津上企钢联商贸有限公司	1000	2015.7.16
973	天津斧鼎文化传播有限公司	800	2015.7.24
974	天津瑞方房地产开发有限公司	3000	1997.6.3
975	天津丽曼生物科技有限公司	5	2014.11.12
976	天津蓝韵生物科技有限公司	3	2014.11.13

续表 16

序号	企业名称	注册资本（万元）	取照时间
977	迈恩德电子有限公司	8000	2014.4.29
978	天津赛柯环保科技有限公司	500	2015.7.28
979	天津五光富明牧业科技有限公司	3000	2015.7.28
980	天津艾维生物科技有限公司	25	2015.7.28
981	中远安泰（天津）科技有限公司	1000	2015.7.27
982	天津汇纯科技有限公司	100	2015.7.30
983	中铁五洲控股集团有限公司	58000	2015.8.3
984	天津汇智光华动力科技有限公司	3500	2015.7.29
985	易生利丰（天津）美容有限公司	50	2015.7.30
986	灵山森林木（天津）科技有限公司	720	2015.1.23
987	鲁南来顺（天津）科技有限公司	860	2015.1.13
988	中天一维（天津）科技有限公司	3000	2015.8.5
989	果多美网络科技（天津）有限公司	500	2015.8.6
990	中油石化建设工程有限公司天津分公司	0	2015.8.4
991	天津天利鼎盛房地产经纪有限公司	100	2015.8.6
992	天津知艺科技有限责任公司	100	2015.7.27
993	天津桃桔商贸有限公司	100	2015.7.23
994	天津君安华天机械设备有限公司	3600	2015.7.24
995	天津好大夫科技有限公司	10000	2015.8.12
996	天津优爱创科技有限公司	100	2015.8.18
997	申缔创展（天津）商贸有限公司	1000	2015.8.18
998	天津诺博福莱科技有限公司	100	2015.8.20
999	天津万达国际电影城有限公司武清店	0	2015.8.21
1000	天津车匠科技有限公司	20	2015.8.27
1001	天津万恒仪表有限公司	500	2015.7.28
1002	天津力邦生物科技有限公司	5	2014.12.23
1003	天津多米杰生物科技有限公司	5	2014.12.23

续表 16

序号	企业名称	注册资本（万元）	取照时间
1004	天津天意达生物科技有限公司	300	2014.12.25
1005	天津丰美食用油有限公司	1000	2014.8.19
1006	穆勒纺织品（天津）有限公司	1000	2014.10.30
1007	天津康盛恒国际贸易有限公司	2000	2015.8.31
1008	天津大卫华娱文化传播有限公司	100	2015.8.27
1009	天津市广纵物业管理有限公司	50	2015.8.31
1010	潍坊子萱经贸有限公司天津分公司	0	2015.8.21
1011	天津佳德华彩劳动服务有限公司	50	2015.9.6
1012	天津市信通瑞银资产管理合伙企业（有限合伙）	150080	2015.9.6
1013	天津岩真企业管理咨询有限公司	10	2015.9.6
1014	天津市印象营销策划有限公司	50	2015.9.8
1015	天津优果水果销售有限公司	50	2015.9.8
1016	天津助尔医疗科技有限公司	100	2015.9.7
1017	指道（天津）网络科技有限公司	100	2015.8.27
1018	郅远印象（天津）科技有限公司	50	2015.9.9
1019	天津市津徽家具销售有限公司	100	2015.9.9
1020	四季能量供应链管理（天津）有限公司	100	2015.9.10
1021	天津拓程生物科技有限公司	1000	2015.9.11
1022	天津皓雅生物科技有限公司	500	2015.9.14
1023	达伦多（天津）国际贸易有限公司	5000	2015.9.16
1024	天津凯科特科技有限公司	500	2015.9.16
1025	天津爱洛斯网络科技有限公司	1000	2015.9.15
1026	上海统嘉劳务服务有限公司天津分公司	0	2015.9.16
1027	上海统嘉汽车零部件加工有限公司天津分公司	0	2015.9.17
1028	天津市圆锐通科技有限公司	200	2015.9.16
1029	天津中北亚金属材料有限公司	1000	2015.9.14

续表 16

序号	企业名称	注册资本（万元）	取照时间
1030	天津中远盛世金属材料销售有限公司	1000	2015.9.14
1031	天津市聚鑫达金属材料有限公司	850	2015.9.16
1032	天津飞思创汇广告设计有限公司	50	2015.9.24
1033	天津汉瑞斯科技有限公司	100	2015.9.22
1034	天津卡莫文化传播有限公司	200	2015.9.22
1035	天津朗瑞斯科技有限公司	100	2015.9.24
1036	天津耀源文化传播有限公司	50	2015.9.24
1037	天津依娜摄影服务有限公司	50	2015.9.23
1038	天津优耐文化传播有限公司	50	2015.9.23
1039	天津优达通供应链管理股份有限公司	1000	2015.4.24
1040	齐鲁猛虎（天津）科技有限公司	800	2015.1.16
1041	敏惠（天津）科技有限公司	880	2015.1.16
1042	天津市天地申通物流有限公司武清分公司	0	2015.9.14
1043	天津盛世起航科技有限公司	100	2015.9.29
1044	天津易博优科技有限公司	100	2015.9.29
1045	天津市汇羽电子商务有限公司	1000	2015.9.29
1046	天津海沿进出口有限公司	100	2015.9.30
1047	天津食安居餐饮管理有限公司	100	2015.9.30
1048	天津洋仓国际贸易有限公司	100	2015.9.30
1049	天津市瑞泰进出口有限公司	100	2015.9.30
1050	天津胡萝卜电子商务有限公司	500	2015.9.30
1051	天津市津水阳光科技有限公司	100	2015.10.12
1052	天津觅商机国际贸易有限公司	100	2015.9.30
1053	天津行道商贸有限公司	50	2015.10.14
1054	天津爱佑康科技发展有限公司	600	2015.10.13
1055	天津成翔隆科技有限公司	50	2015.10.13

续表 16

序号	企业名称	注册资本（万元）	取照时间
1056	天津光大环球科技有限公司	500	2015.10.13
1057	天津中星锐博企业管理咨询有限公司	141.7	2015.10.16
1058	天津市厚生航人餐饮管理有限公司	100	2015.10.14
1059	天津洛安林商贸有限公司	500	2015.10.20
1060	蒙恩（天津）绿化工程有限公司	500	2015.10.21
1061	天津乔西商贸有限公司	500	2015.10.20
1062	实康（天津）生物科技有限公司	200	2015.10.22
1063	天津鸿聚天诚商务信息咨询有限公司	100	2015.10.27
1064	砂橙（天津）园林绿化工程有限公司	6000	2015.10.30
1065	百仕活（天津）商务信息咨询有限公司	6000	2015.11.3
1066	加翎加（天津）环境科技有限公司	1000	2015.10.27
1067	天津普瑞华盛医学检验所有限公司	500	2015.10.9
1068	天津中恒达科技有限公司	10	2015.10.28
1069	神州物联（天津）有限公司	6700	2015.10.30
1070	天津若华机械配件有限公司	100	2015.10.29
1071	天津凯达汽车租赁有限公司	80	2015.11.2
1072	天津信意缘车务信息咨询有限公司	100	2015.11.2
1073	洋世界（天津）国际贸易有限公司	1000	2015.11.3
1074	天津驰外国际贸易有限公司	120	2015.11.3
1075	天津市元亨科技有限公司	100	2015.11.4
1076	大天医学工程（天津）有限公司	2000	2015.11.5
1077	哈克尼斯银幕（天津）有限公司	200	2015.11.4
1078	九三极恒医学工程（天津）有限公司	2000	2015.11.5
1079	天津京安天永科技发展有限公司	1000	2015.11.5
1080	天津市源宇泰和钢材销售有限公司	800	2015.10.19
1081	天津市均达科技有限公司	200	2013.3.15
1082	天津市建电实业有限公司	1000	1999.1.4

续表 16

序号	企业名称	注册资本（万元）	取照时间
1083	天津市普光医用材料制造有限公司	9297.96	2001.9.27
1084	滴滴集运（天津）科技股份有限公司	1000	2007.11.30
1085	天津极欧科技股份有限公司	100	2012.12.6
1086	天津德嘉汽车零配件有限公司	800	2015.11.11
1087	天津市力锐建筑工程有限公司	50	2015.11.11
1088	天津清企助力生产力促进有限公司	300	2015.11.11
1089	天津安华聚众科技合伙企业（有限合伙）	301.5	2015.11.6
1090	天津市和麦秀科技有限公司	1000	2015.9.30
1091	天津市平源房地产经纪有限公司	200	2015.11.12
1092	天津世纪鑫华钢铁有限公司	1000	2015.11.11
1093	天津世纪鑫盛钢铁有限公司	1000	2015.11.11
1094	天津市彩狮广告有限公司	500	2015.11.13
1095	天津汉防生物科技有限公司	600	2015.11.16
1096	天津中禾种业有限公司	10000	2015.11.19
1097	爱乐思（天津）国际贸易有限公司	600	2015.11.20
1098	天津丸幸服装有限公司	1000	2015.11.23
1099	天津市礼兴装饰装修有限公司	100	2015.11.26
1100	天津麦嘉乐餐饮服务有限公司	350	2015.11.26
1101	天津市乐艺佳装饰有限公司	500	2015.11.26
1102	天津米尔斯鸿福楼餐饮管理有限公司	50	2015.11.17
1103	津舆汇（天津）法律服务有限公司	100	2015.11.26
1104	天津浩迪佳和商贸有限公司	500	2015.11.27
1105	天津源鲜洋食品贸易有限公司	100	2015.11.24
1106	国信联（天津）股权投资合伙企业（有限合伙）	125002	2015.12.4
1107	天津心物天使电子商务有限公司	100	2015.12.4
1108	天津集信企业管理咨询中心（有限合伙）	500	2015.12.8

续表 16

序号	企业名称	注册资本（万元）	取照时间
1109	天津天赐劳动服务有限公司	100	2015.12.16
1110	天津金百隆建筑集团鑫禹机电设备安装有限公司	300	2015.12.16
1111	天津俪曼商贸有限公司	50	2015.12.16
1112	天津中世家房地产经纪有限公司	30	2015.12.17
1113	天津武清山姆进出口有限公司	1000	2015.12.15
1114	依友（天津）文化传播有限公司	50	2015.7.17
1115	天津创亿企业管理咨询有限公司	500	2015.7.15
1116	天津誉晟恒达房地产经纪有限公司	100	2015.7.13
1117	海德利森（天津）检测设备有限公司	50	2015.12.22
1118	天津拓八荒科技有限公司	100	2014.12.19
1119	帝倜（天津）网络科技有限公司	200	2015.11.30
1120	天津臻瑗购科技有限公司	50	2015.12.11
1121	泽优（天津）企业管理咨询有限公司	50	2015.12.11
1122	天津荣科房地产经纪有限公司	50	2015.12.24
1123	天津华融商务信息咨询有限公司	50	2015.12.07
1124	三英精控（天津）科技有限公司	1000	2015.12.28
1125	天津顺禾农业科技有限公司	300	2015.12.29
1126	瑞中商务信息咨询（天津）有限公司	100	2015.12.24
1127	天津格美电子商务有限公司	100	2015.12.24
1128	天津汉斯顿电子商务有限公司	100	2015.12.24
1129	天津奔泰电子商务有限公司	100	2015.12.28
1130	天津世纪聚星文化传播有限公司	100	2015.12.30
1131	天津聚星乐成文化传播有限公司	100	2015.12.30
1132	天津有乐文化传播有限公司	1000	2015.12.29
1133	天津塞科凯尔科技有限公司	4000	2015.12.29
1134	华圣蓝金（天津）活性炭有限公司	2005	2015.12.4

续表 16

序号	企业名称	注册资本（万元）	取照时间
1135	天津市梦幻新能源汽车制造有限公司	2000	2015.12.15
1136	天津市墨言生产力促进有限公司	50	2016.1.5
1137	天津旭帆科技有限公司	1000	2016.1.5
1138	天津选啥网络科技有限公司	100	2016.1.6
1139	天津安达倍信企业管理咨询有限公司	100	2016.1.6
1140	天津美源星商贸有限公司	1000	2016.1.5
1141	天津天宝光碟有限公司	4406	1992.7.31
1142	天津天宝电子科技有限公司	800	1998.1.22
1143	中天高科特种车辆有限公司	9600	2001.5.14
1144	爱尚泓久（天津）文化传播有限公司	100	2015.12.7
1145	巴伐朗尼（天津）玻璃机械有限公司	100	2015.11.11
1146	天津百众祥餐饮服务有限公司	200	2015.9.23
1147	唱咏医药科技（天津）有限公司	100	2015.10.30
1148	天津大玺商贸有限公司	500	2016.1.7
1149	天津菲世生物科技有限公司	100	2015.10.26
1150	天津国之帅物业服务有限公司	100	2015.11.3
1151	天津晗夫圣科技有限公司	100	2015.11.3
1152	天津市黄金屋装饰工程有限公司	100	2015.9.8
1153	天津杰睿龙网络科技有限公司	200	2015.11.3
1154	天津聚万鑫信息科技有限公司	100	2015.10.28
1155	天津乐农电子商务有限公司	10	2015.10.14
1156	天津路图信息科技有限公司	300	2015.12.7
1157	七彩石（天津）科技有限公司	50	2016.1.6
1158	天津齐家物联网科技有限公司	500	2015.9.16
1159	天津市通特信息科技有限公司	200	2015.10.13
1160	天津微焦点文化传播有限公司	100	2015.12.16
1161	天津孝爱格天文化传播有限公司	50	2015.12.21

续表 16

序号	企业名称	注册资本（万元）	取照时间
1162	天津邢成教育科技有限公司	10	2015.10.15
1163	天津市盈爱网络科技有限公司	200	2015.12.28
1164	宜德（天津）科技有限公司	200	2015.9.22
1165	天津义隆祥建筑工程有限公司	500	2015.11.11
1166	天津雅亭文化传播有限公司	100	2015.11.17
1167	天津盈赫商务信息咨询有限公司武清分公司	0	2015.12.16
1168	天津金雷展翼机电设备安装有限公司	50	2016.1.11
1169	天津非池中电子商务有限公司	100	2016.1.11
1170	天津海鸟城进出口贸易有限公司	10000	2016.1.8
1171	中企联企业管理咨询（天津）有限公司	500	2016.1.13
1172	天津华创瑞风空调设备有限公司	2000	2015.9.25
1173	天津唯拓科技有限责任公司	101	2016.1.21
1174	天津君浩餐饮管理有限公司	100	2016.1.21
1175	天津志天家具有限公司	20	2016.1.21
1176	渤润（天津）外贸综合服务有限公司	5000	2016.1.29
1177	天津原野装饰工程有限公司	1000	2016.1.25
1178	天津市焱林电子商务有限公司	100	2016.1.28
1179	天津有梦信息技术有限公司	50	2016.1.18
1180	天津金百隆建筑集团飞宏建筑工程有限公司	400	2016.1.14
1181	天津杰唯文化传播有限公司	100	2016.2.2
1182	天津逗友文化传播有限公司	100	2016.2.2
1183	天津奇异果汽车租赁有限公司	200	2016.1.29
1184	天津编客广汇企业管理咨询中心（有限合伙）	60	2016.1.22
1185	天津汇速通企业管理咨询中心（有限合伙）	100	2016.1.28

续表 16

序号	企业名称	注册资本（万元）	取照时间
1186	天津渤海志成企业管理咨询合伙企业（有限合伙）	100	2016.2.2
1187	天津渤海志昇企业管理咨询合伙企业（有限合伙）	100	2016.2.2
1188	天津森普沃科技发展有限公司	5	2016.2.3
1189	亦昭生物医药科技（天津）有限公司	1000	2015.9.11
1190	天津联慧企业管理咨询中心（有限合伙）	200	2015.8.24
1191	天津智韵衡谊新能源科技有限公司	100	2015.12.9
1192	志诚鸿瑞（天津）新能源科技有限公司	100	2015.12.8
1193	天津市三叶虫岩矿技术服务有限公司	10	2016.2.3
1194	天津瑞安捷财务咨询有限公司	20	2016.1.26
1195	天津汇力致远商务咨询有限公司	50	2016.2.5
1196	天津洪种企业管理咨询中心（有限合伙）	100	2016.2.17
1197	沈阳市天顺路发冷藏物流有限公司天津分公司	0	2016.2.19
1198	天津通泰电子商务有限公司	10000	2016.1.21
1199	天津星创互联传媒科技有限公司	1000	2016.2.26
1200	博爱记忆（天津）科技有限公司	300	2016.3.9
1201	天津溯寻印象科技发展有限公司	200	2016.3.4
1202	天津享远互联科技发展有限公司	200	2016.3.4
1203	天津梦想腾飞科技有限公司	1000	2016.3.4
1204	上奕（天津）营销策划有限公司	500	2016.3.23
1205	天津乐美宇航科技有限公司	200	2016.3.25
1206	天津鑫予梦想科技有限公司	217	2016.3.24
1207	天津昭石科技有限公司	500	2016.3.25
1208	冠蔻纪元（天津）商务信息咨询有限公司	100	2016.3.24
1209	瑞兴隆（天津）钢材销售有限公司	300	2016.3.22

续表 16

序号	企业名称	注册资本（万元）	取照时间
1210	天津宝润利丰商贸有限公司	300	2016.3.28
1211	天津东方天璇商贸中心	100	2016.3.23
1212	天津宏华福康商贸中心	100	2016.3.23
1213	天津祥宏源商贸中心	100	2016.3.23
1214	天津仁和泰康商贸中心	100	2016.3.24
1215	天津富泰海迪商贸有限公司	300	2016.3.24
1216	天津鑫胜运达二手车销售有限公司	100	2016.3.29
1217	天津华商盛泰科技有限公司	300	2016.3.29
1218	天津皇鼎瑞佳科技有限公司	300	2016.3.28
1219	金凯莉（天津）文化传播有限公司	50	2016.3.29
1220	天津市联创耀信环保科技有限公司	300	2016.3.25
1221	天津福顺通家政服务有限公司	50	2016.3.30
1222	中际联合（天津）科技有限公司	1000	2016.2.23
1223	天津铭铨志远科技有限公司	600	2014.12.17
1224	天津燕西装饰工程有限公司	100	2016.3.9
1225	天津云海体育文化传播有限公司	100	2016.3.8
1226	天津斯沃尔自动化科技有限公司	300	2016.3.9
1227	天津荣君混凝土销售有限公司	1000	2016.2.26
1228	天津裂帛天使电子商务有限公司	100	2016.3.2
1229	天津庆丰科技有限公司	100	2016.3.14
1230	天津一通百通信息技术有限公司	500	2016.3.1
1231	天津伯乐无忧劳动服务有限公司	50	2016.2.25
1232	天津焯越商业管理有限公司	1000	2016.3.18
1233	天津宸泰化工有限公司	200	2016.3.15
1234	广州市汉久进出口贸易有限公司天津分公司	0	2016.3.3
1235	天津和琪餐饮服务有限公司	100	2016.3.1

续表 16

序号	企业名称	注册资本（万元）	取照时间
1236	天津洪辉企业管理咨询中心（有限合伙）	100	2016.3.1
1237	联合维克（天津）热能技术有限公司	300	2016.3.8
1238	天津青皮网络科技有限公司	500	2016.3.14
1239	天津瑞诺康生物科技有限公司	1000	2016.3.14
1240	天津泰娅企业管理咨询有限公司	10	2016.3.3
1241	天津智融鸿源科技有限公司	100	2016.3.15
1242	天津中造云商新媒体科技有限公司	300	2016.3.3
1243	天津众乐文化传播有限公司	100	2016.3.15
1244	天津禾谷企业管理咨询有限公司	10	2016.2.24
1245	天津富粮科技有限公司	1000	2016.3.1
1246	天津佳思保科技有限公司	1000	2016.3.21
1247	天津宇斯特装备有限公司	5000	2016.3.21
1248	天津瑞鑫宏达企业管理咨询合伙企业（有限合伙）	50	2016.3.25
1249	天津云仓物流有限公司	100	2016.3.24
1250	天津市墨凡生产力促进有限公司	100	2016.3.18
1251	中投汇金（天津）国际贸易有限公司	500	2016.3.25
1252	中文投影视版权交易中心有限公司	5000	2016.3.18
1253	正大煜恒文化传播（天津）有限公司	2000	2016.3.25
1254	天津璀璨星辰信息技术有限公司	500	2016.3.23
1255	新能（天津）能源有限公司	8000	2016.3.24
1256	天津浦华企业管理咨询有限公司	10	2016.3.24
1257	天津星云天逸网络科技有限公司	1000	2016.3.21
1258	天津中天思源文化传播有限公司	1000	2016.3.22
1259	天津凌和渡科技有限公司	100	2016.3.18
1260	天津颖程科技有限公司	10	2016.3.10
1261	天津本初科技有限公司	20	2016.3.10

续表 16

序号	企业名称	注册资本（万元）	取照时间
1262	天津江树思源科技有限公司	10	2016.3.10
1263	天津君驰科技有限公司	10	2016.3.10
1264	天津璐伟科技有限公司	10	2016.3.10
1265	天津明桐科技有限公司	10	2016.3.10
1266	天津农友农业科技有限公司	10	2016.3.10
1267	天津田苗农业科技有限公司	10	2016.3.10
1268	天津向荣科技有限公司	10	2016.3.10
1269	天津岭龙科技有限公司	10	2016.3.10
1270	天津星睿影视传媒有限公司	300	2016.3.29
1271	天津市蜜笙卤侠坚果有限公司	20	2016.3.28
1272	天津和胜世纪科技有限公司	100	2016.3.28
1273	中鼎创世（天津）国际贸易有限公司	500	2016.3.29
1274	天津浚合商务信息咨询有限公司	30	2016.3.29
1275	天津贝海电子商务有限公司	100	2016.3.14
1276	万泰中联科技（天津）有限公司	1000	2016.3.31
1277	天津华诚磐石环保科技有限公司	100	2016.3.28
1278	天津一元光明科技中心（有限合伙）	300	2016.4.5
1279	康腾（天津）商贸有限公司	1000	2010.11.26
1280	康腾（天津）环保设备有限公司	104	2011.7.20
1281	天津鹏冉房地产经纪有限公司	100	2016.4.8
1282	天津皓宇达电力科技有限公司	100	2016.4.15
1283	天津亿老汇养老服务有限公司	300	2016.4.18
1284	迪诺孚（天津）医学科技有限公司	1000	2016.4.5
1285	晟福（天津）流体自动控制设备有限公司	2000	2016.4.15
1286	君歌多米诺（天津）物联网科技有限公司	358	2016.4.20
1287	天津君歌环保科技有限公司	588	2016.4.19

续表 16

序号	企业名称	注册资本（万元）	取照时间
1288	天津鑫悦宏达科技有限公司	500	2016.4.21
1289	天津幸运星科技有限公司	100	2016.3.31
1290	天津爱多贝贝健康管理服务有限公司	500	2016.4.8
1291	天津中禾生物技术有限责任公司	1000	2016.4.18
1292	内蒙古途家商业管理有限公司天津分公司	0	2016.4.8
1293	天津汇华丰化工设备科技有限公司	50	2016.4.22
1294	天津金捷瑞机电设备科技有限公司	30	2016.4.21
1295	天津埃彼咨石化科技有限公司	510	2016.4.22
1296	海贝（天津）科技有限责任公司	100	2016.4.25
1297	天津嘻哈芒果户外体育文化传播有限公司	50	2016.4.14
1298	天津泰韩国际贸易有限公司	50	2016.4.14
1299	智汇博睿（天津）医药科技有限公司	100	2016.4.8
1300	天津德林宇恒房地产经纪有限公司	50	2016.4.27
1301	天津东方千里马体育文化传播有限公司	60	2016.4.26
1302	天津国明浩辰科技发展有限公司	10000	2016.4.13
1303	天津金百隆建筑集团成骏建筑工程有限公司	500	2016.4.14
1304	天津金蜜蜂企业管理咨询有限公司	1000	2016.4.27
1305	天津润祥生物科技有限公司	118	2016.5.5
1306	天津霖然科技有限公司	100	2016.4.18
1307	汇中盛世信息咨询（天津）有限责任公司	2000	2016.4.21
1308	汇中盛德企业管理咨询（天津）有限公司	500	2016.4.21
1309	天津迅领企业管理咨询有限公司	100	2016.4.15
1310	天津思然妙学教育科技有限公司	50	2016.4.22
1311	埃德瑞（天津）科技发展有限公司	300	2016.4.19

续表 16

序号	企业名称	注册资本（万元）	取照时间
1312	天津沁尔康电子商务有限公司	100	2016.5.5
1313	天津宏图佰翔建筑设计有限公司	100	2016.5.5
1314	天津兢羽生物医药科技有限公司	2000	2016.5.9
1315	天津利顺祥和商贸有限公司	200	2016.5.6
1316	天津市金轮图腾进出口有限公司	100	2016.4.29
1317	天津凌润企业孵化器有限公司	200	2016.4.28
1318	天津市荣安伟业房地产开发有限公司	6000	2016.5.9
1319	天津市荣丰伟业房地产开发有限公司	8000	2016.5.5
1320	易览天下（天津）网络科技有限公司	100	2016.5.6
1321	天津冰河文化传媒有限公司	500	2016.5.9
1322	天津沐恒称重设备科技有限公司	100	2016.3.31
1323	天津仁益顺昌商贸有限公司	3000	2016.3.30
1324	天津荣祥森悦商贸有限公司	3000	2016.3.30
1325	天津富盈益华科技有限公司	300	2016.4.1
1326	天津源鑫盛达商贸有限公司	100	2016.4.22
1327	天津金恒天诚商贸有限公司	100	2016.4.22
1328	天津远达交通设施有限公司	500	2016.4.14
1329	天津东方天璇科技发展有限公司	100	2016.4.13
1330	天津余味餐饮管理有限公司	100	2016.4.15
1331	天津南橡木商务信息咨询有限公司	500	2016.4.11
1332	天津蓝天同创光伏科技有限公司	1000	2016.5.9
1333	天津海乐达装饰工程有限公司	100	2016.5.5
1334	天津昊煜国际贸易有限公司	960	2016.5.13
1335	阿甘(天津)农业科技有限公司	1000	2016.5.12
1336	安宇（天津）装饰工程有限公司	200	2016.5.12
1337	贝力拓（天津）科技发展有限公司	200	2016.5.13
1338	天津露乐国际贸易有限公司	800	2016.5.11

续表 16

序号	企业名称	注册资本（万元）	取照时间
1339	天津梧笛生产力促进有限公司	50	2016.5.13
1340	允通北斗（天津）科技有限公司	2000	2016.5.10
1341	天津中金汇丰科技有限公司	1000	2016.5.20
1342	深圳市明喆物业管理有限公司天津武清分公司	0	2016.5.19
1343	天津博领健康管理有限公司	100	2016.5.19
1344	天津市延中线缆有限公司	500	2016.5.12
1345	天津析北科技有限公司	100	2016.5.17
1346	天津润汇房地产经纪有限公司	20	2016.5.20
1347	艺秋林（天津）广告有限公司	500	2016.5.19
1348	天津联合久利文化发展有限公司	10	2016.5.24
1349	天津雨润文化发展有限公司	10	2016.5.24
1350	天津东景财务咨询有限公司	100	2016.5.24
1351	天津撒可富化肥有限公司	100	2016.5.20
1352	天津芭田化肥有限公司	100	2016.5.24
1353	铁科华铁经纬（天津）信息技术有限公司	4980	2016.5.27
1354	天津寞妃餐饮管理有限公司	30	2016.5.31
1355	天津众享金属材料销售有限公司	20	2016.5.30
1356	天津天弘益商贸有限公司	10	2016.5.31
1357	天津轩耀生物科技有限公司	1000	2016.6.1
1358	天津市艾瑞莉卡服装贸易有限公司	100	2016.5.23
1359	天津市宝信德隆建筑工程有限公司	200	2016.6.1
1360	天津木槿花教育信息咨询有限公司	60	2016.5.24
1361	天津市芃盛文化交流有限公司	100	2016.5.31
1362	天津冉昌科技有限公司	10	2016.6.2
1363	天津市若达科技有限责任公司	100	2016.5.31

续表 16

序号	企业名称	注册资本（万元）	取照时间
1364	天津市旭德房地产经纪有限公司	50	2016.5.26
1365	天津珍玲餐饮管理有限公司	50	2016.5.26
1366	伟益康（天津）生物科技研发中心（有限合伙）	200	2016.6.3
1367	正德诚三生科技有限公司	5000	2016.6.3
1368	天津多摩仕奥瑞家居用品销售有限公司	50	2016.5.26
1369	天津艾达康医疗科技有限公司	500	2016.5.11
1370	天津番茄理想体育文化传播有限公司	100	2016.6.6
1371	天津梵晟嘉和体育文化传播有限公司	50	2016.6.7
1372	天津爱尝鲜商贸有限公司	100	2016.5.23
1373	天津菜菜鸟电子商务有限公司	10	2016.6.1
1374	天津德冠企业管理咨询有限公司	100	2016.5.16
1375	天津广选家电维修有限公司	300	2016.5.17
1376	天津恒飞盛企业管理咨询有限公司	100	2016.5.16
1377	天津聚鑫博远科技有限公司	50	2016.5.26
1378	天津俊涵羽鑫科技发展有限公司	500	2016.5.19
1379	天津陆柒捌电子商务有限公司	10	2016.6.1
1380	天津模咔群星文化娱乐经纪有限公司	100	2016.5.26
1381	天津三好搬家服务有限公司	100	2016.5.19
1382	太悟文化发展有限公司	10000	2016.5.16
1383	天津泰山斗机械设备安装有限公司	100	2016.5.25
1384	天津泰西斯文化传媒有限公司	100	2016.6.2
1385	鑫科瑞（天津）彩钢板销售有限公司	500	2016.5.27
1386	天津煜之缘测控技术有限公司	100	2016.5.27
1387	天津铂雅领航汽车租赁有限公司	50	2016.5.20
1388	天津馨美园日化产品销售有限公司	100	2016.4.21
1389	天津鲍勃科技有限公司	50	2016.6.6

续表 16

序号	企业名称	注册资本（万元）	取照时间
1390	天津昌达通泰科技有限公司	100	2016.6.2
1391	天津万事盛达科技有限公司	100	2016.6.3
1392	天津我能文化传播有限公司	100	2016.6.3
1393	晓瞪羚科技有限公司	10000	2016.6.7
1394	天津兴越酒店管理有限公司	500	2016.5.30
1395	天津旭依鸣科技有限公司	50	2016.6.7
1396	天津海东青环保科技有限公司	1000	2016.4.19
1397	天津爱友科技有限公司	100	2016.4.26
1398	天津春秋服装销售有限公司	300	2016.4.6
1399	天津福气来搬家服务有限公司	50	2016.4.28
1400	天津富文瑞通财务咨询有限公司	100	2016.5.16
1401	天津津泓伟业建筑工程有限公司	500	2016.5.10
1402	大商度（天津）生产力促进有限责任公司	1000	2016.4.26
1403	天津锦诚佳合农业科技有限公司	200	2016.5.24
1404	天津塑创空间装饰工程有限公司	1000	2016.4.18
1405	天津湘腾科技有限公司	50	2016.5.10
1406	天津瑞丰嘉源科技有限公司	300	2016.5.10
1407	天津万博凯建筑工程有限公司	500	2016.5.11
1408	天津万信源化工贸易有限公司	1000	2016.5.3
1409	鑫玺鑫（天津）信息技术开发有限公司	100	2016.4.20
1410	天津盛源信化工贸易有限公司	1800	2016.4.27
1411	天津金鼎鸿泰建材科技有限公司	300	2016.5.24
1412	天津鼎安宏华商贸中心	100	2016.4.5
1413	天津快捷通管道工程有限公司	50	2016.4.25
1414	天津澜訾洺商贸有限公司	100	2016.4.28

续表 16

序号	企业名称	注册资本（万元）	取照时间
1415	北京天元世纪装饰工程设计有限公司天津分公司	100	2016.4.11
1416	天津通泰科技创新产业园有限公司	10000	2016.5.17
1417	中农立华（天津）农用化学品有限公司	3729.53	1997.3.5
1418	海普（天津）制鞋有限公司	12072.6711	2006.11.22
1419	天津富安伟祥商贸有限公司	100	2016.6.20
1420	天津嘉华兴创科技有限公司	100	2016.6.20
1421	天津金丰渤海线缆有限公司	1000	2016.6.17
1422	天津津海腾飞商贸有限公司	80	2016.6.8
1423	天津良辰文化传播有限公司	600	2016.6.16
1424	天津龙源泰顺科技有限公司	100	2016.6.12
1425	天津圣源康科技发展有限公司	100	2016.6.17
1426	天津腾思科技有限公司	200	2016.6.21
1427	忆念信息技术（天津）有限公司	500	2016.6.15
1428	天津织梦圆商贸有限公司	100	2016.6.8
1429	天津佳源伟业商贸有限公司	100	2016.6.23
1430	天津津工泵业有限公司	100	2016.6.27
1431	天津市卡其科技有限公司	50	2016.6.27
1432	天津鲲鹏宏鑫建筑工程有限公司	1619	2016.6.22
1433	天津路德科技有限公司	50	2016.6.24
1434	天津秋叶园餐饮有限公司	500	2016.6.24
1435	天津锐垚科技有限公司	50	2016.6.27
1436	天津哲炎广告有限公司	100	2016.6.28
1437	天津福瑞康科技有限公司	100	2016.6.29
1438	天津汉和聚缘商务信息咨询有限公司	1000	2016.6.28
1439	天津吉悦财务咨询有限公司	100	2016.6.29
1440	天津万克森焊材销售有限公司	50	2016.6.29

续表 16

序号	企业名称	注册资本（万元）	取照时间
1441	安盈数据科技（天津）有限公司	300	2016.6.6
1442	金谷唐科技（天津）有限公司	500	2016.6.14
1443	天津青创汇壹企业管理咨询中心（有限合伙）	25.0001	2016.6.15
1444	北京食圣天下餐饮管理有限公司天津分公司	0	2016.6.14
1445	爱之湾（天津）商贸有限公司	1000	2016.5.24
1446	天津市百通力达电气科技有限公司	100	2016.6.22
1447	天津保信立德生物科技有限公司	300	2016.6.16
1448	北京华创瑞风空调科技有限公司天津分公司	0	2016.6.16
1449	华颂汽车租赁（大连）有限公司天津分公司	0	2016.6.20
1450	康腾水业（天津）有限公司	8000	2016.5.24
1451	天津天智网络科技有限公司	100	2016.6.22
1452	天津顽皮狗科技有限公司	10	2016.6.20
1453	天津万安源盛科技有限公司	100	2016.6.17
1454	天津希尔贝国际贸易有限公司	200	2016.6.12
1455	天津雍联网络科技有限公司	50	2016.6.22
1456	中海外科技（天津）有限公司	3000	2016.5.27
1457	天津英孚机电设备有限公司	1200	2016.6.20
1458	天津开门红农业科技发展有限公司	500	2016.6.27
1459	天津越音速科技有限公司	5000	2016.6.27
1460	明光恒辉能源科技有限公司	5000	2016.6.30
1461	天津金啸科技有限公司	100	2016.7.4
1462	天津猋一餐饮管理有限公司	5	2016.6.20
1463	天津橙阳科技有限公司	3	2016.6.16
1464	天津樱桃良品电子商务有限公司	30	2016.7.4

续表 16

序号	企业名称	注册资本（万元）	取照时间
1465	天津天肽生物科技有限公司	5000	2015.9.7
1466	阿斯特（天津）机械设备技术有限公司	500	2016.6.27
1467	天津安盛华珠宝产业园有限公司	8000	2013.12.20
1468	天津金瑞溢彩实业有限公司	10000	2013.12.12
1469	天津市维乐电子商务有限公司	50	2016.6.29
1470	天津见素抱朴企业管理咨询中心（有限合伙）	539.34	2016.7.4
1471	四川文轩在线电子商务有限公司天津分公司	0	2016.6.6
1472	天津威斯康顿酒店管理有限公司	10	2016.6.27
1473	天津汉秀双禹机电设备有限公司	300	2016.7.12
1474	天津豪贯家科技有限公司	3	2016.7.18
1475	天津沐柯莱进出口有限公司	100	2016.6.28
1476	天津磐星机械设备贸易有限公司	200	2016.6.29
1477	天津平茂科技发展有限公司	500	2016.7.18
1478	天津森谜园林设计有限公司	20	2016.7.11
1479	天津薇拉维卡进出口贸易有限公司	500	2016.2.14
1480	天津茵茵环保科技有限公司	20	2016.7.12
1481	优粉科技（天津）有限公司	500	2016.7.11
1482	天津元牛科技有限公司	2000	2016.7.12
1483	天津泽泽环保科技有限公司	20	2016.7.4
1484	天津翠馨科技有限公司	15	2016.7.18
1485	天津春涛科技发展有限公司	20	2016.7.20
1486	天津市凯翔安泰机械租赁有限公司	200	2016.7.19
1487	迈克博（天津）生物科技有限公司	1000	2016.7.20
1488	天津哲宇科技有限公司	20	2016.7.19
1489	天津卡尔达网络科技有限公司	50	2016.7.20

续表 16

序号	企业名称	注册资本（万元）	取照时间
1490	天津知汇生物技术有限公司	170	2016.7.22
1491	天津美源金服科技有限公司	5000	2016.7.21
1492	景泽科技（天津）有限公司	180	2014.3.11
1493	天津正通万科科技有限公司	100	2016.7.5
1494	天津佰物伽通物流有限公司	100	2016.7.11
1495	天津鹏飞盛祥商贸有限公司	100	2016.7.12
1496	天津润泽建业建筑工程有限公司	2000	2016.7.12
1497	天津新视线文化传播有限公司	1000	2016.7.4
1498	天津焱阳通科技有限公司	100	2016.7.11
1499	天津初见婚庆服务有限公司	100	2016.7.18
1500	天津卓卡科技有限公司	50	2016.7.19
1501	数字点典国际信用评价（北京）有限公司天津分公司	0	2016.7.20
1502	天津允信天达科技有限公司	1000	2016.7.19
1503	天津宇空商贸有限公司	30	2016.7.20
1504	天津雪洋食品有限公司	800	2015.10.29
1505	天津梦马仓储有限公司	500	2016.7.25
1506	格兰富水泵（苏州）有限公司天津分公司	0	2016.7.26
1507	天津青雀岭南文化传媒有限公司	10	2016.7.25
1508	天津市卡漠科技发展有限公司	100	2016.7.26
1509	天津春工教育科技有限公司	50	2016.8.1
1510	天津叁捌零零科技企业孵化器有限公司	100	2016.8.1
1511	天津思齐环保科技有限公司	20	2016.7.25
1512	天津思源科技有限公司	20	2016.7.26
1513	天津远润环保科技有限公司	20	2016.8.1
1514	天津市赛拉维招标代理有限公司	300	2016.7.25

续表 16

序号	企业名称	注册资本（万元）	取照时间
1515	天津宏邦房地产经纪有限公司	50	2016.8.1
1516	天津尚书教育信息咨询有限公司	50	2016.8.1
1517	天津意献科技有限公司	100	2016.8.2
1518	北航（天津武清）智能制造研究院有限公司	200	2016.8.2
1519	天津歌者企业管理咨询中心（有限合伙）	20	2016.8.10
1520	魁元盛（天津）宠物用品有限公司	100	2016.8.10
1521	天津市雍祥市政工程有限公司	1000	2016.8.11
1522	天津面壁企业管理咨询中心（有限合伙）	58	2016.8.10
1523	瀚田工程技术（天津）有限公司	100	2016.8.16
1524	天津天水科技有限公司	30	2016.8.15
1525	天津四九商务信息咨询有限公司	500	2016.8.12
1526	天津恒纪元企业管理咨询中心（有限合伙）	54	2016.8.10
1527	天津瑞盈文化传播有限公司	500	2016.8.11
1528	天津创青春投资管理中心（有限合伙）	1001	2016.8.16
1529	天津市正信劳动服务有限公司	300	2016.8.17
1530	天津鸿顺盈和建筑工程有限公司	100	2016.7.4
1531	天津市双强机械加工有限公司	50	2016.8.18
1532	天津领威科技有限公司	3	2016.8.18
1533	天津沁彤建筑工程有限公司	100	2016.8.9
1534	天津临济企业管理咨询中心（有限合伙）	195	2016.8.9
1535	天津市鼎盛鑫科技有限公司	1000	2016.8.9
1536	天津鑫海文化传播有限公司	100	2016.8.17
1537	北京叁捌零零管理顾问有限公司天津分公司	0	2016.8.23
1538	天津安盛房地产开发有限公司	5000	2016.8.15
1539	天津百恒兴科技有限公司	100	2016.8.23

续表 16

序号	企业名称	注册资本（万元）	取照时间
1540	天津宾祎科技有限公司	200	2016.8.9
1541	天津市博富科技有限公司	500	2016.8.12
1542	春宝网络科技（天津）有限公司	100	2016.8.24
1543	春芳科技（天津）有限公司	100	2016.8.11
1544	天津大翎商务信息咨询有限公司	100	2016.8.2
1545	天津恒波供应链管理有限公司	1000	2016.8.24
1546	吉诺斯广告有限公司	5000	2016.8.25
1547	汇天下（天津）电子商务有限公司	5000	2016.8.17
1548	天津聚吉商务信息咨询有限公司	10	2016.8.15
1549	天津凯杰房地产经纪有限公司	300	2016.8.15
1550	天津乐尚文化传媒有限公司	300	2016.8.16
1551	天津墨戈企业管理咨询有限公司	10	2016.8.2
1552	木舟树（天津）儿童娱乐有限公司	50	2016.8.23
1553	天津帕斯泰克医疗器械有限公司	100	2016.8.18
1554	天津鹏钜商贸有限公司	100	2016.8.23
1555	天津启星计划文化传播有限公司	25	2016.8.22
1556	天津三鼎影视传媒有限公司	300	2016.8.17
1557	腾思彬（天津）商贸有限公司	100	2016.8.5
1558	天津新路文化传播有限公司	50	2016.8.22
1559	天津中传教育信息咨询有限公司	10	2016.8.25
1560	天津易昌新能源科技发展有限公司	500	2016.8.25
1561	天津谦和成仁科技有限公司	3	2016.8.16
1562	天津健超教育科技有限公司	3	2016.8.24
1563	天津三博远志医学检验所有限公司	500	2016.8.23
1564	天津坤坤科技发展有限公司	10	2016.7.26
1565	天津元骏科技有限公司	200	2016.8.25
1566	恒诺（天津）生物医药科技有限公司	200	2016.8.25

续表 16

序号	企业名称	注册资本（万元）	取照时间
1567	爱德瑞低碳科技（天津）有限公司	5000	2016.9.1
1568	天津鑫德冷链物流有限公司	1000	2016.9.1
1569	天津汇达保洁服务有限公司	10	2016.8.31
1570	天津晶选佳品国际贸易有限公司	1000	2016.9.1
1571	天津久龙翔科技发展有限公司	1000	2016.8.30
1572	天津思域企业管理咨询有限责任公司	1000	2016.8.30
1573	天津承鸿伟业建筑工程有限公司	1000	2016.9.1
1574	天津北北商贸有限公司	500	2016.7.26
1575	天津德斯通商贸有限公司	100	2016.7.26
1576	天津恒顺益商贸有限公司	100	2016.7.27
1577	天津市嘉熙科技有限公司	50	2016.7.27
1578	天津巨匠装饰工程有限公司	500	2016.7.25
1579	天津美佳美户保洁服务有限公司	50	2016.7.27
1580	天津市艾弗杰科技有限公司	50	2016.8.9
1581	天津季晨科技有限公司	200	2016.8.16
1582	天津诚百来科技有限公司	500	2016.8.11
1583	天津嘉茂晟达科技有限公司	100	2016.8.11
1584	天津海中金房地产经纪有限公司	369	2016.8.23
1585	天津市津源居房地产经纪有限公司	50	2016.8.17
1586	天津浩洲商贸有限公司	200	2016.8.1
1587	天津京康盟宏大科技有限公司	500	2016.8.9
1588	天津乐淼科技有限公司	50	2016.8.16
1589	天津列星科技有限公司	550	2016.8.22
1590	天津隆轩科技有限公司	100	2016.8.22
1591	天津前途明加油站管理有限公司	20	2016.8.18
1592	天津融天晟商贸有限公司	500	2016.8.23
1593	天津睿一文化传媒有限公司	100	2016.8.12

续表 16

序号	企业名称	注册资本（万元）	取照时间
1594	天津市益惠晟科技有限公司	360	2016.8.16
1595	天津泰文仲鸿科技有限公司	100	2016.8.2
1596	天津又白商贸有限公司	60	2016.8.2
1597	天津宏星丰瑞装饰工程有限公司	500	2016.8.10
1598	天津福腾信风食品销售有限公司	80	2016.8.30
1599	天津清开博远防腐技术有限公司	500	2016.8.31
1600	天津中瑞泽天教育科技有限公司	50	2016.9.1
1601	天津亚日达电子商务有限公司	50	2016.9.6
1602	天津渤港科技有限公司	50	2016.9.6
1603	天津都奉尔鑫商贸有限公司	100	2016.9.5
1604	天津淼嘉装饰工程有限公司	200	2016.9.8
1605	天津荣君科技有限公司	50	2016.9.6
1606	天津庭宇清洁服务有限公司	500	2016.9.7
1607	沃壹度（天津）商贸有限公司	200	2016.9.2
1608	天津鑫学盛教育科技有限公司公司	50	2016.9.1
1609	天津自由行广告有限公司	50	2016.9.7
1610	北京东光物业管理股份有限公司天津分公司	0	2016.8.26
1611	天津多乐朗汽车代驾服务有限公司	20	2016.8.10
1612	涵薇生物科技（天津）有限公司	120	2016.9.1
1613	天津恒运兴业网络科技有限公司	100	2016.8.11
1614	天津景瀚瑞亨商贸有限公司	500	2016.8.25
1615	天津明宜装饰有限公司	100	2016.8.29
1616	天津圣光富商贸有限公司	200	2016.8.29
1617	天津市索利德石油工程技术服务有限公司	500	2016.8.10
1618	天津钰润电子科技有限公司	1000	2016.8.29

续表 16

序号	企业名称	注册资本（万元）	取照时间
1619	奥瀚科技（天津）有限公司	4000	2016.8.29
1620	迪诺安富（天津）环保科技有限公司	500	2016.9.8
1621	迪诺孚（天津）科技企业孵化器有限公司	500	2016.9.8
1622	天津广恒信息技术有限公司	200	2016.9.2
1623	天津瀚数科技有限公司	100	2016.9.2
1624	天津和东能源科技发展有限公司	200	2016.9.7
1625	天津红苹果国际贸易有限公司	10	2016.9.6
1626	尖叫（天津）健康科技有限公司	100	2016.8.30
1627	开财汽车销售有限公司	5000	2016.9.1
1628	天津市立山化工产品销售有限公司	200	2016.8.26
1629	天津龙湾黎明商务信息咨询有限公司	10	2016.9.6
1630	天津奇迹互娱网络科技有限公司	50	2016.9.7
1631	锐澳酒业（天津）有限公司	500	2016.9.5
1632	天津水之归处国际贸易有限公司	1000	2016.9.2
1633	天津拓远科技有限公司	50	2016.9.7
1634	天津物海化工产品销售有限公司	200	2016.9.1
1635	天津永众互联网信息服务中心（有限合伙）	15	2016.9.5
1636	天津耀阳船舶管理有限公司	206	2016.9.8
1637	宜信普惠信息咨询（北京）有限公司天津第四分公司	0	2016.9.6
1638	天津昌格昊特科技发展有限公司	100	2016.8.29
1639	天津鼎瑞商务信息咨询有限公司	10	2016.8.26
1640	天津光茂科技有限公司	500	2016.9.2
1641	天津垒猴科技有限公司	30	2016.9.1
1642	天津沃德昌格科技发展有限公司	100	2016.8.29
1643	天津康韵来科技有限公司	200	2016.9.8

续表 16

序号	企业名称	注册资本（万元）	取照时间
1644	天津瑞赛克环境科技有限公司	5000	2016.9.8
1645	天津才居建筑装饰工程有限公司	10	2016.9.2
1646	昌盛嘉禾（天津）科技有限公司	100	2016.8.29
1647	天津虹绽科技有限公司	5	2016.8.31
1648	天津路许科技有限公司	3	2016.9.14
1649	天津神竺科技有限公司	3	2016.9.14
1650	天基测绘（天津）有限公司	100	2016.9.12
1651	天津市同生赛富科技有限公司	100	2016.9.13
1652	天津市恒源诚信科技有限公司	100	2016.9.12
1653	天津薇薇餐饮管理有限公司	3	2016.9.18
1654	天津一诺企业管理咨询有限公司	50	2016.9.21
1655	天津鸿俊房地产经纪有限公司	100	2016.9.21
1656	荷华众创空间（天津）有限公司	500	2016.9.20
1657	荷中康复科技发展（天津）有限公司	500	2016.9.20
1658	天津壹昭科技有限公司	3	2016.9.18
1659	天津石头剪刀布教育科技有限公司	100	2016.9.18
1660	财隆（天津）科技有限公司	1000	2016.9.19
1661	逸海中欣（天津）影视文化传媒有限公司	1000	2016.9.18
1662	迪诺烯能（天津）照明科技有限公司	400	2016.9.18
1663	天津菲乐教育信息咨询有限公司	5	2016.9.14
1664	天津美女会文化传媒有限公司	100	2016.9.22
1665	天津鑫茂汇科技有限公司	200	2016.9.20
1666	天津知源蓝琪装饰有限公司	30	2016.9.28
1667	天津佰瑞铭岳文化传播有限公司	300	2016.9.14
1668	天津淳治商贸有限公司	1000	2016.9.14
1669	天津鼎弘馨商贸有限公司	500	2016.9.18

续表 16

序号	企业名称	注册资本（万元）	取照时间
1670	天津鑫富和商贸有限公司	500	2016.9.20
1671	天津九方文化传播有限公司	50	2016.10.08
1672	黑羚（天津）科技有限公司	100	2016.9.29
1673	天津海德润金属材料销售有限公司	500	2016.9.26
1674	天津千源进出口有限公司	200	2016.9.27
1675	世纪金光（天津）科技有限公司	1000	2016.9.27
1676	中安合众科技发展有限公司	10000	2016.9.26
1677	天津市源满汇庄商贸有限公司	30	2016.9.13
1678	天津优锐鸿腾科技有限公司	50	2016.9.12
1679	天津万也达商贸有限公司	500	2016.9.21
1680	天津泰和正义建材销售有限公司	1000	2016.9.18
1681	天津世纪同文房地产经纪有限公司	10	2016.9.22
1682	天津品仓科技有限公司	100	2016.9.19
1683	天津乐平津科技有限公司	50	2016.9.18
1684	天津红山红人造花贸易有限公司	50	2016.9.19
1685	天津浩晨建筑工程有限公司	818	2016.9.13
1686	天津富泰园林绿化工程有限公司	500	2016.9.21
1687	天津云渊企业管理咨询合伙企业（有限合伙）	100	2016.10.24
1688	天津益福商贸有限公司	80	2016.10.24
1689	天津引擎商务信息咨询有限公司	1000	2016.10.31
1690	天津三度食品贸易有限公司	100	2016.11.1
1691	天津红都刻章有限公司	100	2016.11.3
1692	天津坤晟科技发展有限公司	800	2016.10.31
1693	天津星品商贸有限公司	20	2016.10.28
1694	天津智兴通讯器材销售有限公司	200	2016.11.3
1695	摩德科技（天津）有限公司	827	2004.11.30

续表 16

序号	企业名称	注册资本（万元）	取照时间
1696	天津牛棚青创企业管理咨询有限公司	10	2016.9.27
1697	北京中环伟业文化发展有限责任公司天津分公司	0	2016.9.29
1698	车酷租车有限公司	5000	2016.9.26
1699	天津大用冷链物流有限公司	1000	2016.10.12
1700	天津贷驾网络科技有限公司	100	2016.10.10
1701	儿时农业科技（天津）有限公司	100	2016.10.8
1702	汉氏联合（天津）干细胞研究院有限公司	2000	2016.09.26
1703	莱特沃德复合材料（天津）有限公司	500	2016.09.30
1704	迈迪济森（天津）科技有限公司	300	2016.10.10
1705	华保鑫诺保险销售有限公司天津第一分公司	0	2016.9.22
1706	天津你爱你家房地产经纪有限公司	100	2016.9.30
1707	天津帕斯盛俊企业管理咨询合伙企业	30	2016.9.22
1708	三英精控（天津）仪器设备有限公司	1000	2016.9.27
1709	北京世纪朗通科技有限公司天津分公司	0	2016.10.9
1710	天津斯汀浩科技有限公司	3	2016.9.27
1711	苏州易德龙科技股份有限公司天津分公司	0	2016.9.23
1712	天津正千环保科技有限公司	500	2016.9.30
1713	天津雪妹商贸有限公司	3	2016.10.18
1714	天津妙语商务信息咨询有限公司	10	2016.10.18
1715	天津冉起教育科技有限公司	100	2016.10.18
1716	天津清净环保科技有限公司	3	2016.10.20
1717	天津市禺心科技有限公司	20	2016.10.19
1718	天津赛唐科技有限公司	100	2016.10.19
1719	天津漾雅商贸有限公司	20	2016.10.25

续表 16

序号	企业名称	注册资本（万元）	取照时间
1720	天津博兴建筑工程有限公司	2480	2016.10.26
1721	天津福泫科技有限公司	100	2016.10.25
1722	天津金亥科技有限公司	100	2016.10.25
1723	天津苒焉科技有限公司	100	2016.10.27
1724	天津昶赢企业管理咨询有限公司	500	2016.10.25
1725	天津瑞佳隆泰企业管理咨询合伙企业（有限合伙）	50	2016.10.19
1726	天津世研国际贸易有限公司	50	2016.10.18
1727	天津亿瑞房地产经纪有限公司	200	2016.10.20
1728	天津市雍信工程技术咨询有限公司	200	
1729	天津稚萃科技有限公司	100	2016.10.19
1730	中发智汇（天津）信息技术有限公司	5000	2016.10.13
1731	中青创服（天津）企业管理咨询有限公司	10	2016.11.1
1732	北京中盛永信科技发展有限公司天津分公司	0	2016.10.21
1733	臻一浤（天津）教育科技有限公司	3000	2016.11.1
1734	天津国晴商贸有限公司	3	2016.10.26
1735	科交汇知识产权代理（天津）有限公司	5000	2016.11.1
1736	天津安浩富佳教育信息咨询有限公司	3	2016.11.1
1737	天津梦宇科技有限公司	3	2016.10.17
1738	兰博文（天津）体育文化有限公司	500	2016.10.31
1739	国评（天津）知识产权评估有限公司	5000	2016.10.31
1740	天津麦多村淘商贸有限公司	3	2016.10.25
1741	天津楠怀商贸有限公司	3	2016.10.20
1742	天津新合文化传媒有限公司	3	2016.10.20
1743	天津红木科技有限公司	3	2016.10.24
1744	天津雨竹商贸有限公司	3	2016.11.4

续表 16

序号	企业名称	注册资本（万元）	取照时间
1745	精传（天津）广告传媒有限公司	1000	2016.11.3
1746	科兴基因技术（天津）有限公司	300	2016.11.3
1747	盾川（天津）科技有限公司	100	2016.10.28
1748	天津焦阳美晶商贸有限公司	3	2016.11.3
1749	天津恩昱科技有限公司	3	2016.10.13
1750	天津顺力科技有限公司	3	2016.10.12
1751	天津馨鑫装饰设计有限公司	100	2016.10.19
1752	迈克博（天津）生物产业研究院有限公司	1000	2016.11.4
1753	中盈科创（天津）知识产权服务有限公司	15000	2016.10.31
1754	丁丁法律服务（天津）有限公司	100	2016.11.8
1755	明佳巴巴（天津）企业管理咨询有限公司	6000	2016.11.10
1756	天津锋芝商贸有限公司	3	2016.11.8
1757	镜面品牌管理（天津）有限公司	75	2016.11.9
1758	名动时代（天津）科技有限公司	100	2016.11.7
1759	天津自由人服饰有限公司	500	2016.11.11
1760	天津天梦服饰有限公司	100	2016.11.11
1761	沛宇（天津）科技有限公司	1000	2016.11.11
1762	纳瑟科技（天津）有限公司	100	2016.11.15
1763	普睿英（天津）科技有限公司	1200	2016.10.19
1764	粤厨鲜（天津）餐饮服务有限公司	100	2016.10.17
1765	中青创投（天津）投资管理有限公司	200	2016.8.26
1766	智语（天津）国际贸易有限公司	1000	2016.11.14
1767	天津明智拓泓企业管理咨询中心（有限合伙）	5500	2016.11.15
1768	天津浪漫小屋儿童娱乐有限公司	50	2016.11.18

续表 16

序号	企业名称	注册资本（万元）	取照时间
1769	天津东润梵建筑工程有限公司	500	2016.11.18
1770	天津永腾室内装饰设计有限公司	3	2016.11.22
1771	天津巴德科技有限公司	3	2016.11.25
1772	天津至诚真合商贸有限公司	200	2016.5.31
1773	天津市达锦商贸有限公司	100	2014.3.4
1774	思瑞原创（天津）科技有限公司	1000	2016.5.25
1775	天津筑宇物业管理有限公司	100	2016.4.21
1776	天津汇天商务信息咨询有限公司	50	2016.10.26
1777	天津市鸿盛信达商贸有限公司	30	2016.11.9
1778	圣火（天津）太阳能设备有限公司	1000	2016.9.8
1779	圣火（天津）环保设备有限公司	1000	2016.9.21
1780	天津坤舆万国企业管理咨询有限公司	100	2016.9.19
1781	天津市溪堃建筑工程有限公司	100	2015.4.28
1782	天津天肽生物科技有限公司	5000	2015.9.7
1783	天津艾祯汐网络科技有限公司	50	2014.11.13
1784	天津融德财务咨询有限公司	100	2016.7.27
1785	威尔罗斯（天津）科技有限公司	100	2016.4.13
1786	天津妙法生物科技有限公司	180	2016.3.23
1787	淳清源（天津）生物科技有限公司	180	2016.3.23
1788	天津宜和东方电子商务有限公司	180	2016.3.23
1789	景泽科技（天津）有限公司	30	2014.3.11
1790	天津三一友泰科技有限公司	100	2014.5.30
1791	天津宏泰国际货运代理有限公司	500	2014.10.20
1792	天津迈珂琳生物科技有限公司	500	2015.7.10
1793	天津林格贝医药科技有限公司	100	2016.12.30
1794	天津尹洛琪食品销售有限公司	300	2016.1.3
1795	天津肌活科技发展有限公司	104.72	2015.6.25

续表 16

序号	企业名称	注册资本（万元）	取照时间
1796	来特威科技（天津）有限公司	500	2015.10.30
1797	上海玺宠商务信息咨询有限公司天津武清分公司	0	2016.12.30
1798	天津金阔商务信息咨询有限公司	300	2016.12.12
1799	天津淘大电子商务有限公司	100	2015.10.27
1800	天津洛莱科技有限公司	100	2016.12.22
1801	天津市欣百伦科技有限公司	3500	2016.12.30
1802	雨田科技（天津）有限公司	100	2016.12.28
1803	盘古啤酒（天津）有限公司	200	2016.12.28
1804	天津查古文化发展有限公司	300	2016.12.27
1805	遇优商务信息咨询（天津）有限公司	200	2016.12.20
1806	天津云飞雨凝科技中心（有限合伙）	100	2016.12.20
1807	中健华科（天津）生物科技有限公司	5000	2016.12.21
1808	天津灵瞳众智科技中心（有限合伙）	100	2016.12.15
1809	凯峰商务信息咨询（天津）有限公司	100	2016.12.20
1810	天津津爱红木家具销售有限公司	1000	2016.12.23
1811	天津普罗斯科技有限公司	50	2016.12.19
1812	天津市华佗建设工程有限公司	10000	2016.11.22
1813	天津月皓广告有限公司	100	2016.11.22
1814	天津惠闪科技有限公司	100	2016.11.30
1815	天津栩栩科技有限公司	500	2016.12.1
1816	京明华（天津）科技发展有限公司	1000	2016.11.30
1817	中善海思（天津）科技有限公司	1000	2016.12.14
1818	天津寰宇地理信息有限公司	1000	2016.12.15
1819	遇优教育科技（天津）有限公司	100	2016.12.14
1820	二五八众创空间（天津）有限公司	100	2016.12.30
1821	天津新耀德辉生产力促进有限公司	200	2016.11.30

续表 16

序号	企业名称	注册资本（万元）	取照时间
1822	天津于蓝生物科技有限公司	3000	2015.11.17
1823	中科日晟（天津）光伏发电设备有限公司	3000	2016.11.18
1824	良日优捷（天津）物流有限公司	100	2013.4.3
1825	红杉软件与技术服务有限公司	5000	2016.12.1
1826	天津共享际科技有限公司	500	2016.11.24
1827	澳普林特（天津）电子材料有限公司	1000	2016.12.14
1828	天津荣元信息咨询中心（有限合伙）	10	2016.12.20
1829	致海通达（天津）商务信息咨询有限公司	10	2016.12.22
1830	天津津瑞祥硕农业科技有限公司	300	2016.12.23
1831	天津天桃农业科技有限公司	1000	2016.11.21
1832	天津恒华瑞诚商业管理有限公司	1000	2016.12.15
1833	拓城必达（天津）企业管理咨询有限公司	500	2016.12.7

第五篇

金　融

20世纪90年代初，武清开发区建立。随着项目的引进，金融、保险业开始在区内建立、发展。国有银行、股份制银行等金融机构相继进入，形成了开发区的金融、保险业。

第一章 银行

中国建设银行、中国农业银行、中国银行、中国工商银行、中信银行、天津农商银行等银行分行在武清开发区设有分支机构，为区内企业办理开户（包括人民币、外币）信贷和各种结算业务。

第一节 中国建设银行武清开发区支行

中国人民建设银行武清支行是最早进入武清开发区的金融机构，于1992年开始筹建，1993年3月正式成立中国人民建设银行天津市分行武清县支行高新技术产业园区办事处，办公地址位于武清高新技术产业园区出口京津公路旁。

1996年随着中国人民建设银行更名为中国建设银行，中国人民建设银行天津市分行武清县支行高新技术产业园区办事处同时更名为中国建设银行天津市分行武清支行高新技术产业园区办事处。2000年改为分理处。2004年12月升格为中国建设银行股份有限公司天津武清开发区支行。至2016年有员工9人。

管理人员变动情况：

1993年3月—1996年8月：主任：关士维，副主任：高会芬

1996年8月—1998年2月：副主任（主持工作）：高会芬

1998年2月—2001年4月：主任：朱永秋，副主任：高会芬

2001年4月—2008年6月：主任（行长）：白雪松，副主任（副行长）：高会芬

2008年6月—2010年3月：行长：周德芝，副行长：梁勇

2010 年 3 月—2012 年 4 月：副行长（主持工作）：梁勇

2012 年 4 月—2012 年 8 月：副行长（主持工作）：李晓东

2012 年 8 月—2016 年 6 月：行长：李晓东 副行长：胡志祥

2016 年 6 月—：行长：孙元锋 副行长：胡志祥

主营业务

中国建设银行天津武清开发区支行紧跟武清开发区总公司招商方向，2000 年前，支行累计向“三区一园”的企业和开发区单位提供贷款 6 亿元，支持园区的标准厂房建设、供水工程、供热供气工程、污水处理工程等多个基础设施建设项目，同时支持区内 13 家创利税好的企业，为 40 家企业办理外汇存贷、汇款、国际结算汇票据的承兑、贴现、外汇担保、结汇、售汇、资信调查、鉴证等业务。几年来累计放外汇贷款 300 万美元。

进入 21 世纪以来，特别是 2013 年开始对公业务营销迎来爆发式增长。在 2013 年至 2016 年间，世界 500 强佛吉亚公司、赛科希德医疗器械研发生产基地项目、中际联合高空安全装备天津项目、中医联合实验室主体公司、艺龙网、赫基集团、经纬集团、新疆生产建设兵团、南海控股集团、欧华美科集团、阿芙精油等相关子公司落户支行。支行积累了大量大客户、集团客户服务经验，且为相关公司搭建现金管理平台、银企直联等系统。

2015 年，开发区支行全口径存款余额 69293 万元，较上年年末增长 3515 万元；其中企业存款时点余额 53351 万元，较上年年末增加 5390 万元，储蓄存款时点余额 15942 万元，较上年年末减少 1875 万元；公司机构类客户账户新增 320 户。

截至 2016 年 12 月 31 日，开发区支行全口径存款余额 79392 万元，较上年末新增 10155 万元。其中企业存款时点余额 57957 万元，较上年年末新增 4606 万元，日均余额 55049 万元，较上年年末新增 803 万元；储蓄存款时点余额 21435 万元，较上年年末新增 5549 万元，日均余额 18973 万元，较上年年末新增 2282 万元。全年新增账户 529 个。

第二节 中国农业银行武清开发区支行

机构

1994 年年初，中国农业银行天津分行武清支行设立武清开发区营业部，并正式开办外汇业务。1996 年农村金融体制改革，武清辖内农村合作金融、商业性金融、政策性金融实行“一分一脱”，信用合作联社从农行分离出去，另组班子，独立经营；同时新组建农业发展银行。至此，农业银行开始从职能和业务发展上向国有商业银行转化。2002 年始，中国农业银行天津分行实行机构升格，武清开发区支行作为武清支行下辖机构的营业单位升格为二级支行，升格后依旧隶属武清支行。

截至 2016 年年底，武清开发区支行拥有在职员工 26 人，党支部书记兼网点负责人，办公地址为杨村街道泉州北路 6 号，紧邻开发区管委会；业务范围较广，涉及经营存款、贷款、国际结算、代理保险、代理收付、代发工资、代理发行国家债券等业务。

主营业务

农行武清开发区支行业务涵盖公司业务、资产业务、国际业务、零售业务，为园区内企事业单位、员工及附近居民提供支付结算、国际贸易、各类贷款、投资理财等全面支持。

1. 公司业务。账户业务：公司账户结算服务，存款人可以办理日常转账结算和现金收付业务；现金管理业务：账户收付款服务，投融资服务、供应链金融服务等；电子银行业务：企业网上银行、掌上银行服务，可为企业提供电子渠道账户管理，电子回单、代发工资、投资理财、票据业务等；电子商务业务：集供应链管理、多渠道支付结算、线上线下协同发展云服务等一体定制化商务金融云服务。

2. 零售业务。为个人客户提供存取款、外汇、信用卡、电子银行、理财、基金、贵金属等服务。

3. 资产业务。为客户提供担保承诺类、投资银行类、融资类业务。

4. 国际业务。跨境结售汇、跨境参融通、内保外贷业务、信用证、押汇业务及外汇票据托收 / 光票托收等。

2010—2016 年农业银行武清开发区支行存、贷款余额统计表

表 17

年份	存款年末余额（万元）		银行贷款年末余额（万元）		
	人民币	美元	人民币		美元
			总额	其中：固定资产贷款余额	
2010	183495	818	317348	288120	133
2011	148638	1950	393939	358046	141
2012	202424	1666	309273	263152	89
2013	220176	1282	211576	197147	70
2014	227066	1116	200517	197782	63
2015	201761	1255	191002	176600	109
2016	224984	1744	294887	247005	17

第三节 中国银行武清开发区支行

中国银行天津武清开发区支行于 1995 年 9 月 22 日获得中国人民银行天津市分行同意设立的批复，1996 年 3 月 8 日正式成立。自成立以来，中行武清开发区支行从无到有，从小到大，资产负债规模和综合收入水平稳步提高。特别是 2007 年以来的十年间，中行武清开发区支行进入了快速发展期。

2012 年，中行开发区支行迁入目前营业行址，截至 2016 年已发展成为兼具储蓄、对公结算、国际业务、中小企业金融服务于一身的综合性服务网点。

2007—2016 年中行武清开发区支行各项指标统计表

表 18　　单位：万元

年份	2007	2008	2009	2010	2011	2012	2013	2014	2015	2016
存款（万元）	40150	44611	49568	55075	61195	67994	75549	83944	93271	103634
贷款（万元）	35390	39322	43691	48546	53939	59933	66592	73991	82212	91347
税前利润	1511	1679	1865	2072	2303	2559	2843	3159	3510	3900

第四节　中国工商银行天津高科技园区支行

中国工商银行股份有限公司天津高科技园区支行成立于 1997 年 7 月 17 日，位于天津市武清开发区福源道北侧金融商务楼，2016 年有员工 19 人，建筑面积 1844.20 平方米。主营业务包括：办理人民币存款、贷款、结算业务；办理票据贴现；代理发行金融债券；代理发行、代理兑付、销售政府债券；买卖政府债券；代理收付款项；代理保险业务；外向储蓄；外币兑换；外汇存款；外汇贷款；外汇汇款；国际结算；办理结汇、售汇业务；通过上级行办理代客外汇买卖业务；个人实盘外汇买卖；代理国外信用卡付款；代收及兑付外币旅行支票；外币票据的承兑和贴现等。

截至 2016 年年底，中国工商银行天津高科技园区支行已为武清开发区园内 1000 余家企业开立了单位结算账户，本外币存款余额已超 43 亿多元。中国工商银行天津高科技园区支行一直秉承“客户至上”的服务理念，为武清开发区园内企业和周边个人客户提供安全、便捷、高效的金融服务。

2012—2016 年天津高科技园区支行存款贷款情况统计表

表 19

年份	存款（万元）	贷款（万元）
2012	354478	263492
2013	388982	314466
2014	426969	333456
2015	434530	484702
2016	431799	551593

第五节　中信银行天津武清支行

中信银行天津武清支行位于武清开发区福源道北侧金融商务楼 1－103、1－203 号，于 2012 年 8 月 23 日正式对外营业。截至 2016 年年底，支行员工 27 人，其中中共党员 11 人。设置对公、零售、会计三个业务部门。支行自开业以来，不断完善管理措施，加强员工培训，提高服务水平，拓展业务渠道，以“服务武清发展、融入武清发展、助推武清发展”为宗旨，充分发挥自身优势，满足区内居民金融需求，支持和服务武清经济建设，为全区百姓、为驻区企业、为武清发展提供最优质的服务。开业以来各项业务快速平稳发展，整体资产质量保持良好，未发生不良贷款情况。

公司业务：政府融资平台资源深度挖掘业绩翻番。2016 年，武清支行进入第四个发展年度，在前三年机构业务形成良好发展态势的基础上，乘势而上，通过“综合融资服务”的方式为区内重点平台客户提供资金支持，拉动支行存款规模大幅提升。公司业务发展模式改革创新效果明显，经过近一年时间的试行，无论是在内部分工协作上，还是在客户营销效果上，均取得了较好的成效。综合盈利能力经济利润规模再创新高，实现了经济利润的大幅增长。

零售业务：积极拓展零售业务，提高服务品质，主要表现在以下几个方面：结合目前发展趋势，加强电子银行业务发展；组织信用卡公私联动、全员营销动员，提高支行信用卡；突破基金销售，取得客户认可；服务品质方面突飞猛进增长，获得社会群众的认可。

管理工作：进一步加强各项党建工作，增强员工的凝聚力和战斗力，为实现武清支行的经营目标，统一了思想，打下了良好的基础。加强风险合规及企业文化建设，将风险文化建设作为一项常态化工作来进行。大力支持运营条线的各项工作，通过梳理内部业务流程，最大限度的避免了道德风险和操作风险的发生。在授信业务方面，贷前要求客户经理对客户做到充分的尽职调查，提高个人工作素质以提升风险识别能力；在操作环节加强内部审批制度以避免操作风险；贷后方面加强了统一管理工作，由专人对贷后工作进行管理，以避免出现贷后风险。

截至 2013 年年底，对公存款时点达到 9.35 亿元，零售管理资产余额达到 3.01 亿元。累计投放人民币贷款 1.8 亿元。

截至 2014 年年底，对公存款时点达到 22.2 亿元，零售管理资产余额 2.91 亿元；各项贷款 8.76 亿元。

截至 2015 年年底，对公存款时点达到 19.86 亿元，零售个人存款时点达到 1.73 亿元；各项贷款 22.16 亿元。

截至 2016 年年底，对公存款时点达到 38.83 亿元，零售个人存款时点达到 1.38 亿元；各项贷款 26.83 亿元。

第六节　天津农商银行武清开发区支行

2001 年 12 月 4 日，依据中国人民银行天津分行下发的《关于天津市武清区开发区农村信用社开业的批复》天津市武清区开发区农村信用合作社成立。

2005 年 12 月，天津市武清区开发区农村信用合作社更名为天津市武清区农村信用合作联社开发区信用社。

2010 年 7 月，天津市武清区农村信用合作联社开发区信用社更名为天津农村商业银行股份有限公司武清开发区支行（简称天津农商银行武清开发区支行），机构地址为天津市武清区开发区卧龙潭公寓公建楼。经营范围：办理经天津农村商业银行股份有限公司授权的吸收本外币公众存款；发放本外币短期、中期和长期贷款；办理国内结算；办理票据承兑与贴现；代理发行、代理兑付；承销政府债券；买卖政府债券、金融债券；从事银行卡业务；代理收付款项及代理保险业务；外汇汇率、外币兑换；经中国银行业监督管理委员会批准的其他业务。

2001—2016 年天津农商银行武清开发区支行经营情况一览表

表 20　　单位：万元

年份	现金收入	现金支出	存款	贷款	利润
2001	346	325	2438	0	1
2002	19162	19161	5797	397	88
2003	32810	32709	12562	9001	22
2004	36741	36772	15657	12855	177
2005	47114	47153	16211	12444	76
2006	48960	48929	20635	12061	526
2007	41153	41132	21439	14728	868
2008	42569	42601	17174	13861	909
2009	40779	40728	40888	11346	715
2010	35336	35381	31502	50625	1158
2011	47973	47932	13376	48478	2449

续表 20

年份	现金收入	现金支出	存款	贷款	利润
2012	28111	28173	18196	40699	1118
2013	38928	37845	241479	25497	1614
2014	40646	40610	36101	64281	2052
2015	34173	34208	45196	115770	4441
2016	51999	52004	25672	75295	2580

第二章　保险

中国人民保险公司、中国平安保险公司、中国太平洋保险公司等保险公司天津分公司和天津市社会保险公司在开发区建立之初即设有分支机构和办事处，为入区企业和干部职工提供货物运输保险（包括海上、陆上、航空运输货物保险）、建筑工程和安装工程保险（一切险）、财产保险（包括财产险、财产一切险）、人身保险、医疗保险、机动车保险、雇主责任保险、职工养老保险等业务。现主要有人保开发区营销服务部。

第一节　中国人民保险公司武清支公司开发区营销服务部

中国人民保险公司天津市武清区公司为全民所有制企业，隶属于中国人民保险公司天津市分公司，经营各种财产保险和人寿保险，是最早在武清恢复办理保险业务的一家保险公司，在全区的保险市场占据着主渠道的作用。经过多年发展，公司取得了长足的进步。

下属单位开发区营销服务部坐落于武清开发区，该部自 2003 年 5 月成立以来，为武清开发区总公司、天狮集团、绫致时装、天鹅湖、麦格昆磁、杰麦、正威等机关、企业单位提供了财产保险、车辆保险、责任保险、船舶货运险、健康意外伤害保险、保证保险等六大类 120 多个险种的风险保障 1200 多亿元，累计支付赔款达 5000 多万元，为园区的快速发展起到了保驾护航、造福企业和职工的良好作用。

第二节　工伤保险

工伤也称职业伤害。是指劳动者在工作或者其他职业活动中因意外事故和职业病造成的伤害或死亡。工伤保险是社会保险的一个组成部分。它通过社会统筹建立工伤保险基金，为因工伤残和患职业病以及由于这两种原因而死亡的职工，遗属提供社会保险。它包括医疗救治、职业康复和必要的物质补偿。

工伤保险有四个特点：一是强制性。它是由国家立法强制执行，在一定范围内的用人单位、职工必须参加；二是非营利性。工伤保险是国家对劳动者履行的社会责任，也是劳动者应该享受的基本权利，工伤保险不以营利为目的；三是保障性。是指劳动者在发生工伤事故后，对劳动者或其遗属发放的工伤待遇要保障其基本生活；四是互助互济性。是指通过征缴保险费建立工伤保险基金，由社会保险机构在人员之间、地区之间、行业之间对费用实行再分配，调剂使用资金。

中国的工伤保险制度首次立法于新中国成立初期。1951 年 2 月 26 日，中国政府为保护工人职员的健康，减轻他们生活中的困难，依据当时经济条件，由政务院公布《中华人民共和国劳动保险条例》（以下简称《条例》）。这部综合性法规主要包括养老保险、医疗保险、工伤保险和生育保险等内容，初步形成了中国的社会保险体系。条例规定"有工人、职员一百人以上的国营、公私合营、私营及合作社经营的工厂、矿场及其附属单位（包括铁路、航运、邮电的各企业单位与附属单位；工、矿、交通事业的基本建设单位；国营建筑公司）的工人与职员（包括学徒）不分民族、工龄、性别和国籍，符合工伤保险条件的，享受工伤保险待遇"。1953 年政务院对该《条例》进行修正公布试行，后来发布的《劳动保险条例实施细则》对工伤保险等问题作了较为详细的规定。这些法规一直沿用至 1996 年 12 月 31 日。计划经济时期，符合《条例》条件的企业执行该《条例》。1985 年起，企业职工工伤费用由所在单位负担，医疗费全额报销，工伤期间工资照发。医疗终结，完全丧失劳动能力的办理退休手续。

根据《劳动法》相关规定，为了保障劳动者在工作中遭受事故伤害和患职业病后获得医疗救治、经济补偿和职业康复的权利，分散工作风险，促进工伤预防，1996 年 10 月 1 日，劳动部制定《企业职工工伤保险试行办法》（劳字 [1996]266 号），《试行办法》实施后，工伤职工待遇有较大提高。

2003 年 4 月 16 日，国务院第 5 次常务会议讨论通过《工伤保险条例》，温家宝总理签署国务院令（第 375 号）予以公布，自 2004 年 1 月 1 日起实行。《工伤保险条例》适用范围涵盖"中华人民共和国境内的各类企业、有雇工的个体工商户（以下称用人单位）"。上述单位"应当依照本条例规定参加工伤保险，为本单位全部职工或者雇工（以下称职工）缴纳工伤保险费"。"中华人民共和国境内的各类企业的职工和个体工商户的雇工，均有依照本条例的规定享受工伤保险待遇的权利"。各省、自治区、直辖市人民政府决定"有雇工的个体工商户参加工伤保险的具体步骤实施办法"。

第六篇

经济综合管理

武清开发区是 1991 年 12 月 28 日经国务院批准建立的首批国家级高新技术产业开发区之一，是天津市高新技术产业园区武清开发区和武清经济开发区的合称。开发区坐落在城区北侧，京津塘高速公路旁。规划总面积 24.8 平方公里，首期开发的 6.4 平方公里由 3 平方公里的高新技术产业区、2 平方公里的经济产业区和为产业区配套的 1.4 平方公里的生活区组成。

开发区遵循“着眼长远，适当超前，综合起步，滚动开发”的发展思路，自 1992 年 4 月正式启动以来，坚持基础设施和招商引资两手抓，在实际运作中做到“征用一片，开发一片，建成一片，收益一片”，由小到大，滚动发展。建区的当年便完成了“五通一平”（即给水、排水、电力、供热、通讯和土地平整）0.96 平方公里。吸引中外企业 43 家，引资 9.2 亿元，其中外资 9100 万美元。至 1993 年，“五通一平”面积扩大到 2.5 平方公里。完成了全区路网、管网综合规划和中心区、生活区规划。发展了国内外招商代理机构，设立了北京招商部，并与国家及京津两市侨联、台联等十几个团体及涉外机构建立了协作关系，吸纳了一批规模大、起点高的企业入区。1993 年新增入区企业 68 家，协议投资 15 亿元，其中外资 1.15 亿美元。

开发区无论是规划、建设，还是对企业的服务，全部围绕着“以经济建设为中心”这条主线开展。在招商中，以吸引产业项目、高新技术项目为主，做到以企业立区、以企业立业、以企业立命。至 2000 年，开发区为投资者提供包括道路、供水、给水、排水、供电、供热、通信、供气等基础设施条件。区内建成棋盘式路网，公路密度 8 公里 / 平方公里。建有地下水和引滦（滦河水）地表水厂各 1 座，可提供标准自来水，日供水能力 7 万立方米。采用雨污分流体系，分别纳入区内雨水系统和污水处理系统。华北、京津塘 2 大电网为开发区提供电力能源。建有 8 万门 IDD 的电信中心，数字微波、光纤电缆、数据专线等现代化手段齐全的通讯系统。海关、工商、税务、公安、金融、保险等部门在区内设有分支服务机构。

2000 年 12 月，开发区管委会进行调整，办公室和总公司下设 7 部 4 个直属公司，即招商部、企业管理部、规划建设部、综合部、财务部、城市管理部、劳动就业部；物业公司、热力公司、自来水公司、园林绿化工程公司。开发区总公司对入区企业提供“一条龙”服务和“一站式”办公，实行“封闭式”管理。随着开发区体量的增大和事业的发展，开发区将管理部门扩大到 16 部、2 中心、2 组、2 处、5 直属公司的格局，实施对开发区全方位的经济技术和行政管理。即党建工作部、综合服务部、招商部、资本运营部、经济运行部、预决算部、招标采购部、规划设计部、工程管理部、科技服务部、人力资源部、企业管理部、安全发展部、城市管理部、二次开发部、法务部，自贸区（武清园）招商服务中心、行政服务中心，生物医药产业重大项目工作组、智能制造产业重大项目工作组，德国代表处、珠三角办事处，自来水公司、绿化公司、热力公司、工业物业公司、开发区物业公司。

在各项经济管理中，各部门强化服务理念，加强信息化建设，依法依规办事，提高工作效率，促进了开发区经济的高速发展。

第一章　计划管理

第一节　五年计划的编制与执行

五年计划编制，以武清区（含原来的县）规划局、统计局为主，开发区内各职能部门配合完成。从武清开发区 1991 年 12 月经国务院批准建立，经过一个八年开发建设时期，至 2016 年，先后编制执行了“十五”“十一五”“十二五”“十三五”四个五年计划。

开发区设有规划设计部，具体负责开发区的总体规划、控制性详细规划、城市设计导则、土地细分导则的制订及控制管理工作；负责区内远景、市政、景观、产业等各专项规划的制订及控制管理工作等。

武清开发区“十五”计划及 2015 年发展规划设想

一、发展现状

武清开发区于 1991 年 12 月经国务院批准建立。规划控制面积 24.8 平方公里，首期开发 6.4 平方公里。经过八年的开发建设，开发区已具一定规模。

1. 投入 6 亿元用于基础设施和配套设施建设。

（1）基础设施：完成了 6.4 平方公里区域的道路、综合管线开发建设，具备了生产经营条件。区内建成 35 千伏安变电站两座，220 千伏安变电站一座；8 万门电讯大楼一座；日供水 6 万吨净水厂和万吨地下水源厂各一座；开凿地热井两眼，供地热水 175 吨 / 小时；建四座供热站，供热能力 150 蒸吨。累计铺架热力管网 44 公里，供热面积达到 45 万平方米；铺设给水管线 34 公里，雨水管道 47 公里，污水管线 43 公里，建设道路 32 公里。

（2）公共服务设施：经国家批准建立了中华人民共和国武清海关，可为区内外进出口企业提供便捷的通关服务；中国银行、建设银行、工商银行、农业银行等金融部门在区内分别设有办事机构；派出所、国税所、地税所已挂牌服务；建筑面积 5000 余平米的创新大楼为开发区高新技术产品的孵化基地。天鹅湖度假村、海关培训中心、白天鹅酒店可提供培训、住宿、餐饮、娱乐等服务。此外，开发区总公司自建的 8 万平方米标准厂房可出租、出售。

（3）居住区配套：开发区 1.4 平方公里的生活区是主要居住区。2016 年，生活区 30 余万平方米的栖仙公寓、别墅已经投入使用。为生活区配套的家乐联锁超市已经开业。英华双语制小学部于 2000 年 8 月 28 日正式开学。

（4）市政、市容：开发区主要道路已实现了夜间照明，主要道路交叉口设立了交通警示灯。开发区东、南两个进出口安装了大型龙门架。开发区建有公建绿地三处，主要道路的绿化、美化工程基本完成。全区绿化面积 100 余万平方米，实现了便道硬化。

2. 招商引资：截至 2000 年 10 月，开发区已吸引来自国内及世界 21 个国家和地区的 320 余家企业入区，其中合资企业 59 家，独资企业 87 家。协议吸引内资 15 亿多元，外资 5.2 亿美元，资金到位率为 80%。世界著名公司，如日本的大真空、住友、丸红、大荣、依都锦，瑞典的斯维达拉集团，丹麦的丹佛斯，美国的麦格昆磁、华兰德，芬兰的瑞特格，加拿大的国际济丰，韩国的 LG，中国（台湾）光宝电子、杰麦集团等在区内注册投资。国内科研机构和大专院校企业，如天津大学三英焊业公司、海华制药公司、新北洋化工公司以及天狮集团、娃哈哈集团、名门饲料等新兴的民营企业在开发区内也得到了健康发展。开发区产业以电子、机电一体化、生物工程、医药、新型建材为主，涌现了一批技术含量高、附加值高的产品，如 VCD、水晶振子、光二级管、变频器、药芯焊丝、钕铁硼、生物制药等。同时，市场占有率较高的乐器、食品、服装等经济型项目也在开发区得到了较大的发展。

3. 经济发展：开业企业 110 余家，累计完成技工贸总收入 90 余亿元，出口额 30 多亿元，缴纳税金 6 亿元，解决就业 17000 余人。

4. 存在问题：基础设施、配套设施功能需进一步完善；人员素质、管理、服务水平有待提高。

二、发展规划

1. 发展思路：以招商引资为中心，注重社会效益和经济效益，重点发展电子信息、新材料和生物与医药三大主导产业。在全面促进入区企业健康发展的同时，侧重扶植已具规模，有市场，有发展潜力的企业向集团化发展。通过建立和引进社会化服务体系，加快高新技术产业化步伐，尽快形成和积聚高新技术产业规模和优势，带动武清区社会经济全面上水平。

2. 阶段性目标：2000 至 2002 年内，按照区委、区政府确定的“二、四、五、十”发展目标，将开发区 6.4 平方公里开发完毕并摆满项目。2003—2005 年，开始沿京津塘高速公路南至逸仙园界区域内发展，初步形成京津塘高速公路产业带上的新技术产业园区。2006—2015 年，按开发区的总体发展规划布局，以京津塘高速公路为对称轴向北发展，不断扩大区域规模。

3. 规划指标：

（1）2000—2005 年

建设：投入建设资金 5 亿元，重点用于完善 6.4 平方公里起步区和二期发展初期的基础设施和配套设施建设。完成工业用地中泉达路以西至逸仙园界 2 平方公里范围内的开发。结合招商引资，建立高标准的电子信息产业园、生物医药产业园和新材料产业园。

招商：2002 年以前，把 6.4 平方公里范围内未出让的 157 万平方米土地全部摆满项目。至 2005 年累计利用外资额达到 8 亿美元。

经济指标：以 2000 年指标为基数，按照年平均增长 10% 的速度，到 2005 年，地区生产总值完成 9.2 亿元，技工贸总收入达到 47 亿元，出口供货额 18 亿元，利润额 2 亿元，上缴税金 2 .9 亿元，区内从业人员达到 2.8 万人，其中大专以上人员 9000 人。

（2）2006—2015 年

以京津塘高速公路为对称轴向北发展，规划建设科研区、展览区、生活配套区等公建设施，吸引京津地区的技术成果和力量，大力发展以电子信息、新材料、生物与医药为主导的高新技术产业。至 2015 年累计利用外资额达到 15 亿美元。各项经济指标以 2005 年指标为基数，按照年平均增长 15% 的速度，地区生产总值达到 37 亿元，技工贸总收入达到 189 亿元，出口供货额 72 亿元，利润总额 8 亿元，上缴税金 11.7 亿元，区内从业人员总数达到 5 万人，使武清开发区成为设施齐全、功能完善、环境优美、高效益的科技园区。

三、措施保证

（一）注重总体规划并以规划为先导，完善基础设施、配套设施建设，突出城市规模和功能，提高环境档次。

1. 规划：完成 24.8 平方公里控制规划；6.4 平方公里供热、供电、通讯、绿化专业规划；完善生活区、中心区详规；着手进行高速路以北生活区、展览区、科研区的规划工作。

2. 基础设施建设: 8.4 平方公里范围内的道路、管网骨架全部建成; 新打地热井一眼、供热站三座，完成 110 千伏安变电站一座，配合陕气入杨工程做好区内供气工程。

3. 配套设施建设: 用 7 年左右的时间把 1.4 平方公里的生活区全部开发、配套完毕。在现有基础上，新增居住面积 30 万平方米；建设高档次中学和幼儿园各一座；完成天鹅湖度假村工程和海关培训中心工程建设，进一步完善中心区整体服务功能；完善中心区科研、信息、配套功能建设，强化科技孵化和产业化服务功能；加大绿化、美化环境投入，新增绿化面积 30 万平方米，完成所有道路标志牌工程。

（二）以招商为中心，注重经济与社会效益，灵活方法，保证招商的可持续发展。

1. 灵活招商方法，用足、用活现有政策，突出实效。充分研究和把握加入 WTO 的历史性机遇，把吸引跨国公司同引入国营大企业、民营企业相结合，把现实注册与长远招商相结合；把全面招商与侧重吸引相结合，加快招商进程。

2. 积极打造品牌，发挥总体环境优越的招商优势。在原有招商网络和信息渠道的基础上，结合开发区的综合环境优势，进行大规模的宣传，树立招商品牌。充分发挥互联网这一资源，加大管理与建设的投入，使网络成为公司对外宣传、对外招商的强有力的阵地。

3. 进一步完善招商走向市场的机制，本着向市场要成果，要效益的原则，加大招商的激励程度，调动招商人员的积极性。同时，招商人员的素质要不断提高，适应新的形势需要。

（三）建立和引进社会化服务体系，全面扶持企业发展，加快高新技术产业化步伐。

通过各种形式建立和引进更多的全面的高水平的服务项目入区。重点建立与引进项目有：

1. 建立和引进科技企业基金，吸引科技成果和科技人才入区。

2. 建立和引进风险投资基金，扶持高科技成果的产品转化。

3. 建立和引进担保基金，为企业开辟融资渠道。

4. 建立和引进信息、人才中心，为企业提供便利。

以上项目可作为招商项目进行招商，适时也可以采用市场项目招标。

（四）继续完善和创新管理机制，保持发展的比较优势。

1. 健全开发区管理服务机构，增强服务功能，提高管理专业化水平。不断学习和借鉴外地成功经验，在实践中摸索现代化城市管理模式。

2. 牢固树立“管理即服务”思想，千方百计扶植企业发展。坚持先放开、后引导，先发展、后受益原则，做到扶植企业发展在前，完善管理在后；让利在前，收益在后。提高对企业服务的主动性、全面性。在全面促进企业发展的同时，有针对性地对已经形成规模，市场前景好，有发展潜力的企业向集团化发展，结合主板、二板市场，帮助这些企业集团上市。

3. 完善开发区招聘、培养、使用的用人机制，强化人的素质培养，突出人的特长，不断调整和注入新的活力，始终保持一支适应开发区发展需要的廉洁、高效、精力旺盛的生力军，保证开发区各项工作的顺利进行。

武清开发区十一五规划

一、指导思想

坚持科学发展观，结合全区及开发区实际，突出抓好招商引资、城市建设、改善环境三个重点，努力创建全国一流开发区，进一步发挥开发区对全区经济和社会发展的带动辐射作用，为武清经济社会发展做出应有的贡献。

二、发展目标

把武清开发区建设成为京津之间最具实力和竞争力的园林式、现代化、科技产业新城区，使开发区真正成为带动辐射全区经济的龙头，对外开放的窗口和武清城区一道靓丽的风景。

全面地、高质量地完成一、二期 13.3 平方公里的开发建设任务，自 2007 年起，开始启动三期建设。2006—2010年，预计招商引资180亿元（注：以2005年实现注册资本20亿元，每年平均递增20%计算）。税收至2010年预计可达14.1亿元(按每年15%增幅计算，2005年实施独立财政体制的基数7亿元)。就业总人数达6万人。

三、发展方向和重点

1. 努力建设环保型、生态型、效益型开发区，提高项目质量，保障持续发展。

2. 实施优势产业带动战略，把五大主导产业、高新技术产业做大做强，提高配套能力，形成产业聚集效应。

3. 实施服务品牌带动战略，树立企业是上帝的理念，从细微处入手，不断提高服务质量和水平。

四、主要措施

1. 抓住机遇期，加大招商引资力度

（1）做好招商引资基础工作。一是加强招商网络建设，充分发挥招商代理人和中介机构的作用。二是通过多种形式进行宣传，扩大武清开发区的知名度。三是有目的地选择一批重点项目和服务业项目进行包装，推向市场。

（2）设置企业准入标准。在保证招商引资数量的基础上，提高入区企业的质量，达到“四个不入区”，即：投资总额在1500万元人民币或150万美元以下的项目不入区；投资强度不够的项目不入区；高耗资源的项目不入区；不环保的项目不入区。

（3）珍惜有限的土地资源。一是重点吸引高新技术、高附加值、高投资强度的项目，投资强度争取突破每亩200万元人民币。二是充分利用闲置土地、厂房和停产企业，挖掘土地潜力。

（4）拓宽招商领域。不但要继续做好工业企业的招商引资工作，还要加大对贸易、服务、基础设施等项目的招商引资力度，促进经济社会共同发展。

（5）研究招商方法，提高引资效果。一是加强政策调研和对经贸形势的分析，及时捕捉新的经济动态和信息，以便指导招商工作。二是进一步规范开发区情况介绍、谈判技巧和谈判程序，使之更加切合投资者实际，更有针对性。三是采取多种形式，将坐等招商与走出去招商结合起来，专业招商与社会招商结合起来，拓宽招商信息源。

2. 以完善城市功能为重点，提高城市化建设水平

（1）制定好几个规划：一是北河滩商业商贸区规划；二是二期公建用地规划；三

是二期软体区规划；四是三期用地规划。通过完善以上规划，使开发区实现健康、持续发展。

（2）分步实施，保证进度。一是北河滩商业商贸区。总建筑面积58.9万平方米，预计投资约23亿元人民币。计划于2005年完成详细规划设计，并启动建设20万平方米，2006年完成建设40万平方米，2007年全部建成。

二是开发区二期公建区。2005年拿出详细规划方案，2006年启动建设，2007年全部建成，总计5万平方米。

三是二期软体区。2005年着手二期软体区规划设计，2007年启动相关基础设施建设，2010年完成招商任务。

四是三期规划用地。2005年拿出三期6平方公里用地总体规划方案，2007年启动基础设施建设，为开发区长远发展备足后劲。力争到2010年基础设施全部完成，摆满项目。

（3）坚持经济发展和社会发展的统一。注重生态建设，确保园区绿化率达到35%以上，打造良好的环境品牌。

3. 以提高管理水平和行政服务水平为重点，优化投资环境

（1）坚持“封闭式”管理、“一站式”办公、“一条龙”服务机制，改善行政服务环境，努力营造“公开、公正、廉洁、透明”的行政氛围。同时，发挥ISO 9000质量管理体系和ISO 14000环境管理体系认证证书的“名片”作用，加快与国际接轨的步伐。

（2）通过多种形式，开展多种活动，主动为企业解难题，办实事，努力营造亲商、安商、富商的良好氛围。

4. 发挥企业协会的作用，分国别、行业等组织区内企业进行交流，增进企业间的沟通。

武清开发区“十二五”时期发展建设规划

一、“十一五”规划执行情况

“十一五”期间，武清开发区在区委、区政府的正确领导下，以建设京津之间最具实力和竞争力开发区为目标，深入贯彻落实科学发展观，务实进取，扎实苦干，经受住了金融危机的严峻考验，圆满完成了“十一五”规划确定的发展目标，全区经济发展龙头和主发动机地位不断强化。

1. 经济实力明显增强。地区生产总值由2005年的35亿元增加到2010年的118亿元，年均递增28%；工业总产值由2005年的82亿元增加到2010年的420亿元，年均递增39%；税收由2005年的10亿元增加到2010年的45亿元，年均递增35%；固定资产投资由2005年的8亿元增加到2010年的74亿元，年均递增56%。外贸出口额由2005年的37亿元增加到2010年的65亿元，年均递增12%。

2. 开发建设顺利推进。二期7.6平方公里开发圆满完成。三期15平方公里开发进展顺利。撤村建居工作圆满完成，共投入16.4亿元，征地19.56平方公里，搬迁11村、3930户、12074人。高端制造业聚集区、国际保税物流园基础设施投入15亿元，2010年年底可完成道路、管线、渠系及厂站工程，实现"十一通一平"；招商工作已经全面展开，并引进一批大项目、好项目。天狮国际大学到年底启动建设。创业总部基地完成基础设施建设，规划的6个区域中心服务区、企业总部区、商务酒店区、服务外包区、综合办公区、专家公寓区建设全面启动，到年底建筑面积16万平米的服务外包区竣工。四期10平方公里开发启动规划工作。完成了远期93平方公里空间发展战略规划。投入15亿元，进一步完善一、二期基础设施建设，其中新建和修缮道路共24公里，新建桥涵10座。

3. 招商引资成果突出。吸引投资由2005年的13.7亿元增加到2010年的80亿元，年均递增42%。五年共引进项目210个，其中内资项目135个，外资项目75个。聚集了一批优质项目，有中粮、英格索兰等世界500强，以及南玻、赛诺、日进、马泰克、奥特莱斯、韦斯伐里亚、蜡笔小新、EKC、伊利、娃哈哈、蓝猫等国内外行业龙头项目。2007年设立了创业拓展中心，预计到2010年年底可吸引注册类企业280个，引进注册资本70亿，实现税收4亿元。

4. 产业结构调整优化。工业项目发展更加侧重环保节能，从电子信息、新型建材、机械制造、汽车及零部件、生物医药五大主导产业，调整优化为电子信息、机械制造、生物医药、汽车及零部件、新材料、新能源六大主导产业。起步发展了文化创意、服务外包、物流等现代服务业。骨干企业支撑作用不断增强，前30家企业纳税额占开发区总量的85%，并培育出了日进汽车、中粮包装、娃哈哈宏振等一批新的经济增长点。

5. 服务环境不断优化。践行"服务他人就是发展自己"理念，坚定实行"封闭式"管理，"一站式"办公和"一条龙"服务。丰富行政服务功能，协调引进了检验检疫部门。加强功能设施建设，建筑面积1.2万平方米、具有出口退税功能的公用型保税仓库、出口监管仓库投入使用；新建标准厂房13万平方米；新建高新公寓8.5万平方米、栖仙温泉公寓西区 22 万平方米；7.6 万平方米的金融商务中心建成投入使用，9000 平方米的东湖俱乐部完成主体建设。新增绿化面积 200 万平米，绿化率由 2005 年的 30% 增加到 2010 年的 40% 以上。

6. 稳定和谐局面进一步巩固。严格落实建设项目“环保三同时”验收，开展环保监督检查工作，依法从严处理了排放超标企业。坚决落实安全生产责任制，五年中未出现任何安全生产责任事故。深入贯彻落实《中华人民共和国劳动合同法》，妥善解决各种劳动争议，维护企业和员工合法利益，保证了用工形势的稳定。就业人数从 2005 年的 3.8 万人增加到 2010 年的 7.6 万人，年均递增 14.9%。

二、“十二五”期间面临的总体形势

（一）面临形势分析

7. 外部环境趋好。世界经济复苏和结构调整的步伐加快，将促进国际直接投资流动加速。国家宏观经济政策的连续性促进国内经济回升向好。环渤海经济圈特别是北京和滨海新区的带动辐射作用强劲。

8. 面对课题崭新。开发区已进入产业结构调整和发展转型升级期，二次创业任务艰巨，发展创意、物流、服务外包、高端产业等面临大量崭新课题，需要通过不断创新予以破解。

9. 肩负责任重大。实现全区“三年倍增”计划和“十二五”规划，开发区作为武清的经济龙头和主发动机，责任重大、任务艰巨。周边开发区竞相发展态势迅猛，竞争异常激烈。

（二）发展优势条件

10. 区位交通比较优势。武清处于环渤海经济圈京津发展主轴的中间节点，经过多年建设，已全面融入京津半小时都市圈。开发区周边海陆空交通网络完善，通达优势明显，已成为汇集京津冀人流、资金流和信息流的重要经济平台。

11. 基础设施和资源优势。保障能力强，基础设施达到“十一通一平”，实现了三水源供水、三气源供气、双电网供电。地耐力高，建设成本低；土质好，绿化成本低；城市处于发展阶段，员工生活成本低。三期开发建设顺利完成，为企业发展提供了广阔空间。

12. 服务环境优势。经过多年发展特别是“十一五”期间的大建设大投入，武清开发区生产条件、生活条件实现了由量变到质变的飞跃。各级政府部门服务意识不断增强，行政服务效率持续提升。

（三）主要问题矛盾

13. 产业亟待升级。在成功实现劳动密集型向资本密集型产业转型的基础上，技术密集型特别是高新技术产业发展还不充分，绿色环保节能等高端新兴产业发展有待加强，现代服务业发展相对滞后。

14. 平台建设层次需进一步提高。对比周边开发区，在整体规划、基础设施、功能设施、生态环境建设等方面有一定比较优势。但与高端产业、高层次企业的需求比，整体建设水平还需进一步提高，以增强吸引力。

15. 服务需进一步与国际接轨。现有服务体系能够较好支撑传统制造业发展，但还不适应高端制造业、现代服务业加快发展。在创意、IT、服务外包、现代物流等产业中，企业经营模式多样，对我们服务的理念、效率、方法提出了许多新要求和更高标准。

三、“十二五”规划的指导思想、发展原则和总体目标

（一）指导思想：

16. 指导思想：“十二五”期间，武清开发区将进入成熟发展期和加快发展期。按照全区“十二五”规划要求，开发区将坚持“高端化、特色化、集约化”方向，深入贯彻科学发展观，开拓创新，奋力拼搏，大力发展高端制造业、现代服务业，升级产业结构，培育产业集群，实现跨越发展，把武清开发区建设成为京津之间最具实力和竞争力的高端绿色园区。

（二）发展原则：

17. 拓展发展空间。科学谋划、超前谋划未来空间发展布局规划，加快基础设施开发建设，为长远发展奠定建设基础。

18. 促进产业转型升级。注重引进高新、环保、节能等新兴产业，发展循环经济、低碳经济。加速劳动型向智力型产业转型，发展科技、创意、文化、物流、服务外包等现代服务业。

19. 实施大项目拉动。坚持项目强区，大力引进投资规模大、科技含量高、带动能力强、发展前景好的优质项目，提高项目对经济发展的贡献率。

20. 提升功能环境。坚持服务立区、服务致胜，以不断创新的精神坚定推进服务环境持续改进，打造具有国际标准的投资环境。

（三）总体目标：

21. 主要指标：到 2015 年，实现地区生产总值 360 亿元，年均增长 25%；工业总产值 1045 亿元，年均增长 20%；财税收入 137 亿元，年均增长 25%；固定资产投资 235 亿元，年均增长 26%；吸引投资 200 亿元，年均增长 20%；平均每年新创造就业岗位 10000 个以上。

四、“十二五”期间主要任务

（一）拓展发展空间，提速开发建设

22. 土地拓展思路。按照市、区两级城市总体规划和土地利用规划，积极主动运作，争取“十二五”期间土地使用指标。坚持规划先行，科学规划拓展区域的战略发展方向，促进建设理性发展。

23. 三期开发建设。遵循“突出特色，明确功能，抢占高点，科学发展”的总思路，打造平台建设新优势。2011 年完成高端制造业聚集区、国际保税物流园市政基础设施收尾工程。2012 年建成还迁小区。天狮国际大学建设 2013 年一期竣工，2015 年建成。

24. 创业总部基地开发建设。2012 年全面完成中心服务区、商务酒店区、专家公寓区、总部经济区和综合办公区工程。

25. 四期开发建设。2011 年完成四期 10 平方公里发展规划并启动撤村建居工作，2012 年完成基础设施建设，2015 年建成。

（二）强化宣传推介，扩大招商引资

26. 招商思路。按照“倍加珍惜土地资源、坚持可持续发展”的思路，探索落实新机制、新招法，确保引进一大批优质项目。加大资金投入，强化项目策划包装，组织大型招商推介活动。利用各级媒体、网络，进行全方位的招商宣传。坚持舍得理念，对优质项目在政策、资金、服务上给予全力支持。

27. 创业总部基地招商。制定落实税收奖励、行业扶持基金、租金补贴、人才引进等相关产业政策。发展总部经济，着力引进企业总部、研发中心、结算中心等高附加值的服务业项目。与北京中关村科技园、专业投资咨询机构、京津冀高校和科研院所密切合作，引进一批高质量服务外包、IT、动漫、游戏、创意、研发和孵化项目。2012 年全面完成招商任务。

28. 高端制造业招商。着眼于高端制造业，引进一大批世界 500 强、国内 500 强和行业龙头企业。以北欧绿色产业园为平台，引进一批高质量外资环保节能产业。2012

年摆满项目。

29. 物流业招商。充分宣传武清及物流园区位、交通优势，发挥公用保税仓库和出口监管仓库功能作用，以及海关、检验检疫服务职能，引进一批国际、国内知名物流地产企业。2012 年摆满项目。

30. 四期招商。坚持高端高质高新化方向，瞄准新兴产业，推进四期招商，到 2015 年全面完成招商任务。

31. 创业拓展中心招商。充分发挥平台作用，对各乡镇和“四园”引进项目提供全方位服务。推动总部经济、楼宇经济加快发展，推进无地招商。确保五年吸引投资 100 亿元。

（三）抓项目促升级，提升经济实力

32. 狠抓项目开工达产。实施项目化管理，强化“一个项目、一名领导、一套班子、一抓到底”的责任机制，建立跟踪反馈机制，加强监督考核，推动项目早落地、早开工、早投产。创新招法多渠道融资，强化建设资金保障。

33. 加快科技型中小企业发展。坚持“内育”与“外引”两手抓，促进高新技术产业和战略性新兴产业的集聚发展，鼓励企业进行技术创新，创造核心技术和新产品。扶持拥有自主知识产权、自主品牌企业发展，打造一批科技型中小企业和科技“小巨人”企业。建设中小型企业科技园、孵化器。积极引导有条件企业上市。支持企业做强、做大增财税。

（四）提升功能支撑，打造国际标准投资环境

34. 加强功能建设。新建开发区招商服务中心，占地 50 亩、建筑面积 4 万平米，2012 年建成并投入使用。完成玉圭园主题公园、佛罗伦萨小镇等大型服务功能项目建设，提升服务支撑能力。以“强有力保障，零缺陷服务”为目标搞好物业、供水、热力等市政服务。扩大金融、法律、信息、咨询等服务机构引进。

35. 建设绿色园区。提升城市园林绿化建设水平，五年新增绿化面积 300 万平方米，使绿化率达到 45% 以上。严格落实建设项目“环保三同时”验收，严格落实节能减排硬性指标。强化“城市环境也是服务”理念，完善落实城市管理长效机制，提升市容环境水平。

36. 强化行政服务。秉承“服务他人就是发展自己”理念，完善服务体系，从项目接洽、落地到建设、投产强化部门之间无缝隙对接。为企业“代言代办”，做到上下一心搞服务、重诺守信求发展。

（五）坚持和谐发展，落实保障举措

37. 强化安全生产。坚决落实安全生产责任制，加强宣传教育，实施分类管理，切实提高监督管理的针对性和实效性，确保不出现安全生产责任事故。

38. 强化就业服务。主动对接企业用工需求，拓宽招用工渠道，做好人才储备，帮助和促进企业延揽人才。多渠道、多层次开发就业岗位。

39. 构筑人才高地。以满足高端制造业、现代服务业和现代物流业发展为目标，优化人才培养、吸引、使用和激励机制，吸引招商引资、规划建设、经济管理、资本运作等方面的创新型、专业化人才。

40. 创新体制机制。按照“小机构、大服务，精简、高效”的原则，在招商引资、重大项目推进、企业服务及内部激励机制上改革创新。建立完善高效运转、保障有力的服务平台。建立完善网络化、专业化的科技创新平台。建立完善多元化、多层次的投融资平台。

41. 确保和谐稳定。加强企业管理，规范企业经营行为。保障企业和员工合法权益，做好劳动争议调解工作。完善突发事件预警和应急处置机制，提高预防和处置能力，抓早、抓小、抓苗头，有效防止重大不稳定事件发生。

武清开发区“十三五”时期发展规划

一、过去五年的发展成就

“十二五”期间，武清开发区以建设京津之间最具实力和竞争力开发区为目标，深入贯彻落实科学发展观，加快转型升级，实施创新驱动，圆满完成了发展目标，经济社会发展上了一个大台阶。

（一）经济实力明显增强。地区生产总值由2010年的118亿元增加到2015年的426亿元，年均增长29.3%；工业总产值由2010年的420亿元增加到2015年的1280亿元，年均增长25%；税收由2010年的45亿元增加到2015年的118亿元，年均增长23.6%；五年累计实现固定资产投资913亿元。

（二）发展空间优化拓展。三期15平方公里中的高端制造业聚集区、保税物流区完成招商建设，天狮国际大学2013年启动规划，2015年可完成市政建设和一期部分主体。四期20平方公里2011年启动开发，其中起步区5平方方公里的市政设施、5万平方米的标准厂房完成建设。创业总部基地120万平方米中的服务外包区、企业总部区和专家公寓区建成，综合办公区、商务酒店区和中心服务区基本建成，基础设施和绿化景观工程全部完成。规划 10 平方公里的京津高村科技创新园 2014 年启动开发 ,2015 年起步区 1.67 平方公里市政工程竣工。占地 335 亩的自贸区武清园 2014 年启动规划，至 2015 年年底跨境物流仓库和楼宇项目可启动建设。大力推进“二次开发”，先后整合、收回土地 630 亩。

（三）招商建设成果突出。五年累计引进项目 821 个、投资 850 亿元，年均增长 18%。其中有国际纸业、德尔福、苏伊士、中化、中交建等世界 500 强 16 个，有信义汽车玻璃、巴克斯酒业、法国库恩、突尼斯柯菲凯博等国内外行业龙头项目，特别是引进哈沃、合宜、莱斯、格力莫、阿玛松等德国项目 30 余个，德企聚集效应显著。借重首都资源，引进了铁科院、北交控、诺禾致源等首都高端项目 135 个。引进了融鑫汇、欧华美科、阿芙精油结算中心、网动科技等总部楼宇项目 306 个。引进了中纺院、中科院微生物研究所、天大前沿院等国家级科研院所近 20 个。五年累计建成佛罗伦萨小镇、亚马逊、韦史伐里亚、维益食品等优质项目 107 个并投产。

（四）资本运营取得实效。积极拓展融资渠道，加强中长期融资，减少短期融资，优选低成本融资，通过银行贷款、企业债券、中期票据、信托、融资租赁、BT 等多种方式融资，保证了园区发展各项资金需求。通过深入调研，确定了开发区上市工作方案。强化资金管理，严格落实工程项目预决算和评审制度，优化了资金使用效率。

（五）体制机制不断创新。着眼于强化规划建设、招商引资和企业服务等主要职能，进一步建设“精炼、统一、高效”的管理体制机制。增加审批职能，成立并高效运行开发区行政服务中心，区工商、发改、国土、规划、人防等职能部门派驻专人现场办公，实施一次性告知、并联审批、限时办结、全程代办等工作机制，项目手续审批办结时间提速 40%，正全力推进承接区级审批权限下放工作。增设了德国海外招商代表处。剥离部分社会管理职能，向区相关部门移交了绿化养管、市政维护、道路保洁、学校管理、社区物业、社区服务等社会管理职能。强化了招商引资、手续办理、规划建设、企业服务无缝对接的产业项目流程化、专业化服务推动机制。完善机关行政管理制度，从 30 项增加到 50 项。进一步规范“三重一大”决策工作的实施办法，全面推进依法治理园区。

（六）创新驱动稳步推进。完成了 11.5 万平米的京津高校武清科技创新园规划，引进产学研用项目 23 个。完善研发服务平台建设，园区内有红日药业抗体药物技术等企业工程技术中心 8 个、光彩圣火等国家级和市级孵化器 4 个、中纺院滤料技术检测等检验检测机构3个，高新技术企业达43家。五年累计引进培育科技型中小企业555家，小巨人企业90家。完成转型升级企业114家。民营市场主体新增1000余家。建立开发区博士后科研工作站、院士工作站和专家服务基地，五年累计引进各层次人才3583人，其中院士11人、长江学者1人、“千人计划”2人、科技部973计划首席科学家2人、“863”项目负责人1人。

（七）生态环境建设取得新进展。实施“四清一绿”工程，新建及改造绿化面积360万平米，绿化率达42%以上。严格实施网格化常态管理。引进并完成华电分布式能源站建设，成为全国首家为工业开发区提供电、热、冷、蒸汽和热水综合性解决方案的能源站。中电投、信义共260兆瓦光伏发电项目实施顺利。推动三期、四期污水处理设施建设，实现了污水达标排放。完成自有3座热力站改造，8家企业煤改燃。积极推进了市级、国家级生态工业园区创建工作。

（八）稳定和谐局面进一步巩固。坚决落实安全生产责任制，未出现重大安全生产责任事故。成立了开发区人民调解委员会、工会法律援助工作站，妥善解决各种劳动争议，维护企业和员工合法利益。就业人数从2010年的7.6万人增加到2015年的14万人，年均增长13%。

（九）党建工作取得新成效。牢牢把握从严管党、治党、建设党的“新常态”，深入开展党的群众路线教育实践、“三严三实”等活动。加强党的基层组织建设和党员教育管理，非公党组织覆盖率由92%提高到96%。建成开发区党建展厅作为党员教育的主阵地。严格落实党风廉政建设责任制，促进全体干部员工廉洁自律。坚决执行中央八项规定和厉行节约反对浪费条例。加强学习型机关和学习型队伍建设，提升队伍素质和服务水平，开发区被评为全国文明单位。

二、“十三五”期间面临的总体形势

（一）面临形势分析

1. 国际产业发展环境有所改善。世界经济仍处后危机调整期，主要经济体增速有所回升。创新全球化深度演进，全球将进入空前的创新密集和产业振兴时代，新能源、新材料以及生物技术、环保技术、物联网等领域正在面临重大技术突破，信息技术广泛运用，服务业和制造业深度融合，不断催生新的商业模式和新兴业态。这为开发区利用国际创新资源，在局部优势领域实现跨越式发展提供了契机。

2. 国内经济环境深刻转变。“新常态”成为新期经济发展的重大逻辑，经济增长速度换挡、结构调整阵痛和前期刺激政策消化的“三期叠加”阶段性特征明显。国家提出“中国制造 2025”战略，大力推进创新驱动、智能转型和绿色发展，加快从制造大国转向制造强国。这为开发区调整产业结构、率先转变发展方式指明了方向。

3. 区域政策环境利于发展。滨海新区开发开放、天津自由贸易试验区、国家自主创新示范区、京津冀协同发展以及“一带一路”五大战略机遇叠加前所未有，作为改革开放的先行区和对外开放的重要窗口，开发区应进一步提高开放的水平，主动探索转型升级的模式与路径，加快实施创新驱动战略，大力推进大众创业、万众创新，建设创新型园区。

4. 开发区面对课题崭新。开发区面临着由速度规模型向质量效益型转变、同质化竞争向特色差异化转变等大量崭新课题，需要通过不断创新予以破解。同时要加快实现由成本优势向产业优势和综合竞争优势转变。

（二）发展优势条件

1. 区位交通优势凸显。经过多年建设，武清开发区已全面融入京津半小时都市圈，周边海陆空交通网络完善，已成为汇集京津冀人流、资金流和信息流的重要经济平台。

2. 服务环境优质高效。经过多年大投入大建设，武清开发区生产条件、生活条件实现了由量变到质变的飞跃。各级职能部门服务意识不断增强，行政服务效率持续提升。

3. 政策叠加优势突出。企业可享受国家级经济技术开发区、国家级高新技术产业园区、天津自由贸易试验区、天津国家自主创新示范区、京津冀协同发展等叠加政策，并享受人才引进、科技型中小企业发展、千企转型升级、民营经济加快发展等扶持政策。

（三）主要问题矛盾

1. 经济结构性矛盾仍然存在。当前现代服务业占地区生产总值 23.5%，占比仍然较低。310 家工业企业产值情况为机械制造占 20.2%、新材料占 12.0%、生物医药占 10.8%、汽车及零部件占 9.1%、电子信息占 8.3%、新能源占 1.5%、其他占 38.1%，经济结构有待进一步优化，新兴产业和高端产业规模偏小。纳税前 30 名企业占总量的 68 %，经济竞争实力和抗风险能力有待进一步提升。另外，目前全部工业用地产值 752 万元 / 亩，规模以上实体企业工业用地产值 1061 万元 / 亩，与先进园区还存在差距。

2. 土地、环境等资源约束愈益明显。经过二十多年发展，园区基本完成了 35 平方公里的开发建设，目前土地供应率超过 94%，可用于开发建设的土地面积所剩不多，资源瓶颈比较突出。目前可供出租的楼宇仅有企业总部区 20 余万平米，标准厂房总建筑面积 46.5 万平米出租率超过 90%，楼宇、厂房容量不足。同时，厂房的产业兼容性有待进一步提高，GMP 车间等标准化公共技术平台资源不足，对高端产业、高层次企业的需求支撑不足。商业休闲功能不强，现代化、国际化的社会服务设施没有形成集聚，富有特色的商业设施比较缺乏。同时，开发区环境承载能力的刚性约束日趋明显，节能减排的压力不断增大。

3. 创新驱动的制约不断凸显。区域创新体系尚不完备，创新链不同环节缺少专业化中介服务机构提供支撑服务。创新型企业实力不强，比重、创新能力有待提高。科技创新平台建设较先进园区存在较大差距。符合转型发展需要的高层次人才比较紧缺，创新型、领军型、复合型人才尤为不足，产业人才的结构与产业转型战略的匹配度有待提高。

三、“十三五”规划的指导思想、发展原则和总体目标

（一）指导思想

“十三五”期间，武清开发区进入转型发展期，要以结构调整、转型升级和创新驱动为主线，保持经济稳定增长，转变经济发展方式，调整优化产业结构，推动创新驱动发展，推进改革体制机制，加强生态文明建设，把武清开发区建设成为京津之间科技、创新、绿色园区。

（二）总体指标

“十三五”末，当年实现地区生产总值 713 亿元，年均增长 11%；工业总产值 2061 亿元，年均增长 10%；财税收入 216 亿元，年均增长 12%；五年累计实现固定资产投资 1000 亿元。

1. 借势“京津冀协同发展”，建成承接北京高端资源的桥头堡。发挥区位优势，依托京津高村科技创新园、欧盟产业园、创业总部基地、京津高校科技创新园等创新创业载体，大力发展先进制造业、生物医药和总部经济三大主导产业，加强与京津高校和科研机构的产学研用合作，构建示范区承接北京技术转移和科技成果转化的重点园区。同时大力发展跨境电子商务、大数据等现代产业，发展绿色低碳循环经济。

2. 转型升级取得突破性进展，建成创新型科技园区和新型工业化园区。制造业的结构和层次明显优化，主导产业支撑作用更加突出，高新技术产业占比明显提高，服务业在区域经济中的比重明显提升，尤其是现代服务业取得较大发展。科技创新迈出新的步伐，在生物医药等产业领域，新建一批国家级、省级重点实验室、工程研究中心和企业技术中心，实现产业核心技术和关键技术的重点突破。与高校、院所、生产

企业建设协同创新发展平台，大力发展“众创空间”，为创业创新搭建新平台。加强国际化人才聚集，鼓励科技人员带科技成果到开发区创新创业。培育发展中小企业、瞪羚企业，使科技企业成为区域创新内生动力。

3. 生态环境优化取得突破性进展，建成生态型服务型园区。环境基础设施更加完善，节能减排、循环经济发展取得新的成效，主要污染物排放得到有效控制，环境质量明显改善，土地等资源集约利用水平进一步提高，可持续发展能力显著增强。优化园区空间布局，完善商业休闲等服务设施，提高园区信息化、智能化水平。积极主动地借鉴先进园区经验，探索园区转型发展新的理念。进一步完善规范、高效的管理体制机制和服务体系。打造具有国际标准的投资环境。

四、“十三五”期间主要任务

（一）优化提升结构，促进产业高端化

实施“强二拓三”战略，以打造生物医药和轨道交通两个“千亿级”产业集群为重点，加快发展以总部、金融、文化、服务外包、第三方物流、商贸旅游为主体的服务型经济。

1. 以现有主导产业为依托，提升发展先进制造业。鼓励驻区装备制造企业增设研发、销售机构，提升在国内外的竞争优势。瞄准产业链的关键缺失环节和急需引进的行业、产品和技术，重点引进发展轨道交通、关键零部件、农用机械设备、智能基础制造设备等先进制造业。进一步完善产业链，提升高端项目在新增项目中的比重。

2. 以生物医药为引领，大力发展新兴产业。根据园区产业基础，结合国家战略，重点布局发展生物医药产业，进一步做大产业规模，发掘上下游产业链，形成一批新兴产业产品群。支持加大研发投入力度，提高研发能力和专利申请数量。提升生物制药产业创新能力，大力发展诊断试剂、新一代基因测序等先进技术，加大力度发展生物医药外包服务业务。积极开拓靶向药、仿制药和新药研发市场。打造完整生物医药产业链条。

3. 以总部经济为突破口，加快发展现代服务业。抢抓京津冀协同发展等机遇，大力发展服务型经济，加快打造现代服务业集聚区。创业总部基地重点引进央企、国企二、三级总部以及国内外大企业的区域管理中心、采购中心等职能性总部，形成区域企业总部经济和特色产业总部经济。自贸区武清园商业部分重点发展融资租赁、金融租赁、离岸结算、商业保理等产业，物流部分重点发展跨境电商、期货交割和高端商品国际物流。京津高村科技创新园以大数据作为主导产业，通过高端引领实现新型科技创新

园区建设。

（二）优化空间布局，加快推进开发建设

结合开发区产业发展重点方向，进一步优化园区空间布局，统筹园区功能、空间布局和城市形态，提升园区空间资源的配置效率。

1. 欧盟产业园。到 2017 年，一期 5 平方公里产业项目全部建成投产。适时启动二期 4.5 平方公里村庄拆迁，拆迁后两年内完成市政开发。

2. 京津高村科技创新园。到 2016 年，一期全部道路建成，形成完整路网系统。到 2020 年，3 平方公里园区全部建成，力争启动远期 7 平方公里开发，形成京津冀高速走廊上的门户形象，成为天津市西北部功能区桥头堡。

3. 自贸区武清园。跨境物流仓库到 2016 年建成 6 万平方米，2020 年增至 10 万平米；建筑面积 10 万平方米的楼宇项目到 2020 年完成建设。成为武清区对外开放新窗口。

4. 创业总部基地。到 2016 年，建成商务酒店区和中心服务区；到 2018 年，建成综合办公区。

5. 二次开发。到 2020 年，推动完成 2.3 平方公里“供而未用”土地开发建设，实现集约发展。开阔思路，精心设计，完成自创区核心区 2.6 万平方米老厂房提升改造。

6. 产业项目建设。天狮国际大学 2016 年完成建筑物主体施工，2017 年完成全部工程建设。红日康仁堂 2016 年竣工投产。绫致服装华北物流中心 2016 年投产。创意米兰 2017 年建成开业。同时，加快其他新签约项目建设，确保项目早开工早建设早投产早达产。

（三）抓招商引资，确保引进高端优质项目。

提高招商项目的科技含量，确保投资强度和税收效益，“十三五”期间引进高端项目 1000 个以上。

1. 强化平台招商。欧盟产业园引进生物医药、先进制造业、新材料等高质高新项目 50 个以上，形成具有绿色生态特点的欧盟产业聚集发展基地。高村科技园要主动承接首都功能疏解和产业转移，围绕大数据和生物医药等主导产业引进项目 300 个。自贸区武清园大力引进跨境电商、融资租赁、商业保理、贸易结算和外资总部结算等产业项目 300 个。创业总部基地要大力引进国企、央企二、三级总部和贸易结算项目 500 个，形成聚集效应，打造“亿元楼宇”10 个。

2. 研究产业发展政策。精心研究经开区、高新区、天津自由贸易试验区、国家自主创新示范区和京津冀协同发展等政策，结合区位、交通、产业、环境等综合优势，制定科学的开发区投资促进政策。

3. 强化宣传推介。坚持举办高水平的集中推介活动和专项招商活动。强化海外招商，进一步建设海外招商办事处及招商合作机构。系统梳理重点项目分出等级，进一步强化重点项目的一对一攻关。加强与普华永道、高力国际等国际知名咨询机构及金融街的深度合作。

（四）集聚创新资源，建成创新型园区

加大科技创新聚焦力度，以掌握核心技术、发展自主知识产权为宗旨，着力建设以企业为主体、市场为导向、政产学研紧密结合的区域科技创新体系，推动科技创新、产业创新、企业创新、市场创新、产品创新。

1. 进一步完善创新主体建设。加快培育引进龙头企业、拳头产品、研发机构、领军人才。大力发展科技型中小企业，助推企业做强做优做大。加强科技攻关，增加资金支持，拿出更多杀手锏产品。推动千企转型，加快改造低散小污粗企业，实现科技发展。做好高新技术企业认定工作，释放更多政策红利。引进高端科研机构和跨国企业研发中心。

2. 进一步完善科技平台建设。着眼提升科技创新源动力，建设生物医药产业研究院等科研平台；生物医药成果转化中心等专业化服务平台；科技型企业孵化器平台；院所技术与企业技术对接平台；进一步集聚一批高水平研发、金融、人才、知识产权中介服务机构，加强专业性服务体系建设。

3. 进一步推动产学研一体化。探索与中关村等在重点合作领域共建跨区域产业技术联盟新模式，融入京津冀三地产业技术创新交流合作，构建以市场需求为导向的技术创新和成果转化机制，鼓励校企合作、院企合作，建设产学研基地和科技成果转化基地。

4. 进一步完善创新投融资体系。引进创业投资基金等科技金融机构，探索建立“银行 + 政府 + 担保 + 保险 + 创投 + 科技服务中介”统一结合的科技金融平台，逐步建立全面覆盖中小企业各发展阶段的金融服务产业链。

5. 加快发展众创空新模式。面向大众创新创业需求，着力培育创客、创新工场等集市场化、专业化、集成化、网络化于一体的新型“众创空间”，建设一批创客空间、创业咖啡、创新工场等新型孵化平台，促进创业者和天使投资人交流定期化、常态化，营造大众创业、万众创新的良好局面。

6. 大力引进培养高层次人才。通过专家服务基地、院士工作站、博士后工作站和引进国内外知名培训机构等，打造多元化、一体化、便利化的产业创新人才培养环境。完善人才公共服务体系，提升园区生产生活水平。依托众创空间、重点实验室、工程技术中心等人才发展平台，完善人才创新创业服务体系。

（五）打造绿色宜居环境，建设生态示范园区

坚定不移实施“四清一绿”行动，实现天蓝地绿水清，完成国家生态示范园区创建。

1. 提高资源集约利用水平。加大节能降耗工作力度，严格控制高耗能项目，加快淘汰落后产能，加强节能技术改造和能源审计。大力发展循环经济，鼓励企业引进和推广资源梯级利用技术、废物综合利用技术，做好中水回用、“煤改燃”等节能减排工作。鼓励太阳能、光伏发电等新能源的示范应用。进一步提高土地投资强度，健全土地集约利用机制，引导高耗能行业和企业等加快优化升级。

2. 加大生态环境保护力度。严格落实网格化管理，强化环境基础设施建设，推进绿化建设和景观优化。加强环境综合整治和生态修复，严格控制主要污染物排放总量。进一步提高环境监管的能力和水平，加强环境信息化建设，健全环境质量监测与污染监管系统、风险预警和环境应急系统，完善环境质量监测体系，做好生态工业宣传普及工作。

（六）加快改革攻坚步伐，增创体制机制新优势

推进创新发展模式改革试验，率先在重点领域和关键环节改革取得突破，构建充满活力、富有效率、更加开放、有利于科学发展的体制机制。

1. 创新行政管理体制。加大简政放权力度，深化行政审批制度改革，完善开发区“一站式”行政服务机构设置。深入推动落实一颗印章管审批、一本绿卡管引才。

2. 深化投融资体制创新。构建市场化、多元化的投资格局，保持基础设施投资规模，积极拓宽融资渠道，探索完善 PPP 模式开发高村园、自贸区。规范融资平台管理，防范风险。推动开发区实现三板上市。支持有条件的区内企业上市。

3. 大力推进园区服务信息化建设。推进建设电子政务，拓展网上政务服务内容，建立简化、快捷的行政服务模式。推进地理信息库的建设。大力推进“互联网 +”工程建设，建设“智慧园区”。

4. 推进企业管理体制改革。学习借鉴国内外先进地区在企业管理、社会服务等方面科学的发展理念和高效的体制机制，努力打造专业、高效的新型企业服务体系。推进开发区管理法制化，明确管理体制、管理权限、发展定位等。确保园区安全稳定。

（七）党的建设

牢牢把握党要管党、从严治党要求，大力加强开发区机关党组织和非公企业基层党组织建设，组织开展专题教育活动，并不断巩固扩大活动成果。加强党的纪律建设，严肃党内政治生活，加强党的基层组织建设和党员教育管理，巩固非公企业阵地建设。严格落实党风廉政建设责任制，不断加强廉政风险防控机制建设，促进全体党员干部员工廉洁自律。

五、实施保障

本纲要提出的产业布局、发展方向和重点，以及在基础设施、资源环境等领域提出的任务，各责任部门要切实履行职责，确保落到实处。

（一）编制和实施专项规划和年度计划。把总体规划纲确定的目标任务、重大建设项目安排进行分解，落实到专项规划、园区规划以及年度计划中，引导各领域的协调发展；各类专项规划必须与本纲要衔接。

（二）组织实施一批重大建设项目。围绕“十三五”经济社会发展总体目标，集中力量，发挥园区主导作用与调控能力，安排一批重大建设项目。

（三）落实目标责任制。对于规划中提出的发展目标、重点任务和重点建设项目，要明确责任部门负责完成；对于规划中提出的政策性内容，相关责任部门要研究制定具体的实施意见加以落实。

（四）加强规划实施的监督考核。建立规范的评估机制，及时总结规划进展情况，解决规划实施过程中存在的问题，并根据未来环境的变化情况适度修订规划内容，确保规划的科学性和指导性。建立规划实施监督考核机制，分年度和中期对规划实施情况进行检查。

第二节　年度发展计划编制与执行

年度发展计划在五年计划指导下，结合实际发展情况进行编制。其主要内容包括对上一年度经济和社会发展状况的总结，本年度经济和社会发展思路、目标、任务、对策和资金收支计划的提出等。从 1992 年至 2016 年，共完成 25 个年度计划。每个年度发展计划均得到贯彻执行，如期实现或提前完成发展计划。

第三节　年度专项计划编制与执行

年度专项计划在年度发展计划指导下进行编制。各专项发展计划，包括固定资产投资计划（含政府投资基本建设投资计划）、利用外资计划、工业计划等。以上各年度专项计划，是执行年度发展计划的基础。年度专项计划编制后，开发区采取积极措施确保计划完成，包括积极争取、协调与上级有关领导部门的业务关系，协助解决基本建设所需资金及项目的区域配套，参与项目的融资、贷款、组织申报相关手续等工作，促进专项计划的如期完成。

第二章　基本建设管理

第一节　项目审批

武清开发区对入区企业项目审批工作，统由行政服务中心（以下简称“中心”）办理，提供高效、快捷、全方位的“一站式办公、一条龙服务”服务。

一、项目审批服务职能

“中心”的建立，是为打造武清开发区优质高效的投资服务环境，由武清开发区与武清区市场监管局、国土局等部门共同组建的审批服务机构。中心遵循“服务至上、优质高效”的原则，采用开发区与职能部门派驻专员联合办公的模式，协助办理开发区项目的注册、规划、国土、建设等各项手续，切实提高办结效率。

“中心”主要为企业提供服务如下：

1. 一次性告知及提醒服务：在一次性告知服务基础上，增加一次性提醒和问题汇总机制，为企业全流程手续所需要件准备工作夯实基础。

2. 参与招商接待，并为企业提供相关手续咨询服务。

3. 为开发区实体项目编制倒排工期时间表，并依据双方定制的手续时限，定时督促、跟进企业手续办理。

4. 针对企业手续推进过程中所遇到的困难，组织各职能部门召开手续对接会，切实为企业解决实际问题。

5. 市场监管委手续服务：协助办理企业名称核准、设立、变更及执照办理过程中相关问题的咨询、报件等。

6. 立项环能评手续：立项、环评、能评咨询服务；协助企业办理相关审批手续；协助组织对接相关审批部门规划手续：协助办理内外资项目规划条件、修详规方案、建筑方案、用地证、门牌号、工程证等手续。

7. 人防手续：协助办理人防报批手续。

8. 施工证手续：协助办理报建备案；勘察文件审查合格证；施工图设计文件审查合格证；监理、勘察、设计、施工招标及合同备案；节能备案；监督备案；施工证；消防设计备案（审核）；不动产权证。

9. 档案管理窗口：负责中心项目全流程档案收录及统计。

10. 集中办公区管理窗口：负责管理园区集中办公区房号申领、统计及传递工作。

二、项目报批服务

1. 企业名称核准、设立、变更的相关手续。

2. 项目用地地籍调查、权属、地类核实、征转组卷、储备证、出让方案等手续。

3. 内外资项目规划条件、修详规方案、建筑方案、用地证、门牌号、工程证等手续。

4. 人防手续：协助企业办理人防报批手续。

5. 建设手续：协助企业办理报建备案；勘察文件审查合格证；施工图设计文件审查合格证；监理、勘察、设计、施工招标及合同备案；节能备案；监督备案；施工证；消防设计备案（审核）；不动产权证。帮助企业办理清欠办、消防支队、房管局等部门相关手续及咨询工作。

三、项目协调服务

1. 国土方面：在未取得土地指标的情况下，提前对接区国土局进行土地征供手续组卷工作。

2. 规划方面：协调修详规方案、建筑方案、工程证等图纸预审。

3. 消防、人防方面：协调武清区消防支队、审批局投资项目科对施工图进行预审。

4. 建设方面：施工许可证等报卷资料预审。

第二节 工程承发包管理

建区初期，武清开发区工程建设项目承发包管理工作，坚持区内外分别负责。其中：对总公司内自建工程，由总公司直接负责组织承发包管理；对入区企业工程建设项目则由管理部门以提供服务的形式，协助搞好承发包管理。自建区以来，区内任何工程建设项目均实行招投标管理办法，从不由某个部门或某个领导独立做主。2000 年 1 月 1 日，《中华人民共和国招标投标法》颁布实施，武清开发区积极遵守、狠抓规范落实。

2016 年成立招标采购部，使工程建设管理步入规范化轨道，为确保工程建设质量，避免工程建设中腐败现象的滋生，发挥了积极作用。

一、管理组织

武清开发区为推进“四个全面”战略布局，加强党风廉政建设，推进依法治区。2016 年 3 月成立武清开发区招标采购部，成立伊始在开发区招标采购领导小组指导下，按照“三重一大”议事规则制定完善了《武清开发区项目招标采购管理办法 (试行)》(以下简称《办法》)，严格依据该办法完成招标项目 200 余个。2017 年 7 月赋予招标采购领导小组办公室职能。

二、指导文件

《武清区人民政府办公室关于规范区属国有企业招标采购工作的通知》《武清开发区项目招标采购管理办法 (试行)》《开发区关于规范自主议标流程的实施意见（试行）》。上述文件为《中华人民共和国招标投标法》及国家、天津市相关部门颁布有关招标投标的政策法规。

三、工作构架

招标采购工作采用横向分权制约机制，即由项目管理部门、预结算部和招标采购部相互监督共同配合完成项目招标采购工作：

一是项目管理部门按照《办法》规定的，通过相应层级的“三重一大”决策程序，确定项目实施。编制项目方案、技术要求、质量标准、工期等内容后，启动项目招标采购程序。二是项目管理部门将项目要求分别送预结算部和招标采购部，预结算部负责与财政局评审中心对接，出具项目招标控制价。三是招标采购部接到招标控制价后启动并协调三个部门共同完成项目招标采购流程。

四、人员构成

招标采购部由总公司副总经理张武民分管，部门人员 2 名，其中部长 1 名（孙波）、员工 1 名（陈国栋）。

五、工作程序

（一）接收项目管理部门提交的项目启动单和技术文件（任务书）；建立项目临时档案，待预结算部提供招标控制价后启动该项目。

（二）接到项目后，在工作台账上登记、建立项目编号，按照项目类型建立项目电子档案。

（三）招标资料齐全后编制项目招标文件：

一是自主邀请项目，按照行业标准、规范编制招标文件。

二是自主公开项目，与代理公司共同核对项目类别、行业规范、资质资格等信息，委托其编制项目招标文件。

三是建设主管部门公开招标项目，与代理公司共同核对项目类别、行业规范、资质资格等信息，委托其协助办理招标备案等建委手续，编制项目招标文件。

（四）招标文件联审联定。招标文件编制完成组织项目管理部门、预结算部联合审核招标文件相关条款，确认无误后报请分管领导批准发布招标公告。

（五）招标公告结束后，统计投标单位名单，传送资本运营部以便开具投标保证金收据。

（六）收集投标单位对项目及招标文件的疑问，组织项目相关部门及投标单位召开招标答疑会，并形成答疑纪要传至各投标单位。

（七）组织项目相关部门参与项目开标会。

（八）开标会后形成项目招投标情况一览表，并向招采领导小组汇报招投标情况。

（九）招投标情况一览表待招采领导小组共同签字确认后转发至项目管理部门。通知招标代理公司发布中标公示，公示结束后向中标单位发中标通知书。

（十）项目招标投标过程所有资料的存档工作。

（十一）每周编制招标项目情况周报表，及时向招采领导小组成员通报各招标采购项目进展情况及重要节点安排。

（十二）不定期组织招标采购领导小组会议。

第三节　工程质量监督

一、工程管理部职责

（一）负责编制年度工程计划，安排建设施工，搞好工程质量监理和现场协调指导；

（二）负责重点建设工程开发进度计划的编制；

（三）负责重点建设工程进度和质量的监督和管理；

（四）负责重点建设工程资料的搜集、管理和归档；

（五）负责区内产业项目催进场及日常服务工作；

（六）负责区内产业项目、自建项目燃气、电力、弱电等配套服务工作；

（七）配合招标采购部、预结算部做好招标前准备工作；

（八）负责提供与建设投资相关咨询和法律法规说明服务；

（九）保障建筑领域安全，做好农民工清欠工作；

（十）完成领导交办的其他事项。

武清开发区部分工程项目一览表

表 21

编号	项目名称	简介	备注
1	创业总部基地	1. 中心服务区占地 130 亩，建筑面积 6 万平方米。 2. 企业总部区 260 亩，建筑面积 32 万平方米 3. 服务外包区占地 160 亩，建筑面积 16 万平方米 4. 酒店服务区占地 70 亩，建筑面积 18.6 万平方米 5. 综合办公区占地面积 200 亩 6. 专家公寓占地 300 亩	
2	高新公寓	建筑面积 15 万平米	
3	中欧产业园	占地 9.5 平方公里，一期 5 平方公里，二期 4.5 平方公里	
4	京津高校科技创新园	规划面积 161 亩，建筑面积 11.5 万平方米	
5	标准厂房	单栋面积 2400~34000 平方米，总建筑面积 50 万平方米	

第四节　项目管理

项目管理主要包括对政府投资开发区的公建项目、基础设施项目进行立项审批，并在项目实施过程中进行监督检查，保证政府投资发挥最大效益。立项审批主要内容包括项目的建设规模、投资规模、资金来源、经济技术可行性、经济效益和社会效益等。对项目的监督检查，贯彻于项目建设全过程，包括对项目招标情况的监督、资金使用情况的检查等。

武清开发区从项目申办到基建程序如下：

1. 项目申办程序

入区企业投资项目申办程序，包括：立项；报批合同章程，领取批准证书；领取工商营业执照；刻章、银行开户、税务登记、财政登记、开业。

2. 用地申办程序

入区企业用地申办程序，包括：项目批文、领取规划用地许可证；填写天津市有偿用地预约申请表；签订国有土地使用权出让合同，领取国有土地使用证。

3. 基建申办程序

入区企业基建申办程序，包括：领取《规划设计条件书》进行初步设计审批；报施工图，领取规划建设许可证；委托工程监理，办理开工许可证；放线开工；竣工验收。

武清开发区对建筑设计规划要求：建筑密度不大于35%，容积率0.8 ~ 1.2以下，绿化面积在30%以上；临主干道退线15米，一般道路10米；临路围墙应采用低通透式，高度一般不超过1.8米。

随着开发区事业的快速发展，为适应任务的增加，开发区设立了工程管理部、招标采购部、预结算部、城市管理部等专业部门加强对基本建设项目的服务与管理。由工程管理部配合招标采购部、预结算部对基建项目做招标前的准备，并安排建设施工、开发进度和对工程的进度、质量进行监理，最后由城市管理部对新建项目及环境状况进行评估验收。

2016年，根据武清区人民政府办公室关于规范区属国有企业招标采购工作的通知，制订了《武清开发区项目招标采购管理办法（试行）》和《武清开发区关于规范“三重一大”决策工作的实施办法》及附件，基本建设项目管理在实践中不断改进、强化，更加趋向严密与科学。

第五节　政府采购

政府采购是20世纪末出现的新政策，第一个率先试行的是在1998年的天津市开发区。当时遵循的是“公平、效率、协商”的原则，采取公开招标、邀请招标等多种方式，政府对项目进行集中招标采购。

武清开发区工委是招标采购工作的最高决策和监督机构，其下成立招标采购领导小组负责此项工作，小组在工委领导下，对招标采购工作实施指导、管理和日常监督。为了适应开发区的管理体制机制，进一步规范招标采购行为，保证招采质量、效益，防范风险，2016 年，开发区成立招标采购部，使招采工作进一步完善。

开发区招采工作管理执行部门及职责：

（一）项目管理部门由开发区工委根据项目情况确定，负责项目方案和实施计划的制定，负责提供项目的技术要求，办理项目前期立项、图纸审查等相关手续，负责投标文件的技术评审；

（二）预结算部负责出具招标控制价、工程量清单等，负责招标文件的商务评审；履行招采领导小组办公室工作职能；

（三）招标采购部负责招标采购工作的实施和流程管理，负责项目招标资信、资格的确定，负责在相关部门提供的项目技术、商务等资料基础上，编制合规的招标文件，招标过程中行使甲方代表职责。配合招采领导小组确定中标单位。

（四）资本运营部负责招标采购过程中的资金往来。

招标采购方式及工作流程：

招标采购方式：

（一）建设主管部门公开招标：必须在建设主管部门监督下，在建设主管部门指定场所，由招标采购部对接招标代理机构依法依规组织公开招标（招标所需资料齐全时，一般完成招标不超过 45 天）。

（二）自主公开招标：由招标采购部对接招标代理机构，依据《招标公告发布暂行办法》（国家发改委第 4 号令），在“中国采购与招标网”上发布招标公告，遵循《中华人民共和国招标投标法》履行招标程序，采用低价中标法进行评估（招标所需资料齐全时，一般完成招标不超过 30 天）。

（三）自主邀请招标：须经招采领导小组批准方可采用。由项目管理部门、预结算部、招标采购部以及其他部门共同推荐符合条件的 3 家以上投标单位，由招标采购部统一发布招标邀请并组织招标，采用低价中标法进行评标（招标所需资料齐全时，一般完成招标不得少于 10 天）。

招标采购工作流程：

（一）招标采购部配合项目管理部门制定项目招标实施方案；

（二）项目管理部门配合招标采购部办理招标审批手续；

（三）招标采购部发布招标公告或招标邀请；

（四）资本运营部收取投标单位保证金；

（五）招标采购部向投标单位发放招标文件、图纸等相关资料；

（六）必要时，招标采购部组织召开招标答疑会；

（七）招标采购部组织招标会；

（八）招标采购部报请招采领导小组确定中标单位；

（九）招标采购部配合资本运营部退还中标单位的投标保证金及未中标单位的投标费用，项目管理部门根据签订合同条款配合资本运营部收取或退还中标单位其他相关费用。

开发区招标采购部自2016年成立以来至年底共接到招采项目申请136个，其中已完成104个（包括1个竞拍项目），正常推进项目11个，因政采新规定暂停的项目10个，发生异常项目11个。已完成的104个项目（招标控制价合计53858.8585万元，中标金额合计50905.53042万元，节省预算资金2953.32808万元，中标金额降幅比率5.4%）。

其中：通过建委公开招标共22个（招标控制价合计40464.1896万元，中标金额合计38825.38162万元，节省预算资金1638.80798万元，中标金额降幅比率4.1%）；通过政采招标共31个（招标控制价合计10107.071万元，中标金额合计9359.6843万元，节省预算资金747.3867万元，中标金额降幅比率7.4%）；通过自主邀请招标共39个（招标控制价合计2077.0326万元，中标金额合计1787.8137万元，节省预算资金289.2189万元，中标金额降幅比率13.9%）；通过自主议标共11个（招标控制价合计1210.5653万元，中标金额合计932.6508万元，节省预算资金277.9145万元，中标金额降幅比率22.95%）。

第六节　统计管理

开发区的统计管理具体部门为经济运行部，根据多年实践，确定该部主要工作职责是：贯彻执行上级统计机关的工作安排和有关国民经济和社会发展、经济运行、统计等工作的法律法规和规章，并组织实施和监督检查；负责统计工作，包括统计资料的收集、整理、汇总和统计报表报送，全面完成各项统计工作；负责拟定经济发展年度计划目标，制定相关制度、措施，确保完成年度发展目标；负责经济运行分析工作，为决策层提供及时、准确、前瞻的信息资料；负责向各部门提供统计数据，配合做好相关工作；负责企业扶持政策资料收集和数据审核工作；负责向税务部门提供入区项目信息资料，管理企业纳税情况；负责建立与财税部门沟通机制，定期组织税收工作分析交流例会；负责开发区经济普查工作；协调税务部门参加招商项目考察、会商和洽谈；配合做好统计法律法规规章的宣传和贯彻执行。

第三章　劳动管理

第一节　机　构

1992 年，武清区开发区管理委员会成立时，下设办公室和开发区总公司。2000 年 12 月，办公室和总公司下设 7 部 4 公司，其中成立了主管劳动的劳动就业部。2016 年，公司进行调整，涉及劳动管理职能的分为人力资源部和安全发展部，有关业务同时接受武清区劳动和社会保障局部门指导。

人力资源部职责主要有：

1. 负责劳动用工平台建设，加强与京、津、冀大中专院校联系，拓宽用工渠道，降低企业用工成本，根据企业需要组织企业参加各类招聘会，协助企业办理用工、退工、人才存档开户等手续。

2. 负责企业人才服务，定期完善企业人才信息库，宣传各级人才政策，协助企业做好各类人才的引进，奖励及落户相关工作，负责本土人才培养工作。

3. 负责专家服务基地、博士后工作站、大学生实习实践基地等人才载体建设，做好博士后的引进、培养和使用工作；加强和大院大所及科研机构联系，协助企业实现创新发展。

4. 负责对企业进行劳动用工方面法律法规政策的宣讲，发挥劳动争议调解委员会作用，及时化解劳资争议，配合区职能部门进行劳动监察、预防和处理群体性事件。

安全发展部涉及劳动管理的主要职责是：

负责劳动生产安全等相关法律法规的宣教；负责安委会办公室各项日常工作，协调开发区安委会各成员部门做好安全生产工作。

第二节　劳动力管理

一、用工制度

武清开发区招工用工严格执行《中华人民共和国劳动法》和天津市有关劳动用工制度的政策规章。

（1）用工单位经报批后，可根据自身生产经营的需要，自行确定招聘人员、自行确定机构和编制。

（2）企业用工实行劳动合同制，签订集体劳动合同报送开发区劳动管理部门审查。

（3）企业及时足额向职工支付工资，工资标准不低于天津市规定的最低限额。

（4）企业依照国家和天津市关于劳动保护的规定，保证职工在安全、卫生的条件下工作。

（5）企业职工依法享受养老、失业等社会保险和法律规定的其他福利待遇。

（6）鼓励和保障科研单位、大专院校和企业、事业单位的科技人员到开发区工作。凡调入武清开发区的外地科技人员，配偶及子女户口可迁入开发区，并享受市区居民户口待遇，配偶是农业户口的可转为非农业户口。

二、员工来源

至 2000 年，武清开发区企业从业人员达 3 万余人。员工主要来自武清和天津市、北京市及周边地区。另外，还有来自全国各地的工程技术人员和管理人员，欧美、韩、日等国家和中国港、澳、台地区的员工等。到 2016 年，吸引直接就业 12 万人。

三、员工素质

武清开发区是国家级高新技术产业开发区，拥有大学毕业、专科毕业、留学生、外籍人员等一大批科研技术人员，素质较高。管理人员中大学毕业的占 90% 以上。生产工人中，以职业学校、中专、高中毕业生为主体，特殊技术工种持证上岗率达到 95% 以上。近年，高学历员工入区呈明显上升趋势。

四、管理情况

积极配合区人力资源和社会保障局有关部门，对开发区内劳动力资源进行统计和管理，发布企业就业岗位信息，组织指导社会劳动力竞争就业，对区内劳动力和外省劳动力进区就业进行管理；帮助企业进行各类职业技能培训和各类保险收缴等。对发生劳动争议情况，协助有关部门共同依法处理等。

开发区在进入21世纪以来，社会保障制度进一步健全，使劳动力管理工作更加完善。2001年，区内有6300人缴纳养老和失业保险，占区内企业从业人数的47.2%；2002年，全区投保企业达74家，比上年度增加15家。投保人数9604人，比上年度增加3304人；至2003年，投保企业又增加21家，达到95家，投保人数增加2816人，总人数达12420人。至2016年，区内投保企业和投保人数基本做到应保尽保。

企业职工的权益一直得到较好的保障，未发生重大用工纠纷事件。近年来，区内制定落实联络员每月普访、职能部门双月联席、班子成员季度走访企业等服务制度。2012年，累计走访企业1900家（次），协调解决问题459个，提供就业岗位11417个，新拓展用工渠道4个，协助企业解决劳动用工2.7万人；2013年走访企业324家（次），解决和答复企业问题336个，组织企业开展各类招聘活动250场，累计录用1.7万人，赴河北、山东等地组织专场招聘，引进劳动力1800余名；2014年走访企业960余家（次），解决问题千余个，新建企业电子交流平台，解答181家各种问题1800余个，累计组织企业参加各类招聘会278场，累计录用1.6万人。2015年走访服务企业900余家（次），协调解决各类问题1900余个；组织招聘会281场，达成就业意向3.2万人。

2016年，走访企业980余家（次），协调解决各类问题1100余个，同步完善高管微信交流平台等企业电子服务平台建设。推动38家企业完成转型升级，兑现扶持资金补贴245.5万元。举办各类招聘会272场，提供就业岗位10.5万个，达成就业意向4.1万个，兑现2015年度人才奖励资金1849.72万元。

第三节　劳动工资

一、工资的宏观管理

开发区所属企业员工的劳动工资由各企业独立自主依据《中华人民共和国劳动法》和市、区法律、法规分配。开发区执行配合武清区人力资源和社会保障局有关工资的规定进行宏观管理。

1994年，企业工资改革实现了计划经济向市场经济的转变，开始落实企业分配自主权，上级部门由微观管理向宏观管理过渡。

1995 年，《中华人民共和国劳动法》实施，境内企业开始实施最低工资制度，并开始建立工资分配宏观指导体系。

2002 年，按照天津市统一要求，对企业自主决定工资水平办法、工资指导线及最低工资标准等工资调控政策进行调整：一是在扩大企业自主决定工资水平办法的实行范围方面，突破国有企业改制后才能自主决定工资水平的限制，规定无论什么性质的企业改制后均可申请实行自主，实行计税工资企业工资集体协商后也可自主决定工资水平；二是完善工资指导线制。当年，武清区政府直接公布工资指导线水平，提高了发布层次，调控力度得到加强。到“十五”期末，全区企业单位从业人员人均劳动报酬是“九五”期末的 1.92 倍，年均递增 13.9%，与全区 GDP 增幅基本同步。

2006 年 6—7 月，武清区劳动和社会保障局对全区企业职工一季度工资收入进行抽样调查，在 7 类企业 496 户 81594 人中，人均月工资为 1544 元。当年，开发区遵照《天津市 2005 年度全市平均工资等有关问题的通知》精神，充分发挥劳动力市场工资指导价位的作用，工资指导线、基准线由 12% 调整为 13%，下线由 5% 调整为 6%，上线由 20% 调整为 22%。

2007 年，区内企业从业人员劳动工资继续提高。一季度，武清区劳动社保局对包括开发区的企业和职工劳动工资进行抽样调查，2006 年度被调查企业月均工资为 1499 元。

2008 年，被调查企业月均工资为 1476 元；到 2009 年企业月均工资突破 2000 元，达到 2033 元。至 2016 年，企业月均工资达到 5265 元。

二、最低工资

天津地区 1993 年 1 月颁布职工平均工资，1995 年开始执行最低工资标准。此后，用人单位内部工资分配制度、分配形式、工资收入水平得以规范，使劳动者的合法权益也得到相应的保障。区内用人企业单位绝大多数能够执行这一标准；个别单位未执行的，在区劳动社保局的监督检查下限期整改，使所有用人单位的劳动者劳动工资均能达到天津市规定的最低工资标准以上。

武清区 20 年内 3 阶段最低工资标准和平均工资表

表 22

年份	平均工资（元 / 月）	月最低工资标准（元）	非全日制用工（元 / 小时）	最低工资执行时间
1996	637	230	—	1996.7.1
2006	1895	650	6.4	2006.4.1
2016	5265	1950	19.5	2016.7.1

第四节　劳动安全与保护

一、安全生产管理机构

武清开发区自建区起十分重视劳动安全与保护，始终坚持“安全第一、预防为主、综合治理”的方针，坚持“安全发展”的理念，坚持“属地管理、分级负责”的原则，积极贯彻落实《中华人民共和国安全生产法》和《天津市安全生产责任制规定》，制定了《武清开发区安全生产工作方案》，并在 2015 年做了进一步修订，实现了“依法整顿、综合治理、巩固提高、强化监管、务求实效”的总体要求，正式组建安全发展部，努力打造开发区安全监管工作的长效机制。

开发区安全生产建有“武清开发区安全生产委员会”，设主任 1 名，作为开发区安全生产工作第一责任人，对开发区安全生产工作全面负责；设副主任 5 人，配合主任开展工作，领导分管部门、公司做好分管范围内的各项安全生产；设委员 10 名，由各部门、公司负责人组成，分管各部门、公司单位的安全生产责任工作。

二、安全生产保护措施

开发区安全生产委员会大力开展安全教育活动，推进多项安全检查，全面排查事故隐患，解决了一批安全生产中的突出问题，完成了安全生产的既定目标。其主要措施:

1. 建立健全安全责任体系

一是制定《安全开发区建设实施意见》，成立领导小组，形成“责任明确、各司其职”的安全监管格局。制定了《武清开发区安全生产“党政同责、一岗双责”实施方案》，按照“管行业必须管安全、管业务必须管安全、管生产经营必须管安全”原则履行安全职责。二是重新修订了《武清开发区安全生产工作方案》，明确实行安全生产工作周汇报制度，做到常抓不懈，警钟长鸣。三是与综合服务部、安全发展部、工程管理部、城市管理部、自来水公司、绿化公司、热力公司、工业物业公司、开发区物业公司共9个负有安全生产责任部门签订安全生产目标责任书，层层压实安全监管责任。四是与区内305家企业签订了安全生产目标责任书，同时要求企业与车间、班组签订目标责任书，将安全责任落实到每道工序、每个岗位。2015年，与区内213家企业签订安全生产责任书；2016年制定风险评估机制和黑名单管理制度，与305家企业签订安全生产目标责任书，强化主体责任。

2. 积极开展安全生产宣传和教育培训

一是多措并举，加强宣传、培训工作，抓好各项法规政策的贯彻落实。通过邀请安全专家开展讲座、组织安全生产月活动、检查、走访等多种形式进行新“安全生产法”“五落实五到位”“党政同责，一岗双责”等宣贯活动。2015年，发放宣传书籍及挂图共1200余份。2016年，协助区安监局、市场监管局、消防支队举办了2016年安全生产月咨询日、职业卫生宣传周、“119”消防安全宣传日等专题活动5次，并组织开展了安全知识竞赛，共发放宣传书籍及挂图1320份。二是认真开展对企业负责人、安全管理人员和特种作业人员进行多样培训。2015年，针对上述人员培训达2400余人次；召开4次安全生产工作会议，700余家次企业参会，对春节、“两会”、“安全生产月”、“十一”等关键节点的安全生产工作进行了安排和部署。组织召开“安全生产工作会议”“安全生产月工作会议”“开发区危险化学品专项整治会议”“开发区大排查大整治专题会议”等共6次会议，及时传达市、区两级有关指示精神，安排部署专题工作，共1500家（次）企业2000人次参加。邀请专家组织开展了5次安全生产专题培训会议，共950家（次）企业1500人次参加。组织企业负责人、安全管理、特种作业人员参加持证上岗培训3次，共培训2000余人。2016年开展安全教育专题培训6次，专题活动5次，持证培训5次，4000余人次参与。

3. 深入排查隐患大力整治

每年开发区都要针对季节特点、重要时段、重要点位开展了多轮次的排查整治活动。2015年，共检查复查企业960余家次，下发整改通知书410余份，发现各类安全隐患1830项，当年整改1720项，整改率达94%。通过开展专项整治活动，有效防范了各类安全事故的发生。2016年，强化专项整治，梳理建立重点部件专项档案，深入排查，聘请专家检查企业 761 家（次），发现隐患 1415 项，整改 1361 项，其余继续推动整改。搭建安全监控平台，实现对 8 家危化企业 24 小时监控。认真开展食品检查，推动 367 家企业开展自查，发现问题 290 项，整改 273 项，其余继续。开展药品巡查 300 余次，检查 230 余家次，未发现问题。

一是多年持续开展安全生产大排查大整治活动。按照“全覆盖、零容忍、严执法、重实效”的总要求，坚持问题导向、防打结合、标本兼治、注重治本、综合施策的原则，对开发区所有企业开展了检查排查整治，整改消除了一批安全隐患。二是集中开展了危险化学品专项整治活动，按照武清区统一部署，开发区聘请危险化学品专家集中开展了危险化学品企业安全排查整治行动，做到横向到边、纵向到底、不留死角。督促贝格、阿托兹、飞博来、强源等 13 家涉及“黄、蓝”表企业进行隐患整改，至 2016 年已全部完成。三是扎实开展各行业、各领域安全专项治理。开发区安委会各成员部门先后开展了消防安全、人员密集场所、粉尘作业、预防硫化氢中毒、特种设备作业和供水、供热、供气等专项检查，同时在元旦、春节、“五一”、“十一”、“两会”等重要时段及马拉松比赛等重要活动期间开展了安全生产大检查，确保了开发区安全生产形势的持续稳定。

2006 年，对区内 12 家排污重点监测企业和 38 家从事危险化学品生产、贮存、使用的企业进行普查，对存在问题企业督促及时整改到位。2007 年对有关企业进行 3 次拉网式普查，督促 27 家存在问题企业整改到位。

2012 年，与区内 206 家企业签订安全生产目标责任书，深入企业进行安全生产检查 684 家次，督促整改安全隐患 804 项。

2013 年重新修订《武清开发区安全生产工作方案》，与区内 164 家企业签订安全生产目标责任书。对企业进行安全检查 634 家（次），整改安全隐患 683 项。举办 4 期企业高管系列培训班。

2014 年，与 112 家重点企业签订安全生产目标责任书，检查企业 790 余家（次），整改隐患 1500 项，依法处罚问题企业 6 家。全年化解各类涉企矛盾 27 件。开发区被评为武清区 2014 年度平安示范园区。

2016 年，围绕季节特点、重要时段、重要点位开展了多轮次的排查整治活动，共检查复查企业 1500 余家（次），下发整改通知书 650 余份，发现各类安全隐患 1415 项。截至 2016 年年底，已整改 1361 项，整改率达 96%。通过开展专项整治活动，有效防范了各类安全事故的发生。一是采取聘请安全专家协助检查的方式，全年开展日常检查和 9 次专项检查，重点推动企业开展粉尘专项评估的大排查大整治。二是对自来水公司、华电福源热电站、百川燃气等供水、供电、供热和供气等涉及公共安全点位开展了 3 次排查，确保生产生活安全，并在春节等重要活动期间开展了安全大检查，确保开发区安全形势稳定。

4. 完善安监体系，提高保障能力

在完善安全监管体系方面，开发区一是对区内有关企业安全生产情况进行全面摸底调查，建立了安全信息数据库。二是建立了危险化学品、职业卫生、特种设备、消防等专项档案，特别是将企业实施分级管理，2015 年设定 281 家企业中，一级企业 86 家，二级企业 121 家，三级企业 74 家。对一级企业实行重点监管，每月检查一次，二级企业每季度检查一次，三级企业每半年检查一次。三是安防网建设稳步推进，如伊利、完达山等 13 家企业进行了终端设备的安装、调试。四是与永安评价公司签订安全服务外包合同，聘请专家每季度协助开发区进行安全生产检查，提高了安全检查的专业性、准确度，制定安全风险评估制度，邀请专家进行把关，从源头上控制了安全风险。

在提高应急保障能力方面，一是聘请安全专家编制了《武清开发区突发事件综合应急预案》，规范突发事件处置程序。二是国家安研中心公司正对开发区安全生产风险全面评估，2017 年 6 月前完成风险评估报告，将据此对重点区域、单位和重要风险源点加强防范，并实现数字化和可视化，为突发事故应急救援提供决策支持。三是督促欧利生、绫致、日丰、大都克、光宝电子等 51 家重点企业开展了消防应急疏散演练，提高企业现场应急处置能力。

5. 落实安全开发区建设六件实事

2016 年，开发区一是与天津赛智理工安全评价公司签订服务合同，聘请专家对企业进行检查，提高了安全检查的专业性。二是制定安全风险评估制度，邀请专家对新入区 45 个项目企业把关，从源头上控制安全风险。三是开发区 8 家涉及危化企业完成安防网一期建设工程，实现 24 小时实时监控。四是树立艾尔姆、伊利、亚马逊、基伊埃 4 家企业分别为职业卫生、涉氨、仓储物流、机械制造方面安全生产示范单位，共组织 127 家同行业企业现场交流，推广好的安全生产工作经验。五是制定“黑名单”管理制度，对纳入“黑名单”的企业办理相关业务予以限制或禁止。六是已对企业巡更系统全面调查，推动 63 家企业设立巡更系统，共有 86 家企业建立巡更系统。

6. 重污染天气的应急保障

近年来，随着污染天气的加重与频发，按照国家、天津市、武清区的法律法规及预案，开发区针对重污染天气实施预警行动、应急响应和污染排放控制。所谓“重污染天气”是指根据《环境空气质量指数（AQI）技术规定（试行）》（HJ633 — 2012），空气质量指数（AQI）级别达到五级（重试污染）及以上污染程度的大气污染。

2016年，开发区成立武清开发区重污染天气应急领导小组（简称“应急领导小组”）。组长由郭新华、张绍锋担任，副组长由张书月、李鹏程、武剑峰担任。成员包括：综合服务部（原综合部）、工程管理部（原建设部）、安全发展部、城市管理部（原城管部）、热力公司、工业物业公司、开发区物业公司、绿化公司。

主要职责是：负责制定并实施重污染天气应急保障实施方案，落实区级应急预案以及各成员部门应急保障预案的各项任务、措施，并将实施方案的执行情况及时上报区应急指挥部。

（1）办事机构及职责

应急领导小组的办事机构是开发区重污染天气应急小组办公室（简称“应急小组办公室”），应急小组办公室作为常设机构，设在安全发展部。应急小组办公室主任由王付华担任。

主要职责是：负责应急小组的日常工作，指导、协调、监督重污染天气预警，督促检查各成员部门应急响应措施的落实情况，汇总各方面情况报上级部门及有关领导。

（2）应急小组成员职责

安全发展部：

承担应急小组办公室的职责。负责按照区应急指挥部发布的预警信息和指示要求，协助环保等有关部门开展空气环境质量监测、重污染天气预警在本区域内的发布、对重点排污企业主要污染物排放情况进行执法检查等，并制定监测预警应急保障预案。负责面向开发区内企业及单位，发布空气重污染日预警信息、健康保护信息、做好减排措施的宣传及推动工作；在空气质量严重污染和极重污染情况下，对开发区内重点及一般排放企业实行限产减排监督并根据实际情况需要下达临时停产指令。

工程管理部：

负责对开发区各建筑工地的扬尘污染控制措施实施监督管理，并按预警分级发布停工令；督促混凝土搅拌站落实扬尘污染防治，并实施监督管理，负责对工程建设项目混凝土和砂浆使用情况进行监管。

城市管理部：

负责协调开发区内建筑垃圾、沙石等散装物料运输管理监管工作；区内道路保洁和按照预警级别洒水；负责垃圾焚烧、秸秆焚烧、城区户外烧烤及餐饮油烟整治。

热力公司：

提高锅炉污染物治理设施运行效率，确保污染物排放符合国家及天津市地方标准。

工业物业公司、开发区物业公司：

负责面向本区内居民、企业员工发布健康保护信息及做好减排措施的宣传及推动工作。

绿化公司：

负责防治养护区域内园林绿化工地的扬尘污染。

综合服务部：

负责组织对应急小组各成员部门重污染天气应急保障实施方案落实情况进行监督检查，对执行不力的成员部门及责任人进行责任追究。

（3）监测预警

区应急指挥部接到市人民政府、市环保局预警信息后，经报请区政府、区应急指挥部主要领导同志同意，由区应急指挥部办公室负责面向全区发布预警信息工作。

重污染天气预警等级分为四级，与重污染天气事件等级分级相对应，分别为Ⅳ级（蓝色）、Ⅲ级（黄色）、Ⅱ级（橙色）、Ⅰ级（红色）预警，Ⅰ级（红色）为最高级别。

Ⅳ级（蓝色）预警：

预测空气质量指数（AQI）日均值（24 小时均值，下同）> 200 且未达到高级别预警条件时。

Ⅲ级（黄色）预警：

预测 AQI 日均值 > 200 将持续 2 天及以上且未达到高级别预警条件时。

Ⅱ级（橙色）预警：

预测 AQI 日均值 > 200 将持续 3 天且出现 AQI 日均值 > 300 的情况时。

Ⅰ级（红色）预警：

预测 AQI 日均值 > 200 将持续 4 天及以上且 AQI 日均值 > 300 将持续 2 天及以上时；或预测 AQI 日均值达到 500 并将持续 1 天及以上时。

安全发展部牵头组织做好开发区内预警信息发布工作。

第一时间通过应急平台短信系统、QQ 群、政务内网等方式向区内各企业单位负责人发送我区空气质量数据和必须采取的重污染天气应急响应措施。

通过网络、电子显示装置、报刊等媒体和微信、手机短信等方式向社会公众发布信息，告知公众主动采取自我防护措施。

随着预警级别的提高，增加信息发布频次。安全发展部、各物价公司等有关部门负责，在学校、医院、体育场（馆）、旅游景区（点）等重点区域和人员密集场所，做好大气重污染预警信息的接收和传播工作。

预警信息内容：重污染天气发生的时间、地点、范围、预警等级、主要污染物浓度范围等。

（4）响应措施

按照“以人为本、预防为主，强化管理、统一领导，加强预警、及时响应，部门联动、社会参与”的原则，根据空气污染情况分别采取相对应的四级响应措施。

发布Ⅳ级预警时，实施Ⅳ级响应。

建议性和健康防护措施。

提醒儿童、老年人和心脏病、肺病患者以及过敏性疾病患者应当留在室内，停止户外运动，一般人群减少户外运动。倡导公众绿色出行和绿色生活，尽量乘坐公共交通工具或电动汽车等方式出行，减少祭祀烧纸等行为。倡导工厂、工地等有关单位积极采取措施，减少工业和扬尘污染的排放。

发布Ⅲ级预警时，实施Ⅲ级响应。

在Ⅳ级响应措施基础上，增加以下强制性措施：

1）重点排污工业企业中除已达到燃气排放标准的燃煤设施外，其余燃煤设施全部采取限产、加强管理等措施，确保二氧化硫、烟（粉）尘、二氧化氮排放量各削减20% 或达到燃气排放标准。

2）一般污染排放企业采取使用低硫优质煤、提高污染治理设施运行效率、压缩生产负荷等措施，确保二氧化硫、烟（粉）尘、二氧化氮排放浓度控制在现行排放标准限值的 80% 以下，不能达到要求的，一律停产。

3）停止室外喷涂、粉刷、切割、护坡喷浆作业。

4）停止所有施工工地的土石方作业（包括：停止土石方开挖、回填、场内倒运、掺拌石灰、混凝土剔凿等作业，停止建筑工程配套道路和管沟开挖作业）。建筑垃圾和渣土运输车、砂石运输车辆禁止上路行驶。

5）所有水泥粉磨站、渣土存放点全面停止生产、运行。混凝土搅拌站和砂浆搅拌站停止生产，站内堆放的散体物料全部苫盖，增加洒水降尘频次。

6）城区及有关镇区主要道路在日常机扫水洗作业的基础上，增加机扫水洗和保洁作业频次。对于可机扫水洗道路，在非冰冻期内每日大水量冲洗 2 至 3 次，在冰冻期内增加吸扫作业频次。

7）加强公交运力保障。

8）城区道路全天实行中型及以上柴油货车限行管理（承担民生保障及急救、抢险等任务的除外）。

发布Ⅱ级预警时，实施Ⅱ级响应。

在Ⅲ级响应措施基础上，增加以下强制性措施：

1）重点排污工业企业中除已达到燃气排放标准的燃煤设施外，其余燃煤设施确保二氧化硫、烟（粉）尘、二氧化氮排放量削减比例各增加至 30% 或达到燃气排放标准。

2）一般污染排放企业采取使用低硫优质煤、提高污染治理设施运行效率、压缩生产负荷等措施，确保二氧化硫、烟（粉）尘、二氧化氮排放浓度控制在现行排放标准限值的 70% 以下，不能达到要求的，一律停产。

3）城区及有关镇区主要道路在日常机扫水洗作业的基础上，增加机扫水洗和保洁作业频次。对于可机扫水洗道路，在非冰冻期内每日大水量冲洗增加到 3 至 4 次，在冰冻期内增加吸扫作业频次。

发布Ⅰ级预警时，实施Ⅰ级响应。

在Ⅱ级响应措施基础上，增加以下强制性措施：

1）停止全区可能产生大气污染的与建设工程有关的生产活动。

2）全区行政区域内道路全天实行机动车（含外埠车辆）单双号行驶。

3）城区及有关镇区主要道路在日常机扫水洗作业的基础上，增加机扫水洗和保洁作业频次。对于可机扫水洗道路，在非冰冻期内持续进行机扫、冲洗和洒水作业；在冰冻期内增加吸扫作业频次。

4）预测 AQI 日均值达到 500 并将持续 1 天及以上时，中小学及幼儿园停课。

5）停止所有户外大型活动。

6）企事业单位实行弹性工作制。

响应终止

预警解除即响应终止，应急指挥部各成员单位、各镇人民政府（街道办事处）负责通知采取响应措施的单位终止响应。

（5）保障措施

1）加强组织领导。

开发区重污染天气应急领导小组负责统一领导重污染天气的预警响应工作。开发区应急领导小组办公室设在安全发展部，负责开发区应急领导小组的日常工作，对接武清区重污染天气应急指挥部，及时报送信息、反馈情况、传达指令，应急小组成员各部部长及公司经理是第一责任人。

2）建立工作机制。

应急准备。开发区应急领导小组办公室牵头组织做好污染排放源清单的建立与更新工作，并报区重污染天气应急指挥部备案。包括：工业排放源及污染控制措施清单、混凝土砂浆搅拌站及水泥粉磨站扬尘排放源及污染控制措施清单、建筑拆迁等施工工地扬尘排放源及污染控制措施清单、粉状物料渣土贮存场扬尘排放源及污染控制措施清单。

方案启动。预警信息发布与应急响应启动同步进行。在接到应急预警信息后，经报请开发区应急领导小组主要领导同意实施本方案，有关各部、公司据职责分工，落实应急响应措施。

监督检查。方案启动 3 小时后，各相关单位根据职责分工，责成专人开始监管检查。方案实施 12 小时后，区应急指挥部督察组采取巡查、抽查的方式进行监督检查。对没有严格落实响应措施的现场纠正、督促落实，检查过程中发现的问题及时报区应急指挥部主要领导。在区应急指挥部启动督查机制后，开发区应急领导小组按要求做好相关工作。

责任追究。应急响应过程中，对拒不执行应急措施的企业，由有关单位依法采取措施立即关闭；对执行不力的企业，要按照高限依法严肃查处。应急响应结束后，应急领导小组办公室要汇总情况、编写专报，上报开发区有关领导。

总结评估。预警解决即响应终止，接到区级指令后，开发区应急领导小组办公室负责通知采取响应措施的单位停止响应，并组织对响应过程和响应措施效果进行总结评估，针对存在问题提出意见建议，经开发区主要领导、分管领导同意后，24 小时内报区应急指挥部。

强化资源保障。开发区应急领导小组办公室要建立完善环境安全应急指挥系统，根据应急工作需要在各相关单位抽调人员参与工作，并制作应急响应联络图，配备必要通讯器材。本方案实施后，各单位相关工作人员接受开发区应急领导小组统一指挥，落实相关措施。各有关企业、单位要安排足够的人力资源和专项经费，确保应急各项工作顺利进行。

加大宣教演练。通过短信、互联网、手册、刊物、宣传画等手段，广泛宣传针对重污染天气的各项应急法律、法规，积极向群众宣传重污染天气的健康防护常识和技能，开发区综合部要协调区内媒体全力协助做好相关工作。同时，开发区应急领导小组办公室每年至少组织 1 次专项演练，组织专家对演练实效进行评估，积累经验、总结教训、弥补不足，并及时对工作进行调整。

第四章　工商管理

第一节　基本情况

2011年6月28日，“泉州路工商所”迁址到武清开发区创业总部基地C01号楼办公。

2012年8月，工商武清分局调整辖区，武清开发区内工商管理全部划归泉州路工商所管辖。

2014年2月28日，天津市市场和质量监督管理委员会成立（原工商、质监、药监合并）。随之镇街市场和质量监督管理所挂牌。泉州路工商所更名为：武清区东蒲洼街市场和质量监督管理所、武清区豆张庄镇市场和质量监督管理所，两所合署办公。

辖区监管范围：武清开发区、商务区、创业总部基地、东蒲洼街、豆张庄镇等。

监管所的业务工作主要是：辖区各类市场主体的日常巡查监管（年度报告、双随机抽查、经营异常名录移出、执法检查数据录入等）；个体工商户的设立、变更、注销登记；食品生产、食品、保健食品经营的监管；食品、保健食品经营、餐饮业个体工商户的食品经营许可证的受理、现场核查、发证；商标、广告、合同监管（指导商标注册、规范广告经营行为、培养“守合同，重信用”单位等）；执法办案、查处违法生产经营行为；消保维权等。

近年来，武清开发区发展迅速。截至2016年年底，各类市场主体总数7000余户（含各镇街、园区招商注册在武清开发区的企业），培养命名“守合同，重信用”企业7家，天津市著名商标3件。

东蒲洼街市场监管所2016年查处各类违法案件43件，罚没款23万元；解决处理消费者投诉举报1021件，为消费者挽回经济损失100余万元。开通了“绫致时装（天津）有限公司”“天津圣朗商业有限公司（佛罗伦萨小镇）”两个“消费维权直通站”，提高了维权效率，有效保护了消费者的合法权益。

第二节 发证企业情况

武清开发区辖区内共有强制性产品认证（3C）获证企业27家。其中，建筑安全玻璃4家；汽车安全玻璃1家；低压成套开关设备（低压配电柜）2家；开关及控制器等1家；音视频录制播放及处理设备1家；汽车灯具1家；电动三轮车1家；汽车改装1家；汽车门铰链1家；汽车内饰件3家；汽车座椅及头枕1家；压缩机1家；空调器2家；消防产品3家；照明灯具1家；混凝土防冻剂1家。

工业产品生产许可证获证企业20家。其中，工业品取证企业11家；电线电缆1家；复合肥1家；危险化学品包装物、容器3家；离心泵1家；助力车（电动自行车）1家；预应力钢绞线1家；制冷设备3家。其中，食品相关产品取证企业9家；食品用塑料包装容器工具等制品7家；食品用纸包装容器等制品1家；餐具洗涤剂1家。

截至2016年底，园区有12家企业的16种产品获得“天津市名牌产品”称号。2014年天津红日药业股份有限公司被认定为第一届天津质量奖提名奖，2016年被认定为第二届天津质量奖。

附：2016年度武清开发区发证企业名单

强制性产品认证（3C）获证企业一览表

（有效证书）

表23

序号	认证项目第二级	认证项目第三级	企业名称	生产地址
1	安全玻璃	建筑安全玻璃	天津南玻节能玻璃有限公司	天津市新技术产业园区武清开发区
2	安全玻璃	建筑安全玻璃	天津信堡玻璃股份有限公司	天津市武清区天津新技术产业园区武清开发区内泉达路31号
3	安全玻璃	建筑安全玻璃	信义玻璃（天津）有限公司	天津市新技术产业园区武清开发区泉发路33号

续表 23

序号	认证项目第二级	认证项目第三级	企业名称	生产地址
4	安全玻璃	建筑安全玻璃	信义光伏产业（安徽）控股有限公司天津分公司	天津市武清开发区广源道北侧
5	安全玻璃	汽车安全玻璃	信义汽车部件（天津）有限公司	天津市新技术产业园区武清开发区广源道南侧信义玻璃工业园
6	安全玻璃	低压成套开关设备	天津博世达电力设备制造有限公司	天津市武清区发达路 4 号
7	安全玻璃	低压成套开关设备	天津市建电实业有限公司	中国天津武清开发区泉旺路 19 号
8	安全玻璃	开关及控制器等	丹佛斯（天津）有限公司武清分公司	天津市新技术产业园区武清开发区泉汇路 9 号
9	音视频设备	音视频录制播放及处理设备	天津华迈科技有限公司	天津市武清开发区福源道泉和路 8 号
10	机动车辆及安全附件	汽车灯具	欧德亮法尔宝汽车灯系统科技(天津）有限公司	天津市新技术产业园区武清开发区新兴路 1 号北欧绿色产业园
11	机动车辆及安全附件	电动三轮车	天津丰腾科技发展有限公司	天津市武清开发区福源道 18 号 511 — 68（集中办公区）
12	机动车辆及安全附件	汽车改装	中天高科特种车辆有限公司	中国天津市武清开发区泉发路西侧
13	机动车辆及安全附件	汽车门锁及门保持件	那美钢（天津）汽配有限公司	天津新技术产业园区武清开发区汇丰路 7 号
14	机动车辆及安全附件	汽车门锁及门保持件	山阳（天津）机械有限公司	天津新技术产业园区武清开发区开源道 56 号
15	机动车辆及安全附件	汽车内饰件	梦达驰汽车系统(天津）有限公司	天津新技术产业园区武清开发区开源道北侧

续表 23

序号	认证项目第二级	认证项目第三级	企业名称	生产地址
16	机动车辆及安全附件	汽车内饰件	丘比克（天津）转印有限公司	天津武清开发区汇丰路 5 号
17	机动车辆及安全附件	汽车内饰件	天津诗兰姆汽车零部件有限公司	天津市武清开发区源道 36 号
18	机动车辆及安全附件	汽车座椅及座椅头枕	宝沃佛吉亚（天津）汽车部件系统有限公司	天津新技术产业园区武清开发区泉明路 8 号 7 号厂房
19	家用和类似用途设备	压缩机	丹佛斯（天津）有限公司	天津市武清开发区福源道 5 号
20	家用和类似用途设备	压缩机	思科普压缩机（天津）有限公司	天津新技术产业园区武清开发区开源道 27 号
21	家用和类似用途设备	空调器	天津奥克斯电气有限公司	天津市武清开发区福源道北侧
22	家用和类似用途设备	空调器	维克（天津）有限公司	天津市武清开发区源和道 16 号
23	消防产品	建筑耐火构件	天津龙甲特种门窗有限公司	天津新技术产业园区武清开发区禄源道 22 号
24	消防产品	建筑耐火构件	天津市龙甲门业有限公司	天津新技术产业园区武清开发区福源道 18 号
25	消防产品	喷水灭火产品	丹佛斯森科（天津）消防设备有限公司	天津新技术产业园区武清开发区泉汇路 9 号
26	照明电器	灯具	莱斯勒斯风电科技（天津）有限公司	天津新技术产业园区武清开发区福源道北侧
27	装饰装修产品	混凝土防冻剂	天津建工特种混凝土材料科技发展有限公司	天津市武清开发区泉华路 9 号

工业产品生产许可证（QS）获证企业一览表

（工业品部分）

表 24

序号	企业名称	产品名称	证书号	注册地址	生产地址	备注
1	天津市津能电线有限公司	电线电线	（津）XK06—001—00010	天津新技术产业园区武清开发区开源道 32 号	武清开发区开源道 32 号	省级发证
2	天津博生源肥料科技发展有限公司	复肥	（津）XK13—001—00031	天津市武清开发区福源道 18 号 531	大良镇武香路 8 号	省级发证
3	深圳华特容器股份有限公司天津分公司	危包	（津）XK12—001—02012	天津市武清开发区禄源道 27 号	武清开发区禄源道 27 号	省级发证
4	天津中粮制桶有限公司	危包	（津）XK12—001—00066	天津新技术产业园区武清开发区丰和路与广源道交口	武清开发区丰和路与广源道交口	省级发证
5	中粮包装（天津）有限公司	危包	（津）XK12—001—00067	天津新技术产业园区武清开发区开源道	武清开发区开源道	省级发证
6	西岛泵（天津）有限公司	离心泵	（津）XK06—003—00031	天津新技术产业园区武清开发区高新路南	武清开发区高新路南	省级发证
7	天津三一友泰科技有限公司	助力车（电动自行车）	（津）XK16—002—00224	天津市武清开发区高新路	武清开发区高新路 7 号	省级发证

续表 24

序号	企业名称	产品名称	证书号	注册地址	生产地址	备注
8	康业钢丝（天津）有限公司	预应力混凝土用钢材钢丝	XK05 — 003 — 00221	天津市武清开发区泉丰路 9 号	武清开发区泉丰路 9 号	国家发证
9	丹佛斯(天津)有限公司	制冷设备	XK06 — 015 — 00891	武清开发区福源道 5 号	武清开发区福源道 5 号	国家发证
10	天加空调（天津）有限公司	制冷设备	XK06 — 015 — 01210	天津新技术产业园区武清开发区开源道 21 号	武清开发区开源道 21 号	国家发证
11	维克（天津）有限公司	制冷设备	XK06 — 015 — 01506	天津市武清开发区源和道 16 号	武清开发区源和道 16 号	国家发证
12	北京华创瑞风空调科技有限公司天津分公司	制冷设备	XK06 — 015 — 01913	天津市武清区开发区泉丰路 9 号第 3 号厂房	天津市武清区开发区泉丰路 9 号第 3 号厂房	国家发证
13	艾默生过程管理（天津）阀门有限公司	防爆电器	XK06 — 014 — 00833		武清开发区	国家发证
14	天地融电子(天津)有限公司	集成电器 IC 卡读写机	XK09 — 008 — 00292		武清开发区泉达路 20 号	国家发证

工业产品生产许可证（QS）获证企业一览表

（食品相关部分）

表 25

序号	企业名称	企业地址	产品名称	负责人	证书号
1	奥普拉（天津）塑料制品有限公司武清分公司	天津新技术产业园区武清开发区泉达路 16 号	食品用塑料包装窗口工具等制品		（津）XK16－204－00137
2	瑞一（中国）科技发展有限公司	天津新技术产业园区武清开发区泉汇路 2 号	食品用塑料包装窗口工具等制品	张明	（津）XK16－204－00028
3	天津市泉塑塑料制品有限公司	天津市武清区开发区福源道北侧	食品用塑料包装窗口工具等制品	张东海	（津）XK16－204－00264
4	天津娃哈哈宏振饮料有限公司	天津市武清开发区福源道北侧	食品用塑料包装窗口工具等制品	宗庆后	（津）XK16－204－00092
5	天津完达山乳品有限公司	天津市武清开发区泉发路 28 号	食品用塑料包装窗口工具等制品	孙红霞	（津）XK16－204－00172
6	天津伊利乳品有限责任公司	天津新技术产业园区武清开发区泉达路 16 号	食品用塑料包装窗口工具等制品	李勇	（津）XK16－204－00107
7	天津丰美食用油有限公司	天津市武清开发区开源道 63 号	食品用塑料包装窗口工具等制品	张铁强	（津）XK16－204－00240
8	天津天狮生物工程有限公司	天津市武清开发区新源道 20 号	餐具洗涤剂	曹满	（津）XK16－114－00005
9	万国食品包装（天津）有限公司	天津市武清开发区泉汇路 16 号	食品用塑料包装窗口工具等制品	何诗敏	（津）XK16－205－00019

武清开发区名牌产品情况表

表 26

序号	申报单位	申报产品	注册商标	备注
1	天津天狮生物工程有限公司	虫草菌丝体胶囊	天狮	
	天津天狮生物工程有限公司	儿童型营养高钙冲剂	天狮	
2	天津市宇刚保温建材有限公司	预制直埋保温管	图形	
3	天津红日药业股份有限公司	血必净注射液	血必净	
	天津红日药业股份有限公司	盐酸法舒地尔注射液	川威	
	天津红日药业股份有限公司	低分子量肝钙注射液	博璞青	
4	天津大华油脂有限公司	小磨香油	芝露坊	
5	天津市普光医用材料制造有限公司	医用无纺纱布	LIGHTS	
6	蜡笔小新（天津）有限公司	果冻	蜡笔小新（图形）	
7	金红叶纸业（天津）有限公司	卫生纸、纸巾纸	清风	
8	乐金华奥斯（天津）有限公司	PVC－U门窗异型材	好佳喜	
9	天津冠芳可乐饮料有限公司	野山楂果汁果肉饮料	冠芳	
10	天津南玻节能玻璃有限公司	中空玻璃	SG（图形）	
	天津南玻节能玻璃有限公司	低辐射镀膜玻璃	SG（图形）	
11	天津市龙甲门业有限公司	防盗门、防火门	龙甲	
12	天津市福厦食品有限公司	巧克力	怡浓（图形）	

第五章　税收管理

第一节　国、地税务

1994年，国家实行税制改革，国、地税机构分设。8月1日，天津市武清县国家税务局开始对外办公。县国税局内设8个职能科室及22个国税所。1996年，增设开发区国税所。

1994年8月1日，天津市地方税务局武清县分局正式成立。下设6个科室和21个税务所。1998年7月设立杨村中心税务所。县地税局负责县直和34个乡镇各类企业、党政机关及事业单位的地方税收征管工作。1997年1月6日，国、地税征管分工调整，开始对在县开发区内注册企业的营业税、个人所得税、车船使用税、印花税、房产税、土地使用税及内资企业所得税进行征管。翌年9月1日，国、地税分工再次调整，开始对全县集贸市场和个体工商户的营业税、个人所得税及其它地方税收进行征管，并开始对各类纳税人随增值税和消费税附征的城市维护建设税、教育费附加、防洪工程维护费进行征管。

开发区的经济运行部负责与税务部门的沟通，提供入区项目信息资料，管理企业纳税情况，定期组织税收工作分析交流例会等。

第二节　税收征稽

1993—2016年开发区地税完成税收情况表

表27　　单位：万元

年份	税种							合计
	营业税	个人	企业	房产税	城镇	土地	其他	
1993	2.27	—	—	—	—	—	6.60	8.87
1994	56.72	22.66	—	—	—	—	2.83	82.21
1995	141.29	—	—	—	—	—	5.11	146.40
1996	365.50	—	—	—	—	—	—	365.50
1997	537.80	1882.70	48.80	172.90	—	—	1273.00	3915.20
1998	585.40	2353.60	241.00	286.00	—	—	703.00	4169.00
1999	887.20	1821.20	1909.10	430.90	—	—	573.51	5621.91
2000	1015.00	2723.00	1137.30	495.00	—	—	339.00	5709.30
2001	3174.76	2957.16	496.90	683.46	8.88	—	403.35	7724.51
2002	6020.84	2321.86	1697.31	834.23	23.43	—	1288.30	12185.97
2003	2233.25	3939.68	1931.76	916.33	—	27.94	1067.29	10116.25
2004	7465.21	8069.39	1013.13	1328.37	41.39	—	1260.69	19178.18
2005	6286.44	9292.76	4454.22	1665.75	62.36	10.22	2233.68	24005.43
2006	14635.69	9163.47	2452.21	2283.44	67.71	2670.46	4796.56	36069.54
2007	24706.39	9313.65	2404.90	4440.09	912.77	338.85	7836.30	49952.95
2008	21681.80	12667.57	4628.99	3078.93	1160.47	502.28	11819.73	55539.77
2009	34041.31	13808.54	4886.10	3390.00	1270.80	1469.53	12807.23	71673.51
2010	49822.16	19783.11	7490.18	3745.73	1793.57	4278.12	16208.84	103121.71
2011	55019.94	26173.73	8797.21	5331.24	1919.63	6528.41	36903.16	140673.32

续表 27

年份	税种							合计
	营业税	个人	企业	房产税	城镇	土地	其他	
2012	100307.46	24363.63	16121.32	7356.39	2518.96	4603.14	53938.71	209209.61
2013	120787.09	30342.73	21221.70	4736.75	2914.00	12488.88	68785.12	261276.27
2014	152413.15	37734.77	39760.02	16539.54	3548.51	12960.02	86999.85	349955.86
2015	177854.08	46233.29	44787.57	12892.14	2747.43	12778.86	85302.35	382595.72
2016	73947.98	47841.75	43182.10	17309.53	2832.98	19706.75	86408.44	291229.53

1993—2016 年开发区国税完成税收情况表

表 28　　　　单位：万元

年份	税种				合计
	增值税	企业所得税	消费税	其他	
1993	78.01	—	—	—	78.30
1994	134.04	—	—	—	134.04
1995	662.38	—	—	—	662.38
1996	1272.03	—	—	—	1272.03
1997	9211.70	303.20	—	—	9514.90
1998	8734.00	522.30	—	—	9256.30
1999	8685.20	483.90	30.20	—	9199.30
2000	10888.00	1431.00	41.00	—	12360.00
2001	16699.08	2856.41	62.23	—	19617.72
2002	20960.56	4352.21	12.68	—	25325.45
2003	33355.79	9608.33	32.99	—	42997.11
2004	32369.09	13558.09	86.18	—	46009.36

续表 28

年份	税种				合计
	增值税	企业所得税	消费税	其他	
2005	38723.27	21658.72	104.84	—	60486.83
2006	56862.73	41683.87	114.06	—	98660.66
2007	82066.69	76650.73	231.59	82.60	159031.61
2008	109854.97	89523.07	400.37	8.73	199787.14
2009	137251.51	108457.26	288.20	37.10	246034.07
2010	154883.29	149068.62	236.35	132.41	304320.67
2011	191602.25	215739.72	188.19	47.74	407577.90
2012	246535.46	217217.95	210.59	418.67	464382.67
2013	318117.94	202241.17	158.77	241.28	520759.16
2014	356089.03	234460.45	232.04	606.42	591387.94
2015	359485.64	257727.67	384.04	7902.10	625499.45
2016	374964.77	193928.68	1256.10	1763.18	571912.73

第六章　外事管理

第一节　出入境管理

一、机构

天津市出入境管理机构为天津市公安局下属的天津市公安局出入境管理局，武清区内尚未设立出入境管理局服务大厅。开发区出入境管理接受天津市及武清区相关机构领导，无专门出入境管理机构。

二、外事交流活动

2011 年 4 月 22 日，中国欧盟商会企业家代表团到武清开发区考察。中国欧盟商会企业家代表团一行 46 人在市商务委副巡视员、市外企协会副会长兼秘书长赵毓民的陪同下，到武清开发区进行考察。代表团一行听取了开发区整体建设发展情况介绍，参观了开发区的建设情况，以及创业总部基地、高端制造业聚集区、保税物流区等重点开发区域和佛罗伦萨小镇、信义玻璃等大项目建设，并深入丹佛斯（天津）有限公司、戴纳派克（中国）压实摊铺设备有限公司进行实地参观考察。通过实地参观考察和听取情况介绍，代表团对武清开发区的区位、交通、环境，以及服务水平等方面给予高度评价。

2012 年 9 月 12 日，中欧经贸合作与可持续城镇化发展论坛在武清开发区举行主题为“优势互补、携手共赢”的 2012 年中欧经贸合作与可持续城镇化发展论坛在天津武清经济技术开发区的天狮国际健康产业园举办。本次活动由中欧经贸合作与可持续城镇化发展论坛组委会主办，中国欧盟商会、中欧商业协会及中国开发区协会协办，武清经济技术开发区承办，欧盟驻华使团、天津市商务委为支持单位。欧盟驻华代表团、天津市政府、中国开发区协会、武清区、欧盟商会领导出席，欧盟企业、投资基金和银行、融资需求企业、国内开发区代表、武清开发区欧盟企业、招商中介机构、行业协会代表200余人参加，40余家主流媒体参与了报道。论坛期间天津市副市长李文喜会见了欧盟联盟驻中国代表团副团长卡门·卡诺一行，并为大会致辞；武清区委书记张勇致欢迎词；欧盟商会建设行业工作组主席马晓利、中国开发区协会副会长黄太和致辞；欧洲联盟驻中国和蒙古国代表团副团长卡门·卡诺做主旨演讲；欧盟商会、国内开发区代表、武清开发区欧盟企业及融资需求企业代表相继发言。

2012年10月19日，中国投资协会外资委员会到武清开发区考察，中国投资协会外资委员会及美国美亚电力、沃尔沃公司等16家国际知名企业代表应邀到武清开发区考察并举行座谈。开发区工委书记、总公司总经理刘东海及相关负责人参加座谈，其间向客人详细介绍了武清及开发区情况。本次考察活动是由武清开发区与中国投资协会外资委员会共同组织，参加企业包括美国美亚电力、太古公司、新世界等16家国际知名企业，双方希望通过此次考察座谈活动，达到增加了解、加强沟通的效果，为今后合作创造机会。

2013年12月12日，武清开发区在北京举行欧盟产业园投资环境说明会。商务部欧洲司、欧洲国家使馆、中介机构、在谈外资项目共50余家、70余人参加。会上，商务部欧洲司副司长翟谦致辞，肯定了武清开发区欧盟产业园为中欧开展经贸合作的全新尝试，希望企业家们积极投资，实现合作共赢。

2014年3月26日，武清开发区举行欧盟产业园投资环境说明会。为进一步推介欧盟产业园投资环境，加大欧盟企业招商引资力度，武清开发区在天狮国际健康产业园奥蓝际德国际酒店举办“2014年中国·天津·武清开发区欧盟产业园投资环境说明会”。区委书记张勇，区长助理余元堂，开发区工委书记、总公司总经理刘东海，商务部欧洲司、部分欧洲国家驻华使馆、已入区企业、重点中介机构、在谈外资项目负责人120余人参加。区长助理余元堂主持会议。

2014年5月15日，武清开发区参加葡萄牙产业园区投资建设推介会。5月15日，武清开发区参加在北京东方君悦酒店举办的“葡萄牙产业园区投资建设推介会”，此次推介会是葡萄牙总统席尔瓦对中国进行国事访问期间一次重要的经济交流活动。推介会以建设葡萄牙中国产业园项目、中国园区投资环境说明为主要内容，来自葡萄牙汽车零部件、食品、信息通信、生物医药、能源、金融等领域的企业家及中方代表约100余人参加了会议。武清开发区作为天津市商务代表团重要成员，在市商务委副主任孙剑楠带队下，与葡萄牙经济部副部长 Pedro GONCALVES 先生、葡萄牙驻华使馆经济顾问 Duarte GONCALVES 先生进行了高峰会面，并在随后的推介会上作为全国两家开发区之一进行了主旨演讲，对武清开发区欧盟产业园做了宣传推介，扩大了影响力。5 月 16 日，武清开发区参加中葡企业行业分组对接会，有针对性的与葡萄牙汽车零部件、电子等行业企业进行了交流沟通，取得了良好效果。

2014 年 7 月 15 日至 24 日，武清开发区组成欧洲招商代表团赴德国、法国、意大利 3 个欧洲国家开展了为期 10 天的招商工作，取得了突破性成果。在欧洲招商期间，拜访推动新项目 7 个，拜访行业协会和金融机构 5 个。在意大利阿尔巴市举办招商推介会，通过座谈形式宣传了武清区整体投资环境及京津冀协同发展为武清区带来的重要机遇和巨大潜力，重点推介了开发区欧盟产业园。参会企业对武清产生了浓厚的兴趣，深入了解了中国经济发展现状以及武清投资环境优势。

2015 年 10 月 30 日，由中国商务部投资促进事务局和武清开发区管委会主办的“2015 年武清开发区中欧产业园投资环境说明会暨欧盟商协会领袖与企业家对话会”在武清开发区举行。商务部投资促进事务局、中国国际投资促进中心、天津市商务委、武清区各职能部门、德国商界领袖及企业家代表、开发区已入区企业、意向客户、服务机构负责人 80 余人参加。仪式上，副区长刘东海与副局长王旭为“武清经济技术开发区中欧产业园”揭牌。

2016 年 4 月 14 日，美国密苏里大学精英班到武清考察调研，其间参观武清开发区部分企业。

2016 年 7 月 12 日至 13 日，在市商务委统一组织下，武清开发区党工委副书记张书月随天津市代表团参加江苏省盐城市承办的第 15 次泛黄海中日韩经济技术交流会议全体会议。泛黄海中日韩经济技术交流会议是三国间唯一由政府、经济团体、企业、大学和科研机构共同参与的次区域合作机制，旨在加强三国泛黄海区域内贸易、投资、技术等各领域交流与合作。2016 年是泛黄海合作机制成立 15 周年，中日韩三国政界、经济界和学界 300 多名代表齐聚盐城，围绕“绿色创新与开放融合”主题，共同参加了泛黄海会议全体会议、产学官大学校长论坛、泛黄海商务论坛、产业园区·特区合作论坛、商务洽谈会等系列会议，并分组进行产业考察，探讨三国共同实现绿色经济与创新发展的新合作模式，进一步密切三国地方间经贸合作关系，全面推进泛黄海区域经济融合发展。

2016 年 9 月 10 日，驻中韩国大使馆携北京韩国中小企业协会及在京韩国企业家代表团一行 30 多人到开发区进行首轮商务考察。代表团一行实地考察了开发区创业总部基地、中欧产业园，走进了乐金华奥斯、日进等韩国代表企业，并对武清新城区及佛罗伦萨小镇等项目进行参观。其间，举行了武清开发区韩国企业投资说明会。驻中韩国大使馆参赞徐旻廷女士、北京韩国中小企业协会会长柳铉先生分别就中韩 FTA 签署背景下中韩经贸关系、韩国中小企业协会情况及投资意向进行了介绍。区招商局、开发区相关招商负责介绍了武清区及开发区发展基本情况，并与考察人员进行了座谈交流，围绕韩国客商关心的问题做了详细地解答，双方就建立长期交流合作关系达成共识。

2016 年 10 月 13 日，第十七届斯诺研讨会（武清站）在武清区举办，斯诺研讨会代表团到武清开发区考察调研，实地考察红日药业等企业。

2016 年 12 月 23 日，香港特别行政区驻北京办事处主任傅小慧一行到武清，就区域投资环境进行考察调研。区委副书记、区长杨令生，副区长刘东海陪同。傅小慧指出，近年来，香港与武清在经贸投资、青年交流等方面开展广泛合作，取得了丰硕成果。武清作为京津冀协同发展中的热点地区，在城市建设、基础设施、服务业发展等方面都取得了显著成就。香港特别行政区驻北京办事处将更好地发挥桥梁纽带作用，推动更多香港企业来武清投资。随后，傅小慧一行实地考察了区行政审批中心、开发区创业总部基地“青创中心”和佛罗伦萨小镇。

第二节　出入境检验检疫

一、机构

武清出入境检验检疫局前身是中华人民共和国天津出入境检验检疫局武清办事处，成立于 2009 年 3 月，2012 年 10 月经中编办批复成立中华人民共和国武清出入境检验检疫局，机构规格正处级，隶属于天津出入境检验检疫局管理，为中央垂直管理单位。该局坐落在武清开发区源泉路 6 号，下设办公室、检务科、工业品科和动植食科，2016 年有干部职工 24 人，

二、职能

主要承担武清区进出口工业产品、食品、化妆品、动植物产品检验检疫、原产地证签证和免于办理强制性产品认证证明审批的业务职能。

武清检验检疫局主要从事进口旧机电、成套设备、服装、玩具、强制性认证商品

和危险化学品等重点敏感商品的检验监管，开展出口工业产品退运追溯调查工作，实施目录外进出口商品监督抽查。在进出口食品化妆品和出境动植物及其产品的检验检疫方面，主要涉及肉制品、保健食品、速冻方便食品、面制品、奶制品、肠衣、饲料、家具、竹木草制品等产品。自2012年开展原产地证书签证以来，采取政策宣传贯彻、服务上门、一对一帮扶等多项举措，及时将各种自贸协定新政策、便利化措施宣传、落实到位。武清检验检疫局年均实施进出口货物检验检疫近1万报检批，货值约9.6亿美元，签发各类原产地证书9000余份。

第七章 海关

第一节 基本概况

中华人民共和国武清海关是国务院1995年5月12日批准设立的处级海关，隶属于天津海关，1996年开始筹建，1997年12月28日经海关总署批准开关。武清海关办公地点位于武清区福源道创业总部基地C03号楼。

一、背景

为了更好地吸引外资来武清投资建厂，方便企业办理进出口业务，促进武清外贸经济的快速发展，1993年5月26日武清县人民政府向天津市人民政府申请设立海关机构。

二、审批

天津市人民政府于1993年《关于在武清县设立海关的请示》向国务院请示在武清县设立海关。国务院于1995年5月12日批复天津市人民政府《国务院关于同意设立武清海关机构的批复》（国函〔1995〕38号）同意设立武清海关，编制规模50名，首期配备40名。海关总署于1995年11月8日向天津海关下发通知《海关总署关于设立武清海关的通知》，决定设立“中华人民共和国武清海关”（正处级），隶属于天津海关。武清海关由天津海关负责筹建，筹建人员编制5名。

三、筹建

根据国务院和海关总署关于设立武清海关的批复与通知，天津海关于1996年1月成立“武清海关筹备处”，正式开始筹建武清海关。经天津海关与武清县人民政府研究协商确定，武清海关办公用房面积（包括附属用房）占地6600平方米，建筑面积4280平方米，家属宿舍20套共计2400平方米（含200平方米单身宿舍），由武清县政府提供。1996年8月28日天津海关与武清县人民政府在武清海关关址共同举行了《武清海关奠基典礼仪式》，天津海关关长赵桂芬、武清县委书记邵久武、县长李树宏和国家科委、市园区有关部门负责人及企业界代表100余人出席奠基仪式。武清海关办公大楼从1996年8月28日开始破土兴建，于1997年10月底基本竣工，历时14个月。1997年11月27日海关总署组成验收小组对海关办公大楼及其他项目进行了验收。

四、开关

1997年12月12日海关总署对《天津海关关于申请武清海关验收开关的报告》作出批复，《海关总署关于同意武清海关开关的批复》，同意武清海关于1997年12月28日开关。

1997年12月28日武清海关举行开关揭牌仪式。海关总署副署长黄汝凤和天津市人民政府副市长朱连康出席揭牌仪式并致辞祝贺，武清县委书记李乃彦、天津海关关长赵桂芬、武清海关副关长肖军（主持工作）等主要领导出席仪式并讲话。海关总署、天津市、国家科委有关部门领导、武清县委、县政府主要领导及有关部门负责人、天津海关领导及处室和分关负责人、天津海关老领导、新闻媒体和企业界代表共计140余人参加了揭牌仪式。中央电视台、新华社、天津电视台和《天津日报》等新闻媒体现场进行了报道。至此武清海关对外正式开始办理海关业务。开关当日，天津海关党组书记、关长赵桂芬为该关题词："打好基础、树好形象、争创一流。"

第二节　机构设置

海关总署1997年12月12日在《海关总署关于同意武清海关开关的批复》中明确规定："武清海关领导干部职数为1正（正处级）1副（副处级）；内设3个科级机构：办公室、业务科、行政财务科。"1997年12月26日经天津海关党组研究决定并报总署人教司同意，任命肖军为武清海关副关长（主持工作）、陈明为武清海关副关长。武清海关开关之初内设3个科室，共有干部、职工16人（其中：干部15名，职工1名；副处领导干部2人，科级干部3人）。之后，随着海关业务量的逐年增长，内设科室和人员也在不断的进行变化和增加。截至到2016年，共有办公室、财务装备科、货运监管科、审批科、核销科、稽查科6个科室，38名干部（其中：处级领导干部2人，科级干部15人）、职工1人。

第三节　业务范围

一、业务管辖范围

海关总署 1997 年 12 月 12 日在《海关总署关于同意武清海关开关的批复》中明确规定，武清海关业务管辖范围是武清县。1998 年 5 月 1 日经天津海关批准，天津经济技术开发区逸仙园科学工业园（驻武清开发区）内所辖企业的海关业务划归武清海关监管。至此，武清全境的海关业务全部归属武清海关监管。

二、业务监管范围

天津海关 1997 年 12 月 11 日下发文件《天津海关关于划分武清海关监管区域及业务分工的通知》，批准武清海关于 1997 年 12 月 16 日对外办公，12 月 28 日正式开关。主要业务范围包括：武清区所辖范围内的外商投资企业、加工贸易企业和其他进出口企业的备案、设备减免税审批；办理加工贸易合同审批、核销；办理进出境货物和商品通关、征收关税和其他税费；查缉走私；编制海关统计和办理其他海关业务。

武清海关1997年12月28日开关以来，在天津海关党组的领导下，始终坚持“高起点、快起步，争创一流”的工作要求，始终坚持“武清兴，海关兴”的发展理念，大力加强业务建设、队伍建设、廉政建设和海关文化建设等基础性工作，积极推进和谐海关和学习型海关建设，走出了一条“依区而立、依区而兴”、独具区域型海关特色的发展之路。建关 19 年来，为武清外贸经济的发展做出了积极的贡献，海关业务从无到有、队伍从小到大、建设从弱到强，事业得到了健康全面发展。

建关 19 年来，连续 5 年荣获“天津市文明单位”称号，2012 年获得“全国文明单位”荣誉称号。分关年年被天津海关评为“基层建设达标先进单位”，党支部（现为党总支）先后 12 次被天津海关机关党委评为“先进党支部”，团支部年年被天津海关团委评为“先进团支部”，货运监管科年年被天津海关评为“文明窗口标兵单位”。稽查科、核销科和办公室先后被评为武清区“青年文明号”。货运监管科于 2006 年 2 月 21 日被团市委授予天津市“青年文明号”称号，稽查科于 2015 年 10 月被团市委授予天津市“青年文明号”称号。

建关 19 年，先后有 140 多人次获得了天津市、海关总署以及天津海关的各种奖励和表彰，有 2 名关员荣立“三等功”，1 名关员被评为天津市劳动模范。同时，向天津海关和兄弟关区输送了30多名优秀人才。其中，1人现担任正厅局级领导职务，1人担任副厅局级领导职务，5人担任处级领导职务，7人担任科级领导职务。

建关19年来，共收到企业表扬信400余封，锦旗260余面，廉政工作始终保持了零投诉、零举报和零发案率。

武清海关历任关长名录

肖　军：任职时间：1997年12月至2000年4月（副关长，主持工作）；2000年4月至2002年5月任关长。

师国旺：任职时间：2002年5月至2003年8月（副关长，主持工作）

叶　刚：任职时间：2003年8月至2005年12月（副关长，主持工作），2005年12月至2006年2月任关长

史新鸣：任职时间：2006年2月至2011年3月

张　明：任职时间：2011年3月2016年1月

孙国利：任职时间：2016年6月至今

2016年主要业务情况

2016年武清海关接受进出口报关单申报共计8403票，监管进出口货物总值8.1亿美元，进出口货运总量5.25万吨，同比下降22%，累计征收税款11.28亿元 。（注：受政策影响，武清区企业出口报关全部在新港海关、机场海关等口岸海关办理。进口方面，在武清海关办理报关的企业约占全区进出口企业的三分之一。）

办理企业注册登记241家，企业信息变更444家，注销企业10家。审批减免税设备25票，设备总货值1498万美元。办理进出口企业减免税设备年报手续14家，设立加工贸易电子化手册417册，审批深加工结转159份，审批外发加工63票。

服务地方经济和企业发展情况

一、优化服务解决企业实际问题

积极开展“双万双服”活动，通过入企指导、电话服务、新媒体网络援助、面对面帮办等一系列举措，搭建海关与企业的“全天候通道”，进一步提高服务效率和精准度；不断优化企业注册备案登记服务，利用“关企合作平台”为企业提供“最短办事途径”，为企业压缩时间、人力、交通成本；引导企业开展AEO认证工作，与武清

区内高资质及重点项目企业建立友好型关企合作关系，真正做到审批更简、监管更强、服务更优。

二、多措并举着力提高服务效率和质量

一是积极开展通关一体化改革，使武清区企业能够及早享受到海关改革的红利。6月1日武清海关正式实行“属地海关申报、口岸海关查验”通关业务模式。该模式每票（集装箱）为武清区企业节省往返武清监管车运输费用约1000元，享受口岸查验免收费政策节省辖区企业查验掏箱费用600余元，武清区企业通关时间较原有模式缩减约一半。

二是进一步缩短工作时限。对无问题、不涉及加工贸易内销补税、核查等情事手册由原来的30天核销期缩短为15天，涉及保证金的手册由专人负责办理核销，尽快使企业办理退保手续，缓解企业资金压力。加工贸易企业申请退还风险类保证金的手续在5个工作日时限内减少1个工作日，缩短为4个工作日。外商投资企业鼓励类项目项下进口设备减免税审批手续提高工作效率一倍，工作时限缩短为5个工作日。

三是实施周六、周日和节假日预约加班制度，满足武清区企业非正常通关时段的合理进口需求。

三、以实际需求为导向提供海关增值服务

一是武清海关领导亲自协调天津海关职能部门来武清，实地走访具有一定知名度的自有品牌企业，了解企业通关需求，现场解答企业归类、缴税及通关时效等方面问题，为忠旺等有需求的企业提供进口大型设备进行预归类、建立归类样品库等便利企业通关的措施，提高通关效率。

二是走访重点企业，宣讲国际服务外包业务进口货物保税监管模式的政策，推动企业转向“生产+服务”型。

三是通过定期向武清区委、区政府报送《关地动态》形式，为地方政府提供辅助决策参考，以实际行动促进地方经济发展。该项工作得到区委、区政府领导的肯定。2016年以来，王小宁书记、戴东强区长先后多次在武清海关报送的《关地动态》上作出批示。在此基础上，武清海关还着力强化与地方经贸主管等部门的沟通协调。互相沟通情况，形成管理合力，实现企业共管、责任共担、信息共享的综合管理格局，着力促进区域经济的快速发展，企业经营的健康有序。

第七篇

党政群团

第一章　中国共产党武清开发区工作委员会

第一节　组织机构

1993年4月28日，成立中共武清开发区支部委员会，由3名委员组成，隶属于中共武清县委直属机关党委。2000年6月，武清撤县设区后，支部委员会更名为中共天津市武清区委开发区支部委员会，隶属于中共武清区委直属机关党委。

2000年12月11日，经区委研究决定，建立中共天津市武清区委开发区工作委员会，虞东文任书记。

2001年1月15日，任命韩淑玲、崔秀杰为开发区工委委员。

2003年9月26日，任命尤国敏为开发区工委委员，任综合部部长。

2005年10月30日，经区委组织部部务会议研究决定，免尤国敏开发区工委委员职。

2006年9月21日，王恩成任区委开发区工委委员、书记；虞东文任开发区管委会办公室正处级调研员，免其区委开发区工委书记、委员职。

2006年11月23日，黄巨山任区委开发区工委委员；李刚任区委开发区工委委员。

2008年11月7日，钟书明任区委开发区工委委员、书记（兼）；张绍锋任区委开发区工委委员、副书记；王恩成任开发区管委会办公室正处级非领导职务，免其区委开发区工委书记、委员职务。

2009年3月20日，王继宾任区委开发区工委委员。

2011年8月17日，张书月任区委开发区工委委员。

2011年12月30日，刘东海任区委开发区工委书记（兼）；免钟书明开发区工委书记（兼）职务。

2012 年 10 月 21 日，李鹏程任区委开发区工委委员；武剑峰任区委开发区工委委员。

2013 年 9 月 30 日，张书月任区委开发区工委副书记；免黄巨山区委开发区工委委员职；免王继宾区委开发区工委委员职务。

2013 年 10 月 24 日，杜瀛涛任区委开发区工委委员；郎聪任区委开发区工委委员。

2015 年 10 月 29 日，郭新华任区委开发区工委委员、书记；免去刘东海区委开发区工委书记、委员职务。

2016 年 3 月 16 日，成立党建工作部，郝鋆任党建工作部副部长，主持工作，试用期一年。

2016 年 5 月 4 日，经区委研究决定，中共天津市武清区委开发区工作委员会更名为中共天津武清经济技术开发区工作委员会，为区委派出机构，原工委领导班子成员转任更名后的相应职务，不再另行办理任免职手续。

2016 年 6 月 13 日，免武剑峰、李鹏程、郎聪、杜瀛涛天津武清经济技术开发区工委委员职务。

中共天津武清经济技术开发区机关总支部委员会

总支书记：张武民　组织委员：王继宾　宣传委员：李鹏程　纪律委员：武剑峰　青年委员：郎聪

表 29

支部名称	支部书记	组织委员	宣传委员	党员	人数
武清开发区机关第一党支部	魏建东	杨少海	殷绍峰	郭新华、石洪波、刘喜鹤、闻琪、孙厚明、徐建桥、赵廷顺、王金龙（预备）	11
武清开发区机关第二党支部	张武民	裴洪亮	孙 波	张绍锋、刘文香、王凤丽、程克顺、伊虹、徐松、李建伟、贾朴、王志敏、陈国栋、范北斗（预备）	14.

续表 29

支部名称	支部书记	组织委员	宣传委员	党员	人数
武清开发区机关第三党支部	王继宾	王金祥	王 玉	朱瑞林、许贤、苑广伟、刘福伟、饶晓光、苏晓吉、刘俊平、段然、王继伟、李孟赢、劳卫、焦兴盛	14
武清开发区机关第四党支部	郎 聪	王秀丽	李 杰	孙浩、徐宁、王永苹、韩泷	7
武清开发区机关第五党支部	李鹏程	张秀启	丁 丽	王凤刚、李洪宇、杨雷、王付华、杨超、王树柠、徐立程、王君健、薄国兵、高妍、冯涛（安全）、郝帅、张洪姣、刘思含、王志杰、陈鹏、李瑞光、果建伟、刘娜、闫蕾蕾、于建营、肖达（预备）	25
武清开发区机关第六党支部	武剑峰	王福东	崔洪年	杨英、刘健、陈文振、侯杰、肖仓、李海朋、沙佩建、武宝铎	11
武清开发区机关第七党支部	虞东文	汤雯雯	于雪松	王恩成、任瑞才、谭昕、王德成	7

武清开发区工委下设党组织一览表

表 30

序号	基层党支部名称	支部书记	党务工作者	成立时间	专职党员
1	武清开发区机关党总支	张武民	闻琪	2016.5.30	144
2	武清开发区机关第一党支部	魏建东	李馥伶	2016.5.30	19
3	武清开发区机关第二党支部	张武民	董诗怡	2016.5.30	17

续表 30

序号	基层党支部名称	支部书记	党务工作者	成立时间	专职党员
4	武清开发区机关第三党支部	王继宾	刘俊平	2016.5.30	15
5	武清开发区机关第四党支部	郎聪	韩泷	2016.5.30	7
6	武清开发区机关第五党支部	李鹏程	高妍	2016.5.30	20
7	武清开发区机关第六党支部	武剑峰	武宝铎	2016.5.30	20
8	武清开发区机关第七党支部	虞东文	李丽丽	2016.5.30	46
9	天狮集团党委	黄小江	张喆	2012.2.12	108
10	天狮集团第一党支部	李炳云	张喆	2001.7	25
11	天狮集团第二党支部	秦惠玲	张喆	2001.7	11
12	天狮集团第三党支部	刘灿辉	张喆	2001.7	10
13	天狮集团第四党支部	李德华	张喆	2014.3	6
14	天狮集团第五党支部	董根苓	张喆	2014.3	7
15	天狮集团第六党支部	冯樯	张喆	2014.3	24
16	天狮集团第七党支部	王飞	张喆	2014.3	25
17	红日药业股份有限公司党总支	张广明	张毅	2013.6	96
18	红日药业集团行政党支部	翁益坤	张毅	2013.11	26

续表 30

序号	基层党支部名称	支部书记	党务工作者	成立时间	专职党员
19	红日药业生产质量党支部	张军军	张毅	2013.11	25
20	红日药业营销中心党支部	王未沫	张毅	2013.11	29
21	红日药业技术研发党支部	常淑梅	张毅	2013.11	16
22	中粮包装（天津）有限公司党总支（双重管辖）	冯凯	张欣	2011.11.18	95
23	办公职能党支部	张丽丽	张欣	2011.12	31
24	工厂党支部	郑功昊	张欣	2011.12	44
25	两片罐党支部	李俊山	张欣	2011.12	20
26	诺禾致源生物信息科技有限公司党委	王琪峰	王妍妍	2015.10.29，2016.12 升党委	114
27	第一党支部	张扬	王妍妍	2016.12	38
28	第二党支部	谷月娇	王妍妍	2016.12	37
29	第三党支部	周晓炜	王妍妍	2016.12	39
30	东蒲洼市场和质量监督管理所党支部	窦玉成	韩超	2012.9.15	11
31	武清渤海报关行党支部	杨钰	杨钰	2003.5.1	52
32	中天高科特种车辆有限公司党支部	张顶云	魏进	2003.10.22	40

续表 30

序号	基层党支部名称	支部书记	党务工作者	成立时间	专职党员
33	天津翰桥车体制造有限公司党支部	孙国强	王伟	2012.9.26	5
34	天津市宇刚保温建材有限公司党支部	王秀华	刘海英	2012.5.28	4
35	天津市三英焊业股份有限公司党支部	张乃民	闫焕娜	2012.5.18	11
36	信义玻璃（天津）有限公司党支部	韩雪梅	韩雪梅	2011.6.27	11
37	龙甲门业有限公司党支部	蒋立莉	蒋立莉	2002.5.3	6
38	玻石机械（天津）有限公司党支部(芬兰)	张素杰	郑志体	2012.5	3
39	天津凯涛奇食品有限公司党支部	孙凤桐	刘全发	2012.9.28	11
40	天津伊利乳品有限责任公司党支部	陈天杰	杨威瀚	2014.3.7	7
41	玉圭园（天津）文化娱乐有限公司党支部	张有德(离职)	韩永军	2014.3.07	3
42	中天高科防务技术有限公司党支部	王金龙	杨文超	2015.12.25	3
43	天津优达通供应链管理股份有限公司党支部	薛丽迁	杨钰	2016.5.18	3
44	天津怡和嘉业医疗科技有限公司党支部	孙薇	张浩琳	2016.6.13	8
45	天津武清泉达医院有限公司党支部	刘洪宇	赵艳丽（非）	2016.6.20	4
46	巴克斯酒业（天津）有限公司党支部	刘帅	郭亮(非)	2016.8.2	3
47	敏华家具（中国）有限公司党支部	戴志锋	陈均华	2015.6.20	5

续表 30

序号	基层党支部名称	支部书记	党务工作者	成立时间	专职党员
48	维克（天津）有限公司党支部	孙健	郭晓辉	2015.8.14	35
49	天大领先制药有限公司党支部	李河	赵宝雨	2015.6.1	3
50	日丰企业（天津）有限公司党支部	郭金祥	郭金祥	2015.6.10	2
51	启联（天津）科技股份有限公司党支部	朱学华	朱学华	2015.12.28	1
52	嘉吉饲料（天津）有限公司党支部（美国）	李梦如	李梦如	2015.9.21	2
53	EKC 工业（天津）有限公司党支部（印度）	平小路	平小路	2014.3.7	2
54	天津博耐特电子有限公司党支部	王钦山	张燕	2015.5.29	1
55	天津和治药业有限公司党支部	谢迎飞	谢迎飞	2015.6.10	1
56	北京裕昌置业集团天津投资有限公司党支部	陈姗姗	宋潇文	2013.5.20	1
57	蜡笔小新（天津）有限公司党支部	陈晨	陈晨	2011.6.30	1
58	马克菲尔（天津）柔性支挡有限公司党支部（意大利）	汲海波	汲海波	2014.3.20	1
59	天津君歌集团有限公司党支部	刘凤宝	曹路	2016.11.23	1
60	国能飞腾有限公司党支部	冯俊江（已转走）	李政佳	2012.7.12	1
61	艾尔姆风能叶片制品党支部（丹麦）	张建超	张建超	2015.4.15	1

续表 30

序号	基层党支部名称	支部书记	党务工作者	成立时间	专职党员
62	天津光彩圣火科技企业孵化器有限公司党支部	王丽丽	唐春秀	2015.9.21	1
63	天津赛诺制药有限公司党支部		郝静	2014.3.18	0
64	光效影业管理有限公司党支部	穆建宝	张海悦	2015.6.12	0
65	天地融（天津）有限公司党支部	翁玮	翁玮	2015.7.2	0
66	味千食品发展（天津）有限公司党支部（香港）	戚园丽	戚园丽	2015.9.21	0
67	天津天宝光碟有限公司党支部	李建臣	小崔	2015.9.21	0
68	天津大真空有限公司党支部(日本)	谢建红		2012.11.2	0
69	金红叶纸业（天津）有限公司党支部	郭铭炜	郭铭炜	2014.5.20	0
70	华住金属有限公司党支部（日本）	韩裔	韩裔	2012.5.28	0
71	三卓韩一橡塑科技股份有限公司党支部	甄江山	付天娜（非）	2015.11.20	0
72	创意米兰党支部(朗霆国际贸易有限公司)	谢德亮	钟颖	2016.9.30	0
73	合众创亚（天津）包装有限公司党支部（新加坡）	李凤艳	李凤艳	2016.11.22	0

续表 30

序号	基层党支部名称	支部书记	党务工作者	成立时间	专职党员
74	天津鸿佳地毯有限公司党支部(港澳台)	杨宝旺	董召贤	2016.11.22	0
75	德尔福派克电气系统有限公司党支部（美国）	康伟	田娜	2016.11.23	0
76	宾德科机械设备（天津）有限公司党支部（奥地利）	康静	康静	2016.11.23	0
77	西岛泵（天津）有限公司党支部（日本）	高婵媛	刘泉	2016.11.23	0
78	天加空调（天津）有限公司党支部	马莉	马莉	2016.12.9	0
79	天津中禾种业有限公司党支部	吕国喜	刘洪波	2016.12.6	0
80	莱斯安全阀门（天津）有限公司党支部			2016.12.16	0
81	麦格昆磁（天津）有限公司党支部（美国）		高倩	2016.12.16	0
82	欧德亮法尔宝汽车灯系统科技（天津）有限公司党支部（德）	王婉	王婉	2016.12.16	0
83	山阳（天津）机械有限公司党支部（日）		谢春明	2016.12.16	0
84	万可电子（天津）有限公司党支部（德）			2016.12.16	0
85	功学社（天津）商贸有限公司党支部（台湾）		齐赛月	2016.12.30	0
86	泰坦爱迪姆机械制造（天津）有限公司党支部（意大利）			2016.12.30	0

续表 30

序号	基层党支部名称	支部书记	党务工作者	成立时间	专职党员
87	天津武清区天鹅湖温泉度假村有限公司党支部	乔海涛	袁静	2016.12.30	0
88	沃斯坦热力设备（天津）有限公司党支部（荷兰）		梅文颖	2016.12.30	0
89	光宝电子（天津）有限公司（港澳台）		刘会红	2016.12.16	0
90	艾默生过程管理（天津）阀门有限公司（美国）		连春燕	2016.12.16	0
91	LG 化学 (天津) 工程塑料有限公司党支部		曹君	2016.12.20	0
92	奥帕汽车配件（天津）有限公司党支部	穆怀勇		2016.12.20	0
93	天津杰麦多乐器有限公司党支部		陈付霞	2016.12.20	0
94	天津西马格特宝机械有限公司党支部	李智勇	王平	2016.12.20	0
95	大都克电接触科技（中国）有限公司党支部		王立影	2016.12.20	0
96	瑞一（中国）科技发展有限公司党支部	云杨	李娜	2016.12.20	0
97	天津浔兴拉链科技有限公司党支部	刘拥华	万萌	2016.12.20	0
98	天津同力重工有限公司党支部	马荣涛	裴丽红	2016.12.20	0
99	西斯密(天津)电机有限公司(意大利)		毕瑞丹	2016.12.16	0

续表 30

序号	基层党支部名称	支部书记	党务工作者	成立时间	专职党员
100	天津富禄通信技术有限公司党支部（韩）		金月寿	2016.12.16	0
101	非公企业第一联合党支部	陈国栋	陈国栋	2016.11.9	0
102	非公企业第二联合党支部	李海朋	李海朋	2016.11.9	0
103	非公企业第三联合党支部	侯杰	侯杰	2016.11.9	0
104	非公企业第四联合党支部	冯涛（安）	冯涛（安）	2016.11.9	0
105	非公企业第五联合党支部	王志杰	王志杰	2016.11.9	0
106	非公企业第六联合党支部	张萌	张萌	2016.11.9	0
107	非公企业第七联合党支部	张强涛	张强涛	2016.11.9	0
108	非公企业第八联合党支部	劳卫	劳卫	2016.11.9	0
109	非公企业第九联合党支部	李林杰	李林杰	2016.11.9	0
110	非公企业第十联合党支部	徐松	徐松	2016.11.9	0
111	非公企业第十一联合党支部	李建伟	李建伟	2016.11.9	0
112	非公企业第十二联合党支部	苏晓吉	苏晓吉	2016.11.9	0

第二节 学习教育

武清开发区成立后，在招商引资的同时，重视宣传思想工作。1993—1994 年，学习宣传邓小平关于建设中国特色的社会主义理论，用特色理论武装全区党员干部。1995 年，开展学习宣传孔繁森先进事迹活动。还开展了忠心献给祖国、爱心献给社会、关心献给他人、孝心献给父母、信心留给自己的“五心”活动。1996 年，全区继续深入开展“六爱两评”活动。同时，开展以“六杯”“三日”（“六杯”即公仆杯、文明杯、环境杯、敬业杯、新风杯、成才杯；“三日”即机关干部周末读书日、科技传播日、青年志愿者义务奉献日）为载体的系列精神文明创建活动。

1999 年，通过开展“三讲”教育，推动领导班子、领导干部提高自身素质，加强党性修养，端正思想作风，认真实践全心全意为人民服务的宗旨，大力弘扬求真务实、言行一致的工作作风。有重点地解决领导干部中存在的突出问题，努力做到思想上有明显提高，政治上有明显进步，作风上有明显转变，纪律上有明显增强。

2000 年，总公司所属党组织集中进行“三讲”（讲学习、讲政治、讲正气）教育。公司党组把“三讲”集中教育作为党的思想政治工作的重中之重，严格按照中央确定的指导思想和工作部署，稳步推进。“三讲”集中教育结束后，又开展“回头看”活动。领导班子和领导干部在思想上有明显提高、政治上有明显进步、作风上有明显增强。

认真学习党中央和市委规定的系列文件，广泛听取了意见，认真查找了自身存在的问题，制定了整改措施，明确了努力方向。通过“三讲”教育和“回头看”活动，进一步锻炼了党性，增强了班子的凝聚力和战斗力，促进了工作的发展。同时，大力推进精神文明建设。开展了以“六杯三日”活动为载体的精神文明建设活动。以撤县建区和迎接新世纪为契机，开展了多种健康有益的活动，公司上下呈现出良好的精神风貌。

2001 年，在全体党员干部中先后开展“三个代表”重要思想集中学习教育。在学习教育中，对规定篇目组织学习，撰写读书笔记和心得体会，部分同志在大会或中心组会议上发言、交流，对自身存在的问题，有针对性地写出反思材料，经群众民主评议，最后制定整改措施。全体党员、干部加深了对党的性质、任务和宗旨的认识，坚定了理想和信念，找出了存在的差距与不足，制定和完善了措施，并在各项工作中加以改进。

2002 年，以学习邓小平理论、“三个代表”重要思想为重点，以提高党员领导干部理论水平和执政能力为落脚点，在党员领导干部中开展以读一本理论著作、讲一次党课、写一篇调研报告为主要内容的“三个一”活动，开展领导干部学理论征文和优秀党课讲解评选活动。在党员干部中积极开展“立党为公，执政为民”的思想教育。帮助党员干部树立正确的权力观，牢记“为人民服务”的宗旨。

2003 年，加强党员干部理论学习，做好党员发展工作。总公司所属党组织通过“三会一课”的形式，加强党员干部的理论学习。如认真学习党的路线、方针、政策，学习“WTO”有关知识，学习“三个代表”重要思想和中共中央总书记江泽民“5·31”重要讲话及中共十六大精神，通过学习提高了思想认识，武装了头脑，保证了与党中央思想的统一。在党风廉政建设中注重加强党群干群关系，提高群众参与程度，如不定期地召开各种类型的座谈会、进行问卷调查等倾听群众的呼声，虚心听取群众的意见，树立了党员干部在群众中的良好形象。

对基层党员干部进行政治理论和业务能力培训；积极发扬党内民主，进一步健全党内生活制度；扎实推进机关党支部的思想作风建设，在改革发展中创先进、争优秀。

2004 年，按照上级党委要求，总公司所属党组织利用“三会一课”“座谈会”等形式组织党员干部任职学习任长霞、牛玉儒等先进楷模的事迹；学习宣传贯彻《中国共产党党员权利保障条例》，教育和引导广大党员干部牢固树立“立党为公、执政为民”的观念，增强了总公司所属党组织的凝聚力、向心力和战斗力。

2005 年，总公司所属党组织按照党委关于开展保持共产党员先进性教育活动的安排与部署，认真组织党员开展教育活动。通过“学习动员”“分析评议”和“整改提高”三个阶段的理论学习、思想剖析和分析评议、制定整改措施，提高了广大党员的素质，增强了党支部的创造力、凝聚力和战斗力，有效地促进了公司各项工作的开展。

认真抓好党员集中学习教育、撰写党性自我分析材料、开好民主生活会、征求群众意见和建议、制定整改方案、组织群众满意度测评等六个环节。在学习动员阶段，领导动员讲话、制定实施方案、统一日程安排，确定集中学习教育辅导人，每个党员均有学习笔记，保证集中学习时间不少于 40 小时。在分析评议阶段，每个党员写好党性自我分析材料，在民主生活会上开展批评与自我批评；以问卷和座谈会的形式征求群众的意见和建议，进行梳理归纳后上报党组。在整改提高阶段，针对群众的意见和建议，制定整改方案，组织群众满意度测评。

2006 年，在党员干部中积极开展“立党为公，执政为民”的思想教育。按照党委的要求，公司支部利用“三会一课”“座谈会”“收看录像”等形式组织党员干部认真学习先进典型事迹报告；学习宣传贯彻《中国共产党党员权利保障条例》，教育和引导广大党员干部牢固树立“立党为公、执政为民”的观念，增强了总公司所属党组织的凝聚力、向心力和战斗力。

2007年，总公司党组织就加强自身建设作出决定：1. 切实加强学习，不断提高理论素质和工作水平。把加强学习作为履行职责的第一需要，不断更新和完善知识结构，拓宽知识领域，丰富知识储备。2. 保持政治坚定，不折不扣地执行中央的决策部署和方针政策。不断增强政治敏锐性、政治鉴别力和政治坚定性，善于从政治上观察问题、分析问题、处理问题，在关键时刻和重点问题上立场坚定、旗帜鲜明，经得起风浪考验。3. 坚持与时俱进，创造性地开展工作。坚持把中央的方针政策与具体实际相结合，研究新情况，解决新问题，努力在新的起点上，开创工作的新局面。积极培养创新意识，倡导创新精神，完善创新机制，形成鼓励创新的氛围，最大限度地激发创造活力。4. 改进工作作风，求真务实真抓实干。发扬求真务实精神，大兴求真务实之风，脚踏实地，埋头苦干，少说多干，创造实实在在的工作成果。5. 践行党的宗旨，坚持立党为公，执政为民，把实现好、维护好、发展好最广大人民的根本利益作为一切工作的出发点和落脚点，把爱民、为民、富民作为价值取向和义不容辞职责，高度关注民主、重视民生、保障民生、改善民生。6. 牢记“两个务必”，弘扬艰苦奋斗的优良传统。切实增强忧患意识、公仆意识、节俭意识，培养良好的生活作风和健康的生活情趣，自觉抵制拜金主义、享乐主义和奢靡之风。在各项工作中贯彻勤俭节约原则，投到群众直接受益的事情上。7. 大力发扬民主，增强班子的团结统一和活力。坚持民主集中制的各项制度和规定。建立健全新工作机制和运行方式。完善党组议事规则和决策程序，健全完善集体领导与个人分工负责相结合的制度，坚持民主生活会制度。8. 坚持清正廉洁，永葆共产党人的政治本色。自觉遵守党纪国法，严格执行领导干部廉洁从政各项规定，带头落实党风廉政建设责任制。是年，总公司党组成员思想建设成效显著，党组战斗力、凝聚力进一步增强。

2008年，加强班子自身建设，增强党组织凝聚力，在实践中，充分发挥支部战斗堡垒作用。如何增强党支部的建设，充分发挥党支部的战斗堡垒作用，是支部工作的重点。支部班子是工作的核心，核心作用好坏，事关企业兴衰，事业成败的大问题。为此，总公司党组织始终把狠抓支部班子自身建设放在党建工作的首位。在思想建设上，注重加强对班子思想观念、宗旨意识、事业心、责任感、党性原则的教育；在组织建设上，坚持群众路线，遵守民主集中制原则，重大事情的决策上，统一思想、统一认识，在工作中分工明确、各司其职、既分工又合作，实现了真正意义上的和谐统一；在作风建设上，密切联系群众，倾听群众呼声，虚心听取建议，随时接受群众的监督，在党员群众中树立了威信。尤其在重点工程中发挥了支部班子心往一处想，劲往一处使的干劲，带领广大党员干部抢抓机遇、开拓进取，想在先，干在前，以身作责，率先垂范，以自身的模范行为影响和教育每一名党员干部职工。

2009 年，集中开展深入学习实践科学发展观活动。坚持抓紧抓实抓好。公司党组制定实施方案，召开全公司动员大会，作出全面部署。成立由主要领导参加的领导小组，多次召开公司党组会议和领导小组会议，听取工作汇报，研究解决问题。党员领导干部根据工作分工，分别建立联系点，调研指导工作，推动学习实践活动深入开展。加强指导检查，使学习实践活动成为推动事业科学发展、促进社会和谐的强大动力。坚持领导干部带头宣讲、带头调研、带头整改。领导干部深入联系点和基层单位，联系实际宣讲，做专题学习报告。党组召开专题民主生活会，深入查找班子和个人存在的突出问题，认真开展批评与自我批评，明确科学发展的思路和举措。

2011 年，开展学习实践科学发展观活动。重点抓三个方面：1. 搞好学习培训。采取集中学习和个人自学相结合，专题辅导与讨论交流相结合等形式进行，学习内容主要是《科学发展观党员干部读本》。2. 撰写党性分析材料。从理想信念、宗旨意识、大局观念、创新精神、廉政勤政等方面入手，每名党员全面总结思想、工作和作风等方面的情况，重点检查存在问题。3. 召开专题党员民主生活会，开展批评与自我批评。4. 抓好整改提高。一是对照检查和民主评议中反映的问题，每个党员认真制定有针对性的整改措施，明确重点，确定时限，落实责任，认真进行整改。二是以“三会一课”为主要载体，抓好党员教育制度落实。每季度对党员进行一次党课教育；党员每季度向党小组汇报一次思想和工作情况；党支部每季度召开一次党员思想分析会；党员干部及时参加培训会或轮训会。三是结合“学习实践科学发展观”教育，开展“立党为公、执政为民”教育活动，强化宗旨意识，切实转变工作作风，使广大党员干部成为刻苦学习、自觉实践科学发展观的模范。

建立健全机关学习制度，明确政治理论学习每月不少于一次，业务知识学习每月不少于两次，切实提高机关干部学习的自觉性。推进规范化建设。认真贯彻执行民主集中制，重大决策和重要工作坚持集体讨论决定，确保决策的民主化、科学化。认真执行党内“三会一课”制度，按时召开支部大会和民主生活会，按时组织上好党课，进一步加强党组织的凝聚力和战斗力。加强对党员干部组织的领导，充分调动一切积极因素，为全面完成 2012 年任务而发挥重要作用。

继续加强对党员干部的教育。一、抓紧抓好党员干部政治理论学习和教育，做到时间、内容、人员、效果四落实，同时对上级党组织的重大决策及时传达贯彻。组织参加多种形式的学习、讨论、交流、培训。二是实行党员目标管理。开展民主评议党员活动，对党员的管理做到有目标、有督查、有落实，年终有考评。三是做到按时交纳党费，党费收缴有专人管理，四是积极完成总公司党组织交给的各项任务。

2014 年群众路线活动启动以来，在学习教育、听取意见阶段，按照规定动作不能少的原则，给每位领导和机关各科室定制学习“菜单”、印发学习资料等。同时，印制征求意见表、设置征求意见箱，广泛征求意见建议。在查摆问题、开展批评阶段，完成了党委领导班子及个人的对照检查材料汇总，问题清单梳理等专题民主生活会的前的各项准备工作，保证了生活会顺利召开。在整改落实、建章立制阶段，整理上报了党委班子整改措施、整改工作任务书、建章立制工作任务书、专项整治工作落实任务书等。

2016 年开展“两学一做”做“四讲四有”合格党员活动。

主要做了以下几个方面工作：

一、全面深入系统学习党章党规 通过认真学习《中国共产党廉洁自律准则》《中国共产党纪律处分条例》《中国共产党党员权利保障条例》等党内法规，掌握廉洁自律准则规定的“四个必须”：即必须坚定共产主义理想和中国特色社会主义信念，必须坚持全心全意为人民服务根本宗旨，必须继承发扬党的优良传统和作风，必须自觉培养高尚道德情操，努力弘扬中华民族传统美德，廉洁自律，接受监督，永葆党的先进性和纯洁性。把握“四个坚持”：即坚持公私分明、先公后私、克己奉公，坚持崇廉拒腐、清白做人、干净做事，坚持尚俭戒奢、艰苦朴素、勤俭节约，坚持吃苦在前、享受在后、甘于奉献。通过熟读和学习纪律处分条例，掌握各类违纪行为的情形和处分规定。通过重温党章党规，进一步明确做合格党员的基本标准，提升全体党员尊崇党章党规、敬畏党章党规、遵守党章党规的思想和行动自觉，守住为人、做事的底线。

二、全面深入系统学习系列讲话 全体党员学习习近平总书记系列重要讲话，在全面、系统和深入上下功夫，坚持读原著、学原文、悟原理，紧紧围绕坚持和发展中国特色社会主义这个主题，联系中共十八大以来党的理论和实践创新进程，联系改革发展稳定、内政外交国防、治党治国治军的新要求，全面准确把握习近平总书记系列重要讲话的重大意义、科学内涵、基本观点、精神实质和实践要求。深入学习《习近平总书记系列重要讲话读本（2016年版）》，明确各篇章的具体内容。同时，把学系列讲话与学党章党规统一起来，在学系列讲话中加深对党章党规的理解，在学党章党规中深刻领悟系列讲话的基本精神。把学习习近平总书记系列讲话同学习马克思列宁主义、毛泽东思想、邓小平理论、“三个代表”重要思想、科学发展观结合起来，深入领会党的科学理论既一脉相承又与时俱进的内在联系，切实坚定道路自信、理论自信、制度自信、文化自信。

坚持“带着问题学、针对问题改”，把解决问题贯穿学习教育全过程。一是强化问题导向，认真查摆存在问题。区委和开发区工委印发的“非公企业‘两学一做’指导方案”中明确了要突出解决的问题。对于每个党员来说，要结合各自实际对这些问题再对照、再聚焦、再细化。在查摆问题过程中，做到“三个结合”，即与“两学”相结合，带着问题学党章党规、学系列讲话，不断解开思想扣子、纠正认识偏差；与个人思想工作实际相结合，对照党纪国法，对照正反两方面典型，把自己摆进去，把问题找准、找实；与教育实践活动和“三严三实”专题教育整改落实情况相结合，往深里找、往细处查，既找共性问题，也找个性问题，持之以恒对照查摆，推动作风建设不断取得新成效。二是强化整改落实，着力解决突出问题。企业党组织以解决问题为牵引，坚持边学边改、即知即改，改好一个个具体问题，做好一件件具体事情，狠抓整改落实。三是强化领导带头，以上率下层层示范。企业党支部书记和中高级管理层党员要在学习教育中走在前面、深学一层，坚持做到“六个带头”，即：带头参加学习讨论；带头谈体会、讲党课、作报告；带头参加组织生活会、民主评议；带头立足岗位作贡献；带头坚持边学边改、整改问题；带头严格执行双重组织生活等基本制度。四是强化融入中心，立足岗位争做贡献。“学”得怎么样，“做”的是否合格，最终还要体现在推动企业的中心工作上。企业党组织要结合各自行业领域实际，搭建实践载体，开展形式多样的主题活动，组织引导党员立足岗位、履职尽责。

三、坚持“抓在日常、严在经常”，推动党的思想政治建设常态化　按照中央部署、区委和开发区工委的要求，非公企业党组织全力以赴做好“两学一做”学习教育的方法措施，具体从以下几方面按步骤开展。

一是及时接转党员组织关系并组建党的组织。全面排查掌握非公企业中的失联党员和“口袋”党员底数，逐一登记造册。7月上旬前，要将党员的党组织关系转接到所在的非公企业党组织。要结合党员组织关系集中排查，进一步摸清非公企业从业人员中的党员情况。

二是研究制定具体方案（7月底前）。非公企业党组织要结合各自实际，研究制定开展学习教育的具体方案。非公企业中的党员一般要按照党员组织隶属关系，参加组织关系所在地党组织的学习教育；非公企业中的流动党员，由工作单位和党员组织关系所在地协商确定参加学习教育的党组织。各非公企业要落实每名党员参加学习教育的党组织。

三是围绕专题学习讨论（11月底前）。要按照“业余、小型、灵活、分散、实效”的原则，结合党员队伍实际，采取编印口袋书、制作微党课微视频、开展体验式教育、运用网络媒体等形式开展学习教育。同时把个人自学和集中学习结合起来，企业支部要参照工委发放的《学习计划》，指导支部党员制定个人的学习计划，引导党员读原著、学原文、悟道理。紧紧围绕四个专题组织党员开展讨论学习。具体为6月底前开展专题一《讲政治、有信念，做政治合格的明白人》的学习讨论；7月底前开展专题二“讲规矩、有纪律，做纪律合格的明白人”的学习讨论；9月底前开展专题三：“讲道德、有品行，做道德合格的明白人”的学习讨论；11月底前开展专题四：“讲奉献、有作为，做发挥作用合格的明白人”的学习讨论。企业党组织班子成员和企业决策层、管理层中的党员要在学习讨论中发挥表率作用，要求职工党员学习掌握的内容自己要熟知尽知，要掌握好与履职尽责密切相关的规定和要求。特别是要系统学习掌握中央、市委、区委和开发区工委对加强非公企业党建工作的政策要求，带头参加所在党支部的学习讨论，带头交流宣传，积极给予指导。

四是创新方式讲党课（全年）。党支部要结合专题学习讨论，非公企业党组织书记要结合专题学习讨论，结合开展纪念建党95周年活动为党员讲党课，要注重联系企业党组织实际，做到党课内容生动鲜活、能产生共鸣；党组织中的普通党员要为支部其他党员讲党课；普通党员要围绕“听党课、找差距、谈感想、做榜样”主题撰写心得体会。

五是召开专题组织生活会（12月底前）。年底前，企业党支部要以“两学一做”为主题，年底前召开专题组织生活会。会前，采取个人查、组织帮、党员提、大家议等多种方式，广泛征求意见，对照“五好党支部”和“四讲四有”合格党员标准，认真查找党组织和党员存在的突出问题和薄弱环节，自觉“对号入座”，撰写支部班子和党员个人简要对照检查材料。班子成员之间开展严肃的批评和自我批评，针对查摆出的问题和薄弱环节制定整改措施。

六是开展民主评议党员（12月底前）。以党支部为单位召开全体党员会议，对党员进行民主评议，可安排与专题组织生活会一并进行，开发区工委将会全程监督把关。支部开展评议时要对照党员标准，按照个人自评、党员互评、民主测评、组织评定的程序组织评定，评定要确定评议等次。结合民主评议，支部书记或班子成员要与每名党员谈心谈话，对优秀的予以表扬；对有不合格表现的，按照党章和党内有关规定，区别不同情况，稳妥慎重给予组织处置。

七是深入开展“五好党支部”创建活动。坚持从支部抓起，从支部强起，结合学习教育，积极开展“五好党支部”创建，即“支部班子好、党员管理好、组织生活好、制度落实好、作用发挥好”。要采取学习讨论查摆问题、摸清底数分类定级、清单管理整改落实、严格标准考核评定、选树典型总结经验5个步骤推动创建活动。针对非公企业工作特点，紧紧围绕凝聚群众、激发活力、促进发展主题，在企业党员中普遍开展以“开展一次特色党日活动、培养一批入党积极分子、进行一次入党生涯座谈交流、开展一次志愿服务、提出一批发展建议”为主要内容的“五个一”工程，充分发挥非公企业党组织政治核心作用，使党建工作与非公企业发展同频共振。

八是深入开展六项专项整治。坚持问题导向，强化底线思维，聚焦解决非公企业党组织、党员队伍、党的组织生活、党员教育管理中存在的突出问题，深入开展6项专项整治：1. 集中整治党员组织关系排查不深入、不落实的问题；2. 集中整治基层党组织应覆盖未覆盖的问题；3. 集中整治基层党组织到期不换届的问题；4. 集中整治党的组织生活制度不健全不落实的问题；5. 集中整治党员不主动按时足额交纳党费的问题；6. 集中整治党组织班子作用发挥不充分的问题。

九是立足岗位做贡献。要把党组织活动与非公企业生产经营行为深度融合，积极探索为非公企业发展所需要、为党员群众所欢迎的活动载体，引导广大党员在企业发展中当先锋作表率。要结合企业生产经营，广泛开展业务竞赛、岗位示范、技术创新、诚信经营等主题活动，促进企业持续健康发展。

四、坚持“区分层次、分类指导”，不断增强学习的针对性和实效性 这次学习教育主要是面向全体党员，层级多、领域广，各种类型党组织和党员之间，情况都各有不同，甚至千差万别，要坚持从实际出发开展教育，防止形式主义，要坚持“一把钥匙开一把锁”，防止“大水漫灌”，防止一刀切、一锅煮。所谓“区分层次”主要是，针对企业中高级管理层党员和普通员工党员等不同情况作出安排。对党员，学习内容要精当适用，学党章党规重点是工委发放的《党员党规党章学习读本》列出的范围，学系列讲话重点是《习近平总书记系列重要讲话读本（2016年版）》，学习方式可以灵活多样，个人学、集体学、“线下”学、“线上”学，总的是要符合实际、管用有效；做合格党员的要求，就是要践行党章，把“四讲四有”即“讲政治、有信念、讲规矩、有纪律，讲道德、有品行，讲奉献、有作为”落到实处。对中高级管理层党员来说，要学得更多更深一些、要求更严更高一些，在全面、系统、深入上下功夫。所谓“分类指导”主要是，在企业内部，要注重区分不同工作性质的特点，明确学习教育的重点内容、组织方式，做到具体化、精确化、差异化。

第三节　宣传工作

1992 年

8 月 7 日上午　武清县人民政府在北京人民大会堂召开了“天津新技术产业园区武清开发区及天津市武清经济开发区新闻发布会”。县长梁文忠，县人大常委会主任刘金铎，县政协主席程振江，县委副书记王成全，县委常委、宣传部长何俊田，县人大常委会副主任杨作莹，县长助理王树培及开发区管委会的全体成员参加。会议邀请了新华社李继成主任及中央人民广播电台、中央电视台、人民日报等二十余家新闻单位的记者 30 余人。会上，县长梁文忠就武清的投资环境作了简要介绍，县长助理、开发区管委会副主任王树培作了两区情况的说明。与会记者对武清开发区的投资环境表示了极大关注。

1993 年

8 月 14 日至 15 日　“首都新闻记者俱乐部”成员一行 10 人，到武清开发区进行了为期两天的专题采访。

1996 年

2 月 7 日　新华社记者刘志杰，经济日报记者童之奇，经济参考报记者肖德木，人民日报记者王惠敏到武清开发区进行采访。

2000 年

10 月 18 日　“中国天津武清开发区之窗”—www.tjuda.com 改版开通。开发区之窗包括“开发区概览”、“投资指南”、“管理服务”等背景资料以及“新闻”、“公告”、“配套信息”、“统计公报”等动态信息栏目。

2003 年

3 月 24 日 台商报专版宣传《武清开发区情况综述》。

9 月 新华每日电讯专稿《一座园林式、现代化的科技工业新城区——天津武清开发区》。

2004 年

3 月 1 日 新华社采访《武清开发区吸引世界目光》。

7 月 6 日 天津电视台采访《武清开发区上半年招商及经济运行形势喜人》。

2006 年

制定庆祝建区十五周年新闻宣传工作方案：1. 区内媒体组织系列报道。在《武清资讯》12 月份每期报纸头版显著位置刊登宣传稿件，在区电视台 “武清新闻”节目中设置“开发区 15 年发展巡礼”专栏。2. 在天津日报、今晚报等市内平面媒体，“新农村”版或第二版刊发大篇幅新闻稿，并在一版刊发短消息。在天津电视台和电台报道开发区成绩。3. 组织新华社、人民日报、中国日报、中央电视台、中央人民广播电台、经济日报、中华工商时报等国家、市级媒体记者 12 月份到开发区进行集中采访，撰写新闻通稿《武清开发区建区 15 年硕果累累》，根据各自媒体特点，多角度报道并刊发。

2007 年

制定纪念武清开发区奠基 15 周年宣传工作方案：

6 月 18 日—23 日，在区电视台《武清新闻》中开设专栏，集中报道开发区发展成果。

6 月 19 日，在《武清资讯》上刊发专版，刊登反映开发区发展成果的文稿和图片。

6 月 26 日，在《武清资讯》副刊上用专版刊发歌颂开发区发展建设成就的散文、诗歌、书法、绘画等作品。为此，拟在 6 月中旬，组织区内文艺、文化工作者到开发区集中采风。

6 月份适当时间，以集中、全面反映开发区发展历程为目标，召集相关人员，启动开发区发展史相关资料搜集整理工作。

2008 年

赞助在武清体育馆举行的中波女排对抗赛、美国女篮 vs 天津女篮对抗赛。

2009 年

3 月 31 日，召开“绿色北欧——安徒生产业创意园”建设规划发布会，多家媒体对此次活动进行了集中宣传报道：

一、中央电视台四套 4 月 1 日 15：00《中国新闻》。

二、人民网 3 月 31 日《各地要闻》。

三、中国日报 4 月 2 日《中国在线》。

四、天津日报 4 月 2 日第 9 版。

五、今晚报 4 月 6 日第 12 版。

六、天津电视台 4 月 1 日《天津新闻》。

七、天津人民广播电台 4 月 1 日《区县联盟广播》。

八、网易 3 月 31 日《新闻中心》。

九、北方网 4 月 1 日《天津要闻》。

十、搜狐 4 月 2 日《新闻中心》。

另外，中国泰国商会网、中关村创意产业网、渤海论坛、天津信息网等多家网站也对活动进行了报道。

2010 年

4 月 12 日，《经济日报》天津武清区：打造高端化高新化产业集群。

4 月，《天津日报》报道“干事创业群英谱”展示开发区和园区企业良好形象。

9 月，《中国日报》刊发武清开发区宣传专稿。

10 月，《香港商报》报道“天津武清开发区 10 年引资 350 亿”。

2011 年

6 月 9 日，佛罗伦萨开业仪式 时任天津市副市长任学峰致辞 百余家媒体报道。

10 月，参展中国国际矿业大会。

12 月，天津市政府召开国家级开发区授牌仪式，时任天津市副市长任学峰主持仪式并为武清开发区授牌，市级媒体广泛报道。

12 月 15 日，在香港《香港商报》进行特别报道《中国武清开发区 20 年与全球客商携手共赢》。

12 月 28 日，在香港《大公报》进行专版宣传《中国武清开发区理想投资地》。

2012 年

3 月 5 日，在全国两会期间在《人民政协报》做整版宣传，之后连续 6 年在该时段、该报纸做专版宣传，2016 年、2017 年都进行了 4 个整版的大篇幅宣传。

5 月 26 日，开发区冠名赞助 “天津武清开发区杯国际马拉松赛”，此后连续五届都冠名赞助该赛事，提高了知名度，展示开发区拼搏奋发向上的精神。

10 月，在《中国品牌》杂志刊发“天津武清开发区：‘筑巢引凤’谋发展”报道。

9 月，开发区赞助“中华人民共和国第九届大学生运动会”，进一步提高知名度。

12 月 15 日，武清开发区举行“京津高校（武清）科技创新园”、“天津大学（武清）前沿技术研究院”揭牌仪式。市委常委、教育工委书记朱丽萍，天津大学校长李家俊出席。市级以上媒体争相报道。

2013 年

3 月，完成开发区视频宣传片制作。在《中国商务年鉴》刊载“国家级开发区”宣传彩页，在《新天津新发展蓝皮书》刊载宣传报道。

4 月，《天津新闻》采访开发区借重首都资源招商。在《旅客报》刊载“理想投资地：中国武清开发区”专版宣传。

7 月，承办商务部部分国家级经济技术开发区座谈会。

10，在《天津市区县年鉴》刊载宣传彩页。

2014 年

4 月，在《商务部投资指南》刊载宣传彩页。

6 月 1 日，创办发行武清开发区第一份报纸——《武清开发区时讯》，月刊，每月发行 600 份，以总公司内部、园区企业为主要阅读对象。宣传武清开发区自身发展动态和阶段性成果，宣传开发区文化、企业文化，凝聚广大园区全体职工的智慧和力量。

7月，在《天津区县志》刊载宣传彩页。

8月28日，外国媒体驻北京记者开展“达沃斯采访季暨京津冀协同发展采访活动”，英国天空新闻、美国之音、德国新闻社、意大利太阳报、半岛电视台、香港卫视等13家媒体集中采访了园区高校园、天大前沿院、丹佛斯、中欧产业园。

10月20日—24日，中宣部组织中央媒体采访团围绕“京津冀大气污染防治”主题到天津市就大气污染防治思路举措和进展成效进行集中采访，并将推出系列报道。

12月，在《中国世界贸易组织年鉴》刊载宣传彩页。

2015年

3月，在《德国机械联合会杂志》刊载宣传资料。

4月，参加北京春季房展。

7月，接受《经济日报》采访“对接首都资源和打造产业承接平台”主题。

10月，台湾无线卫视电视台拍摄佛罗伦萨小镇。

10月30日，2015年武清开发区中欧产业园投资环境说明会暨欧盟商协会领袖与企业家对话会举行，中欧产业园揭牌，天津日报进行了报道。

此外，举办创业总部基地、中欧产业园等集中推介活动10余次，参加相关领域专项活动30余次。与搜狐焦点网、中国招商网、京津冀投资网等媒体合作开展网络宣传，进一步扩大在业内及京津冀地区的知名度。

12月，达伦多跨境商品直购体验中心试开业，共有包括央级媒体、境外媒体、网络媒体、京津冀地区主流媒体和区属“两台一报”在内的30家媒体、38名记者参加，累计在市级及以上媒体发稿32篇，全媒体转发转载达400余篇次。

2016年

1月1日，将《武清开发区时讯》改版升级为《协同先锋报》，进一步突出重点、服务大局，发行扩大到4000份。

1月1日，在北京电视台卫视频道《气象服务》栏目、财经频道《商务气象》栏目投放广告，提高北京地区知名度，扩大影响力、助力招商引资。

2月，新华社《国家财经周刊》采访佛罗伦萨小镇。

3月，在《瞭望》杂志两会特刊制作宣传广告彩页。

4 月 8 日，完成武清开发区微信公众号建设，正式对外推广。

6 月，在天津航空 26 家飞机上投放小桌板宣传广告，提高品牌影响力，锁定各阶层精英群体，助力招商。

6 月 21 日，中央外宣媒体记者团到武清采访，采访开发区信义玻璃和园区领导。

7 月，在《中国统计年鉴》刊载宣传彩页。

8 月，人民日报、新华社、中新社、中央人民广播电台等央级媒体采访团到武清采访创新驱动发展。

10 月，文化创意产业园签约在北京晚报、京华时报、中国商报等 15 家市级以上媒体和腾讯、凤凰等 20 家主流网站进行了报道。

11 月，新华社采访开发区京津冀协同发展成果。

第二章　武清开发区管理委员会

第一节　机构

武清开发区工委、开发区管委会、开发区总公司下设22个部门、5个直属公司，是对开发区实行统一行政管理的机关，主要职能是：根据国家法律，法规和有关规定，制订开发区的行政管理办法，编制开发区经济发展规划，并组织实施；按审批权限审批开发区内的投资项目；统一管理开发区的财政、税收业务；处理开发区涉外事务；管理和审批开发区的土地使用和建筑设计；直辖市区内各职能机构的工作关系；兴办教育、文化、卫生等公益事业，维护开发区的社会秩序；保护开发区企业的合法权益等。

1990年11月8日，根据武清县人民政府[1990]90号文件精神决定建立天津武清新技术产业园区，并成立园区开发建设领导小组。组长：梁文忠；副组长：邵久武、冯祥生、李乃彦；成员：武文宏、李本贵、尤兰英、杨守旭、甄玉鑫、张友平、何宪臣、吴汉发、赵俊起、杨思富、张珍、李学鹏、张树林、曹建伦、肖同福。办公室主任：张树林(兼职)；副主任：张玉。工作人员由建委、经委、外经贸委各派出一名科长或主任科员组成，办公地点在县政府院内。

1991年12月28日，国家科委[91]国科发火字958号文件正式批准建立天津新技术产业园区。天津新技术产业园区由政策区和武清新建区两部分组成，武清新建区为3平方公里。

1992年3月9日，天津市科学技术委员会将武清新建区正式命名为“天津新技术产业园区武清开发区”。

1992年3月9日，根据第三次县长办公会纪要，成立武清县经济开发区管理委员会，梁文忠任主任，邵久武、杨作莹任副主任，王树培、武文宏、李本贵、甄玉鑫为成员。成立开发区总公司。王树培任总经理，下设综合部、招商部、建设部。

1992 年 7 月 14 日，经天津市政府 (津) 政字 [1992]70 号文件，成立天津新技术产业园区武清开发区和天津市武清经济开发区管理委员会，梁文忠任主任，邵久武、杨作莹、王树培任副主任。委员有：武文宏、李本贵、甄玉鑫、虞东文。

1992 年 8 月 8 日，武清县人民政府 (武政发 [1992]086 号) 同意成立天津市武清经济开发总公司 (集体所有制)，公司实行总经理负责制，任命虞东文为总经理。

1992 年 8 月 12 日，武编发 [1992]45 号文件确定：天津新技术产业园区武清开发区和武清经济开发区管理委员会实行两块牌子一套人马：管委会下设办公室和开发区总公司，也实行一套人马两块牌子：管委会办公室和开发区总公司的规格为县属局级；管委会办公室和开发区总公司下设综合部、招商部、建设部、企业管理部、财务部。

1993 年 1 月，聘任王恩成为开发区总公司副总经理。

1993 年 2 月 8 日，开发区总公司办公地点迁至曹园。

1993 年 3 月 4 日，总公司设立驻京招商处，地点在北京保利大厦。

1993 年 12 月 28 日，总公司办公地点迁至开发区一号别墅楼。

1995 年 12 月，成立物业管理部，何建发任物业管理部副部长职务。

1996 年，成立城市管理部，撤销物业管理部，任命王春东为城市管理部副部长，免何建发物业管理部、建设部副部长职务。

1996 年 5 月 20 日，任命韩淑玲为企业管理部部长，免综合部部长职务，汲向春负责综合部工作，免崔秀杰企业管理部副部长职务。

1996 年 8 月 26 日，总公司聘任任瑞才、谭昕为总经理助理，任命崔秀杰为企业管理部副部长。

1996 年 10 月 18 日，经县长办公会 1996 年 11 月 7 日 (第十次) 批准成立开发区劳动就业部。

1996 年 12 月 2 日，总公司正式成立开发区自来水公司、热力公司、物业公司，各公司属部级单位，设独立法人、实行独立核算，任命邱学峰为热力公司经理、李富国为副经理；李洪宇任供水公司副经理、王春东兼任物业公司经理；杨宜峰任劳动就业部副经理；汲向春任综合部副经理。韩淑玲任综合部部长，免其劳动就业部经理职。

1996 年 12 月 17 日，任命安友霞为招商部副经理，免齐明招商部副经理职务。

1997 年 1 月 1 日，设立武清开发区劳动就业部。杨宜峰任劳动就业部副部长。

1997 年 1 月，成立武清开发区劳动争议调解委员会。

1997 年 8 月 13 日，任命邱学峰为热力公司经理；李富国为物业公司经理；汲向春为城市管理部副经理；免汲向春综合部副部长职务；免王春东城市管理部副部长职务。

1998 年 4 月 30 日，总公司研究决定，任命闫仕林为物业公司副经理，李富国为物业公司经理，免其物业公司副经理、热力公司副经理职务。

1998 年 11 月 19 日，经全体员工民意测评结果，人事进行调整。任命邱学峰为招商部部长；韩晓明为规划建设部部长；李富国为热力公司经理；闫仕林为物业公司经理；肖同博为绿化公司经理。免任瑞才规划建设部部长职务；免邱学峰热力公司经理职务；免李富国物业公司经理职务；免杨宜峰劳动就业部副经理职务，调企业管理部工作。免汲向春城市管理部副部长职务，园林绿化公司工程公司副经理职务，调综合部工作。免安友霞招商部副部长职务；免李洪宇自来水公司副经理职务。取消城市管理部代管园林绿化工程公司职能；城市管理部工作由企业管理部代管；劳动就业部由尹国华负责；自来水公司由李洪宇负责。

1998 年 12 月 3 日，经总经理办公会研究决定，任命王泉洪为招商部副部长。

2000 年 1 月 4 日，任命谭昕为总公司总会计师。

2000 年 6 月 27 日，任命汲向春为综合部副部长。

2000 年 11 月 17 日，任命杨宜峰为招商部部长，黄玉广为招商部副部长。免邱学峰招商部部长。

2000 年 12 月 12 日，经区政府研究决定，任命张宗启为开发区管委会办公室主任、开发区总公司总经理。免虞东文开发区管委会办公室主任、开发区总公司总经理职务。

2001 年 1 月 2 日，任命崔秀杰为企管部部长。

2001 年 9 月 3 日，任命尹国华为招商部副部长，杨宜峰为广东办事处主任，黄玉广为上海办事处主任，杜瀛涛为福建办事处主任，安有霞为天津办事处主任，马桂新为北京办事处主任，王洪亮为北京办事处副主任。免汲向春综合部副部长。

2001 年 11 月 29 日，任命梁晓芬为企管部副部长。

2002 年 1 月 14 日，任命梁晓芬为企管二部部长，免其企管部副部长。

2002 年 4 月 27 日，任命张军为财务部副部长。梁晓芬为企管部部长，免企管二部部长。杨宜峰任就业部部长，兼企管二部部长。

2002 年 5 月 28 日，任命崔秀杰为城管部副部长。

2002 年 8 月 19 日，任命李洪宇为工业物业公司副经理，免其自来水公司副经理。杨永生任净水中心经理，兼任自来水公司经理。

2002 年 12 月 31 日，经区政府研究决定，郭宝联任武清开发区管委会办公室主任、总公司总经理；聘任李良君为开发区总公司副总经理；免张宗启武清开发区管委会办公室主任、总公司总经理职务。

2003 年 1 月 1 日，经区委研究同意，由总公司聘任李良君为副总经理。

2004 年 2 月 18 日，成立城区开发领导小组办公室，韩晓明任主任，免其建设部部长职务。杨永生任建设部部长，免其净水中心经理职务。崔秀杰任企管部部长，免其城管部副部长职务。王凤刚任净水中心经理，免其物业公司副经理职务。王秀丽任财务部副部长。王福东任城管部副部长。

2004 年 4 月 16 日，经区政府研究决定，免刘满授武清开发区管委会办公室副主任、总公司副总经理职务务。

2005 年 2 月 18 日，任命李洪宇为工业物业公司经理。苗俊喜任司机班班长。

2005 年 4 月 18 日，免王福东城管部副部长职务。

2005 年 9 月 3 日，李良君辞去开发区总公司副总经理职务。

2005 年 11 月 5 日，任命崔秀杰为招商部部长，免其企管部部长职务。黄巨山任企管部副部长。李刚任综合部副部长。免尤国敏综合部部长职务。免尹国华招商部副部长职务。

2005 年 11 月 18 日，经区政府研究决定，钟书明任开发区管委会办公室主任、总公司总经理。免郭宝联开发区管委会办公室主任、总公司总经理职务。免任瑞才开发区总公司总工程师职务。

2005 年 12 月 7 日，任命李富国为规划建设部部长，免其热力公司经理职务。杨永生任劳动就业部部长，免其规划建设部部长职务。聘任曹式龙为热力公司经理（工资及福利待遇按热力公司标准执行）。

经总经理办公会议研究决定，对总公司招投标工作小组调整如下：王恩成任组长，谭昕任副组长，组员包括李富国、聂光炎、武剑峰、赵剑波、杨雷。

2006 年 3 月 22 日，崔秀杰任总经理助理，兼任总公司企业管理部部长，分管劳动就业部工作；李富国任总经理助理，兼任公公司规划建设部部长，分管城市管理部工作；黄巨山任总公司招商部副部长，暂时主持工作；免去崔秀杰总公司招商部部长职务；免黄巨山总公司企业管理部副部长职务。

2006 年 5 月 1 日，经总经理办公会会议研究，恢复王福东总公司城市管理部副部长职务。

2006年9月22日，经总经理办公会议研究决定：聘任黄巨山为总经理助理，兼任总公司招商部部长；聘任李刚为总经理助理，兼任总公司综合部部长；聂光炎任总公司规划建设部部长；武剑峰任总公司规划建设部副部长；安有霞任总公司企业管理部副部长，暂时主持工作；王洪亮任总公司招商部副部长；杜瀛涛任总公司综合部副部长；聘任苗俊喜为工业物业公司副经理（工资及福利待遇按工业物业公司标准执行），免李富国总公司总经理助理、规划建设部部长职；免崔秀杰总公司总经理助理、企业管理部部长职务。

2006年9月24日，经总经理办公会议研究决定，对总公司招投标工作小组调整如下：组长：李富国，副组长：谭昕，组员：聂光炎、武剑峰、赵剑波、杨雷、郑洪来。

2006年9月25日，经总经理办公会议研究决定：张秀启任总公司司机班班长，享受副部长级待遇。免苗俊喜总公司司机班班长职务。

2007年3月19日，武桂宝任工业物业有限公司副经理（待遇参照总公司副部长标准执行）。

2007年5月11日，黄巨山任总公司企业管理部部长；李洪宇任总公司城市管理部部长；张武民任总公司财务部部长；安有霞任总公司招商部副部长。免黄巨山总公司招商部部长职务；免李洪宇工业物业有限公司经理职务；免安有霞总公司企业管理部副部长职务。总公司招商部由副部长王洪亮主持日常工作；工业物业有限公司由副经理武桂宝主持日常工作。

2007年10月31日，谭昕任开发区管委会办公室副处级调研员。

2007年11月12日，免黄巨山总公司企业管理部部长职务；由副部长李鹏程主持企业管理部工作。

2007年12月5日，张绍锋任开发区管委会办公室副主任；李富国任开发区管委会办公室副主任；免谭昕开发区总公司总会计师职务。

2007年12月14日，聘任黄巨山为武清开发区总公司副总经理。

2007年12月16日，总公司增设城市开发部，聂光炎任城市开发部副部长（主持工作）；武桂宝任总公司规划建设部副部长（主持工作）；李洪宇任工业物业有限公司经理；免李洪宇总公司城市管理部部长职务；免聂光炎总公司规划建设部副部长职务；免武桂宝工业物业有限公司副经理职务；总公司城市管理部由副部长王福东主持日常工作。

2008年5月18日，杨永生任自来水有限公司经理；王凤刚任园林绿化有限公司经理；王继宾任武清开发区创业拓展中心主任；免杨永生总公司劳动就业部部长职务；免张雨田园林绿化公司经理职务。

2008 年 11 月 8 日，聂光炎任城市开发部部长；王洪亮任招商部部长；武桂宝任规划建设部部长；李鹏程任企业管理部部长；王福东任城市管理部部长；王秀丽任劳动就业部部长；裴洪亮任财务部副部长；杨永生任热力有限公司经理；李洪宇任自来水有限公司经理；韩洪斌任工业物业有限公司副经理，暂时主持工作；免聂光炎城市开发部副部长职务；免王洪亮招商部副部长职务；免武桂宝规划建设部副部长职务；免李鹏程企业管理部副部长职务；免王福东城市管理部副部长职务；免王秀丽财务部副部长职务；免杨永生自来水有限公司经理职务，免李洪宇工业物业有限公司经理职务；免安有霞招商部副部长职务；免曹式龙热力有限公司经理职务。

2008 年 12 月 2 日，黄巨山任开发区管委会办公室副主任（试用期一年）；聘任李刚天津武清区开发区总公司副总经理；免张绍锋开发区管委会办公室副主任职务。

2008 年 12 月 12 日，张书月任综合部部长；免李刚综合部部长职务。

2009 年 1 月 13 日，郎聪任招商部副部长。

2009 年 5 月 6 日，杜瀛涛任武清开发区创业拓展中心副主任。

2009 年 10 月 14 日，王德成任开发区管委会办公室副主任（正处级）。

2009 年 12 月 9 日，黄巨山任开发区管委会办公室副主任。

2010 年 3 月 30 日，韩洪斌任工业物业有限公司经理，免其工业物业有限公司副经理职务。

2010 年 4 月 25 日，王继宾任招商部部长；杜瀛涛任武清开发区创业拓展中心主任；免王继宾武清开发区创业拓展中心主任职务；免王洪亮招商部部长职务；免杜瀛涛武清开发区创业拓展中心副主任职务。

2010 年 8 月 15 日，刘东海任开发区管委会办公室主任；免钟书明开发区管委会办公室主任职务。

2010 年 10 月 18 日，聘任翟伟为武清开发区总公司副总经理。

2010 年 10 月 19 日，总公司城市开发部职能并入规划建设部。王继宾任武清开发区创业拓展中心主任；聂光炎任热力有限公司经理；王福东任工业物业有限公司经理；杜瀛涛任招商部部长；韩洪斌任城市管理部部长；免王继宾招商部部长职；免聂光炎城市开发部部长职务；免杨永生热力有限公司经理职务；免王福东城市管理部部长职务；免杜瀛涛武清开发区创业拓展中心主任职务；免韩洪斌工业物业有限公司经理职务。

2010 年 11 月 22 日，撤销规划建设部，设立规划部和建设部。武桂宝任建设部部长；杜瀛涛任武清开发区创业拓展中心主任；武剑峰任规划部部长；郎聪任招商部部长；免王继宾武清开发区创业拓展中心主任职；免武桂宝规划建设部部长职务；免杜瀛涛招商部部长职务；免武剑峰规划建设部副部长职务；免郎聪招商部副部长职务。

2011 年 2 月 21 日，张武民任开发区总公司总会计师。

2011 年 4 月 7 日，裴洪亮任财务部部长；王晓学任财务部副部长；免张武民财务部部长职务；免裴洪亮财务部副部长职务。

2011 年 12 月 31 日，经区委研究决定，张勇任天津新技术产业园区武清开发区和武清经济技术开发区管委会主任。

2012 年 3 月 25 日，总公司招商部门拓展为招商一部、二部、三部、四部和创业拓展中心等五个部门，相关部门人员调整如下：郎聪任招商一部部长；韩洪斌任招商二部部长；王金祥任招商三部副部长，主持工作（试用期一年）；许贤任招商四部副部长，主持工作（试用期一年）；张秀启任城市管理部副部长，主持工作（试用期一年）；李宝江任司机班班长，享受副部长级待遇（试用期一年）。免韩洪斌城市管理部部长职务；免张秀启司机班班长职务。

2012 年 7 月 6 日，李富国任开发区管委会办公室调研员；黄巨山任开发区管委会办公室调研员。

2012 年 10 月 27 日，设立总部基地物业公司，杨雷任总部基地物业公司副经理，主持工作（试用期一年）；韩洪斌任建设部部长；崔洪年任规划部副部长（试用期一年）；刘玉柱任企业管理部副部长（试用期一年）；免武桂宝建设部部长职务；免韩洪斌招商二部部长职务。

2013 年 5 月 12 日，郑洪来任建设部副部长（试用期一年）；杨少海任财务部副部长（试用期一年）；孙波任综合部副部长（试用期一年）；孙竹任招商二部副部长，主持工作（试用期一年）；王玉任招商五部副部长，主持工作（试用期一年）；王金祥试用期满，任招商三部副部长，主持工作；许贤试用期满，任招商四部副部长，主持工作；张秀启试用期满，任城市管理部副部长，主持工作；李宝江试用期满，任司机班班长，享受副部长级待遇。

2013 年 10 月 24 日，聘任张武民为天津新技术产业园区武清开发区总公司副总经理；聘任王继宾为天津新技术产业园区武清开发区总公司副总经理；免去王德成开发区管委会办公室副主任（正处级）职务。

2014年4月29日，撤销服务部、栖仙物业公司，成立开发区行政服务中心，崔洪年任行政服务中心主任，免其规划部副部长职务；王福东任建设部部长，免其工业物业公司经理职；闫世林任工业物业公司经理，免其栖仙物业公司经理职；张秀启任城管部部长，免其城管部副部长职务；王金祥任招商三部部长，免其招商三部副部长职务；许贤任招商四部部长，免其招商四部副部长职务；刘玉柱任企管部部长，免其企管部副部长职务；杨雷任开发区物业公司经理，免其优达物业公司副经理职务；孙波任综合部副部长，主持工作；杨英任规划部副部长，主持工作（试用期一年）；张士硕任建设部副部长（试用期一年）；免张书月综合部部长职务；免李鹏程企管部部长职务；免武剑峰规划部部长职务；免韩洪斌建设部部长职务；免郑洪来建设部副部长职务。

2014年8月25日，免去张勇天津新技术产业园区武清开发区和武清经济技术开发区管委会主任职务；免去李富国天津新技术产业园区武清开发区管委会办公室调研员职务；免去黄巨山天津新技术产业园区武清开发区管委会办公室调研员职务。

2014年10月15日，撤销武清开发区创业拓展中心，其职能转入开发区行政服务中心，成立招商六部和武清开发区德国代表处。王金祥任招商一部部长，免其招商三部部长职务；许贤任招商二部部长，免其招商四部部长职务；孙波试用期满，任综合部副部长，主持工作；王玉试用期满，任招商三部副部长，主持工作，免其招商五部副部长职务；杨少海试用期满，任财务部副部长；苑广伟任招商四部副部长，主持工作（试用期一年）；王小萌任招商五部副部长，主持工作（试用期一年）；劳津任武清开发区德国代表处主任，副部长待遇，主持工作（试用期一年）；杜瀛涛免其创业拓展中心主任职务；郎聪免其招商一部部长职务；孙竹免其招商二部副部长职务；汪志红通知挂职担任天津新技术产业园区武清开发区管委会办公室副主任。

2014年10月17日，解聘黄巨山天津新技术产业园区武清开发区总公司副总经理职务；解聘刘东海天津新技术产业园区武清开发区总公司总经理职务；免李富国天津新技术产业园区武清开发区管委会办公室副主任职务；免黄巨山天津新技术产业园区武清开发区管委会办公室副主任职务。

2014年12月29日，刘福伟任招商部副部长，负责侨梦苑招商工作（试用期一年）；李杰任招商六部副部长，主持工作（试用期一年）。

2015年7月7日，孙波任综合部部长，免其综合部副部长职务；王玉任招商三部部长，免其招商三部副部长职务；杨英试用期满，任规划部副部长，主持工作；张士硕试用期满，任建设部副部长。

2015 年 11 月 19 日，郭新华任天津武清经济技术开发区管理委员会主任；张绍锋任天津新技术产业园区武清开发区总公司总经理；朱瑞林任天津新技术产业园区武清开发区总公司副总经理；刘东海不再担任天津武清经济技术开发区管理委员会办公室主任职务。

2016 年 1 月 11 日，聘任张绍锋为天津新技术产业园区武清开发区总公司总经理；聘任朱瑞林为天津新技术产业园区武清开发区总公司副总经理；聘任张武民为天津新技术产业园区武清开发区总公司副总经理；聘任王继宾为天津新技术产业园区武清开发区总公司副总经理。

2016年2月1日，李子树挂职担任天津新技术产业园区武清开发区总公司副总经理，挂职时间（2016 年 2 月至 2016 年 11 月）。

2016 年 3 月 16 日，成立党建工作部，郝鋆任党建工作部副部长，主持工作，试用期一年；预结算部，杨少海任预结算部部长，试用期一年，免其财务部副部长职；招标采购部，孙波任招标采购部部长，试用期一年，免其综合服务部部长；科技服务部，李杰任科技服务部副部长，主持工作，免其招商六部副部长职务；二次开发部，赵岩任二次开发部副部长，主持工作，试用期一年；综合部更名为综合服务部，魏建东任综合服务部部长，试用期一年；规划部更名为规划设计部；建设部更名为工程管理部；财务部更名为资本运营部；劳动就业部更名为人力资源部；东疆武清产业园筹备工作领导小组办公室更名为东疆招商部；刘福伟任招商六部副部长，主持工作，免其招商部副部长职；丁丽任企业管理部副部长，主持工作，试用期一年；李伟任东疆招商部副部长，主持工作，试用期一年。

2016年7月19日，聘任孙浩为天津新技术产业园区武清开发区总公司副总经理（列张武民之后），不再担任京津高村科技创新园（天津）有限公司副总经理职务；聘任武剑峰、李鹏程、郎聪为天津新技术产业园区武清开发区总公司副总经理。

2016 年 7 月 26 日，撤销李伟东疆招商部副部长职务。

2016 年 8 月 1 日，成立开发区生物医药产业重大项目工作组，郭新华任组长，孙浩任副组长，王永苹为组员，日常工作由孙浩负责；成立开发区智能制造产业重大项目工作组，张绍锋任组长，李鹏程任副组长，王树柠为组员，聘任雷彦斌为顾问，日常工作由李鹏程负责。成立经济运行部、法务部。杨英任规划设计部部长，免其规划设计部副部长职；刘文香任经济运行部副部长（试用期一年），主持工作；王凤丽任经济运行部副部长（试用期一年）；殷绍峰任法务部副部长（试用期一年），主持工作；石洪波任综合服务部副部长（试用期一年）；王金祥任东疆招商部部长，免其招商一部部长职务务；王玉任招商一部部长，免其招商三部部长职务；苑广伟任招商三部副部长，免其招商四部副部长职务；王小萌任招商四部副部长，免其招商五部副部长职务；刘福伟任招商五部副部长，免其招商六部副部长职务；沈晓菁任招商六部副部长（试用期一年），主持工作；肖仓任行政服务中心副主任（试用期一年）；徐立程任安全发展部副部长（试用期一年）；王君健任企业管理部副部长（试用期一年）；刘健任工程管理部副部长（试用期一年）；徐宁任人力资源部副部长（试用期一年）；杨超任工业物业公司副经理（试用期一年）；程克顺资本运营部副部长待遇；王永苹任开发区生物医药产业重大项目工作组组员，副部长待遇；王树柠任开发区智能制造产业重大项目工作组组员，副部长待遇；免李伟东疆招商部副部长职务。

2016 年 8 月 15 日，成立珠三角办事处，取消招商五部、招商六部，东疆招商部更名为自贸区（武清园）招商服务中心。王金祥任自贸区（武清园）招商服务中心主任（正部长级），免其东疆招商部部长职务；刘福伟任珠三角办事处主任，主持工作（副部长级），免其招商五部副部长职务；沈晓菁任招商一部副部长，免其招商六部副部长职务。

2016 年 11 月 1 日，刘庆时任天津武清经济技术开发区管理委员会调研员。

2016 年 11 月 25 日，苗俊喜任热力公司副经理，免其工业物业公司副经理职务，待遇不变。

2017 年 1 月 18 日，郭新华不再担任武清经济技术开发区管理委员会主任职务。解聘孙浩天津新技术产业园区武清开发区总公司副总经理职务。

第二节　各部门职责

在建设发展中，不断建立完善总公司所属各部门的制度化建设，建立健全岗位责任制，提高了员工素质，加强了队伍建设，使总公司逐步步入了制度化管理轨道。

一、党建工作部职责

（一）负责党的建设、思想政治建设、作风建设、党风廉政建设和精神文明建设；

（二）负责党组织和党员队伍建设工作，保证党员发展质量，开展党员教育和管理，组织党员开展各种活动，开展民主评议党员工作；

（三）负责非公党建工作，推进党的组织和工作覆盖，建立健全基层党支部的组织生活制度，灵活多样开展创先争优活动，探索总结适合企业特点的非公党建工作方法和经验；

（四）负责中层干部考察、考核，完善干部选拔任用工作的内部监督机制。负责对领导班子和领导干部落实党风廉政建设责任制情况进行考察、考核及评价；

（五）负责纪检监察工作，检查机关及相关单位在遵守和执行法律、法规以及相关决定、命令中的问题。受理对机关各部门人员违反纪律行为的控告、检举以及对处分决定不服的申诉并负责调查处理。承担法律、法规规定由监察机关履行的其他职责；

（六）负责机关人事工作，负责员工招聘、劳动合同签订和户档转存工作。负责员工的信息管理、职称、培训工作；

（七）负责员工培训及拓展训练组织工作；

（八）负责共青团、工会、妇联相关工作；

（九）完成领导交办的其他事项。

二、综合服务部职责

（一）办公室职责

1. 负责年度工作会、工委办公会、部长例会组织筹办工作；

2. 负责机关综合性文件起草等文秘工作，负责文件的收发、传阅等工作；

3. 负责保密工作。加强保密教育和相关法律法规培训，制定保密管理办法，确保机关无失密案件发生；

4. 负责档案管理工作。按期收集、及时归档，确保完整、安全和备查；

5. 负责督查各部门贯彻落实工委各项决策部署情况；负责协调督办各项重点工程、工作及领导交办的重点事项；

6. 负责开发区对外公共关系和形象设计与维护工作；

7. 负责信息宣传工作，策划与投放开发区对外宣传广告，统一制作对外宣传品；

8. 负责绩效考核工作；

9. 负责机关信息化和智慧开发区建设工作；

10. 负责政务信息的收集与发布；

11. 负责机关物业工作，负责食堂、办公设备、办公用品、卫生等日常管理工作；

12. 负责车辆、车务、驾驶员管理，负责车辆的日常调配工作；

13. 负责协助企业筹备开业、奠基等相关活动，协助招商部门筹备项目签约、推介活动等工作；

14. 负责机关印章办法的制定、完善和实施，负责日常印章管理；

15. 负责机关各项行政管理制度的实施和监督；

16. 完成领导交办的其他事项。

（二）法务职责

1. 负责制定开发区合同管理办法，起草标准合同文本；规范开发区所有合同、协议的签订、管理、归档；

2. 负责开发区规范性文件、对外文件、管理制度和重大决策的合法性审核，参与相关会议、讨论，了解有关决策及经济活动的相关背景；

3. 制定完善各项行政管理制度；

4. 负责与常年法律顾问对接合同审核及开发区涉法、涉诉案件工作；

5. 负责依法治区相关工作和法治开发区建设，负责法律法规培训，对区内企业进行普法宣传；

6. 完成领导交办的其他事项。

三、招商部职责

（一）负责招商引资工作；

（二）负责招商队伍管理，建设高效、专业、廉洁团队；

（三）负责制定招商引资相关政策及办法；

（四）负责拓展招商引资渠道，搜集项目信息；

（五）负责项目接待、洽谈、考察、追踪、落地等；

（六）负责投资协议、房屋租赁合同等合作文件起草；

（七）负责牵头并会同其他部门对项目进行综合评审，对达标项目提出入区意见和申请；

（八）完成领导交办的其他事项。

四、东疆招商部职责

（一）负责自贸区、天津港、东疆港有关部门协调工作；

（二）负责自贸区武清园筹备期内运营主体的设立、变更工作；

（三）负责自贸区相关项目的引进及服务工作；

（四）负责自贸区相关政策研究，并提供政策咨询；

（五）处理与自贸区武清园相关的其他事项；

（六）完成领导交办的其他事项。

五、资本运营部职责

（一）资本运营职责

1. 负责制定并落实财务管理制度，严格执行财经纪律和财经法规，确保管理规范，安全运行；

2. 负责总公司、二级公司的财务管理、会计核算、资金收支审核监督和审计工作；

3. 根据各部门资金预算编制年度资金收支计划，按照要求编制合理的融资方案，落实融资渠道，确保资金需求和高效运转；

4. 负责编制理财方案，在确保资金安全的基础上，增加收益，实现保值增值；

5. 负责申请、落实与财政部门的各项资金拨款工作；

6. 定期向主要领导报送财务收支、财务分析报告；

7. 负责内部审计和委托审计，对接上级部门审计监督；

8. 协助制定对外投资管理办法，协助做好对外投资项目的批复工作；

9. 负责工程及采购资金的审核、申请和拨付。兑现项目扶持政策。审核支付各项资金；

10. 负责固定资产投资工作；

11. 负责核算工会会费，按照规定及时返还；

12. 督促各部门催收应收款项；

13. 负责员工薪资计算、发放，及时缴纳员工保险、公积金；

14. 负责金融创新，为企业提供融资服务；

15. 完成领导交办的其他事项。

（二）经济运行职责

1. 贯彻执行有关国民经济和社会发展、经济运行、统计等工作的法律、法规、规章，并组织实施和监督检查；

2. 负责拟定经济发展年度计划目标，制定相关制度办法和措施，确保完成年度发展目标；

3. 负责统计工作，包括统计资料的收集、整理、汇总和统计报表报送，全面完成各项统计任务；

4. 负责经济运行分析工作，包括税收、工业产值、服务业收入、固投等，为决策层提供信息资料；

5. 负责向各部门提供统计数据，配合做好相关工作；

6. 负责企业扶持政策兑现申请；

7. 负责向税务部门提供新项目资料，监控企业纳税情况；

8. 协调税务部门参加招商项目考察、会商和洽谈；

9. 负责建立与财税部门沟通机制，定期组织税收工作分析交流例会；

10. 负责开发区经济普查工作；

11. 负责开发区企业上市咨询、服务和推动落实；

12. 完成领导交办的其他事项。

六、预结算部职责

（一）负责所有招采项目的预算编制和结算审核，严格执行国家预结算法规和有关制度，确保预结算工作依法依规。负责制定、完善公司预结算管理办法、工作程序；

（二）负责监督、审核第三方造价咨询公司预结算评审工作；

（三）负责与区财政局评审中心对接沟通，报件并协调评审中心出具项目招标控制价，负责服务类和自主招采项目的招标控制价编制，负责向招标小组汇报相关评审结果；

（四）参与招标文件审议，参加项目招标会，对招标工作流程提出合理化建议，参与审核商务标，参与主要设备和材料供应商的考察，参与招采项目合同或协议的审核，参与项目增减项现场见证及计量，监督增减项的真实性与必要性，参与项目竣工验收、评议等工作；

（五）负责收购项目土地和建（构）筑物价格评估，联系对接第三方评估机构工作；

（六）协助招商做好企业建设投资造价咨询等工作；

（七）向招标领导小组汇报项目预结算工作；

（八）完成领导交办的其他工作。

七、招标采购部职责

（一）严格执行招标投标有关法律法规和相关制度，确保招投标工作依法依规；

（二）负责制定、完善开发区招采管理办法和工作流程，并负责解释说明；

（三）协助项目主管部门制定招标所需相关技术文件和资信文件，组织联审会确定招标文件；

（四）负责与区相关部门沟通，推动落实招标采购工作；

（五）负责招采过程组织工作，监督第三方招标代理机构的代理行为；

（六）负责组织召开项目招标答疑会及会议纪要的联审；

（七）负责组织招采合同或协议的审核；

（八）参与主要设备和材料供应商考察；

（九）向招标小组汇报相关工作；

（十）完成领导交办的其他事项。

八、行政服务中心职责

（一）负责配合招商部门做好项目落地前的相关咨询工作；

（二）负责办理企业的工商营业执照、发改委立项、环评、能评、人防、建委及各类前置后置审批工作；

（三）负责汇总企业各项审批工作办理情况并及时汇报；

（四）负责企业涉及规划的咨询、预审、审批工作；

（五）负责办理买地企业的土地征转、招拍挂、确权等工作；

（六）负责办理买地企业的房产确权工作；

（七）负责企业与各职能部门之间的协调工作；

（八）负责收集并整理归档与审批相关的文件；

（九）负责协助资本运营部做好固定资产投资统计上报相关工作；

（十）负责对违法用地企业进行管控、处理并做好与国土资源局的对接工作；

（十一）负责证后监管工作；

（十二）负责配合二次开发部做好审批工作；

（十三）完成领导交办的其他工作事项。

九、规划设计部职责

（一）负责开发区总体规划、控制性详细规划、城市设计导则、土地细分导则的制订及控制管理工作；

（二）负责区内远景、市政、景观、产业等各专项规划的制订及控制管理工作；

（三）负责自建项目方案及施工图设计任务书编制、方案汇报、设计对接及组织施工图联审工作；

（四）负责协调设计单位为自建项目提供现场服务并办理相关手续；

（五）负责搜集整理设计前期资料、最终方案、施工图等相关资料，建立设计专项档案；

（六）协助招标采购部拟定招标文件并参加开标评审工作；

（七）协助审查、签订设计合同；

（八）负责为招商部门及入区企业提供用地红线图、能源接口图、规划设计条件等相关资料和咨询服务；

（九）参与企业新建、扩建总平图、鸟瞰图、外立面效果图规划审批；

（十）参与企业报送的路由申请、厂区开口、临建申请等规划审批；

（十一）负责对新建及扩建企业进行规划巡查，对发现问题的企业下发整改通知，并递交城管部；

（十二）负责对企业开工前，联系相关单位进行控制点、定桩、放线、验线工作，并在企业竣工后组织相关部门进行竣工验收；

（十三）负责提供其他部门所需的规划设计数据、图纸文件以及其他资料，并负责企业分布图、鱼图等现状图纸的更新；

（十四）完成领导交办的其他事项。

十、工程管理部职责

（一）负责编制年度工程计划，安排建设施工，搞好工程质量监理和现场协调指导；

（二）负责重点建设工程开发进度计划的编制；

（三）负责重点建设工程进度和质量的监督和管理；

（四）负责重点建设工程资料的搜集、管理和归档；

（五）负责区内产业项目催进场及日常服务工作；

（六）负责区内产业项目、自建项目燃气、电力、弱电等配套服务工作；

（七）配合招标采购部、预结算部做好招标前准备工作；

（八）负责提供与建设投资相关咨询和法律法规说明服务；

（九）保障建筑领域安全，做好农民工清欠工作；

（十）完成领导交办的其他事项。

十一、科技服务部职责

（一）负责区内高新技术企业认定、科技型中小企业等咨询及申报工作；

（二）负责园区和区内企业科技项目，包括企业工程中心、重点实验室、专利试点、创新资金等咨询及申报工作；

（三）负责国家级高新区、国家自主创新示范区工作的全面推进；

（四）负责高端制造、生物医药两个千亿级产业集群顶层设计、方案制定和重点推进；

（五）负责科技创新载体，包括生物医药产业研究院、众创空间、孵化器等平台的搭建、管理及提升；

（六）负责高校院所、科研机构等资源及国际科技合作项目的引进工作；

（七）负责产业政策研究和发展战略谋划；

（八）负责引导基金的设立、管理及使用；

（九）完成领导交办的其他事项。

十二、人力资源部职责

（一）负责劳动用工平台建设，加强与京津冀大中专院校联系，拓宽用工渠道，降低企业用工成本，根据企业需要组织企业参加各类招聘会，协助企业办理用工、退工、人才存档开户等手续；

（二）负责企业人才服务，定期完善企业人才信息库，宣传各级人才政策，协助企业做好各类人才的引进、奖励及落户相关工作，负责本土人才培养工作；

（三）负责专家服务基地、博士后工作站、大学生实习实践基地等人才载体建设，做好博士后的引进、培养和使用工作；加强与大院大所及科研机构联系，协助企业实现创新发展；

（四）负责对企业进行劳动用工方面法律法规政策的宣讲，发挥劳动争议调解委员会作用，及时化解劳资争议，配合区职能部门进行劳动监察，预防和处理群体性事件；

（五）完成领导交办的其他事项。

十三、企业管理部职责

（一）落实《武清开发区企业服务工作方案》中的各项企业服务措施，安排落实每季度领导班子成员走访工作、组织企业协会各项联谊活动、组织企业高管培训会、组织区内职能部门与企业的联席会议；

（二）负责企业服务工作，做好企业普访，及时了解企业生产经营中的各方面情况，协调相关部门解决企业生产经营过程中遇到的问题；组织企业办理工商年度报告，协助企业办理一般纳税人认定；负责中小微企业融资补偿机制相关工作；协助企业办理各项变更手续，统计、汇总企业基本情况及增资、变更、资金到位情况；负责“促惠上”活动的组织推动；

（三）负责企业档案整理工作，与招商部的后期衔接，收集、建立企业档案，更新完善企业简介、企业名录信息、官网信息；负责企业标准厂房租赁合同的续签工作；

（四）负责管委会的 ISO 9001、ISO 14001 体系认证的监督审核工作；

（五）负责企业服务手册和企业产品信息的编制及更新改版工作；

（六）负责推动现有企业总部或区域总部、结算中心、采购中心、销售中心的设立；

（七）负责建立园区公交系统，对接交通主要枢纽；

（八）负责推动企业转型升级，促进民营企业发展，搜集整理并协助企业享受市、区各项政策；推动企业品牌创建；

（九）负责政协相关工作；

（十）完成领导交办的其他事项。

十四、安全发展部职责

（一）负责生产安全、食品药品安全相关法律法规的宣传教育培训工作；监督、指导企业开展安全“三同时”工作；

（二）对企业进行生产安全、食品药品安全监督检查，对违法违规的企业进行依法处理；指导企业应急救援体系建设和应急救援工作，组织应急预案的备案和演练；

（三）负责安委会办公室各项日常工作，协调开发区安委会各成员部门做好安全生产工作；

（四）负责环保相关法律法规的宣传贯彻工作；监督、指导企业开展环保“三同时”工作；对企业进行环保监督检查，对违法违规的企业进行依法处理；

（五）鼓励企业使用节能、环保设备，推动企业进行循环化改造，做好国家生态示范园区申报有关工作；

（六）组织协调各部门做好“美丽开发区·一号工程”中各项工作；

（七）完成领导交办的其他事项。

十五、城市管理部职责

（一）负责市容环境治理和道路、交通、水利、电力、监控设施的养管单位年度“养管协议”签订和监督、管理，组织养管单位季度验收并配合养管费申报，以及上述养管项的中小修工程申报；

（二）负责协调和配合街（镇）综合执法单位对违法、违规事项进行管制和查处；

（三）负责对所有建设项目施工现场进行巡查核实，对未履行规划审批手续的责令停工或拆除；

（四）负责防汛及清融雪工作的协调和监管；

（五）负责施工单位“环境责任书”的签订和监管以及环境卫生保障金的预收及返还；

（六）负责质保到期的新建项目（道路、水利、交通、电力、监控及配套设施）的验收、养管移交和新建道路环境治理工作的移交；

（七）负责雨污水接口、企业门牌号码编制、标识牌匾及精神堡垒设置的审批；

（八）负责武清开发区交通安全小组的相关工作，主要涉及企业七座以上及运输车辆的年检审核和签章；

（九）负责起草、签订“生活垃圾清运协议”和清运费催缴，以及生活垃圾清运工作的安排与实施；

（十）完成领导交办的其他事项。

十六、二次开发部职责

（一）负责制定土地二次开发的工作方案、制度及流程；

（二）负责宣传、贯彻、落实《中华人民共和国物权法》《中华人民共和国土地管理法》《中华人民共和国城市房地产管理法》《天津市土地管理条例》等法律、法规，及土地供应政策；

（三）负责建立企业闲置用地、低效用地，闲置厂房，闲置办公楼宇等空间资源的数据库；

（四）负责与构成闲置土地的企业进行洽谈，通过多种方式实现土地二次开发；

（五）负责与“僵尸企业”进行洽谈，在多兼并、少破产的前提下，通过多种方式实现土地二次开发；

（六）完成领导交办的其他事项。

十七、自来水公司职责

（一）负责供水设施的日常管理维护；

（二）负责新增供水设施的管理并提供相关咨询服务；

（三）负责企业供水费用收取并提供相关咨询服务，接受社会监督；

（四）保障供水、用水安全；

（五）完成领导交办的其他事项。

十八、热力公司职责

（一）负责供热设施的日常管理维护；

（二）负责新增供热设施的建设管理并提供相关咨询服务；

（三）负责企业供热费用收取并提供相关咨询服务，接受社会监督；

（四）保障供热安全，让用户满意；

（五）完成领导交办的其他事项。

十九、绿化公司职责

（一）负责参与区内绿化工程规划方案制定及图纸会审，并负责办理招标前期手续，配合组织招标实施和合同签订；

（二）负责绿化工程的工期、质量、验收等协调管理，监督施工合同的履行；

（三）负责企业开门、开口、工程施工等破坏绿地审批、费用测算以及恢复督办；

（四）完成领导交办的其他事项。

二十、工业物业公司职责

（一）负责人才公寓入住咨询、管理、服务；

（二）负责人才公寓房屋查验、设施维修、环境卫生和安全稳定；

（三）负责人才公寓商业配套设施的招租运营管理；

（四）负责标准厂房的房屋交接、日常巡查及用电负荷核准，装修改造、绿化和环境卫生的监管，协调房屋产权单位对厂房进行维修维护等物业管理和服务工作；

（五）完成领导交办的其他事项。

二十一、开发区物业公司职责

（一）负责创业总部基地企业的物业管理服务；

（二）负责创业总部基地楼宇日常维护和维修、安全保卫和环境卫生；

（三）负责创业总部基地内自营服务项目的招商、管理；

（四）负责创业总部基地各外包单位的监督、协调；

（五）完成领导交办的其他事项。

二十二、德国代表处职责

（一）参与德国中心的日常工作；

（二）联系和沟通各类德国及欧洲的商务组织；

（三）负责在谈项目的追踪、接待、洽谈；

（四）搜集德国和欧洲的新项目信息，对接招商部门；

（五）负责德国和欧洲已落户企业的回访，相关新项目跟进，上下游相关企业的联系和沟通；

（六）参加展会及相关活动，拓展招商渠道；

（七）负责组织和接待来访的国内外客人；

（八）完成领导交办的其他事项。

第三章　群众团体

第一节　工会

武清开发区工会组织成立于1992年5月，开发区工会紧紧围绕经济发展大局，健全工委领导工会工作机制，大力实施强基创先工程，探索加强工会活力建设，在经济建设主战场、维权工作、帮扶工作、组织建设等方面，取得了较好成绩。荣获武清区工人先锋号荣誉。

开发区工会始终把企业建会工作作为基础工作。通过广泛开展工会政策宣传和丰富多彩的活动，拥有职工25人以上的57家实体企业独立建会率达100%。

加强政策宣传，强化走访力度，指导具备入会条件的200家中小企业全部加入开发区小型非公企业工会联合会。目前各入会企业工会工作开展形式良好，取得明显成效。

筹办了面向外企管理者的联谊活动，组织企业到已建会外企参观了解工会在，激发职工工作热情、创造性和解决劳资纠纷等方面的积极作用，提升大多数外企高管的建会支持。今年推动德尔福（美国）、哈蒙（比利时）、合宜锻造（德国）等外资企业顺利建立了独立基层工会。

2015年6月，完成了开发区人才公寓二期装修，新增居住面积6.6万平米，均为标准间设计，双人，厨卫俱全，并提供24小时空调通讯热水等服务，同时人才公寓完善了银行、超市、社区医院、健身房等生活配套设施。截至目前新入住职工1000余人。

一是支持完善硬件设施，对有意愿建设优秀职工之家典型的企业提供了资金支持6.6万元。

二是发挥典型引领作用。培育了凯涛奇、华电福源等职工之家典型，组织企业负责人、工会主席、职工代表参观、交流，全面推动所有企业“职工之家”建设。

进一步完善开发区高新公寓职工书屋功能，为丰富新入住的1000名职工业余文化生活，职工书屋更新各类书籍 3000 册，并适当延长开放时间至晚 8:00，为职工提供了学习便利。

利用 3 月份“工资集体协商宣传月”，集中进行工会政策宣讲，进一步使企业经营者了解工资集体协商协议对维持用工稳定的作用，使职工了解工资集体协议对维护自身经济利益的保护作用。

开发区工会结合实际，开展了面向企业、行业和区域的分类协商与协议签订工作。目前已签订单独工资集体协商协议 57 家，签订区域工资集体协商协议 7 份、涵盖企业 200 家，签订新能源行业工资集体协商协议 4 家。建会企业工资集体协议签订率达到 100%。

通过定期走访，鼓励引导企业加入劳动关系和谐企业的创建活动，在保障职工工资福利、职工参与企业民主管理、劳动争议调解等具体工作上开展指导。今年新增劳动关系和谐企业 4 家（合宜锻造、友元办公、哈蒙、德尔福）。开发区劳动关系和谐企业达 57 家，其中天狮集团被评为全国模范劳动关系和谐企业，中粮包装被评为天津市 AAA 级劳动关系和谐企业，红日药业、赛诺制药被评为天津市 AA 级劳动关系和谐企业。

进一步发挥开发区人民调解委员会作用，全年累计走访企业 956 家次，接听答复各类咨询、投诉电话 1800 余个，协调解决和答复了企业提出的各类问题近 700 个。妥善处理了国际纸业转卖涉及 180 名职工经济补偿问题，科威金属 50 名员工 100 万工资问题，保证开发区企业用工的稳定。

开发区工会积极组织做好会员卡的宣传与管理工作，使职工会员服务卡真正成为职工会员的“福利卡”。截至目前，辖区内实际职工人数约 3.5 万人，分三批次办理工会会员卡共有 130 余家企业约 2.5 万人。此外，开发区工会与天津银行一同到企业完成持卡会员的开卡服务，协助会员职工真正享受到工会带来的全方位、“一条龙式”服务。实施工会卡救助保障以来，开发区共有 6 名职工分别因火灾、重大疾病等原因受惠，共获救助资金 45580 元。

积极开展困难职工帮扶工作，面向全部企业工会摸排困难职工情况，建立困难职工数据库并及时更新。

敦促企业为困难职工提供安全、稳定的工作环境。鼓励企业为困难家庭和职工提供适合的工作岗位。

完善机制，实现因重大变故或大病造成生活困难的职工可随时向帮扶站申请临时资助，在儿童节、重阳节期间困难职工子女、父母予以助学、敬老等领取资助。2014年春节前对100余名在统困难职工累计补助16.3万元。

为天狮大学、信义玻璃等20家企业的施工场地及一线职工送藿香正气水、蚊不叮、加多宝等避暑用品。

与中国人民大学培训学院合作，每月邀请清华大学、北京大学等培训师，组织企业高管培训。累计为区内350家次重点企业的近500名高管进行培训，为提高企业骨干综合管理能力。

组织开发区足球队、篮球队、羽毛球队、乒乓球队、瑜伽队等体育运动队伍，积极组织企业职工定期参与各队活动，改善职工健康状况。

艾尔姆组织家庭日活动、伊利组织趣味运动会等活动。丹佛斯创建了劳模（技能人才）创新工作室，组织了技能提升培训大讲堂等活动10余次。

2015年开发区企业上缴工会经费4072.77万元，增长6.1%，超任务近100万元。在工会经费不断增加的同时，开发区工会加强了经费使用和审计保证了工会经费的合理、合规使用。

2016年是“十三五”发展的开局之年，是加快建设京津卫星城、美丽新武清的起步之年。开发区工会在区委的坚强领导和区总工会的有力指导下，紧紧围绕经济发展大局，健全工委领导工会工作机制，全面深入开展“当好主力军，建功‘十三五’”主题实践活动，进一步推进工会活力建设，助力园区经济发展。

（一）抓基层工会组建，夯实工会活动基础

1. 督导企业独立建会。开发区工会始终把企业建会放在园区工会工作的首要位置。今年以来，通过广泛的宣传和政策引导，开发区现已拥有职工25人以上独立建会企业64家，同比增加12.3%，实现增长的同时，又保证了独立建会率100%。

2. 强化小企业工会联合会建设。加强政策宣传，强化走访力度，指导具备入会条件的196家中小企业全部加入开发区小型非公企业工会联合会。目前各入会企业工会工作开展形式良好，取得明显成效。

3. 推进集团型企业下属分公司建会。与天狮集团有限公司企业负责人及工会有关领导取得联系，宣传工会相关政策、组织有关人员到已建会企业学习参观工会的日常运行，深入了解企业工会在激发职工工作热情、创造性和解决劳资纠纷等方面起到的积极作用，从而赢得企业的建会支持。今年天狮集团下属分公司天狮生物工程、天狮生命源、天狮生物发展、奥蓝际德国际旅行社、天狮学院等5家企业实现了独立建会，进一步完善了天狮集团基层企业工会的组织架构。

（二）抓职工服务平台建设，增强工会凝聚力、影响力

1. 强化职工活动平台建设，打造“职工之家”。一是支持完善硬件设施，今年开发区工会对有意愿建设优秀职工之家典型的企业提供了资金支持 1.5 万元。二是发挥典型引领作用。培育了中天高科、瀚侨车体、完达山等职工之家典型企业，组织企业负责人、工会主席、职工代表到有“建家”经验的企业参观走访、交流经验，促进开发区“职工之家”建设全面发展。

2. 强化职工生活品质提升，完善基层工会平台建设。今年 7 月，对作为全国“职工书屋”示范点的高新公寓职工书屋进行了图书更新和设备改造升级。除本单位新增图书 3000 余册外，还向上级工会递交了职工书屋示范点补配图书申请报告，预计于 2017 年年初配发到位；11 月底，推举我区市级劳模创新工作室典型单位红日药业参加 2016 年天津市十大示范性劳模创新工作室评选活动；12 月，推动开发区“星级工会法律援助工作站”申报、评选以及审查评定工作，不断提高园区工会法律援助工作专业化水平。

（三）抓工资集体协商，和谐企业劳动关系

1. 强化政策宣传。年初集中开展“工资集体协商要约行动”，向企业和职工进行有关工资集体协商方面的政策宣讲，进一步使企业经营者了解工资集体协商协议对维持用工稳定的作用，使职工了解工资集体协议对维护自身经济利益的保护作用。

2. 注重任务落实。开发区工会结合实际，开展了面向企业、行业和区域的分类协商与协议签订工作。目前已签订工资协议 76 份，覆盖企业 258 家、涵盖职工 37225 人，签订覆盖率达 100%。其中 25 人以上企业单独签订 64 份、涵盖职工 34231 人；行业性协议 5 份，覆盖企业 39 家、职工 522 人；区域性协议 7 份，覆盖企业 157 家、职工 2472 人。签订率达到 100%，圆满完成年初制定的工作目标。

3. 主抓行业协商。开发区全年共签署行业性工资集体协议 5 份，涵盖企业 39 家。其中，新增行业类型 4 个，包括有：生物医药、现代服务、房地产、批发零售等不同领域，加上原有的新能源行业，形成了类别齐全、各具特点、典型突出、覆盖广泛的行业性集体协商新模式。

（四）抓和谐企业创建，优化园区企业发展环境

完善劳动关系和谐企业创建机制。通过定期走访，鼓励引导企业加入劳动关系和谐企业的创建活动，在保障职工工资福利、职工参与企业民主管理、劳动争议调解等

具体工作上开展指导。年内新增劳动关系和谐企业 14 家。开发区劳动关系和谐企业达 121 家，其中天狮集团被评为全国模范劳动关系和谐企业，中粮包装被评为天津市 AAA 级劳动关系和谐企业，红日药业被评为天津市 AA 级劳动关系和谐企业。

（五）抓工会卡服务工作，实现园区企业全覆盖

开发区工会积极组织做好会员卡的宣传与管理工作，使职工会员服务卡真正成为职工会员的“福利卡”。截至目前，共有 130 余家企业分四批次办理工会会员卡，涉及职工人数超过 2.6 万人。此外，开发区工会与天津银行一同到企业完成持卡会员的开卡服务，协助会员职工真正享受到工会带来的全方位、“一条龙式”服务。2016 年全年，开发区共有 12 名职工分别因火灾、重大疾病等原因受惠，共获救助资金 12 万元。

（六）抓困难帮扶工作，为企业及职工排忧解难

1. 积极发挥开发区困难职工帮扶站作用。积极开展困难职工帮扶工作，面向园区企业工会摸排困难职工情况，建立困难职工数据库并进行实时数据更新。

2. 积极实施困难资助计划。2016 年，开发区工会先后于 7 月初和 9 月初组织并开展了“夏送凉爽”和“金秋助学”两项职工帮扶活动，为职工送去实惠、为企业排忧解难，赢得了企业及职工的一致好评。据统计“夏送凉爽”活动支出工会经费 35926 元、“秋季助学”活动支出工会经费 22200 元，共计支出 58126 元，惠及企业 40 余家，职工近万人，重点帮扶困难职工 44 人，用爱心和福利缓解了他们的工作和生活压力。此外，在 12 月上旬开展的“冬送温暖”帮扶活动中，开发区工会共报送困难职工 167 人，涉及企业 40 家。预计帮扶补贴金额将达到 20 余万元。

（七）抓职工文体、培训及竞赛活动，提高职工知识水平、改善健康状况

积极开展职工活动，为企业提供人才支持。广泛开展“当好主力军，建功‘十三五’”主题活动，开展多样性的职工文体活动和交流活动，积极组织企业职工定期参与各队活动，改善职工健康状况；组织开展多层次的企业职工培训，开展园区企业高管培训和企业职工学历教育，不断提高开发区企业管理水平；组织园区企业职工参与武清区“五比一创”劳动技能竞赛、职工职业知识大赛等活动，在今年的职工职业知识大赛中，开发区企业中粮包装、艾尔姆风能分获冠亚军，开发区工会获优秀组织奖。丰富多彩的职工活动教育引导职工立足岗位学习新知识、钻研新技术、创造新工艺、掌握新技能，为开发区科技创新、企业发展提供保证。

（八）抓工会经费征收管理，保障工会工作顺利开展

2016 年开发区企业上缴工会经费 4158.23 万元，增长 2%。在工会经费不断增加的

同时，开发区工会加强了经费使用和审计保证了工会经费的合理、合规使用。

建立工会企业名称

天津同力重工有限公司
天津天宝光碟有限公司
天津国财有限责任会计师事务所
功学社(天津)商贸有限公司
天津澳普林特通讯器材组件有限公司
天津浔兴拉链科技有限公司
天津中粮制桶有限公司
马克菲尔(天津)钢纤维有限公司
天津南玻工程玻璃有限公司
中粮包装(天津)有限公司
天津运城制版有限公司
天津市宝利德空调设备有限公司
天津华电福源热电有限公司
天津市建电实业有限公司
天津市武清开发区腾龙印业有限公司
天津市龙甲门业有限公司
那美钢(天津)汽配有限公司
天津鸿佳地毯有限公司
天津磁化电子有限公司
天津艾天电池有限公司
天津红日药业股份有限公司
乐金华奥思(天津)有限公司
丹佛斯(天津)有限公司
绫致时装(天津)有限公司
优派克精密机械(天津)有限公司
中天高科特种车辆有限公司

天津瀚侨车体制造有限公司
光宝电子(天津)有限公司
日丰建材(天津)有限公司
德尔福派克电气系统有限公司天津分公司
信义玻璃(天津)有限公司
天津大真空有限公司
蜡笔小新(天津)有限公司
天津市普光医用材料制造有限公司
高新公寓
天津凯涛奇食品有限公司
麦格昆磁(天津)有限公司
天津天狮集团有限公司
天津天狮生物工程有限公司
天津天狮生物发展有限公司
天津天狮生命源有限公司
天津天狮学院
天津奥蓝际德国际旅行社有限公司
天津阿托兹精细化工有限公司
欧利生涂料(天津)有限公司
天津华迈科技有限公司
西湖(天津)橡塑制品有限公司
天津渤海联合物流有限公司
天津名门动物食品有限公司
天津市腾龙职业培训学校
爱姆卡(天津)工业五金有限公司
天津天大领先制药有限公司
莱生天津天然保健品开发有限公司
天津格瑞新金属材料有限责任公司
天津市海正泰克塑胶制品有限公司
国际纸业(天津)包装有限公司

友元办公联盟(天津)有限公司
康赛斯(天津)空调有限公司
天津龙甲特种门窗有限公司
天津市宇刚保温建材有限公司
赫英木结构制造天津有限公司

第二节　共青团

武清开发区共青团组织成立于1992年5月，多年来开发区团支部一直是一个朝气蓬勃，充满生机和活力的基层团组织，具有很强的号召力和凝聚力。在武清开发区工委的领导下，团支部始终做到组织健全，核心作用好；团员青年队伍富有朝气，积极进取，勇于开拓；紧紧围绕开发区重点工作，开展适合团员青年特点的主题活动；制度健全，注重落实，成为工委的得力助手。

一、抓好政治学习，提高政治思想素质

1. 定期组织团员青年学习党的路线方针政策，特别是中共十八大召开以后，及时组织团员青年收听收看十八大新闻，开展专题讨论，组织知识竞赛等，使团员青年不断加深对党的十八大精神的理解和认识，始终站在改革开放的第一线，在日常工作中发挥带头作用，使十八大精神的学习贯彻不断深入，在工作和学习中找到了实际的契合点和定位。

2. 定期举办团员理论学习交流会，在团员青年中宣传党的知识和历史，结合新形势的发展，交流思想，畅谈体会。

3. 定期从报纸、杂志及网络上摘录国际与国内的政治信息，提供给团员青年阅读，并互相交流意见和观点。

4. 团支部有计划、有重点的向党组织推荐思想，政治进步的优秀团员，作为党组织的后备力量。通过学习，使广大团员青年的政治思想素质不断提高。截至目前，共有22名青年团员向党组织递交了入党申请书，许多同志自觉按党员标准要求自己，定期向组织汇报思想。

二、组织活动

团支部积极组织了各种活动，促使广大团员青年在完成本职工作的同时，加强学习，

不断实践，从工作中积累经验，以满足业务不断发展的要求。

1. 定期组织内部业务交流，每周各部门内部例会，每月公司组织全体会议，将在工作中遇到的问题及获得的经验互相交流，互相学习，提出新的意见和建议，共同发展，共同提高。

2. 每季度组织一次服务政策与招商业务知识培训，促进了团员青年知识水平与业务水平的整体提高。

3. 团支部针对团员青年的不同情况和工作需要，帮助他们寻找适合的学科专业和深造渠道。繁忙的工作并没有影响大家的学习热情。部分团员青年都利用业余时间参加了硕士研究生、博士研究生等课程的学习，并有部分团员参加了司法考试、计算机考试、职称考试，使他们在学历与能力上都有不同程度的提高。

三、团员青年模范带头作用

在党支部的领导和团支部的组织下，广大团员青年立足本职工作，发扬青年的奉献精神，积极投身于开发区的经济发展。

1. 招商引资是开发区经济发展的基础，全体团员青年始终坚持以服务招商工作为重点，密切关注开发区招商项目，积极主动，采取全程跟踪服务方式，先后为赖斯安全阀、正美玻璃、中投证券、天房等多家入区企业提供涉及土地使用权出让转让、厂房租赁等服务。在为企业提供服务过程中，坚持高效、快捷的原则，做到一次告知、二次受理、三次办结；遇有企业有特殊要求时，则加班加点，保证当天办结。高效率的服务赢得了入区企业对开发区服务作风的高度赞扬。

2. 在开发区设置了困难职工帮扶站，先后共帮扶 40 余家企业的 101 位困难职工，帮扶资金 14 万余元。其中团员青年积极行动，先后共捐助 1.8 万元。

3. 开发区团支部响应团区委的号召，在青年职工中征集志愿者 50 余人次，为两届国际马拉松比赛提供志愿者服务。

四、开展主题活动，丰富业余文化生活。

青年人的活力是团组织的特点，也是开展工作的基础和推动力。团支部始终贯彻一个工作重点就是：发挥团组织的核心作用，开展多种形式的文体娱乐活动，丰富团员青年的业余文化生活。组织团员青年积极参加团区委、区工会组织的各类文体竞赛。篮球比赛、羽毛球比赛、乒乓球比赛、国际礼仪座谈会、劳动技能竞赛、单身青年联席等。通过组织活动，极大地调动了团员青年的工作热情，增强了团队凝聚力。开发区团支部决心在机关团委的正确领导下，紧紧围绕开发区工委的中心工作，积极工作，开拓进取，为建设美丽武清，美丽开发区做出更大的贡献。

开发区团支部获奖情况一览表

表 31

获奖名称	年度	企业名称	备注
武清区新长征突击队	2016	武清开发区	武清开发区行政服务中心
区级新长征突击手		武清开发区	郝鋆
武清区新长征突击队	2015	武清开发区	武清开发区管委会安全发展部
区级新长征突击手		武清开发区	王金祥
区级新长征突击手		武清开发区	王小萌
武清区优秀共青团员	2014	武清开发区	苑广伟
			王小萌
武清区优秀团干部		武清开发区	丁 丽
武清区先进进城务工人员	2013	南玻集团	靳宝树
			王东刚
			李天秀
市级新长征突击队		武清开发区	招商一部
区级新长征突击队		武清开发区	建设部
区级新长征突击手		武清开发区	丁 丽
武清区青年科技创新带头人		信义玻璃	单晓义
			史小明
			杨大伟
优秀共青团员		武清开发区	丁 丽
武清区新长征突击手		红日药业	于 晶

第三节　妇联

一、妇女工作

武清开发区妇联组织成立于1992年5月，园区妇联组织紧紧围绕改革、发展、稳定的总方针，创造性开展妇联工作，在创业上求成效，在创造上寻发展，在创新上谋出路，推动"巾帼建功"，"双学双比"等活动向纵深开展，促使妇女维权与社会发展齐头并进，五好文明家庭创建跃上新台阶，各项工作取得新进展。

（一）培训

定期不定期开办"巾帼新女性大讲堂"，开展妇女教育培训、技能培训（卫生、政策），提升妇女形象和发展能力。2013年园区妇联累计组织了6次讲座，有800余人参加。另外2013年7月份组织了劳动技能竞赛，有5家28人参加（叉车、焊工、钳工）。2015年，聘请人民大学教授组织6次企业高层次管理人员培训，培训480人次，培训课程包括高效能人士的七个习惯、品绩管理、创新管理与创新思维。与区人社局、外企服务公司等第三方培训机构合作，组织了8次人事经理培训，累计886家企业2200余人参加培训；另外，根据《武清区人民政府关于实施技能人才培训福利计划意见》，组织区内1797名在职职工报名参加各类技能培训，其中女性职工占90%以上。

（二）就业

为了促进妇女就业，推动妇女自我价值的实现和提升。园区妇联走入社区、乡镇以及劳动力、人才2个市场，为就业女性搭建交流平台，2013年度累计组织招聘273场，录用1.8011万人（女性9000人），2015年组织招聘281场，达成就业意向3万余人（其中：女性1.6万人），参加招聘的企业都是经过园区妇联层层把关、筛选，从工资、福利待遇等方面进行比较，保障女性体面就业、尊严就业 。

（三）服务

设立未婚青年联谊会、集体婚礼、生育服务（独生子女）、免费健康体检、春风送暖等五个板块。有针对性的开展各项服务。2013年9月15日妇联和工会在奥蓝际德为300余名未婚男女举办了一次联谊会（女130人），在7月和团市委为56对男女在郊野公园举办了运河之恋牵手人生大型集体婚礼（8对），另外，2013年为区内女职工办理了31份生育服务证、5份独生子女证。4月为农民工家属发放免费体检卡200

余张（418元，团委）；1月为39名困难女职工送去每人1000元慰问金。除此，对于外来女职工孩子入学（小学、初中）也都是对口、免费入学，通过上述一系列的活动，减少了女职工后顾之忧，让务工人员感受到家的温暖，使她们全身心投入到工作中去，从而更有力推动了企业和谐发展。2015年，会同工会金秋助学帮扶20个困难家庭共计1.52万元；帮扶了24家企业103名困难职工共计16.3万元；帮扶对口大碱厂困难户13户3.6万元；补助杰麦患癌职工及西湖火灾职工共1.3万元；开展送凉爽到一线活动，到天狮大学、绫致物流园等20个施工现场或企业慰问一线工人，除此，还积极开展爱心储蓄罐义卖活动，积极为贫困母亲筹措资金。

（四）维权

通过社会化的专业服务，一方面为广大妇女提供情绪发泄和心理倾诉的空间，另一方面也为有需要的妇女提供个别化政策辅导，引导妇女情绪压力合理释放。通过倾诉、倾听、调解等，进而解决妇女受侵害案件。2012年园区发生劳动争议50余件，经过调解，全部解决，调解成功率达100%。2015年，接听各类咨询、投诉电话1450余个，在妇联创办的服务平台上回答各类问题1120余个，调解劳动争议89件，调解成功率达100%，女职工的权益得到维护，无集体上访事件，保障了社会以及家庭的和谐稳定。

（五）创新

2016年，针对开发区非公企业女职工组织基础薄弱以及女职工干部兼职化的趋势，在抓同步组建的同时，探索如何使非公企业组织建起来以后能够运转。为此，园区妇联就女职工组织建设状况、发挥作用情况、存在问题和解决措施等进行了深入调研，总结各企业女职工组织在实践中创造的经验，明确了健全女职工组织、加强女职工干部队伍建设、建立和完善女职工工作机制、维护女职工合法权益和特殊权益、创新女职工工作方法，提出了组织健全、人员到位；建立制度，规范工作；民主参与、依法维权；开展活动，服务女职工的工作目标，有效地推动了区内非公企业女职工的工作。

二、开发区妇联历年获得的荣誉

（一）个人荣誉

2011—2012年度，郎聪、王秀丽获得区级“三八红旗手”；

2013年度，许贤、杨英获得区级“三八红旗手”；

2015 年度，王玉获得区级“三八红旗手”；

2015 年度，王秀丽获得“全国巾帼建功标兵”，李杰获得区级“城乡妇女岗位建功先进个人”。

2016 年度，闻琪获得区级“三八红旗手”。

（二）团体荣誉

2013 年度，武清开发区总公司就业部被评为区级“三八”红旗集体。

2016 年度，武清开发区总公司生物医药产业重大项目工作组荣获 2016 年度巾帼建功先进集体。

第八篇

科技 教育 文化

第一章 科技

围绕产业链部署创新链，强化科研成果推广和产业链关联项目培育，推动智能制造、轨道交通等创新产业集群发展，加快实现科研优势向产业优势转化。打造高水平的协同创新平台和研发转化基地。加快战略性新兴产业发展，努力引进一批带动力强、关联度高的优质产业项目。截至2016年，有国家级科研院所近30个，企业、工程技术中心11个，检验检测机构5个，国家级和市级孵化器3个、市级众创空间1个，科技型中小企业1000余家，超亿元企业100余家，市级以上高新技术企业80家。产业基金、融资平台等科技金融服务完善。建有武清开发区博士后科研工作站、院士工作站和专家服务基地，高端人才、创新人才加速聚集。同时，以突出特色、完善功能、提高效益为重点，提升科技创新和公共服务功能。

以提升科技创新能力为核心，支持高校院所、龙头企业等各类主体建设技术创新平台，引导社会机构建设创业孵化平台，提升创新创业服务能力。

建立以工研院为代表的技术创新平台。依托创业总部基地和京津高校科技创新园打造"产业创新谷"，引进京津冀等地大院大所以及市场化运作的科研平台，建成北航智能制造研究院、物理医学与健康产业技术研究院等。支持区内龙头企业牵头成立产业技术研究院，突破产业共性技术，提升产业整体创新能力。吸引世界500强企业、中央企业、行业龙头企业在开发区设立研发机构。建设一批国家级、市级重点实验室、工程中心、企业技术中心等研发平台。

建设开放式创新平台。紧抓京津冀协同发展国家大学创新园区建设机遇，支持开发区企业与京津高校院所建立全面战略合作，探索联合开发、优势互补、成果共享、风险共担的产学研用合作新机制。支持众创、众包、众扶、众筹"四众"平台建设，推动线上线下服务相结合。

建设众创空间和孵化器。完成以双创特区示范基地建设为抓手，贴紧产业升级和科技创新，自下而上探索，在自主创新示范区建设上实现突破。依托创业总部基地打造“众创空间集聚区”。围绕生物医药、高端装备领域建设专业孵化器，支持民营企业、创投机构、高校院所等建设新型孵化载体，完善创业辅导、天使投资等服务。加强与美国布瑞奇孵化器等全球高端创新创业机构合作，推进海外创新成果孵化中心建设。建设加速器和专业园，建成生物医药产业园。

第一节　科技创新园

一、高校科技创新园

自从京津冀协同发展提升为国家战略以来，武清开发区积极做好面向京津冀地区大院大所的引进入驻工作，通过招财引智打造京津冀科技创新高地。

2014 年以来，结合大院大所的引进工作，重点打造京津高校武清科技创新园，园区位于武清开发区高端制造业聚集区，规划占地 161 亩，建筑面积 11.5 万平方米，总投资 3.4 亿元，由丹麦著名规划设计师秉承绿色、环保、可持续发展理念设计，园区的发展定位是致力提高原始创新、集成创新和引进消化吸收再创新能力，借助区位交通优势，面向京津百余所高校和科研机构，加强产学研用结合，打造国家级重大研究课题技术成果转化的创新平台。

坐落在京津高校武清科技创新园的中科院微生物研究所诺科生物科技企业孵化器，占地 2000 平方米，总投资 800 万元，该企业孵化器主要面向具有自主知识产权的生物医药、生物试剂以及相关的生物领域企业，在今后三年，这个孵化器将引入企业 30 家以上。

中科院微生物研究所研究员刘文军说：“武清区的优势是非常明显的，它跨越京津之间，人文的文化氛围非常好，整个的教育水平都非常高，总的设计来讲，我们对这个产业是看好的，它是一个高科技型的企业，它投入的成本可能会高，但是产出可能是比较明显的。同时开发区已经有了像天狮集团、红日药业这些企业，我们看到它的发展空间是非常大的。”

除了来自北京的大专院校、科研院所选择在京津高校武清科技创新园坐落自己的孵化企业之外，来自天津的一些高等院校也选择在这里来建立自己的科技成果转化基地。天津大学武清前沿技术研究院 2012 年底挂牌入驻，总投资 2.4 亿元，是天津大学与武清区共建具有国际标准的科技创新、产业促进、技术服务、战略咨询与人才培养的协同创新平台和“政产学研用”合作基地。前沿院依托天津大学优势学科与重大科技课题主要建设四个机构，涉及生物医药、化工材料、先进制造、精密测试、新能源、绿色建筑、海洋、环保等领域前沿技术的研究，其专利技术优先提供武清区企业甄选和使用，每年将在当地注册企业5家，培育项目5个，技术服务企业100家，该研究院的技术转移中心，每年将在武清区对接项目100个。

截至2016年，武清开发区京津高校武清科技创新园已成果入驻天津大学前沿院、中科院微生物研究所、诺科生物科技企业孵化器、中国农业大学现代富博智能装备三家创新型企业院所，一批大院大所和高新技术企业入驻，为武清开发区打造京津冀科技创新高地，奠定了坚实的基础。

二、高村科技创新园

2014年

7月3日，市人大常委会组成人员履职学习班来京津高村科技创新园调研，区委书记张勇，区人大常委会主任韩胜军陪同。

7月11日，北京市通州区区长岳鹏率通州区党政代表团来京津高村科技创新园调研，区委常委、常务副区长李建成，副区长刘广生陪同。

7月31日，在北京市中国科技会堂举行“协同京津冀、决战大数据”2014论坛暨京津·高村科技创新园推介会，区委常委、常务副区长李建成，开发区工委书记、总公司总经理刘东海参加。

8月14日，国铁道科学研究院副院长聂阿新、董守清、赵有明等一行8人到武清区考察调研，开发区工委书记、总公司总经理刘东海陪同。

8月19日，生物产业园项目、嘉丰达智汇中心项目举行投资协议签约仪式，副区长尤天成，武清开发区工委书记、总公司总经理刘东海参加。

8月21日，区政府办公室相关科室到京津高村科技创新园考察调研。

8月28日，区政府办公室相关科室到京津高村科技创新园考察调研。

9月16日，区级老领导邵久武、李乃彦、李树宏等一行8人到京津高村科技创新园考察，区委书记张勇、区委副书记郭宝琴陪同。

9月26日，区委、区政府主要领导带队实地检查京津高村科技创新园建设情况，并听取了园区管委会副主任刘东海同志关于园区基础设施建设情况、落地项目建设情况及明年安排的汇报。区政府领导就协调解决项目建设过程中存在的问题、加快工程建设、保障施工安全等方面强调了意见。

10 月 12 日，在区行政中心会议楼举行武清区人民政府和北京电影学院的战略合作框架协议签约仪式，区委书记张勇、副区长李伯怀、开发区工委书记刘东海出席。

10 月 23 日，新兴际华集团有限公司董事长、党委书记刘明忠等一行 9 人到武清区实地考察项目情况，武清开发区工委书记刘东海陪同。

10 月 28 日国家发改委城市和小城镇改革发展中心李铁主任一行到武清学习考察，区委书记张勇，区委常委、常务副区长李建成，区委常委、副区长钟书明，副区长刘广生陪同。

10 月 28 日，天津市武清区通信与信息化成果展示大会暨太平洋电信天津数据中心开业典礼举行，区委书记张勇，区政府党组成员、开发区工委书记刘东海参加。

11 月 25 日，部分市人大代表到京津高村科技创新园进行会前视察，区委书记张勇，区人大主任韩胜军，区委常委、副区长钟书明参加。

11 月 27 日，国家统计局、市统计局一行 40 人到京津高村科技创新园调研。

11 月 27 日，参加第二届天津华侨华人回国创业培训班座谈会，并组织来自 9 个国家地区的近 30 位创业负责人到太平洋电信参观考察，副总经理孙浩陪同。

12 月 19 日，在京举办高村助力产业升级——2014 智慧城市产业链与生态圈建设研讨会，首都工作部部长张朝阳参加。

2015 年

1 月 13 日，“千人计划网”负责人周宇煜一行到武清考察并实地察看京津高村科技创新园，区委常委、组织部长周惠军陪同。

1 月 18 日，召开《国务院关于清理规范税收等优惠政策的通知》（国发 [2014]62 号）文件专题学习研讨会。

1 月 20 日，武清挂职锻炼的任丘市领导到园区考察。

1 月 31 日，京津冀规划编制项目组就京津冀协同发展的相关规划问题来武清调研，并到京津高村科技创新园太平洋电信项目实地考察，区委常委、常务副区长李建成，副区长刘广生，区政协副主席、开发区工委书记刘东海陪同。

2月13日，组织召开园区2014年度工作经验总结会。

3月2–3日，铁科院一行来武清调研。

3月6日，京津高村科技创新园与天津神州浩天科技有限公司举行企业综合服务平台入驻暨投资签约仪式，区政协副主席、开发区工委书记刘东海参加。

3月16日，区委书记王小宁来园区调研。

3月20日，千人计划专家来园区实地调研。

4月8日，京津高村科技创新园与北京华财会计股份有限公司举行企业入驻暨共建“华财·网商众创公社”合作签约仪式。

4月21日，武清区人民政府与中国牧工商（集团）总公司在武清区政府区行政中心会议楼签订战略合作签约，区委常委、常务副区长李建成，区委常委、副区长李文运出席。

4月21日，武清区投资环境恳谈会暨大项目集中签约仪式在武清区天狮国际宴会中心举行，区委副书记郭宝琴，副区长尤天成，区政协副主席、武清开发区工委书记刘东海出席。其中，搜房网等企业代表发言。

5月15日，举行京津高村科技创新园与清华大学数据科学研究院签约仪式暨园区产业规划开题评审会，区政协副主席、开发区工委书记刘东海出席。

5月19日，邀请区委讲师团，组织召开园区2015年度第一次宣讲授课《新常态 新机遇 新发展 新武清》。

5月26日，北京通州区乡镇（街道）党政正职研修班学员到武清进行专题调研，区委副书记郭宝琴、区委常委、组织部长周惠军陪同。

5月29日，中国国际友人研究会合作小组到京津高村科技创新园考察，区发改委主任韩松龄陪同。

6月12日，组织召开2015年度第二次宣讲授课《积极落实政策，促进经济发展》。6月12日，召开园区“三严三实”专题教育党课。

6月16日，组织召开2015年园区年中重点工程工作推动会。

6月24日，与清华大学数据科学研究院在北京清华大学联合举办大数据助力京津冀协同发展高峰论坛暨2015京津·高村科技创新园推介会，武清开发区总公司副总经理李富国参加。会上，园区受聘为清华大数据产业联合会的理事会员单位。

6月30日，第二届服务贸易与现代服务业投融资论坛暨京津·高村科技创新园“华财网商众创公社”推介会在北京大学英杰交流中心成功举办，武清区科企办、招商局、人力社保局相关负责同志参加。

7月10–11日，在创业在武清——“千人计划”专家产业沙龙暨绿博行活动中，园区与智汇邦签订战略合作协议，发起成立智汇邦－武清大数据创新创业基地。11日，专家们到园区调研。

7月15日，武清区人民政府与搜房网签署全面战略合作协议，搜房网总部园区正式落户武清，市委常委、常务副市长段春华，市政协副主席王治平、区委书记王小宁出席。区政协副主席、武清开发区工委书记刘东海主持签约仪式。

7月21日，区委书记王小宁同志在区行政中心会见了澳大利亚电信集团董事总经理 Martijn Blanken 贝闵添先生一行。区委常委、常务副区长李建成同志，区政协副主席、武清开发区工委书记刘东海同志及高村镇、京津高村科技创新园主要领导参加座谈。

8月4日，组织全体干部员工集中观看了“三严三实”教育专题片《杨善洲》、《沉沦》。

8月11日，京津高村科技创新园2015年武清区高校研究生社会实践活动圆满结束。

8月27日，区委领导带领区安监等相关部门负责同志视察我园区安全生产工作。

8月28日，市侨办领导到园区考察访问。

8月31日，复旦大学研究院客人到园区考察。

10月15日，北京市计算中心常务副主任刘彤一行7人到我园区进行实地参观考察，区科协副主席、科企办副主任孙铁陪同。

10月，园区协同创新服务平台落成并运营，为首届“双创周"献礼。

10月28日，京津高村科技创新园与新兴重工集团举行新兴重工国际贸易总部项目签约仪式，区委书记王小宁，区委常委、区委办公室主任王志强，区政协副主席、武清开发区工委书记刘东海出席。

11月15日，联合清华大学数据科学研究院在京举办“2015京津高村科技创新园大数据产业规划研讨会暨大数据助力京津冀协同发展高峰论坛（冬季论坛）”

12月4日，组织全体干部员工集中观看《“三严三实”先进典型巡回报告会（武清区专场）》。

2016年

2月19日，天津市科委生物医药处处长孙文秀一行3人到园区考察指导工作，区科协副主席、科企办副主任孙铁陪同。

3月4日，刘东海副区长来京津高村科技创新园调研并进行座谈交流。

3月15日，苏宁副区长带队深入京津高村科技创新园，就“四清一绿”工程建设和园区企业发展情况进行专题调研。

3月23日，曲海富副区长、科企办副主任孙铁到园区实地考察并进行座谈交流。

4月8日，武清区投资环境恳谈会暨大项目签约活动举行，市政协副主席王志平，市投资促进办公室主任孙虎军，区委书记王小宁，区委副书记、区长杨令生出席。此次集中签约投资项目75个，涉及高端装备制造、生物医药、科技研发、机器人、电子商务、网络传媒、众创空间、融资租赁、商贸物流等领域，预计总投资49亿元。其中，美房网北方总部、小马奔腾华北总部、合生堂医疗、中实道路、智慧图科技5家企业落户京津高村科技创新园。

4月19日，刘东海副区长、开发区工委书记郭新华、开发区总公司总经理张绍锋来园区调研。

4月19日，京津高村科技创新园和买律网签订战略合作协议，合作搭建法律电商服务平台。园区总经理李富国、副总经理杜瀛涛，买律网董事长王岳、顾问赵文生出席仪式。

4月22日，由清华大学数据科学研究院联合清华大数据产业联合会共同策划的“大数据在清华——数据科学高峰论坛”在清华大学隆重召开。论坛上，京津高村科技创新园与清数D-LAB举行共建数据创新孵化基地合作签约仪式，京津高村科技创新园副总经理杜瀛涛、清数D-LAB主任邱东晓分别代表双方签署协议。

5月9日，“京交会”组委会组织人民日报、新华社、中国日报、北京电视台、香港商报等10余家境内外主流媒体赴园区展开实地采访。

5月26日，京津高村科技创新园党支部成立。

5月30日，京津高村科技创新园联合中国服务贸易协会共同在京举办了第四届“京交会”中国服务创新·创业论坛,副区长曲海富出席。

6月1日，京津高村科技创新园与北京瀚海智业投资管理集团签署战略合作协议。

8月2日，京津高村科技创新园举行重大投资项目签约仪式，能源站、水处理两项目正式落户京津高村科技创新园，副区长刘东海出席。

8月11日，常务副区长孙剑楠实地查看京津高村科技创新园项目建设情况，并围绕园区创新发展展开座谈交流。

9月3日，联合清华信息科学与技术国家实验室、清华大学数据科学研究院医疗健康大数据研究中心、清华大数据产业联合会在津举办首届清华京津冀医疗健康大数据高峰论坛。

10月12日，举行京津高村科技创新园创新创业沙龙暨瀚海智业“海外高端项目中国行”项目对接会。

10月27日，宁夏回族自治区中卫市副市长祝增坤一行3人到京津高村科技创新园考察。

10月27日，在武清举行投资环境恳谈会暨项目签约仪式上，汇通博远机器人项目、金晖集团武清有限合伙项目落户京津高村科技创新园，总投资3.4亿元。

11月30日，举行首都项目集中签约仪式，副区长刘东海出席，区工经委、招商局相关负责同志参加。

12月21日，园区控股子公司天津市京津新城科技发展股份有限公司成功在天交所创业板挂牌。

12月28日，天津市京津新城科技发展股份有限公司在津举办挂牌鸣锣仪式。

第二节　科技型中小企业

截至2016年，开发区有科技型中小企业961家，占开发区入驻企业近50%。科技型中小企业以灵活的经营理念，守诚信，创名牌，赢得了声誉，为武清经济社会的发展做出了贡献。

第三节　专利

2016年，开发区拥有PCT专利31项，其中丹佛斯天津有限公司14项，艾默生过程管理（天津）阀门有限公司4项，戴纳派克（中国）压实滩铺设备有限公司4项，玻实机械（天津）有限公司3项，天津红日药业股份有限公司4项，天津红日药业股份有限公司中国人民解放军第三军医大学第一附属医院1项，天津天狮生物发展顾有限公司1项。

2016 年开发区拥有 PCT 专利情况一览表

表 32

序号	申请单位组织机构代码	申请单位统一社会信用代码	申请单位名称	PCT 专利名称	PCT 申请号
1	600891927	911202226008919279	丹佛斯天津有限公司	监控装置和监控方法	PCT/CN2016/081066
2	600891927	911202226008919279	丹佛斯天津有限公司	测量润滑油稀释度的方法、传感器和检测油位的方法	PCT/CN2016/081256
3	600891927	911202226008919279	丹佛斯天津有限公司	涡旋压缩机	PCT/CN2015/100149
4	600891927	911202226008919279	丹佛斯天津有限公司	涡旋压缩机	PCT/CN2014/095831
5	600891927	911202226008919279	丹佛斯天津有限公司	动铁芯组件及使用其他的电磁阀	PCT/CN2013/082053
6	600891927	911202226008919279	丹佛斯天津有限公司	用于压缩机的温控设备及方法、压缩机组件和制冷系统	PCT/CN2013/074246
7	600891927	911202226008919279	丹佛斯天津有限公司	SOLENOID VALVE	PCT/CN2012/078496
8	600891927	911202226008919279	丹佛斯天津有限公司	SOLENOID VALVE	PCT/CN2012/078494

续表 32

序号	申请单位组织机构代码	申请单位统一社会信用代码	申请单位名称	PCT 专利名称	PCT 申请号
9	600891927	911202226008919279	丹佛斯天津有限公司	BALL VALVE	PCT/CN2012/078495
10	600891927	911202226008919279	丹佛斯天津有限公司	CHECK VALVE	PCT/CN2012/078493
11	600891927	911202226008919279	丹佛斯天津有限公司	内置式永磁电机的转子和使用其得内置式永磁电机	PCT/CN2012/085164
12	600891927	911202226008919279	丹佛斯天津有限公司	密封装置和阀	PCT/CN2009/074914
13	600891927	911202226008919279	丹佛斯天津有限公司	SIGHT GLASS ASSEMBLY	PCT/CN2008/071714
14	600891927	911202226008919279	丹佛斯天津有限公司	PROCESS OF JOINING STAINLESS STEEL MENBER AND GLASS MEMBER BY SINTERING	PCT/CN2008/071715
15	700447997	911202227004479976	天津天狮生物发展有限公司	含有五色果蔬精华的咀嚼片剂及其制备方法	PCT/CN2009/075048

续表 32

序号	申请单位组织机构代码	申请单位统一社会信用代码	申请单位名称	PCT 专利名称	PCT 申请号
16	754802368	91120222754802368E	艾默生过程管理（天津）阀门有限公司	HYDRAULIC ACTUATING DEVICE FOR A SLIDING STEM CONTROL VALVE ASSEMBLY	PCT/CN2010/080404
17	754802368	91120222754802368E	艾默生过程管理（天津）阀门有限公司	METTHOD OF JOINING A CERAMIC PLUG TIP AND A SETEL SUPPORT MEMBER USING A THREADED JOINT AND AN ADHESIVE	PCT/CN2010/079341
18	754802368	91120222754802368E	艾默生过程管理（天津）阀门有限公司	VALVE TRIM APPARATUS HAVITY TO RECEIVE CONTAMINATES SEALING SURFACE	PCT/CN2010/073212
19	754802368	91120222754802368E	艾默生过程管理（天津）阀门有限公司	MULTIPLE STAGE ANTI-SURGE VALVES	PCT/CN2015/092088

续表 32

序号	申请单位组织机构代码	申请单位统一社会信用代码	申请单位名称	PCT 专利名称	PCT 申请号
20	718211771	911202227182117712	戴纳派克（中国）压实摊铺设备有限公司	OIL-SAVING AUTOMATIC CONTROL SYSTEM FOR MILLING MACHINE , MILLING MACHINE AND CONTROL METHOD THEREFOR	PCT/CN2014/092284
21	718211771	911202227182117712	戴纳派克（中国）压实摊铺设备有限公司	LOCKING DEVICE FOG MATERIAL CONVEYOR AND MATERIAL CONVEYOR THEREOF	PCT/CN2014/092283
22	718211771	911202227182117712	戴纳派克（中国）压实摊铺设备有限公司	WATER SPRINKLING CONTROL SYSTEM OF MILLING MACHINE AND CONTROL METHOD THREFOR	PCT/CN2014/092281
23	718211771	911202227182117712	戴纳派克（中国）压实摊铺设备有限公司	ANTI-SEGREGATION AUGER DISTRIBUTOR AND PAVER	PCT/CN2014/077526
24	727515857	91120222727515857Q	玻石机械（天津）有限公司	平板材料上片装置	PCT/CN2012/087773

续表 32

序号	申请单位组织机构代码	申请单位统一社会信用代码	申请单位名称	PCT 专利名称	PCT 申请号
25	727515857	91120222727515857Q	玻石机械（天津）有限公司	平板材料的切割设备及其工作方法	PCT/CN2012/087768
26	727515857	91120222727515857Q	玻石机械（天津）有限公司	一种热强化玻璃板的热处理方法和热处理设备	PCT/CN2012/082105
27	10409702X	9112000010409702XT	天津红日药业股份有限公司	法舒地尔化合物的用途、方法及其药物组合物	PCT/CN2009/000509
28	10409702X	9112000010409702XT	天津红日药业股份有限公司	苦柯胺 B 盐及制备方法和用途	PCT/CN2011/000479
29	10409702X	9112000010409702XT	天津红日药业股份有限公司	BENZOHETEROCYCLIC COMPOUNDS, PREPARATION METHODS AND USES THEREOF	PCT/CN2011/072816
30	10409702X	9112000010409702XT	天津红日药业股份有限公司 中国人民解放军第三军医大学第一附属医院	苦柯胺 A 和苦柯胺 B 的用途	PCT/CN2011/000478
31	10409702X	9112000010409702XT	天津红日药业股份有限公司	具有抗 Xa 因子活性的磺酸化五糖化合物	PCT/CN2016/095464

2016 年开发区获得的荣誉、称号、命名一览表

表 33

序号	荣誉称号	颁发单位	试点工作周期	申报时间	获取时间
1	国家知识产权质押融资试点园区	国家知识产权局	三年	2016 年 4 月	2016 年 8 月
2	国家知识产权试点园区	国家知识产权局	2017 年 1 月至 2019 年 12 月	2016 年 10 月	2016 年 12 月
3	天津市专利试点园区	天津市知识产权局	2016 年 1 月至 2018 年 12 月	2016 年 4 月	2016 年 6 月
4	天津市级专利导航项目（基因工程产业专利导航）	天津市知识产权局	2016 年 8 月 1 日至 2017 年 7 月 31 日	2016 年 5 月	2016 年 9 月
5	天津市留学人员创业园	天津市外国专家局	两年	2016 年 5 月	2016 年 6 月
6	天津市小型微型企业　创业创新示范基地	天津市中小企业局	无期限	2016 年 11 月	2016 年 12 月

第二章 教育

武清开发区内拥有国家职业学校2所和大学3所。在建天狮国际大学占地3000亩，建筑面积210万平方米。借助区位和交通优势，能够接受京津两地百余所大学和科研机构的人才辐射，京津高校武清科技创新园目前已入驻天津大学前沿技术研究院、高校科技创新成果转化武清中心、中国农业大学、中科院微生物研究所、南开大学吸附分离技术工程中心等产、学、研、用项目。

英华国际学校，提供从幼儿园到高中的全寄宿制双语教育和国际高中、留学预科教育，与英国、加拿大、澳大利亚、韩国等国家高等院校建立了留学“直通车”。

第一节 天津英华国际学校

一、基本情况

英华学校占地163.65亩，建筑面积87409.6平方米，分为小学、中学两个校区。课程设置主要包括国内普通教育课程和中加、剑桥国际教育课程，其中国内教育课程涵盖幼儿、小学、初中、高中四个学段，共56个教学班，2088名学生；国际教育课程主要是中加、剑桥国际高中，留学生部，共25个教学班，624名学生。学校有教职员工427人，其中，专任教师250人，外籍教师46人。学校先后获全国优秀民办中小学、全国最具办学特色国际学校、天津市先进民办学校、天津市魅力学校等荣誉称号。

二、办学历史

开发区于2000年全资建设了天津雍阳英华学校（小学校区），2003年全资建设了天津英华学校（中学校区），总投资约2.19亿元。2000年9月至2003年7月11日期间，由第一届董事会负责学校（英华小学）管理，董事会成员为，董事长王胜林，董事郭保联、李良军、孙克林、张福增。

2003年7月，区教育局下属天津利达贸易公司与广州华美教育投资集团以货币形式出资，联合成立了天津英华教育投资管理有限公司。其中利达公司出资490万元，持股49%；华美集团出资510万元，持股51%。同年，天津英华教育投资管理有限公司与武清开发区总公司签订了《英华中小学合作办学协议》，合作举办天津英华国际学校。2003年7月—2006年7月，第二届董事会负责学校管理，董事会成员为，董事长张克强，副董事长程致平，董事叶立强、陈金龙、孙克林。2006年7月—2009年4月，第三届董事会负责学校管理，董事会成员为，董事长张克强，副董事长程致平，董事林向阳、陈金龙、张景玲。

2009年4月，天津利达贸易公司按政策要求，将其在天津英华教育投资管理有限公司49%的股份转让给开发区总公司，由开发区总公司与广州华美教育投资集团联合成立天津英华教育投资管理有限公司。天津英华教育投资管理有限公司作为乙方与开发区总公司共同建立天津英华国际学校。

2015年3月10日，开发区总公司与天津英华教育投资管理有限公司续订合作办学协议，合作有效期至2027年6月30日。2009年至2016年，第四届董事会负责学校管理，董事会成员为，董事长张克强，副董事长程致平，董事林向阳、陈金龙、张绍锋，2015年10月任命林向阳为执行董事。

三、学校管理体系

英华学校实行董事会领导下的校务委员会负责制，校务委员会执行董事会决议，对董事会负责。校务委员会负责制定学校的发展规划，统筹管理教学、人事、财务等方面工作。2016年，董事会成员由华美集团方面代表和武清方面代表组成，华美集团代表张克强任董事长，林向阳、陈金龙任董事；武清代表程致平任副董事长，张绍锋任董事。校务委员会成员10人，分别是林向阳、约翰·埃文斯(剑桥高中部校长)、李子胜、王克坤、孙连富、努兹奥·罗曼诺（中加国际高中部加方校长）、许桂芝、张景玲、张涛、钟文辉、刘文祥。

四、办学理念

学校以中共十八届三中全会精神为指导，立德树人，依法治校，坚持以“教育要立足中华文明的‘根’，面向现代化、面向世界、面向未来”为总体指导思想，秉承“东西并融·爱·启程未来”的办学宗旨，恪守“在英华，发现我自己”的办学理念，确定了“美丽英华”“品质英华”“智慧英华”“幸福英华”四个维度的建设目标，明确了英华未来发展的30年愿景：致力通过“做大、做实、做精、做优、做特”五个六年规划目标，一步一个脚印，稳步扎实地向把英华建成为一所“具备中华文化底蕴并融合国际先进教育理念的中国名校”。

英华学校获得了全国优秀民办中小学、全国最具办学特色国际学校、天津市先进民办学校、天津市魅力学校等荣誉称号。

五、普通教育

普通教育包括幼儿、小学、初中、高中四个学段。2016年，在校生小学21教学班，学生735人；初中16个教学班；普通高中19个教学班，学生851人。

小学坚持素质教育特色不动摇，形成了一套独特的育人模式，是全国小学生日常英语教学实验学校、中国少年科学院科普基地、武清区教学质量优秀单位。

初中自2011年独立出来后，建立了“学科+英语+人文”三大特色育人体系，全面提升教育教学质量，综合促进学生个性发展、协调发展。中考成绩连年稳中有升，优生比率远超区内平均水平。2014年、2015年、2016年连续三年培养出郝泽陈、薛博文、王泽龙同学成为武清区中考状元。2016年中考，38名毕业生的中考分数进入武清区前100名（562.5分），545分以上高分段学生170人，占该届毕业生52.1%。

普通高中部高考本科上线率现已达到90%以上，有23名毕业生考入清华和北大（不含留学生）。2016年高考，学校普通高中在校考生249人。总体一本率65.3%；总体二本率92.7%；实验班一本率100%。理科680分以上4人，600分以上56人；文科最高分647分，600分以上3人。其中，李睿、张轩鹤同学被清华大学录取，张开宣同学被北京大学录取。

六、国际教育

（一）国际高中教育

国际高中教育有中加国际高中、剑桥国际高中共21个班，学生556人。

中加国际高中是英华学校与加拿大安大略省教育部合作的国际高中。把中国高中课程与加拿大高中课程有效整合，毕业生凭学校考核成绩，直接升入海外大学。自创办至2016年，实现了中国高中毕业率、加拿大高中毕业率、国外大学录取率和签证率四个100%。世界百强大学录取率已达到86%。

剑桥国际高中2013年由英国剑桥大学国际考试委员会授权设立。该项目执行

IGCSE 和 A Level 课程教学与考试评价体系。该项目自开办以来，发展势头强劲，已成为国内第七所具有“牛津大学、剑桥大学入学考试”考点资质的学校。该部小班教学，精致管理，纯英语教学，2016 年有教学班 8 个，学生 171 人。2016 届（首届）12 名毕业生中，2 名学生被牛津大学录取，1 名学生被剑桥大学录取，毕业生全部被英国帝国理工学院、伦敦大学学院，美国纽约大学、卫斯理女子学院、UCLA 大学等世界排名前 100 强的名校录取。

（二）留学生教育

留学生教育有 4 个班，学生 68 人。

学生来自韩国、日本、乌兹别克斯坦、泰国、俄罗斯、哈萨克斯坦、加拿大、美国等多个国家，本科升学率始终保持 100%，年年有学生考上清华北大等名校，是天津市拥有留学生最多的基础教育类国际学校，是天津市唯一一所国家汉语办公室确定的“汉语水平考试”的中学考点。

七、师资队伍

教师队伍整体素质不断提高，人员相对稳定。2016年，全校教职员工共427人，其中，专任教师 250 名。专任教师中，武清公职教师 56 名。专任教师的学历为本科 238 人、大专 11 人；职称为高级 62 人、中级 69 人。省市级教学骨干教师 15 人。来自加拿大、美国、英国、韩国等国家的外教 46 人 。

八、学校特色与经济效益

自建校以来，学校牢牢把住国际化特色不放松，即使普通教育也同样渗透强化国际化特色，使不论哪个学段的英华学生，既掌握了中国优秀的学习方法，学到了中国教育特有的扎实的基础知识，又了解了西方先进的理念和能力。

随着学校办学特色的形成，求学者增加，提升了生源质量，生源综合录取比例目前已达到 10∶1，优质教育成果赢得更高的社会美誉。如此良性循环，同时带来了一定的经济效益。建校至 2008 年，英华在完成区委区政府规定办学目标的基础上，基本了实现盈亏平衡。

过去十三年，学校一直执行稳健的财务政策。在紧密围绕学校发展所需要提供的财务支持的基础上，不断强化资金管理，保障学校资产的保值增值。学校一切利润效益均投入于学校硬件设施升级、教职工薪酬福利的改善以及学校整体办学质量的品质化提升，致力于促进学校未来长远的可持续发展。

第二节 天狮学院

一、基本情况

学院地处京津黄金走廊，具有极好区位优势。学院现占地 668 亩，校舍面积 16 万多平方米，学校分东西两个校区，东校区占地 668 亩，建设中的西校区占地 3.2 平方千米 (4800 亩），建筑面积 210 万平方米，拥有舒适的学生宿舍，实行公寓化管理。学院教学设施先进，建有现代化多媒体教室、语音室和仿真实验实训室 40 个，拥有千余台计算机确保学生上课用机。还拥有标准的田径运动场、体育馆、游泳馆、运动馆。馆藏图书 58 万多册，其中电子图书 30 万册。学院千兆主干校园网的 2000 余个信息点广布校园。

天狮学院的办学宗旨是立足天津、面向全国、服务环渤海经经济圈，以培养应用型高技能人才为主。学院在重点实施本科教育的同时，仍举办专科层次的高等职业教育。学院现设经济管理系、电子计算机系、外国语系、艺术设计系，开设以财经管理类学科专业为主，涵盖工学电气信息类、人文社科类等适应市场需求的 14 个热门学科专业。学院现有 5507 多名在校生，来自全国 23 个省、市、自治区。

学院实行董事会领导下的院长负责制。天津天狮集团有限公司总裁李金元任学院董事长，天津市原副市长陆焕生教授任学院副董事长和名誉院长，天津城市建设学院原院长朱世和教授任院长，学院领导班子其他成员均由长期从事高等院校教学及管理工作的专家教授组成。

天津天狮学院拥有一支具有丰富教学经验的以专职教师为主、专兼职结合的师资队伍。2016 年，有教师 213 人，其中具有副高级以上职称的占 50.3%。学院还聘请了优秀全职外籍教师授课。

学院建立健全了奖助学金制度，完善了“帮扶”系统，为贫困生求学成长提供了强有力的保障。仅 2007 年就有 68 名学生获国家和市级奖学金。天狮集团每年投入 200 万元为贫困生和优秀生设置了“金元奖学金”和“金元助学金”，受资助学生达 40%，最高资助金额达万元。董事长李金元和学院的巨额资助，激励了广大学生奋发努力、刻苦学习，其中的优秀者，有的考取了北京大学等名牌高校研究生，有的进入了政府机关、事业单位和知名企业，成为了国家和社会的栋梁之材。2008 年，凡超过当地本科录取线 50 分以上并第一志愿报考天狮学院者免除考生 4 年学费，超过 100 分以上者，在免除 4 年学费的基础上，天狮集团保证为其提供全球就业机会。

天津天狮学院被评为 2015 天津市最佳民办大学。

二、办学理念

学院坚持以服务为宗旨，以就业为导向，走产学研结合发展道路，培养高级应用型技术人才为办学理念，以素质教育为核心，以培养技术应用能力为主线，使学生德智体美全面发展。

学院与天狮集团在理念、信息、人力资源、设备资源、科研条件、实训基地、国际资源和文化等方面实行“八个共享”，及“一体化办学”和“订单式教育”，把课堂教学与增强学生动手实践能力紧密结合，突出能力培养，使教学质量不断提高，一大批优秀学子在天狮集团就业发展。同时，学院大力建设校外实训基地，与微软、天津天地伟业数码科技有限公司等 28 个知名企业建立了合作办学关系，为学生实习实训和就业开辟了绿色通道。学院设立了经济管理类、计算机类、电子类、IT 类专业技术职业技能鉴定站，具有 27 个职业资格考试认证权，双证书率达 85.5%，为学生创造了职业准入条件。

学院坚持国际化办学，举办英语强化班和聘请外教来校授课，强化了英语教学，增强了学生英语运用能力和国际交往能力。学院董事长李金元还专为有志于出国留学的师生设立了专项奖学金，为成绩优秀且家庭贫困的师生提供资助。学院与英国斯旺西大学等建立了校际合作交流关系，努力推动学院国际化进程。

学院坚持“严谨治学、严格管理”的方针，形成了师德高尚、教学严谨、诲人不倦、教书育人的教风勤奋刻苦、认真钻研、积极进取、勇于创新的学风。学院不断深化教学改革，完善了“多方向、模块型、组合型”的教学模式和课程体系，建立了科学的实践教学体系和全程的教学质量监控体系，促进了教学质量的提高。学院教师和学生在各级各类竞赛中屡获殊荣。

学院坚持“以学生为本”，以素质教育为核心，严格要求与人文关怀紧密结合，坚持对每个学生成长成才负责，营造良好育人环境，培养具有较高综合素质的合格人才。学院明确了“一个底线（道德底线）、四个合格（政治合格、学习合格、身心健康合格、遵纪守法合格）”为学生思想政治工作的基本目标。严格按照国家规定配齐了辅导员和班主任。在学生中大力开展了爱国主义、理想信念、荣辱观教育、感恩教育和诚信教育。着力加强校风学风建设，实行“半军事化”管理，制定了“十提倡”和“十不准”制度，设立了“校园文明监督岗”，发挥了学生自我教育、自我管理、自我约束和自我服务功能。广泛开展了科技、文化、社会实践活动，营造良好的校园文化氛围，全面提高了学生综合素质，为学生德智体美全面发展奠定了坚实基础。

三、历任领导

1999—2003 院长武善谋教授 原天津市高教局局长。

2003—2006 院长杨渝钦教授 原天津大学党委书记。

1999—2006 副院长齐世闻教授 原天津理工大学副院长。

1999—2005 副院长侯国荣教授 原天津师范大学校长。

2005—2009 副院长 刘志明 教授 原河北工业大学党委书记。

2008—2011 副院长 李杨威 副研究员。

2011—2016 院长 朱世和 教授 原天津城建学院院长。

2016—至今 副院长（主持工作）范顺成 原河北工业大学教务处。

第三节　博士后科研工作站

建立武清开发区博士后科研工作站，是武清开发区培养、引进、使用高端人才，为开发区建设发展建立的新机制。博士后科研工作站是指在企业、科研生产型事业单位和特殊的区域性机构内，经批准可以招收和培养博士后研究人员的组织。博士后科研工作站的设立，反映了全区较强的科研能力、业务水平及综合实力，为进一步吸纳、培养和使用高层次、高学历专业型人才、创新型人才提供了新的平台和广阔的空间。

2013 年，经人力资源和社会保障部、全国博士后管理委员会批准，武清经济技术开发区管理委员会博士后科研工作站在天津开发区系统率先建立。当年，12 月 13 日，武清开发区博士后工作站举行授牌仪式。区领导张勇、李建成、周惠军、刘东海出席。相关职能部门、博士后分站负责人共 100 余人参加。活动中，区人才发展专项资金给予开发区博士后工作站一次性经费补助 30 万元，对区中医院、京滨工业园和红日药业 3 个分站分别给予一次性 10 万元经费补助。同时，3 个分站分别与相应的博士后流动工作站、进站博士三方签署了《联合培养博士后协议书》。武清开发区博士后科研工作站的设立，实现了武清区博士后建站工作零的突破，是实现人才强区战略的一座重要里程碑。

2017年1月18日，天津市滨海新区人力资源和社会保障局发出《关于天津经济技术开发区等7个博士后科研工作站增设分站有关问题的通知》，就有关博士后科研工作站的工作开展、职能定位等做了明确规定。

通知指出，根据《全国博士后管委会办公室关于批准在天津经济技术开发区博士后工作站增设天津膜天膜科技股份有限公司等分站的通知》和《全国博士后管委会办公室关于批准在天津市武清经济技术开发区管理委员会博士后工作站增设天津钢研海德科技有限公司分站的通知》精神，天津经济技术开发区管理委员会等7个博士后科研工作站获准增设19个分站。

通知要求，各新设站单位要根据《国务院办公厅关于改革完善博士后制度的意见》（国办发〔2015〕87号）及原人事部、全国博士后管委会《博士后管理工作规定》（国人部发〔2006〕149号）要求，结合本单位实际，做好以下工作：

一、抓紧建立博士后工作体系。要制定切实可行的博士后工作管理制度，加强规范化管理。建立由单位主管领导牵头负责，人力资源、科技、财务等相关部门协同配合的博士后工作领导小组，设立日常工作部门，安排专人从事博士后日常管理工作。

二、充分发挥博士后创新优势。要认真做好博士后的引进、培养和使用工作，年底前，各新设站单位至少招收1名博士后进站。要积极与全国已设立博士后科研流动站的高校、科研院所联系，尽早确定联合招收单位和博士后合作导师。要以多种渠道、多种方式发布博士后招收信息，对申请从事博士后研究工作的人员进行认真遴选。要为博士后创造良好的工作和生活环境，围绕博士后建立创新团队，充分发挥博士后在企业科技创新中的智力优势。按照要求，人社部和市人力社保局将定期开展博士后科研工作站评估工作，对评估优秀的单位将予以表彰，对评估不合格的单位依照有关规定处置。

三、积极参与博士后活动。要积极参与国家、我市和所在区人力社保部门开展的各项博士后活动，积极申报中国博士后科学基金、天津市企业博士后创新项目择优资助计划、天津市优秀博士后国际化培养计划等资助项目，并主动加强与我市其他博士后科研流动站、工作站设站单位的交流合作。

这一通知，使武清开发区博士后科研工作站步入了规范化管理轨道。

第三章 文化

第一节 企业文化建设

开发区总公司始终坚持利用文化体育活动为载体与园区企业建立联系，凭借着开发区管委会丰富的企业资源优势和强大的企业组织能力，每年都会组织多种形式的文体活动来丰富园区企业业余文化生活，并取得了广泛的企业影响和良好的社会效应。

第一，以活动带动企业职工能力提升。2015 年开发区先后组织了多场针对园区企业职工的培训活动，借以提升园区企业职工职业技能，增强职业素养，提高工作效率，与中国人民大学培训学院合作，每月邀请清华大学、北京大学等培训师，组织企业高管培训，累计为区内 350 家次重点企业的近 500 名高管进行培训，从根本上提高了企业骨干综合管理能力；组织召开了题目为“新世纪职场素养全面提升”培训会，邀请全国知名人力资源专家为广大职工传授职场生存技巧，全面提升职工职业素养和责任心，找回职业动力与热情；为满足开发区企业劳动技能人才提升需求，开发区总公司在园区范围内广泛开展劳动技能竞赛活动，为此专门成立了劳动竞赛活动领导小组，每年组织专题活动，2015 年先后参与筹备了中粮、华电福源、金红叶等多家企业涵盖企业 90% 以上职工参与的劳动竞赛活动，通过技能竞赛、知识竞赛、素质拓展竞赛等形式，进一步激发了广大职工的创新潜能和创造活力，提升了企业自主创新能力，为企业发展注入了活力。

第二，以活动丰富企业职工业余文化生活。2015 年，依托开发区足球队、篮球队、羽毛球队、乒乓球队、瑜伽队等体育运动队伍，积极鼓励并组织企业职工定期参与各队活动，改善职工健康状况。其中最具代表性的赛事如：“国环杯”篮球赛、“迎春杯”职工象棋大赛、“金泰丽舍杯”职工乒乓球比赛、“联通杯”职工羽毛球比赛等，开发区每届都会组织园区企业派出代表队参加比赛并取得了不俗的成绩；在“五一劳动节”

和“十一黄金周”期间，开发区与看购电影合作，先后组织并开展了2次面向开发区企业职工的集体观影活动，用看电影这一简单轻松的方式为职工业余生活带去欢乐。此外，开发区还联合园区企业组织并开展了“牵手职场情缘，共建美丽武清”职工交友联谊活动，切实为广大职工解难题、办实事；开发区还积极鼓励企业依托基层企业工会自发组织各类型文体活动。2015年，在开发区总公司的大力支持下，艾尔姆组织了“家庭日活动”、伊利组织“趣味运动会”等系列文体活动。此外，丹佛斯依托劳模（技能人才）创新工作室，组织开展了技能提升培训大讲堂等活动10余次，华电福源则依托先进职工之家资源优势，举办企业运动会、职工读书会和企业职工交友联谊会等企业活动。此类活动的成功开展极大地丰富了职工业余文化生活，拉近了企业与职工之间的距离。

第二节　活动方案

一、足球队活动方案

（一）活动人员

领队1人；队长1人，副队长1人；队员34人：总公司、高村园、东疆园及下属公司正式职工，共计：37人

（二）活动时间

每周四下午18：00—20：00或周六早8：00—10：00

（三）活动地点

绿茵地带室内球场或杨村十五小

（四）活动安排

1. 队长、副队长负责活动组织及所需物品准备工作，包括足球、饮用水、必备药品；

2. 队长、副队长负活动场地预定、活动情况及出勤记录。

（五）注意事项

1. 文明活动。活动中队员需团结友善，不得与他人发生冲突，不得做出有损开发区形象的行为。

2. 活动前要做好准备热身活动，避免受伤。

（六）活动经费

1. 场地费：室内球场 240 元 / 两小时（每周一次）

室外球场 300 元 / 两小时（大场，每两周一次）

2. 矿泉水：40 元 / 两箱（注：每次活动 2 箱）

总计：430 元 / 周

计划 11 和 12 月活动 8–10 次，活动总费控制在 3440 元内。若费用出现剩余自动补充下季度继续使用。

二、羽毛球活动方案

（一）活动人员

队长 1 名，副队长 1 名，队员 29 名，共计 31 人。

（二）活动时间

每周六或周日下午 2∶00—4∶00。

（三）活动地点

杨村第三中学体育馆。

（四）活动安排

1. 队长及副队长负责活动前补给工作，包括羽毛球、饮用水、必备药品；

2. 队长及副队长负活动场地预定、活动情况及出勤记录。

（五）注意事项

活动前要做好准备活动，尤其肩、肘、手腕等关节部位，否则很容易受伤。

（六）活动经费

1. 场地费：160 元（注：两个塑胶场地，一个木地板场地，共三个场地，使用两个小时）

2. 矿泉水：20 元 / 箱（注：每次活动 2 箱）

3. 羽毛球：66 元 / 筒（注：每桶球可供活动 2 次使用）

总计：266 元 / 次

每季度活动 12 次，活动总费用为 3192 元 / 季度。每季度费用出现剩余自动补充下季度继续使用。

三、乒乓球活动方案

（一）活动人员

队长 1 名，副队长 1 名，队员 29 名，共计：31 人

（二）活动时间

每周六或周日下午 2：00–4：00。

（三）活动地点

杨村第三中学体育馆。

（四）活动安排

1. 队长及副队长负责活动前补给工作，包括乒乓球、饮用水、必备药品；

2. 队长及副队长负活动场地预定、活动情况及出勤记录。

（五）注意事项

活动前要做好准备活动，尤其肩、肘、手腕等关节部位，否则很容易受伤。

（六）活动经费

1. 场地费：60 元（注：三个乒乓球案，使用两个小时）

2. 矿泉水：20 元 / 箱（注：每次活动 2 箱）

3. 乒乓球：40 元 / 盒

总计：140 元 / 次

计划每季度活动 12 次，活动总费用为 1680 元 / 季度。每季度费用出现剩余自动补充下季度继续使用。

四、瑜伽队活动方案

（一）活动目的

为增强职工身体素质、缓解工作压力、改善亚健康状态，武清开发区为职工定期开展瑜伽课程，让职工在工作之余得到放松。

（二）活动时间

每周二、周五两次瑜伽课程，春、夏、秋季中午 12:15—13：15，冬季暂定每次中午 12：00—13：00。

（三）活动纪律

每位成员都要积极参与瑜伽课，如有事无法上课的，请提前在微信群中告知。

（四）活动分工

队长：主要负责组织安排瑜伽课程，联系瑜伽老师，制定活动预算等工作。

副队长：主要负责预定活动场地，通知队内成员各项事宜，做好出勤记录等工作。

（五）活动经费

场地费每次 125 元，老师课时费每次 150 元，一周两次课程，每季度总计 6600 元。

（六）活动注意事项

1. 每次上课前半小时内，尽量少吃，避免饱腹状态上课，课程结束后一小时内不要吃饭。

2. 练习瑜伽的过程中要注意安全，不勉强自己做有难度的动作，达到力所能及的程度即可。

3. 各队员自备瑜伽服、瑜伽垫。

第三节　资助举办国际马拉松赛

武清开发区积极参与国际性体育赛事，于2012年至2017年主动资助中国田径协会、天津市体育局、武清区政府，连续举办了六届“天津武清开发区杯国际马拉松赛”。由于所资助社会举办的国际性赛事均实行央视对国内外数十个国家直播，收到了一举多得的显著效果。一是宣传了武清开发区，增强了招商引资吸引力，促进了园区建设发展。二是开阔了武清人的视野、激发了武清人参与体育、开展全民健身活动的热情。三是扩大了武清在国内外的影响力，对于推动武清进一步扩大开放、开发及各项事业的发展，都发挥了重要作用。

第一届　2012 年 5 月 26 日上午，天津武清开发区杯国际马拉松赛隆重举行。经过两个多小时激烈争夺，来自肯尼亚的选手蒂奥尼和普盖蒂奇分别夺得男、女马拉松赛冠军。

本次比赛经国家体育总局和天津市政府批准，由中国田径协会、天津市体育局、武清区人民政府共同主办。比赛吸引了来自 23 个国家和地区的 10244 名选手参加了男、女全程马拉松，男、女 10 公里和男、女 5 公里的比赛。蒂奥尼夺得男子全程马拉松冠军的成绩为 2 小时 16 分 16 秒，女子冠军成绩为 2 小时 37 分 22 秒。中国选手马拉松比赛的最好成绩是王晓姝以 2 小时 41 分 16 秒，夺得女子马拉松赛第三名。其他比赛冠军为邬淑红 (个人、女子 5 公里)、金铭铭 (天津工业大学、女子 10 公里)、李少壮 (大连理工大学、男子 5 公里)、博卡 (埃塞俄比亚、男子 10 公里)。

第二届 2013年5月25日上午，第二届武清开发区杯天津国际马拉松赛武清区成功举办。

赛事共设男、女全程马拉松，男、女10公里，男、女迷你马拉松(5公里)，全程接力赛等项目。截至报名结束，本次马拉松赛报名参赛运动员总计15923人，其中全程马拉松报名人数1883人，男子1656人，女子227人，包括国内注册运动员男子2人，女子3人。马拉松接力报名参赛队伍共63支，其中男子接力队46支，女子接力队17支。十公里报名人数1597人，其中男子1193人，女子404人。迷你马拉松(五公里)12128人，其中男子6669人，女子5459人。

此次马拉松赛路线起终点均为区政府前广场，具体路线为：区政府前广场（起点）→沿雍阳西道向西（直行）→（左转）翠亨路→（左转）前进道→（左转）京津公路→（左转）福源道→至新平路口（折返）→福源道（直行）→（右转）京津公路→（右转）前进道→（右转）翠亨路→（右转）雍阳西道→区政府前广场（终点），路线途经的区域主要包括主城区、运河沿线、开发区等。

第三届 2014年10月28日上午，“2014天津武清开发区杯国际马拉松赛”在天津市武清区行政中心前鸣枪起跑，来自12个国家和地区的1万余名运动员同场竞技。经过两多小时角逐，最终，一名埃塞俄比亚选手以2小时17分33秒的成绩率先冲过终点获得男子组冠军，两名肯尼亚选手分获男子组二、三名。女子组前三名分别被中国天津选手王晓姝及两名肯尼亚选手收入囊中。中国籍运动员马拉松特别奖分别被男子组第六名的张喜财及女子组冠军王晓姝获得。

第四届 2015年9月13日上午，“2015天津武清开发区杯国际马拉松赛”在区行政中心前广场鸣枪开赛。全国24个省市运动员报名参赛，来自16个国家和地区的17528名运动员同场竞技，为广大观众和体育爱好者呈现了一场精彩的体育盛会。经过两个多小时的激烈角逐，埃塞俄比亚选手包揽男女马拉松赛冠军。

本届赛事较之上一届在马拉松和迷你马拉松的基础上，增设了半程马拉松项目。奖项设有马拉松名次奖、中国籍选手马拉松特别奖和半程马拉松名次奖，马拉松名次奖最高可获得150000元人民币。本届马拉松赛的报名参赛人数也创下历届“天马”之最，其中马拉松报名人数2609人、半程马拉松3449人、迷你马拉松11470人，总计17528人，其中包括37名外籍运动员。比赛路线在去年路线的基础上进行了进一步优化设计，以备战、“练兵”2017年全运会，主要集中在雍阳西道、翠亨路、前进道、京津公路、福源道等武清城区主干道，道路平坦宽阔、风景优美宜人。CCTV-5和乐视网分别通过录播和直播的方式向广大观众全景呈现了赛事的精彩盛况，观众在感受马拉松赛独特魅力的同时，也看到了一个美丽和谐、宜居宜业的武清和一个日新月异、飞速发展的新天津。

第五届 2016年5月15日上午，“2016年天津武清开发区国际马拉松赛”在区行政中心前广场鸣枪开赛。此次赛事包括马拉松、半程马拉松和迷你马拉松三个项目，奖项设有马拉松名次奖和半程马拉松名次奖，奖励金额较之上届有了大幅度的提高。参加全国马拉松锦标赛的运动员比赛成绩同时计入天津国际马拉松赛成绩，同时按照有关规定享受相应奖励。最终来自肯尼亚的选手基普克雷尔获得男子组冠军。

为全面备战、对接2017年天津全运会，打造更具观赏性的高端体育盛会，此次赛事在竞赛项目、比赛规程等方面进行了进一步优化和规范，并在固定赛道的基础上不断提升绿化美化效果，为广大参赛选手创造了良好的竞技环境。

赛事设计规模为20000人，其中马拉松项目报名人数限4000人，半程马拉松项目报名人数限2000人，迷你马拉松项目报名人数限14000人。

第六届 2017年4月29日上午，第十三届全国运动会马拉松赛暨2017天津（武清）国际马拉松赛在天津市武清区举行，除专业组之外，本届赛事还增设了群众组比赛。这是本届全运会进行的第一个决赛项目。

本届全运会马拉松比赛最终参赛人数为4248人，其中专业组24个队120人，群众组4128人，参赛单位覆盖全国31个省市区。

为保证比赛秩序及安全，比赛采取分区站位、分枪出发。赛道沿途提供充分饮水、饮料、降温喷淋设备供给，并安排充足的志愿者提供服务，同时加大了医疗救护设置密度，保证选手的生命安全。

经过激烈比拼，河北省老将王佳丽以2小时33分36秒第一个冲过终点，获得专业组女子冠军。专业组男子项目冠军则由来自云南队的董国建摘得，耗时2小时18分45秒。山东选手运艳桥以2小时32分45秒夺得群众组男子冠军，这也是全运会历史上第一块群众组金牌。群众组女子冠军的获得者是山东选手唐辉，成绩为2小时55分51秒。女子专业组团体前三名分别归属了内蒙古队、江苏队和云南队。

第九篇

政　法

第一章 公安

第一节 机构设施

1995年10月，组建开发区民警办公室，由武清区公安局内保科负责管理。办公地点在丹佛斯公司东侧平房里，办公桌椅是临时借用的，出警骑自行车，条件较为艰苦。

1996年9月，经天津市公安局批准，武清开发区派出所成立，钟有善任所长，苏建兴任副所长，两名内勤民警，一名治安民警。办公地点移到开发区禄源道9号一座三层小楼，使用面积近300平方米，另有三间平房宿舍，两间车库，两间食堂。

1997年3月，成立开发区保安大队，归属开发区派出所管理，从复员军人中，挑选出38名优秀者作为第一批开发区保安员，分配到丹佛斯、大真空、伊都锦、华住四个单位负责保卫任务。1997年12月，开发区派出所下设逸仙园民警办公室，由一名副所长和两名联防队员负责管理。

2003年9月，开发区派出所在紫微宫二楼办公，办公室设在二楼大厅，面积300余平方米，冬季无供暖设备，条件较为艰苦。

2004年7月，开发区派出所迁入禄源道17号增1号三层办公小楼，使用面积1300平方米，办公条件大为改善。

2010年10月，开发区派出所新楼建成投入使用，新办公楼整体四层，建筑面积3000平方米，办公条件进一步改善。

第二节 社会治安

2014年，以“抓防控、降发案”为主线，深入开展夏季治安百日行动、严打严防百日行动等工作，助推辖区经济发展，全力维护开发区的稳定。全年共接处警3899起，其中110报警3650起，发刑事案件135起，破案65起，其中，破积案78起，刑事处理28人，其中网上在逃人员7名；发治安案件870起，破案822起，行政拘留20人，调解纠纷728起；登记暂住人口1803人。同比，接处警上升11%，刑事案件发案上升17%，破案上升10%，破积案上升49%，治安案件发案上升24%，破案上升26%，行政拘留人数上升66%，调解纠纷上升9%。其中“两抢一盗”案件下降30%，盗窃企业和工地案件下降30%，入户盗窃下降50%，盗窃非机动车案件案件下降11%，电信诈骗案件上升98%。

2015年，开展“解矛盾、破小案、防事故、保民安”专项行动、夏季破案会战、打侵财、治隐患等专项行动，助推辖区经济发展，全力维护开发区的稳定。1至11月共接处警3672起，其中110报警3433起，发刑事案件219起，破案39起，其中，破积案18起，刑事处理36人，其中网上在逃人员7名；发治安案件811起，破案690起，行政拘留16人，调解纠纷451起；登记暂住人口1795人。同比，接处警上升10%，刑事案件发案上升44%，治安案件发案与2014年同期持平。实现全年队伍无违纪、无信访案件发生。全年收取支助警70余万元。

2016年，以“抓防控、降发案”为主线，深入开展“治乱保安”专项行动、“打击盗抢骗”、“打现行、强基础、保平安”等专项行动，助推辖区经济发展，全力维护开发区的稳定。全年共接处警3430起，其中110报警3250起。发刑事案件256起，破案55起；其中破积案20起。刑事处理44人，其中网上在逃人员8名。发治安案件651起，破案500起，调解纠纷509起；行政拘留20人、登记流动人口1765人。同比，接警量下降了6%；刑事案件发案上升11%，破案率上升41%，刑事打处上升22%；治安案件下降了19%，实现全年队伍无违纪、无信访案件发生。

一、惩治刑事犯罪

2014年，破获梁某在高新公寓钻窗入室强奸女员工案件；运城制版员工张某某利用回收废料诈骗案件；快侦快破，20小时内破获汪某盗窃高新公寓超市案件；破获崔某非法持有枪支案件，破获吴某某在高新公寓抢劫等暴力案件；破获张某盗窃三星手机电池案件，涉案金额6000余元；打掉一个团伙，破获周某等三人盗窃EKC公司钢瓶案件，涉案金额4.96万元；破获陈某盗窃亚马逊公司库房案件，涉案金额2万余元。以上一大批案件的破获，给犯罪嫌疑人以沉重的打击，打出了公安机关的声威、打出了人民警察的气势，有效维护了辖区的稳定。

2015年，坚持严打不动摇，保持高压态势。年内打掉4个犯罪团伙，接连破获多起涉企案件，为企业挽回经济损失150余万元，其中破获顾某某、马某某、贾某某团伙盗窃麦格昆磁铁锭、废磁环等材料案件；破获李某某、朱某某、刘某某团伙盗窃麦格昆磁公司滤网废料案件；破获郭某某、路某某、吕某某团伙等盗窃三星公司二十辆电动车案件，破获王某、刘某某、金某某团伙等敲诈勒索案件；破获亚马逊公司库房被盗案件；破获绫致服装有限公司退货部5万余元服装被盗案；破获天津日进汽车系统有限公司库房价值10万余元轴承被盗案件；破获发生在开发区农行门前的往年重伤积案。通过流动人口清理清查、巡逻盘查检查、深入企业走访排摸、大情报推送信息等多种形式深挖线索，抓获网上在逃人员6名，其中包括1名往年网上在逃人员，1名外省网上在逃人员。破获的三星视界有限公司电动车被盗案件、麦格昆磁企业原料被盗案件先后被平安天津、平安武清官方微信宣传报道。分局以简报的形式对开发区派出所“解矛盾、破小案、防事故、保民安”专项行动开展情况进行了宣传。

2016年，打掉3个犯罪团伙，接连破获多起涉企案件，为企业挽回经济损失85余万元，其中破获团伙盗窃平和汽车配件案件；破获牛某某、王某某等团伙盗窃麦格昆磁公司滤网废料案件；破获高某某、张某某、陈某、李某某、张某某等团伙等盗窃亚马逊公司价值20余万元托盘案件，破获韩某某、王某某、吴某某、李某某、周某某、齐某某故意伤害案件；破获司某、夏某某、祝某某等团伙诈骗案。通过流动人口清理清查、巡逻盘查检查、深入企业走访排摸、大情报推送信息等多种形式深挖线索，抓获网上在逃人员8名，其中包括6名外省网上逃犯。破获的绫致公司被诈骗案件、三星公司更衣柜被盗案件、高新公寓宿舍被盗窃案件、联合协创物业公司30万元被诈骗案件以及成功拦截一起电信诈骗案件等先后被平安天津、平安武清官方微信、天津电视台法制频道宣传报道。

二、创建平安辖区

2014年，开发区派出所会同总公司、消防、安监、劳动、电力等部门，对辖区企业单位开展6次联合安全大检查，重点检查企业安保组织、制度不落实、警卫人员不能发挥作用的问题。对涉及煤水电气、剧毒及反恐重点单位采取定期检查与集中抽查相结合的方法，共检查企业200余家，发现安全隐患56处，督促其整改，及时堵塞了漏洞。盗窃企业案件比2013年同期下降30%。经梳理分析，电信诈骗案件相对高发，为有效控制发案，针对电信诈骗、企业内更衣室、宿舍侵财犯罪，专门刻录宣传光盘

500余张，发放到各企业单位，利用各企业单位的广播系统每天播放，对员工天天教育、时时提醒。同时在高新公寓、金融中心、天狮学院等地开展了10次针对防抢、防盗、防电信诈骗的集中统一宣传活动，发放宣传资料1300余份。针对砸车玻璃、盗窃工地、街头诈骗等犯罪制作多种宣传材料2000余份，发放到区内企业，提高其防范意识，落实好人防、技防措施。自9月底市局开通平安天津微信、改版平安天津警务微博以来，开发区派出所进行了广泛深入的推介和宣传工作，辖区内683人订阅平安天津微信和微博，及时了解警务资讯和安全防范知识。通过大量的宣传和防范工作的开展，提高了辖区企业和群众的安全防范意识。全年发生大的盗窃企业和工地的案件，入户盗窃案件大幅下降。做好开发区视频监控建设和技防检查工作。协调总公司，争取资金，大力推进开发区内高清视频监控建设。督促20余家企业对技防设施升级改造，修复摄像头300余个，做到重点部位监控不留死角，提前完成分局下达的本年度技防标定任务数。

2015年，对辖区企业单位开展12次联合安全大检查，重点检查企业安保组织、制度不落实、警卫人员不能发挥作用的问题。对涉及煤水电气、剧毒及反恐重点单位采取定期检查与集中抽查相结合的方法，共检查企业200余家，发现安全隐患56处，督促其整改，及时堵塞了漏洞。年内盗窃企业案件比2014年同期下降30%。加强重点反恐单位和涉危企业、行业场所的管理。建立民警每周对4家重点反恐单位和8家涉危企业进行安全检查的工作制度，在“9·3”阅兵和中共十八届五中全会安保期间，组织民警每天进行检查，排除隐患4起，保证重点反恐单位和涉危企业不出问题。采取定期、突击检查相结合的方式，对旅店、歌舞娱乐、电子游艺场开展检查，实现场所全年无黄赌毒等丑恶现象。处罚不按规定登记旅客的旅店2家，批评教育6家。做好人口管理工作。辖区常住人口1656人，流动人口多，外来务工人员居住以公寓和企业宿舍居住为主。为有效加强人口管理，将私房出租情况纳入视线，将公寓式居住和企业宿舍居住人员相结合管理，深入了解辖区内常住人口和暂住人口动态，做到底数清，情况明，对有违法犯罪嫌疑的，做到发现得了，控制得住，争创平安辖区。广泛开展防范宣传，提升自防意识和能力。一是利用双微平台宣传。针对嫌疑人利用网络平台诈骗的动向，大力推进平安天津、平安武清官方微信订阅工作，同时所领导与企业中高层领导互动、社区民警与企业行政管理和安全负责人互动，通报辖区最新治安状况，宣传防电信诈骗、防盗、防抢和安全防范等知识，通过延伸宣传渠道，提高辖区企业员工的安全防范意识。二是逐人逐车提醒。针对盗油案件高发，开发区派出所组织三次打击盗油专项行动，盘查嫌疑车辆，挤压犯罪空间。在巡逻中向大货车司机逐人提醒，逐人发放防范提示单，现盗油案件正呈逐步下降趋势。三是利用广播系统宣传。专门刻录宣传光盘500余张，利用各单位的广播系统每天播放，对员工天天教育、时时提醒。四是繁华地区集中宣传。在高新公寓、金融中心、天狮学院等地开展了10次针对防抢、防盗、防电信诈骗的集中统一宣传活动，发放宣传资料2600余份。五是加强矛盾纠纷排查化解工作，处理影响辖区稳定的事件39起。会同总公司、分局相关职能部门、开发区人民调解委员会等部门，妥善处置科威金属员工堵门讨薪、宁夏“小白帽”到天狮大学工地等恶意讨薪、金侨大道农民工、天狮大学城农民工爬塔吊讨薪等39起涉稳事件，处置非正常死亡事件7起，切实维护了辖区的社会治安稳定。六是精心组织，周密安排，确保警卫任务、大型活动安全。为确保国际自行车比赛、国际马拉松比赛顺利进行，所领导组织民警多次实地查看线路，制定缜密的安保方案，为分局领导决策提供准确详实的数据。全年执行京沪铁路、京山铁路、高速公路、两会、国际自行车赛、国际马拉松、天狮年会、绿博会等警卫任务79次，出动警力600余人次，圆满完成了各项警卫任务，未发生影响警卫任务安全的事件。

2016年，创建人民满意的平安辖区。1.开展联合安全大检查，提升企业防范能力。对辖区企业单位开展12次联合安全大检查，重点检查企业安保组织、制度不落实、警卫人员不能发挥作用、财务室、保险柜、仓库等重点部位的人防技防落实不到位问题。对涉及煤水电气、剧毒及反恐重点单位采取定期检查与集中抽查相结合的方法，共检查企业230余家，发现安全隐患56处，督促其整改，及时堵塞了漏洞。2.加强重点反恐单位和涉危企业、行业场所的管理。建立健全22家反恐重点单位档案，民警定期对反恐单位和10家涉危企业进行安全检查，在中共十八届六中全会安保期间，组织民警每天进行检查，排除隐患4起，保证重点反恐单位和涉危企业不出问题。采取定期、突击检查相结合的方式，对旅店、歌舞娱乐、电子游艺场开展检查，查处吸毒案件1起，查处赌博案件1起，有效打击了黄赌毒等社会丑恶现象，净化了辖区空气。3.做好人口管理工作。2016年辖区常住人口2966人，流动人口多，外来务工人员居住以公寓和企业宿舍居住为主。为有效加强人口管理，将私房出租情况纳入视线，将公寓式居住和企业宿舍居住人员相结合管理，深入了解辖区内常住人口和暂住人口动态，做到底数清，情况明，对有违法犯罪嫌疑的，做到发现得了，控制得住。4.加强矛盾纠纷排查化解工作，处理影响辖区稳定的事件45起。年内会同总公司、分局相关职能部门、开发区人民调解委员会等部门，妥善处置天元工地民工堵门、瑞宜新公司工人讨薪、新马港公司堵门讨薪、天狮集团天津籍经销商因“超越计划”投资失败到集团讨要说法、天狮集团赤峰7名女经销商以及吉林、宁夏等地因“超越计划”投资失败欲跳楼、裸奔和组织集会讨要说法等事件，成功劝阻25名山东籍经销商到市政府上访事件，成功制止1名山西籍经销商跳楼事件。经协调工作发放工人工资500余万元。切实维护了辖区的社会治安稳定。5.精心组织，周密安排，确保警卫任务、大型活动安全。为确保国际自行车比赛、国际马拉松比赛顺利进行，所领导组织民警多次实地查看线路，制定缜密的安保方案，为分局领导决策提供准确详实的数据。全年执行京沪铁路、京山铁路、高速公路、两会、国际自行车赛、国际马拉松等警卫任务45次，出动警力469人次，圆满完成了各项警卫任务，未发生影响警卫任务安全的事件。

三、服务经济发展

开发区派出所牢固树立服务理念，主打服务品牌，助推经济发展。继续坚持“三必到”制度和三级走访制度：一是“三必到制度” 即企业有困难必到、企业发案必到、企业提出需求必到。二是三级走访制度，即所领导下访制度、所领导接访制度、民警上门走访服务制度，所领导、民警每周不少于三个半天下企业走访，每周走访不少于8家企业。2014年，奥克斯公司、信义公司有为保安人员培训的要求，派出所组织民警和保安队长，对企业的60余名保安员进行为期5天的培训。做好天狮学院新生入学的安保工作，同时定期给学生上法制课，提高学生的法制意识。

四、外资企业、外国人员管理和服务

一是对外资企业、外国人采取动态管理。2014年为90余家外资企业建立档案。掌握界内300余位外国人工作、生活情况，做到人来登记，人走注销，掌握外国人的轨迹和动态，实现对涉外企业和外国人的动态管理。及时掌握各类不安定因素，将矛盾纠纷化解在萌芽状态。二是快侦快破涉及外资企业和外国人案件。2014年快侦快破麦格昆磁公司生产废料被盗、三星公司电动车被盗案件、一韩国人被敲诈勒索案件，亚马逊公司商品被骗案、绫致公司服装案、日进公司轴承被盗案，帮助巴基斯坦一商人协调处理购物纠纷，维护了外资企业的正常经营秩序，保护了外国人的合法权益。

第二章　法务

第一节　法务工作

一、健全制度，夯实基础

建立健全公司内控制度、完善公司法人治理、法律事务管理，逐步形成依法治区的框架体系，规避经营风险。拓展法律服务领域、不断创新与完善方式方法，构建支撑公司发展战略的法务工作体系。完善法务管理办法和法务审核流程，明确各部门、关键岗位在风险管理中的职责，推动将风险管理纳入各项业务管理流程，努力实现法务介入的“及时性、全面性、实效性、前置性”。

二、强化管理，防控风险

通过参与公司重大经济合同事前论证、合同签订跟踪、执行过程监控、后续事项的处理及完成效果的评估，防控全过程风险。通过建立合同管理台账、重大合同动态跟踪制度，及时发现合同管理和公司经营管理中存在的问题，提出改进意见和建议。收集各部门日常签订的常用合同，通过事前的修改和完善，以合同范本指导业务部门进行合同签订。面向业务经办部门经办人开展法律知识培训，使风险关口前移，减少纠纷争议。加强对重点业务、重大项目的法律风险研究。

三、整合资源，提高效能

诉讼案件做到认真负责、及时完成，保证公司利益最大化，必要时邀请顾问律师参加诉讼仲裁的起诉、应诉，做好诉讼前与对方当事人协调谈判工作，争取双赢。对重大、复杂案件，通过整合相关资源来解决，发现重大法律问题立即向公司报告相关案情，使领导迅速作出决策。加强业务知识学习，加强与公司各部门交流，更好的为公司各项业务提供切合实际的法律服务。

第二节 武清开发区法务管理办法

第一条 为规范武清开发区法务管理工作，确保合同、规范性文件、管理制度、重大决策的合法性，防范法律风险，按照国家相关法律法规，结合开发区实际情况，特制定本管理办法。

第二条 法务审核文件范围。

（一）合同，指总公司及总公司参股公司与其他平等主体的自然人、法人或其他组织之间，所签订的书面合同及补充 / 更正协议。主要包含：招商类合同、建设工程类合同、金融类合同、服务类合同以及采购类合同等；

（二）以总公司名义对外发布的声明、公示函、警告函、公告等文件；

（三）授权书、备忘录、承诺书、意向书等各项证明文件；

（四）对外制定发布的条例、规定、通告、办法、决定；

（五）行政管理制度；

（六）“三重一大”（重大决策、重要干部任免、重大项目安排、大额度资金使用）相关决策。

第三条 合同文本分类。

（一）示范文本，指由国家、相关部委或职能部门制定的文本，必须使用现行有效的示范文本；

（二）标准文本，指总公司制定的内部通用文本；

（三）协商文本，指与相对方共同协商后，主要由我方起草的文本；

（四）对方文本，指由对方起草的文本。

第四条 合同文本的格式及填写要求。合同文本整体干净整洁，字体、字号、行间距应一致；合同主体应真实存在且名称准确；同一主体在合同中的称谓应保持一致；合同应填写完整，不适用条款明确写明不适用；填写建设工程合同相关示范文本应认真阅读通用合同条款；填写页码；按类别编号。

第五条 合同文本的起草。合同、协议的起草以遵守相关法律法规及总公司相关规定为前提，由经办部门或相对方起草，规范性文件、管理制度、重大决策由经办部门起草。注意以下重点事项：

（一）采购类和建设工程类合同。预付款一般按合同金额的10%支付，最高不超过合同金额的30%，并在工程进度款中予以抵扣。有预付款的合同必须要求承包方缴纳履约保证金或履约保函。合同款按定期支付的，承包人应按定期实际完成的工程量向发包人或监理人提交付款申请。合同款按工程进度分段支付的，承包人应按照专用条款约定的工程进度或完成的工程量并依据专用条款约定的格式、内容，向发包人或监理人提交付款申请。合同约定的拨付资金比例不得超过工程进度的 80%。最后一笔进度款应在竣工结算审核完成后进行拨付，结算审核期限按项目大小及难易情况而定。项目竣工验收后，应保留不低于工程合同价的 5% 作为质量保证金。待质保期满由承包方向工程管理部门申请，工程管理部门会同监理部门验收合格后出具证明进入清算程序。

（二）招商类合同。

1. 购地类投资协议应明确投资总额、税收承诺（每亩纳税不少于 50 万元）、承诺考核时间及方式、未达承诺的解决办法、土地手续完成后的进场时间和建设周期、土地预留定金及违约责任等条款。

2. 租赁类投资协议应明确投资总额、税收承诺（标准厂房每平方米纳税不少于 1500 元，办公楼宇每平方米纳税不少于 5000 元）、承诺考核时间及方式、未达承诺的解决办法、投产时间及违约责任等条款。

3. 租赁合同应明确租赁期限、租赁保证金、租金标准，享受优惠租金的条件、承诺考核时间及方式、未达承诺的解决办法、水电暖及物业费用的收取及违约责任等条款。

4. 招商代理类协议应明确引进项目个数、代理服务费的标准、考核办法、支付时间与进度比例及违约责任等条款。

5. 孵化器类协议原则上应明确引进项目个数、引进项目的税收贡献、税收考核时间及方式、违约责任等条款。

6. 重大投资及功能类等特殊项目有突破以上约定的经领导班子会研究决策。

第六条 资本运营部预先资金使用审核。合同中涉及资金支付的，应预先提交资本运营部就支付金额及付款进度是否符合公司整体资金预算计划进行审核。

第七条 法务审核流程。经办人应当将待审文件纸质及电子文本、《法务审核意见书》（以下简称“《意见书》”见附件一）、资本运营部出具的审核意见、必需资质文件同时提交法务部。

审核具体流程：经办部门负责人及分管领导签署送审意见→法务、律师审核→律师出具《律师意见书》→针对律师意见经办部门负责人签署修改意见（对未采纳的律师意见要逐条进行说明）→经办部门分管领导签署意见→法务部分管领导签署意见→

总经理签署意见并决定是否授权有关分管领导签署合同。

第八条 法务审核内容。

（一）文本是否规范；

（二）必需资质文件：营业执照、生产许可证、经营许可证、建筑工程资质证、装修资质证等相关法定证件；委托代理手续；证明合同签订人身份的相关证件等是否齐全；招投标类合同是否包含招标书、投标书、投标报价表、中标通知书、物资描述简表、证明投标人资格及物资质量合格性的文件；

（三）相对方姓名或名称、法定代表人、住所等主体信息是否填写完整且准确；

（四）标的、价款、结算方式和付款方式、数量、质量、履行期限、地点和方式、违约责任、解决争议的办法是否明确且书写规范；

（五）需经过招标采购的项目招标后送审的合同文本是否与招标书要求的范本一致；

（六）合同有附件或补充协议的，是否在条款中注明；

（七）是否有违反法律法规、社会公共利益及经济秩序的条款；

（八）各方权利与义务关系是否平等，是否有对总公司明显不利的条款。

第九条 法务审核时限。示范文本及标准文本合同，审核时限不超过三个工作日；其他类合同、规范性文件、管理制度和重大决策，不超过五个工作日；较复杂的、涉及重大项目的及有特殊情况的文件，审核时限酌情加急或延期。

第十条 合同签订。签订合同必须采用书面形式且有必要的场面要求，任何部门和个人不得以口头形式达成协议或私下签署协议。合同的签订、规范性文件、管理制度及重大决策的发布均须有经总经理签字的《法务审核意见书》。

经办部门在合同签订前必须按照本办法规定进行法务审核，禁止倒签补签合同。

在签订合同时，除特殊情况加盖总公司公章和法定代表人印章的合同外，必须加盖合同专用章，以及法定代表人或法定代表人授权的分管副职亲笔签名。其中合同专用章仅用于总公司对外签订合同使用，由法务部负责管理。其余各类用章均由综合服务部统一管理；相对方为法人或其他组织的，必须加盖法人或其他组织公章和法定代表人亲笔签名（或印章）或委托代理人亲笔签名；对方为自然人的，必须有当事人亲笔签名，并按指印（必要时留存身份证复印件或身份证号码）。前述盖章位置应同时写明合同签订日期。超过一页的合同均须加盖骑缝章。

第十一条 合同归档。

（一）合同归档范围。合同原件、补充 / 更正协议、资质文件、会议纪要、《法务审核意见书》等相关法律文件；其他需保管、归档的重要法律材料；

（二）合同编号格式。总公司简称 - 部门首字母 - 年份月份 - 编号 - 补充 / 更正协议编号。例如：综合服务部 2015 年 9 月合同编号：UDA-ZH-1509-001，此合同的补充协议编号：UDA-ZH-1509-001-01；

（三）归档要求。合同原件由经办部门、法务部各留存一份。涉及收付款及扶持政策兑现的需同时将合同原件送交资本运营部存档（扶持政策、备忘录原件还应送交经济运行部）。合同经办部门必须在合同签订后三日内将原件及补充 / 更正协议、资质文件、会议纪要、《法务审核意见书》、《律师意见书》等相关法律文件交法务部归档。

第十二条 合同传递。合同经办部门必须在合同签订后三日内将合同副本及相关资料传递相关部门。

(一)招商购地建厂类合同协议副本需传递至行政服务中心、规划设计部、工程管理部、资本运营部、经济运行部、工业物业公司、企业管理部、城市管理部、综合服务部。

（二）租赁标准厂房类合同协议副本需传递至行政服务中心、规划设计部、工程管理部、资本运营部、经济运行部、工业物业公司、企业管理部、城市管理部、综合服务部。

（三）租赁办公楼宇类合同协议副本需传递至行政服务中心、规划设计部、工程管理部、资本运营部、经济运行部、优达物业公司、企业管理部、城市管理部、综合服务部。

（四）注册类合同协议副本需传递至行政服务中心、资本运营部、经济运行部、企业管理部、综合服务部。

（五）经过招标采购后签订的合同协议副本及中标通知书（复印件）、公开招标领导签字单（复印件）、预结算结算单（复印件）需由各经办部门传递至资本运营部。

（六）涉及收款、付款条款的合同，各经办部门应及时将合同副本传递至资本运营部。

第十三条 合同文件执行。

（一）经办部门负责落实并监督合同的履行、规范性文件、管理制度和重大决策的执行。并于每年六月和十二月将所签合同的实际履行情况送法务部备案。

（二）法务部门负责对经办部门提出的合同履行过程中相关法务问题提出处理建议。

（三）涉及税收承诺类的合同由经济运行部根据承诺税收完成的实际情况，统计报送。

（四）工业物业公司对租赁标准厂房的租金等费用进行收缴和催收。

（五）优达物业公司对楼宇租金等费用进行收缴和催收。

（六）工程项目管理部门对其管理项目的工程进度、质量等依据合同条款分别落实。

（七）租赁办公楼宇类合同的续签由原招商部门负责，对照新政策予以续签或清退，经济运行部配合提供必要数据。

（八）租赁标准厂房类合同的续签由企业管理部负责。

第十四条 责任追究

（一）法务责任。应严格对合同、规范性文件、管理制度和重大决策进行合法性审核，承担审核责任。

（二）经办部门负责人及分管副职责任。经办部门负责人及分管副职负责对合同相对方的真实性、合法性、可靠性及履约能力负责；保证合同签订事由及各方权利义务关系符合各方谈判及协商的本意；确保合同、规范性文件、管理制度和重大决策顺利实现。未履行上述责任的要追究经办部门负责人及分管副职责任。

（三）未按此办法执行，私自签订合同及未经法务审核程序签订合同的严格追究经办人、经办部门负责人和分管副职责任，给开发区造成重大经济损失的予以辞退并保留追究相关人员法律责任的权利。

（四）在合同执行过程中，经办部门、优达物业公司、工业物业公司及工程管理部门对合同执行、监管不力造成损失的将追究相关责任人责任。法务部、经济运行部应严格按照此办法做好合同落实情况统计汇总工作，并及时将汇总情况报送领导。

第十五条 简易程序。对合同条款相对单一、履约风险较低且需重复性签订的合同，经主要领导确认后送法务部备案，该类经备案的合同可适用简易程序直接签订。

第十六条 本办法自公布之日起试行。

第十篇

商　务　区

武清商务区（以下简称商务区）成立于2012年2月18日。是武清区委、区政府抢抓国家经济转型升级契机，制定的“园区化、集约化、高端化”发展现代服务业的战略举措，有效推动了现代服务业和工业“双轮”驱动发展。2017年11月20日并入武清开发区，隶属武清开发区统一管理。

第一章　概况

2012年创建之初，商务区的发展定位是：计划总投资规模500亿元，建设国家级的生态经济示范区，使其成为“园区化、集约化、高端化”的现代服务业聚集区。

区域位于天津市武清城区西部核心区。开发面积5平方公里，总体规划建筑面积600万平方米。园区周边10分钟车程内，有京津塘、京津、京沪、滨保4条高速公路的5个出入口，京津城际铁路经停站1处，以及103、104国道，区位交通优势明显。园区市政基础设施全面实现“十一通一平”。

商务区是武清区的生态先行示范区，在借鉴中新天津生态城模式的基础上，指标体系、生态规划、绿色技术等均达到国际一流水平，园区内绿化率40%以上，区内建筑全部达到国家绿建标准。已建成的700亩中央公园，开阔水面、湿地风格的城市林地，营造了一个恬静闲适、充满自然情趣商务休闲区。同时，按照未来智慧城市需求，整合城市运行核心资源，全面打造开放便捷的智慧园区。

国际企业社区是商务区自建工程，总规划占地300亩，建筑面积40万平方米。已建成西区33栋楼宇，包括2栋高层，31栋多层，建筑面积17万平方米。全面按照花园式办公社区打造，建筑均按照国家绿色建筑三星标准建设，已获住建部绿色建筑三星级标识认证（国内绿色建筑最高等级）。园区重点发展新一代信息技术、金融、文化创意、生物医药等产业。

商务区借鉴国内外成熟的CBD经验，强化区内功能的多元混合，打造了功能完善的配套体系。

几年来，商务区生态环境建设凸显，载体功能日臻完善，服务水平不断提高，已成功吸引中兴通讯、太平洋电信、V1 汽车世界、诚通集团、招商局集团、中信金石、武汉大学研究院、天津科学技术研究院、京津科学技术研究院等 1000 余家国内外知名企业在区域内落户、创业发展。

第二章 机构

武清商务区总公司成立于2012年2月18日，2017年11月20日并入武清开发区管理。其领导机构曾建立有区委书记、区长，主管商务区的区委常委、副区长兼任的天津市武清商务区管理委员会，管委会下设办公室、商务区工委、商务区总公司。但由于管委会设置时间较短，且由区级领导兼任，日常工作则由商务区工委、总公司主持运行。因此，此章只对历任党政领导班子及领导成员、工作分工分别给予记述，对曾经建立的管委会领导机构不再赘述。

第一节 园区领导机构

自园区建立至并入武清开发区管理以来，在五年多的时间里历经两任党政领导核心。分别如下：

一、第一任领导人员与工作分工

（2012.2—2014.10）

张绍锋　商务区工委书记，武清商务区总经理。

翟　伟　商务区工委委员，武清商务区常务副总经理。

李 震　商务区总公司副总经理，分管财务部、企业管理服务部。

张耐民　商务区总公司副总经理，分管建设部、城市管理部。

励贺林　商务区总公司副总经理，分管招商部。

武桂宝　商务区总公司副总经理，分管招商部、招商服务部。

二、第二任领导人员与工作分工

（2014.110—2015.11）

翟　伟　商务区总公司总经理 主持公司全面工作。

李　震　商务区总公司副总经理 分管财务部。

张耐民　商务区总公司副总经理 分管建设部、城市管理部。

武桂宝　商务区总公司副总经理 分管招商部。

励贺林　商务区总公司副总经理 分管招商部。

胡新兵　商务区总公司副总经理 分管招商部（外交部派遣挂职人员）。

第三任领导人员与工作分工

（2015.11—2017.11）

张福旺　商务区工委书记、总公司总经理，主持全面工作。

李　震　商务区工委副书记、总公司副总经理，分管党建工作部、财务部、企业管理服务部。

张耐民　商务区工委委员、总公司副总经理，分管建设部、城市管理部、安全生产监督管理站。

励贺林　商务区工委委员、总公司副总经理，分管招商四部、招商五部、招商六部、招商服务部。

武桂宝　商务区工委委员、总公司副总经理，分管企业发展促进中心、科技人才服务部、物业公司。

胡新兵　商务区总公司副总经理（外交部派遣挂职人员），分管招商一部、招商二部、招商三部。

闫文杰　商务区工委委员，分管综合部、协管党建工作部。

冯立军　商务区工委委员，分管规划部、协管招商一部、招商二部、招商三部。

第二节　部门设置及职责

商务区根据建设发展的实际需要，逐步建立了覆盖各项工作的18个部、一个中心、两个公司。各部门名称及职责工作范围分别是：

1. 党建部：协助党工委管理园区各级党组织，负责组织开展园区党的建设相关工作，加强党风廉政建设。

2. 综合部：负责总公司调研、督办、文秘、接待等工作，负责文件的审阅、起草、管理工作，负责后勤保障共组，负责新闻宣传工作。

3. 招商一部：负责招商引资、主导产业培育工作，负责投资协议、房屋租赁合同的起草工作，负责招商引资政策的制定。

4. 招商二部：负责招商引资、主导产业培育工作，负责投资协议、房屋租赁合同的起草工作，负责招商引资政策的制定。

5. 招商三部：负责招商引资、主导产业培育工作，负责投资协议、房屋租赁合同的起草工作，负责招商引资政策的制定。

6. 招商四部：负责招商引资、主导产业培育工作，负责投资协议、房屋租赁合同的起草工作，负责招商引资政策的制定。

7. 招商五部：负责招商引资、主导产业培育工作，负责投资协议、房屋租赁合同的起草工作，负责招商引资政策的制定。

8. 招商六部：负责招商引资、主导产业培育工作，负责投资协议、房屋租赁合同的起草工作，负责招商引资政策的制定。

9. 首都工作部：负责面向北京招商引资、主导产业培育工作，负责投资协议、房屋租赁合同的起草工作，负责招商引资政策的制定。

10. 招商服务部：协助招商部，办理企业前期手续，向企业提供咨询服务，做好与企业的前期对接；认真做好企业档案管理与传递、招商数据统计工作。

11. 规划部：负责商务区城市设计、控规导则的编制，以及各专项规划编制工作，负责总体规划控制管理工作，协助投资方办理规划许可证、土地使用证、房产确权证等工作。

12. 建设部：负责商务区工程管理工作，协助企业办理项目图纸审查、招标备案、施工许可证、房产确权证，协助解决建设、消防、环保等方面的问题。负责农民工管理、城市管理、安全生产工作。

13. 城管部：负责园区市容和环境卫生的管理工作，负责园区户外广告、生活垃圾、特种垃圾和建筑垃圾的行业管理工作。

14. 安监站：负责商务区的安全生产状况，对园区内容易发生重大生产安全事故的生产经营单位进行严格检查，发现事故隐患，进行及时处理。

15. 财务部：负责财务管理工作，制定并落实各项财务管理制度，制定资金使用计划，编制年度资金预算，负责融资管理工作，负责财务审计工作，负责工程预决算管理工作。

16. 预决算部：负责商务区项目开发过程中的成本控制与管理，参与建设工程的招投标工作，负责工程招标的标底编制和审定。

17. 企业发展促进中心：负责规范企业的运行管理，确保各项工作开展与公司的战略目标保持高度一致，促进企业的可持续发展。

18. 科技人才部：负责商务区科技创新发展工作，负责与科研机构、高校院所、国际合作项目的合作对接，负责人才引进工作，负责科技招商工作。

19. 企业管理服务部：负责国民经济和社会发展、经济运行、统计的规划编制工作，并抓好落实；负责商务区企业服务工作，负责企业劳动争议调解协商仲裁工作，协助做好政策兑现、人员招聘、积分落户、社会保障、劳资纠纷等工作。

20. 赛得物业公司：按照国家对物业管理的标准，全面做好国际企业社区房屋、设备设施、环境等维护管理。采取有效措施，为业主和房屋使用者在公共区域内的人身财产安全提供保障。

21. 赛得酒店运营公司：负责赛得商务会议中心、赛得酒店、园区餐厅、绿色建筑展示中心的日常运营，满足园区及周边企业住宿、会议以及聚餐等企业经营的工作需求，企业运营的基础设施保证。

第三章　建设历程

根据商务区历年有关资料记载，区域内的建设发展历程及其成果，除2012年初建、2017年并入武清开发区管理不再详细赘述外，其他各年度情况分别记述如下：

第一节　奋发起步

2013年，是商务区建设发展的第二年，也是奋发起步之年。全年累计吸引注册资金29亿元，固定资产投资20.3亿元，税收5108万元，引进科技型中小企业52家。

一、招商引资

全年引进项目150余个，总投资超过300亿元，包括V1汽车世界、兴天通讯、民生银行中民交通管理中心、中绿创投基金、世纪博爱等。形成了“信息技术、金融产业、高端商贸、总部经济、文化创意”五大主导产业。

1. 新一代信息技术。借助中兴通讯、太平洋电信优势，打造了信息技术产业链，引进项目50余个，其中商务区7个，迅联时代新媒体产业园、随锐科技、鹏博士、正祥科技、安康科技、福泽科技和维讯电子；兴天通讯公司引进30余个，太平洋电信公司引进10余个。信息技术产业预期总价值已超过150亿元，环渤海IP价值洼地效应显现。成立了天津市云计算产业联盟。

2. 金融产业。金融产业聚集效应初显，引进金融项目6个，包括民生银行中民交通投资管理中心、中信集团金石基金管理公司、中绿创投基金、天津武清村镇银行、朗润投资，总投资超过50亿元。重点追踪项目10余个。

3. 高端商贸。坚持高端化、优质化、规模化，引进项目5个，V1汽车世界、梦金园珠宝等全国最大的旗舰店，总投资超过60亿元。重点追踪10余个。

4. 总部经济。依托区位交通优势，大力发展总部经济，引进项目2个，海达集团总部、格威特集团。重点追踪10余个。

5. 文化创意。大力发展时尚创意产业，引进项目4个，同沅文化和伯乐聚星影视公司等，总投资超过10亿元。重点追踪10余个。

以上成绩得益于三项举措。一是坚持深耕首都，积极追踪首都大院大所、科研机构、央企国企，引企总数占整体一半，特别是引进了一批行业顶层的科技项目；二是狠抓产业链招商，依托北斗、中兴、太平洋电信3家龙头企业，分别组建专门招商队伍，强力攻坚，科技园区初具规模；三是强化拓展招商范围，在借重用好京津资源的同时，拓展长三角、珠三角、以及海外招商渠道，与100余家中介机构建立了长期合作关系，为引资突破奠定了坚实基础。

二、规划建设

1. 规划设计。与中新生态城签署了合作建设生态园区协议，确定了建设方案，完成了指标体系和生态规划编制初稿。与兴天公司合作组建了智慧园区建设管理机构，启动了智慧园区建设。完成了西部新区景观、道路绿带、南东路绿化带和水街区域全专业施工图设计。完成了西部新区亮化规划、湖区标识系统、城市家具和夜景亮化工程设计。完成了国际企业社区建筑方案及全专业施工图设计，完成了绿建三星设计咨询。完成了西部新区和太平洋项目道路、管线全专业施工图设计，以及太平洋数据中心两条道路绿化景观方案。

2. 市政基础设施建设。总投资14.1亿元。完成湖区景观工程，铺设草坪9万平方米，种植乔灌木9000株，种植花卉3.7万平方米，铺设漫跑路4500平方米，高耐竹4800平方米，修建观景塔1座、观景盒4个、观景连廊400米，修建水浪构筑物8个、风车12个。修建道路8.4万平方米，管线近5万延米，道路绿带19万平方米。水系工程，安装水闸5个，驳岸修复500米。太平洋项目，修建道路两条，共8000平方米。

3. 产业项目。14个项目启动规划建设。太平洋数据枢纽中心完成了主体施工，正在进行外檐装修；完成了展示中心基础；正在扎实推进110千伏电站建设；二期桩基完工，正在进行基础施工。兴天花园云谷和海达总部大厦桩基完工，正在进行基础施工。国际汽车园、世纪博爱、中绿创投基金、格威特、格瑞德完成了概念性方案，正在进行施工图设计。迅联时代新媒体产业园、北斗奥吉通、朗润、金鹏瑞翔正在进行概念性方案设计。

三、商务区管理

1. 组织机构建设。成立了“天津市武清商务区管理委员会”，区委书记张勇任管委会主任，区委常委、副区长钟书明任管委会副主任。成立了“共青团天津市武清商务区工作委员会”。新建了招商服务部、企业管理服务部、城市管理部三个部门，内设部门达到8个。注册成立了赛得房地产、赛得商贸、赛得物业和赛得园林绿化四家子公司。

2. 廉政建设。按照中央“八项规定”，修订了财务管理、招投标管理、工程建设管理、车辆管理和办公用品管理5项制度，并将制度执行情况与考核挂钩。强化招标小组对招投标过程的审核监管，实行招投标全过程公开。严格执行资金使用计划，提高资金合理性，降低了财务成本。严格控制考察接待，明确考察人数和经费预算，精简接待。实行了采购、报销分部门执行机制。

3. 员工管理。实行了员工绩效考核制度，按照重点工程（工作）、日常表现按月考核，考核结果公开公示。组织了三轮员工招聘，共招聘新员工16人、厨师3人。建立了商务区人才档案专用账户。定期员工培训，有效提高了员工业务能力。修订了公司行政管理制度。

四、发展环境

1. 企业服务工作。实行了企业服务首问责任制，对企业问题专人限时办理，全年协助企业办结事项40余件。针对信息技术、金融、商贸等产业，实行专人专职服务。协助企业开通了沟通区内职能部门的绿色通道。制定了《招商服务管理手册》，实现了签约、注册到建成投产的标准化服务，“标准化服务·高效贴心”被评为区级“满意在武清”服务品牌。实现了督办工作常态化，按周统计工程进展，按月进行现状分析，为工程正常推进提供了数据支撑。实行了督查专报制度。

2. 宣传工作。在国内外新闻媒体加大宣传力度，累计发稿150余篇。其中，在《人民日报》、《光明日报》各1篇，《人民日报》稿为全区仅有的3篇之一。《天津日报》头版头条2篇，《武清资讯》头版头条2篇。在《经济日报》《北京晨报》《天津日报》《今晚报》《每日新报》《旅客报》《中国信息化》杂志等主流平面媒体实现发稿。网络媒体发稿100余篇。公司被评为2013年度区级精神文明建设工作先进集体、区级宣传思想工作先进集体、区级新闻报道工作先进集体。制作了商务区招商宣传片。网站点击率超过33万次。

3.融资工作。全年融资8.2亿元，包括绿化景观4.2亿元，太平洋数据中心一期4亿元。

第二节　新的跃升

2014年，是商务区各项事业协调发展，实现新的跃升之年。全年实现服务业销售收入31.3亿元，同比增长213%；引资到位50.6474亿元，增长74.5%；税收1.4亿元，增长176%；固定资产投资59.04亿元，增长193%；新增科技型中小企业51家。

一、产业发展的战略集群效应日益凸显

年内引进项目769个，其中，投资200亿元项目1个，超亿元项目11个，购地项目9个，租赁办公楼宇项目65个，注册项目692个。

1.新一代信息技术产业战略发展集群初步形成。成立了新一代信息技术产业研究中心，以及天津大学姚建铨院士牵头的云计算与物联网研究院。依托招商局兴天云谷、太平洋电信信息服务产业园等，引进项目450余个，包括，真讯康科技、云腾科技、荣信伟业、统御科技、峥嵘年华、汇缘科技、一凡科技、中福科技、中科卫士、易寻方达、中卫科技、时空经纬、北斗新时空、北斗车卫士、中文投、中搜网、中移联、合纵时代、淘游天下、微点科技、嘉业智德等，初步形成了云计算、导航、移动互联网三个主要板块。

2.新产业拓展成效显著。其中，金融产业，引进了中民交通投资管理中心、中融投融资租赁有限公司、嘉业财富投资管理有限公司、杨帆鸿运投资咨询有限公司；高端商贸，引进了伍尔特、重庆商会、久旭商贸、雄鹰酒店管理、瑞远实业、艾珂服装、码头王餐饮、瑞福轩、一山消防设备、汉威阀门、速航进出口贸易；生物医药产业，引进了红日康仁堂、元宝枫生物医药、德泽景华健康咨询公司、子时合丰医疗科技。文化创意产业，引进了文化传媒商会、博雅知远、汇众天下。

3.科技创新能力大幅提升。引进了中关村创业学院、微软创投加速器、诚通人力、宝蓝股份、863科技孵化器、北京高校创业基地、NCO中小企业服务平台等项目，为园区以科技创新驱动发展搭建了高水平平台。

4.原有企业增资效果明显。2014年全年老企业增资共5.26亿元，其中，V1汽车世界3.65亿元、中绿创投0.5亿元、太平洋电信0.2亿元、简耀广告0.01亿元。另外，完成了中瑞新能源股份制改造。

二、产业发展的配套功能环境全面跃升

1.“生态、智慧”主题特色日益凸显。加速推进了生态园区建设，借鉴中新生态城模式，高标准编制了生态园区指标体系并进行了分解，完成了可再生能源专项规划；按照零碳标准，启动了绿色建筑展示中心建设；将国际企业社区作为生态示范项目，按照绿建三星的国内最高标准建设，目前已完成绿建三星设计标识评价。扎实推进智慧园区建设，制定了工作方案，完成了可研报告专家评审；正在制定主干光纤网铺设方案，以及重点区域 wifi 无线覆盖和视频监控系统方案；启动了国际企业社区智能化施工，17 个子系统全部进场；扎实推进了中央公园智慧化方案设计。

2. 市政景观环境全面优化。坚持把生态环境作为提升园区核心优势的关键来抓，严格执行“美丽武清 · 一号工程”网格化机制，建立了商务区网格化管理体系，确定了每个网格的网格员。实施中央公园景观提升工程，补植乔木 883 株，花灌木 956 株，新植大柳树 117 株，完成湖区挡车石更换及部分标识安装；实施了灯光亮化工程，完成了灯具选型及施工图优化设计；完成了湖区标识系统方案及施工图设计。实施了道路绿化景观提升工程，完成了 7 条新建道路绿化、7 条道路景观提升，共种植苗木 1.51 万株，铺设地被草皮 3.3 万平方米。启动了湖区配套卫生间及管理用房建设。

3. 国际企业社区建设进展顺利。园区占地 300 亩，共计 40 万平方米，启动了占地 129 亩的西区建设，建筑面积 17 万平方米，包括两栋高层（15 层）、31 栋多层（2 至 4 层）。2016 年，两栋高层全部完成了主体及二次结构施工，正在进行外檐装修；多层区楼宇施工基本完成，正在进行附属管线、道路、景观施工。涵玉干细胞、随锐科技、天使街、文化传媒商会、爱链科技等企业正在装修设计，物业服务中心正在装修。

三、产业项目建设加速推进

1. 太平洋电信数据中心。一期数据中心，总投资 5.5 亿元，包括，2.2 万平方米数据中心、2100 平方米展示中心、1500 平方米 110 千伏电站，以及院区景观、300 亩整体绿化，和柴发、暖通、消防、电梯、精装、10 千伏变电设备、电力外线、弱电等专业，工程全部竣工，正在移交。二期数据中心完成了主体、二次结构及部分外檐装修。

2. 招商局兴天云谷。包括 1 栋展示中心、3 栋研发楼、39 栋云联盟楼宇及部分商业项目，分三期建设。一期，展示中心和研发 1# 楼，展示中心已完成主体及外檐施工，正在进行精装修；研发 1# 完成主体，正在进行二次结构施工。二期，研发 2#、4# 楼和 14 栋商务办公楼宇，已完成施工图设计，正在进行桩基施工。三期，占地 200 亩，

将建设17栋高层、19栋多层，总建筑面积26万平方米，正在进行规划设计。

3. 其他在建项目情况。一是海达总部大厦，建筑面积2.1万平方米，已完成主体及二次结构施工，正在进行外檐装修。二是金鹏瑞翔，建筑面积7.6万平方米，正在进行桩基施工。三是V1汽车世界，完成了概念性方案设计及赛道区建筑方案设计，完成了700亩场地整平，正在进行赛道区施工图设计及工程进场手续办理。

四、产业发展的配套服务环境日益优化

1. 深入开展党的群众路线教育实践活动。按照中央、市委、区委要求，开展了三个环节的教育实践活动，总公司上下全员参加。一是扎实做好基层基础工作，对照中央“八项规定”和反对“四风”要求，修订完善制度23项、新建制度12项，规范了差旅、接待、用车管理；组织了民主生活会、组织生活会，全体党员干部进行了对照检查和自我党性分析。二是提升了党员干部素养，学习了教育实践活动全部规定篇目，邀请区委党校政策研究室副主任高怀霞进行了六个专题的教育讲座，围绕“如何在教育实践活动中坚持两不误、两促进，切实推进改革发展稳定、建设美丽武清”组织了专题讨论。三是形成了活动特色，坚持开门征求意见，组织了三次基层座谈会、三轮企业调研，发放征求意见信100余份，累计征求企业意见建议150余条，全部实现即知即改；根据意见建议修订了《企业服务管理手册》，在网站开通了企业服务专区，开通了企业服务微信平台，畅通了企业服务绿色通道。

2. 机关建设有效加强。用党的建设统领机关建设，深入落实“下基层、解难题、交朋友”“五个一批”等活动，建立了党建宣传区，发展新党员3人。审批了企业联合党支部1个。成立了商务区工会。成立了招商五部、六部，完善了招商团队，公司内设部门达到13个。修订完善了员工考核方案。完成了商务区网站改版。商务区被评为市级文明单位、区级宣传思想工作先进集体、精神文明建设先进集体，商务区机关党支部被评为区级优秀党组织。

3. 财务管理有效加强。完成了太平洋电信2亿元、国际企业社区7亿元融资。启动了太平洋电信数据中心一期移交运行工作。启动了发行企业债工作。完成了股权变更。

4. 企业服务水平显著提升。全年累计走访企业100余次，协助企业解决各类问题150余件。建立了商务区调解委员会。完成了第三次全国经济普查商务区核查工作。完成上报民营企业776家。引进了世界顶尖物业顾问公司戴德梁行，为入区企业提供高水平的物业管理服务。

第三节　提速前行

2015年，是商务区建设提速前行之年。全年实现服务业增加值65.87亿元，同比增长60%；引资到位50.0038亿元；税收2.708亿元，同比增长74%；固定资产投资73.07亿元，同比增长24%；新增科技型中小企业55家，完成了3家高新技术企业、1家小巨人企业认定。

一、招商引资

全年累计引进项目444家，其中上报招商局150家，产业项目1个，总部办公项目15个。

1. 产业聚集实现新提升。主攻新一代信息技术、金融、文化创意等产业，引进新一代信息技术产业项目100余个，包括快手网络、并行科技、爱链科技、炬联众慧、家有购物、微贰、中美计桥、彩虹蜗牛、欧德玛诺等；金融产业项目8个，包括瑞领资本、信筹通达、信使APP等，涵盖了基金、股权众筹、银行等领域；文化创意产业项目20余个，包括津商文化、美库原创等。另外，还引进了一批生物医药、商贸类项目。实现了中瑞新源在新三板挂牌上市。

2. 平台招商效果明显。国际企业社区年内引进总部办公项目17家，办公面积近3万平方米，入驻率达27%；招商局网谷·企业街区，实现了招商局网谷、兴天通讯双向发力，年内引进信息技术产业项目28个；启动了海达大厦招商。

3. 科技创新步伐加快。借助国家大众创业、万众创新契机，全面实施了科技创新驱动战略，打造了“智慧硅谷·众创空间”，由智慧硅谷公司负责运营，目前在孵项目10余个。承办了“中华之梦”创业大赛，在全国5000余个项目中遴选的120个优秀项目在武清参加了两季复赛，决赛在中央电视台举行，有21个项目落户商务区，在谈项目20余个，落实创业投资4亿元，同时借助大赛影响力有效宣传了商务区。扎实推进了国家级自主创新示范区、市级留学人员创业园申报。组织了两个年度的“春晖杯”海外获奖人才武清行活动，30余个获奖项目在武清进行了路演。

二、规划建设

1. 市政配套日益优化。完成了智源东道、广场东路、通源道、达源道、新昌路、新平南路的选址和立项。完成了T型路及附属桥梁的全专业施工图设计。实施了景观提升工程，按照零碳标准，建成了1700平米的绿色建筑展示中心，完成了中央公园及园区道路景观提升。完成了电力规划设计及论证、中压排管施工图设计。开通了567路公交车。

2. 扎实推进了国际企业社区建设。投资11亿元，完成了西区建设，占地129亩，建筑面积17万平方米，其中，地上11.4万平方米，地下5.6万平方米，包括2栋高层、31栋多层。全部建筑获住建部绿色建筑三星级标识认证，是国内最大的绿建三星建筑群。完成了智慧化建设，铺设了“一个中心、三个平台、十七个子系统”，以及“统一数据光纤和园区WLAN无线”两张网。启动了二期建设，扎实推进了规划设计和手续办理工作，年后各工种全面进场。

3. 全面推进了产业项目建设。招商局网谷·企业街区，一期展示中心、研发中心1号楼竣工实现运营，二期8栋完成了主体及二次机构施工，正在进行内外檐施工。海达大厦竣工实现运营。建成了金辉中心主体，正在进行二次结构施工。V1汽车世界，完成了规划设计及赛道区8宗地的土地手续。完成了君利项目土地摘牌。正在办理涵玉国际抗衰中心、金轮挂牌手续。完成了伍尔特、中绿创投建筑方案初稿，正在进行完善修订。

三、机关管理

1. 扎实推进了党的建设。深入开展了“三严三实”专题教育活动，制定了《工作方案》，组织了“严以修身，坚定理想信念”“严以律己，严守政治纪律”“严以用权，始终勤政廉政”三个专题学习讨论活动。组织领导班子成员在广泛调研的基础上，联系自身思想、工作、生活和作风实际，讲了党课，开展了三次学习讨论活动。查摆了领导班子成员个人问题清单、制定了整改任务书，已全部整改到位。继续深入推进了党的群众路线教育实践活动。组织了“牢记为人民服务宗旨”主题教育活动。扎实推进工委中心组学习。完成了领导干部个人事项报告，完成了领导班子及新任科级干部“一报告两评议”。审批了“招商局兴天云谷党支部”，正在加紧推动迅联、彩虹蜗牛两个非公党组织建设。审批了3名党员。

2. 深入做好了人员管理。深入实施了员工两级培训制度，先后邀请清华大学、人民大学、张盈律师事务所有关教授专家，对全体员工、部分企业负责人进行了素质提高培训。狠抓业务培训，各部门分别自行组织，双周一次，综合部每月进行了考核。

组织了丰富多彩的员工文体活动，组建了足球、篮球、乒乓球、羽毛球、太极拳、跑步六个俱乐部，每周开展活动。

3. 有效加强了资金管理。完成了中国银行 2 亿元、天津银行 8000 万元、齐鲁银行 6000 万元融资。启动了太平洋电信数据中心回购。

四、发展环境

1. 企业服务工作有效加强。明确了“一中心、五平台”服务体系，启动了企业综合服务中心招商，美通云动、诚通人力、横秋财务、墨言知识产权、企兴知识产权、众合天下、恒信达企业管理、张盈律师事务所 8 家机构确定进驻。组织了 2 次银企对接会，完成了中小微企业风险补偿资金 4.41 亿元。组织 5 家企业与瑞领资本进行了金融对接。协助招商局网谷、兴天通讯、家有购物、美通云动等 12 家企业招聘员工 500 余人，为企业解决员工住宿 70 余人，协助 4 名人才落户武清。组织招商局网谷、兴天通讯、迅联等 8 家企业建立了工会。

2. 赛得物业实现正常运营。依托戴德梁行国际化的物业管理经验，推动赛得物业公司全面进驻国际企业社区，完成机构设置、人员招聘，确定了国际企业社区楼宇租赁费、水电费、制冷供热费价格，实现正常运营。督促社区内 8 家企业完成了装修，实现运营。赛食汇园餐、简坐时尚餐厅实现运营。

3. 打造了安全和谐稳定局面。严格执行“美丽武清·一号工程”网格化管理，实行了市容环境监管常态化机制，园区环境有效加强。全面完成了“六五”普法工作。针对建设施工、交通运输、人员密集场所、有限空间作业、用电安全等重点领域，全面开展了安全生产大检查，在 9 家企业排查出安全隐患 35 项，已督促企业全部整改完成。

第四节　跨越发展

2016 年，是商务区实现跨越发展之年。全年实现服务业增加值 90 亿元，同比增长 37%；三级财政收入 4.64 亿元，同比增长 71.3%；一般预算收入 1.6 亿元，同比增长 84%；固定资产投资 90.01 亿元，同比增长 23.18%；完成科企认定 61 家，股改上市 4 家。

一、产业体系

1. 主导产业加速发展。信息技术、现代金融、文化创意等主导产业呈现良好发展态势，整体订单额120亿元，利税突破25亿元，同比增长67%。围绕上述产业，年内引进新项目167家，引资到位30.669亿元，其中实体46个，北京企业100家。包括，互联网舆情平台、智橙科技、云测、51社保网、逸行网等信息技术项目36个，胖猪猪商业保理、美联盛航、厚朴征信等金融项目6个，墨言、森淼教育、璀璨宝熙等文化创意项目17个。骨干企业的核心作用日益突出，康仁堂、中信金石2家企业纳税突破1亿元，诚通人力3000万元、鹏博士1000万元。企业员工总数超过2000人。

2. 招商平台不断优化。商务区被批准为国家级生态示范区、天津市留学人员创业园，纳入了国家自主创新示范区，有力的提升了商务区平台规格。与中国科技网、中关村民营科技企业家协会、互联网协会等10余家机构签署了招商代理协议，累计搭建招商中介平台66个。以商招商氛围逐步形成，通过红日康仁堂、同赢文化、张盈律师事务所等，引进企业17家，年承诺税收1000余万元。设立了首都工作部，首都招商工作全面推进。

3. 科技创新全面加强。智慧硅谷被批准为市级众创空间，按照独立板块，组建了运营团队，启动了孵化运营管理。引进了武汉大学天津空间信息研究院、京津科学技术研究院、中科院理化所新材料基地、北京语言大学国际交流服务中心4个院所项目。中瑞新源、随锐科技、并行科技成功在新三板挂牌上市，锦华园林在天津OTC挂牌，实现再融资5亿元。

4. 国际企业社区招商顺利。规范了国际企业社区扶持企业发展政策，入驻企业41家，累计办公面积6万余平方米，入住率55%。

二、发展平台

1. 扎实推进国际企业社区建设。扎实做好西区运营管理，完成了园区绿化景观、指引标示、logo墙的设计安装，完成了不动产权证办理，规范了物业管理，启动了篮球场、健身区建设，形成了富有特色的发展载体，年内接待参观1500余人次。启动了东区建设，占地162亩，建筑面积23万平方米，共39栋多层，3栋高层，完成了设计及手续办理，完成了桩基施工，总包队伍进场，确定了国家三星级绿色建筑技术实施方案。

2. 进一步完善了市政基础设施。按照全国文明城区建设标准，实施了绿化景观提升工程，以中央公园为重点，种植了142亩波斯菊主题花海，完成了255亩草坪铺装，补植换植乔木910株、灌木1237株、水生植物15.3万株，安装发光座椅13个、高灯2个、垃圾桶57组，铺设彩色沥青1.38万平米；完成了道路绿带景观提升，安装文明宣传围挡；强化了大气、扬尘治理，组建了专门队伍，采购了2辆喷洒车、1辆清扫车，不间断进行清理。完成了中压排管施工图设计及施工。完成了4个市政道路口的交通信号灯和安防设施安装。启动了园区空间导视系统设计，安装了2个边界形象柱。

3. 大力推进产业项目建设。招商局网谷·企业街区，完成了主体及二次结构施工，完成了外檐、水暖、电气、消防部分施工。金晖中心完成了主体、二次结构施工，正在进行外檐施工。扎实推进了V1汽车世界、中绿创投、伍尔特、金轮等项目的方案设计及手续办理。

三、发展环境

1. 服务配套功能大幅跃升。拓展了"一中心，六平台"服务体系，企业发展促进中心全方位协调企业服务功能，扎实推进了企业服务中心建设，完成了H2主题酒店样板间装修，启动了绿建展示中心改造工程。与各大银行对接，启动了ATM机布点工作。研究了通勤车运营路线，正在与交通局对接合作协议。落实中小微风险补偿资金12.263亿元。

2. 企业服务向精细化发展。以"促惠上"为抓手，重点走访了156家企业，梳理在融资、用工、市场、配套等方面的问题218个，已落实196项，22项正在办理。协助兴天通讯落实国家服务业发展引导资金200万元。协助企业兑现人才奖励资金9万元，完成了15名新引进人才落户手续办理工作。按照主动专项服务标准，对纳税大户实施了高标准服务，促使中信证券、诚通人力2个重点企业实现了税收促进翻倍。

3. 物业服务工作不断加强。充分借助戴德梁行先进的物业管理经验，全面优化企业国际企业社区物业服务，组织了园区消防、治安检查2轮。扎实做好了工程查验及运营维护工作。采购了4辆电动观光车。完成了D1、A3、A2及H2部分楼宇装修，正在推动B1、B4等5栋楼宇、H2高层部分楼宇装修。

4. 有效巩固了安全稳定局面。全面提升了安全生产管理层级，实施了安全生产不良信用"黑名单"、24小时巡查、每月集中排查等制度，所有施工单位、企业均列入考核范围，督促其严格落实安全生产责任。委托中智国际安全中心，搭建了完善的安全体系，组织了12轮安全技能培训、现场安全检查等。健全完善了安全设施，安装了新开路、新安路与畅源道、来源道交口交通信号灯、安全技防设施。

四、机关建设

1. 扎实推进了党的建设。加强党员干部思想建设，开展了群众路线教育和"三严三实”“回头看”，有效巩固了教育成果。按照区委安排，狠抓了“两学一做”学习教育，完成了四个专题教育活动，组织了“四查四找四学习”和六项专项整治，干部员工政治意识、大局意思、核心意识、看齐意识全面增强。优化基层党组织，新成立党支部4家，布置特色党员活动室3个。狠抓从严治党，深化了《准则》和《条例》落实，制定了“两个责任”清单，强化了“三重一大”决策，组织开展廉政宣传和警示教育活动2个批次。完成了商务区选区的区级党代表、人大代表、政协委员、团区委委员换届工作。

2. 有效加强了队伍管理。以提高效率和规范管理为目标，制定了总公司专题会议、招商项目会商、员工因公外出申请3项制度。进一步完善了招商引资考核办法。实施了员工两级培训制度，邀请人民大学培训团队组织了5次专业素质培训。组织了员工拓展训练。

3. 体制机制创新成效明显。优化了部门职责，新建了党建工作部、企业发展促进中心、科技人才服务部、招商服务部，对综合部、企业管理服务部职责进行了调整。加大了重点工程（工作）的督办力度，实行了《每周动态》制度，起草了37期、督查专报12期。重新设计了商务区logo、VI标识系统，组织了大型推介活动8次，在国内各级媒体发稿200余篇，有效提升了商务区形象品味，拓展了在国内重要区域的影响力。

第五节　驻区企业

商务区创建以来，利用优越的区位优势、政策优势，以及完善的配套设施、优美的生态环境、快捷、良好的服务，通过园区员工的不懈努力，招商引资力度不断加大，吸引了国内外大批企业来园区入驻。到2017年年底，入驻企业、注册企业总数达2313家，其中驻区企业达500余家。现将入住的部分重点企业收录于下：

一、注册企业名录（2017年）

1　易维宝（天津）科技有限公司　国际企业社区H2号楼706室–55（集中办公区）

2　天津恒润达企业管理咨询有限公司　国际企业社区H2号楼706室–74（集中办公区）

3　天津虹运教育科技有限公司　国际企业社区H2号楼706室–23（集中办公区）

4　猎人无忧（天津）企业管理咨询有限公司　国际企业社区H2号楼706室–75（集

中办公区）

5 天津一三九实业有限公司 国际企业社区 H2 号楼 706 室 -42（集中办公区）

6 天津快客科技有限公司 国际企业社区 H2 号楼 707 室 -01（集中办公区）

7 天津乐园华林商贸有限公司 国际企业社区 H2 号楼 603 室 -52（集中办公区）

8 万可建筑工程（天津）有限公司 国际企业社区 H2 号楼 707 室 -02（集中办公区）

9 九州冷域（天津）科技孵化器有限公司 国际企业社区 H2 号楼 502 室

10 中路轨道交通设备（天津）有限公司 国际企业社区 H2 号楼 707 室 -04（集中办公区）

11 天津家乐科技发展有限公司 国际企业社区 H2 号楼 707 室 -05（集中办公区）

12 中科诺森（天津）环保工程技术有限公司 国际企业社区 H2 号楼 707 室 -09（集中办公区）

13 齐鲁（天津）科技发展有限公司 国际企业社区 H2 号楼 707 室 -12（集中办公区）

14 盛仕鑫财务咨询（天津）有限责任公司 国际企业社区 H2 号楼 707 室 -13（集中办公区）

15 中友（天津）文化发展有限公司 国际企业社区 H2 号楼 707 室 -07（集中办公区）

16 金坤时代财务咨询（天津）有限责任公司 国际企业社区 H2 号楼 707 室 -10（集中办公区）

17 天津君盟泽科技发展有限公司 国际企业社区 H2 号楼 707 室 -17（集中办公区）

18 天津财商财务咨询有限公司 国际企业社区 H2 号楼 707 室 -08（集中办公区）

19 天津仁正信房地产经纪有限公司 国际企业社区 H2 号楼 707 室 -14（集中办公区）

20 天津鑫昇房地产经纪有限公司 国际企业社区 H2 号楼 707 室 -15（集中办公区）

21 天津鸿杰园林工程有限公司 国际企业社区 H2 号楼 707 室 -20（集中办公区）

22 天津恒鑫汇达企业管理咨询有限公司 国际企业社区 H2 号楼 707 室 -21（集中办公区）

23 天津汇集诚通科技有限公司 国际企业社区 H2 号楼 707 室 -22（集中办公区）

24 天津旗洋自行车贸易有限公司 国际企业社区 H2 号楼 707 室 -23（集中办公区）

25 睿地势（天津）规划设计有限公司 国际企业社区 H2 号楼 707 室 -24（集中办公区）

26 天津武云聚安科技中心（有限合伙） 国际企业社区 H2 号楼 707 室 -18（集

中办公区）

27 天津市浩大物流有限公司　国际企业社区 H2 号楼 707 室 –27（集中办公区）

28 天津宝庆物流有限公司　国际企业社区 H2 号楼 707 室 –28（集中办公区）

29 天津水舞时代科技有限公司　国际企业社区 H2 号楼 707 室 –35（集中办公区）

30 天津航雅文化传播有限公司　国际企业社区 H2 号楼 707 室 –25（集中办公区）

31 天津富日天宸科技发展有限公司　国际企业社区 H2 号楼 707 室 –26（集中办公区）

32 天津欧洛奇信息技术有限公司　国际企业社区 H2 号楼 707 室 –34（集中办公区）

33 斯德尔电气技术（天津）有限公司　国际企业社区 H2 号楼 707 室 –39（集中办公区）

34 瑞盈凯（天津）文化传媒有限公司　国际企业社区 H2 号楼 707 室 –41（集中办公区）

35 天津火山文化传媒有限公司　国际企业社区 H2 号楼 707 室 –67（集中办公区）

36 君博伟利（天津）科技有限公司　国际企业社区 H2 号楼 707 室 –30（集中办公区）

37 天津田氏恒瑞科技有限公司　国际企业社区 H2 号楼 707 室 –29（集中办公区）

38 天津恒天远通科技有限公司　国际企业社区 H2 号楼 707 室 –36（集中办公区）

39 天津市惠国环保科技有限公司　国际企业社区 H2 号楼 707 室 –44（集中办公区）

40 德宇企业管理咨询（天津）有限公司　国际企业社区 H2 号楼 707 室 –50（集中办 公区）

41 天津玟芳商务信息咨询有限公司　国际企业社区 H2 号楼 707 室 –43（集中办公区）

42 天津汇坤恒商务信息咨询有限公司　国际企业社区 H2 号楼 707 室 –45（集中办公区）

43 天津容晟法律咨询有限公司　国际企业社区 H2 号楼 707 室 –47（集中办公区）

44 海秀智慧（天津）农业发展有限公司　国际企业社区 H2 号楼 707 室 –48（集中办公区）

45 天津速派汽车贸易有限公司　国际企业社区 H2 号楼 707 室 –53（集中办公区）

46 智合新天（天津）科技有限公司　国际企业社区 H2 号楼 707 室 –42（集中办公区）

47 天津星创互娱文化传播有限公司　国际企业社区 H2 号楼 707 室 –52（集中办公区）

48 霞客行（天津）文化传播有限公司　国际企业社区 H2 号楼 707 室 –57（集中办公区）

49 鼎怡瑞禾（天津）文化传播有限公司　国际企业社区 H2 号楼 707 室 –61（集中办公区）

50 天津市丹恩液压机械贸易有限公司　国际企业社区 H2 号楼 707 室 –40（集中办公区）

51 天津沐和物业管理有限公司　国际企业社区 H2 号楼 707 室 –55（集中办公区）

52 天津恒数科技有限公司　国际企业社区 H2 号楼 707 室 –51（集中办公区）

53 天津昴芯科技发展有限公司　国际企业社区 H2 号楼 707 室 –58（集中办公区）

54 天津津昌人力资源服务有限公司　国际企业社区 H2 号楼 707 室 –49（集中办公区）

55 万源通汇（天津）商务服务有限公司　国际企业社区 H2 号楼 707 室 –62（集中办公区）

56 天津盈丰世纪科技有限公司　国际企业社区 H2 号楼 707 室 –32（集中办公区）

57 天津妙境科技有限公司　国际企业社区 H2 号楼 707 室 –33（集中办公区）

58 天津赛得智谷众创空间有限公司　国际企业社区 A9 号楼 101 室

59 天津知行合一企业管理咨询有限公司　国际企业社区 H2 号楼 707 室 –73（集中办公区）

60 天津魔力工坊科技有限公司　国际企业社区 H2 号楼 707 室 –56（集中办公区）

61 凡视（天津）科技有限公司　国际企业社区 H2 号楼 5 层 507 室

62 天德地顺（天津）服装有限公司　国际企业社区 H2 号楼 707 室 –38（集中办公区）

63 天津豫通津装饰工程有限公司　国际企业社区 H2 号楼 707 室 –75（集中办公区）

64 天津信义企业管理咨询有限公司　国际企业社区 H2 号楼 707 室 –74（集中办公区）

65 天津乐成教育科技有限责任公司　国际企业社区 H2 号楼 707 室 –64（集中办公区）

66 天津龙马联盟文化传播有限公司　国际企业社区 H2 号楼 707 室 –68（集中办公区）

67 天津链城农业科技有限公司　国际企业社区 H2 号楼 707 室 –65（集中办公区）

68 天津金审优享企业管理咨询合伙企业（有限合伙）　国际企业社区 H2 号楼

707 室 –66（集中办公区）

69 天津企美盛和科技有限公司 国际企业社区 H2 号楼 707 室 –60（集中办公区）

70 天津市泓至泽企业管理咨询有限公司 国际企业社区 H2 号楼 707 室 –06（集中办公区）

71 天津格瑞特网络科技有限公司 国际企业社区 H2 号楼 707 室 –72（集中办公区）

72 天津伟捷祥机电设备安装有限公司 国际企业社区 H2 号楼 707 室 –69（集中办公区）

73 天津超琪科技有限公司 国际企业社区 H2 号楼 707 室 –70（集中办公区）

74 天津达行天下科技有限公司 国际企业社区 H2 号楼 708 室 –12（集中办公区）

75 天津克尔图斯信息技术有限公司 国际企业社区 H2 号楼 708 室 –13（集中办公区）

76 天津元朗教育信息咨询有限公司 国际企业社区 H2 号楼 708 室 –07（集中办公区）

77 天津丰源和顺空调制冷设备安装有限公司 国际企业社区 H2 号楼 708 室 –02（集中办公区）

78 天津市江瑞建筑劳务有限公司 国际企业社区 H2 号楼 708 室 –03（集中办公区）

79 斐海（天津）科技有限公司 国际企业社区 H2 号楼 708 室 –06（集中办公区）

80 天津市弘泽盈达商贸有限公司 国际企业社区 H2 号楼 708 室 –16（集中办公区）

81 海峡（天津）众创空间有限公司 国际企业社区 H2 号楼 707 室 –71（集中办公区）

82 天津厦达商务信息咨询中心（有限合伙） 国际企业社区 H2 号楼 708 室 –08（集中办公区）

83 天津全息律见企业管理咨询有限公司 国际企业社区 H2 号楼 708 室 –09（集中办公区）

84 天津博钊建筑装饰工程有限公司 国际企业社区 H2 号楼 708 室 –10（集中办公区）

85 天津智优文化传播有限公司 国际企业社区 H2 号楼 708 室 –23（集中办公区）

86 奕昕博机械零配件制造（天津）有限公司 国际企业社区 H2 号楼 708 室 –11（集中办公区）

87 天津至善环保科技有限公司 国际企业社区 H2 号楼 708 室 –04（集中办公区）

88 自然数（天津）文化传播有限公司 国际企业社区 H2 号楼 708 室 –25（集中

办公区）

89 天津行有尚教育科技有限公司　国际企业社区 H2 号楼 708 室 –17（集中办公区）

90 天津米步科技有限公司　国际企业社区 H2 号楼 708 室 –19（集中办公区）

91 天津佑民环保科技有限公司　国际企业社区 H2 号楼 708 室 –05（集中办公区）

92 天津汉斯德清洁服务有限公司　国际企业社区 H2 号楼 708 室 –29（集中办公区）

93 北京联合创宇房地产经纪有限公司天津分公司　国际企业社区 H2 号楼 708 室 –22（集中办公区）

94 天津市东兴鼎昊酒店管理有限公武清分公司　国际企业社区 H2 号楼 708 室 –18（集中办公区）

95 天津晋冠融通企业管理咨询中心（有限合伙）　国际企业社区 H2 号楼 708 室 –33（集中办公区）

96 天津盛元普惠商务信息咨询中心（有限合伙）　国际企业社区 H2 号楼 708 室 –41（集中办公区）

97 天津通源企业管理咨询有限公司　国际企业社区 H2 号楼 708 室 –30（集中办公区）

98 天津市溢鸣电子商务有限公司　国际企业社区 H2 号楼 708 室 –35（集中办公区）

99 天津阿朵拉信息科技有限公司　国际企业社区 H2 号楼 708 室 –38（集中办公区）

100 欢娱（天津）文化传播有限公司　国际企业社区 H2 号楼 708 室 –24（集中办公区）

101 天津市腾辉物业服务有限公司　国际企业社区 H2 号楼 708 室 –32（集中办公区）

102 天津市花渡花卉销售有限公司　国际企业社区 H2 号楼 708 室 –31（集中办公区）

103 天津佳影文化传播有限公司　国际企业社区 H2 号楼 708 室 –39（集中办公区）

104 菲思（天津）装饰设计有限公司　国际企业社区 H2 号楼 708 室 –28（集中办公区）

105 菲思（天津）企业管理咨询有限公司　国际企业社区 H2 号楼 708 室 –26（集中办公区）

106 菲思（天津）人力资源服务有限公司　国际企业社区 H2 号楼 708 室 –27（集中办公区）

107 胜吉（天津）国际贸易有限公司　国际企业社区 H2 号楼 708 室 –20（集中办公区）

108 溢贸（天津）国际贸易有限公司　国际企业社区 H2 号楼 708 室 –21（集中办公区）

109 天津赛得酒店有限公司　国际企业社区 H2 号楼 1301 室

110 艺泓（天津）文化传播有限公司　国际企业社区 H2 号楼 708 室 –44（集中办公区）

111 雍信（天津）企业管理咨询有限公司　国际企业社区H2号楼708室–45（集中办公区）

112 天津市商橙网络技术有限公司　国际企业社区H2号楼707室–46（集中办公区）

113 天津市君仕达车务信息咨询有限公司　国际企业社区H2号楼708室–34（集中办公区）

114 菲思（天津）电子商务有限公司　国际企业社区H2号楼708室–36（集中办公区）

115 菲思（天津）汽车维修有限公司　国际企业社区H2号楼708室–37（集中办公区）

116 天津市盛景科技有限公司　国际企业社区H2号楼708室–40（集中办公区）

117 天津红方商务信息咨询有限公司　国际企业社区H2号楼707室–11（集中办公区）

118 天津创捷机电设备有限公司　国际企业社区H2号楼708室–47（集中办公区）

119 天津骆途科技有限公司　国际企业社区H2号楼706室–61（集中办公区）

120 天津市道宽集成房屋科技有限公司　国际企业社区H2号楼708室–53（集中办公区）

121 天津海正泰合企业管理咨询有限责任公司　国际企业社区H2号楼708室–52（集中办公区）

122 天津岩帕科技有限公司　国际企业社区H2号楼708室–48（集中办公区）

123 天津智美珍源商务信息咨询有限公司　国际企业社区H2号楼708室–50（集中办公区）

124 天津逸迈轮胎销售有限公司　国际企业社区H2号楼708室–49（集中办公区）

125 建设在线（天津）网络科技有限公司　国际企业社区H2号楼708室–60（集中办公区）

126 天津青悠慧创科技发展有限公司　国际企业社区H2号楼708室–56（集中办公区）

127 四八三二（天津）信息科技有限公司　国际企业社区H2号楼708室–58（集中办公区）

128 天津金洁利企业管理咨询中心（有限合伙）　国际企业社区H2号楼708室–46（集中办公区）

129 天津绿氧科技发展有限公司　国际企业社区H2号楼708室–59（集中办公区）

130 天津圣耀企业管理咨询有限公司　国际企业社区H2号楼708室–61（集中办

公区）

131 天津大道自然光科技有限公司　国际企业社区 H2 号楼 708 室 –57（集中办公区）

132 天津揣通科技有限公司　国际企业社区 H2 号楼 708 室 –51（集中办公区）

133 天津宏鑫汽车销售有限公司　国际企业社区 H2 号楼 709 室 –03（集中办公区）

134 天津乾升优旺财务咨询有限公司　国际企业社区 H2 号楼 709 室 –04（集中办公区）

135 天津众恒丰财务咨询有限公司　国际企业社区 H2 号楼 709 室 –05（集中办公区）

136 天津青谷企业管理咨询中心（有限合伙）　国际企业社区 H2 号楼 708 室 –62（集中办公区）

137 天津百人行房地产经纪有限公司　国际企业社区 H2 号楼 708 室 –71（集中办公区）

138 天津市津晨线缆有限公司　国际企业社区 H2 号楼 708 室 –68（集中办公区）

139 国玑企业管理咨询（天津）有限公司　国际企业社区 H2 号楼 708 室 –67（集中办公区）

140 国本医院管理（天津）有限公司　国际企业社区 H2 号楼 708 室 –66（集中办公区）

141 天津弘高伟业商贸有限公司　国际企业社区 H2 号楼 708 室 –70（集中办公区）

142 天津耀光教育信息咨询有限公司　国际企业社区 H2 号楼 708 室 –69（集中办公区）

143 天津忙格景观规划设计有限公司　国际企业社区 H2 号楼 708 室 –65（集中办公区）

144 嘉富（天津）企业管理咨询有限公司　国际企业社区 H2 号楼 708 室 –74（集中办公区）

145 黑龙江源泉国土资源勘察设计有限公司天津分公司　国际企业社区 H2 号楼 708 室 –15（集中办公区）

146 天津道诚科技有限公司　国际企业社区 H2 号楼 708 室 –75（集中办公区）

147 汉能（天津）环保科技有限公司　国际企业社区 H2 号楼 708 室 –73（集中办公区）

148 天津鑫盛源房地产开发有限公司　国际企业社区 H2 号楼 709 室 –07（集中办公区）

149 天津百亮科技有限公司　国际企业社区 H2 号楼 708 室 –64（集中办公区）

150 天津中南锦清房地产开发有限公司　国际企业社区 H2 号楼 709 室 –15（集中

办公区）

151 天津市瑞丰线缆有限公司　国际企业社区 H2 号楼 709 室 –13（集中办公区）

152 天津小路网络科技有限公司　国际企业社区 H2 号楼 709 室 –21（集中办公区）

153 天津维尔玛机器人有限公司　国际企业社区 H2 号楼 709 室 –01（集中办公区）

154 天津元生星辰科技发展有限公司　国际企业社区 H2 号楼 709 室 –45（集中办公区）

155 五色糖（天津）文化传播有限公司　国际企业社区 H2 号楼 709 室 –46（集中办公区）

156 天津朗御文化传播有限公司　国际企业社区 H2 号楼 709 室 –06（集中办公区）

157 国壮(天津)文化传媒有限公司　国际企业社区 H2 号楼 709 室 –08(集中办公区）

158 通弘燕达（天津）信息科技有限公司　国际企业社区 H2 号楼 709 室 –12（集中办公区）

159 天津熙漫民情商务信息咨询有限公司　国际企业社区 H2 号楼 709 室 –18（集中办公区）

160 天津永利健康信息咨询有限公司　国际企业社区 H2 号楼 709 室 –19（集中办公区）

161 天津大智杰人力资源服务有限公司　国际企业社区 H2 号楼 709 室 –16（集中办公区）

162 水淋广告设计(天津)有限公司　国际企业社区 H2 号楼 709 室 –20(集中办公区）

163 天津魔法星球文化传播合伙企业(有限合伙）　国际企业社区 H2 号楼 709 室 –17（集中办公区）

164 天津中科理化新材料技术有限公司武清分公司　国际企业社区 A3 号楼 401 室

165 异启互娱(天津)科技有限公司　国际企业社区 H2 号楼 709 室 –24(集中办公区）

166 天津皇亿生物科技发展有限公司　国际企业社区 H2 号楼 709 室 –28（集中办公区）

167 天津智瑞达科技合伙企业（有限合伙）　国际企业社区 H2 号楼 709 室 –32（集中办公区）

168 越凡同辉（天津）教育科技有限公司　国际企业社区 H2 号楼 709 室 –31（集中办公区）

169 天津蜗牛星人教育科技有限公司　国际企业社区 H2 号楼 709 室 –30（集中办

公区）

170 克伦斯（天津）轨道交通技术有限公司　国际企业社区 H2 号楼 709 室 –29（集中办公区）

171 天津实科众联科技有限公司　国际企业社区 H2 号楼 709 室 –23（集中办公区）

172 天津望海科技有限公司　国际企业社区 H2 号楼 709 室 –33（集中办公区）

173 天津蕊新炀科技有限公司　国际企业社区 H2 号楼 709 室 –34（集中办公区）

174 天津楠瑞兴昇科技有限公司　国际企业社区 H2 号楼 709 室 –41（集中办公区）

175 天津亚加文乐科技有限公司　国际企业社区 H2 号楼 709 室 –42（集中办公区）

176 天津星亚南晨科技有限公司　国际企业社区 H2 号楼 709 室 –43（集中办公区）

177 天津必昂迪科技发展中心（有限合伙）　国际企业社区 H2 号楼 709 室 –35（集中办公区）

178 天津盈启企业管理咨询中心(有限合伙）　国际企业社区 H2 号楼 709 室 –36(集中办公区）

179 天津托普纳驰企业管理咨询中心(有限合伙）　国际企业社区 H2 号楼 709 室 –37（集中办公区）

180 天津天德福凤鸣科技有限公司　国际企业社区 H2 号楼 709 室 –39(集中办公区）

181 天津市锦业房地产经纪有限公司　国际企业社区 H2 号楼 709 室 –44（集中办公区）

182 云开（天津）供应链管理有限公司　国际企业社区 H2 号楼 709 室 –40（集中办公区）

183 天津南文升象影视传媒有限公司　国际企业社区 H2 号楼 709 室 –51（集中办公区）

184 天津奇优致安信息技术有限公司　国际企业社区 H2 号楼 709 室 –49（集中办公区）

185 昶信科技（天津）信息咨询有限公司　国际企业社区 H2 号楼 709 室 –50（集中办公区）

186 天津易税互联科技合伙企业(有限合伙）　国际企业社区 H2 号楼 709 室 –57(集中办公区）

187 天津宝乐文化传媒有限公司　国际企业社区 H2 号楼 709 室 –38（集中办公区）

188 中玑企业管理咨询（天津）有限公司　国际企业社区 H2 号楼 709 室 –53（集

中办公区）

189 国本科技（天津）有限公司　国际企业社区 H2 号楼 709 室 –54（集中办公区）

190 天津中安矿山机械维修有限公司　国际企业社区 H2 号楼 709 室 –56（集中办公区）

191 天津正半圆科技有限公司　国际企业社区 H2 号楼 709 室 –52（集中办公区）

192 天津诺行商贸合伙企业（有限合伙）　国际企业社区 H2 号楼 709 室 –64（集中办公区）

193 天津云税互联科技合伙企业（有限合伙）　国际企业社区 H2 号楼 709 室 –66（集中办公区）

194 天津智育文化传播中心（有限合伙）　国际企业社区 H2 号楼 710 室 –01（集中办公区）

195 康童宝贝（天津）商贸有限公司　国际企业社区 H2 号楼 710 室 –02（集中办公区）

196 天津伊特新材料科技有限公司　国际企业社区 H2 号楼 710 室 –03（集中办公区）

197 天津市洪宇建筑装饰工程有限公司　国际企业社区 H2 号楼 710 室 –06（集中办公区）

198 天津丰源鑫诺进出口贸易有限公司　国际企业社区 H2 号楼 710 室 –12（集中办公区）

199 天津景阳生物科技有限公司　国际企业社区 H2 号楼 710 室 –15（集中办公区）

200 天津慧瑞科技有限公司　国际企业社区 H2 号楼 710 室 –22（集中办公区）

201 天津琼影科技有限公司　国际企业社区 H2 号楼 710 室 –17（集中办公区）

202 天津君侠科技有限公司　国际企业社区 H2 号楼 710 室 –18（集中办公区）

203 天津安荣科技有限公司　国际企业社区 H2 号楼 710 室 –25（集中办公区）

204 天津百莱脑商务信息咨询有限责任公司　国际企业社区 H2 号楼 710 室 –26（集中办公区）

205 天津明德联创科技中心（有限合伙）　国际企业社区 H2 号楼 710 室 –05（集中办公区）

206 天津京才联商务信息咨询有限公司　国际企业社区 H2 号楼 710 室 –08（集中办公区）

207 天津北大联创科技中心（有限合伙）　国际企业社区 H2 号楼 710 室 –19（集中办公区）

208 天津虹进科技发展有限公司　国际企业社区 H2 号楼 710 室 -14（集中办公区）

209 天津惠成科技有限公司　国际企业社区 H2 号楼 710 室 -07（集中办公区）

210 天津建峰智航科技有限公司　国际企业社区 H2 号楼 710 室 -16（集中办公区）

211 天津可览嘉联科技合伙企业(有限合伙)　国际企业社区 H2 号楼 710 室 -34(集中办公区)

212 天津凯思商贸有限公司　国际企业社区 H2 号楼 710 室 -36（集中办公区）

213 天津启平科技合伙企业（有限合伙）　国际企业社区 H2 号楼 710 室 -10（集中办公区）

214 天津遥兮科技有限公司　国际企业社区 H2 号楼 710 室 -23（集中办公区）

215 天津南宇科技合伙企业（有限合伙）　国际企业社区 H2 号楼 710 室 -09（集中办公区）

216 中航天元防务技术（北京）有限公司天津分公司　国际企业社区 H2 号楼 A5 号楼

217 天津品控建筑装修有限公司　国际企业社区 H2 号楼 709 室 -62（集中办公区）

218 一米乡愁（天津）电子商务有限公司　国际企业社区 B2 号楼 301 室

219 天津明朝万达科技有限公司　国际企业社区 H2 号楼 707 室 -59（集中办公区）

220 杭州今元标矩科技有限公司天津武清分公司　国际企业社区 H2 号楼 709 室 -70（集中办公区）

221 天津市建峰人力资源服务有限公司　国际企业社区 H2 号楼 709 室 -75（集中办公区）

222 天津市雅琪装饰工程有限公司　国际企业社区 H2 号楼 709 室 -55(集中办公区）

223 天津紫晶导电材料有限公司　国际企业社区 A3 号楼 402 室

224 天津威远企业管理咨询有限公司　国际企业社区 H2 号楼 709 室 -14（集中办公区）

225 天津数介科技有限公司　国际企业社区 H2 号楼 710 室 -20（集中办公区）

226 天津九域工程项目管理有限公司　国际企业社区 H2 号楼 710 室 -30（集中办公区）

227 杭信通商贸(天津)有限公司　国际企业社区 H2 号楼 710 室 -38(集中办公区）

228 天津中创汇影文化传播有限公司　国际企业社区 H2 号楼 710 室 -28（集中办公区）

229 天津成东科技有限公司　国际企业社区 H2 号楼 710 室 –29（集中办公区）

230 天津健海物业管理有限公司　国际企业社区 H2 号楼 710 室 –31（集中办公区）

231 天津中盈工程技术咨询有限公司　国际企业社区 H2 号楼 710 室 –39（集中办公区）

232 天津利是贸易有限公司　国际企业社区 H2 号楼 710 室 –41（集中办公区）

233 天津美达财地商贸有限公司　国际企业社区 H2 号楼 710 室 –44（集中办公区）

234 天津汉邦服装设计有限公司　国际企业社区 H2 号楼 710 室 –35（集中办公区）

235 天津华实科技有限公司　国际企业社区 H2 号楼 710 室 –37（集中办公区）

236 天津万泉汇海企业管理咨询有限公司　国际企业社区 H2 号楼 710 室 –32（集中办公区）

237 光盒（天津）网络科技有限公司　国际企业社区 H2 号楼 710 室 –48（集中办公区）

238 天津云阶梯企业管理咨询有限公司　国际企业社区 H2 号楼 710 室 –21（集中办公区）

239 味肆网络科技（天津）有限公司　国际企业社区 H2 号楼 407 室

240 海川人力资源（天津）有限公司武清分公司　国际企业社区 H2 号楼 710 室 –43（集中办公区）

241 天津市永新软道科技有限公司　国际企业社区 H2 号楼 710 室 –49（集中办公区）

242 意仕爱（天津）商贸有限公司　国际企业社区 H2 号楼 710 室 –45（集中办公区）

243 天津市盖德电子科技有限公司　国际企业社区 H2 号楼 710 室 –56（集中办公区）

244 天津奥创思拓广告有限公司　国际企业社区 H2 号楼 710 室 –57（集中办公区）

245 天津市天骏伟业科技有限公司　国际企业社区 H2 号楼 710 室 –66（集中办公区）

246 天津万年兴广告有限公司　国际企业社区 H2 号楼 710 室 –59（集中办公区）

247 天津市安途广告有限公司　国际企业社区 H2 号楼 710 室 –54（集中办公区）

248 天津蓝酷科技有限公司　国际企业社区 H2 号楼 709 室 –22（集中办公区）

249 天津汇承恒商务信息咨询有限公司　国际企业社区 H2 号楼 709 室 –25（集中办公区）

250 天津圣邦兴业科技有限公司　国际企业社区 H2 号楼 709 室 –26（集中办公区）

251 天津义如同丰科技有限公司　国际企业社区 H2 号楼 709 室 –27（集中办公区）

252 天津欧世邦汽车销售有限公司　国际企业社区 H2 号楼 707 室 –63（集中办公区）

253 北京归斓房地产咨询服务有限公司天津分公司　国际企业社区 H2 号楼 708

室 -14（集中办公区）

254 天津龙淳科技发展有限公司　国际企业社区 H2 号楼 708 室 -42（集中办公区）

255 天津智寻科技有限公司　国际企业社区 H2 号楼 708 室 -43（集中办公区）

256 天津姬美祯科技有限公司　国际企业社区 H2 号楼 708 室 -54（集中办公区）

257 天津枫航科技有限公司　国际企业社区 H2 号楼 709 室 -10（集中办公区）

258 德赛英创（天津）科技有限公司　国际企业社区 H2 号楼 709 室 -48（集中办公区）

259 “天津米欢顺世企业管理咨询合伙企业（有限合伙）”　国际企业社区 H2 号楼 709 室 -58（集中办公区）

260 天津晟博德雅建筑工程有限公司　国际企业社区 H2 号楼 709 室 -59（集中办公区）

261 天津壹竖文化传播有限公司　国际企业社区 H2 号楼 709 室 -60（集中办公区）

262 天津朗艺广告有限公司　国际企业社区 H2 号楼 709 室 -61（集中办公区）

263 天津金谷粒企业管理咨询中心（有限合伙）　国际企业社区 H2 号楼 709 室 -63（集中办公区）

264 天津金麦粒企业管理咨询中心（有限合伙）　国际企业社区 H2 号楼 709 室 -65（集中办公区）

265 龙舟（天津）企业管理咨询合伙企业（有限合伙）　国际企业社区 H2 号楼 709 室 -67（集中办公区）

266 天津华德实业有限公司　国际企业社区 A4 号楼

267 天津晟顺尧建筑安装有限公司　国际企业社区 H2 号楼 709 室 -68（集中办公区）

268 天津市澜鑫宏伟科技有限公司　国际企业社区 H2 号楼 709 室 -69（集中办公区）

269 北京沃达管理咨询有限公司天津分公司　国际企业社区 H2 号楼 709 室 -71（集中办公区）

270 天津斯沃特企业管理咨询有限公司　国际企业社区 H2 号楼 709 室 -72（集中办公区）

271 天津德寿临餐饮管理有限公司　国际企业社区 H2 号楼 709 室 -73（集中办公区）

272 天津憬悟文化传播有限公司　国际企业社区 H2 号楼 709 室 -74（集中办公区）

273 天津吉祥商服科技有限公司　国际企业社区 H2 号楼 710 室 -13（集中办公区）

274 天津鼎翊时澜科技发展合伙企业（有限合伙）　国际企业社区 H2 号楼 710 室 -24（集中办公区）

275 天津快道科技有限公司　国际企业社区 B1 号楼 301 室

276 天津市五环新能源有限公司　国际企业社区 H2 号楼 710 室 –46（集中办公区）

277 天津唐顿科技有限公司　国际企业社区 H2 号楼 710 室 –58（集中办公区）

278 健融（天津）医药科技有限公司　国际企业社区 A9 号楼 106 室

279 天津华宇有志科技合伙企业（有限合伙）　国际企业社区 H2 号楼 710 室 –61（集中办公区）

280 岭东聚力（天津）科技发展有限公司　国际企业社区 H2 号楼 710 室 –62（集中办公区）

281 天津宸泰精测环保科技有限公司　国际企业社区 H2 号楼 710 室 –69（集中办公区）

282 天津尚观博文教育科技有限公司　国际企业社区 H2 号楼 710 室 –70（集中办公区）

283 天津市辰瑞税务师事务所有限公司　国际企业社区 H2 号楼 709 室 –47（集中办公区）

284 天津光宇电力成套设备有限公司　国际企业社区 H2 号楼 707 室 –37（集中办公区）

285 天津小鹅科技合伙企业（有限合伙）　国际企业社区 H2 号楼 710 室 –52（集中办公区）

286 天津天茂健康信息咨询有限公司　国际企业社区 H2 号楼 710 室 –67（集中办公区）

287 天津湘云生物科技有限公司　国际企业社区 H2 号楼 710 室 –68（集中办公区）

288 天津弘毅国文教育科技有限公司　国际企业社区 H2 号楼 710 室 –55（集中办公区）

289 天津博立硕装饰工程有限公司　国际企业社区 H2 号楼 710 室 –64（集中办公区）

290 北京国恒保险代理有限公司天津分公司　国际企业社区 H2 号楼 710 室 –27（集中办公区）

291 天津众英科技有限公司　国际企业社区 H2 号楼 710 室 –73（集中办公区）

292 天津泓阳广告有限公司　国际企业社区 H2 号楼 710 室 –74（集中办公区）

293 天津深茂企业管理咨询有限公司　国际企业社区 H2 号楼 710 室 –75（集中办公区）

294 天津普强电子商务有限公司　国际企业社区 H2 号楼 801 室 –01（集中办公区）

295 天津怡远企业管理咨询有限公司　国际企业社区 H2 号楼 801 室 –03（集中办公区）

296 天津维源国际贸易有限公司　国际企业社区 H2 号楼 710 室 –40（集中办公区）

297 北京正言征信有限公司天津分公司　国际企业社区 H2 号楼 801 室 –04（集中办公区）

298 天津睿博点金科技有限公司　国际企业社区 H2 号楼 801 室 –05（集中办公区）

299 天津市蒲公英科技发展有限公司　国际企业社区 H2 号楼 801 室 –06（集中办公区）

300 天津市神草科技发展有限公司　国际企业社区 H2 号楼 801 室 –07（集中办公区）

301 天津华安派天下企业管理咨询合伙企业（有限合伙）　国际企业社区 H2 号楼 801 室 –10（集中办公区）

302 天津币合餐饮管理中心（有限合伙）　国际企业社区 H2 号楼 710 室 –47（集中办公区）

303 天津可瑞优电子商务有限公司　国际企业社区 H2 号楼 801 室 –16（集中办公区）

304 天津市聚华阳科技发展有限公司　国际企业社区 H2 号楼 801 室 –13（集中办公区）

305 天津运通津商商务信息咨询有限公司　国际企业社区 H2 号楼 710 室 –42（集中办公区）

306 天津圣德恩环保科技有限公司　国际企业社区 H2 号楼 801 室 –09（集中办公区）

307 天津长胜企业管理咨询有限公司　国际企业社区 H2 号楼 801 室 –14（集中办公区）

308 天津市弘珍科技有限公司　国际企业社区 H2 号楼 710 室 –04（集中办公区）

309 中核中汇（天津）科技有限公司　国际企业社区 H2 号楼 801 室 –18（集中办公区）

310 天津禄灼华科技有限公司　国际企业社区 H2 号楼 801 室 –08（集中办公区）

311 兰特光电科技（天津）有限公司　国际企业社区 H2 号楼 710 室 –71（集中办公区）

312 天津腾标科技有限公司　国际企业社区 H2 号楼 710 室 –72（集中办公区）

313 天津金盈企业管理咨询中心（有限合伙）　国际企业社区 H2 号楼 710 室 –63（集中办公区）

314 天津燚森中文化传媒有限公司　国际企业社区 H2 号楼 801 室 –11（集中办公区）

315 天津优澜房地产咨询有限公司　国际企业社区 H2 号楼 801 室 –15（集中办公区）

316 天津市伟创鑫杰科技有限公司　国际企业社区 H2 号楼 801 室 –28（集中办公区）

317 天津博智尚观教育科技有限公司　国际企业社区 H2 号楼 801 室 –24（集中办公区）

318 天津润诚赢智教育科技有限公司　国际企业社区 H2 号楼 801 室 –25（集中办公区）

319 天津广进聚源财务咨询有限公司　国际企业社区 H2 号楼 801 室 –27（集中办公区）

320 天津宝津企业管理咨询合伙企业（有限合伙）　国际企业社区 H2 号楼 801 室 –19（集中办公区）

321 天津信策商务服务有限公司　国际企业社区 H2 号楼 801 室 –12（集中办公区）

322 嘉富瑞华实业有限公司　国际企业社区 H2 号楼 801 室 –17（集中办公区）

323 壹信融（天津）科技有限公司　国际企业社区 H2 号楼 801 室 –23（集中办公区）

324 天津亮力商贸有限公司　国际企业社区 H2 号楼 801 室 –20（集中办公区）

325 天津行镇商贸有限公司　国际企业社区 H2 号楼 801 室 –21（集中办公区）

326 天津美和商贸有限公司　国际企业社区 H2 号楼 801 室 –22（集中办公区）

327 天津橙橙文化传播有限公司　国际企业社区 H2 号楼 801 室 –30（集中办公区）

328 天津伟文企业管理咨询中心（有限合伙）　国际企业社区 H2 号楼 801 室 –33（集中办公区）

329 贝思（天津）文化科技合伙企业（有限合伙）　国际企业社区 H2 号楼 801 室 –35（集中办公区）

330 信树育人（天津）教育科技合伙企业（有限合伙）　国际企业社区 H2 号楼 801 室 –36（集中办公区）

331 天津齐悦信息技术中心（有限合伙）　国际企业社区 H2 号楼 801 室 –41（集中办公区）

332 天津志也科技有限公司　国际企业社区 H2 号楼 801 室 –37（集中办公区）

333 天津海达家乐超市有限公司新开路店　国际企业社区 H2 号楼一层西侧

334 嘉仕伦（天津）科技有限公司　国际企业社区 H2 号楼 801 室 –38（集中办公区）

335 天津希尔康生物科技有限公司　国际企业社区 H2 号楼 801 室 –42（集中办公区）

336 天津安恒商贸有限公司　国际企业社区 H2 号楼 801 室 –43（集中办公区）

337 天津龙腾科技有限公司　国际企业社区 H2 号楼 801 室 –44（集中办公区）

338 天津国融进化科技合伙企业（有限合伙）　国际企业社区 H2 号楼 801 室 –45（集中办公区）

339 瑞禾（天津）家居有限公司　国际企业社区 H2 号楼 801 室 –34（集中办公区）

340 社宝通人力资源（北京）有限公司天津分公司　国际企业社区 H2 号楼 801 室 –02（集中办公区）

341 麦迪贝克生物科技发展（天津）有限公司　国际企业社区 H2 号楼 802 室 –01（集中办公区）

342 麦杰渥特环保科技（天津）有限公司　国际企业社区 H2 号楼 802 室 –02（集中办公区）

343 天津体之源体育科技有限公司　国际企业社区 H2 号楼 802 室 –03（集中办公区）

344 天津梅兰商务信息咨询有限公司　国际企业社区 H2 号楼 802 室 –11（集中办公区）

345 天津光亮企业管理合伙企业（有限合伙）　国际企业社区 H2 号楼 801 室 –40（集中办公区）

346 天津亿米影视文化传媒有限公司　国际企业社区 H2 号楼 801 室 –46（集中办公区）

347 天津安云信科技发展有限公司　国际企业社区 H2 号楼 801 室 –32（集中办公区）

348 天津全安商贸有限公司　国际企业社区 H2 号楼 801 室 –49（集中办公区）

349 龙船（天津）科技有限公司　国际企业社区 H2 号楼 801 室 –31（集中办公区）

350 天津网林永创科技有限公司　国际企业社区 H2 号楼 801 室 –39（集中办公区）

351 天津新港中企业管理咨询中心（有限合伙）　国际企业社区 H2 号楼 802 室 –12（集中办公区）

352 首泰（天津）科技有限公司　国际企业社区 H2 号楼 802 室 –04（集中办公区）

353 颐贤工程科技（天津）有限公司　国际企业社区 H2 号楼 802 室 –14（集中办公区）

354 天津爱培优聚贤企业管理咨询合伙企业（有限合伙）　国际企业社区 H2 号楼 802 室 –15（集中办公区）

355 天津学策企业管理咨询合伙企业（有限合伙）　国际企业社区 H2 号楼 802 室 –16（集中办公区）

356 天津毅达环保科技发展有限公司　国际企业社区 H2 号楼 801 室 –46（集中办

公区）

357 天津蓝湖信息科技有限公司　国际企业社区 H2 号楼 802 室 –17（集中办公区）

358 天津北鲁肴科技有限公司　国际企业社区 H2 号楼 801 室 –47（集中办公区）

359 天津丰海知识产权服务有限公司　国际企业社区 H2 号楼 802 室 –18（集中办公区）

360 天津乾为天财务咨询有限公司　国际企业社区 H2 号楼 802 室 –05（集中办公区）

361 知与行（天津）科技合伙企业（有限合伙）　国际企业社区 H2 号楼 802 室 –06（集中办公区）

362 天津兴迪大数据科技有限公司　国际企业社区 H2 号楼 802 室 –29（集中办公区）

363 天津新港中不动产网络有限公司　国际企业社区 H2 号楼 802 室 –24（集中办公区）

364 玖富为办（天津）企业管理咨询有限公司　国际企业社区 H2 号楼 802 室 –13（集中办公区）

365 天津新达智控科技发展有限公司　国际企业社区 H2 号楼 801 室 –26（集中办公区）

366 城投创展（天津）置业有限公司　国际企业社区 H2 号楼 801 室 –29（集中办公区）

367 天津易众学教育信息咨询有限公司　国际企业社区 H2 号楼 801 室 –48（集中办公区）

368 夏牧日出（天津）餐饮管理有限公司　国际企业社区 B1 号楼 401 室

369 福尧（天津）汽车服务有限公司　国际企业社区 H2 号楼 802 室 –07（集中办公区）

370 天津远威体育文化发展有限公司　国际企业社区 H2 号楼 802 室 –08（集中办公区）

371 嘉则（天津）国际贸易有限公司　国际企业社区 H2 号楼 802 室 –09（集中办公区）

372 天津市正茂科技发展有限公司　国际企业社区 H2 号楼 802 室 –19（集中办公区）

373 天津杰图学亚科技有限公司　国际企业社区 H2 号楼 802 室 –20（集中办公区）

374 天津知书科技有限公司　国际企业社区 H2 号楼 802 室 –21（集中办公区）

375 天津富顺杰科技有限公司　国际企业社区 H2 号楼 802 室 –22（集中办公区）

376 天津乐瑞陈音科技有限公司　国际企业社区 H2 号楼 802 室 –23（集中办公区）

377 天津薪易融科技有限公司　国际企业社区 H2 号楼 802 室 –25（集中办公区）

378 双海昌盛（天津）商贸有限公司　国际企业社区 H2 号楼 802 室 –26（集中办公区）

379 天津智捷科技发展有限公司　国际企业社区 H2 号楼 802 室 –28（集中办公区）

380 天津锐科莱达科技有限公司　国际企业社区 H2 号楼 802 室 –30（集中办公区）

381 天津观正科技有限公司　国际企业社区 H2 号楼 802 室 –31（集中办公区）

382 天津中升之宝汽车销售服务有限公司　国际企业社区 H2 号楼 802 室 –32（集中办公区）

二、重点企业简介

1. 招商局网谷 · 企业街区。2012 年，由中兴通讯集团投资的云计算产业基地项目落户商务区，计划总投资 40 亿元，建设占地 350 亩，为建筑面积 50 万平方米的云计算产业基地。2014 年，兴天通讯公司与招商局蛇口工业区签署合作协议，共同投资建设该项目，项目最终定名为“招商局网谷 · 企业街区”，项目包括 1 栋展示中心、2 栋研发中心和 39 栋云联盟楼宇。2016 年，一期展示中心、研发 1 号楼已建成实现运营；二期 8 栋商务办公楼宇已完成主体及二次结构施工，年内实现运营。

2. 金晖中心。由金鹏瑞翔公司投资建设，占地 35.1 亩，共有 5 栋楼宇，包括 3 栋多层，2 栋高层，总建筑面积为 7.7 万平方米。楼宇除金鹏瑞翔公司自用外，剩余楼宇已启动招商工作，村镇银行已确定进驻。2017 年，已完成主体施工，年内实现运营。

3. 随锐科技。该项目成立于 2006 年 1 月 23 日，是一家专注于高清视频通信产品及视频云平台设计、研发、销售和服务的高科技公司。作为国内高清视频通信产品及视频云服务提供商，公司始终坚持自主创新，坚持走“以创新科技产品驱动公司发展”的道路，为客户提供“五位一体、互联互通”的视频云服务。

4. 并行科技。该项目成立于 2007 年，立足于高性能计算领域，提供数据中心设计、建设、在线运维、运营大数据采集分析、业务运行优化等全方位服务。拥有自主研发的数据中心在线运维软件和运营大数据分析软件，是一家专注于高性能计算和大数据分析领域的全内资高新技术企业。

5. 家有购物北方呼叫中心。该项目属区域总部项目。家有购物集团（国内三大电视购物平台之一）在园区现有内呼业务基础上，拓展设立 900 坐席外呼中心，占用 2500 平米（1 栋楼），运营后年税收 500 万元以上。

6. 彩虹蜗牛。该项目属互联网 + 教育项目。该公司是幼少青素质教育综合解决方案的提供商。入驻高层区，占用 500 平方米，预计年税收 300 万元、100 人入驻。

7. 诚通人力。该项目属央企二级区域总部和互联网 + 项目。诚通集团在园区设立

互联网 + 人力资源平台，从事人才综合服务业务。占用 2500 平方米（1 栋楼），9 月份正式启动业务，预计今年税收 2000 万元、40 人入驻。

8. 百康芯生物。该项目属生物医药项目。该公司致力于自动化核酸检测系统的研发、生产和销售的科技公司。注册资本 1000 万元，占用 1500 平方米，预计年纳税 700 万。

9. 张盈律师事务所武清分所。该项目是由全国优秀律师事务所张盈律师事务所设立的项目，办公面积 900 平方米，目前引进优秀律师 8 名，今年该分所累计处理各类案件 100 多起，成为武清当地该行业第一所。

10. 炬联众慧。该项目属新一代信息技术项目。该公司是通过数字化工具，帮助企业完成从研发到制造一体化实施工业 4.0 解决方案提供商。入驻高层区，预计年税收 300 万元。

11. 美联盛航保险代理。该项目属金融保险项目。拥有全国经营资质的大型金融保险代理有限公司。注册资本 1000 万元，预计年纳税 200 万元。

12. 墨言知识产权。该项目是国内规模最大的品牌运营一站式服务商东灵通集团在武清设立的独资子公司，主要从事品牌运营、专利申请、商标注册等业务，2015 年入住国企企业社区，发展迅猛，2016 年有办公人员 22 名，业务收入突破千万元。

13. 量化派结算中心。该项目属大数据和互联网 + 项目。量化派是基于大数据业务的金融消费服务提供商，客户为金融机构和企业（个人）。占用 2500 平方米（1 栋楼），预计 10 月入驻，年营业额 20 亿元、税收 1000 万元。

14. 蚁安居网络科技。该项目属电子商务项目。是华耐家居集团下属的家装 O2O 平台，计划三年内“新三板”上市。预计年纳税 500 万元。

15. 京津科学技术研究院（北京科学技术研究院）。该项目是由天津市科委、北京市科学技术研究院、武清区政府牵头，北京科力新技术发展总公司、北方技术交易市场、武清商务区总公司三方共建，投资总额 400 万元，旨在建成中国先进的科学技术研究高地和科研成果转化与产业转化的示范基地，为京津两地科研项目合作与经济发展做出巨大贡献，预计三年内引进近百个高科技项目。目前三方已经签署战略合作协议，预计明年年初实现正式运营。

16. 武汉大学天津空间信息研究院。该项目是天津市武清区政府与武汉大学合作项目。2015 年 11 月 11 日，区政府与武汉大学签署了合作协议。武清商务区与武汉大学遥感测绘信息工程国家重点实验室负责落实协议内容。研究院将涵盖四方面职能：一是先进激光雷达产业化基地，发展先进激光雷达产业，推动激光雷达设备国产化。二是卫星遥感大气监测京津冀研究中心，主要开展天空地多平台大气校正方法与遥感技术研究。三是智慧城市研究中心，实现城市大规模三维场景快速三维建模。四是专业技术及继续教育培训中心，打造全国性空间信息培训基地。目前该已完成装修，并正式入驻办公。

17. 伯乐聚星。该项目 2013 年在武清商务区成立天津伯乐聚星影视文化传播有限公司，目前正在国际企业社区筹备设立天津伯乐聚星影视艺术交流中心，专注于影视创作交流、影视人才培训、动画艺术创意制作等。北京伯乐聚星影视文化传播有限公司成立于 2006 年，公司系专业从事影视剧拍摄、制作、发行为一体的专业机构；公司具备业内一流资质、营业性演出许可证、电视栏目制作许可证等。至 2016 年年底该公司已成功拍摄电影 11 部，电视剧 187 集，微电影 5 部。

18. 海达集团总部。该项目建筑面积为 2.1 万平方米，注册资本为 1 亿元，建成后每年可实现税收 5000 万元。

19.V1 汽车世界。该项目位于武清城区西南部，由美国威特集团投资建设，占地 738 亩，规划建筑总面积 60 万平方米，总投资 50 亿元。定位为汽车创新生态园、汽车产业基地、赛车运动及时尚生活体验综合体，将成为国内首家涵盖汽车服务、休闲娱乐和汽车运动等业态的目的地项目，为汽车品牌、专业用户和消费者提供首选的一站式汽车服务解决方案。

第四章 管理制度

商务区自建立以来，主动借鉴国内外先进的管理经验，参照武清开发区管理制度，根据本部门工作开展的实际，建立健全了较为科学严谨的多项管理制度。2014 年 9 月，将各项管理制度正式编制了《武清商务区总公司机关行政管理制度汇编》，并开始实施。使商务区各项工作纳入了制度化、规范化管理的轨道。

第一节 会议组织

一、总经理办公会制度

（一）会前筹备

1. 参会人员。总经理办公会议由公司领导班子成员参加，综合部部长列席，根据会议需要可要求相关部门部长列席。

2. 议题确定。各分管副职需提交的议题，由综合部收集报总经理审定，总经理根据议题确定是否召开。

3. 材料报送。列入会议研究的议题材料，由相关部门起草，经分管副职审定后送综合部。对于篇幅较长、问题较为复杂或有其它特殊要求的议题材料，相关部门要在会议召开前 1 天送班子成员审阅。

4. 会议通知。会议时间、地点、议题确定后，由综合部通知参会人员。班子成员因特殊情况不能参会，应向总经理请假。

（二）会中服务

1. 会议正式开始前，综合部分发会议议题材料。

2. 综合部做好会议记录，确保记录完整、清晰、准确。

3. 综合部负责会务工作。

（三）会后工作

1. 综合部及时整理会议纪要，由分管副职审核、总经理签发，一般情况下会后 1 天内整理、印发完毕。

2. 会议纪要发至班子成员，需要扩大发放时由总经理决定。

3. 会议记录、纪要按文档管理规范分别存档。会议记录不得复印、摘抄、外传。

二、总经理周例会制度

(一) 会前筹备

1. 会议时间。为提高工作效率，加强沟通协调，促进公司工作及时、有序开展，由总经理召集召开总经理周例会，原则上每周一召开 1 次。

2. 参会人员。总经理周例会由公司领导班子成员参加，综合部部长列席。

3. 资料准备。会前 1 天，每名班子成员将本周工作计划反馈综合部，综合部汇总形成《领导班子成员每周工作计划表》在会议时发放。

(二) 会中议事

1. 各分管副职通报各自分管联系领域重点工作上周推进情况，提出本周主要工作安排意见。

2. 各分管副职提出分管联系领域需要提请审议和报告的重要工作事项、问题和建议。

3. 总经理进行前段工作小结，安排本周重点工作。

三、部长例会制度

（一）会前筹备

1. 会议时间。每月月初召开部长例会，具体时间总经理确定。

2. 参会人员。会议由总经理主持，公司领导班子成员、各部门部长参加。

3. 会议组织。综合部通知会议时间、地点，安排会场。

4. 材料准备。各部门会前撰写当月工作总结和下月工作计划，会前交综合部汇总，会议开始前提交班子成员。

（二）会议内容

1. 听取各部门的上月工作完成情况及本月重点工作计划汇报。

2. 总经理对上月工作完成情况进行点评，对出现的问题提出意见并责成有关部门研究改进。

3. 确定本月重点工作，对完成有困难的工作研究解决办法。

（三）会务工作

1. 各部门在每月 25 日前将当月工作完成情况、下月重点工作计划报综合部汇总。

2. 综合部整理完成本月重点工作计划一览表，在公司内网上公布。

四、会议纪律制度

（一）参会人员必须提前 10 分钟到达会场，不得无故缺席或迟到、早退。

（二）各部门要按会议要求安排出席会议人员，未经主持会议领导同意，不得缺席或安排其他人员代替参会。每次会议要做好签到工作。

（三）参会人员进入会场后应对随身携带的通信工具作消声处理；不准在有重要领导出席的任何会议上接打手机。会议期间禁止会客，禁止无关人员进入会场。

（四）讨论发言或议题汇报，要充分准备，简明扼要，态度鲜明，认真负责；插话要切合主题，不得随意打断别人的发言。

（五）会议决定的事项，凡未确定对外公布的，参会人员要严格保密。会议文件要妥善保管，不宜扩散的散会前要退回。

第二节　工作管理

一、首问负责制度

（一）首问负责制是指第一位接受来访、来电、来信的公司工作人员，必须负责接待、解答、受理或者引导办理有关事项，使有关事项得以及时有效处理。

（二）首问责任人是指服务对象来反映情况、咨询业务、联系工作，本单位第一位被咨询人就是首问责任人；当有两个以上工作人员在一起被询问时，职务高者为首问责任人。

（三）首问责任人要热情礼貌、用语文明；要熟悉本岗位职责和工作流程；要牢固树立服务意识，切实为前来办事人员着想；要体现机关工作人员良好的职业道德和精神风貌。

（四）首问责任人的责任：

1. 属于首问责任人职责范围内的事项，首问责任人要主动询问来访人员咨询事项；属于本部门职责范围的，当具体经办人不在时，首问责任人应先接受下来，并记下前来办事人员的联系方式，再交具体经办人处理。

2. 不属于本单位或本部门职责范围的，首问责任人应告知或尽可能帮助联系承接部门或告知责任人联系方式。

3. 属于电话咨询的，首问责任人应按照上述原则给予答复；属于举报或投诉的，首问责任人应将反映的事项、举报或投诉人姓名、联系电话等要素记录在册，及时向相关领导报告。

4. 首问负责人不得推诿应付，不得拒办职责范围内的事项，不能越权办理职责范围以外事项，更不能违反法律法规和公司相关规定办事。

5. 对首问负责人违反本制度造成工作失误的，按有关规定追究其责任。

二、限时办结制度

（一）限时办结制是指服务对象到公司办事，在符合法律法规和有关规定以及手续齐全的前提下，经办部门或经办人应在规定或承诺的时限内办结其所诉求事项。

（二）各部门要根据职责要求，本着急事急办、特事特办的原则，以法律法规为依据、以公开服务承诺的时限为标准，科学、合理地确定所承办事项的办理时限，严格时间观念，讲诚信，讲效率。

（三）工作人员应举止端庄，服务热情，不准刁难服务对象。

（四）对服务对象要求办理的事项，手续完备、材料齐全、符合规定的，承办人必须严格按照有关规定及时办理；因故不能及时办理的，要向服务对象说明原因。

（五）法规已明确办理时限的，能提前则尽量提前办结。对外已明确承诺办理期限的，必须在承诺时限内办结。

（六）上级机关和领导批示件应按照要求在规定时限内办结，并保证办理质量。

（七）机关工作人员对确需延时办理的事项，应报相关领导审批，并告知诉求人延时办理的理由。

（八）工作人员不准推诿应付，不准拒办职责范围内的事项。

（九）对办事拖拉、无故超过办事时限的，将按照有关规定追究相关责任人的责任。

三、一次性告知制度

（一）对来公司办事（电话咨询）的服务对象，要一次性告知有关的办事程序和要求。

（二）服务对象前来办理事项，承办人应当场审核其有关材料。材料不齐全或不符合要求的，应一次性告知其所需补正的材料。办事人按照告知的要求补正后，承办人员应按时予以办理。

（三）服务对象办理的事项如涉及多个部门，或对相应法律法规不明确等特殊情况，承办人应及时告知，解答或帮助咨询，使其知悉有关情况。

（四）一次性告知应坚持服务对象至上、热情服务，为服务对象提供便利的原则。

（五）对未能一次性告知清楚，致使服务对象跑第二趟而引起投诉的，将按照有关规定追究相关责任人的责任。

四、督查制度

（一）督查内容。包括公司年度重点工程工作、公司承担的各项区级重点工程工作、总经理办公会议定的重点工程工作、部长例会议定的每月重点工程工作、公司主要领导交办的督查项目。

（二）督查责任。实施逐级负责机制，责任部门对分管副职负责，分管副职对总经理负责。

（三）督查联络员。各部门须指定唯一督查联络员，报综合部备案，负责本部门督查项目进展情况汇总和报送。

（四）督查程序

1. 立项。一是年度重点督查项目。每年初综合部根据公司工作要点梳理一批重点工程工作，明确项目名称、主要内容、阶段性目标、完成时间、责任部门、责任领导，经总经理办公会审定后确定为督查项目。二是会议议定重点督查项目。总经理办公会、总经理周例会、部长例会、现场联查等会议结束后 2 天内，综合部将会议议定重要事项和主要领导交办事项。三是区督查部门发办项目。

2. 发办。一是综合部根据《年度重点工程工作细化分解表》进行全年督查。二是综合部汇总会议议定重点督查项目形成《督查专报》发各部门和分管副职。三是综合部收到区督查部门发办项目后，经请示总经理，分发相关部门。

3. 催办。一是年度重点督查项目，每月 25 日综合部整理当月项目进展情况，对突出问题形成督查建议，以书面形式报公司主要领导。二是会议议定重点督查项目，各督查联络员要根据每期《督查专报》及时自行梳理本部门督查项目，并分别于每月 25 日将进展情况报送综合部。综合部汇总后报公司主要领导。三是区督查部门发办项目，各相关部门要做好督办事项办理，督查联络员配合综合部做好向区督查部门事项回复工作。

4. 督促。综合部对每个督查项目进行跟踪督查，特别是做好关键时期和关键节点的督查。

5. 反馈。综合部及时将公司主要领导指示精神及时反馈到各相关分管副职和责任部门，根据时限要求进行催促和检查。

第三节 综合管理

一、厉行节俭制度

（一）严格财产购置、办公用品购置、招待费、差旅费的审批。

（二）节约用水。全体员工树立节约用水意识，杜绝浪费，爱护用水设施，遇到漏水现象及时报修。

（三）节约耗材。提倡双面用纸，推进无纸化办公，提倡修旧利废，强化文印耗材管理。

（四）节约用车。工作期间，尽量减少不必要公务车出驶台次，提高使用效率，对于集体活动，由综合部统一安排乘车。

（五）节约餐桌。量食而取，不得浪费。

二、用电管理制度

（一）为保证公司机关日常用电需要，最大限度地节约用电成本，减少电能的直接和间接损耗，实现合理利用和发挥用电效率之宗旨，根据公司实际，制定本办法。

（二）本办法用电范围主要包括办公区照明用电、电脑用电、饮水机用电及会议室、走廊、宿舍用电等。日常用电管理对象包括各类灯具、打印设备、电动工具、饮水机、空调等。

（三）各部门各自负责本区域内的用电工作。办公用电、电脑用电、饮水机、会议室用电实行各部门专人负责制。

（四）注意节约用电，尽量使用自然光。不用时随手关灯，人少时关闭部分照明灯。不准在办公室里使用任何个人用大电量电器。公司所有办公场所要根据日光照度的变化和实际需要开关照明灯，及时关闭电源开关，白天日光充足情况下一般不开灯或分区开灯办公，杜绝“长明灯”现象。下班后，工作人员尤其是最后一个离开工作场所的，要自觉检查并关闭空调、电脑、照明灯等所有用电设备，以杜绝浪费。

（五）空调开启后不可开门办公，离开办公室时要关好空调器开关、关上门。夏季室温不高于 26 度，不可以开启空调设备。

（六）不得擅自改装、加装、拆卸供电设施。禁止私拉、乱接电源和宽带网线。办公室严禁乱拉、乱接照明灯具，严禁更换和接电源、插座等违章用电行为；严禁在办公场所使用大功率耗电设备，需要时应向综合部申请办理。

（七）禁止随意动用和损坏公共场所配电箱、开关或灯具等用电设施，如有违反规定造成损失或事故的，除加倍赔偿外要追究相应责任。

（八）各部门发生用电故障时要立即通知综合部，不得私自处理，由综合部联系物业管理公司进行处理解决。

（九）结合公司实际情况，综合部每月不定时、不定期对各区域用电情况进行督查，其中会议室、接待室、宿舍、廊灯、饮水机、机房等为重点督查点。在检查中如发现用电隐患应立即上报部门或公司领导。

（十）考核办法。

1. 公司用电由综合部负责日常检查和考核。

2. 综合部对违规用电的相关部门及责任人，进行温馨提醒、个别交流、书面告知、经济处罚等处理。

3. 综合部对待违规用电行为的考核纳入到绩效管理中。

三、会议室使用管理制度

（一）各部门使用会议室前，需在会议召开前 1 ~ 2 天内在公司内网“会议安排”栏目预订，并说明会议内容、时间、人数和使用要求，由综合部统一做出会务安排。特殊情况下需急用的，可告知综合部即时协调，并在内网补录相关情况。

（二）各部门在内网预订会议室时应首先进行查看，避免会议室预订冲突，如取消预订要及时清空网上预订内容，并告知综合部。

（三）会议室使用完毕，使用人要自觉将灯、窗、空调关好，座椅摆放整齐，以维持会议室的整洁。并及时通知服务人员对会议室进行清理、复位，补充消耗品，做到随用随清。

（四）会议室一切公物未经综合部许可，不得随意搬离会议室。

（五）会议室内的各种音像设备由专业人员进行操作。招商部门全体人员及各部门相关人员经培训后可独立进行操作。为延长多媒体会议室设备使用寿命，除重大接待服务人员提前开启多媒体设备外，其余接待在会议开始时自行开启多媒体，并在使用完毕后及时关闭。

四、办公用品管理制度

（一）公司办公用品由综合部统一购置、管理与发放，并指定保管人，保管人不得超标发放，严格履行入库和领物登记手续，做到账目清楚，入、出相符。

（二）各部所需专用设备，按公司财务审批权限报相应领导批准后再行购置。购置后，报财务部备案。

（三）公司的影音设备、共用办公设备由专人使用和保管，其他人不得随意动用。

（四）各部门要控制和合理使用办公用品，杜绝浪费现象。

五、宣传品管理制度

（一）综合部负责宣传品购置、管理。

（二）宣传品的购置或定制要根据公司对外开展业务的需要，由相关部门提出，综合部制定方案，经总经理批准后实施。

（三）采购的宣传品应与公司定位及企业文化相符合，达到提升对外形象的目的；在宣传品的选材和品种上追求简单实用，但要体现公司特色。

（四）宣传品应标有公司 Logo 等公司标志。

（五）宣传品入库、出库应如数登记，注明领用人、领用用途、数量。领取宣传品后因故未送出的，应及时退回综合部，重新登记。

（六）综合部每季度对宣传品进行清点，年底时要进行一次全面盘点。在宣传品数量不足时及时提出补充需求。

六、印章管理制度

（一）管委会、管委会办公室印章为一级管理，须经总经理批准方可使用。商务区总公司印章、天津赛得投资发展有限公司印章为二级管理，经分管副职批准方可使用。

（二）印章使用程序。

1. 合同、协议类及行文文件，经总经理或分管副职签署的可直接到综合部用印，由各部门签署的需填写印章使用申请表，需经分管副职签字到综合部用印。确须紧急用印，须经分管副职通过电话与综合部确认，然后补报印章使用申请表。

2. 为提高效率，各部制定需经常使用印章的文件和事项目录，专人申报，经总经理审批签字后报综合部备案。综合部接各部门专人用章需求后需与备案目录核对，确定无误后填写印章使用登记表，并监督用章。

（三）原则上所有印章均不得携带外出。确需携印章外出办事的，填写印章借用申请表，经分管副职批准后送综合部存档。携印章外出，必须有除司机外的两名公司正式员工同时在场方可使用，用毕及时送还。非公司工作人员不得使用公章。

（四）严禁在空白文档上加盖印章。

（五）因违反印章管理制度给公司造成损失的，视情况给予经济处罚、人事处分直至辞退。

七、档案管理制度

（一）文书、照片、音像和实物等档案由综合部设专人管理，负责档案收集、归档、保存、使用，各部门形成的上述档案应及时送交综合部存档。

（二）公司各部设专人负责本部门的档案收集。凡工作活动中形成的具有保存价值的文件材料均由各部门整理、立卷、归档，并于每年 6 月底前向公司档案室移交上一年度档案。移交时要清点、核实，履行交接手续。

（三）档案查阅必须严格遵守保密法和相关规定，履行借阅手续，按时归还。如需要摘录、复制档案，经有关领导批准后方可进行。要保证案卷的清洁，禁止拆卷、剪裁、涂改、逾期不还，更不得损坏、遗失。因个人原因造成档案损失的，视情况予以经济处罚、人事处分直至辞退。

（四）非工作人员不得随便进入档案库房。档案管理人员要认真落实档案防护措施，保持库房清洁。管理人员应熟悉与档案库有关的水电设施，经常检查。离开库房注意关门落锁，切断照明电源。

八、车辆管理制度

（一）公司车辆由综合部统一管理和安排使用。

（二）各部门业务用车需在公司内网预订，注明用车性质、时间、路线和车型，网上预定后告知综合部。由综合部按“先订先派”原则调度。如因招商工作需要，不论预订先后都予先派。特殊情况下，部门公车统筹使用。

（三）用车人员不准假公济私擅自改变用车性质和行车路线，如有此种行为，司机有权拒绝执行。

（四）严格公车使用。本着主要负责同志保证工作用车，其他班子成员根据工作需要统一调剂使用的原则进行安排。公务用车夜间一律不得在居民区等公共场所停放。不准将公务用车用于私家旅游、接送子女上学、探亲访友、学习驾驶、参与婚丧喜庆等非公务活动。

（五）严禁公车私用。司机本人公车私用或协助其他员工公车私用的，发现一次予以经济处罚和人事处分，发现两次予以辞退。

（六）司机要准时出车，热情服务，及时返程。夜间车辆必须放入地下停车场，保证车辆安全。未经批准司机不得将车开出公司。除公事外，车辆不准在外过夜。因私自将车辆在外过夜造成损失的，视损失情况给予经济处罚直至辞退。

（七）司机要做好车辆的管理和保养。每日收车要认真检查、清洗车辆、加足燃料，使车辆始终保持良好状态，保证随时出车。

（八）车辆修理、购件，必须经分管副职批准。车辆用油实行单车考核，杜绝油料流失。

（九）司机应严格遵守交通规则，不准开斗气车、带病车。出车期间不准饮酒，更不准酒后驾车。由司机原因造成事故的，由个人负经济责任和刑事责任，发生重大事故的予以辞退。

（十）司机以外工作人员不得驾驶公司内车辆。如因违反此规定所引起的一切后果均由个人承担，并给予人事处分直至辞退。

九、精简会议制度

（一）严格会议审批制度。各部门召集企业会议必须报总经理同意，能不开的会议坚决不开，可以合并的合并召开。

（二）与会者须做好会前准备。会议涉及的相关资料要准备充分，力戒空话、套话。要简明扼要，立足实际，具有可行性。

（三）简化会议程序，坚持开短会、讲短话。

（四）严格控制会议支出，压缩会议经费，工作会议一律不摆放花草、不制作背景板。

（五）公司领导不出席一般性的庆祝会、纪念会、表彰会、博览会、研讨会及各类论坛。

十、精简文件制度

（一）严格控制文件发送范围，根据文件内容予以区分，厉行节约，减少发文份数。

（二）可以通过非文件形式传达贯彻的，不发文；缺乏具体意见和措施、不解决实际问题的，不发文；在领导分管范围内已作部署的，不发文；内容相近、体例相似、可以合并的，不单独发文。

（三）提高各类文件质量和效率。各部门下发企业的文件通知，坚持短而精的原则。

（四）加快机关信息化建设，逐步实现文件、通知等公文网络传输和网上办理。

十一、规范出访制度

（一）为加强和规范商务区总公司国内差旅费管理，推进厉行节约反对浪费，参照《党政机关厉行节约反对浪费条例》，制定本制度。

（二）差旅费是指工作人员临时到常驻地以外地区公务出差所发生的城市间交通费、住宿费、伙食补助费和市内交通费。

（三）出差必须按规定报经单位领导批准，从严控制出差人数和天数；严格差旅费预算管理，控制差旅费支出规模；严禁无实质内容、无明确公务目的的差旅活动，严禁以任何名义和方式变相旅游，严禁异地部门间无实质内容的学习交流和考察调研；如有借款需求，出差申请人提前通知财务部，以便财务部进行资金准备。

（四）城市间交通费是指工作人员因公到常驻地以外地区出差乘坐火车、轮船、飞机等交通工具所发生的费用；出差应考虑安全、效率和经济等因素选择合适的交通工具，不论是选择飞机、火车、汽车或其他任何交通工具，均须在出差申请单上列明，并经过批准；出差员工的主要行程主要交通工具（包括飞机票，火车票等）应通过公司指定的部门指定的供应商进行购买并统一报销。特殊情况必须经过主管副总经理和总经理批准后可以自行购买；到出差目的地有多种交通工具可选择时，出差人员在不影响公务、确保安全的前提下，应当选乘经济便捷的交通工具；乘坐飞机时，民航发展基金、燃油附加费可以凭据报销；乘坐飞机、火车、轮船等交通工具时，每人次可以购买交通意外保险一份。所在单位统一购买交通意外保险的，不再重复购买。

1. 选择飞机出行时，应选择经济舱；

2. 选择高铁 / 动车出行时，应选择二等座。全列软席列车二等软座；

3. 选择火车出行时，应选择普通座；

4. 选择轮船出行时，应选择三等舱；

5. 其他交通工具，凭据报销；

6. 未按规定等级乘坐交通工具的，超支部分由个人自理。

（五）住宿费是指工作人员因公出差期间入住宾馆（包括饭店、招待所）发生的房租费用；出差人员应当根据安全、经济、便捷的原则，选择三星以下宾馆及快捷酒店住宿；如果公司可以提供统一的酒店预订的资源，或者接待公司有提供价格优惠的签约酒店时，员工应使用该公司的资源。

（六）伙食补助费是指对工作人员在因公出差期间给予的伙食补助费用，早餐报销每餐上限为20元，午餐和晚餐的报销上限为每餐50元，每人每天120元包干使用；伙食补助费按出差天数计算，按规定标准包干使用；出差人员应当自行用餐。凡由接待单位统一安排用餐的，应当向接待单位交纳伙食费；如果酒店的费用不含早餐，员工可以报销每餐上限为20元的早餐费用；如果接待方提供了接待或工作餐，则不给予报销该餐的餐费；海外出差的情况，员工可以凭有效的书面证据报销合理数额的餐费。

（七）市内交通费是指工作人员因公出差期间发生的市内交通费用；市内交通费按出差天数计算，每人每天80元包干使用；出差人员由接待单位或其他单位提供交通工具的，应向接待单位或其他单位交纳相关费用。

（八）报销管理：城市间交通费按乘坐交通工具的等级凭据报销，订票费、经批准发生的签转或退票费、交通意外保险费凭据报销。住宿费在标准限额之内凭发票据实报销。伙食补助费按出差目的地的标准报销，在途期间的伙食补助费按当天最后到达目的地的标准报销。市内交通费按规定标准报销。未按规定开支差旅费的，超支部分由个人自理。

（九）工作人员出差结束后应当及时办理报销手续。差旅费报销时应当提供出差审批单、机票、车票、住宿费发票等凭证。财务部门应当严格按规定审核差旅费开支，对未经批准出差以及超范围、超标准开支的费用不予报销。

（十）出差人员不得向接待单位提出正常公务活动以外的要求，不得在出差期间接受违反规定用公款支付的宴请、游览和非工作需要的参观，不得接受礼品、礼金和土特产品等。

（十一）出差人员外出参加会议、培训，举办单位统一安排食宿的，会议、培训期间的食宿费和市内交通费由会议、培训举办单位按规定统一开支；往返会议、培训地点的差旅费按照规定报销。

十二、规范接待制度

（一）参照《党政机关厉行节约反对浪费条例》《党政机关国内公务接待管理规定》

《天津市党政机关公务接待管理办法》等有关规定，根据商务区实际，制定本制度。

（二）公务接待费，是指为保障员工出席会议、考察调研、执行任务、学习交流、请示汇报工作等国内公务活动确需开支的必要费用，包括住宿费、餐费、交通费、会议费及其他费用。

（三）因正常业务需要接待外部访客时，承办部门应当会同财务部门根据规定的接待范围和标准，拟定接待计划并报主管副总审批。对能够合并的公务活动应统筹接待；

（四）接待活动实行接待清单制度。接待活动结束后，接待部门如实填写接待清单，并由主管副总审签。接待清单包括接待对象的单位、姓名、职务和公务活动项目、时间、场所、费用等内容，作为接待费报销的凭证；

（五）公务接待要与差旅费、会议费管理的有关规定有效衔接。凡是被接待人能够通过差旅费和会议费解决的费用，由被接待人自理，接待费中不得重复开支；

（六）接待对象的住宿应当严格执行差旅、会议管理的有关规定，选择三星以下宾馆及快捷酒店住宿，在定点饭店或内部接待场所安排，执行协议价格。住宿用房以标准间为主，不得超标准安排接待用房，不得额外配发洗漱用品；

（七）确因工作需要，接待单位可提供接待一次，人均不得超过 60 元，并严格控制陪餐人数，接待对象在 10 人以内的，陪餐人数不得超过 3 人；超过 10 人的，陪餐人数不得超过接待对象人数的三分之一；

（八）公务接待用餐应当提供家常菜，不得提供鱼翅、燕窝等高档菜肴和用野生保护动物制作的菜肴，不得提供香烟和高档酒水，不得使用私人会所、高档消费餐饮场所；

（九）公务接待中确需接待单位安排交通工具的，应当安排集中乘车，合理使用车型，严格控制随行车辆；

（十）不得超标准接待，不得私客公待，不得将非公务活动纳入接待范围；不得组织旅游和公务活动无关的参观；不得组织到营业性娱乐场所、健身场所活动；不得安排专场文艺演出；不得以任何名义赠送礼金、礼品、有价证券、纪念品和土特产等；

（十一）如果需要申请人现金结算，申请人必须向用餐地索要发票，并在接待发生后 5 个工作日内报销费用；

（十二）严格执行公务接待费的开支范围和标准，严格控制公务接待费支出总额。不得在公务接待费中列支应当由接待对象承担的差旅、会议、培训等费用；不得以举办会议、培训为名列支、转移、隐匿接待费开支；不得以公务接待名义列支其他支出；

（十三）公务接待费报销凭证应包括财务票据、接待清单等。按规定严格审核，经总经理审批后方可报销。对超标准、超范围开支的公务接待费，一律不予报销。

第四节　人事管理

一、用人管理制度

（一）用人原则：实行聘任制，面向社会、公开招聘、双向选择、能进能出。

（二）新录用员工与公司订立书面劳动合同，个人档案存入区政府人事人才服务部门。

（三）公司负责办理员工职称评定、职务工资定级和调级手续，并将有关材料及时存入员工个人档案。

（四）公司按照国家有关政策规定为员工缴纳社会保险和公积金。

（五）员工有以下情形之一的，依照相关劳动法律法规，经总经理办公会议研究决定予以撤职或辞退：专业知识、技能及实际工作表现被证明不符合继续留用条件的；严重违反总公司规章制度的；严重失职，营私舞弊，给总公司造成重大损失的；不服从公司整体工作安排，工作效率低，影响公司整体工作进度的；服务态度粗劣，刁难企业，严重损害开发区形象和声誉的；同时与其他用人单位建立劳动关系，或虽未与其他用人单位建立劳动关系但存在劳动事实并领取酬金，以致对完成总公司工作任务造成严重影响的；被依法追究刑事责任的。

二、员工考核制度

（一）考核内容：根据总经理办公会研究，按照季度、半年、全年对员工进行考核。其中，第一季度、第三季度为单季度考核；半年、全年为总体考核。考核内容分为两部分：

1. 重点工程（工作）进展情况。年初将重点工程（工作）细化分解，各项任务核配至各部门，落实唯一责任人。考核前对重点工程进展情况进行梳理汇总，形成报告，报总经理办公会议研究。

2. 对全体员工进行民主评议。

（二）考核原则：考核本着公平、公正、公开的原则，考核结果面向全体员工公示。

（三）考核办法：员工考核总分值 100 分，其中，重点工程（工作）完成情况 70 分，民主评议 30 分。

1. 重点工程（工作）完成情况

每年初，由领导班子对各部门承担的重点工程（工作）核定分值。考核前，综合部对各部门重点工程（工作）执行情况进行核准，形成报告，报总经理办公会议研究。凡亏进度项目，由各部门部长向总经理办公会做情况说明，总经理办公会研究打分。

2. 民主评议

按照德、能、勤、绩四项进行评议。评议结果含总经理办公会议评议、部门评议、员工互评三项。

部门评议。由主管副总经理和部长进行评议，分别画票，权重各 10%。

员工互评。全体员工互评打分，取平均值，权重 20%。

总经理办公会议评议。将以上评议结果合并汇总，提交总经理办公会，同时提请总经理办公会评议，权重 60%。

计分方式：员工民主评议考评分数 = 总经理办公会评议分数 ×60%+ 主管副总经理评议分数 ×10%+ 部长评议分数 ×10%+ 员工互评平均分 ×20%

将按以上程序所得民主评议考评分数乘以 30%，所得分数为民主评议的最终分数。

3. 突出贡献奖。

此奖金根据工作绩效情况，由总经理办公会议决定发放范围及金额。

（四）考核结果与绩效奖金挂钩。

（五）考核结果面向全体员工公示。

三、岗位培训制度

（一）培训范围：包括公司全体在岗人员。

（二）培训组织实施：全员培训由综合部统一安排、落实并实施。

（三）培训形式：

1. 入职教育：对新入职人员进行入职教育，了解公司的企业文化、经营理念、发展历程、管理规范和经营业务等。

2. 岗位技能培训：根据公司的发展规划及各部门工作的需求，按专业分工不同对员工进行岗位技能培训，可视实际情况合并举办。

3. 部门内部培训：由各部门根据实际工作需要，对员工进行小规模的、灵活实用的培训。

4. 外派培训：培训地点在公司以外，包括参加各类培训班、管理人员及专业业务人员外出考察等。

（四）参加岗位培训的人员应按时参加学习，做好学习记录。培训过程前、中、后所有记录和数据，由综合部统一收集、整理、存档。

（五）公司投入的培训费用应严格按照培训计划实施，杜绝浪费。

四、考勤管理制度

（一）员工考勤严格依据个人打卡记录计算。

（二）员工每天上午上班、下午下班时各须打卡一次。忘打卡、因公未按时打卡须由当事人写清原因，经部门经理签字后报综合部备案，视为打卡。忘打卡而未备案的，忘打卡一次，按事假半天计算；一日忘打卡两次，按事假1天计算。

（三）员工请假需填报请假单。1个工作日由分管领导审批，2个工作日及以上由总经理审批。批准后的请假单送综合部备案。如遇特殊情况，来不及填报请假单的，事后要补办手续。

（四）员工因公出差不能打卡，须事先写明情况，由分管领导签字后报综合部备案，作为考勤统计依据。

（五）旷工连续2个工作日或全年累计5个工作日的，经总经理办公会研究，给予经济处罚、人事处分直至辞退。

（六）员工有下列情况之一者，视为旷工，经总经理办公会研究，给予经济处罚、人事处分直至辞退：

1. 未经请假或请假未获批准擅离职守者；

2. 请假期满，未续假或续假未获批准而逾期不归者；

3. 请假理由或证明与事实不符者；

4. 不服从分配调动，未按指定时间到职者；

5. 未经批准，擅离岗位从事与本职工作无关的活动者。

五、休假管理制度

（一）病假

1. 病假申请程序、所需证明

员工请病假须填报《请假单》，半个工作日由所在部门部长审批，1个工作日由分管副总审批，2个工作日及以上由总经理审批。员工请病假须提供公司指定的区、县级以上医院的诊断证明，证明需在看病后3个工作日内，附已批准的请假单后递交综合部备案。凡提供虚假材料，一经查出，按旷工处理。

2. 员工休病假期间，公司可以不定期安排员工到指定医院检查，以跟踪员工病情。员工治疗结束或医疗期满的，根据检查结果或劳动能力鉴定结果，公司有权要求员工立即恢复工作或为其重新安排工作岗位上班。员工提供相关依据表明既不能胜任原先从事的工作也不能胜任重新安排的工作，公司将根据国家相关规定予以进一步处理。

3. 病假工资待遇

员工当月休病假累计 10 个工作日以内（含 10 个工作日），按天扣除绩效工资；超过 10 个工作日的，扣除当月全部绩效工资。

（二）事假

1. 事假申请程序

员工请事假须填报请假单，半个工作日由部门经理审批，1 个工作日由分管领导审批，2 个工作日及以上由总经理审批，批准后的请假单在休事假前或休事假后 1 个工作日之内送综合部备案，否则按旷工处理。

2. 事假工资待遇

员工因个人或家庭原因需要，可以向公司申请事假，事假为无薪休假，员工休事假扣除当天全部工资、绩效奖金。

全年（即：1 月 1 日至 12 月 31 日）累计休事假 20 个工作日(含 20 个工作日)以上，不足 60 个工作日的，年终奖金发放 50%；累计休事假 60 个工作日以上(含 60 个工作日)的，年终奖金全部扣除。

（三）带薪年假

1. 带薪年假时间（休假日期不包含法定节假日和公休日）

员工累计工作已满 1 年不满 10 年的，年休假 5 天；已满 10 年不满 20 年的，年休假 10 天；已满 20 年的，年休假 15 天。

下列情形，员工不享受当年的年休假

（1）累计工作满 1 年不满 10 年的员工，请病假累计 2 个月以上的；

（2）累计工作满 10 年不满 20 年的员工，请病假累计 3 个月以上的；

（3）累计工作满 20 年以上的员工，请病假累计 4 个月以上的。

2. 带薪年假申请程序

员工休带薪年假需填写休假申请单，由部长、主管副总经理、总经理逐层审批，并提前半个月将批准的休假申请单送综合部备案。

3. 带薪年假待遇

单位确因工作需要不能安排员工休年假的，经员工本人同意，可以不安排员工休年假。对员工应休未休的年休假天数，单位按照该员工日工资收入的300%支付年假工资报酬。单位安排职工休年假，但是员工因个人原因未申请年假的，单位只支付其正常工资。

（四）婚假、丧假、产假（休假日期包含法定节假日和公休日）

1. 婚假

员工结婚给予3天婚假，晚婚（男25周岁、女23周岁，以结婚证日期为准）给予10天婚假。

2. 丧假

员工的直系亲属（父母、配偶和子女、兄弟姐妹、配偶父母）去世，给予丧假5天（不含路途时间）；非直系亲属（祖父母、外祖父母、兄弟姐妹的配偶、配偶的兄弟姐妹、父母的兄弟姐妹等）去世，给予丧假3天（不含路途时间）。

根据路程远近，由总经理批准，酌情另给予路程假。

3. 产假

产假假期为98天，其中产前休息15天，产后休息83天。晚育（女方24周岁以上生育第一个子女），增加产假30天；难产（剖宫产以及产程中使用吸宫器、产钳等非正常顺产的平产手术者，并需有医院证明），增加产假15天；多胞胎生育，每多生育一胎，增加产假15天。

女方产假期间给予男员工7天的护理假。

有不满一周岁婴儿的女员工，单位每天给予两次哺乳（含人工喂养）时间，每次三十分钟（不含往返途时间）。多胞胎生育的，每多哺乳一个婴儿，每次哺乳时间增加三十分钟。女员工每天两次的哺乳时间，可以合并使用。哺乳时间和往返途中的时间，算作出勤时间。

女员工怀孕流产的，所在单位应当根据医务部门的证明，给予一定时间的产假。女职工怀孕不满4个月流产时，给予15天至30天的产假；怀孕满4个月以上流产者，给予42天产假。

4. 婚假、丧假、产假待遇

婚假、丧假、产假期间工资、奖金照发。超出以上规定时限的，按事假处理。

（五）考核办法

月度工资、奖金依据每月员工考勤统计发放。

带薪年休假补贴、年终奖金依据员工年度考勤汇总情况发放。

第五节　职责标准

一、劳动制度

（一）全体员工要恪守“廉诚、守信、务实、进取”的总要求，自觉加强职业素养，做到爱岗敬业，忠于职守，顾全大局，团结同事，具有奉献精神和创新精神。

（二）作风严谨正派，严守公司秘密。注重仪表，举止文明，严格遵守社交规范和工作语言规范。

（三）守时守约，严格遵守作息时间，按时上班。工作时间不得脱岗、空岗、串岗、闲谈及大声喧哗，不允许做上网购物、浏览无关网页等与本岗无关的事情。临时外出要告知上一级领导。保持通讯 24 小时畅通。

（四）爱护公司财物，损坏公物照价赔偿，故意损坏公物的加倍赔偿。

二、着装制度

（一）员工在工作时间内要佩戴胸卡，注意仪容仪表，总体要求是得体、大方、整洁、颜色搭配协调。

（二）男员工必须着西装，穿正装皮鞋，参加招商接待活动时需戴领带，从事建筑工程类室外工作时，可着便装；不得蓄须、蓄长发。

（三）女员工必须着职业套装，不得穿休闲服、运动服、超短裙或其他有碍观瞻的奇装异服，不允许穿凉拖鞋，可以化淡雅、清新、自然的工作妆。

（四）工作服与便服不得混穿，不得出现披衣、挽袖、卷裤腿等不文雅行为；饰物的佩戴应得当。

（五）着装检查由综合部负责，各部门负责人认真配合，督促部内员工遵守本规定。

三、值班制度

（一）日常值班及节假日值班，由综合部统一安排。值班人员未按时值班的，按旷工处理。因故不能值班者，应委托他人代值并提前向带班领导说明。被委托人未能上岗的，视为委托人空岗。

（二）值班人员负责值班期间公司的安全保卫，处理来访、来文、来电和各种突发事件，遇紧急情况值班人员应妥善处理并及时向带班领导请示报告。

（三）值班人员一律在值班室值班，保持值班室内卫生，并须在公司食堂倒班用餐，不得空岗。值班人员不得带领、容留公司以外的人员在公司内活动。

（四）每天早上 8:00 交接班，值班人员要认真做好值班记录，并将未尽事宜及时交办给接班人员或相关部门。接班人员应提前 10 分钟到岗。

（五）每天下午下班后，值班人员关闭楼梯间各楼层门窗。

（六）按谁值班谁负责的原则，值班人员必须按照规定时间到岗，如擅自离岗，发生事故，要追究带班领导和值班人员的责任。

（七）值班人员请事假，须提前换班并向带班领导汇报，否则按空岗处理。

（八）综合部负责督查值班情况，并定期通报。

四、卫生制度

（一）各部员工保持本部门办公室和所属卫生区清洁。早晨班前 15 分钟为卫生打扫时间。要求做到及时对办公桌椅、电话、电脑、饮水机及室内设施进行除尘与擦拭；个人用品码放整齐，桌面不杂乱；及时倾倒纸篓，更换垃圾袋；及时开窗换气，保持空气清新，无异味；办公室地面应用挤干的拖把清洁，应无积水、无污迹；门窗玻璃及时清洁，视线范围内无污点、印迹及灰尘。

（二）专职保洁人员负责楼道、卫生间等公共区域的卫生保洁工作。

（三）商务中心服务人员负责总经理、副总经理办公室（含休息室）及各会议室的卫生保洁工作。

（四）综合部督促检查专职保洁人员、商务中心服务人员的卫生保洁工作。同时，不定期协调组织各部门员工，对各部办公场所和所属卫生区进行检查评定，将检查结果及共性问题、个性问题在内网上进行通报，通报后三日内对整改情况进行复查，检查结果纳入月考核。

五、保密制度

（一）公司按照《中华人民共和国保守国家秘密法》的有关规定，严格控制秘密知悉范围。全体员工要严守公司内部秘密。对涉及公司的秘密，不该问的不问，不该说的不说。

（二）公司设专职保密员负责公司的定秘、保密工作。

（三）公司建设工程招标资料、招商数据、在谈项目、企业经营状况、财务情况、内部管理制度以及具有保密性质的上级文件均在保密范围内，应由各部门妥善进行保管，任何人不得私自向外公布、泄露。

（四）坚决杜绝门户网站、计算机、存储介质失密、泄密事件发生。

（五）各部门重要数据、资料、文件应在年底由部门整理后于次年六月移交档案室集中保存。

（六）需向上汇报或向外宣传的各种数据，由综合部统一收集整理，经总经理批准后，一口对外。

（七）各部门打印或复印具有秘密性质的文件所产生的废件要及时进行粉碎销毁，不得按普通废品处理。

（八）对违反公司保密制度的人员，给予通报批评、警告直至辞退，情节严重的依照《中华人民共和国保守国家秘密法》的有关规定追究刑事责任。

六、安全保卫制度

（一）总公司安全保卫工作必须贯彻“管理从严、预防为主”的方针，按“谁分管、谁负责”的原则，实行公司统一管理，部门分工负责，人防与技防相结合的综合管理办法。

（二）下班时，要关闭窗户，锁好门窗，现金和贵重物品不得存放在办公室内，发生失窃责任自负。

（三）各部门在工作期间，不准长时间滞留其他人员闲谈或闲转，夜间一律不准在公司留宿他人。

（四）财务部要保证各项技防设备的正常使用，保险柜要严格按规定存放现金或有价证券。

（五）综合部要经常检查防火、防盗设施。夜间和中午值班，要加强楼内和院内各处防护检查。发现可疑现象要立即向值班人员报告，果断处理。对来客来访做到热情接待、严格管理，禁止闲杂人等进入办公楼。

（六）严禁将毒品和易燃、易爆等危险品带入楼内。

（七）综合部负责对安全保卫工作情况进行定期或不定期检查。

七、计算机管理制度

（一）为降低办公成本，最大限度发挥网络支撑服务作用，公司提供开放的计算机网络环境和统一管理服务；员工要服从统一管理，不得擅自调整网络相关设置，不得擅自删除、修改计算机中的程序及文件。

（二）重要数据和文件须保存在公司数据服务器的部门文件夹中，目录设置要条理清晰、检索方便。

（三）保持良好使用习惯，严禁做与工作、学习无关的事，严禁登陆内容不健康的网站。

（四）充分发挥公司内网办公平台作用，积极参与不断完善丰富相关内容。

（五）每天下班时必须关闭计算机。平时注意保持计算机及相关设备的清洁。

第六节　其他

一、机关食堂管理制度

（一）食堂厨师职责

1. 服从领导，准时开饭，服务态度积极、热情、主动。

2. 搞好个人卫生，定期洗澡、理发、剪指甲；操作间内不准吸烟；工作期间着装戴帽并按时清洗。

3. 保持操作间、饭厅地面、墙壁、门窗卫生，做到窗明几净；保持碗柜、冰箱、面板、盆、碗等日常用品的清洁；公用餐具及时消毒。

4. 操作间、餐厅不得有苍蝇、老鼠出现。

5. 保证食品卫生，不用过期及散装调料、食油，生熟分置。

6. 提高厨艺水平，粗菜细做，实行食谱制。

7. 禁止非操作人员进入操作间及仓库，食堂开放时做好岗位职守。

8. 在保证日常时间就餐的同时，保证因公外出人员就餐。

（二）食堂就餐制度

1. 用餐时间：早 6：50—7：45；中 11：45—12：30；晚 17：30—18：10。午餐按综合部规定实行错峰用餐。

2. 用餐人员须排队打饭，不得进入操作间和仓库。

3. 食堂用餐时不得打闹和大声喧哗，讲究个人卫生，维护食堂卫生，爱护餐桌、餐椅等公共设施。

4. 食堂用餐不得饮酒。

5. 公用餐具不得带出餐厅。

（三）客饭申请制度

各部门有客人需要在食堂用餐时，需向综合部申请，同意后方可通知食堂管理人员安排客饭。如遇客人较多应提前一天申请。

二、钥匙管理制度

（一）总公司各类钥匙由综合部统筹管理、复制，公共部位由综合部统一管理；各部门钥匙由部门负责人管理。

（二）如因公需使用公共钥匙，须向综合部说明使用目的，用毕后应立即归还。

（三）各部门负责人负责本部门管理钥匙的使用，不得任意复制或借予非本部门人员使用，钥匙遗失时应立即报备。

三、治丧管理

（一）总公司员工本人（包括离退休人员）、配偶及本人和配偶的父母去世，由总公司副经理以上干部前去吊唁，并以总公司名义敬献花圈或花篮。

（二）吊唁活动由综合部负责组织。

第五章　要闻纪略

2012 年

2 月 18 日，中国天津武清商务区成立，招商引资、规划建设、公司筹建全面启动。

3 月 10 日，商务区领导分别赴天津滨海新区、上海陆家嘴金融贸易区、上海虹桥商务区，以及北京望京科技园，针对园区开发建设、经营模式等进行考察。同期，与部分会计师事务所、学院教授、咨询公司、银行，就园区公司化运作模式进行探讨，初步确定了园区发展模式

4 月 27 日，中兴通信融合通信全球云计算产业基地项目落户商务区。项目规划用地 450 亩，包括产业用地 350 亩，总投资 40 亿元，建成后年销售收入 100 亿元，税收 10 亿元以上，可吸纳 5000 人就业。

5 月 17 日，丹麦驻华大使裴德盛一行考察商务区，与区委书记张勇，区委常委、副区长钟书明，以及商务区主要领导，就生态园区建设进行了探讨。

6 月 11 日，国际汽车园建设协议签署，该项目由美国威特集团投资 50 亿元建设，项目总占地 680 亩，规划建筑面积 54 万平方米，将建设成为集汽车博览、销售、后市场服务、文化体验等多功能于一体的综合汽车园。

6 月 12 日，世纪博爱项目由开发区转入商务区，该项目由北京世纪博爱公司建设，规划用地 70 亩，总投资 10 亿元，规划建设五星级酒店、医疗研究所和信息中心各 1 个。

8 月 8 日，商务区作为协办方，参加了武清开发区在北京主办的投资环境推介会，这是商务区首次参与举办区外招商推介活动。

8 月 22 日，娃哈哈集团董事长宗庆后考察商务区，现场察看了娃哈哈商超地块情况，区委常委、副区长钟书明，商务区总公司总经理张绍锋等陪同。

8 月 23 日，中兴通讯公司与武清区政府签署了合作建设《智・惠武清项目协议》。

11 月 6 日，中共天津市武清区委商务区工作委员会成立，张绍锋任首任工委书记，

翟伟、李震、张耐民任工委委员。

11月22日，由商务部主办、武清商务区承办的国家级经济技术开发区生态园国际合作经验交流会在商务区举行，17家来自各省市的园区负责人参加了交流。

12月5日，题为“大数据背景下的绿色信息服务——下一代数据中心高峰论坛暨太平洋电信信息枢纽中心签约仪式”在天狮健康产业园举行。工业和信息化部、天津市经信委、国内外电信企业专家参加了论坛，国内外30余家主流媒体参与了报道。太平洋电信集团将在商务区建设占地300亩的“天津信息服务产业园”，园区规划建筑面积38万平方米，预计总投资100亿元，可吸引5000名高端人才就业，建成后年税收7亿元。

2013年

3月11日，中国卫星导航定位协会与武清商务区签署战略合作协议，国家战略性科技产业“北斗新兴战略产业园”落户武清商务区。项目占地375亩，重点发展卫星导航、授时、通信等导航系统高新技术产业，吸引一批应用终端机元器件制造、核心芯片研发、应用软件开发及北斗卫星应用配套的相关产业，带动形成上下游产业链，打造产学研一体化的高科技园区。天津市人大常委会副主任荀利军、人大教科文卫委副主任张志方，国家测绘地理信息局党组成员、纪检组长、卫星导航协会会长张荣久，天津市勘察院院长李文春，区领导张勇、李建成、钟书明，卫星导航协会领导周星、苗前军、范京生等出席签约仪式。

4月7日，鹏博士项目落地。该企业主要从事计算机网络技术、电子信息技术、光电一体化技术的开发、咨询、转让业务。

5月21日，团区委批准成立商务区团工委，李晓婷为首任团工委书记。

5月29日，格威特集团落户商务区，拟在商务区打造商务写字楼及沿湖商业街项目，建筑面积约9万平方米，总投资为10亿元，建成后每年可实现税收1亿元。

5月31日，迅联时代新媒体产业园落户商务区签约仪式在武清商务区举行，项目占地约60亩，其中一期迅联博纳和机器人项目科技研发总部占地30亩，二期产业园项目占地30亩，总投资约为6亿元，建成后每年可实现税收1亿元。此项目将国际化理念与本地市场需求相结合，专注网络整合营销传播服务，包括网络营销策略、媒介计划及购买、视觉创意设计等数字营销服务。

6月5日，中绿创投基金落户商务区，该项目主要投资具有上市潜力的科技型的成长型中小企业。项目一期占地 40 亩，二期占地 40 亩，总投资约 5 亿元，建成后每年可实现税收 2 亿元。

7 月 8 日，中信集团金石基金管理公司落户商务区，项目一期注册资本 1 亿元，二期计划注资 50 亿元，筹集并管理客户资金进行股权投资，同时为客户提供股权投资的财务顾问服务。

8 月 28 日，由武清商务区主办、天津鑫隆股权投资基金有限公司承办的“资润武清·创富天下”武清区企业香港上市融资论坛在天鹅湖国际会议中心举行。活动中，10 余位业内专家发表了主题演讲，200 余家企业代表参加了活动。区委书记张勇发表致辞。

11 月 11 日。商务区生态示范园区建设启动，该项目全面借鉴中新生态城模式。武清区政府与中新天津生态城管委会签署《合作建设武清生态示范园区战略合作协议》，区委常委、副区长钟书明代表武清区政府签约。同时，武清商务区总公司与天津生态城投资开发有限公司签署《合作建设武清商务区生态示范园区框架协议》。

11 月 19 日，武清商务区举行哈尔滨工业大学研究所天津研发中心揭牌仪式。该研发中心将主要在工业机器人和工业自动化领域为企业提供技术咨询与服务，根据企业实际情况，制定配套设备研发方案，并帮助企业联系对接机器人生产厂家。

12 月 6 日，天津市武清商务区管理委员会成立，由区委书记张勇任管委会主任，区委常委、副区长钟书明任管委会副主任，管委会办公室设在商务区总公司。

12 月 7 日，商务区企业兴天花园云谷品牌推介活动举行，来自全国多个行业的专家悉数到场，数十家媒体齐聚一堂，作为兴天公司在武清首发的全新科技园区项目“花园云谷”举行了盛大的品牌发布会。会后，30 余家企业与兴天公司签订合作协议，启动注册 10 余家。

12 月 28 日，商务区总公司与北京随锐科技有限公司签约。该公司为国内领先的“三网融合”平台视频通信产品提供商、基于三网融合公共网的视频云平台及视频云服务的提供商。

是年，商务区全年累计吸引注册资金 29 亿元，固定资产投资 20.3 亿元，税收 5108 万元，引进科技型中小企业 52 家。其中，招商引资成效显著，全年引进项目 150 余个，总投资超过 300 亿元，其中，50 亿元以上项目 1 个，娃哈哈商超；10 亿元以上 5 个，分别为国际汽车园、奥吉通“导航定位公共服务平台”、民生银行中民交通管理中心、中绿创投基金、世纪博爱。

是年，商务区服务品牌“标准化服务，高效贴心”，被评为区级“满意在武清”服务品牌。商务区被区委评为区级宣传思想工作先进集体、区级精神文明建设工作先进集体、区级宣传报道先进集体。

2014 年

1 月 28 日，商务区总公司与美通云动科技有限公司签约，合作打造移动互联网产业基地。将利用三年时间，推动 1 千个样板移动端网站成为国内最有影响力的移动营销样板，并推动北方地区不少于 3 万家企业利用相应移动端网站进行营销。同时，共同筹建“微软创投孵化器”（云适配大厦），孵化器企业年税收不低于 3000 万元。

2 月 25 日，张盈（武清）律师事务所举行揭牌仪式，商务区“企业中介服务中心”启动运营。张盈律师事务所与商务区合作建设企业服务中心，将为企业提供法律和财会、翻译等多元服务，加速提升商务区服务功能环境。

3 月 10 日，武清商务区总公司与华贸置地签订战略合作协议。该项目包括互联网生态研发基地、网商生态体验式仓储物流中心及智能生态生活社区三部分。互联网生态研发基地占地 740 亩，将以国际领先的设计理念，建设生态、个性化的创意办公场所，并通过与配套的生活区和体验式仓储区建设统一的互联网平台，实现办公、生活与社交线上、线下的互动体验。占地 1500 亩的生态体验式仓储物流中心，主要是在为研发基地办公的网商提供现代仓储和配送物流中心的基础上，与网商线下体验区、创意餐饮、现代物流体验式旅游相结合的新兴物流中心。智能生态社区为生活区，占地 840 亩，是为研发基地办公人员打造的及智能住宅和 O2O 社区商业为一体的互联网生活社区，社区建立了统一的互联网平台，实现对住宅安全、生活设施的远程控制和互动，在线订餐与送餐，线上、线下购物与社交体验，提供给互联网研发人员需要的生活环境。

4 月 10 日，武清商务区总公司与国内四家顶级招商中介机构签署合作协议。分别为德勤华永会计师事务所、天津滨海柜台交易市场股份公司、天津中天对外服务有限公司、长江证券公司。

7 月 18 日，武清商务区与北京 MBA 联盟签约成立“北京 MBA 联盟创业孵化基地”，双方将共同为北京 MBA 联盟成员搭建创新创业平台和交流学习中心，并提供工商注册、咨询引导、政策扶持、投资奖励等一系列配套服务。

7 月 19 日，天津武清商务区举办“天津移动互联网产业基地”揭牌仪式。天津移动互联网产业基地是天津武清商务区与云适配－美通云动（北京）科技公司联手打造的高科技产业基地项目。

8月23日，京津自主创新高峰论坛暨中关村·武清创业学院揭牌仪式在武清商务区举行。活动由武清商务区与中关村自主品牌创新发展协会联合主办，区委书记张勇，区委常委、副区长钟书明，以及发改委、商务委、工商局、招商局、商务区负责人出席。

9月26日，第六届金鼎创意传播国际大奖终审在天津武清商务区精彩谢幕。来自北京、上海、广州、香港以及台湾地区等极具影响力和专业水准的21位评审老师经过12个小时奋战，共有56件案例从318件有效案例中脱颖而出，获奖比17.61%。大奖立足“科技改变传播”，金鼎创意传播国际大奖以其精准的定位和视角成为业内颇具特色的奖项，参赛案例侧重新技术应用和新传播手段。

10月27日，天津武清商务区与天津涵玉生物科技有限公司正式签定投资建设合作协议。计划投资6亿元建设涵玉干细胞研发基地，建成后，每年实现税收1亿元。

12月20日，中瑞新源能源科技（天津）股份有限公司股份制改造完成，这是商务区第一家完成股份制改造的企业，该企业改造由知名券商长江证券股份有限公司辅导完成。

2015年

1月1日，招商局网谷·企业街区建设加速推进。由招商局蛇口工业区与中兴通讯下属网信集团合作，共同投资在武清商务区建设集研发孵化、商务办公为一体的云计算产业基地，包括1栋展示中心、3栋研发楼、41栋云联盟楼宇及部分商业项目。兴天通讯公司为园区新一代信息技术业务运营公司，主要研发云计算、智慧城市、大数据等产业。先后参与了天津市建设全国供热示范城市的供热计量信息化工程、武清区智·惠武清建设、杨村一中智慧校园、武清文博馆智慧化系统、商务区国际企业社区的智慧化建设等。

5月2日，举办了中华之梦创业大赛。此次大赛是在“大众创业、万众创新”时代大背景下，依托国家“互联网+”行动计划，打造的最富活力的创智投三方深度合作平台。“开放、融资、融智”是此次大赛主题。大赛由商务区联合中搜网络、华普亿方和洪泰基金联合主办，活动覆盖了全国20个省市，有超过3000个项目参与。红杉、IDG资本、中搜创投等上千家投资机构将为大赛提供过亿元的资金支持。活动共举办了两个赛季，按照初评、复赛、决赛三个阶段进行，商务区承担两个赛季的复赛阶段比赛，决赛在中央电视台举行。活动邀请了10位明星级创业导师、以及300余位导师评审团，为创业者出谋划策。商务区是“中华之梦”创业大赛的产业孵化基地，其17万平方米的国际企业社区成为创新创业企业的孵化载体。共有21个参赛项目落户商务区，落实创业投资资金4亿元。

6月19日，扎实推进“三严三实”专题教育活动。严格按照上级党组织工作部署，全面深入开展了“三严三实”专题教育活动，既作为群众路线教育活动延展深化，也是持续深入推进总公司思想政治建设和作风建设的重要举措。活动开展与开发建设等中心工作有机结合起来。狠抓了思想政治教育，针对区委书记王小宁讲党课内容，工委召开了专题会议进行学习讨论，对商务区专题教育活动进行了动员部署。工委书记、各位工委委员先后在分管部门范围内讲了党课，班子成员的党课紧贴实际，深入浅出的讲解了“三严三实”专题教育的重大意义和深刻内涵。学习期间，集中研讨了焦裕禄、孔繁森、杨善洲等先进典型，以及周永康、薄熙来、徐才厚，天津市的武长顺、沈东海、马白玉等反面事例，从正反两方面汲取教训、自警自省。按照区委安排，深入组织开展了三个阶段的专题学习研讨活动，每一个阶段，班子成员均根据自身工作，深入企业进行调研，调研中累计召开座谈会12次、发放征求意见信200余封，共征求基层意见60余条，经汇总为17项，有针对性的制定了整改措施。同时，针对三个专题，先后组织班子成员进行了研讨，有力推动了专题教育活动下延至基层。各位班子成员结合专题研讨情况，对照党章，以及正反两方面典型，联系个人思想、工作、生活和作风实际，深入查摆了自身存在的“不严不实”问题八个方面15项，全部实现即知即改。

7月1日，海达大厦竣工。海达大厦是商务区首个竣工产业项目，项目占地18.75亩，建筑面积2.1万平方米。为海达集团投资建设，建成后将该集团总部及下属子公司行政办公迁入。

8月1日，赛得物业公司实现运营。天津赛得物业服务有限公司是天津赛得投资发展有限公司的全资子公司。2015年起，全面接管国际企业社区物业管理服务，为国际企业社区物业设施提供管理，为入驻国际企业社区的企业提供一流物业服务。该公司服务标准全面借鉴物业管理巨头——戴德梁行丰富的全球化物业管理经验。公司内设综合部、客服部、秩序部、保洁部、工程部5个部门，员工24人，全部公开招聘；秩序及保洁人员91人，专业外委管理，为国际企业社区达到物业一级服务标准提供了强有力保障。

8月1日，智慧硅谷众创空间启动运营。“智慧硅谷·众创空间”由微天下（天津）科技孵化器公司负责运营，该项目注册资金30万元，多家投资人共同发起设立，是具有金融属性的创新型企业孵化平台。该公司致力于帮助创业企业实现级待遇私有数据中心的全IT运营环境，助力其在创业初期即实现管理、财税、人力、专利、数据资源等保障体系标准化的高速发展。为投资人和投资机构提供标准化财账数据交换接口，已实现投前项目信息分析、投中尽职调查信息披露、投后的实时财务监管。至2016年在孵项目10余个。

9月12日，组织了“港京汽车拉力赛武清行”暨V1汽车世界项目启动仪式。拉力赛车队自9月12日从香港发车，经深圳、韶关、长沙、武汉、郑州、保定各站的比赛后，于 9月24日抵达武清，25日天津至北京赛段比赛发车。同时，启动了V1汽车世界项目建设，该项目建成后将拥有超过50万平方米的建筑面积，其中包括一条长4公里的国际汽车联合会认证的G2赛道；集合了多个世界知名品牌汽车的4S / 2S店，一条800米的具有路况选择系统的专属四驱越野试驾体验车道；以及私人尊享的高端汽车俱乐部；还有最先进的活动设施，以及许多其他汽车相关业务。V1汽车世界将成为中国第一个以汽车行业发展为主题的项目，主要着重于独家限量的汽车休闲和娱乐领域。私人尊享的高端汽车俱乐部的入会机制采用邀请制，将配套建造会员专属大厦，具有温度调节功能的高科技停车场区域，并且直接连接赛道。此外V1汽车世界还配备了专业级的卡丁车跑道，汽车主题的豪华精品酒店，大型的会议、展览中心以及汽车文化主题博物馆，馆内将展出经典款式且极具标志性品牌的老爷车等，通过这些现代化设施的建设完善了V1汽车世界的功能性。随着赛车运动在中国的崛起，V1汽车世界将成为这项运动发展的主流平台。赛道将会给无论是普通车主还是专业赛车手带来令人血脉贲张的赛车体验。对于赛车运动的初学者也不必担心，V1专业安全驾校用于培训下一代的专业赛车手。

9月15日，天津市委、市政府领导考察商务区。9月15日，市领导到武清商务区国际企业社区视察。仔细听取园区规划建设情况，要求园区明确主导产业，引进重点研究院所和龙头企业，带动集群发展。在智慧硅谷众创空间，市领导来到并行科技、爱链科技等企业，与企业负责人进行了交流，详细了解创业思路，勉励并行科技公司扎下根来，充分运用大数据分析、人才等优势，成为该领域领军者。在爱链科技公司，市领导观看了声控机器人应用展示，希望创业者紧盯市场，拓展业务，用好扶持政策，尽快发展壮大。随锐科技股份有限公司从事视频通讯设备的研发、设计、服务等业务，市领导认真察看了企业创新成果展示后，希望将智慧视频广泛应用于远程教育、安全生产监控等方面，更好实现经济效益和社会效益。

11月11日，武汉大学天津研究院落户商务区 。武清区政府与武汉大学签署合作仪式。科技合作重点涵盖科技成果转化、技术研发和产业升级、创建众创空间、高层次人才培养、推动科研项目和人才交流等方面。武汉大学将就“先进彩色激光雷达产业化基地”和“卫星遥感大气监测京津冀研发中心”两个重大科研成果转化，与武清商务区进行研究，并就将武清商务区建设成为武汉大学产业化转移基地进行规划设计。先进彩色激光雷达产业化基地，是对彩色三维扫描激光雷达技术进行产业化发展，投产后将实现三维空间信息与地物色彩信息的同步获取。该技术是智慧城市的重要技术革新，目前处于国际领先地位，也是光电产业的升级发展，可拉动上下游产业聚集，完善商务区新一代信息技术产业链条。卫星遥感大气监测京津冀研发中心，是依托京津冀一体化协同发展国家战略，结合交通、大气治理等一体化需求，开展遥感探测硬件技术产品、卫星遥感和大气监测系统应用、相关数据处理和分发等研发工作，同时，为“智慧武清”建设提供高标准的大气污染监测网络和管理系统。

12月3日，中瑞新源在“新三板”挂牌上市。中瑞新源于12月3日在“新三板”挂牌上市，长江证券为其主办券商。中瑞新源能源科技（天津）股份有限公司是由国家发改委、财政部审批备案的一家专业节能服务公司；天津节能协会理事单位，是西门子、施耐德电气的战略合作伙伴，并与天津大学有着长期的友好合作，凭借西门子、施耐德电气在全球100多个国家提供整体解决方案的能力，尤其是在能源与基础设施、工业过程控制、楼宇自动化和数据中心与网络等市场处于世界领先地位，也借助着天津大学等高校的科研能力，为天津及全国的工业和建筑企业客户提供安全、可靠、高效的能源管理、楼宇自控和安防服务。

2016年

4月12日，由北京市科学技术研究院、天津市科委、武清区政府合作建设的京津科学技术研究院，首批25家北京科学技术研究院院属企业考察团到开发区商务区考察。考察团听取了商务区对园区发展、相关政策、办公服务的情况介绍，实地考察了京津科学技术研究院选址现场，以及商务区的发展环境。北京市科学技术研究院条件处、北京市电加工研究所、北京营养源研究所、北京富迪创业科技、北京北斗融科5家院属企业和部门初步确定入驻研究院。

5月26日，武清商务区被市人才工作领导小组、市人力社保局、市外国专家局联合批准为“天津市留学人员创业园”，成为全市现有的17家留创园之一。此次被评为

市级留创园之后，可享受国家、市级科技扶持、人才奖励、项目推介等多重优惠政策，

1—6 月，商务区突出高端定位，狠抓产业聚集，实现了时间过半、任务超过半。累计完成一般预算收入 1.143 亿元，完成全年任务的 51.7%，同比增长 34.11%；三级财政收入 3.03 亿元，完成全年任务的 50.5%，同比增长 19.52%；服务业增加值 45.63 亿元，完成全年任务的 35.1%，同比增长 13.06%；固定资产投资 57.62 亿元，完成全年任务的 52.38%，同比增长 11.45%；引资到位额 36.08 亿元，完成全年任务的 120%，引进科技型中小企业 45 家。重点做好了三项工作：一是狠抓创业生态，以市级留创园、市级众创空间为抓手，重点抓实留学人员创业、众创空间孵化、高校院所孵化等工作，引进海外创业项目 7 家，众创空间孵化 5 家、毕业 2 家，院所孵化 4 家。二是狠抓主导产业聚集，引进信息技术、文化创意等产业项目 30 余个、现代金融项目 6 个，金融产业规模首次突破 160 亿元。三是狠抓载体平台提升，扎实推进了国际企业社区东区、招商局网谷、V1 汽车世界等项目建设，开竣工面积 60 余万平方米。

7 月 19 日，商务区总公司与北京光盒力量动漫科技有限公司签订合作协议，该企业的动漫产业基地落户商务区。光盒力量有限公司是总部位于北京，高速成长且极具潜力的动漫及文化娱乐产业公司，是中国最大的以内容为驱动的少儿动漫内容提供商。公司主营业务为动画及游戏产业，高品质动画年产量达 6000 分钟，拥有国内最顶尖的制作团队及最先进的引擎动画制作专利技术。光盒力量此次入驻商务区国际企业社区，预计可实现年税收 1500 万元，研发人员 200 人，项目的引进，丰富了商务区科技研发产业业态。

7 月 25 日，商务区与金柚网签署合作协议，金柚网北方结算中心落户商务区，全面负责该公司在北方的结算业务，预计可实现年税收 1000 万元。

8 月 1 日，商务区与中航天元防务技术（北京）有限公司签署合作协议，中航天元研发中心和结算中心正式落地商务区。该项目将入驻商务区国际企业社区 A5 号楼，办公面积 2500 平方米，办公人员 90 人，预计可实现年销售额 2 亿元，税收 1500 万元。

8 月 15 日，商务区总公司安全生产形势健康稳定，各项安全管理工作有序展开。一是开展“夏季安全大检查”、启动“深入开展安全生产大检查”以来，完成辖区 39 处企业、工地等责任主体 3 次全覆盖检查，发现隐患问题 153 处，全部完成整改或已制定整改计划，实现隐患闭环管理。二是完成安全生产教育培训、职业健康培训、预防夏季灾害性天气培训等多种教育培训，发放宣传材料 300 余份，组织 100 余人次进行应急救援演练。三是投资 19 万元购买第三方安全技术服务，至 2016 年年底辖区安

全风险评估已进入收尾阶段。

8月18日，为给企业提供良好的法律援助服务，提高企业的服务水平，优化园区服务环境，商务区在张盈律师事务所举办了“双万双服”大型座谈会。会上，邀请地税、司法、质量监督、妇联、团委等部门，对与会的50余家企业进行了现场专业培训，同时与企业负责人就企业发展中的问题进行了座谈，企业共提出各类问题21余件，现场解决17件。

8月23日，商务区认真落实区重点工作推动会议精神，在深入学习区领导重要讲话精神的基础上，对照全年重点工作，总结分析，谋划部署，提出确保全年目标任务完成的四项举措。一是继续推动产业聚集，丰富项目信息，优化招商网络，确保年内国际企业社区一期摆满，新引进项目200家以上，新增税收1亿元以上。强化大项目攻坚，重点追踪推动中核电、中能建、中国通广电子等央企次级总部落地，确保年内引进3家以上。二是狠抓京津冀协同发展，突出楼宇土地空间和综合环境优势，努力在聚集科技文创等轻资产总部型项目上取得优势。三是着力提高园区服务质量，以落实“双万双服”活动为总抓手，促进康仁堂、诚通人力、中信金石基金等纳税20强企业稳增长，推动美联盛航、并行科技等初创型企业快速发展，搭建优质的税收梯队。强化产业项目服务，推动V1汽车世界完成赛道核心区建设，促进金晖中心、招商网谷、君利大厦等5个加快建设，确保国际企业社区二期年底投入运营，新增楼宇空间50万平方米以上。四是狠抓党建保障，持续深入学习中共十八届六中全会和市委第十一次党代会精神，牢固树立“四个意识”，切实履行好“两个责任”，落实“两学一做”常态化制度化学习教育，抓好区委巡查意见整改，用风清气正的政治生态为发展提供坚强的组织和纪律保障。

9月20日，至善环保科技与商务区签订合作协议，落户武清商务区。至善环保科技是一家主要研发生产激光设备、激光清洗、工业水处理、热力设备等。

9月28日，北京快道网络有限公司与商务区签署合作协议，落户国际企业社区，办公面积1200余平方米，预计年税收1000万元。快道网络互联网服务平台是由北京快道网络科技公司投资建设的互联网加盟经济服务平台公司，该项目专注于为投资创业者提供匹配优质的加盟连锁中介服务。该公司在国内率先提出了“加盟经济”的服务模式，通过分析研判创业者数据及投资喜好，精准匹配优质加盟连锁项目，并提供创业者保障服务，至年底该公司年营业额超过5亿元，是该领域国内的龙头企业。

第十一篇

人　物

第一章　人物名录

第一节　开发区历任管委会主任、副主任名录表

表 34

届次	姓名	职务	任职时间
第一任	梁文忠	主任	1992.8—1994.7
	邵久武	副主任	1992.8—1994.7
	杨作莹	副主任	1992.8—1994.7
	王树培	副主任	1992.8—1994.7
第二任	邵久武	主任	1994.7—1997.12
	李树宏	副主任	1994.7—1997.12
	王树培	副主任	1994.7—1997.12
第三任	李乃彦	主任	1997.12—2002.11
	王树培	副主任	1997.12—2002.11
第四任	王树培	主任	2002.11—2008.3
	袁桐利	副主任	2002.11—2008.3
第五任	袁桐利	主任	2008.3—2011.11
	李宝锟	副主任	2008.3—2010.6
	张　勇	副主任	2010.6—2014.8
第六任	张 勇	主任	2011.12—2014.8
第七任	郭新华	主任	2015.11—2017.8
第八任	张绍锋	主任	2017.9—

第二节 开发区总公司历任总经理、副总经理名录表

表 35

届次	姓名	职务	任职时间
第一任	王树培	总经理	1992.3—1992.5
第二任	虞东文	总经理	1992.5—2000.12
	王恩成	副总经理	1993.10—2000.12
	刘满授	副总经理	2000.9—2000.12
第三任	张宗启	总经理	2000.12—2002.12
	王恩成	副总经理	2000.12—2002.12
	刘满授	副总经理	2000.12—2002.12
第四任	郭宝联	总经理	2002.12—2005.11
	王恩成	副总经理	2002.12—2005.11
	刘满授	副总经理	2002.12—2004.04
	谢志申	副总经理	2002.12—2005.11
	李良君	副总经理	2012.12—2005.8
第五任	钟书明	总经理	2005.11—2010.8
	王恩成	副总经理	2005.11—2006.9
	李富国	副总经理	2006.10—2010.8
	黄巨山	副总经理	2007.12—2010.8
	李 刚	副总经理	2008.12—2010.8
第六任	刘东海	总经理	2010.8—2014.10
	李富国	副总经理	2010.8—
	黄巨山	副总经理	2010.8—2014.10
	李 刚	副总经理	2010.8—
	翟 伟	副总经理	2010.10—

续表 35

届次	姓名	职务	任职时间
第七任	张绍锋	总经理	2015.11—2017.9
	朱瑞林	副总经理	2015.11—2017.9
	张武民	副总经理	2015.11—2017.9
	王继宾	副总经理	2015.11—2017.9
	孙 浩	副总经理	2016.7—2017.9
	武剑峰	副总经理	2016.7—2017.9
	李鹏程	副总经理	2016.7—2017.9
	郎 聪	副总经理	2016.7—2017.9
第八任	张福旺	总经理	2017.9—
	朱瑞林	副总经理	2017.9—
	张武民	副总经理	2017.9—
	王继宾	副总经理	2017.9—
	孙 浩	副总经理	2017.9—
	武剑峰	副总经理	2017.9—
	李鹏程	副总经理	2017.9—
	郎 聪	副总经理	2017.9—

第三节 中共武清开发区工委历任书记、副书记名录表

表 36

届次	姓名	职务	任职时间
第一任	虞东文	工委书记	2000.12—2006.9
第二任	王恩成	工委书记	2006.9—2008.11
第三任	钟书明	工委书记	2008.11—2011.12
	张绍锋	工委副书记	2008.11—2011.4

续表 36

届次	姓名	职务	任职时间
第四任	刘东海	工委书记	2011.12—2015.10
	张书月	工委副书记	2013.9—2015.10
第五任	郭新华	工委书记	2015.10—2017.1
	张书月	工委副书记	2015.10—2017.8
第六任	张绍锋	工委书记	2017.9—
	张书月	工委副书记	2017.9—

第四节　区级党代会代表、人大代表、政协委员、市级劳动模范

武清开发区自建立以来，历届管委会主任、工委书记、总经理都是武清区（县）的党代会代表，或是人代会代表、政协委员。其中，首任总经理王树培是县长助理、区政府办主任兼任，均是当年的党代会代表、人大会代表。接任王树培总经理职务的虞东文曾是武清区第一二届的区政协委员。王恩成担任开发区工委书记期间还被授予“天津市劳动模范”荣誉称号。张宗启担任总经理期间还是天津市政协委员。驻区企业——天狮集团总裁李金元,则是政协武清区一、二届政协常委,三、四届的政协副主席。本节对 2016 年年底和 2017 年年初，分别召开的武清区五届党代会、人大会代表和政协会委员名单列表如下：

武清区（开发区）五届党代会代表一览表

表 37

序号	姓名	职　务
1	郭新华	开发区工委书记、开发区管委会主任
2	张绍锋	开发区工委委员、天津新技术产业园区武清开发区总公司总经理
3	张书月	开发区工委副书记
4	张广明	天津红日药业股份有限公司党总支书记、总裁助理

续表 37

序号	姓名	职　务
5	王斌斌	中粮包装（天津）有限公司机修工
6	张　喆	天狮集团第六党支部党办副主任、宣传委员

武清区（商务区）五届党代会代表一览表

表 38

序号	姓名	职　务
1	张福旺	商务区工委书记、总公司总经理
2	郑世鹏	兴天通讯技术有限公司方案规划总监

武清区五届人代会代表一览表

表 39

序号	姓名	职　务
1	张绍锋	开发区工委委员、天津新技术产业园区武清开发区总公司总经理

武清区（开发区）五届政协委员一览表

表 40

序号	姓名	职　务
1	张武民	武清开发区总公司副总经理、总会计师
2	王　玉	武清开发区总公司招商一部部长
3	王小萌	武清开发区总公司招商四部副部长
4	赵　岩	武清开发区总公司二次开发部副部长
5	杨志华	滴滴集运（天津）科技股份有限公司董事长

续表 40

序号	姓名	职　务
6	张 斌	麦格昆磁（天津）有限公司副总裁
7	杨 逸	信义玻璃集团副总裁、集团建玻系统分管领导、信义天津事业部负责人
8	方 亮	天津诺禾致源生物信息科技有限公司财务部职员
9	康文宇	维益烘焙产品（天津）有限公司工厂长
10	许德惠	丹佛斯（天津）有限公司总经理

武清区（商务区）五届政协委员一览表

表 41

序号	姓名	职　务
1	李震	商务区工委副书记、总公司副总经理
2	高雷	商务区总公司科技人才服务部副部长（主持工作）
3	刘晓蓉	商务区总公司企业管理服务部员工
4	白冰	兴天通讯技术有限公司，副总裁
5	李治平	天津珞雍空间信息研究院有限公司副院长

天津市劳动模范一览表

表 42

序号	姓名	职　务	荣誉称号	授予单位
1	王恩成	开发区工委书记	天津市劳动模范	天津市人民政府

附：市级劳动模范王恩成简介

1953年12月生于武清。曾任武清区梅厂镇企经委主任。1993年10月调入武清开发区工作，历任副总经理、中共武清开发区工委书记等职。多年来，他党性强、工作勤奋、团结同志、时时处处发挥模范带头作用，成绩显著。尤其在武清开发区工作期间，他积极带领员工在建设开发区工作中，坚持改革创新、艰苦创业、严格管理、科学发展。仅十几年的时间，就在一片荒芜的土地上，建起了环境优美、设施功能齐全、服务高效快捷、经济发展迅速的全市国家级一流园区。成为武清对外开放的窗口、经济发展的“重中之重”、就业再就业的基地。2004年5月，他被评为天津市2004年度市级劳动模范，受到市有关部门的表彰。

第五节　高级职称人员

自建区以来，开发区总公司在招聘、任用管理人员方面，根据建设发展的需要，不断从科研单位、大专院校以及社会各界吸纳了大批高学历、高职称、高素质的人员，加强了员工队伍建设，为开发区健康、稳步发展奠定了坚实的组织基础。

总公司市级职称人员统计表

表43

姓名	职务	职称
张书月	工委副书记	中学高级教师
张耐民	副总经理	高级工程师
武剑峰	副总经理	高级工程师
闫文杰	工委委员、部长	中学高级教师
冯立军	工委委员、部长	高级工程师
魏建东	综合服务部部长	中学高级教师

续表 43

姓名	职务	职称
杨少海	预结算部 部长	高级工程师
杨 英	规划设计部部长	高级工程师
王福东	工程管理部部长	高级工程师
王秀丽	人力资源部部长	高级纳税筹划师
杜文野	工程管理部二级员工	高级工程师

第二章　人物简介

第一节　开发区历任管委会主任简介

梁文忠

1946年11月生于武清。历任河北省兴隆县五指山林场技术员，天津市武清县农林局林业科科长，武清县杨村公社党委书记，天津市武清县副县长，天津市武清县委常委、常务副县长，天津市武清县委副书记、代县长、县长；1992年8月—1994年7月任天津市武清县委书记、县长兼武清开发区管委会主任；天津市农委常务副主任（正局级）；1996年9月任天津市纪委副书记，市监察局局长。天津市人民代表大会常务委员会内务司法办公室主任。市第十四届人大常委。

邵久武

1939年5月生于武清。历任武清县政府办公室主任，武清县委常委、组织部部长，武清县委副书记、县长，1994年7月—1997年12月任武清县委书记兼武清开发区管委会主任。

李乃彦

1946年3月年生于武清。历任东蒲洼乡党委书记，武清县监察局局长，武清县委常委、副县长，1997年12月—2002年11月任武清县委书记、武清区委书记，兼武清开发区管委会主任，天津市政协常委。

王树培

1953年12月生于武清。历任天津市武清县泗村店中学、城关中学教师，天津市武清县政府办公室干部、主任科员，天津市武清县政府办公室副主任，天津市武清县大沙河乡、梅厂镇党委书记，天津市武清县政府办公室主任，天津市武清县县长助理，兼武清开发区总经理；天津市武清县副县长，天津市武清县委常委、副县长，天津市武清县委副书记、县长，天津市武清区委副书记、区长，2002年11月—2008年3月任天津市武清区委书记兼武清开发区管委会主任。天津市委商务工委书记、市商务委员会主任，市外商投资服务中心主任。

中共十七大代表。第八届、九届天津市委委员。天津市第十六届人民代表大会常务委员会委员。

袁桐利

1965年8月生于武清。历任天津远洋公司职员；共青团天津市武清县委干事、常委、副书记、书记；武清县汉沽港乡、杨村镇党委书记；天津市武清县副县长；天津市武清县委常委、副县长；天津市武清区委常委、副区长；天津市武清区委副书记、副区长；

天津市武清区委副书记、区长，天津市武清区委书记、区长、区委书记，2008 年 3 月—2011 年 5 月任武清区委书记期间兼武清开发区管委会主任。后任天津市政府秘书长，武清区委书记；天津市政府秘书长；天津市委常委、市政府秘书长；天津市委常委、滨海新区区委书记；天津市委常委、政法委员会书记、市总工会主席；河北省委常委、省政府副省长、党组副书记；雄安新区筹备工作委员会临时党委书记。

中共十九大代表。

张　勇

1965 年 12 月出生，天津市人，经济学博士后，正高级工程师。历任天津市地铁建设发展公司经理助理，天津地铁管理处副处长、党委委员，天津市地铁总公司副总经理、党委委员，天津市地铁总公司副总经理、地铁投资公司总经理，天津市房地产开发经营集团有限公司常务副总经理，天津市房地产开发经营集团有限公司总经理；2010 年 6 月武清区委副书记、区长。2011 年 5 月任武清区委书记期间兼任武清开发区管委会主任。

郭新华

1966 年 12 月生于武清。历任武清区委办公室副主任、大王古庄镇党委书记，2015 年 11 月—2016 年 12 月武清开发区管委会主任，现任武清区委常委、区委办公室主任。

张绍锋

1971年5月生于武清。历任武清区委办公室秘书科科长，杨村街道办事处副主任、工委委员、工委副书记、政法委副书记、社会治安综合治理委员会副主任，武清开发区管委会办公室副主任、工委副书记，豆张庄镇党委书记、人大主席（兼），武清区商务平台公司筹备组负责人，武清商务区工委书记、总公司总经理，武清开发区总公司总经理、工委书记，2017年8月任武清开发区管委会主任。

第二节　开发区历任总经理简介

王树培

1953年12月出生于武清。历任天津市武清县泗村店中学、城关中学教师；天津市武清县政府办公室干部、主任科员；天津市武清县政府办公室副主任；天津市武清县大沙河乡、梅厂镇党委书记；1992年3月—1992年5月任天津市武清县政府办公室主任、兼武清开发区总公司经理；天津市武清县县长助理，兼武清开发区总经理；天津市武清县副县长；天津市武清县委常委、副县长；天津市武清县委副书记、县长；天津市武清区委副书记、区长；天津市武清区委书记；天津市委商务工委书记、市商务委员会主任，市外商投资服务中心主任。

中共十七大代表。第八届、九届天津市委委员。天津市第十六届人民代表大会常务委员会委员。

虞东文

1951年10月生于武清。历任武清县石各庄镇镇长、党委书记，1992年5月—2000年12月任武清开发区总公司经理，2000年12月—2006年9月任武清开发区工委书记。

张宗启

1961年12月生于武清。历任飞鹰集团公司总经理、董事长；石各庄镇党委副书记、企管办主任；镇党委书记。2000年12月—2002年12月，任武清开发区管委会办公室主任、开发区总公司总经理；天津市武清区副区长；天津市林业局（天津市绿化委员会办公室）局长（主任）。天津市农村工作委员会副主任、兼任天津市林业局（天津市绿化委员会办公室）局长（主任）。

郭宝联

1952年7月出生于武清。历任共青团武清县委副书记、县委宣传部副部长、大碱厂镇党委书记、武清区外经贸委主任；2002年12月—2005年11月任武清区开发区总经理。后任武清区人大常委会副主任。

钟书明

1963 年 7 月生于武清。历任县政府财贸办科员，县政府办公室科员、科长、副主任，上马台镇镇党委书记。2005 年 12 月—2010 年 8 月任区长助理、武清开发区管委会办公室主任、开发区总公司总经理；区委常委、宣传部部长，开发区工委书记、管委办主任、总公司总经理。后任天津市武清区委常委、政府副区长、区委副书记；天津市东丽区政协主席，天津市农业科学院副院长（正院长级）。

刘东海

1968 年 8 月生于武清。历任县委统战部主任科员，梅厂镇党委副书记，杨村街道办事处主任、党委书记；2010 年 8 月任武清开发区总经理；武清开发区工委书记。后任武清区政协副主席、武清区副区长。

张绍锋

1971 年 5 月生于武清。历任武清区委办公室秘书科科长，杨村街道办事处副主任、工委委员、工委副书记、政法委副书记、社会治安综合治理委员会副主任，武清开发区管委会办公室副主任、工委副书记，豆张庄镇党委书记、人大主席（兼），武清区商务平台公司筹备组负责人，武清商务区工委书记、总公司总经理，武清开发区总公司总经理、工委书记，2017 年 8 月任武清开发

区管委会主任。

张福旺

1980年4月生于武清。历任武清区委办公室秘书科科长，外经贸委副主任，共青团天津市武清区委员会书记，上马台镇党委副书记、镇长，商务区工委书记、总公司总经理，2017年7月任武清开发区工委委员、总公司总经理。

附　　录

一次重要的历史性抉择

冯品清

朋友，当你看到今天的中国武清开发区蒸蒸日上、满目辉煌的时候，当你赞美这座京津走廊崛起的科技新城的时候，当你在享受这一新城成果带来生活日益提高变化的时候，你一定会很想知道当年县委、县政府的决策者们为什么要建开发区的诸多往事吧？中国武清开发区建立20周年前夕，在与当年许多当事人反复深入的采访中，我找到了这次事关武清发展的重要的历史性抉择的答案。

驱动来自加快发展的责任感

20世纪80年代末，与中国农村同行的武清，随着改革开放的深入，市场经济大潮的涌动，特别是家庭联产承包责任制的实行，极大地激发了广大农民的热情。作为津郊农业大县，虽然武清农业生产跨入全国先进行列，粮食播种面积占全市四分之一，产量就占了天津郊县的三分之一。但农民的生活也只是步入了衣食无忧的“温饱型”。想寻求更多的收入、奔小康，靠传统的农业生产已经不行了。

面对这一现状，武清县委、县政府一班人在县委书记徐景树、县长梁文忠的带领下，怀着对武清还要大发展，人民生活水平还要再提高的责任感、紧迫感，在步入“温饱型’的基础上，又在苦苦追寻着新的发展之路。他们带领全县干部群众先是按照中央提出的发展乡镇企业的号召，找路子、筹资金、跑项目，轰轰烈烈搞起了乡镇企业，后又借鉴发达地区兴办开发区的经验，在城区北郑庄搞起了“招商场”的开放、开发试验。结果，乡镇企业由于技术含量低、管理水平低、效益低，数量虽然很大，但效果极差。有的甚至负债累累、亏损倒闭。“招商场”也因只招了一批规模小、效益差商贩，以实验效果不大而停滞。县委、县政府一班人意识到，如无新路可走，武清不仅发展慢，在天津区县中也有落后的危险。如何寻求到新的又好又快发展之路，走在天津区县前列？深感责任重大、压力沉重。县委书记徐景树这个从农村基层党支部书记走上县级领导岗位，并曾经创造过全国农业战线一面旗帜的他，更是不服输。日日夜夜地苦苦思索着，探寻着武清新的发展之路。

老市长指点迷津

1986年8月，中国改革开放的总设计师邓小平到天津视察开发区后不久的一天，时任天津市委副书记、市长的李瑞环同志在听取了徐景树同志关于“巩固农村联产承包责任制、乡镇企业发展情况”的汇报后，提出了武清要利用区位、交通优势，想办法发展自己的建议。

1987年8月，徐景树同志赴日本考察，参观了红小豆的生产加工、与美国硅谷齐名的筑波新技术产业园区，令他大开眼界。也使他想起李瑞环市长的指点。不久，天津市绿化工作现场会在武清召开。李瑞环同志及副市长刘晋峰、顾问毛昌五莅临武清。会议中间，与会同志参观了武清港北森林公园。在回城区的路上，徐景树主动向李瑞环提起赴日本考察的感想，并大胆地提出了进一步改革开放，寻求武清发展的想法。李瑞环同志听了连连点头，称赞他思路新、想法好，鼓励他尽快拿出成熟想法，真抓实干。

1989年6月的一天，当选为中共中央政治局常委、书记处书记后的李瑞环同志去北京上任前夕，途经梅厂镇与武清县委、县政府主要领导话别时，李瑞环同志再次提出武清应利用距离北京较近的优势，抓住一些科技专家想进北京又暂时进不去的状况，吸引全国各地科技专家带技术、带项目到武清来发展。武清要想办法为他们搭建平台，寻求新的发展之路的要求。并热诚地表示：“发展中有啥困难，到北京找我，我会尽力帮助解决”。这叫徐景树同志既进一步打开了思路，又十分感动，也为他后来决定申办开发区奠定了重要的思想基础，同时也给在场的武清县其他领导以极大的鼓舞和力量。

机遇源自火炬计划

1990年10月8日，在武清县秋季商品交易会上，前来参加交易会开幕式的市委常委、市科委主任王成怀在与县长梁文忠谈话间透露：国家正在实施的《火炬计划纲要》中要在全国建一批高新技术产业园区，目前全国许多省市自治区都在积极争取，天津也准备申办。并说，武清如果有想法，可以考虑一起申办。梁文忠同志听了后，当天找到县委书记徐景树同志，汇报了王成怀同志透露的这一信息。

徐景树同志听了非常振奋。他说："火炬计划是一项国家实施科技兴国的战略部署，是发挥我国技术力量的优势和潜力，以市场为导向，促进高新技术成果商品化、产业化、国际化的重要载体"。

"火炬计划的重要内容之一，就是发展高新技术产业开发区"。

"它的重点发展领域是，电子信息、新材料、生物技术、光机电一体化、新能源、高效节能与环保"。

……

说到火炬计划，徐景树同志甚至把计划中实施的一些具体措施、如何认定高新技术项目等内容说得十分详细具体。采访中梁文忠介绍说，徐书记虽然文化水平不高，可他对党和国家政策的学习总是那么认真、细致。加上他那过目不忘超人的记忆力，重要文件只要看一遍或听一遍，几乎就印在脑子里了。特别是他对党的不同时期政策的理解能力、与地方实际的结合能力，更显得超群过人，这一点我们这些和他一起工作过的人都心里佩服。所以，这次当梁文忠把市委常委、市科委主任王成怀同志透露的信息汇报给他说到"火炬计划"时，他对火炬计划了解得如此细致也并不奇怪，说明他对火炬计划早已细致认真研究过了，并且有了自己的想法。为此，他当即对梁文忠说："成怀同志给我们带来的信息很重要，这是一次千载难逢的好机遇，我们寻求加快武清发展的出路很可能就在这里"。说着，他大手一挥坚定地说："文忠，申办高新技术产业开发区，我们干"。接着，他又就如何做好这件事说了自己的一些具体打算和想法，并要求立即组织实施行动。

事后不久，县委书记徐景树就主持召开了县委常委扩大会议，由他说了申办开发区的想法，统一了思想，决定申办建立武清开发区。当年11月8日，县政府正式组建了申办开发区专门机构，即园区领导小组、园区办公室。11月28日，县政府责成副县长冯祥生同志带领部分人员到江苏昆山经济技术开发区学习考察，为申办积累经验。

12 月 28 日，在县政府第二会议室召开园区领导小组成员会议，研究了部门任务与人员分工，提出了必须跑步前进，全面迅速开展工作的要求。从此，紧锣密鼓般地拉开了申办武清开发区的序幕。

摘录 作家出版社《京津走廊崛起的科技新城》

徐书记引领我们申办武清开发区

杨作莹

时间飞逝，斗转星移。转眼间，中国天津武清开发区已经到了它的20岁生日。今天，在这片改革开放充满青春活力的热土上，到处工厂林立、人流如织，一派生机盎然。然而，为了它的诞生，作为县里申办工作者之一的我和当年那支团队，既经受了长达近一年的奔波之苦，也亲身感受到了作为创建武清开发区的决策者、时任县委书记的徐景树同志，对申办武清开发区倾注的心血与付出。往事如烟，20年过去了，件件往事却一直在我的脑海里旋绕显现。

接受任务

时间：1991年3月的一天。

地点：坐落于武清城区雍阳东道的县委大院西会议室。

武清县常委扩大会议召开。我作为县人大常委会副主任、县委常委扩大会议成员之一，参加了这次会议。会议结束前，县委书记徐景树同志代表县委核心领导饶有兴致地讲起了要在武清建设开发区的事。介绍过程中，他在详细分析了全县改革、开放、经济社会发展面临的新形势的基础上，大胆提出了武清应当借国家进一步改革开放的大势，利用京津之间强有力的区位优势和人才聚集优势，建设一个开发区的构想，力求使武清经济有一个更快更好的发展。据我所知，当时武清全县的经济发展形势并不乐观，由于受国家经济调控，银根紧缩的影响，刚刚兴起的红红火火的乡镇企业开始萎缩滑坡，较有优势的农业生产也只能解决人们的温饱问题。武清经济发展的速度在区县中也不靠前，居中游位置，即使有些比我们差的区县，也随时有超过我们的可能。

县委书记徐景树同志在武清发展遇到困惑的关键时刻，果断提出了创建武清开发区的设想，让与会人员都觉得是件寻求全县经济发展的好事。当时，国内建开发区的不多，而县、市级还没有一家提出建设开发区的。普遍认为县委书记徐景树同志提出的这件事站得高，看得远，纷纷表示赞成支持。可开发区到底是个什么样子，创建开发区如何的申报审批，怎样去运作管理？大家谁也不清楚。就是在这次会议上，徐书记明确提出由我负责带领几个人去申办开发区的审批项目。我听到后感到责任重大，又想到自己从大学毕业参加工作后，虽然做过农业科技、乡镇、县妇联、县人大等多项工作，就是没具体做过经济工作，对跑申办开发区的审批手续工作，心里更是没底。感到压力很大，当即提出意见，希望领导考虑其它人选。可徐书记却笑笑说："你是县几大领导机关中唯一的女同志，做这项工作你有优势、有魄力。你先去跑，工作中有啥困难和我说，我和你们一起商量。"做工作一直想得周到细致的老书记，对我鼓励一番后继续说："明天你就上岗组织力量去跑。你所负责的县领导包乡分工的下朱庄乡由我接替，人大分管工作交待一下。其他事什么也不要再干了，就一门心思组织人去跑开发区申办。"听到书记的鼓励，想到书记连我今后工作都做了调整安排，我再无选择，只得答应了，但怎么才能跑成创建开发区，我心里却是一片茫然。

在我参加工作后多年的磨砺中，逐步养成了一种习惯，凡是领导交办的事，只要答应了就一定想尽办法地去完成，再加上自己干起工作来是个急脾气，第二天就到了申办开发区的工作岗位，地点在雍阳东道老县政府办公大楼后的第一排平房。并很快组织了有县政协办公室副主任的张建国、县妇联的魏玉红、建委的孟宪强等同志参加的临时筹建开发区办公室人员，投入了武清开发区申办工作之中。

迅速启动

搞开发区申办工作，对于我们这支刚刚组建起来的团队来说，简直是一项"白纸"工程。

起初，由于大家都是从各单位抽调来的，谁也不知道建开发区的申报手续从哪入手，审批程序怎么运作。我们只能摸着石头过河，想一步，就向徐书记汇报一步。徐书记同意了，我们就干一步。而工作紧张忙碌的徐书记，对筹建工作十分支持。每次汇报，他都认真地听取，详细地询问，主动帮我们出主意、想办法。还时常鼓励我们说："建开发区是事关武清发展的大事，又是个新生事物，难度很大。一定要大胆地想，大胆地闯，要想方设法把开发区跑成，为全县人民谋福祉”。这些，让我和工作人员都很感动，决心克服困难，竭尽全力做好工作，完成县里交给我们的任务。

随着工作不断的深入开展，我和几名工作人员逐步领悟到，创建武清开发区是县委书记徐景树从武清未来发展的高度，抓住国家改革开放的好时机，借助全国二十几个省市申报建设高新技术产业园区的机遇，率先在武清县也建设一个国家级开发区。可当时全国想建开发区的省市，有的早已做出完整的规划，有的已先斩后奏地干起了征地、招商引资，边干边跑审批手续。而我们既无现成的规划，又无明确的建设地点，更没有展开招商引资的工作。我逐步感悟到，原来，是徐书记为了实现全县经济发展，在让我们同他一起做一篇“无中生有”的创新发展的大文章呢。领导的意图明确了，我们的工作劲头就有了，思路也随之越来越清晰了。

要想找有关部门审批创建开发区，首先应当有个让领导认可的整体规划。于是，我们迅速找到市政府、市建委和市规划设计院的有关部门负责同志和专业技术人员，邀请他们到武清听取县领导同志的建设开发区的意图想法，并在反复进行实地考察的基础上，几易其稿，很快义务地为武清搞出了一个较为系统完整的创建开发区的规划。

规划做出后，我们按照工作程序，在县委书记徐景树、县长梁文忠的带领下，先后找到了当时任市政府秘书长的房凤友，市委常委、市科委主任王成怀，市科委副主任梁肃等领导同志，很快得到了市有关部门领导的认可支持。并告诉我们要到负责全国开发区审批手续的国家科委所属“火炬计划”办公室沟通，按照国家有关部门要求做好审批手续的准备工作。不久，我们在市、县有关领导的带领下，赴京到开发区审批主管部门的国家科委“火炬计划”办公室，提出了随天津市高新技术产业园区的规划一起，创建天津市高新技术产业园区武清开发区的申请报告。当我们了解到，当时全国有 25 个省市（包括天津高新技术产业园区）待批，而审批手续十分严格，既要符合国家建设开发区的整体规划，又有自我发展的有利条件才能批准，作为申报创建国家级开发区的部门，武清是全国唯一的县级单位，申报工作会难上加难。

了解这一情况后，我们当即向徐书记做了汇报。他听后，沉思了片刻说：“创建国家级的开发区很难，能否跑成我也心里没底。可我们只要有一分希望，也要用百分之百的力气去跑，不跑就死路一条，只有跑成了武清才有大发展的希望啊。”当徐书记听我们介绍，国家负责开发区项目审批的是分管全国“火炬计划”实施，且有着“火炬司令”之称的国家科委副主任李绪鄂同志时，几乎用命令的口气向我们提出要求。他说：“一定要想办法与负责项目审批的国家科委副主任李绪鄂同志联系上，直接向他汇报、沟通，争取得到他的同情、理解和支持。这样，我们就可能由被动变为主动。”

按照徐书记要求，我们决定想办法到北京与李绪鄂主任挂上钩，争取他的支持。后来，我们通过县体委主任刘文林同志，知道他认识的一位国家科委退下来的老干部和李绪鄂主任住邻居，就毫不迟疑地到了北京，在那位老干部的指引下，找到了李绪鄂主任家。事情很不凑巧儿，李绪鄂主任没有在家，我们没有马上退出，而是主动和他的老伴郝大姐聊了起来。当郝大姐知道我们从武清来时，激动地说：“武清我知道，我还在天津工作过呢。那时，从天津到北京经常路过你们杨村”。听到郝大姐曾经有过在天津工作的经历，我们立即续缘，说大家还是老乡呢。顿时气氛活跃了许多，热情好客的郝大姐听了我们要找李绪鄂主任申报创建开发区的事后，不但答应待老伴回来后立即转达，并告诉我们与他家联系的电话号码。

听到我们和主管创建开发区审批手续的李绪鄂主任联系上后，徐书记十分高兴，主动找到市委常委、市科委主任王成怀，并同县长梁文忠一起，带领我们一起到北京李绪鄂主任家，当面汇报武清创建开发区的想法，恳请老领导给予支持。面对市、县领导干部对创建开发区的诚恳态度和热望，这位高级知识分子出身的正部级领导干部很受感动，表示，只要条件具备就给予支持，并答应有机会到武清亲自考察看看。

值得一提的是，创建武清开发区赢得了全县各有关部门的大力支持。县计委、科委等部门通力协作、紧密配合，在规划制定、工作联系等方面都做了大量卓有成效的工作。尤其是时任县计委主任的武文宏、科委主任甄玉新等同志还几次同我们一起奔波，协助我们开展工作。

初见端倪

5月7日的上午，暖风习习，风和日丽。

这一天，国家科委副主任李绪鄂应武清县委、县政府的邀请，决定来武清进行首次实地考察。上午九时，当市长聂璧初，市委常委、市科委主任王成怀等市有关部门领导和徐书记、梁县长等县领导到京津塘高速公路杨村出口迎接时，却迟迟未到，打电话同北京联系，说早上八点就已准时出发了，车从北京到武清走京津塘高速公路半小时就可到达，路上发生了什么谁也不知道，人们为此十分焦急。直到十点多钟，李绪鄂副主任的车队才缓缓驶出京津塘高速公路杨村出口。见面后，才知道随从车队中一辆工作人员乘坐的轿车在高速公路上飞速行驶时爆胎了，但车子和乘坐在车上的工作人员都安然无恙，没有任何损伤。李绪鄂副主任风趣地说："此次来武清有惊无险，武清福地呀。"一句话，很快使在紧张惊恐的人们中间引发出了一阵轻松的欢笑。这一次，县委书记徐景树同志同县长梁文忠一起，首先详细向李绪鄂副主任一行汇报了创建武清开发区的具体规划，而后陪同李绪鄂副主任一行实地察看了拟建开发区规划区的地理位置、环境条件等情况，还考察了武清的杨村第二小学、县医院、商业大厦等城区基础设施建设情况。这次考察，给国家科委火炬计划办公室的同志留下了较为深刻的印象。此后，我们筹建办公室的几个人时常以报送有关材料、询问申报手续等为由，到北京李绪鄂副主任的家中，了解有关部门对武清创建开发区的态度。那时，李副主任在家时我们向他询问，李副主任不在家时，我们就和其老伴郝大姐聊。尤其是和郝大姐聊得很投机，郝大姐弄清我们的来意后，还经常在我们和李副主任谈话时不时插话，支持我们的想法。就这样，在我们的工作队伍里又增添了一份力量。后来，我们了解到李绪鄂副主任开始时对武清创建开发区是持否定态度的。只是后来看到天津市领导大力支持，武清县党政负责同志决心大，工作人员反复进京锲而不舍的态度，才渐渐感动了他，使他逐步转变看法的。

任何事情都不是一帆风顺的，申办开发区也不时传来跌宕起伏、令人担忧的消息。入夏后的一天，国务委员兼国家科委主任宋健一行来到天津，在天津高新技术产业园区筹建处的会议室里，听取市有关部门负责同志汇报，我也被通知参加了这次汇报会。当市有关部门负责同志介绍了武清也在积极筹建开发区时，宋健同志当即指出："国家科委暂不批准县级建科技园区，天津的塘沽有港口和开发区的优势，可以考虑"。市有关部门的负责同志听后忙插话说："塘沽目前还没有提出要求，武清倒要求很迫切"。宋健主任听了没有表态，也没有做出任何解释。这使正在参加汇报会的我和同去的几个人心里感到一片茫然，觉得武清创建开发区的事悬了。回到县里后，我如实把情况向徐书记做了汇报，可他仍不灰心，继续鼓励我们克服困难，想尽办法地接着去跑。

事情到了当年的 11 月，国家有关部门对创建开发区的审批仍然没有动静，作为筹建工作的我们有些焦急。11 月 5 日，当我们听到国家科委的李绪鄂副主任正在河北省沧州地区考察的消息后，立即向徐书记做了汇报。他要求我们尽快去趟沧州，一是向李主任问问创建开发区的审批情况，二是邀老主任返京时顺路来武清做客。这天的下午四点，按照徐书记的安排，我和县长梁文忠同志，在市委常委、市科委主任王成怀、副主任梁肃同志带领下，毫不迟疑，立即驱车前往，并于当天晚上 11 点多钟赶到了河北沧州，找到了国家科委李绪鄂副主任，这使他非常感动。见面后，我们再次汇报武清创建开发区的筹备情况，并邀请李副主任一行在返京途中到武清停留一天。这次“夜闯沧州”的汇报很有成效，李副主任明确表态，原则同意武清创建开发区，让我们看到了希望。第二天，由于工作繁忙，李绪鄂副主任没有到武清来，只是在他们返京时，我们随车队一直把李副主任一行送到京津塘高速公路杨村出口处，才相互告别返回武清。

就这样，经过几个月反反复复的奔波沟通，创建武清开发区的事儿不时传来好消息。北京审批部门的工作人员不时打来电话，或提出对原申报报告修改的补充意见，或询问我们上报文件中弄不清的问题，大有“山雨欲来风满楼”之感。大家都觉得国家有关部门领导快要研究了，创建武清开发区的事儿有希望了，我们每天都期望着会有好消息的传来。一天，国家科委火炬办公室工作人员突然来电话，要求我们对申报报告中的有些文件再做些修改补充，我们向徐书记汇报后，他立即指示我们，按照上级要求抓紧时间办理迅速上报北京，绝不允许让事儿耽误在我们手里。得到徐书记指示后，我们组织有关人员连夜修改、补充申报报告中的有关文件。第二天，也就是 1991 年 12 月 24 日，正当我们准备将修改、补充的文件资料送往北京时，天突然下起了漫天大雪，开汽车去北京雪大、路滑很危险，进京的京津塘高速公路也已封闭。为了不耽误时间，我们只得到杨村火车站乘火车去京报送相关文件资料，到北京后又转乘市区公共汽车，终于赶在审批部门工作人员下班前，顶风冒雪把所需文件交到了有关同志手里，有关部门工作人员对此十分感动，热情地为我们端上热茶，帮我们拍打身上的冰雪。

喜获成功

1991 年 12 月 28 日。

这一天，是我们创建武清开发区筹备组工作人员最激动难忘的日子，也是每个关注申办武清开发区的市、县领导最难忘的日子。喜讯传来，国家有关部门正式批准了全国 25 个省、市、自治区的 26 家国家级开发区的建立。而武清开发区则是此次批准的全国开发区中唯一县办的国家级开发区。当我们把这一消息告诉徐书记时，看得出，他很激动，眼睛里含着激动的泪花，动情地说：“大家没白忙活，总算跑成了，够棒，够棒！说实话，有一段时间我都有些失望了。这回好了，武清今后发展的希望也可能就在这里。”接着，市委常委、市科委主任王成怀，市科委副主任梁肃等领导同志也分别给我们打来电话，表示祝贺。

此时，心潮起伏、激动不已的我，想到了九个月来为申办开发区，市领导的关注与支持，想到了县委徐景树书记一次又一次的断然决策和精心谋划，想到了全县各部门的积极配合，想到了筹建办公室几名工作人员克服种种困难、千辛万苦的奔波，心中久久不能平静，几乎彻夜未眠。同时我也想到，作为创建开发区的决策者的徐书记，此时此刻绝不仅仅是兴奋激动，他会比我们想得更深更远。武清开发区的批准建立，给他带来的还将是如何建设好开发区的新的重担和更大的压力。

随着创建武清开发区的批准，开发区开始步入了奠基准备和建设阶段，我也完成了当初县常委扩大会上交给我的申办工作任务。不久，我当选为县委常委、宣传部部长，也随之离开了火热的开发区建设岗位。但是，我很快听到了县委书记徐景树同志对开发区建设新决策和构想，目睹了在徐书记带领下从 1992 年 6 月 23 日开发区奠基到建设发展的艰难经历，和取得的一个又一个成绩。

如今，武清开发区从批准建立到目前已二十个年头了，二十年来，历届区（县）委、区（县）政府领导继承老书记的遗志，把武清开发区越做越大，越做越强，迎来了 1000 多家国内外企业入驻，年创税收几十个亿，安置 8 万余人就业，成为武清对外开放的重要窗口，经济发展的主发动机，带动产业升级的龙头，安置就业的重要基地。同时，随着武清开发区的日益发展壮大，拉动了武清经济社会、城市化建设的全面发展，跨入了全市发展的“第一集团军”行列，并向着建设京津之间最具实力和竞争力地区的目标昂首挺进。

每当看到武清这些年发生的可喜变化，总是情不自禁地想起了我们的已故县委书记徐景树同志，想到了他当年带领我们申办开发区的往事。试想，如果没有当年以徐书记为核心的县委、县政府的果断决策，没有当年艰苦的付出，就没有武清开发区建设发展的今天，也就没有武清跨越发展、迅速崛起的今天。现在，令人尊敬的老书记徐景树同志已经离开我们九年了，可我们这些曾经和他一起工作奋斗过的人们不会忘记他，我相信所有的武清人也不会忘记他。在武清区发展的历史上，将永远记住他为创建武清开发区所做出的贡献。

摘录 作家出版社《京津走廊崛起的科技新城》

令人难忘的岁月

——访武清开发区第一任总经理王树培

高元勃

时间：2011年3月15日。

地点：中国·天津武清开发区。

阳光灿灿，暖风习习。在中国武清开发区批准建立20周年前夕，走近曾经在这里担任过第一任总经理和管委会主任长达17年之久的原武清区委书记、现任天津市商务工委书记、商务委主任的王树培同志，倾听了他对武清开发区饱含深情的叙述，记下了在那令人难忘的岁月里，他与开发区的一个个感人故事。

拼抢得来的发展机遇

如果把建立武清开发区作为武清发展史上一次千载难逢机遇的话，那么，面对这一机遇武清人又是怎么奋起抢抓，并为之做出了哪些艰辛的努力与付出呢？

时间回放到1991年。

随着改革开放、农村家庭联产承包责任制的实行，作为津郊农业大县的武清，耕地面积占整个天津农业区县的四分之一，粮食产量占三分之一，且有了“津沽粮仓”的美誉和“全国粮食生产先进县”的桂冠。但是，却只是步入了“温饱型”境地，想要更加富裕、实现小康生活，还只是个追寻的梦幻。武清要发展，实现新的跨越，靠种粮、种菜的传统农业不行，靠满腔热情地跑贷款、抓项目办乡镇企业也不行。此时，深圳特区的崛起，珠江三角洲、长江三角洲经济的迅速发展，乃至全国部分地区开发区的建立，似乎让苦苦追寻发展的武清人看到了一丝光亮。

然而，机遇与挑战并存，它不仅需要领导者远见卓识的果断决策，较好的发展基础，还要国家有关部门的认可批准，建立开发区谈何容易？但是，武清人硬是凭着加快发展的强烈责任感，凭着百折不挠、奋力拼搏的精神，经过近一年艰辛的努力，终于让武清人梦想成真，抢到了这一机遇。1991 年 12 月 28 日，经国家科委批准建立“天津市高新技术产业园区武清开发区”，成为全国第一个办在县上的国家级开发区。

回忆当年武清开发区能够得到批准建立，王树培同志告诉我们，至少有这样几个关键条件：

首先是时任县委书记的徐景树同志。是他，审时度势，以加快武清发展的强烈责任感、紧迫感，果断、大胆地提出了建立武清开发区的构想，带领县委、县政府一班人统一思想、做出决策。并组织强有力的工作班子，亲自指挥，想方设法、千方百计争取这一项目的申报批准。

其次是，市领导和市有关部门的热情支持。时任天津市委常委、市科委主任的王成怀同志，从开发区申报的路径，到规划的制定，审批手续的办理，都给予了积极有力的热情帮助指导，并协调市有关部门具体帮助操作办理。与此同时，他还身体力行，亲自带领县有关领导和工作人员到国家有关部门，找主管项目审批的领导同志介绍情况、做审批前的沟通工作。整个审批过程中，他一路走来，无论是紧张忙碌的会议室里谋划与研究，还是建设基地的实地考察现场，无不留下了他的倾心关注与辛劳的身影。

再次是，时任县长的梁文忠同志和县人大常委会副主任的杨作莹同志，以及筹建工作人员的不懈努力。那时，开发区的审批工作，既没有成熟的经验可以借鉴，又没有任何现成的规划、办理手续的方法可以参考。就是在这一无所有的“白纸”工程上，他们一路碰壁，一路探寻，无数次地上京下卫，汇报情况、争取项目。当年 11 月 5 日，事情到了成败的关键时刻，当外出考察的国家科委副主任李绪鄂同志路经并留宿河北沧州时，他们即刻在市委常委、市科委主任王成怀同志的带领下，一起前往沧州，留下了“夜闯沧州”的佳话。也许是武清人创办开发区执着的精神感动了“上帝”，也许是长途跋涉深夜追寻领导汇报工作的行动打动了这位把握审批权的领导者的心，李绪鄂主任竟当场表示了“可以考虑批准”的明朗态度，同时也给前来争取项目的天津市领导和武清人下了一道：“办不好，我要摘牌子”的“震慑令”。让他们既感到振奋，又深感建设开发区的巨大压力。

经过不懈的拼搏努力，1991 年 12 月 28 日，国家科委正式批准建立“天津市高新技术产业园区武清开发区”。

沿着“南巡路”迈出第一步

1992年。

这一年的春天似乎比往年来的更早，中国改革开放总设计师邓小平同志南方谈话的春风，吹醒了祖国大地，也吹暖了每个中国人的心，全国上下又一次唱响了“春天的故事”。刚刚得到批准建立首个县办国家级开发区的武清人，在春风得意的日子里更显得踌躇满志、激情澎湃。

春节刚过，在县委书记徐景树同志的“举全县之力，尽快建设好武清开发区”的号召下，县长梁文忠就带领开发区筹备组负责人杨作莹、县政府办公室主任王树培，以及丁连喜等同志组成的开发区建设考察组，乘上南去的列车，到改革开放的前沿珠江三角洲考察。他们跑深圳、看珠海，踏上了探寻如何建设发展自己的开发区之路。所到之处，给考察组传递的信息是：“小平同志刚走”和小平同志“发展是硬道理”“改革开放的胆子再大一些，步子迈得再快一些……”等鼓舞人心的讲话精神。看到了改革开放前沿人进一步寻求更好更快发展的满怀激情，学到了建设开发区的经验与方法，也使每个考察组成员对自己即将建设的开发区充满信心和力量，憧憬着武清开发区美好的前景与未来。考察组返回的头一天晚上，一向谦和、民主的县长梁文忠就把大家就地召集在一起，询问每个人此行的收获与体会，急切地请大家说说自己对开发区怎么建设、从哪里起步的意见和想法。说到开发区基础设施从哪起步时，有人建议在离城区较近的六支渠北侧建起，有人则主张在京津塘高速公路杨村出口处建设，甚至争论得面红耳赤。回到武清后的第二天，考察组一行就集体跑到开发区现场进行实地勘察，准备在县委常委扩大会上汇报考察结果时，更加准确地说出考察组的具体想法。实地勘察使大家达成了共识，确定了从京津塘高速公路杨村出口处作为开发区起步区的构想。认为，选择这一地区作为起步区，虽然距离城区较远，但它至少有三大优势：一是紧邻103国道和京津塘高速公路出口，有较大的交通优势；二是这里是县里的废弃砖瓦厂，没有农田，不需从农民手里征地，可以尽快投入建设开发；三是位置明显。建设项目一旦开工，就可以让南来北往来的人们看到热火朝天开发区建设的情景，起到对外广告宣传的作用，有利于招商引资。考察组的这一想法很快在不久召开的“开发区建设如何起步”县委常委扩大会专题会议上，得到了赞同批准。

小平同志南方谈话的春风，也给雄心勃勃、寻求新发展的武清注入了强劲动力，激发了武清人建设好开发区的信心和力量。3月初，在县委召开的一次常委扩大会议上，县委书记徐景树同志提出了“举全县之力，尽快建设好武清开发区”的总体要求。并决定由时任县政府办公室主任的王树培兼任开发区第一任总经理。就是在这次会议上，他以新任总经理的身份述说了开发区在未来发展中“着眼长远、适度超前、综合起步、滚动开发”的16字发展方针和具体想法，并向与会同志做了“三年可看，五年可赚”发展目标的承诺。

随着起步区的确立和组织机构的建立，经过一段紧张忙碌的谋划准备，武清开发区很快步入了实质性建设阶段。

6月23日，中国天津武清开发区在起步区内举行了奠基仪式。市委代理书记、市长聂璧初及市有关部门领导参加，为武清开发区剪彩奠基。接着，开发区第一条公路——“开源道”在这里铺开。建筑面积10000平方米的一号标准厂房，在这里动工兴建，拉开了开发区建设发展的序幕。

8月7日，开发区在首都北京人民大会堂内召开新闻发布会。新闻发布会上，除数十家国内外新闻媒体记者参加外，还有众多国家的驻华使节、办事处负责人出席，打开了武清对外开放的窗口，吹响了武清对外招商引资的进军号角。

新机制带来新的活力

“要建设成现代化的高质量的开发区，就必须有一套完整的现代化水平的管理机制作保障，武清开发区正是在这种全新的管理机制运行中迅速建设发展的。”在谈到武清开发区建设管理的话题时，王树培同志深有体会地说：在开发区建立初期，县委书记徐景树同志在与他担任总经理后的一次谈话中表示，县委只任命一个总经理，其他一律由总公司自主决定。他深知，这无疑是对他这个总经理无限的信任，也给这个刚刚建设起步的新区，提供了宽松的政策和大胆改革创新的发展空间。

组织领导机制。本着精干、高效的原则，由国家批准建立的天津市高新技术产业园区武清开发区，以及由市政府批准建立的武清经济开发区，两个开发区一块牌子、一套人马，统称武清开发区。开发区设管委会，管委会主任、副主任由县主要领导兼任，开发区总经理兼任管委会办公室主任。这一组织机构及其领导机制的形成，既体现了开发区在全局发展中的地位与权威性，又实现了开发区在贯彻执行县委、县政府决策谋略与建设发展步伐，以及在对外交往等方面的一致性。同时，开发区的群团组织一律不设，只设综合部、招商部、城管部、建设部、财务部，呈现出一心一意搞管理、抓建设的组织管理格局。

工作人员聘任制。开发区自建区以来，除特殊人才外，在用人上始终采取企业管理式的聘任制，根据工作需要所录人员，一律采取自愿报名、统一考试、集体决定、择优录用的原则，任何部门、任何领导都无权安插工作人员。就这样，开发区建区20年来，从区级领导机关到开发区总公司领导，无一人擅自安排子女或亲属到开发区上班。同时在区内工作人员灌输“职工没有退路，开发区才有出路”的理念，制订了“廉诚守信，务实进取”的区训。实行能上能下、能进能出、不适应辞退的用人机制，确保了每个工作人员尽职尽责、奋发向上的良好的精神状态。开发区建立初期，工作人员很长一段时间保持在18个人左右，大家心往一处想，劲往一处使，各部门相互支持配合，不分昼夜、不分份内份外地工作。逐步形成了分外团结、极富战斗力的集体，区内的18名工作人员，被人们称为“18棵青松”。严格有力的用人机制，也使开发区成为培养干部的“摇篮”。如今这些人中，有的步入区级领导岗位，有的成为乡镇局主要领导干部，有的成为武清其他迅速发展的经济园区领军人物或骨干力量，他们都在武清经济社会发展中发挥了重要作用，做出了卓越贡献。

分配激励机制。即“模糊工资”。开发区工作人员每月的工资收入，除每人统一的生活费公开外，其他一律根据工作质量好差、贡献大小，由部门负责人排队、主管经理核定发放奖金福利数额，总公司核心领导集体讨论决定，率先在全区砸了“铁饭碗”，不再吃“大锅饭”。解决了干多干少、干好干坏一个样的问题。有个锅炉采购项目，一位职工5天没跑下来，而另一名职工只用了2天，且购买价格下降了40%。同一工作中出现的两种截然不同的结果，总公司给了两个人不同的奖励标准，既鞭策教育了两个职工的工作态度，使其心服口服，也教育了大家，激发了全体员工做好工作的积极热情。

招投标机制。上世纪九十年代初的工程建设，项目由谁干、工钱让谁赚，大都是项目工程单位负责人说了算，即使有简单的招投标，也是走形式，存在着严重的漏洞。开发区基础设施建设开始后，在一个自来水管道铺设工程项目洽谈过程中，120万元工程造价迟迟谈不下来，使工程建设项目洽谈陷入僵局。被迫实行工程招投标后，同样是最初接洽的那家建设单位中标，却使工程造价减少了三分之二，只用了40万元。修建开发区第一条柏油马路，由县领导出头，讲了一大套政治意义，工程造价每平米84元，而修建另一条路时，实行招投标后，却使每平米减到了47元。事实很快使开发区的领导层下决心改变传统的工程承包建设方式，一切工程都实行招投标，并坚持“最低标价中标”的原则，从此避免了工程浪费和腐败现象的滋生。在许多地区开发区工程建设项目中屡屡出现贪污腐败的大潮中，武清开发区20年建设工程项目数不胜数，投入建设资金近百亿元，却无一人被染。

封闭式管理。在武清区内，承担行政管理、行政执法的部门和单位大大小小足有几十家，如果这些部门每天都到企业里指手划脚地“开展工作”，势必给企业带来应接不暇、难以承受的压力。为了让入区企业一心一意抓生产、搞经营，县委、县政府制定文件，明确规定开发区内企业实行“封闭式管理”，任何部门、单位都不许以任何理由私自进入开发区，对开放区所属各企业从事检查工作、收取费用等项活动。确需进入企业工作的，必须在开发区总公司工作人员带领下进行。凡必须收取的行政事业性费用，一律由开发区年内一次性统一付给。封闭式管理，真正让区内企业有了宽松的生产经营环境。难怪许多在这里的投资者，纷纷夸赞“在武清开发区干事业心里踏实、有安全感”。

如果说开发区的管理机制的建立，创造了一个现代化的建设团队，保证了区内各项工作的健康有序运行的话？那么，国家有关部门通过的ＩＳＯ９００１质量管理体系认证，就足以说明武清开发区已经步入了与国际接轨的现代化管理轨道。

为投资者服务是永恒的主题

如何保持开发区持续不断地、又好又快地发展？王树培的回答是：“不断优化环境，更好地为投资者服务，是开发区永恒的主题。”在他领导经历的武清开发区十几年间，服务理念不断深化，也推动着开发区各项工作不断向高速、优质发展。

武清开发区是国家有关部门通过的ISO 14001环境管理体系认证的单位。为此，他们从为投资者创造良好的软硬服务环境入手，做出了一系列卓有成效的工作。

硬环境建设做“大手笔”。不说在区内发展的水、电、路、通讯等硬环境建设，也不说从建区初期的“五通一平”到现在的“十一通一平”，只是说说根据开发区建设发展的需要，所做的几项大的环境工程建设，就足以证明开发区人的用心良苦。

——为了确保区内有足够的高质量的水资源供给，投资亿元搞起了“引滦入杨”

工程，把源源不断甘甜洁净的滦河水引入了开发区。

——当陕气入津工程在武清境内通过时，又积极与有关部门联系，投资一亿多元，实施了“陕气入杨”工程，很快让入区企业用上了环保、价廉的燃气。

——在积极同有关部门争取的基础上，投资数千万元建起了环境优美、办公设备现代化的武清海关，为入区企业架起了报关、通关服务桥梁，大大减轻了部分企业的奔波之苦。

——为解决外籍子女入学的困难，培养更多的现代化实用人才，投资一亿多元，建起了从幼儿、小学到初高中的与世界教育接轨的双语制教育学校。

——投资两亿元建起了环境优美、设施配套齐全的“高新公寓”，为外来打工者安了一个温馨的新家园。

这些，无疑给开发区的环境建设提升了档次，增添了靓丽的光彩。

在服务软环境建设方面，开发区从提高工作人员素质入手，首先提出了“投资者是上帝”的理念，并要求每个工作人员充分认识到“上帝是没错的，如果有错误就是我们”的道理。同时提出，每个工作人员面对投资者不许说“不”“不行”“不能”的话，要想方设法、满腔热情、周到细致地为投资者搞好服务。

一次，天狮集团公司在建设初期某工地施工时与总公司工作人员产生了矛盾，天狮公司总经理在不了解真实情况下找到了开发区，总公司不做任何辩解，主动向投资者赔礼道歉，承担全部责任。不久，当天狮老总明白事情真相，发现本公司也存在一定问题时，心中充满感激，更加坚定了他在武清开发区建设发展的决心，直至发展成为今天国内外颇具影响力的跨国集团公司，并每年为武清提供数亿元的税收。台湾世界最大的乐器生产商杰麦集团公司询问投资税收减免政策时，总公司一名工作人员错误地把50年经营一次性减免3年税收，说成每10年减免3年，50年可减免15年税收。即使是这一错误答复，总公司硬是以12年连续每年为该公司代交8万元的免税额为代价，保持了承诺不变，使投资企业倍受感动。

近年来，开发区进一步深化服务，提出了“服务他人就是发展自己”的理念，并把这一理念逐步在全区推广。良好的服务软硬环境赢得了投资者。20年间，逐步形成了电子信息、生物制药、新型建材、机械制造、汽车及零部件五大支柱产业，吸引世界1000多家企业入驻，其中世界500强企业14家，引资总额超过700亿元。

艰辛中闯出稳步健康之路

同全国大大小小的开发区一样，武清开发区也走过了一条艰难跋涉之路，克服了种种难以想象的困难，度过了一个个激流险滩，逐步步入了健康稳步发展的轨道。

招商关。每个开发区人都心里清楚，如果千辛万苦投资建起的开发区没有投资者进入，就成了“无水之源、无本之木”。怎么招商？招那些商家进入？武清开发区为此想尽了办法，奔跑到了大江南北、世界各地。制定了“内资外资，以外资为主；独资合资，以独资为主”的招商引资方针，创造了“以商招商、中介招商、代理招商、网上招商、跟踪招商、领导招商”等多种招商方法。逐步摸索出了一整套如何识别招商骗局、避免盲目招商的经验。为了扩大开发区的知名度及影响力，增强招商引资的吸引力，他们一面走出去召开新闻发布会、开展大型宣传活动，一面把媒体请进来介绍推销自己。同时在北京建起了有众多国内外新闻记者参加的“首都记者俱乐部”，保持了与宣传媒体的紧密联系，加大了宣传的力度。准确的招商引资定位，多种形式的招商引资方法和媒体宣传，很快打开了招商引资的局面。

土地关。合理有效地使用土地，是开发区避免盲目开发、增强发展效益的关键。开发区在土地使用上制定了“项目决定土地出让”的原则。没有项目，任何单位和个人不能购买征用开发区内的一分土地。然而，曾有一时，全国各地开发区或急功近利、或盲目运作，无论有无项目都大量出让土地，有的甚至把土地卖给打着统一招商的“二道贩子”，致使卖出的土地迟迟不能开发建设，甚至长期荒芜，开发区也得不到应有的效益。受其影响，有人也曾主张武清开发区卖地赚钱。一些想打土地赚钱主意的人，甚至托领导、走后门囤积土地。面对来自各方面的影响干扰，武清开发区的决策者们始终保持清醒的头脑，坚持“项目决定出让土地”的原则不动摇。开发区内每出让一块土地，就必须有一个经营生产项目落地。就这样，仅几年的时间，在首期开发的6.9平方公里的土地上就摆满了企业，保证了区内没有一处荒芜的土地，也没有一个“落地黄”的企业，开发区也因此收到了应有的效益。1995年，开发区建设发展的第三年就有了2700万元的收入，第四年收入超亿元。提前实现了开发区建区初期对县委、县政府“三年可看，五年可赚”的承诺。此外，把好土地关也为开发区长期合理布局、未来发展奠定了坚实的基础。建设初期，他们就在综合起步区邻近京津公路西侧，划出了“休闲度假”与“高端软体”两个区的地域空间。才有了几年后美丽“天鹅湖温泉度假村”的出现，有了十几年后高楼林立、豪华气派的“总部基地”的诞生。

资金关。开发区在建设发展过程中，特别是建设初期，资金紧缺成为制约建设发展的一大难题。而他们却凭着巧妙多样的融资渠道，度过了一道又一道难关。一是高利息吸揽周边村街征地补偿款。由于县里明确规定，为保证群众的长期根本利益，各村街拿到的开发区征用土地补偿资金一律不许动用。开发区就主动出击，与得到征用土地款的村街协商，把钱放在开发区使用，开发区给予高息补偿。这样做，既解决了开发区基础建设中资金短缺的燃眉之急，也让村街群众得到了实惠。二是充分利用进区企业征用土地缴纳的资金，实行“滚动开发”。三是在开发区生活区内适时进行了居民住宅区建设，为开发区基础设施建设筹集了部分资金。四是利用各种渠道广泛吸揽社会闲散资金。仅利用北京记者俱乐部渠道，就吸引了北京地区大量的可用资金。据了解，20 年来，用于开发区建设投入的资金近百亿元，都得到了及时的解决，保证了开发区各项建设的有序进行。

不断开拓新的发展空间

发展是硬道理。主动出击、迎难而上，克服来自方方面面的干扰与挑战，不断拓展地域的发展空间，是开发区发展的不竭动力。

如今，武清开发区的地域发展空间，已由建区初期的 6.9 平方公里，逐步增加到 30 平方公里。区内开发也由“一期”向着“二期、三期、四期”不断地延伸拓展，逐步形成强势规模。2002 年，国家实施宏观调控，部分地区开发区出现萎缩，有的甚至大有被砍掉的危险。武清开发区在发展的困境中，虽然以良好的区位优势、高质量的服务质量，保持了良好发展之势。但是，由国家和市政府批准的一期 6.9 平方公里区域已经摆满企业，土地已成了制约继续发展的当务之急。要扩大开发区的建设使用面积，市政府和国家已经严格控制，不会再批。让开发区和每个关注开发区发展的人都陷入了苦苦思索之中，要想发展，只能等待机遇，再做争取。

一个台湾招商团，以 200 家投资企业同时来大陆发展，一次性投资总额超过 10 亿美金为条件，在从南到北考察无果的情况下来到了武清，即刻引起了武清区委、区政府的高度重视，也让苦苦思索的武清人看到了发展的希望与机遇。立即组织力量，与来访者进行了紧锣密鼓般的磋商洽谈，大胆地提出了引资发展、为招商团提供发展空间的构想。并主动出击，积极与市有关部门联系，寻找发展路径。区委、区政府主要领导还多次亲自和市主要领导汇报，希望把这一事关天津发展的大项目引入落地。很快得到了市领导的高度重视，并带领市有关部门来武清调研协调。经过几个月的积极努力，一个6平方公里的新的园区竟奇迹般地得到了批准，为开发区进一步发展拓展了空间，也让苦苦寻求发展的武清人柳暗花明，看到了更快、更大、更好发展的希望。新的园区地域批准不久，闻名中外的南玻工程玻璃有限公司总经理曾南率先走进这一地域，围着这一地域转了一圈，风趣地说："这里地理位置好，地域开阔。听，这树上的喜鹊已经喳喳地叫了，我们就在这建厂"。仅一年多的时间，投资数亿元的项目就在这里建成投产了。此后，有着世界500强之称的中粮集团、投资数十亿元的天狮国际健康中心等大项目纷纷在这里落地生根。从此，以大项目、好项目为特点的开发区二期建设工程，在这里如火如荼地发展起来了，把武清开发区的发展进一步推向了新的高潮。

在武清城区规划发展区域内，以加快城市化建设进程步伐，彻底改善城区农民生活居住条件为前提的"撤村建居"工程，也为开发区发展进一步开拓了新的地域发展空间。从2003年起至今，区委、区政府在东蒲洼街道20几个村中，在群众自愿的基础上，分两批实施了撤村建居工程，随着撤村建居居民"亨通花园小区"、"翠景花园小区"的建成，以及正在建设中的新的居民住宅小区的开工建设，又给开发区的三期发展提供了更加广阔的发展空间。

瞄准两个效益不动摇

把开发区建设发展与全区城市化建设捆在一起，瞄准社会与经济两个效益不动摇，让开发区与城区建设同步发展，办一个让武清人民受益的开发区，这是武清开发区建设发展中始终不渝追求的目标。实践证明，只有这样，开发区才有今天，武清城区才有今天。谈起这些，这个曾经长期担任过开发区领导者、决策者的他，至今仍感情深重。

一定要建一个环保型的开发区。

说起这个话题，王树培同志作了这样一段表述："英国、德国、美国等发达的资本主义国家早就办过'工业园'、'汽车城'。但是，由于工业的污染，环境的破坏，也使工业园很快成了'死城'、'鬼城'。我们要牢牢记住这些发达国家曾经有过的教训。如果因为建开发区给武清人民留下一座'死城'、'鬼城'，我们将是武清历史的罪人。保护环境、控制污染，是开发区建设一条高压线、铁门槛儿，任何人、任何情况下也不能动摇。"

为此，开发区做出了坚持不懈的努力。

建区初期，韩国一家印染企业以投资3000万美元为条件，到开发区建厂发展。面对这一大项目，即使处于招商引资艰难时期的开发区，首先想到的是有无污染，没有立即盲目引进，而是派人亲自到韩国实地考察。当得知这一项目确有污染时，洽谈人员果断给予回绝。不久，一个号称“全国百个亿元开发项目”之一的负责人找到了县主要领导，要求进开发区建设发展。同样，了解到这一项目属于污染企业时，开发区坚决给予否决，拒不接收。有着世界最大乐器生产商的台湾杰麦公司来开发区建厂时，当得知该公司的电镀车间有污染时，便果断提出污染车间不能建在开发区的要求，并主动在区外为他们联系了建设电镀车间的地点，既保证了对方正常建设投产，又堵住了污染企业入驻园区。于是，这里就有了“从天津到北京，要看蓝天在武清”的佳话。果断坚决地堵住污染企业入驻开发区的行动，保住了开发区这一片净土，不仅为源源不断的入驻企业保持了良好的发展环境，也为建设京津最佳“宜居地”奠定了坚实基础，给世世代代生活在这里的武清人留下了环保洁净、舒适安宁的生存空间。一次，国家环保局局长解振华来天津视察，当王树培同志用武清开发区的事例，说环保也是发展资源时，连连点头称是，夸赞他站得高、看得远、理念新。

关注民生，成了开发区建设发展的一大主题。

企业的最终目标是利润似乎是千古不变的真理。而作为企业式管理运营的开发区，却偏偏早在建设初期就给自己定了“要税收也要就业”的两项指标。也就是说，武清开发区建设发展想到的是，既要给地方财政、全区建设发展提供税收和强有力的资金保障，又要关注着社会的就业再就业、居民群众生活收入水平的提高。多年来，不仅总公司成立了就业部，保持与企业的密切联系，为社会不断提供较多的就业岗位。与此同时，还积极与区人才市场、劳动力市场协作，多渠道开展就业安置工作。目前，已有8万多人在开发区就业，如果按每人月薪2500元计算，当地就业居民每年从这里得到的收入就达20亿元。前些年，许多城市出现了就业再就业难，而武清人却在开发区随时能找到满意的工作，得到稳定的工资收入。开发区为武清的社会稳定、居民就业增收起到了重要的作用。

吃水不忘挖井人

在武清开发区20年建设发展的历程中，社会各界的许多单位和个人，为它的成长做出了积极的贡献。那么，武清人今天最不能忘记的是什么？王树培同志动情地说："武清开发区能有今天，既有从中央到地方各级领导的鼎力支持，历届区（县）委、政府领导和广大群众的关注与支持，又有开发区人自身的积极努力。'吃水不忘挖井人'，对于这些所有关注与支持和参与开发区建设发展的人们，我们都永远不能忘记。"接着，他又扳着手指认真地数了起来。

我们的已故县委书记徐景树同志不能忘。他是武清开发区建立的提出者、决策者、建设者。为了开发区建设，即使从领导岗位上退下来，他也始终关注，积极参与，直到离开我们。客观地看、历史地看，在某种意义上讲，没有景树同志，就没有今天的武清开发区。

国家科委已故的李绪鄂副主任，为武清开发区的批准建立说了破例的话，做了大量的工作，我们是不能忘记的。还有原市委常委、市科委主任王成怀同志，为开发区的审批做了大量的与国家有关部门的沟通工作，也帮助我们做了大量的具体工作。曾经担任过天津市代理市委书记、市长的聂璧初同志，在开发区创办最困难的初期，甚至遭到许多非议的关键时刻，是他带领市有关部门的领导来到武清，参加了我们的奠基剪彩，用行动表明了市委、市政府对武清开发区的态度，给了我们莫大的支持和鼓舞，我们永远感激他。

创建开发区时我们的县长，后来担任市纪委副书记、监察局局长的梁文忠同志，我们不能忘记。是他，坚定不移、勤勤恳恳，为开发区的批准建立奔波劳碌，做了大量卓有成效的工作。邵久武同志、李树宏同志、李乃彦同志、袁桐利同志，以及历届区（县）委、政府的领导同志，都为武清开发区的发展做出了重大的贡献。还有当时负责项目申办的县人大常委会副主任杨作莹同志，为开发区的审批，她付出了千辛万苦的努力。此外，还有在开发区工作过的虞东文、张宗启、郭宝联、钟书明、王恩成、任瑞才、刘满授、谭昕，以及许多在开发区工作过的同志，我们都应记住他们为开发区建设所作出的各种努力和贡献。

对于曾经为开发区做过贡献的许多老同志，过去我们经常逢年到节地去登门看望，有时把他们请来看看开发区的发展。今后，我们也应永远记住他们，保持与他们长期的联系来往。说到武清人的不能忘记，王树培同志还动情地给我们讲了这样一件事儿。过去，每年武清都把老市长聂璧初同志、王成怀同志请来做客，看看武清开发区的发展。他调到市商委工作后，由于工作变动没能再请一些老领导来开发区视察做客。2010 年春节，当他和市领导一起代表市政府慰问老市长时，聂璧初同志握着他的手说："树培，我们远了”。过去在数十里以外的郊县工作，现在调到市区，工作单位与老市长近在咫尺，怎么远了呢？这让在场的许多同志不解。可他却很快明白了，老市长说的不是自己工作单位与他的远近，而是他长期以来与武清开发区的感情，还在关注着武清和武清开发区的建设发展。于是，他立即趴在老市长耳边孩子般地轻声说：“明年我一定再来看您”。结果，2011 年春节前，他想到春节期间应走访的第一个人，就是要代表武清、代表武清开发区去看看老市长聂壁初同志，向老领导汇报武清和武清开发区新的发展变化。说到这里，王树培同志的眼睛湿润了。

深切地寄予厚望

中国·天津武清开发区建立发展的 20 年，在武清发展的历史长河中，虽然只是“弹指一挥间”，但却创造了武清发展史上的奇迹。如今，已成为武清对外开放的窗口，全区经济发展的主发动机，带动产业升级的龙头，安置城乡劳动力就业再就业的基地，京津之间崛起的一座科技新城。一位市级领导看过武清开发区后，曾把武清开发区和天津滨海新区放在一起，形象地比作是天津“骏马”图上经济发展的左右两翼，是值得天津人骄傲、对外展示天津发展的靓丽风景。

采访结束时，当我们说，您在武清工作多年，担任过武清开发区的第一任总经理，即使担任县长、区长、区委书记后，也一直担任着开发区的管委会副主任、主任，长达 17 年之久，为武清开发区的建设与发展呕心沥血、身体力行，做了那么大的贡献。其实，武清开发区能有今天的辉煌成就，全区人最不能忘记的是您！王树培同志听后沉思了片刻，说：“纵观武清发展的历史，无论是上溯到年代悠久的古泉州与古雍阳，还是唐天宝元年定名武清以来的 1200 多年的历史进程，乃至新中国成立至今的 60 多年来的发展经历，值得武清人骄傲自豪的当属中国·天津武清开发区的建设发展。中国改革开放的时代赐予了武清这一千载难逢的机遇，正是我们抓住了这一历史性机遇，才有了武清开发区今天这样世人瞩目的可喜成果，写下了武清发展史上最为辉煌的一页。历史是人民创造的，是武清开发区是历届区（县）委、政府‘举全区（县）之力’，带领全区（县）干部群众抢抓机遇、拼搏进取、共同努力的结果，我只是这支战斗队伍中的一员普通战士，做了我应当做的事”。

我们请他谈谈对武清开发区今后的希望与要求，他饱含深情地说：“武清开发区从国家科委批准的天津市高新技术产业园区武清开发区，到前不久国务院正式批准国家级经济技术开发区，已经成了天津唯一、全国为数不多的国家级“双料”开发区。武清在开发区建区 20 年之际总结它的发展经历，意义深远重大，总结是为了实现今后的发展。希望武清开发区踏着时代的脚步，继续向着新的发展高端大步前进。不断优化环境，更好地为投资者服务，这是武清开发区永恒的主题，武清开发区的明天会更美好！”

摘录 作家出版社《京津走廊崛起的科技新城》

一位成功的拓荒者

——访武清开发区第二任总经理虞东文

杨振关

多年的写作经历，让我觉得追寻辉煌时期的历史足迹，探寻创业者的成功发展之路，是自己人生的一大享受。中国武清开发区 20 岁生日前夕，采访在这里曾任总经理的虞东文，倾听武清开发区拓荒者的艰辛经历及其事业发展恢弘的收获，着实令我心动并享受着。

白纸上面绘蓝图

1992 年 5 月的一天，虞东文从石各庄镇党委书记的岗位上调出，任武清开发区总公司总经理。从此，他便与这里结下了不解之缘。

走马上任的第二天，他便骑着自行车实地察看开发区现场，看到了自己所面临的困难。这是在一张白纸上绘制蓝图：没经验，一切都要摸着石头过河；没机构，总公司仅有的几名员工除他之外都是从县直机关临时抽调的；没启动资金，所以也别讲条件，办公地点设在县政府楼后的两间平房里，距开发区起步区足有十来里路，交通工具就是自备的每人一辆自行车。来到开发区，眼前的景象同样令他吃惊，这里没有一处建筑，撞入眼帘的是一片连着一片的庄稼和荒草，还有砖瓦厂废弃后遗留下的碎砖烂瓦和一个个大大小小的水坑。从遍地野鸟叫，一片蛙鸣声中，他感觉到建设开发区任重而道远，一张白纸，满写着的，都是困难。

而办公桌上的会议记录，又使他看到了县委、县政府战胜困难的信心和决心。那天晚上，他没回家，翻看着会议记录，越看越心情激动，他数了数，仅在他上任前的三月份，市、县领导为创办武清开发区，曾先后六次召开专题会议研究部署：

——3 月 4 日，在市科委二楼会议室召开武清园区工作研究会。市委常委、市科委主任王成怀主持，市科委副主任梁肃、市园区办王士喜、佟玲、武清县县长梁文忠、县人大常委会副主任杨作莹、县政府办公室主任兼开发区总公司总经理王树培等参加会议。

——3 月 8 日，在县政府第二会议室召开第三次县长办公会议，县长梁文忠主持，副县长邵久武、李乃彦和县人大副主任杨作莹参加。会议听取了开发区办公室关于起步区期工程详细规划草案、项目审批和招商办法以及 1992 年工作安排意见的汇报，并就开发区建设的有关具体问题进行了研究。

——3 月 10 日，副县长李乃彦在县政府第二会议室主持召开园区征地工作协调会议。杨村镇、徐官屯乡、东蒲洼乡主要领导参加。

——3 月 14 日，县长梁文忠在政府第二会议室主持召开各银行行长会议，就开发区起步区第一期工程投资问题进行了议定。

——3 月 16 日，县长梁文忠在政府第二会议室主持召开开发区“五通一平”建设协调会和开发区优惠政策协调会。对各项工程建设的规模、标准、工期等问题进行了研究定义。

——3 月 30 日，县长梁文忠在政府大会议室主持召开“武清开发区工作情况通报会”，各部委办、县直各单位及驻武清单位、部队的领导同志参加了会议。会上，县人大常委会副主任杨作莹简要介绍了武清开发区成立的意义、过程和武清开发区的优势，县长助理、县政府办公室主任兼开发区总公司总经理王树培介绍了开发区工作进展情况。县长梁文忠强调指出：“举全县之力，办好开发区。”

“举全县之力，办好开发区。”可见县委县政府的决心之大。虞东文仿佛从那力透纸背的言词中，洞悉了开发区紧张有序的开始和未来美好的明天。

6 月 23 日上午，天津市新技术产业园区授牌及天津市新技术产业园区武清开发区奠基仪式在武清开发区举行，市领导聂璧初、王成怀、张好生，国家科委副主任李效时、秘书长宋必信及国家、市等有关部门的领导出席了授牌及奠基仪式。武清的党政机关领导及各企事业单位代表共 500 余人参加了授牌及奠基仪式。市长聂璧初为武清开发区开工铲土奠基，国家科委副主任李效时受国务院委托代表国家科委向天津市新技术产业园区授“国家高新技术产业开发区”牌。现场红旗招展，鼓乐齐鸣，气氛隆重热烈，昭示着开发区这一颗闪亮的明珠，在京津之间对外开放的黄金通道上熠熠生辉。

开发区的建设如火如荼地开展起来。国家批准的天津新技术产业园区武清新建区的区域范围为3平方公里，涉及杨村、徐官屯、东蒲洼3个乡镇15个村街。被征用土地村街的广大群众识大体，顾大局，无怨无悔地出让了土地，使这一工作在预期内圆满完成。征地工作第一炮打响后，遵循“着眼长远、适当超前、综合起步、滚动开发”和“先开发招商，后逐步规范”的发展思路，坚持基础设施和招商引资两手抓，在实际运作中做到“征用一片，开发一片，建成一片，收益一片。”

举办新闻发布会，向外界广泛地宣传武清，推介武清开发区，是武清开发区招商引资的一项重大举措。经过一段紧锣密鼓的准备，武清县人民政府于1992年8月7日上午，在北京人民大会堂召开了“天津新技术产业园区武清开发区及天津市武清经济开发区新闻发布会”。县长梁文忠，县人大常委会主任刘金铎，县政协主席程振江，县委副书记王成全，县委常委宣传部部长何俊田，县人大常委会副主任杨作莹，县长助理王树培及开发区总公司有关同志参加了会议，会议邀请了新华社、中央人民广播电台、中央电视台、《人民日报》等20余家新闻单位的记者30余名。会上，县长梁文忠就武清的投资环境作了简要介绍，县长助理、开发区管委会副主任王树培作了两区情况的说明。与会记者对武清开发区的投资环境表示了极大的关注，并在各大新闻媒体进行了广泛宣传推介。新闻发布会后，县政府、开发区管委会、县委统战部又于8月18日邀请天津市各民主党派及社会团体负责人来武清听取经济开发区和高新技术产业园区建设情况介绍。市政协副主席肖元、赵今生出席会议并讲话。会上，县长梁文忠介绍了武清经济发展形势、有利条件及今后工作思路。县长助理王树培介绍了两区开发建设招商情况和优惠政策。与会民主党派及社会团体代表纷纷表示要发挥自己人才智力优势，提供信息咨询服务，为引进项目、资金牵线搭桥。

很快，一个招商引资活动在全县范围内广泛开展起来：

——10月9日，县长助理、开发区管委会副主任王树培乘飞机到美国考察招商。

——10月21日，总经理虞东文赴韩国考察招商。

——总公司在北京保利大厦设立驻京招商处，女员工武凤玲只身闯北京招商引资。

——全县各机关，企事业单位，乡镇农民，纷纷行动起来，有线索找线索，有关系托关系，人人献计出力。

与此同时，开发区的基础设施软硬件建设，也热火朝天地进行。逐步实现了以水、电、路、热、通信、土地平整为内容的“五通一平”的标准。招商引资工作也逐步展开。

强化服务　精心筑巢

随着招商引资步伐的加快，开发区的日益发展，总公司自身建设也日臻完善，由初建时的七八名员工发展到“十八棵青松”，再到后来较为规范的部室明确分工，各司其职。相互间虽有变化，然而万变不离其宗，那就是搞好服务，对客户服务，对企业服务。明确提出了“投资者是上帝。不许对上帝说‘不’。上帝没有错”的要求。

要创造一个良好的服务环境，软硬件都要上去，“要两手抓，两手都要硬”。抓硬件，抓“五通一平”。首先是路，路要修，可钱没有，找县交通局，提出目前开发区资金紧张的现状，请他们先出资修路，最后一总算账。对于如此大的一笔垫资，交通局一时也难以周转，然而为了开发区的发展，为了武清的腾飞，他们最后还是选择了把困难留给自己，四处筹措资金，在很短的时间内，使开发区内的公路条条宽阔平坦，纵横交措。为了确保工程质量，总公司的员工与施工队伍一道，肩扛摄相机，钻地下管道拍照存档、记录数据，排查隐患，一经发现质量问题，立即与施工方协商解决，确保工程的百年大计。

1993年10月13日，召开开发区供电规划审核会议，天津电力设计院、天津电力局、武清供电局开发区电力公司等单位有关领导及专家20余人参加了论证会，专家们在开发区供电规划的原则上，提出重视低压可行性论证及开发区远近期规划结合。经过几个月的紧张施工，到1994年3月31日，武清开发区35千伏变电站正式启动，主变及全套配电设备经试验运转正常，已具备向区内送电能力。

供热规划论证会于1993年11月6日召开，天津纺织设计院、天津经济开发区供热公司、天津市劳动局锅炉检验所、武清县劳动局锅炉科等单位有关专家及领导对天津市化工设计院设计的武清开发区供热规划进行了全方位的论证。12月9日，开发区一号地热井进行试井调试，已达正常供水供热，每小时出水量达80至100吨，水温74℃。该地热井可供给5.6万平方米范围内的采暖和洗浴用水。1994年1月4日开始向区内企业鸿发电子有限公司供热。当时受入区企业限制，搞供热工程属于大马拉小车项目，投资大回报小，然而为了创建服务的大环境，在一号热力站投入运营后，又于1994年5月22日举行了二号热力站设备安装招标会。铁道部第十八工程局在六家单位共同投标的情况下，以带资100%，提前预交保证金20万元的优惠条件下一举中标。该工程于6月10日开工，工期仅用了120天，10月11日进行烘炉测试，并一次点火成功。二号供热站位于开发区东部，面积 2914 平方米，有 2 台 10 吨采暖锅炉及附属管网组成，采暖面积 10 万平方米。二号热力站的建成，标志着武清开发区起步区 65 万平方米的供热问题全部得到解决。

经过拼搏努力，到 2000 年，全区井字形路网已四通八达，区内建成 220KV 变电站一座、35 千伏变电站两座，由华北和京津唐两大电网引入双电源供电，10KV 出线送到企业。电站充分采用了自动调压、微机联控、远动通讯等现代化的操作和控制系统，供电质量达到国际先进水准。区内自建 8 万门电讯大楼一座，拥有数字微波、光纤电缆等先进设施和通讯手段。开发区现有日供水能力万吨的地下水源厂一座，原水水质较好，经净化处理，可向用户提供标准自来水。排水采用雨、污分流体系，分别纳入区内雨水和污水处理系统。供热采用集中供热和自办、联办相结合的方式，目前已有四座供热站投入使用，可为用户提供 0・8MPA 压力的饱和蒸汽和 95℃的采暖用水。

配套设施建设日臻完善。0.8 平方公里的中心区是开发区的多功能服务区，海关、银行、税务、公安等服务体系完善，创新大楼、天鹅湖度假村、海关培训中心、两个国际标准网球场等设施为投资者提供孵化基地、休闲、娱乐、餐饮、培训等服务场所；1.4 平方公里的生活区集居住、生活、教育娱乐于一体。15 万平方米的栖仙公寓、别墅投入使用，建起了双语制英华小学。同时，开发区还投入大量资金用于绿化、美化。 在不断完善硬环境的同时，武清开发区还努力营造符合国际惯例的投资软环境。开发区设有开发区管委会和开发区总公司，两块牌子一套人马。设七部四公司，两个办事处（北京、天津）。对入区企业实行“封闭式”管理和“一条龙”服务，“一站式”办公体系。入区企业只要提供必要的资料，一切手续都可以由开发区总公司无偿代为办理，直到领取营业执照、动土、开工。

招商引资　风落梧桐

建开发区，重中之重的工作是招商引资。县委、县政府之所以不惜血本地搞软硬件服务环境，其中心目的还是项目的引进。经济的增长靠项目，解决社会上就业的难题同样离不开项目，没有项目就没有开发区的未来，也没有武清经济社会的稳步增长。

为了尽快引进项目，尤其是大项目，好项目，县委、县政府多次出台优惠政策，层层动员，群策群力。县委、县政府领导还亲自挂帅，带领相关人员远赴海外招商引资。1995 年 4 月 18 日至 5 月 5 日，副县长、开发区管委会副主任王树培带领虞东文等一行4人，赴韩国、日本等招商引资，17天的行程，排满了时间，其中召开说明会6次，先后接触两国工商界人士116人，接触新的投资意向者10余人。此后，两国工商界人士陆陆续续到武清考察、立项。其中有一个韩国项目，已经洽谈了几次，仍没能确定下来。对方以时近春节为由，结束洽谈回国。虞东文将此事向副县长王树培进行了汇报。王树培当即提出，他们撤了我们追。腊月二十八那天，虞东文就带上翻译，登机起程。总经理的突然造访，使韩方企业大受感动，最后终于确定了投资意向。1995年10月20日至11月1日，县委书记邵久武带领武清开发区招商团一行三人赴澳大利亚悉尼市、柏斯市进行考察招商。在澳期间，接触了13家企业，拜访了2家商会和贸促会，加入了纽省国际会并成为其主要负责成员之一，聘请了开发区驻澳代表人，初步确定悉尼市布拉斯莱尔公司咖啡组装机等4家企业的投资意向，开拓了武清开发区新的招商区域。并于10月14日在悉尼市举行了“中国天津武清开发区投资洽谈会”，共有17个企业集团参加此次会议。当地的《澳洲新报》在显著位置对此次活动进行了报道，扩大了武清开发区在海外的影响。1996年5月25日，副县长、开发区管委会副主任王树培带领开发区招商团一行3人对丹麦、美国进行14天的招商考察，期间，招商团先后拜访了丹麦LFU基金会、丹麦丹佛斯公司、美国总商会纽约商会及福特汽车公司。通过相互加深沟通，加深了了解，交流了感情，发展了关系，增进了友谊，坚定了投资者在武清投资增资的信心。此次考察开辟了新的招商渠道，结识了新朋友，取得了预期效果。中美总商会纽约商会随后对武清进行了考察。

对来武清开发区进行考察的客户，无论投资意向如何，都能做到热心接待，全程服务，不但以环境和政策的优势打动对方，更以热诚的服务感动对方。在服务中寻找商机，然后抓住不放，紧追不舍。开发区纳税大户，绫致服装公司的入驻，就是在这种情况下促成的。开发区在为入区企业——丹佛斯集团服务的过程中，得知丹麦还有个大公司——绫致服装集团公司，董事长王配德的哥哥娶了个中国女人做妻子，与开发区员工安友霞认识。虞东文得知这一线索后，找到安友霞，让她以朋友身份联络王配德的中国嫂子，以加深感情，然后再通过王配德嫂子争取董事长王配德来武清开发区投资建厂，一次不行两次，两次不行三次，心诚则灵。随后，虞东文数次进京，与安友霞去王配德在北京的办事处，讲武清开发区的投资环境和优惠政策。县里的有关领导也十分重视绫致集团的入驻，在对方来武清考察时亲自安排布置，热情接待，最终使该集团下决心在武清开发区投资。不但自身的经济效益雪球般越滚越大，而且对武清的贡献近年来在开发区也独占鳌头。

丹麦的“丹佛斯公司”，是丹麦最大的精密机械制造集团，来武清开发区进行投资意向谈判时，光条款就写满了40几页纸。谈判从晚上六点开始，逐个条款进行，一直持续到第二天早晨七点。开发区中层以上干部几乎全员上阵，除参与谈判外，还努力做好服务，给客人准备夜宵，准备方便面和啤酒。让客人不但对谈判的结果满意，更对开发区上上下下的服务满怀感激。正因为留有好的印象，1996年9月18日，丹佛斯集团在世界各地的高层管理人员为期4天的工作会议在武清开发区召开。《工商时报》、《天津日报》、《今晚报》、天津电台等新闻媒体对会议进行了报道，不但宣传了丹佛斯，也宣传了武清，扩大了武清开发区在外界的影响。

经过多年的发展建设，至2000年12月，虞东文离开总经理位置，从事党务工作止，有来自世界近20个国家和地区的300余家企业在区内落户，投资总额近50亿元，其中外资4.5亿美元。投资领域主要集中在电子信息、新型建材、生物工程、机电一体化、磁性材料、医药、食品等行业。丹麦丹佛斯公司，芬兰瑞特格集团，美国麦格昆磁，日本东棉、丸红、三井、住友、伊都锦，台湾光宝、功学社等世界著名公司都在区内投资建厂。随着越来越多入驻企业的建成投产，开发区的社会效益和经济效益日趋显著，2000年实现税收2亿元，占全县财政收入的35%，并带动了全县建筑建材业、加工配套业和服务业的综合发展。园区安置就业1800人，有效地缓解了社会就业压力。

采访虞东文，倾听他讲述武清开发区从无到有、从弱到强的发展经历，仿佛让我听到了一首旋律优美的“拓荒者之歌”，感人肺腑、动人心弦。感悟到了“开发人”为武清发展辛勤耕耘、拼搏奋进的宝贵精神，热血沸腾、令人陶醉！

摘录作家出版社《京津走廊崛起的科技新城》

在希望的田野上奋进

——访武清开发区第三任总经理张宗启

袁文洪

2000年10月。张宗启由石各庄镇党委书记调任武清开发区总经理。从一个农民企业家到镇党委书记，又将主持开发区工作，他深感责任重大。从此，他便以满腔的热情、全身心地投入火热的武清开发区建设发展之中。近日采访了他，机敏、朴实，善谋实干的他，没有讲他自己波澜壮阔的经历、惊天动地的事件，而是更多地讲了他和他率领的团队在区委、区政府领导下，尽心尽力做好开发区工作一个个感人肺腑的故事。

突破瓶颈

张宗启到任后面临的首要问题是开发区一期开发用地项目基本摆满，要发展，必须想办法拓展发展空间。于是，土地问题成了制约开发区发展的一大瓶颈。

土地，是老百姓的命根子。征地拆迁，涉及千家万户的切身利益。又谈何容易！但是，要发展就得占地。俗话说：没有梧桐树引不来凤凰鸟。经过深入细致地调查研究，按照区领导的意见，总公司拿出规划，决定启动开发区二期建设。

但是，问题并不是想象的那么简单。

当时，武清的招商势头进入一个新的发展阶段。许多外商看中了滨海新区发展的态势，也看中了武清开发区的得天独厚的地理位置，高速快捷的交通优势，优惠的政策，良好的建设发展的软硬环境。而此时的开发区一期地段企业已经摆满，急需拓展新的发展区域空间。要拓展新的发展地域空间，只有按照武清城区发展建设规划，动员城区附近的村街居民拆迁腾地。可征地拆迁涉及面广、难度大、工作量大。按照开发区规划，用半年时间全部完成，而且基础设施全部跟上；一年内出形象、见效果。可以想象，涉及东蒲洼街道、南蔡村镇十个村、近5000个农户。要在这么短的时间内完成，时间紧、任务重。征地拆迁、撤村建居，区领导关注，群众关心，一时间成了全区最敏感的话题，工作稍有不慎，既有可能引发“群体事件”，给工作带来麻烦，也会给开发区整体发展造成影响。

关键时刻，区委、区政府高度重视，一面制定相关政策、措施，一面组织有关乡镇、街道干部深入群众之中，广泛宣传相关政策、深入做思想工作，动员群众识大体、顾大局，为开发区建设和全区发展做贡献，很快得到了群众的理解与支持。历经半年，征地拆迁任务竟奇迹般地全部完成。

紧接着，进行基础设施建设，边建设，边招商。当时，有几家外商来开发区考察，看到二期开发动作这么快、力度如此大，纷纷提出投资意向。加快开发区二期建设，提升速度，事关招商引资大局，迫在眉捷。

为了确保基础设施建设时间、质量，公司倒排工期、给任务、压担子，全体工作人员加班加点，各项工程有条不紊、整体推进，终于如期完工，迅速达到了“十一通一平”的标准。开发区这种想事、干事、干成事的工作作风和建设环境吸引了投资者，很快呈现了快速发展的良好势头。南玻公司率先投资建厂。

千里急电

招商！招商！招商！

开发区所有工作人员心里时刻装着招商两个字。因为，他们清楚：只有招商，才能引资；只有招商引资，才能加快开发区发展；只有开发区发展，才能增加税收，才能为全区经济社会的发展提供强有力的支撑。然而，在市场经济的形势下，全国开发区四起，处处都在招商引资。各地“土地转让0地价”“建设贷款给贴息”等优惠政策满天飞，竞争十分激烈。面临严峻的招商形势，开发区总公司不断拓宽思路，不断深化“舍得”理念，创造性地开展工作，在服务上动脑筋、想办法、找出路、求发展。

中天特车正计划在开发区投资。按照当时的地价，每亩8万～10万元，企业由于资金问题，表示不好接受，希望再优惠一些。是打破惯例、降低地价，留住投资者，还是坚持原价，放弃这次招商机会？问题摆在开发区人面前。正是从“舍得”理念上悟出的哲理，开发区果断拍板：只要企业发展好、有前景、能安排就业、能增加税收，就要千方百计留下来。于是，招商部人员立即拨通了企业负责人的电话。但是，企业负责人却远在千里之外，而且表示已经去过廊坊、北辰、塘沽等开发区。如何把“中天特车”引进来，事情紧迫，叫人一板。开发区总公司连夜召开会议，集中大家的智慧，一致认为：这个企业有发展前景，既能安排就业，又能增加税收，而且通过多方了解，得知这个企业有可能会带动其它产业的发展。因此，很有必要灵活运用“舍得”理念，养鱼给水、种花施肥，从长远发展的角度，对这个企业给予大力支持。当时定下的原则是：全力搞好扶植服务，不错过这次招商引资的机会。具体方法是：土地价格可以让步，先不要那么多钱，用地款替贷款，等企业正常运转后再还账。这样，既不损失开发区利益，又缓解了企业资金周转问题，可谓“双赢”。研究决定以后，招商部工作人员立即与企业负责人联系。对方给予的答复是：可以考虑，等待回复。

情况未定。为了珍惜这次招商引资机会，公司总经理办公室和招商部安排专门人员，时刻准备接听电话。一周后的晚 11 点，办公室的电话铃声骤响，工作人员抄起电话，终于接到了“中天特车”项目同意落户武清开发区的回音。这个项目 2001 年立项动工，投产见效后的一年左右时间，所欠地款，包括利息全部还清。

跑在时间前面

开发区的建设者在建设和发展的工作和实践中，对“开发区”有了全新的认识和理解。开发区，意在“开发”。而要真正做到“大开发”，必须有思想上的“大解放”，发展上的“大思路”，措施上的“大动作”，也就是说“人”是关键，“人”是根本。因此，面临新的招商引资形势，坚持“以人为本”，才是开发区之所以发展的决定因素。

开发区把发现人、培养人和使用人，始终贯穿于开发区教育管理和招商引资工作的全过程，使开发区不但成为全区经济发展的主力军、税收的重要支柱，而且是培养人才的摇篮。因此，坚持生活上照顾，工作上支持，政治上关心。

为了提高干部员工的素质，开发区把解放思想、开阔眼界、提高服务水平摆在更加突出的位置。面临开发区二期建设的新形势、新任务，公司领导认为：要尽快出形象、上规模、见效果，必须提高开发区全体工作人员的素质和服务水平，包括思想观念、开发开放意识、工作效率等等，努力培养和打造一支能打、善打硬仗的干部职工队伍，进一步解放思想，打破固步自封，重点走好两步棋：一是“请进来”，请国内外有关领导和理论专家来公司培训，充电、给氧；二是“走出去”，不管是负责招商的，还是不负责招商的，总公司统一安排，分期去全国各地开发区考察学习，在学习外地先进经验的同时，查找自身存在的问题与不足。这些都收到了很好的效果。特别是工作人员在无锡参观考察时，企业的几条横幅引起了他们共同的关注："思想认识每提高一步，经济就发展一步"。"鱼，往往不是大的吃小的，而是动作快的吃动作慢的"，大家很受启发，感觉其中蕴含着通俗易懂的哲学思想和辩证法观点，并成了全体工作人员思想和行动上的座右铭。

提到工作效率，这里面有一段与时间赛跑的故事。

韩国的一家生产化学和建材的企业，当时进区时间不长，规模也不大，不但没盈利而且赔钱。开发区工作人员还得知，远在韩国的总部对这个企业抱的希望不大，而且给这个企业扭亏为盈的期限已到。

要留住这个企业，没有更多的犹豫时间。开发区总公司的领导经过认真的分析，果断决策：立即赶赴韩国。总经理亲自带领招商部工作人员马不停蹄、辗转奔波，到了企业总部，总部正在召开董事会，正要做出撤出中国市场的决定。开发区领导和招商部人员的到来，让韩国总部的人又感动又吃惊。开发区的领导和招商部工作人员，帮助韩国企业总部分析了中国的建材市场和韩国企业生产、销售中存在的问题。当韩国企业总部了解了中国的建设发展现状，建材行业有很大的市场需求的情况后，做出了继续在中国发展的决定。经过两年的发展，这个企业在开始单一品种的基础上又增加了新的品种，企业利润、税收也有了大幅增长。

六进大馆

开发区二期工程建设进入高潮，全体干部员工情绪高涨，建设工地一派热火朝天的喜人景象。开发区的形势鼓舞人心、催人奋进。武清京津之间的区位优势、路网建设、城区改造、环境服务等优势更加凸显，与周边地区的开发区，形成千帆竞发，百舸争流的局面。开发区的建设和发展，得到社会的广泛关注。

面对新的发展形势，开发区决策者清醒的认识到，招大项目、好项目、有前景的项目、能扩大就业和增加税收的项目势在必行。因此，招商引资的任务依然很重。开发区加强基础设施建设，加大招商引资力度，自加压力，负重奋进，确定税收年增长 30% 以上的发展速度和目标。要完成这个目标，对于正在二期工程建设中的开发区人来说，又是一种新的考验，无异于急行军中又来一个大冲锋。

增速多快，只是计划；完成多少税收，只是目标。要确保计划目标的实现，必须在措施上动真格的，在行动上有大的动作。这是关键。

通过认真的分析和思考，结合“由东南亚向欧美地区发展”的基本工作思路，开发区领导和招商部工作人员同时想到，外商到大陆投资，大都经过本国的驻华使馆，各国使馆的商务参赞是个关键。要想到国外，特别是欧美地区招商引资，走访各国大使馆无疑是一条有效的途径。

开发区工作的实践，尤其是南方企业“大鱼吃小鱼理念”，使开发区招商工作人员形成了一条潜规则，即：凡是公司定下来的事就坚决照办，凡是能增加税收、对公司发展有利的事不打折扣、雷厉风行。经过公司精心策划、妥善安排、充分准备，由总经理带队，走访各国大使馆，闯出一条招商引资的新路子。

大使馆并不是随便出入的地方。开发区领导和招商部工作人员不辞辛苦、不畏艰难，经过多番打听，几经周折，通过武清籍在京乡友和中国大使馆的一名商务参赞取得联系，又通过这名商务参赞和瑞典大使馆的一名参赞取得联系，瑞典商务参赞当时表示极大兴趣。但，由于种种原因，约了5次，都没能与瑞典大使馆的商务参赞见面。招商部工作人员没有灰心，终于第六次约见成功。当瑞典大使馆的商务参赞了解武清、了解了武清开发区以后，表示愿意为两国的招商引资搭建平台、提供信息和交流合作的机会，并全力搞好服务。时间不长，瑞典一家企业落户武清开发区。招商部人员借鉴瑞典大使馆的经验，又与几十个国家的大使馆商务参赞取得了联系，引进了韩国的LG电子、丹麦的LM风力发电机叶等一批高科技项目。

据了解，张宗启在开发区工作的两年多日子里，开发区的建设发展、管理、招商引资、环境以及经济效益等各方面，都取得了长足进展。共引进企业，包括注册企业一百六十多家；引资28个亿，安排就业超过一万人，年税收近4.4亿。开发区进入了一个新的历史发展阶段，为今后发展打下了一个很好的基础。采访中他深有感触地说：开发区所以取得显著的成绩，是区委、区政府带领全区干部群众“举全区之力”共同奋斗的结果。作为开发区总经理和开发区的团队，只是怀着对武清、对开发区建设发展的紧迫感、责任感，做了我们应当做的工作。

2003年初，张宗启在武清区 二届人大一次会议上当选武清区人民政府副区长，离开了火热沸腾的武清开发区，走上了新的领导岗位。

摘录作家出版社《京津走廊崛起的科技新城》

用心传递“接力棒”

——访武清开发区第四任总经理郭宝联

李克山

中国改革开放的时代，是机遇与挑战并存的年代，是区位、人才、市场与环境等条件大比拼的赛场。如果把武清开发区20年的建设发展经历比作是这个时代的一场“接力赛”的话，现任区人大副主任的郭宝联，应当是这一接力赛的第四任老总。那是一个春光明媚的上午，他接受了我的采访，满怀激情地回顾了他与开发区团队3年来日夜奔波的故事。

用心干事　成就事业

2002年年底，恰逢武清开发区建区11周年之际，郭宝联同志从区外经贸委主任的岗位上调入开发区，正式走马上任，成为武清开发区的第四任总经理。面对这一新的使命，面对这座京津之间已经崛起的正在蒸蒸日上的科技新城，他既感到振奋又感到重任在肩，开篇锣鼓怎样敲响，如何点燃干部员工的斗志激情，使开发区在原有的基础上以更快的速度向前发展，如同每一位新上任的老总一样，他沉浸在深深思索之中。

开发区建区十一周年，也是武清撤县建区刚刚两年，区长王树培同志在接收国内外新闻媒体采访时提出的从“田园”、“菜园”到“花园”，直至把武清建成京津之间最佳“宜居地”的构想，成了人们追求美好未来的强大动力。开发区总公司的领导者们，决定以此为契机，通过回顾创业历程、总结创业经验，来明确方向、凝聚人心、鼓舞士气，来增强干部员工的责任感、紧迫感，为武清迅速进入经济发展的快车道，早日建成现代科技新城做出新的贡献。

正如预想的那样，庆祝会之后，整个团队团结一致、热情高涨、拼搏努力，发展区位优势，擦亮“服务”品牌，集中精力用心干事，就像运河水后浪推前浪一样，在武清富饶的大地上，在招商引资澎湃的洪流中，奔涌不息，滚滚向前。

正确的战略构想确定之后，还必须深入细致实实在在地抓好落实。细节决定成败，要想干一番事业，要想成就某件事情，必须集中精力，深思熟虑，动用心力，即所谓“用心干事”。

开发区从“招商引资”到“招商选资”，这是一个飞跃。说明武清开发区建设已经有了突破性进展，已经显示出它的强大与宏伟，已经吸引了众多中外客商的眼球，也说明区领导、总公司领导——这些蓝图绘画者们立足武清开发区发展实际，审时度势、科学谋划、大胆决策所取得的成果，更凝聚着他们辛勤耕耘的滴滴汗水。

交谈之间，郭宝联主任满怀深情地回忆起了当年区委书记王树培关注开发区建设、参与招商引资的动人故事。

作为有着 84 万人的区委书记王树培，虽说不上日理万机，也是每天忙得不可开交，但只要开发区有事，特别是招商中的一些重大事情，他都要亲自参加，为开发区的发展出谋划策，经常没黑没白，没年没节地工作着，“亲商”，才能“安商”、招商，才能发展自己。而招商能否取得成功的关键，在于诚信与用心干事。记得有一家外资企业，投资规模较大，来开发区落户较早，在人员就业与税收方面对武清的贡献也较大。该企业先后换了两任总经理，在欢送这两位总经理卸任时，树培书记亲自题词，制成锦旗。前任题词是“创业功臣”，这四个字，实际上就是武清对该总经理在任期间的肯定与赞许；后任题词是“发展功臣”，这既符合事实，又有别于前，同样会使对方感到无比荣耀。面对这样独特的精神奖励，两位总经理深受感动，连连鞠躬致谢，从而促进了该企业的进一步发展。

王书记的故事在开发区成为美谈，用心干事也成了每一位开发区领导工作上的一种境界和追求。对于郭总来说，最令他难忘的一件事儿，可谓“三去顺义”。

顺义有一家做“玻璃幕墙”的企业，计划来武清开发区建厂，该企业占地 50 亩，厂区外表可谓“朴实无华”，是租用别人的厂房。但这家企业管理一流，产品过硬，尤其是研发等软件条件，在全国名列前茅。它更有一个气壮山河的名字——“江河集团”！而我们的“选商”原则，不单是看厂子的大小，投资的多少，还要看产品的质量，有无更大的发展力度，以及经营者的人品素质等。公司的经理是个年纪不大的小伙子，他知识广博，精明能干，精通技术，讲究信义。所以，先是总公司的副总去，后是总经理去。区委书记王树培听了几位总经理的汇报后，觉得小伙子是个可以信赖、不可多得的人才，因此又一次前往考察。小伙子被感动了，于2004年秋带领其中层以上干部来武清回访。王树培书记对此十分重视，与郭宝联总经理分头准备礼品：郭宝联为其买了一套精装本《孙子兵法》；王树培则请著名书法家刘炳森写了四个字——“厚德载旺”，这四个字来源于“厚德载物”，他为何将“载物”改成“载旺”呢？因为小伙子名字叫“刘载旺”。一字之改，便赋予了四字特别动人的含义。而王树培书记的惊人之举，则是他写给“江河集团”的一首气势磅礴的长诗——《江河之歌》！并且在欢迎会上满怀激情亲自给与会者朗诵：

浩浩汤汤，
曲曲折折，
奔涌不息，
上下求索。
凝聚了乾坤的灵气，
激荡着神州的魂魄。
啊，向前！
啊，向前！
黄河——长江，
长江——黄河！

冰雪覆盖的山原，
孕育了你的生命；
高山大地的臂弯，
呵护了你的稚弱。
坚冰造就你不挠的品质，
风暴磨砺出你铿锵的性格。
啊，江河！
当你冲下高原的时候，
带走了黄天厚土的期望与重托。

起伏陡峭的山峦，
锻造了你的筋骨。
跌宕不测的峡壑，
强健了你的体魄。
险滩在你呼啸中低头，
绝壁在你怒吼中惊破。
啊，江河！
当你涌出大川的时候，
峰头东指 淋漓酣畅 大气磅礴。

郁郁葱葱的原野，
吮吸着你的乳汁。
纵横交错的阡陌，
跳动着你的脉搏。
浓墨重彩写就古老的文明，
生生不息托起崭新的中国。
啊，江河！
当你奔向大海的时候，
际会五洲风云 引领潮起潮落。

浩浩汤汤，
曲曲折折，
奔涌不息，
上下求索。
你将东方的神奇融入世界，
又把世界的精彩带给中国。
向前，向前，永远向前，
浩瀚的长江
滚滚的黄河，
你是中华民族不朽的歌！

这抑扬顿挫的诗句，已经大大超越了招商引资的空间，跨越了文化艺术的沟通与交流的界域。而是一位领导者与84万武清人民海纳百川博大雄怀的坦露，是招商引资双方情感与艺术融汇的海洋。这诗，从此伴随着悠扬的乐曲在美丽的天鹅湖度假村缭绕，在雍阳广袤灵秀的大地上空飞翔。这不只是颂扬“江河集团”的诗章，同时也是唱给跨越发展的武清的赞歌！不是吗，有了党的改革开放的好政策，有了区委、区政府践行科学发展观的好领导，广大人民群众为早日把武清建成现代科技新城，正以百倍的热情，昂扬的斗志，如同浩荡的江河，拼搏奋进，势不可挡，奔涌向前！

诚心服务　促进发展

“服务他人就是发展自己”的理念，源于武清开发区的创造与实施，延伸拓展于全区的经济发展之中。这里既充分体现出武清区委、区政府坚持科学发展观的英明决策，又体现着全区在招商引资中凝聚力量、行之有效的操作方法。这里所说的“他人”，主要指来武清的投资者，为他们“服务”，就是在政策允许的情况下为其提供各种便利条件，使之畅通无阻尽快投产早日富起来，水涨船高，商家富起来，我们的财政收入增加，也会随之富起来。相反，商家经营不景气甚至关门倒闭，我们的富又从何谈起呢？至于环境，它包括和谐稳定的社会环境和幽雅舒适的生活环境，毋庸多言，对已经富起来的投资客商来说，优化的服务软环境也是吸引他们投资的法宝。

“绫致时装公司”，是丹麦的一家独资企业，规模从小到大，发展较快，在世界上已经崭露头角，渐成武清开发区的纳税大户，更解决了一批待业者的就业问题。开发区总公司有时很担心这样的企业会被外省市从我们这里“拉”走，郭总觉得，经商办企业虽讲“信义”为先，但人往高处走，如果在服务上不如人家，甚至与人家相差悬殊，多好的朋友心也会慢慢地冷下来，也会离开。为拴心留人，除平时为他们精心搞好服务外，2004年开发区自己动手盖厂房，并将3万多平方米的厂房以优惠价格租给了该企业，为绫致公司着实安了一个家。使该企业坚定了在武清发展立业的信心。同时，为了沟通感情，在区委主要领导去该企业调研时，还送给该企业老板“穆桂英挂帅”“贵妃醉酒”两件戏剧人物工艺品，以示纪念。礼薄情义重，虽然没花几个钱，老板却视为珍宝，爱不释手，觉得武清人真好，表示绝对不离开武清这块风水宝地。

世界五百强企业之一的“中粮集团”，看中了武清，计划在武清开发区投资建厂，“中粮”老总及相关人员来开发区考察时，有两个“意想不到”的事：一是树培书记率开发区人员亲自到高速路出口迎接；二是在划地建造厂房时，区委书记王树培亲自陪同对方来到城区外，踏着高低不平杂草丛生的荒地，抹着额头上的汗水，一会儿东一会儿西，和大家一起认真测量勘察。集团老总见此情景，深深地被打动了，多么难得的区领导，多么诚挚的武清人啊！老板当即拍板，投资4亿元，决定在武清创业发展。

随着改革开放步伐的加快，以及人们现代意识的不断增强，许多外来投资企业已经不满足于给点儿优惠政策，而对投资环境愈加关注。因此，武清开发区内除实现了水、电、路、通讯、土地的“十一通一平”，区内还建起了“行政服务中心”，实行了“一站式办公”、一条龙服务。尤其是生态型开发区域环境，使外来者无不交口称赞，车行园区内，会感到蓝天碧水、道路宽阔，绿树成荫、鲜花簇簇、鸟儿飞鸣、空气清新，花园式的厂区比比皆是。2004和2005年，分别有几家投资在几亿元或几十亿元的企业，打算在开发区投资建厂，有关工作人员通过对这些企业认真考察，发现有不同程度的污染，区领导忍痛割爱，毫不犹豫地放弃了这些企业。此后，在招商过程中凡发现有污染的项目，一律免见免谈。是啊，坚持高科技、环保型服务，就不能见利忘义，只有“舍得”，才能“获得”；只有“舍得”，才能“高端”，事业才会大踏步地向前迈进。

开发区领导靠“服务他人就是发展自己”的新理念，靠远见卓识和敬业精神，深深赢得了投资者的信赖，也赢得了本区广大人民群众的声声赞誉，使开发区永葆旺盛的活力和不断获得更大的发展。

齐心合力　攀登高峰

国内外颇具影响力的武清开发区，是一本记载武清创业史的大书，需要用心解读，它的发展和建设凝聚着几任区（县）委、政府以及开发区领导的心血和汗水。

招商引资是一门学问，要做好这门学问并非易事。当笔者问郭宝联，招商选资有什么具体的标准？他说了个“三要三不要”，我觉得很精辟：“三要”即高新、高质、高端；“三不要”即高耗能、有污染、投资强度小。当笔者又问郭总，听说各级领导为了招商，“没黑没白，没年没节，没皮没脸……”是这样吗？郭宝联笑笑说：这是常人难以体验得到的。他没做过多的解释，却告诉我还有几个“千”呢：千山万水、千辛万苦、千言万语、千方百计……对此他也没做过多的解释，但我通过采访体验，对开发区创业者们所经历的苦辣酸甜已经有了一定的感悟，对几个“千”所包含的内容，是能想象出来的。当笔者再问郭总，武清开发区发展如此之快，主要靠什么？郭总几乎脱口而出说出“四个好”来：好的领导、好的团队、好的机制、好的环境。我想，通过上边所摆的一些事实，这“四个好”人们会不说自明的。

郭宝联总经理在几任开发区总公司总经理中，似乎是任职较短的一个，只有三年的时间。然而，成绩的大小和个人的付出又怎能用时间的长短来计算？更不能脱离历史的积累而割裂地来看。郭总的一番话说得透彻，开发区之所以能够攻艰克难快速发展，主要得益于党和国家改革开放时期的好政策，得益于区委、区政府践行科学发展观和正确决策，得益于整个团队的齐心合力和拼搏苦干。

在我的文章即将结束之时，又想起《江河之歌》中的两句诗：“你将东方的神奇融入世界，又把世界的精彩带给中国。”武清开发区之所以能如旭日东升、大放异彩，神奇之处在于区决策者制定的可持续发展的战略，以及在“亲商”“安商”“富商”中如何取得对方的信任、得到对方的肯定，并产生无尽的人格魅力，而这些靠的却又不仅仅是优惠政策。

武清开发区这本大书需要我们用心继续解读，而如何用心传递好“接力棒”，则是全区 84 万人民的热切期望，它象征着武清科技新城的形象与光明美好的未来。

摘录作家出版社《京津走廊崛起的科技新城》

潮头涌动踏歌行

——访武清开发区第五任总经理钟书明

李蔚兰

引言

古老、寂寥的武清，在历史的红尘中默默伫立了不知多少个世纪，它拥有一片广阔的土地，却少了一支书写精彩史诗的笔。斗转星移，日升月隐，经过沧海桑田的变迁，就在近20年中，改革的浪潮把一块无人问津的荒草地冲刷成了一片金银滩，于是一群英才捎笔走到它的身边，饱蘸智慧之墨，开始书写武清开发区建设的恢弘史诗。20年，开发区经历了一段波澜壮阔的历程：大机遇、大变革；大挑战、大跨越。海市蜃楼的神话从这里诞生；大开发、大发展，思想的芯片，在这里发芽成长。一片又一片的现代化工厂拔地而起，一片又一片厂房拔节向上。

“大风起兮云飞扬”，那含蓄着深厚人文品格的旋律和着美丽天鹅湖水的拍击声，组成了一首大气磅薄的千古绝唱！

迎风踏浪涛头立

阳春三月，春光明媚。走进武清开发区，当这里工作的同志知道我要采访区委常委、开发区第五任总经理钟书明时，有人告诉我说，钟总在这里带领开发区这支永不言败的团队，已经五年多了。

五年，不过是人类历史短暂的一瞬。在历史的长河中，有许许多多这样的一瞬，就那么毫无声息地逝去了。可刚刚过去的这五年，对武清开发区来说却是“天翻地覆慨而慷”的一瞬，是“数风流人物还看今朝”的一瞬。这五年，砥砺奋进，春华秋实，是武清开发区历史的节点；这五年，日新月异，壮美如歌，是开发区发展的跨越；这五年，武清开发区以优质的投资环境，跨越式的经济发展增幅，成为中国国家级经济技术开发区的领跑者。国内生产总值由2005年的35亿元增加到2010年的118亿元；税收由2005年的10亿元增加到2010年的45亿元；吸引投资由2005年的13.7亿元增加到2010年的80亿元。电子信息、机械制造、生物医药、汽车及零部件、新材料、新能源六大主导产业已经成为它建设的恢弘胜景。中粮、英格索兰、赛诺、日进、马泰克、韦斯伐里亚、蜡笔小新、伊利、娃哈哈、玉柴、蓝猫、奥特莱斯、凯旋王国等为代表的中外210个项目，如翩舞的金凤垂青于雍阳这片热土。如今武清开发区在仅占武清1%的土地上创造了50%的地区生产总值，奏响了转型跨越的最强音，更展示了“十一五”的猎猎雄风。在武清开发区20年发展的历史上，及至中国开发区的历史上，武清开发区这五年的发展历程显得格外精彩、前行的脚步显得如此豪迈！人们不禁为开发区的崛起而惊叹！

武清开发区在近五年1800多个日子里，靠什么实现了如此巨大的跨越？是什么力量在支撑开发区人？是什么力量铸就了开发区如此辉煌的伟业？在总经理钟书明的办公室，让我很快找到了答案。

时间回溯到2005年。这一年，武清开发区迎来了成长历程中的一个标志性事件：开发区发展的内部、外部环境发生了重大变化，特别是我国加入WTO后，国际化进程大大加快，国家加强土地管理等，国家对开发区政策差异化优势逐渐弱化。这不是一个个体的问题，而是国际国内形势的发展变化给所有开发区提出的新课题和挑战。

就在这样的形势下，钟书明走马上任武清开发区总公司总经理。2005年11月1日，是很平常的一天，但它却让钟书明的记忆瞬间定格。时任区委书记王树培在谈到由他挂帅任开发区总经理时，对他说：“开发区是武清经济发展的发动机、火车头，是武清未来发展的希望所在。担子不轻，责任很重，区委相信你一定能干好。”话语不多，却让他顿时感到组织对他的无限信任。

品着淡淡的香茶，笔者简单浏览了手边的资料：钟书明，1963年出生于武清，1985年毕业于天津财经学院商业经济系。先后在县政府财贸办公室、县政府办公室担任科员、科长、副主任、上马台镇党委书记。这种经历，使他身上既具备了政府工作人员严谨的工作作风，又具备了基层工作吃苦耐劳的品格。而他在担任上马台镇党委书记的三年里，为了能够造福一方，他全身心地投入到乡镇经济区的建设当中。在他的努力下，包括台湾、韩国等多家中外企业陆续在此落地并开花结果。他亲历了招商引资之种种，也见证了经济区发展壮大的全过程。这不仅使他对经济区的发展有着非常深入的了解，积累了丰富的招商工作经验，同时，在多年的经济工作实践中，使他更有机会对我国经济发展问题进行更加深入的理性思考，形成了符合经济发展要求的正确的思想认识，特别是对国际国内形势突变的新形势下，中国经济开发区的走向也形成了一定的见解。

虽然是这样，但他还是觉得这副担子沉甸甸的。人们清楚地记得，上任第一天的欢迎会上，他没有发表慷慨激昂的就职演说，只对他的同事讲了以下三句话：我要给大家创造一个和谐的工作环境，给大家创造一个能充分发挥自己才能的平台，还要让大家有一个相对满意的回报。语调不高，话语间透着亲切，透着真诚，让人心底油然感动。这分明是一种融合，一种让人尊敬的大气。原来，他要的是一个团结奋进的团队，一个求真务实的集体呀！

凝聚效应最给力

深夜，天边的弦月如钩。此时，总经理的办公室内静静的，烟灰缸里的烟蒂冒了尖，他来回不停地踱步，历史的波涛已然真切地将他推上了全区经济发展的前沿阵地，况且他清醒地知道，当下国内各省、市等待着“凤凰涅槃”的开发区，正以千帆竞技的姿态争夺有限的资源和生产要素。周边的开发区之间竞技势头越来越强劲，每一个好的外资项目进入中国要经过几十个省、市的争夺，进入天津市也要经过几个甚至十几个回合的较量才能最终落地。望着窗外那壮观奇伟、浩瀚无银的星空，他久久地凝视着、思索着……武清开发区怎么办？耳边不断传来区委、区政府决策者的“举全区之力，建设好开发区”的声音，这声音如同一道炽亮的闪电劈开了他一整天风起云涌的天空，让他心潮澎湃，信心倍增。从何踢开第一脚的思路已然在他心中形成。

领导者的责任是对事业的高瞻远瞩的谋划，率领团队作战的凝聚力和指挥能力。而凝聚力、号召力却往往靠的是领导者自身行动的带动力和影响力。于是，他从这个星期天开始，听汇报、开座谈会、搜集信息、实地调研、跟踪考察……这也充分体现了他的工作风格：想事周到、细致、雷厉风行；行事日程满、节奏快、毫不间歇……

敢闯、敢试、敢为，是开发区团队优秀品质最突出的部分。“跑”和“争”成了开发区这五年的关键词。他们主动与国家部委、市直部门和大型国企加强联系，搜集、跟踪项目信息，有针对性地寻找目标客户。并全力推行中介招商。把外国驻华机构、商社、行业协会作为招商中介，通过与他们保持密切联系，广泛了解全球投资信息，及时掌握企业发展动向。一个又一个的“漂亮仗”亮相招商舞台。他们抓住现有的50余家国内外行业龙头企业为代表的一批重点项目，利用其投资链条长、配套项目多的特点，通过深入走访、联谊等形式，加强与龙头企业和其配套企业的交流，促成这些龙头项目增资增项，配套项目加速跟进，同时加强对外宣传推介。利用国家和市级媒体、专业招商网、外资商会等多种媒介，加强多角度、多层次、多形式招商宣传。一个个马不停蹄的行动在开发区的这片土地上蔚然成风……

带团队需要亲和力，招商引资同样需要亲和力。亲和力是什么，是人与人之间信息沟通，情感交流的一种能力。你具有亲和力，你就会积聚旺盛的人气。特别是领导干部，你具有很强的亲和力，就可以团结一切可以团结的力量，赢得人发自内心的信任和拥戴。了解他的人都知道，正是这种与生俱来的亲和力，时时处处自然而然地滋润着亲人、朋友、同事，在他那里没有丝毫矫饰和造作，全是本色使然，天性自然流露，好像他天生就是一个干招商的料，与陌生人打交道能很快拉近彼此的距离，熟人更是愿意与他相交。于是就有了开发区人“不抛弃、不放弃”的拚劲；有了盯紧项目不放松，不达目的不罢休的狠劲。出现了踏破铁鞋跑项目，区领导带队谈项目，争分夺秒抢项目，以情动人、以诚感人留项目等一个个精彩的招商故事。于是就有了蜡笔小新、韦斯伐里亚、伊利、娃哈哈……有了中国水利水电集团、北京住总集团等一批重点企业的落地开花。

没有一股顽强拼搏的劲头，没有一股争创一流的精神，便没有开发区今天的辉煌成就。说来有人可能不相信，即使是遭遇了2008年末的那场撼动全球的国际金融危机，来武清投资的项目依然踏破门槛，仅2009年上半年就引进企业36家，平均每5天引进一家；吸引投资总额40.04亿元，其中外资1.81亿美元；实现税收18.77亿元，同比增长43%，各项经济指标在本市同类开发区中名列前茅，成功实现了“弯道超越”。

面对如此不可思议的数字，我一脸惊讶的表情。钟总却十分平静地这样说：“越是困难的时候，越有超越的机遇，关键是要树立挺过风雨，迎接彩虹的勇气”。我一时无言以对。我知道，在这位总经理的心中，成就从不是他曲终迎接掌声的享受，而是又一曲新的茹苦含辛演奏的拼搏进行曲。

温馨换来春满园

开发区之间招商引资竞争日益激烈的客观现状，决定了一个成功的开发区必须是“全能运动员”、是“内外兼修的高手”。如果一个开发区仅仅能够提供空洞的“巢穴”(硬件)，缺少个性化、人性化的服务，它的吸引力将大打折扣。因此，能否成功地将开发区与企业间生硬的房东”、“房客”关系转化为无微不至的亲人朋友关系，显得尤为重要！服务软环境是吸引投资的核心，真心交朋友的感情投资更被钟书明提到了议事日程。

在武清，多年形成的“服务他人就是发展自己”的理念早已深入人心。开发区职能工作少不了服务，总公司更担负着服务企业、服务项目、服务群众的重任。于是，一种真诚温馨为入区项目实行“保姆式”服务的氛围应运而生，各部门主动将自身发展与园区企业的利益挂钩，想企业之所想，急企业之所急，提出了服务的“三个转变”。一是变被动服务为主动服务。二是变低层次服务为高层次服务。将服务由局限在办理执照、接水接电等简单劳务，向能够提供政策法规咨询和经贸信息等高层次服务转变。三是变初期服务为全程、全方位服务，从公司总经理到公司里的每一名员工，都怀着一颗热忱之心，不分薄厚走访区内企业，一时间，亲商、安商、富商的浓浓氛围，如沐阳光温暖着入区企业的人心。为了帮助韩国中央电子公司拓宽产品销路，他们一同与企业到广东、上海进行调研与推广；他们把瑞特格公司的钢板散热器和丹佛斯公司的温控产品率先在区内栖仙温泉公寓中使用，并向其他住宅小区进行推荐；2006年，投资1.2亿元，启动建设了8万多平方米的集住宿、餐饮、文化娱乐、医疗等配套生活服务设施为一体的高新公寓。不仅为给8000名外来人才创造了一个渴望体贴与温暖的“家”，也为入区企业高水平发展提供了重要的功能支撑。.

日历翻到了2008年。受国际金融危机影响，开发区内众多企业遇到了前所未有的困难。为帮助企业渡过难关，武清开发区及时出台了帮扶企业渡难关的十二项措施，成立了专门的“保增长、渡难关、上水平”活动领导小组和十余个帮扶工作组，采取召开座谈会、走访慰问、个别谈话、公开联系电话或邮箱等多种形式，直接听取企业呼声，面对面地了解企业需求，现场答复、解决企业遇到的各种疑难问题，用贴心的服务，携手企业共度“寒流”。那一年，开发区管委会共走访企业210多家，解决各类问题120余个。非常时期做出了非常之举。通过减免特种设备费用，调整能源价格等措施，降低企业经营成本；通过灵活的用工机制、困难企业补助、员工培训补贴等办法帮助企业摆脱经营困境。

资金周转问题是企业普遍存在的困难，开发区便与多家金融机构签订合作协议，通过提供流动资金贷款支持中小企业发展，由区中小企业信用担保中心利用贷款担保专项资金提供担保，为大批企业解决了资金周转问题。担保中心累计批准 8 家企业的担保申请共计 2930 万元，为他们渡难关提供了强大的后援支持。

在开发区采访，我有一个深切的体验那就是，在种种变化的背后，没变的、而且发扬光大的是开发区人团结一心，开拓创新、拚搏奋起、勇争一流的精神；不变的、一直恪守的是“服务他人就是发展自己”的理念。这无疑就成了开发区这五年跨越发展的支点。

举旗跨越铿锵行

历史的车轮驶入 2009 年底，全球经济开启了新一轮发展高潮，通过深入透析国际国内经济发展大势，区委书记袁桐利审时度势对武清开发区提出了 “坚持高起点，打造高端化、高新化产业集群”的要求。这让开发区的每个决策者、建设者视野越加开阔，胆略和气魄越来越大。生命的拼图尚未完成，前行的脚步也会在此刻提速前行。钟书明同志这样对我说，“我最大的快乐就是在招商的搏弈中胜出。”一种历史和社会的使命感在他身上彰显，他要抓住当前开发建设投资成本低的有利时机，寻路突击，完美转型。

人常说：创业难，守业难，嬗变发展更难。进入 2010 年，似乎是武清开发区最为繁闹的时节，伴着开发区人铿锵有力的足音，前进的号角一次又一次地吹响……一个占地 15 平方公里的三期开发工程井然有序。在这 15 平方公里的土地上，将为我们呈现三个模块，即：高端制造业聚集区、保税物流区和创业总部基地。其中，高端制造业聚集区占地 10 平方公里，将坚持高端高质高新化方向，吸引高科技、高收益且能带动产业链形成的龙头项目，促进产业集群发展。预计招商引资 400 亿元以上，年实现地区生产总值 100 亿元以上，税收 30 亿元以上。保税物流区占地 2.4 平方公里、投资 50 亿元、建筑面积 120 万平方米。将建成立足天津、服务京冀、辐射环渤海的物流服务基地。建成后年实现地区生产总值 50 亿元以上，税收 10 亿元以上。创业总部基地占地 1.26 平方公里，建筑面积 120 万平米，总投资 60 亿元。主要发展文化创意、动漫游戏、服务外包、金融、研发孵化等现代服务业和总部经济。建成后每年可实现地区生产总值 100 亿元以上，税收 20 亿元以上。

在大项目、好项目纷纷落地的同时，开发区的开发建设也在加快推进。总建筑面积23万平方米的北欧绿色产业园一期正在进行基础施工；建筑面积7万平方米的绫致标准厂房、6万平方米的招商中心、32万平方米的创业总部基地机声隆隆、彩旗飘飘；奥克斯高新技术产业基地、信义节能环保玻璃生产基地、凯旋王国、伊利酸奶奶酪生产基地、红日药业中试基地等产业项目建设全面推进，佛罗伦萨小镇·京津名品奥特莱斯开业在即；人人乐、中纺凯泰、国能飞腾、大连机床、维益食品、蓝猫动漫科技园等项目建设顺利进行。这是历史与未来的握手，伴着阳春三月的脚步，用眼睛看，用脚步去量，用精神去称。武清开发区正经历着脱胎换骨、羽化成蝶的华丽转身。它带给我们的是“武清速度”，是标杆的力量，视觉的冲击以及内心的震撼。

回首五载春秋，钟书明感触颇深：“如果说武清开发区近五年是取得一些成绩的话，是历届区（县）委、政府果断决策、正确领导指挥的结果，是各级领导、全区社会各界广泛关注支持的结果，是一代一代开发区人努力奋斗、不懈追求的收获。我和我的团队只是20年接力赛奔跑中的一棒而已。把事业当日子过这既是我们的工作态度，同时也是我们的工作职责。”他把“职责”两字说得很清淅，语调明显在加重。望着他如此坚定的眼神，我感觉到，每个开发区建设者的血管里涌动着的是一股永不停息、与时代脉搏共搏的澎湃激情。呈现给我们的终将是这支团队迎风破浪踏歌行的精彩人生。

尾　声

事业的征程没有尾声，辉煌的篇章又是开始的首页。过去的五年，是开发区建设发展的一座里程碑，站在“十二五”发展的起跑点上，放眼大江南北百舸争流、千帆竞发的发展大势，开发区的规划者未雨绸缪，蓄势待发，精心描绘了一个整体发展的“十二五”蓝图：拓展发展空间、升级产业结构，培育产业集群，实现跨越发展，把武清开发区建设成为京津之间最具实力和竞争力的高端绿色园区……

无人可比的自然秉赋，政府的前瞻性规划，加上开发区人的热情、执着和创造，可以预想，未来五年内在这片土地上将会再崛起一个以特色产业高地为标志的绿色开发区。那一簇簇现代化高端建筑集群，将是搏击长空引领城市发展的雄鹰。

摘录作家出版社《京津走廊崛起的科技新城》

未来 剑指全国一流

——访第六任总经理刘东海

高元勃

火热的六月。

走进沸腾的中国武清开发区，与第六任总经理刘东海采访对话，总有一种催人奋进、激情澎湃之感。这位从杨村街道工委书记来到开发区领导岗位仅一年多时间的他，说起开发区过去的经历，有感动更有豪情；谈到未来的发展，有激情更有力量。特别是他那“利用几年的时间，把武清开发区建成全国国家级一流开发区”掷地有声的话语，着实让人感动、受鼓舞。

过去—— 深刻的感受

6 月 20 日上午，武清开发区总公司总经理办公室。

一阵紧张忙碌的处理日常工作之后，总经理刘东海接受了我的采访。按照事先想好的采访计划，我想请他谈谈来中国武清开发区工作一年后的经验与成果。可一向思维敏捷、工作虎虎生气的他却谦逊地说：“我刚刚来开发区工作一年，没有什么经验成绩可言。要说工作，也是在区委、政府领导下，在区委常委、开发区工委书记钟书明同志带领下，和开发区几十名员工一起做了一些我应该做的工作。”

接着，他动情地说：“还是说说我来开发区一年工作的感受吧。”他说，武清开发区从无到有、从小到大、从弱到强的 20 年发展经历，的确令人瞩目，着实写下了武清发展史上最辉煌的一页。据我了解，我们的开发区即使在全国 122 个国家级开发区中，像武清开发区这样能够以管理水平高、效益好，同时获得高新技术产业园区和经济技术开发区两个国家级牌子的也为数不多，令每个武清人感到骄傲自豪。武清所以有今天的开发区，我的感受很多，但让我感受最深的是：

首先是，得益于历届区（县）委、政府的科学决策和正确领导，得益于从中央、国家各部门到市委、市政府和有关部门的关注与支持，得益于武清开发区人不懈的追求和奋斗，得益于全区广大干部群众、各个部门、包括驻军各部队和驻区企业在内的，社会各界的共同努力。

其次是，有一个非常好的规划。从基础设施配套载体功能到建设工程质量，从区域发展空间到布局划分调整，都富于超前性。我们20年前修的路、搞的环境建设项目至今还跟得上发展的需要。建区初期，就在一期开发区域内预留出一块最好的土地，作为发展现代服务业。近年来，在这块1.26平方公里的预留地上建设的"创业总部基地"，不仅使产业结构实现了升级调整，而且获得了很高的经济回报，未来三年可实现税收10亿元以上，五年有望实现又一个现有开发区的税收效益。

再次是，开发区在多年建设发展中逐步建立了一整套完善、科学的管理机制。无论是用人机制、工资奖金分配机制，还是工程招投标、封闭式管理机制等，都发挥了应有的作用。以工程招投标为例。这么多年，那么多项工程，始终坚持招投标制度。不仅坚持了公开、公平、公正的原则，而且节约了不少建设资金、保证了工程质量，保持了开发区廉诚守信的良好形象。

四是，逐步锻造一支高素质、高效率、能打硬仗的队伍。到武清开发区工作，迎面扑来的是一种武清发展、开发区发展的强烈的责任感、紧迫感气息促动着你，是高效率、快节奏的浓烈的氛围包容着你，让你自觉地和这支团队"5+2""白加黑"地去拼搏奋进。现在的开发区虽然只有六十几名员工，却肩负着几十平方公里、上千家企业服务管理工作，无不体现着开发人良好的精神状态，吃苦耐劳、无私奉献的精神风貌。

五是，良好的服务理念。从"投资者是上帝"到"服务他人就是发展自己"理念的树立，从"一站式办公，一条龙服务"到行政许可服务中心服务体系的形成，想方设法、真情实意地为入区企业提供了热情周到的全方位服务，亲商、安商、富商形成氛围，让投资者在开发区感受到了真情和家的温馨。难怪许多投资者都说，在武清投资发展安心、踏实。甚至不断增资建设，带亲戚朋友、合作伙伴来共同发展。

正是这些种种努力，我们的开发区才有了生机勃发的今天，才有了她在武清经济社会发展中的积极作用与奉献。

今天——争创全国一流

谈到武清开发区的未来建设与发展，刘东海饶有兴致地告诉我们：武清开发区建区20周年，恰逢我国“十二五”计划的开局之年。我们自加压力，给自己提出了新的发展目标。到2015年，实现地区生产总值360亿元，工业总产值1045亿元，财税收入137亿元，固定资产投资235亿元，吸引投资200亿元，几项经济指标年平均增幅都在20%以上。同时，每年新创造就业岗位一万个。到“十二五”末，武清开发区要成为全国一流国家级开发区，走在改革开放和经济发展的前列。

他说，为了保证实现这一目标，我们将努力做好这样几件事：

——拓展开发区发展空间。按照区委、区政府既定的城市建设整体规划的要求，实施“撤村建居”、推进城市化进程的战略性措施，在现有30平方公里的基础上，启动20平方公里的“四期”开发建设。目前7平方公里的起步区已步入实质性操作阶段。

——加大招商引资力度。把招商引资作为立区之本，展开强大的招商引资攻势，招大项目、招好项目。加快“创业总部基地、高端制造业集聚区、保税物流区、金融商务区、文化产业园区”等高端产业项目建设，做好产业升级换代，使开发区产业结构逐步实现质的飞跃。

——进一步加强环境建设。把开发区环境建设作为“立区之源”，在努力做好基础设施配套建设、增强载体功能建设的同时，进一步践行“服务他人就是发展自己”的理念，以国际化标准和一流的服务助推企业发展，打造国际一流的绿色园区。

——把引资与引智结合起来。在想方设法多渠道引进高端人才的同时，整合教育资源，促动2.6平方公里面积、投资200亿元的“天狮大学城”项目建设，尽早投入使用、产生效应，为开发区可持续发展提供足够的人才保证。

未来——充满信心力量

听着刘东海总经理对武清开发区“十二五”规划的宏伟蓝图，以及一个个振奋人心项目的引进建设情况，我们不禁问起开发区将如何面对新形势、采取有力措施，保证计划目标的实现？他沉思了片刻说：“凡事都是机遇与挑战并存，优势与劣势同在，把握时机、审时度势、拼搏奋进，我们就会稳步快速前进”。

接着，他又详细谈了对未来形势的分析。他说，经过20年的拼搏努力，武清开发区这个平台已经到了日趋成熟、各种优势集聚期，目前在全国同时有两块国家级开发区牌子的不多，这既是我们多少年来的可喜成果，也是我们未来发展的最好基础、希望所在；我们有地处京津之间背靠北京、依托天津的得天独厚的区位优势，特别是京津两大都市的产业外溢的新形势，为我们加快发展带来了千载难逢的商机；还有四通八达的海、陆、空交通优势，全区 5 条高速公路、17 个出入口，京津城际轨道，和“九横九纵”的路网体系，形成了便捷高速的路网，又为我们提供了强有力的支撑；生态型的基础设施环境与良好的服务软环境，以及水、汽、土地、住宿等企业低成本的运营条件，为我们寻求发展奠定了坚实的基础。这些，都是我们潜在的集聚优势，对于招商引资都有磁石般的吸引力。与此同时，他还客观地说出了我们再发展中存在的困难和问题。他说，在今后开发区建设发展中我们还有不少“短板’的地方。如，我们现在发展的地域空间与大开放、大开发的形势不匹配。产业结构还要不断调整、升级，服务外包、文化等一些高端产业还要进一步引进开发。环境功能，包括软硬环境建设，还有待于进一步提升。这些问题不解决，会直接制约、影响着我们的建设发展。很快，他便话锋一转满怀信心地说，机遇和优势是我们发展的主流，问题和困难是前进发展中的不足。我们深信，有区委、区政府的正确领导，有社会各界的鼎力支持，有开发人的积极努力，武清开发区一定会以建区 20 年为契机，抢抓机遇、变劣势为优势、攻坚克难、乘势而上，建设好全国一流的开发区，为实现武清经济社会又好又快发展做出新的贡献。

摘录作家出版社《京津走廊崛起的科技新城》

编 后 记

经过一年多的努力，《中国·天津武清开发区志》终于完成编纂任务。作为编修者，能为正在建设的“京津卫星城美丽新武清”记录历史，为京津走廊崛起的科技新城——武清开发区建设发展书写精彩，我们深感欣慰。

编纂《中国·天津武清开发区志》，是武清开发区管委会、总公司为记录历史、传承文明、推动自身未来发展，所做出的一项建设性决策。盛世修志，是中华民族的优良传统。正是在我们祖国改革开放日益深入、中华民族伟大复兴、武清经济社会全面协调发展、开发区建设热火朝天的形势下，武清开发区管委会、总公司满怀责任感、使命感，从2016年11月起，组建了志书编委会，邀请原武清区委宣传部副部长兼《天津日报·武清资讯》主编高元勃，原武清区文化馆馆长、研究馆员王毅，原武清区地方志办公室主任杨振关组建了志书编纂班子，展开了志书编纂总体谋划、主题框架提纲商定、召开区内部门协调会议、史料搜集、文稿撰写，编辑整理、书稿审定、出版印刷等一系列卓有成效的工作。到2017年10月，志书的初稿完成。

在编辑此书过程中，我们按照志书编纂要求，一是尊重史实，以科学严谨的态度，挖掘、撰写、编辑志书。志书中记录的历史沿革、重要事件、重大活动及人物等，都做了大量调查研究工作，坚持有据可查。凡事做到总公司内有资料记载的按照原史料书写；公司资料不全的，到各级档案、图书馆查寻；年代较远又无资料可查的，则采取社会调查的形式，找老同志座谈回忆，尽力使历史准确、清晰。二是在目前撰写有关开发区志书较少、可借鉴的经验不多的情况下，我们主动借鉴天津《泰达志》，以及深圳、珠海等开发区的经验，力求从谋篇布局、记录内容、写作手法等方面，写出一部具有开发区特点的志书。三是在反映史实的基础上，我们深入挖掘武清开发人胸怀广阔、肯于吃苦、乐于为武清建设发展积极奉献的内心世界，在书写辉煌成就的同时，倡导正能量、弘扬时代精神，为今后未来建设发展提供有力的精神动力。四是在书稿完成后，我们主动向有关部室、老领导、老同志及有关部门，核实史实、征询意见、反复修改，并聘请了经验丰富的校对，确保志书的科学、严谨。五是选择方志出版社帮助出版印刷，既通过了专业出版部门有关专家对志书的严格把关、稿件的审定修改，又保证了志书的规范与质量。

一部志书的完成，绝不是少数编纂者所能做到的，而是经过多方面努力、社会各界广泛的帮助支持来实现的，是集体智慧的结晶。在编纂过程中，武清区委、区政府、区人大、区政协等领导机关及各有关部委办部门给予了很大关注支持。天津市开发区（泰达）、方志出版社、武清区档案局、文广局、《天津日报·武清资讯》编辑部等部门在资料搜集、编辑出版等方面都给予了多方面的帮助与支持。尤其是武清开发区的领导及各部门，在办公条件、史料提供、编辑出版等方面更给与了鼎力支持。在志书出版之际，我们一并深表诚挚的谢意。

由于我们的编辑水平、工作能力所限，加之反映的年代时间较长、内容较多，编纂时间较短，书中一定会有纰漏不足之处，敬请谅解。

编　者

2018 年 8 月